Formulation, Implementation, and Control of Competitive Strategy

Formulation, Implementation, and Control of Competitive Strategy

Eleventh Edition

John A. Pearce II
Villanova School of Business
Villanova University

Richard B. Robinson, Jr.
Moore School of Business
University of South Carolina

Boston   Burr Ridge, IL   Dubuque, IA   Madison, WI   New York   San Francisco   St. Louis
Bangkok   Bogotá   Caracas   Kuala Lumpur   Lisbon   London   Madrid   Mexico City
Milan   Montreal   New Delhi   Santiago   Seoul   Singapore   Sydney   Taipei   Toronto

McGraw-Hill
Irwin

FORMULATION, IMPLEMENTATION, AND CONTROL OF COMPETITIVE STRATEGY
Published by McGraw-Hill/Irwin, a business unit of The McGraw-Hill Companies, Inc., 1221 Avenue of the Americas, New York, NY, 10020.

1 2 3 4 5 6 7 8 9 0 DOW/DOW 0 9 8

ISBN   978-0-07-336812-2
MHID   0-07-336812-1

Editorial director: *Brent Gordon*
Publisher: *Paul Ducham*
Senior sponsoring editor: *Michael Ablassmeir*
Editorial coordinator: *Kelly Pekelder*
Senior marketing manager: *Anke Braun Weekes*
Project manager: *Bruce Gin*
Senior production supervisor: *Debra R. Sylvester*
Lead designer: *Matthew Baldwin*
Senior photo research coordinator: *Jeremy Cheshareck*
Photo researcher: *Keri Johnson*
Senior media project manager: *Susan Lombardi*
Cover design: *Kami Carter*
Typeface: *10/12 Times New Roman*
Compositor: *Hurix*
Printer: *R. R. Donnelley*

Library of Congress Cataloging-in-Publication Data

Pearce, John A.
    Formulation, implementation, and control of competitive strategy / John A. Pearce II,
Richard B. Robinson, Jr.—Eleventh ed.
      p. cm.
    Includes index.
    ISBN-13: 978-0-07-336812-2 (alk. paper)
    ISBN-10: 0-07-336812-1 (alk. paper)
    1. Strategic planning. 2. Strategic planning—Case studies. I. Robinson, Richard B.
(Richard Braden), 1947–II. Title.
  HD30.28.P3385 2009
  658.4'012—dc22

                      2007052592

www.mhhe.com

To Susan McCartney Pearce, David Donham Pearce, Mark McCartney Pearce, Katherine Elizabeth Robinson, Corporal John Braden Robinson, and Chance Robinson—for the love, joy, and vitality that they give to our lives.

About the Authors

John A. Pearce II *Villanova University*

John A. Pearce II, Ph.D., holds the Villanova School of Business Endowed Chair in Strategic Management and Entrepreneurship at Villanova University. In 2004, he was the Distinguished Visiting Professor at ITAM in Mexico City. Previously, Professor Pearce was the Eakin Endowed Chair in Strategic Management at George Mason University and a State of Virginia Eminent Scholar. He received the 1994 Fulbright U.S. Professional Award, which he served at INTAN in Malaysia. Dr. Pearce has taught at Penn State University, West Virginia University, the University of Malta as the Fulbright Senior Professor in International Management, and at the University of South Carolina where he was Director of Ph.D. Programs in Strategic Management. He received a Ph.D. degree in Business Administration and Strategic Management from the Pennsylvania State University.

Professor Pearce is coauthor of 36 books and has authored more than 250 articles and refereed professional papers. The articles have appeared in journals that include *Academy of Management Executive, Academy of Management Journal, Academy of Management Review, Business Horizons, California Management Review, Journal of Applied Psychology, Journal of Business Venturing, Long-Range Planning, Organizational Dynamics, Sloan Management Review,* and *Strategic Management Journal.* Several of these publications have resulted from Professor Pearce's work as a principal on research projects funded for more than $2 million. He is a widely recognized expert in the field of strategic management, with special accomplishments in the areas of strategic planning and management, including strategy formulation, implementation, and control, mission statement development, environmental assessment, industry analysis, and tools for strategy evaluation and selection.

Professor Pearce is the recipient of several awards in recognition of his accomplishments in teaching, research, scholarship, and professional service, including three Outstanding Paper Awards from the Academy of Management and the 2003 Villanova University Outstanding Faculty Research Award. A frequent leader of executive development programs and an active consultant to business and industry, Dr. Pearce's client list includes domestic and multinational firms engaged in manufacturing and service industries.

Richard B. Robinson, Jr. *University of South Carolina*

Richard B. Robinson, Jr., Ph.D., is a Moore Fellow at the Moore School of Business, University of South Carolina. He also serves as Director of the Faber Entrepreneurship Center at USC and Assistant Director of the Center for Manufacturing and Technology in USC's College of Engineering and Computing. Dr. Robinson received his Ph.D. in Business Administration from the University of Georgia. He graduated from Georgia Tech in Industrial Management.

Professor Robinson has authored or coauthored numerous books, articles, professional papers, and case studies addressing strategic management and entrepreneurship issues that students and managers use worldwide. His research has been published in major journals including the *Academy of Management Journal, Academy of Management Review, Strategic Management Journal, Academy of Entrepreneurship Journal,* and the *Journal of Business Venturing.*

Dr. Robinson has previously held executive positions with companies in the pulp and paper, hazardous waste, building products, lodging, and restaurant industries. He currently serves as a director or adviser to entrepreneurial companies that are global leaders in niche markets in the log home, building products, animation, and visualization software industries. Dr. Robinson also advises more than 250 students each year that undertake field consulting projects and internships with entrepreneurial companies worldwide.

Preface

This eleventh edition of *Formulation, Implementation, and Control of Competitive Strategy* is a comprehensive revision designed to accommodate the needs of strategy students worldwide in our fast changing twenty-first century. These are exciting times, and they are reflected on the many new developments in this book and the accompanying McGraw-Hill supplements. This preface describes what we have done to make the eleventh edition uniquely effective in preparing students for strategic decisions in tomorrow's fast-paced global business arena. They include:

- A chapter dedicated to corporate social responsibility and business ethics
- A chapter dedicated to structuring effective 21st century organizations
- Extensive coverage of globalization as a central theme integrated and illustrated throughout this book and in a separate, updated chapter of the global business environment
- A major section on leadership including numerous examples and illustrations that help provide practical guidelines young, emerging leaders can use

- A NEW chapter on innovation and entrepreneurship
- "Top Strategist" boxes highlighting the world's best new leaders as strategists
- 100 NEW *BusinessWeek* Strategy in Action boxes

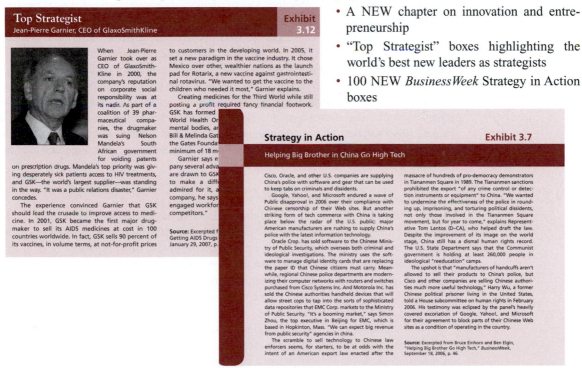

Top Strategist — Exhibit 3.12
Jean-Pierre Garnier, CEO of GlaxoSmithKline

When Jean-Pierre Garnier took over as CEO of GlaxoSmith-Kline in 2000, the company's reputation on corporate social responsibility was at its nadir. As part of a coalition of 39 pharmaceutical companies, the drugmaker was suing Nelson Mandela's South African government for voiding patents on prescription drugs. Mandela's top priority was giving desperately sick patients access to HIV treatments, and GSK—the world's largest supplier—was standing in the way. "It was a public relations disaster," Garnier concedes.

The experience convinced Garnier that GSK should lead the crusade to improve access to medicine. In 2001, GSK became the first major drugmaker to sell its AIDS medicines at cost in 100 countries worldwide. In fact, GSK sells 90 percent of its vaccines, in volume terms, at not-for-profit prices

to customers in the developing world. In 2005, it set a new paradigm in the vaccine industry. It chose Mexico over other, wealthier nations as the launch pad for Rotarix, a new vaccine against gastrointestinal rotavirus. "We wanted to get the vaccine to the children who needed it most," Garnier explains.

Creating medicines for the Third World while still posting a profit required fancy financial footwork. GSK has formed [...] World Health Or [...] mental bodies, an [...] Bill & Melinda Gat [...] the Gates Founda [...] minimum of 18 m [...]

Garnier says [...] pany several adva [...] are drawn to GSK [...] to make a diffe [...] admired for it, a [...] company, he says [...] engaged workfor [...] competitors."

Source: Excerpted f [...]
Getting AIDS Drugs [...]
January 29, 2007, p. [...]

Strategy in Action — Exhibit 3.7

Helping Big Brother in China Go High Tech

Cisco, Oracle, and other U.S. companies are supplying China's police with software and gear that can be used to keep tabs on criminals and dissidents.

Google, Yahoo!, and Microsoft endured a wave of public disapproval in 2006 over their compliance with Chinese censorship of their Web sites. But another striking form of tech commerce with China is taking place below the radar of the U.S. public: major American manufacturers are rushing to supply China's police with the latest information technology.

Oracle Crop. has sold software to the Chinese Ministry of Public Security, which oversees both criminal and ideological investigations. The ministry uses the software to manage digital identity cards that are replacing the paper ID that Chinese citizens must carry. Meanwhile, regional Chinese police departments are modernizing their computer networks with routers and switches purchased from Cisco Systems Inc. And Motorola Inc. has sold the Chinese authorities handheld devices that will allow street cops to tap into the sorts of sophisticated data repositories that EMC Corp. markets to the Ministry of Public Security. "It's a booming market," says Simon Zhou, the top executive in Beijing for EMC, which is based in Hopkinton, Mass. "We can expect big revenue from public security" agencies in china.

The scramble to sell technology to Chinese law enforcers seems, for starters, to be at odds with the intent of an American export law enacted after the

massacre of hundreds of pro-democracy demonstrators in Tiananmen Square in 1989. The Tiananmen sanctions prohibited the export "of any crime control or detection instruments or equipment" to China. "We wanted to undermine the effectiveness of the police in rounding up, imprisoning, and torturing political dissidents, not only those involved in the Tiananmen Square movement, but for year to come," explains Representative Tom Lantos (D–CA), who helped draft the law. Despite the improvement of its image on the world stage, China still has a dismal human rights record. The U.S. State Department says that the Communist government is holding at least 260,000 people in ideological "reeducation" camps.

The upshot is that "manufacturers of handcuffs aren't allowed to sell their products to China's police, but Cisco and other companies are selling Chinese authorities much more useful technology," Harry Wu, a former Chinese political prisoner living in the United States, told a House subcommittee on human rights in February 2006. His testimony was eclipsed by the panel's heavily covered excoriation of Google, Yahoo!, and Microsoft for their agreement to block parts of their Chinese Web sites as a condition of operating in the country.

Source: Excerpted from Bruce Einhorn and Ben Elgin, "Helping Big Brother Go High Tech," *BusinessWeek*, September 18, 2006, p. 46.

- NEW coverage of the pros and cons of outsourcing and the reality of what is now a truly global economy
- 14 NEW *BusinessWeek* end of chapter cases providing practical, interesting, contemporary applications of chapter topics
- NEW coverage and illustration of franchising as a major global economic trend
- NEW cases and illustration modules about companies founded and run by women and minorities
- NEW chapter material, cases, and illustrations examining the accelerating pace of global and technological change and its impact on companies, markets, and whole industries

- NEW coverage of specific companies that have responded to the need for improved business ethics in a manner that provides solid illustration and practical guidance to future business leaders using this book today
- NEW illustrations of renewal, growth, and enhanced profitability among companies in established, mature industries including airlines, pet care, automotive, food, retail, and consumer products
- Comprehensive supplemental material and industry-leading e-book support
- Comprehensive Web site for both the student and the instructor
- A proven model-based treatment of strategic management that allows for self-directed study, easy-to-understand presentation—in a package that represents the most cost-effective book on the market today. Professors and students receive all the advantages of the most expensive books for the lowest price of any major text
- A proven author team recognized with more than 20 research awards from various professional organizations including five "Best Paper" awards from the prestigious Academy of Management

The eleventh edition of *Formulation, Implementation, and Control of Competitive Strategy* is divided into 14 chapters. They provide a thorough, state-of-the-art treatment of the critical business skills needed to plan and manage strategic activities. While the text continues a solid academic connection, students will find the text material to be practical, skills oriented, and relevant to their jobs and entrepreneurial aspirations.

We were thrilled to have access to the world's best business publication, *BusinessWeek*, to create examples, illustration modules, and a wide variety of chapter-ending cases. The result is an extensively enhanced text and chapter discussion cases benefiting from hundreds of contemporary examples and illustrations provided by *BusinessWeek* writers worldwide. You will see *BusinessWeek*'s impact on our discussion case feature, our Strategy in Action modules, and our Web site. Of course, we are also pleased with several hundred examples blended into the text material, which came from recent issues of *BusinessWeek* or *www.businessweek.com*.

AN OVERVIEW OF OUR TEXT MATERIAL

The eleventh edition uses a model of the strategic management process as the basis for the organization of the text material. Adopters have identified this model as a key distinctive competence for our text because it offers a logical flow, distinct elements, and an easy-to-understand guide to strategic management. The model reflects strategic analysis at different organizational levels as well as the importance of innovation in the strategic management process. The model and parallel chapter organization provides a student-friendly approach to the study of strategic management.

The first chapter provides an overview of the strategic management process and explains what students will find as they use this book. The remaining 13 chapters cover each part of the strategic management process and techniques that aid strategic analysis, decision making, implementation, control and renewal. The literature and research in the strategic management area have developed at a rapid pace in recent years in both the academic and business press. The eleventh edition includes several upgrades designed to incorporate major developments from both these sources. While we include cutting-edge concepts, we emphasize straightforward, logical, and simple presentation so that students can grasp these new ideas without additional reading. The following are a few of the elements of the text that deserve particular note:

Corporate Social Responsibility and Business Ethics

Because of the public's heightened sensitivity to the behavior of strategic managers, we developed a new chapter for the eleventh edition that focuses on Corporate Social

Responsibility and Business Ethics. Always important in our text, we are pleased to bring these important issues into the foreground of informed classroom instruction. A key feature of the new Chapter 3 is its emphasis on "naming names." We identify dozens of corporations who are taking steps to assure that their stakeholders are properly represented in their communities and the world. Our goal is to help students to understand how Corporate Social Responsibility and Business Ethics can be managed properly.

Sarbanes-Oxley in 2010 and Beyond

Responding to highly publicized corporate and executive misconduct in recent years, the Sarbanes-Oxley Act was passed by the U.S. Congress requiring certifications for financial statements, new corporate regulations, disclosure requirements, and penalties for failure to comply. Chapter 3 provides in-depth coverage of the act, including discussions of the provisions restricting the corporate control of executives, accounting firms, auditing committees, and attorneys. Particular attention is given to its impact on the governance structure of American corporations, including the heightened role of corporate internal auditors who now routinely deal directly with top corporate officials, after its initial years in existence.

Agency Theory

Of the recent approaches to corporate governance and strategic management, probably none has had a greater impact on managerial thinking than agency theory. While the breadth and measurement of its usefulness continue to be hotly debated, students of strategic management need to understand the role of agency in our free enterprise, capitalistic system. This edition presents agency theory in a coherent and practical manner. We believe that it arms students with a cutting-edge approach to increasing their understanding of the priorities of executive decision making and strategic control.

Resource-Based View of the Firm

One of the most significant conceptual frameworks to systematize and "measure" a firm's strategic capabilities is the resource-based view (RBV) of the firm. The RBV has received major academic and business press attention during the last decade, helping to shape its value as a conceptual tool by adding rigor during the internal analysis and strategic analysis phases of the strategic management process. This edition provides a revised treatment of this concept in Chapter 6, Internal Analysis. We present the RBV in a logical and practical manner as a central underpinning of sound strategic analysis. Students will find several useful examples and a straightforward treatment of different types of "assets" and organizational capabilities culminating in the ability to determine when these resources create competitive advantage. They will see different ways to answer the question "what makes a resource valuable?" and be able to determine when that resource creates a competitive advantage in a systematic, disciplined, creative manner.

The Value Disciplines

A new approach to generic strategy centers on delivering superior customer value through one of three value disciplines: operational excellence, customer intimacy, or product leadership. Companies that specialize in one of these disciplines, while simultaneously meeting industry standards in the other two, gain a sustainable lead in their markets. Chapter 7, Long-Term Objectives and Strategies, provides details on these approaches with several examples of successful company experiences.

Bankruptcy

Many revisions in this book are driven by changes in business trends. Nowhere is that more evident than in our discussion of company bankruptcy. In the 1980s bankruptcy was treated as a last option that precluded any future for the firm. In the first decade of the 2000s the view has dramatically changed. Bankruptcy has been elevated to the status of a strategic option, and executives need to be well versed in its potentials and limitations, as you will see in Chapter 7, Long-Term Objectives and Strategies.

Executive Compensation

While our text has led the field in providing a practice-oriented approach to strategic management, we have redoubled our efforts to treat topics with an emphasis on application. Our revised section on executive compensation in Chapter 10, Implementation, is a clear example. You will find an extended discussion of executive bonus options that provides a comparison of the relative merits of the five most popular approaches, to include the current debate on the use, or overuse, of stock options and the need to accurately account for their true cost.

Outsourcing

"Outsourcing" of jobs and functions has become a global business necessity in the majority of companies in the U.S., Europe and indeed throughout the world today. It has moved from simply seeking low cost manufacturing options to having product development, product design, and indeed core innovation sought by some of the world's best known companies actually done outside that company by an "outsourced" provider. Chapter 11, Organizational Structure, along with an excellent special *BusinessWeek* case, reviews the pros and cons of outsourcing along with a practical look at the post-outsourcing reality of an interconnected global economy.

Structuring Effective Organizations

The accelerating rate of change often driven by the sudden emergence of opportunities in global market niches demanding quick decisions and immediate action places unprecedented demands on an organization's use of people and resources. Forward thinking entrepreneurs and business leaders have responded to this new reality by crafting organizational structures that are fluid, open, virtual networks of people, expertise and knowledge. Doing so is absolutely essential in implementing twenty-first century strategies. Chapter 11, Organizational Structure, has been created to help students understand how to structure effective organizations in these types of market settings. We identify numerous organizations that illustrate effective structures, and explore ways to incorporate key advantages associated with traditional organizing principles into organizational structures that are at the same time ambidextrous, fluid, boundaryless, and comprehensively responsive. And we examine Web-enabled virtual organizations that are rapidly emerging as new "structureless" business organizations.

Leadership

Developments of the last few years that highlight corporate and executive misconduct along with the unprecedented challenge faced by companies seeking to survive and prosper in a dynamic, constantly changing global business environment highlight the critical need for solid leadership more than ever before. Chapter 12, Leadership and Culture, provides a completely new examination of leadership, the critical things that good leaders do, and a look at ways young operating managers can develop specific skills that will help them become outstanding future leaders in what will be an incredibly dynamic global economy.

Innovation and Entrepreneurship

In a global economy that allows everyone everywhere instant information and instant connectivity, change often occurs at lightning speed. So leaders are increasingly looking for their firms to embrace innovation and entrepreneurship as essential foundations from which to respond and find opportunity in overwhelming uncertainty. Indeed this rapid change and steady uncertainty is the ideal setting within which start-up entrepreneurs and disruptive technologies typically thrive. Chapter 14, Innovation and Entrepreneurship, examines innovation, different types of innovation, and the best ways to bring more innovative activity into a firm. It examines the entrepreneurship process as another way to build innovative responsiveness and opportunity recognition into a firm, both in new venture settings and in large business organizations. Finally, it looks at the Web-enabled ways businesses are linking worldwide with people who are not a part of their organizations, yet are key players helping to innovate and create their businesses' future.

Strategic Control

Rapid change necessitates control that is at once loose and flexible yet also tight and focused. Chapter 13 examines four ways strategists create "steering" controls over a firm's overall direction to keep its long-term objectives in focus. Conversely, operating activities and periodic review seek to dissect performance so as to ensure efficient and effective use of company resources. Chapter 13 provides new treatment of approaches to do this including the latest on the Balanced Scorecard approach, Six Sigma, CCC21, continuous improvement and the evaluation of deviations in short-term performance.

OUR STRATEGIC ALLIANCE WITH *BUSINESSWEEK*

We have long felt *BusinessWeek* to be the unquestionable leader among business periodicals for its coverage of strategic issues in businesses, industries, and economies worldwide, and we are proud to include articles which illustrate relevant and compelling examples that resonate with students and instructors alike.

Personal surveys of collegiate faculty teaching strategic management confirmed our intuition: While there are many outstanding business magazines and new publications, none match the consistent quality found in *BusinessWeek* for the coverage of corporate strategies, case stories, and topics of interest to students and professors of strategic management. Through this partnership, we get unconditional access to *BusinessWeek* material for this book and the use of their cutting-edge stories and topical coverage. From our point of view, this is a unique four-way win-win; teachers, students, authors, and *BusinessWeek* all stand to gain in many ways. The most direct way you can see the impact of the *BusinessWeek* alliance is in three book features: discussion cases, Strategy in Action modules, and hundreds of examples woven into each chapter's narrative.

Strategy in Action Modules

Another pedagogical feature, Strategy in Action modules, has become standard in most strategy books. We have drawn on the work of *BusinessWeek* field correspondents worldwide to fill 100 new *BusinessWeek* Strategy in Action modules with short, hard-hitting current illustrations of key chapter topics. We are energized by the excitement, interest, and practical illustration value our students tell us they provide.

Chapter Discussion Cases

As professors of strategic management, we continually look for content or pedagogical developments and enhancements that make the strategy course more valuable. We have been concerned for some time about a need for short cases at the end of each text chapter. So each chapter in this book is followed by at least one short case from *BusinessWeek* to play a role in learning about strategic management by providing a springboard for a brief discussion of "real time" situations involving chapter topics, perhaps supplemented by

Web site and Internet-derived information. These short cases generate useful class discussions or serve as supplements and sources of variety to accompany the text material. They are designed for self-study use in the event they are not discussed in class.

OUR WEB SITE

A substantial Web site has been designed to aid your use of this book. It includes areas accessible only to instructors and areas specifically designed to assist students. The instructor section includes supplement files, which include detailed teaching notes and PowerPoint slides, which keep your work area less cluttered and let you quickly obtain information. Students are provided company and related business periodical (and other) Web site linkages to aid and expedite their research and preparation efforts. Practice quizzes are provided to help students prepare for tests on the text material and attempt to lower their anxiety in that regard. Access to *BusinessWeek.com* articles that update the chapter discussion cases and key illustration modules in the book are provided. We expect students will find the Web site useful and interesting. Please visit us at www.mhhe.com/pearce11e.

SUPPLEMENTS

Components of our teaching package include a revised, comprehensive instructor's manual, test bank, PowerPoint presentation, a large collection of videos designed to complement many of the concepts in the book, and a computerized test bank. These are all available to qualified adopters of the text. Professors can also use a simulation game as a possible package with this text: the Business Strategy Game (Thompson/Stappenbeck). The Business Strategy Game provides an exercise to help students understand how the functional pieces of a business fit together. Students will work with the numbers, explore options, and try to unite production, marketing, finance, and human resource decisions into a coherent strategy.

Acknowledgments

We have benefited from the help of many people in the evolution of this project over eleven editions. Students, adopters, colleagues, reviewers, and business contacts have provided hundreds of insightful comments, suggestions, and contributions that have progressively enhanced this book and its supplements. We are indebted to the researchers and practicing managers who have accelerated the development of the literature on strategic management.

Several reviewers provided feedback to us for the eleventh edition. We are grateful for their honest and compelling suggestions, which facilitated the revisions to this edition:

Mitch Ellison
Quincy University

Sally Fowler
Kogod School of Business, American University

Richard L. Jines
Oakland City University

Timothy S. Kiessling
Eastern Kentucky University

Michael D. Meeks
San Francisco State University

Michael D. Pfarrer
University of Maryland, College Park

Michael W. Pitts
Virginia Commonwealth University

Douglas E. Thomas
University of New Mexico

Marta Szabo White
Georgia State University

Scott Williams
Wright State University

Beth Woodard
Belmont University

The development of this book through eleven editions has benefited from the generous commitments of time, energy, and ideas from the following colleagues. The valuable ideas, recommendations, and support from these outstanding scholars, teachers, and practitioners have added quality to this book:

Mary Ackenhusen, *INSEAD*; A. J. Almaney, *DePaul University*; James Almeida, *Fairleigh Dickinson University*; B. Alpert, *San Francisco State University*; Alan Amason, *University of Georgia*; Sonny Aries, *University of Toledo*; Katherine A. Auer, *The Pennsylvania State University*; Henry Beam, *Western Michigan University*; Amy Vernberg Beekman, *University of Tampa*; Patricia Bilafer, *Bentley College*; Robert Earl Bolick, *Metropolitan State University*; Bill Boulton, *Auburn University*; Charles Boyd, *Southwest Missouri State University*; Thomas Boyle, *Seton Hill University*; Jeff Bracker, *University of Louisville*; Dorothy Brawley, *Kennesaw State College*; James W. Bronson, *Washington State University*; Eric Brown, *George Mason University*; Robert F. Bruner, *INSEAD*; William Burr, *University of Oregon*; Gene E. Burton, *California State University–Fresno*; Edgar T. Busch, *Western Kentucky University*; Charles M. Byles, *Virginia Commonwealth University*; Jim Callahan, *University of LaVerne*; James W. Camerius, *Northern Michigan University*; Sam D. Cappel, *Southeastern Louisiana University*; Richard Castaldi, *San Francisco State University*; Gary J. Castogiovanni, *Louisiana State University*; Jafor Chowdbury, *University of Scranton*; James J. Chrisman, *University of Calgary*; Neil Churchill, *INSEAD*; J. Carl Clamp, *University of South Carolina*; David R. Conley, *Louisiana State University at Alexandria*; Earl D. Cooper, *Florida Institute of Technology*; Louis Coraggio, *Troy State University*; Jeff Covin, *Indiana University*; John P. Cragin, *Oklahoma Baptist University*; Larry Cummings, *Northwestern University*; Peter Davis, *University of North Carolina-Charlotte*; William Davis, *Auburn University*; Julio DeCastro, *University of Colorado*; Kim DeDee, *University of Wisconsin*; Philippe Demigne, *INSEAD*; D. Keith Denton, *Southwest*

Missouri State University; F. Derakhshan, *California State University–San Bernardino*; Brook Dobni, *University of Saskatchewan*; Mark Dollinger, *Indiana University*; Jean–Christopher Donck, *INSEAD*; Lon Doty, *University of Phoenix/San Jose State University*; Max E. Douglas, *Indiana State University*; Yves Doz, *INSEAD*; Julie Driscoll, *Bentley College*; Derrick Dsouza, *University of North Texas*; Thomas J. Dudley, *Pepperdine University*; John Dunkelberg, *Wake Forest University*; Soumitra Dutta, *INSEAD*; Harold Dyck, *California State University*; Raed Elaydi, *University of North Carolina–Chapel Hill*; Norbert Esser, *Central Wesleyan College*; Forest D. Etheredge, *Aurora University*; Liam Fahey, *Babson College*; Mary Fandel, *Bentley College*; Mark Fiegener, *University of Washington–Tacoma*; Calvin D. Fowler, *Embry-Riddle Aeronautical University*; Mark Fox, *IUSB*; Debbie Francis, *Jacksonville State University*; Elizabeth Freeman, *Southern Methodist University*; Mahmound A. Gaballa, *Mansfield University*; Donna M. Gallo, *Boston College*; Diane Garsombke, *Brenau University*; Betsy Gatewood, *Wake Forest University*; Bertrand George, *INSEAD*; Michael Geringer, *Southern Methodist University*; Manton C. Gibbs, *Indiana University of Pennsylvania*; David Gilliss, *San Jose State University*; Nicholas A. Glaskowsky, Jr., *University of Miami*; Tom Goho, *Wake Forest University*; Jon Goodman, *University of Southern California*; Pradeep Gopalakrishna, *Hofstra University*; R. H. Gordon, *Hofstra University*; Barbara Gottfried, *Bentley College*; Peter Goulet, *University of Northern Iowa*; Walter E. Greene, *University of Texas–Pan American*; Sue Greenfeld, *California State University–San Bernardino*; David W. Grigsby, *Clemson University*; Daniel E. Hallock, *St. Edward's University*; Don Hambrick, *Pennsylvania State University*; Barry Hand, *Indiana State University*; Jean M. Hanebury, *Texas A&M University*; Karen Hare, *Bentley College*; Earl Harper, *Grand Valley State University*; William B. Hartley, *SUNY Fredonia*; Samuel Hazen, *Tarleton State University*; W. Harvey Hegarty, *Indiana University*; Edward A. Hegner, *California State University–Sacramento*; Marilyn M. Helms, *Dalton State College*; Lanny Herron, *University of Baltimore*; D. Higginbothan, *University of Missouri*; Roger Higgs, *Western Carolina University*; William H. Hinkle, *Johns Hopkins University*; Charles T. Hofer, *University of Georgia*; Alan N. Hoffman, *Bentley College*; Richard Hoffman, *Salisbury University*; Eileen Hogan, *Kutztown University*; Phyllis G. Holland, *Valdosta State University*; Gary L. Holman, *St. Martin's College*; Don Hopkins, *Temple University*; Cecil Horst, *Keller Graduate School of Management*; Mel Horwitch, *Theseus*; Henry F. House, *Auburn University–Montgomery*; William C. House, *University of Arkansas–Fayetteville*; Frank Hoy, *University of Texas–El Paso*; Warren Huckabay, *Sammamish, WA*; Eugene H. Hunt, *Virginia Commonwealth University*; Tammy G. Hunt, *University of North Carolina–Wilmington*; John W. Huonker, *University of Arizona*; Janice Jackson, *Western New England College*; Stephen R. Jenner, *California State University*; Shailendra Jha, *Wilfrid Laurier University–Ontario*; C. Boyd Johnson, *California State University–Fresno*; Troy Jones, *University of Central Florida*; Jon Kalinowski, *Mankato State University*; Al Kayloe, *Lake Erie College*; Michael J. Keefe, *Southwest Texas State University*; Kay Keels, *Brenau University*; James A. Kidney, *Southern Connecticut State University*; John D. King, *Embry-Riddle Aeronautical University*; Raymond M. Kinnunen, *Northeastern University*; John B. Knauff, *University of St. Thomas*; Rose Knotts, *University of North Texas*; Dan Kopp, *Southwest Missouri State University*; Michael Koshuta, *Valparaiso University*; Jeffrey A. Krug, *The University of Illinois*; Myroslaw Kyj, *Widener University*; Dick LaBarre, *Ferris State University*; Joseph Lampel, *City University–London*; Ryan Lancaster, *The University of Phoenix*; Sharon Ungar Lane, *Bentley College*; Patrick Langan, *Wartburg College*; Roland Larose, *Bentley College*; Anne T. Lawrence, *San Jose State University*; Joseph Leonard, *Miami University–Ohio*; Robert Letovsky, *Saint Michael's College*; Michael Levy, *INSEAD*; Benjamin Litt, *Lehigh University*; Frank S. Lockwood, *Western Carolina University*; John Logan, *University of South Carolina*; Sandra Logan, *Newberry College*; Jean M. Lundin, *Lake Superior State University*; Rodney H. Mabry,

Clemson University; Jennifer Mailey, *SUNY Empire State College*; Donald C. Malm, *University of Missouri–St. Louis*; Charles C. Manz, *University of Massachusetts*; John Maurer, *Wayne State University*; Denise Mazur, *Aquinas College*; Edward McClelland, *Roanoke College*; Bob McDonald, *Central Wesleyan College*; Patricia P. McDougall, *Indiana University*; S. Mehta, *San Jose State University*; Ralph Melaragno, *Pepperdine University*; Richard Merner, *University of Delaware*; Linda Merrill, *Bentley College*; Timothy Mescon, *Kennesaw State College*; Philip C. Micka, *Park College*; Bill J. Middlebrook, *Southwest Texas State University*; Robert Mockler, *St. John's University*; James F. Molly, Jr., *Northeastern University*; Cynthia Montgomery, *Harvard University*; W. Kent Moore, *Valdosta State University*; Jaideep Motwani, *Grand Valley State University*; Karen Mullen, *Bentley College*; Gary W. Muller, *Hofstra University*; Terry Muson, *Northern Montana College*; Daniel Muzyka, *INSEAD*; Stephanie Newell, *Eastern Michigan University*; Michael E. Nix, *Trinity College of Vermont*; Kenneth Olm, *University of Texas–Austin*; K. C. Oshaughnessy, *Western Michigan University*; Benjamin M. Oviatt, *Georgia State University*; Joseph Paolillo, *University of Mississippi*; Gerald Parker, *St. Louis University*; Paul J. Patinka, *University of Colorado*; James W. Pearce, *Western Carolina University*; Michael W. Pitts, *Virginia Commonwealth University*; Douglas Polley, *St. Cloud State University*; Carlos de Pommes, *Theseus*; Valerie J. Porciello, *Bentley College*; Mark S. Poulous, *St. Edward's University*; John B. Pratt, *Saint Joseph's College*; Oliver Ray Price, *West Coast University*; John Primus, *Golden Gate University*; Norris Rath, *Shepard College*; Paula Rechner, *California State University–Fresno*; Richard Reed, *Washington State University*; J. Bruce Regan, *University of St. Thomas*; H. Lee Remmers, *INSEAD*; F. A. Ricci, *Georgetown University*; Keith Robbins, *Winthrop University*; Gary Roberts, *Kennesaw State College*; Lloyd E. Roberts, *Mississippi College*; John K. Ross III, *Southwest Texas State University*; George C. Rubenson, *Salisbury State University*; Alison Rude, *Bentley College*; Les Rue, *Georgia State University*; Carol Rugg, *Bentley College*; J. A. Ruslyk, *Memphis State University*; Ronald J. Salazar, *Human Skills Management, LLC*; Bill Sandberg, *University of South Carolina*; Uri Savoray, *INSEAD*; Jack Scarborough, *Barry University*; Paul J. Schlachter, *Florida International University*; Greg Schultz, *Carroll College*; David Schweiger, *University of South Carolina*; John Seeger, *Bentley College*; Martin Shapiro, *Iona College*; Arthur Sharplin, *McNeese State University*; Frank M. Shipper, *Salisbury State University*; Rodney C. Shrader, *University of Illinois*; Lois Shufeldt, *Southwest Missouri State University*; Bonnie Silvieria, *Bentley College*; F. Bruce Simmons III, *The University of Akron*; Mark Simon, *Oakland University*; Michael Skipton, *Memorial University*; Fred Smith, *Western Illinois University*; Scott Snell, *Michigan State University*; Coral R. Snodgrass, *Canisius College*; Rudolph P. Snowadzky, *University of Maine*; Neil Snyder, *University of Virginia*; Melvin J. Stanford, *Mankato State University*; Romuald A. Stone, *DeVry University*; Warren S. Stone, *Virginia Commonwealth University*; Ram Subramanian, *Grand Valley State University*; Paul M. Swiercz, *George Washington University*; Robert L. Swinth, *Montana State University*; Chris Taubman, *INSEAD*; Russell Teasley, *Western Carolina University*; James Teboul, *INSEAD*; George H. Tompson, *University of Tampa*; Melanie Trevino, *University of Texas–ElPaso*; Howard Tu, *University of Memphis*; Craig Tunwall, *Empire State College*; Elaine M. Tweedy, *University of Scranton*; Arieh A. Ullmann, *Binghamton University*; P. Veglahn, *James Madison University*; George Vozikis, *University of Tulsa*; William Waddell, *California State University–Los Angeles*; Bill Warren, *College of William and Mary*; Kirby Warren, *Columbia University*; Steven J. Warren, *Rutgers University*; Michael White, *University of Tulsa*; Randy White, *Auburn University*; Sam E. White, *Portland State University*; Cleon Wiggins, *Park University*; Frank Winfrey, *Lyon College*; Joseph Wolfe, *Experiential Adventures*; Robley Wood, *Virginia Commonwealth University*; Diana Wong, *Eastern Michigan University*; Edware D. Writh, Jr., *Florida Institute of Technology*; John Young, *University of New Mexico*; S. David

Young, *INSEAD*; Jan Zahrly, *Old Dominion University*; and Alan Zeiber, *Portland State University*.

We are affiliated with two separate universities, both of which provide environments that deserve thanks. As the Villanova School of Business Endowed Chair at Villanova University, Jack is able to combine his scholarly and teaching activities with his coauthorship of this text. He is grateful to Villanova University, Dean James Danko, and his colleagues for the support and encouragement they provide.

Richard appreciates the support provided within the Moore School of Business by Mr. Dean Kress. Mr. Kress provides multifaceted assistance on projects, classes, and research that leverages the scope of what can be accomplished each year. Moore School colleagues in the management department along with Dean Joel Smith and Program Director Brian Klass provide encouragement while staff members Cheryl Fowler, Susie Gorsage, and Carol Lucas provide logistical support for which Richard is grateful.

We want to thank Dr. Ram Subramanian, Montclair State University, for his outstanding contributions in the instructor's manual and ancillaries for this eleventh edition. His dedication and attention to detail make this a better book. Likewise, we are most grateful to Dr. Amit Shah, Frostburg State University, for his excellent earlier contributions to this project.

Leaders at McGraw-Hill/Irwin deserve our utmost thanks and appreciation. Gerald Saykes, John Black, John Biernat, and Craig Beytein contributed to our early success. The editorial leadership of Doug Hughes and Michael Ablassmeir helps to assure that it will continue in this eleventh edition. Editorial coordinator Kelly Pekelder and project manager Bruce Gin helped us to produce a much improved book. The McGraw-Hill/Irwin field organization deserves particular recognition and thanks for the amazing sales record of this text.

We also want to thank *BusinessWeek,* which is proving to be an excellent strategic partner.

We hope that you will find our book and ancillaries all that you expect. We welcome your ideas and recommendations about our material, and we wish you the utmost success in teaching and studying strategic management.

Dr. John A. Pearce II
Villanova School of Business
Villanova University
Villanova, PA 19085–1678

Dr. Richard Robinson
Moore School of Business
University of South Carolina
Columbia, SC 29208

Brief Contents

Table of Contents

Part One

Overview of Strategic Management

The first chapter of this book introduces strategic management, the set of decisions and actions that result in the design and activation of strategies to achieve the objectives of an organization. The chapter provides an overview of the nature, benefits, and terminology of and the need for strategic management. Subsequent chapters provide greater detail.

The first major section of Chapter 1, "The Nature and Value of Strategic Management," emphasizes the practical value and benefits of strategic management for a firm. It also distinguishes between a firm's strategic decisions and its other planning tasks.

The section stresses the key point that strategic management activities are undertaken at three levels: corporate, business, and functional. The distinctive characteristics of strategic decision making at each of these levels affect the impact of activities at these levels on company operations. Other topics dealt with in this section are the value of formality in strategic management and the alignment of strategy makers in strategy formulation and implementation. The section concludes with a review of the planning research on business, which demonstrates that the use of strategic management processes yields financial and behavioral benefits that justify their costs.

The second major section of Chapter 1 presents a model of the strategic management process. The model, which will serve as an outline for the remainder of the text, describes approaches currently used by strategic planners. Its individual components are carefully defined and explained, as is the process for integrating them into the strategic management process. The section ends with a discussion of the model's practical limitations and the advisability of tailoring the recommendations made to actual business situations.

Chapter **One**

Strategic Management

After reading and studying this chapter, you should be able to

1. Explain the concept of strategic management.

2. Describe how strategic decisions differ from other decisions that managers make.

3. Name the benefits and risks of a participative approach to strategic decision making.

4. Understand the types of strategic decisions for which managers at different levels of the company are responsible.

5. Describe a comprehensive model of strategic decision making.

6. Appreciate the importance of strategic management as a process.

7. Give examples of strategic decisions that companies have recently made.

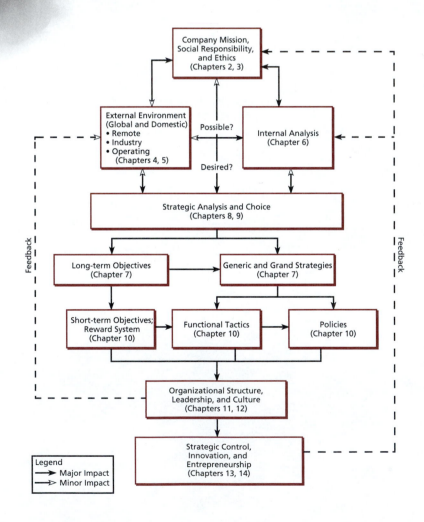

THE NATURE AND VALUE OF STRATEGIC MANAGEMENT

Managing activities internal to the firm is only part of the modern executive's responsibilities. The modern executive also must respond to the challenges posed by the firm's immediate and remote external environments. The immediate external environment includes competitors, suppliers, increasingly scarce resources, government agencies and their ever more numerous regulations, and customers whose preferences often shift inexplicably. The remote external environment comprises economic and social conditions, political priorities, and technological developments, all of which must be anticipated, monitored, assessed, and incorporated into the executive's decision making. However, the executive often is compelled to subordinate the demands of the firm's internal activities and external environment to the multiple and often inconsistent requirements of its stakeholders: owners, top managers, employees, communities, customers, and country. To deal effectively with everything that affects the growth and profitability of a firm, executives employ management processes that they feel will position it optimally in its competitive environment by maximizing the anticipation of environmental changes and of unexpected internal and competitive demands.

To earn profits, firms need to perfect processes that respond to increases in the size and number of competing firms; to the expanded role of government as a buyer, seller, regulator, and competitor in the free enterprise system; and to greater business involvement in international trade. Perhaps the most significant improvement in these management processes came when "long-range planning," "planning, programming, budgeting," and "business policy" were blended with increased emphasis on environmental forecasting and external considerations in formulating and implementing plans. This all-encompassing approach is known as strategic management.

strategic management
The set of decisions and actions that result in the formulation and implementation of plans designed to achieve a company's objectives.

Strategic management is defined as the set of decisions and actions that result in the formulation and implementation of plans designed to achieve a company's objectives. It comprises nine critical tasks:

1. Formulate the company's mission, including broad statements about its purpose, philosophy, and goals.
2. Conduct an analysis that reflects the company's internal conditions and capabilities.
3. Assess the company's external environment, including both the competitive and the general contextual factors.
4. Analyze the company's options by matching its resources with the external environment.
5. Identify the most desirable options by evaluating each option in light of the company's mission.
6. Select a set of long-term objectives and grand strategies that will achieve the most desirable options.
7. Develop annual objectives and short-term strategies that are compatible with the selected set of long-term objectives and grand strategies.
8. Implement the strategic choices by means of budgeted resource allocations in which the matching of tasks, people, structures, technologies, and reward systems is emphasized.
9. Evaluate the success of the strategic process as an input for future decision making.

strategy
Large-scale, future-oriented plans for interacting with the competitive environment to achieve company objectives.

As these nine tasks indicate, strategic management involves the planning, directing, organizing, and controlling of a company's strategy-related decisions and actions. By **strategy,** managers mean their large-scale, future-oriented plans for interacting with the competitive environment to achieve company objectives. A strategy is a company's game plan.

Although that plan does not precisely detail all future deployments (of people, finances, and material), it does provide a framework for managerial decisions. A strategy reflects a company's awareness of how, when, and where it should compete; against whom it should compete; and for what purposes it should compete.

Dimensions of Strategic Decisions

What decisions facing a business are strategic and therefore deserve strategic management attention? Typically, strategic issues have the following dimensions.

Strategic Issues Require Top-Management Decisions   Because strategic decisions overarch several areas of a firm's operations, they require top-management involvement. Usually only top management has the perspective needed to understand the broad implications of such decisions and the power to authorize the necessary resource allocations. As top manager of Volvo GM Heavy Truck Corporation, Karl-Erling Trogen, president, wanted to push the company closer to the customer by overarching operations with service and customer relations empowering the workforce closest to the customer with greater knowledge and authority. This strategy called for a major commitment to the parts and service end of the business where customer relations was first priority. Trogen's philosophy was to so empower the workforce that more operating questions were handled on the line where workers worked directly with customers. He believed that the corporate headquarters should be more focused on strategic issues, such as engineering, production, quality, and marketing.

Strategic Issues Require Large Amounts of the Firm's Resources   Strategic decisions involve substantial allocations of people, physical assets, or moneys that either must be redirected from internal sources or secured from outside the firm. They also commit the firm to actions over an extended period. For these reasons, they require substantial resources. Whirlpool Corporation's "Quality Express" product delivery program exemplified a strategy that required a strong financial and personnel commitment from the company. The plan was to deliver products to customers when, where, and how they wanted them. This proprietary service uses contract logistics strategy to deliver Whirlpool, Kitchen Aid, Roper, and Estate brand appliances to 90 percent of the company's dealer and builder customers within 24 hours and to the other 10 percent within 48 hours. In highly competitive service-oriented businesses, achieving and maintaining customer satisfaction frequently involve a commitment from every facet of the organization.

Strategic Issues Often Affect the Firm's Long-Term Prosperity   Strategic decisions ostensibly commit the firm for a long time, typically five years; however, the impact of such decisions often lasts much longer. Once a firm has committed itself to a particular strategy, its image and competitive advantages usually are tied to that strategy. Firms become known in certain markets, for certain products, with certain technologies. They would jeopardize their previous gains if they shifted from these markets, products, or technologies by adopting a radically different strategy. Thus, strategic decisions have enduring effects on firms—for better or worse. For example, Commerce One created an alliance with SAP in 1999 to improve its position in the e-marketplace for business to business (B2B) sales. After taking three years to ready its e-portals, Commerce One and SAP were ready to take on the market in 2002. Unfortunately, the market changed. The "foolproof strategy" got to the market too late and the alliance failed.

For years, Toyota had a successful strategy of marketing its sedans in Japan. With this strategy came an image, a car for an older customer, and a competitive advantage, a traditional base for Toyota. The strategy was effective, but as its customer base grew older its strategy remained unchanged. A younger customer market saw the image as unattractive and began to seek out other manufacturers. Toyota's strategic task in foreign markets is to formulate and implement a strategy that will reignite interest in its image.

Strategic Issues Are Future Oriented Strategic decisions are based on what managers forecast, rather than on what they know. In such decisions, emphasis is placed on the development of projections that will enable the firm to select the most promising strategic options. In the turbulent and competitive free enterprise environment, a firm will succeed only if it takes a proactive (anticipatory) stance toward change.

Strategic Issues Usually Have Multifunctional or Multibusiness Consequences Strategic decisions have complex implications for most areas of the firm. Decisions about such matters as customer mix, competitive emphasis, or organizational structure necessarily involve a number of the firm's strategic business units (SBUs), divisions, or program units. All of these areas will be affected by allocations or reallocations of responsibilities and resources that result from these decisions.

Strategic Issues Require Considering the Firm's External Environment All business firms exist in an open system. They affect and are affected by external conditions that are largely beyond their control. Therefore, to successfully position a firm in competitive situations, its strategic managers must look beyond its operations. They must consider what relevant others (e.g., competitors, customers, suppliers, creditors, government, and labor) are likely to do.

Three Levels of Strategy

The decision-making hierarchy of a firm typically contains three levels. At the top of this hierarchy is the corporate level, composed principally of a board of directors and the chief executive and administrative officers. They are responsible for the firm's financial performance and for the achievement of nonfinancial goals, such as enhancing the firm's image and fulfilling its social responsibilities. To a large extent, attitudes at the corporate level reflect the concerns of stockholders and society at large. In a multibusiness firm, corporate-level executives determine the businesses in which the firm should be involved. They also set objectives and formulate strategies that span the activities and functional areas of these businesses. Corporate-level strategic managers attempt to exploit their firm's distinctive competencies by adopting a portfolio approach to the management of its businesses and by developing long-term plans, typically for a three- to five-year period. A key corporate strategy of Airborne Express's operations involved direct sale to high-volume corporate accounts and developing an expansive network in the international arena. Instead of setting up operations overseas, Airborne's long-term strategy was to form direct associations with national companies within foreign countries to expand and diversify their operations.

Another example of the portfolio approach involved a plan by state-owned Saudi Arabian Oil to spend $1.4 billion to build and operate an oil refinery in Korea with its partner, Ssangyong. To implement their program, the Saudis embarked on a new "cut-out-the-middleman" strategy to reduce the role of international oil companies in the processing and selling of Saudi crude oil.

In the middle of the decision-making hierarchy is the business level, composed principally of business and corporate managers. These managers must translate the statements of direction and intent generated at the corporate level into concrete objectives and strategies for individual business divisions, or SBUs. In essence, business-level strategic managers determine how the firm will compete in the selected product-market arena. They strive to identify and secure the most promising market segment within that arena. This segment is the piece of the total market that the firm can claim and defend because of its competitive advantages.

At the bottom of the decision-making hierarchy is the functional level, composed principally of managers of product, geographic, and functional areas. They develop annual objectives and short-term strategies in such areas as production, operations, research and development, finance and accounting, marketing, and human relations. However, their

EXHIBIT 1.1
Alternative Strategic Management Structures

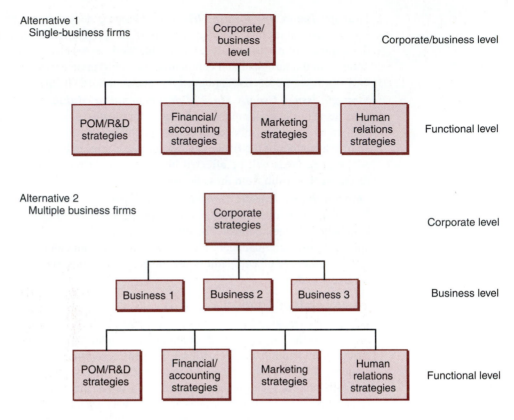

principal responsibility is to implement or execute the firm's strategic plans. Whereas corporate- and business-level managers center their attention on "doing the right things," managers at the functional level center their attention on "doing things right." Thus, they address such issues as the efficiency and effectiveness of production and marketing systems, the quality of customer service, and the success of particular products and services in increasing the firm's market shares.

Exhibit 1.1 depicts the three levels of strategic management as structured in practice. In alternative 1, the firm is engaged in only one business and the corporate- and business-level responsibilities are concentrated in a single group of directors, officers, and managers. This is the organizational format of most small businesses.

Alternative 2, the classical corporate structure, comprises three fully operative levels: the corporate level, the business level, and the functional level. The approach taken throughout this text assumes the use of alternative 2. Moreover, whenever appropriate, topics are covered from the perspective of each level of strategic management. In this way, the text presents a comprehensive discussion of the strategic management process.

Characteristics of Strategic Management Decisions

The characteristics of strategic management decisions vary with the level of strategic activity considered. As shown in Exhibit 1.2, decisions at the corporate level tend to be more value oriented, more conceptual, and less concrete than decisions at the business or functional level. For example, at Alcoa, the world's largest aluminum maker, chairman Paul O'Neill made Alcoa one of the nation's most centralized organizations by imposing a dramatic management reorganization that wiped out two layers of management. He found that this effort not only reduced costs but also enabled him to be closer to the front-line operations managers. Corporate-level decisions are often characterized by greater risk,

EXHIBIT 1.2 **Hierarchy of Objectives and Strategies**

Ends (What is to be achieved?)	Means (How is it to be achieved?)	Strategic Decision Makers			
		Board of Directors	Corporate Managers	Business Managers	Functional Managers
Mission, including goals and philosophy		✓✓	✓✓	✓	
Long-term objectives	Grand strategy	✓	✓✓	✓✓	
Annual objectives	Short-term strategies and policies		✓	✓✓	✓✓

Note: ✓✓ indicate a principal responsibility; ✓ indicates a secondary responsibility.

cost, and profit potential; greater need for flexibility; and longer time horizons. Such decisions include the choice of businesses, dividend policies, sources of long-term financing, and priorities for growth.

Functional-level decisions implement the overall strategy formulated at the corporate and business levels. They involve action-oriented operational issues and are relatively short range and low risk. Functional-level decisions incur only modest costs, because they depend on available resources. They usually are adaptable to ongoing activities and, therefore, can be implemented with minimal cooperation. For example, the corporate headquarters of Sears, Roebuck & Company spent $60 million to automate 6,900 clerical jobs by installing 28,000 computerized cash registers at its 868 stores in the United States. Although this move eliminated many functional-level jobs, top management believed that reducing annual operating expenses by at least $50 million was crucial to competitive survival.

Because functional-level decisions are relatively concrete and quantifiable, they receive critical attention and analysis even though their comparative profit potential is low. Common functional-level decisions include decisions on generic versus brandname labeling, basic versus applied research and development (R&D), high versus low inventory levels, general-purpose versus specific-purpose production equipment, and close versus loose supervision.

Business-level decisions help bridge decisions at the corporate and functional levels. Such decisions are less costly, risky, and potentially profitable than corporate-level decisions, but they are more costly, risky, and potentially profitable than functional-level decisions. Common business-level decisions include decisions on plant location, marketing segmentation and geographic coverage, and distribution channels.

Formality in Strategic Management

formality
The degree to which participation, responsibility, authority, and discretion in decision making are specified in strategic management.

The formality of strategic management systems varies widely among companies. **Formality** refers to the degree to which participants, responsibilities, authority, and discretion in decision making are specified. It is an important consideration in the study of strategic management, because greater formality is usually positively correlated with the cost, comprehensiveness, accuracy, and success of planning.

A number of forces determine how much formality is needed in strategic management. The size of the organization, its predominant management styles, the complexity of its environment, its production process, its problems, and the purpose of its planning system all play a part in determining the appropriate degree of formality.

In particular, formality is associated with the size of the firm and with its stage of development. Some firms, especially smaller ones, follow an **entrepreneurial mode.** They are basically under the control of a single individual, and they produce a limited number of

entrepreneurial mode
The informal, intuitive, and limited approach to strategic management associated with owner-managers of smaller firms.

planning mode
The strategic formality associated with large firms that operate under a comprehensive, formal planning system.

adaptive mode
The strategic formality associated with medium-sized firms that emphasize the incremental modification of existing competitive approaches.

products or services. In such firms, strategic evaluation is informal, intuitive, and limited. Very large firms, on the other hand, make strategic evaluation part of a comprehensive, formal planning system, an approach that Henry Mintzberg called the **planning mode.** Mintzberg also identified a third mode (the **adaptive mode**), which he associated with medium-sized firms in relatively stable environments.[1] For firms that follow the adaptive mode, the identification and evaluation of alternative strategies are closely related to existing strategy. It is not unusual to find different modes within the same organization. For example, ExxonMobil might follow an entrepreneurial mode in developing and evaluating the strategy of its solar subsidiary but follow a planning mode in the rest of the company.

The Strategy Makers

The ideal strategic management team includes decision makers from all three company levels (the corporate, business, and functional)—for example, the chief executive officer (CEO), the product managers, and the heads of functional areas. In addition, the team obtains input from company planning staffs, when they exist, and from lower-level managers and supervisors. The latter provide data for strategic decision making and then implement strategies.

Because strategic decisions have a tremendous impact on a company and require large commitments of company resources, top managers must give final approval for strategic action. Exhibit 1.2 aligns levels of strategic decision makers with the kinds of objectives and strategies for which they are typically responsible.

Planning departments, often headed by a corporate vice president for planning, are common in large corporations. Medium-sized firms often employ at least one full-time staff member to spearhead strategic data-collection efforts. Even in small firms or less progressive larger firms, strategic planning often is spearheaded by an officer or by a group of officers designated as a planning committee.

Precisely what are managers' responsibilities in the strategic planning process at the corporate and business levels? Top management shoulders broad responsibility for all the major elements of strategic planning and management. They develop the major portions of the strategic plan and reviews, and they evaluate and counsel on all other portions. General managers at the business level typically have principal responsibilities for developing environmental analysis and forecasting, establishing business objectives, and developing business plans prepared by staff groups.

An executive who understands and excels at the strategic management process is Richard Lenny, CEO of Hershey. You can read about the challenges he faced, the strategies he led, and the successes he achieved in Exhibit 1.3, Top Strategist.

A firm's president or CEO characteristically plays a dominant role in the strategic planning process. In many ways, this situation is desirable. The CEO's principal duty often is defined as giving long-term direction to the firm, and the CEO is ultimately responsible for the firm's success and, therefore, for the success of its strategy. In addition, CEOs are typically strong-willed, company-oriented individuals.

However, when the dominance of the CEO approaches autocracy, the effectiveness of the firm's strategic planning and management processes is likely to be diminished. For this reason, establishing a strategic management system implies that the CEO will allow managers at all levels to participate in the strategic posture of the company.

In implementing a company's strategy, the CEO must have an appreciation for the power and responsibility of the board, while retaining the power to lead the company with the guidance of informed directors. The interaction between the CEO and board is key to

[1] H. Mintzberg, "Strategy Making in Three Modes," *California Management Review* 16, no. 2 (1973), pp. 44–53.

Top Strategist
Richard Lenny, CEO of Hershey

**Exhibit
1.3**

An ambitious restructuring plan and a move into new-product lines such as premium chocolate and snacks for nutrition-conscious consumers have Hershey predicting a sweet future. CEO Richard Lenny has also bolstered sales of higher-margin, single-serve snacks aimed at on-the-go consumers and is making changes in distribution by expanding the brand's presence beyond grocery stores and mass merchant chains to home improvement and other specialty stores. Overseas, Hershey faces strong competition from Mars and Cadbury Schweppes, but a venture with Korea's Lotte Confectionery will help it make inroads in China and other Asian markets. To increase its competitiveness, Hershey plans to cut its workforce by 10.7 percent or 1,500, and shift more of its production overseas. These moves should bring savings of $170 million to $190 million by 2010.

Source: Reprinted with special permission from "The *BusinessWeek* 50—The Best Performers," *BusinessWeek,* March 26, 2007. Copyright © 2007 The McGraw-Hill Companies.

any corporation's strategy. Empowerment of nonmanagerial employees has been a recent trend across major management teams. For example, in 2003, IBM replaced its 92-year-old executive board structure with three newly created management teams: strategy, operations, and technology. Each team combined top executives, managers, and engineers going down six levels in some cases. This new team structure was responsible for guiding the creation of IBM's strategy and for helping to implement the strategies once they were authorized.

Benefits of Strategic Management

Using the strategic management approach, managers at all levels of the firm interact in planning and implementing. As a result, the behavioral consequences of strategic management are similar to those of participative decision making. Therefore, an accurate assessment of the impact of strategy formulation on organizational performance requires not only financial evaluation criteria but also nonfinancial evaluation criteria—measures of behavior-based effects. In fact, promoting positive behavioral consequences also enables the firm to achieve its financial goals. However, regardless of the profitability of strategic plans, several behavioral effects of strategic management improve the firm's welfare:

1. Strategy formulation activities enhance the firm's ability to prevent problems. Managers who encourage subordinates' attention to planning are aided in their monitoring and forecasting responsibilities by subordinates who are aware of the needs of strategic planning.

2. Group-based strategic decisions are likely to be drawn from the best available alternatives. The strategic management process results in better decisions because group interaction generates a greater variety of strategies and because forecasts based on the specialized perspectives of group members improve the screening of options.

3. The involvement of employees in strategy formulation improves their understanding of the productivity-reward relationship in every strategic plan and, thus, heightens their motivation.

4. Gaps and overlaps in activities among individuals and groups are reduced as participation in strategy formulation clarifies differences in roles.

5. Resistance to change is reduced. Though the participants in strategy formulation may be no more pleased with their own decisions than they would be with authoritarian decisions, their greater awareness of the parameters that limit the available options makes them more likely to accept those decisions.

Risks of Strategic Management

Managers must be trained to guard against three types of unintended negative consequences of involvement in strategy formulation.

First, the time that managers spend on the strategic management process may have a negative impact on operational responsibilities. Managers must be trained to minimize that impact by scheduling their duties to allow the necessary time for strategic activities.

Second, if the formulators of strategy are not intimately involved in its implementation, they may shirk their individual responsibility for the decisions reached. Thus, strategic managers must be trained to limit their promises to performance that the decision makers and their subordinates can deliver.

Third, strategic managers must be trained to anticipate and respond to the disappointment of participating subordinates over unattained expectations. Subordinates may expect their involvement in even minor phases of total strategy formulation to result in both acceptance of their proposals and an increase in their rewards, or they may expect a solicitation of their input on selected issues to extend to other areas of decision making.

Sensitizing managers to these possible negative consequences and preparing them with effective means of minimizing such consequences will greatly enhance the potential of strategic planning.

THE STRATEGIC MANAGEMENT PROCESS

Businesses vary in the processes they use to formulate and direct their strategic management activities. Sophisticated planners, such as General Electric, Procter & Gamble, and IBM, have developed more detailed processes than less formal planners of similar size. Small businesses that rely on the strategy formulation skills and limited time of an entrepreneur typically exhibit more basic planning concerns than those of larger firms in their industries. Understandably, firms with multiple products, markets, or technologies tend to use more complex strategic management systems. However, despite differences in detail and the degree of formalization, the basic components of the models used to analyze strategic management operations are very similar.

Because of the similarity among the general models of the strategic management process, it is possible to develop an eclectic model representative of the foremost thought in the strategic management area. This model is shown in Exhibit 1.4. It serves three major functions: (1) It depicts the sequence and the relationships of the major components of the strategic management process. (2) It is the outline for this book. This chapter provides a general overview of the strategic management process, and the major components of the model will be the principal theme of subsequent chapters. Notice that the chapters of the text that discuss each of the strategic management process components are shown in each block. (3) The model offers one approach for analyzing the case studies in this text and thus helps the analyst develop strategy formulation skills.

Components of the Strategic Management Model

This section will define and briefly describe the key components of the strategic management model. Each of these components will receive much greater attention in a later chapter. The intention here is simply to introduce them.

EXHIBIT 1.4
Strategic
Management Model

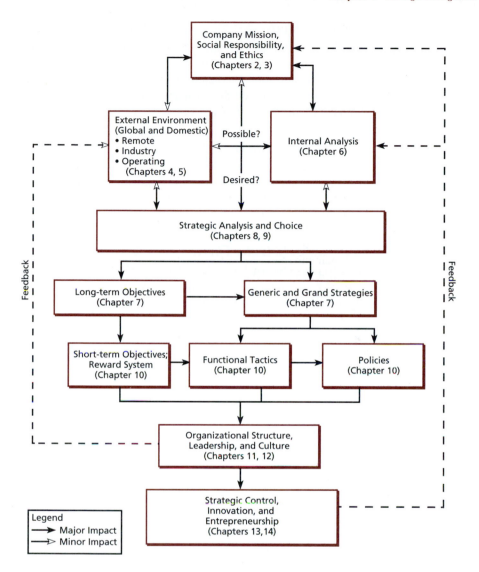

Company Mission

company mission
The unique purpose that sets a company apart from others of its type and identifies the scope of its operations.

The mission of a company is the unique purpose that sets it apart from other companies of its type and identifies the scope of its operations. In short, the **company mission** describes the company's product, market, and technological areas of emphasis in a way that reflects the values and priorities of the strategic decision makers. For example, Lee Hun-Hee, the new chairman of the Samsung Group, revamped the company mission by stamping his own brand of management on Samsung. Immediately, Samsung separated Chonju Paper Manufacturing and Shinsegae Department Store from other operations. This corporate act of downscaling reflected a revised management philosophy that favored specialization, thereby changing the direction and scope of the organization.

Social responsibility is a critical consideration for a company's strategic decision makers since the mission statement must express how the company intends to contribute to the societies that sustain it. A firm needs to set social responsibility aspirations for itself, just as it does in other areas of corporate performance.

Internal Analysis

The company analyzes the quantity and quality of the company's financial, human, and physical resources. It also assesses the strengths and weaknesses of the company's management and organizational structure. Finally, it contrasts the company's past successes and traditional concerns with the company's current capabilities in an attempt to identify the company's future capabilities.

External Environment

A firm's external environment consists of all the conditions and forces that affect its strategic options and define its competitive situation. The strategic management model shows the external environment as three interactive segments: the remote, industry, and operating environments.

Strategic Analysis and Choice

Simultaneous assessment of the external environment and the company profile enables a firm to identify a range of possibly attractive interactive opportunities. These opportunities are *possible* avenues for investment. However, they must be screened through the criterion of the company mission to generate a set of possible and *desired* opportunities. This screening process results in the selection of options from which a *strategic choice* is made. The process is meant to provide the combination of long-term objectives and generic and grand strategies that optimally position the firm in its external environment to achieve the company mission.

Strategic analysis and choice in single or dominant product/service businesses center around identifying strategies that are most effective at building sustainable competitive advantage based on key value chain activities and capabilities—core competencies of the firm. Multibusiness companies find their managers focused on the question of which combination of businesses maximizes shareholder value as the guiding theme during their strategic analysis and choice.

Long-Term Objectives

long-term objectives
The results that an organization seeks to achieve over a multiyear period.

The results that an organization seeks over a multiyear period are its **long-term objectives.** Such objectives typically involve some or all of the following areas: profitability, return on investment, competitive position, technological leadership, productivity, employee relations, public responsibility, and employee development.

Generic and Grand Strategies

generic strategies
Fundamental philosophical options for the design of strategies.

grand strategies
The means by which objectives are achieved.

Many businesses explicitly and all implicitly adopt one or more **generic strategies** characterizing their competitive orientation in the marketplace. Low cost, differentiation, or focus strategies define the three fundamental options. Enlightened managers seek to create ways their firm possesses both low cost and differentiation competitive advantages as part of their overall generic strategy. They usually combine these capabilities with a comprehensive, general plan of major actions through which their firm intends to achieve its long-term objectives in a dynamic environment. Called the **grand strategy,** this statement of means indicates how the objectives are to be achieved. Although every grand strategy is, in fact, a unique package of long-term strategies, 15 basic approaches can be identified: concentration, market development, product development, innovation, horizontal integration, vertical integration, joint venture, strategic alliances, consortia, concentric diversification, conglomerate diversification, turnaround, divestiture, bankruptcy, and liquidation.

Each of these grand strategies will be covered in detail in Chapter 7.

Short-Term Objectives

**short-term
objectives**
Desired results that
provide specific
guidance for action
during a period of one
year or less.

Short-term objectives are the desired results that a company seeks over a period of one year or less. They are logically consistent with the firm's long-term objectives. Companies typically have many **short-term objectives** to provide guidance for their functional and operational activities. Thus, there are short-term marketing activity, raw material usage, employee turnover, and sales objectives, to name just four.

Action Plans

Action plans translate generic and grand strategies into "action" by incorporating four elements. First, they identify specific actions to be undertaken in the next year or less as part of the business's effort to build competitive advantage. Second, they establish a clear time frame for completion of each action. Third, action plans create accountability by identifying who is responsible for each "action" in the plan. Fourth, each "action" in a plan has one or more specific, immediate objectives that identify outcomes that the action should generate.

Functional Tactics

tactics
Specific actions that
need to be undertaken
to achieve short-term
objectives, usually by
functional areas.

Within the general framework created by the business's generic and grand strategies, each business function needs to undertake activities that help build a sustainable competitive advantage. These short-term, limited-scope plans are called **tactics**. A radio ad campaign, an inventory reduction, and an introductory loan rate are examples of tactics. Managers in each business function develop tactics that delineate the functional activities undertaken in their part of the business and usually include them as a core part of their action plan. **Functional tactics** are detailed statements of the "means" or activities that will be used to achieve short-term objectives and establish competitive advantage.

functional tactics
Short-term, narrow
scoped plans that detail
the "means" or activities
that a company will use
to achieve short-term
objectives.

Policies That Empower Action

policies
Predetermined decisions
that substitute for
managerial discretion
in repetitive decision
making.

Speed is a critical necessity for success in today's competitive, global marketplace. One way to enhance speed and responsiveness is to force/allow decisions to be made whenever possible at the lowest level in organizations. **Policies** are broad, precedent-setting decisions that guide or substitute for repetitive or time-sensitive managerial decision making. Creating policies that guide and "preauthorize" the thinking, decisions, and actions of operating managers and their subordinates in implementing the business's strategy is essential for establishing and controlling the ongoing operating process of the firm in a manner consistent with the firm's strategic objectives. Policies often increase managerial effectiveness by standardizing routine decisions and empowering or expanding the discretion of managers and subordinates in implementing business strategies.

The following are examples of the nature and diversity of company policies:

A requirement that managers have purchase requests for items costing more than $5,000 cosigned by the controller.

The minimum equity position required for all new McDonald's franchises.

The standard formula used to calculate return on investment for the 6 strategic business units of General Electric.

A decision that Sears service and repair employees have the right to waive repair charges to appliance customers they feel have been poorly served by their Sears appliance.

Restructuring, Reengineering, and Refocusing the Organization

Until this point in the strategic management process, managers have maintained a decidedly market-oriented focus as they formulate strategies and begin implementation through action plans and functional tactics. Now the process takes an internal focus—getting the work of the business done efficiently and effectively so as to make the strategy successful. What is the best way to organize ourselves to accomplish the mission? Where should leadership come from? What values should guide our daily activities—what should the organization and its people be like? How can we shape rewards to encourage appropriate action? The intense competition in the global marketplace has made this traditionally "internally focused" set of questions—how the activities within their business are conducted—recast themselves with unprecedented attentiveness to the marketplace. *Downsizing, restructuring,* and *reengineering* are terms that reflect the critical stage in strategy implementation wherein managers attempt to recast their organization. The company's structure, leadership, culture, and reward systems may all be changed to ensure cost competitiveness and quality demanded by unique requirements of its strategies.

The elements of the strategic management process are evident in the recent activities at Ford Motor Company. In 2006, Ford undertook to create a strategy to lower costs, increase efficiency, improve designs, and increase brand appeal. These improvements were needed to keep cash flows up to cover rising pension costs. For Ford to accomplish this new strategy it had to improve operations. New executives were brought in to lead product development and financial controls. To break down the bureaucratic boundaries, a committee was created that included employees from the major functional areas, and it was given the assignment to reduce the time needed to develop a new-concept vehicle.

Strategic Control and Continuous Improvement

strategic control
Tracking a strategy as it is being implemented, detecting problems or changes in its underlying premises, and making necessary adjustments.

Strategic control is concerned with tracking a strategy as it is being implemented, detecting problems or changes in its underlying premises, and making necessary adjustments. In contrast to postaction control, strategic control seeks to guide action on behalf of the generic and grand strategies as they are taking place and when the end results are still several years away. The rapid, accelerating change of the global marketplace of the last 10 years has made continuous improvement another aspect of strategic control in many organizations. **Continuous improvement** provides a way for managers to provide a form of strategic control that allows their organization to respond more proactively and timely to rapid developments in hundreds of areas that influence a business's success.

continuous improvement
A form of strategic control in which managers are encouraged to be proactive in improving all operations of the firm.

In 2003, Yahoo!'s strategy was to move into the broadband and Internet search markets. However, even in its early implementation stages the strategy required revisions. Yahoo! had formed an alliance with SBC to provide the broadband service, but SBC had such limited capabilities that Yahoo! had to find new ways to reach users. Yahoo! also needed to continuously improve its new Internet search market, given competitors' upgrades and rapidly rising customer expectations. Additionally, for Yahoo! to increase its market share, it needed to continually improve its branding, rather than rely largely on its technological capabilities.

Strategic Management as a Process

process
The flow of information through interrelated stages of analysis toward the achievement of an aim.

A **process** is the flow of information through interrelated stages of analysis toward the achievement of an aim. Thus, the strategic management model in Exhibit 1.4 depicts a process. In the strategic management process, the flow of information involves historical, current, and forecast data on the operations and environment of the business. Managers evaluate these data in light of the values and priorities of influential individuals and groups—often called **stakeholders**—that are vitally interested in the actions of the business. The interrelated stages of the process are the 11 components discussed in the previous section. Finally, the aim of the process is the formulation and implementation of strategies that work, achieving the company's long-term mission and near-term objectives.

stakeholders
Influential people who are vitally interested in the actions of the business.

Viewing strategic management as a process has several important implications. First, a change in any component will affect several or all of the other components. Most of the arrows in the model point two ways, suggesting that the flow of information usually is reciprocal. For example, forces in the external environment may influence the nature of a company's mission, and the company may in turn affect the external environment and heighten competition in its realm of operation. A specific example is a power company that is persuaded, in part by governmental incentives, to include a commitment to the development of energy alternatives in its mission statement. The company then might promise to extend its research and development (R&D) efforts in the area of coal liquefaction. The external environment has affected the company's mission, and the revised mission signals a competitive condition in the environment.

A second implication of viewing strategic management as a process is that strategy formulation and implementation are sequential. The process begins with development or reevaluation of the company mission. This step is associated with, but essentially followed by, development of a company profile and assessment of the external environment. Then follow, in order, strategic choice, definition of long-term objectives, design of the grand strategy, definition of short-term objectives, design of operating strategies, institutionalization of the strategy, and review and evaluation.

The apparent rigidity of the process, however, must be qualified.

First, a firm's strategic posture may have to be reevaluated in response to changes in any of the principal factors that determine or affect its performance. Entry by a major new competitor, the death of a prominent board member, replacement of the chief executive officer, and a downturn in market responsiveness are among the thousands of changes that can prompt reassessment of a firm's strategic plan. However, no matter where the need for a reassessment originates, the strategic management process begins with the mission statement.

Second, not every component of the strategic management process deserves equal attention each time planning activity takes place. Firms in an extremely stable environment may find that an in-depth assessment is not required every five years. Companies often are satisfied with their original mission statements even after a decade of operation and spend only a minimal amount of time addressing this subject. In addition,while formal strategic planning may be undertaken only every five years, objectives and strategies usually are updated each year, and rigorous reassessment of the initial stages of strategic planning rarely is undertaken at these times.

A third implication of viewing strategic management as a process is the necessity of feedback from institutionalization, review, and evaluation to the early stages of the process. **Feedback** can be defined as the analysis of postimplementation results that can be used to enhance future decision making. Therefore, as indicated in Exhibit 1.4, strategic managers should assess the impact of implemented strategies on external environments. Thus, future planning can reflect any changes precipitated by strategic actions. Strategic managers also should analyze the impact of strategies on the possible need for modifications in the company mission.

A fourth implication of viewing strategic management as a process is the need to regard it as a dynamic system. The term **dynamic** characterizes the constantly changing conditions that affect interrelated and interdependent strategic activities. Managers should recognize that the components of the strategic process are constantly evolving but that formal planning artificially freezes those components, much as an action photograph freezes the movement of a swimmer. Since change is continuous, the dynamic strategic planning process must be monitored constantly for significant shifts in any of its components as a precaution against implementing an obsolete strategy.

Changes in the Process

The strategic management process undergoes continual assessment and subtle updating. Although the elements of the basic strategic management model rarely change, the relative

feedback
The analysis of post-implementation results that can be used to enhance future decision making.

dynamic
The term that characterizes the constantly changing conditions that affect interrelated and interdependent strategic activities.

emphasis that each element receives will vary with the decision makers who use the model and with the environments of their companies.

A recent study describes general trends in strategic management, summarizing the responses of more than 200 corporate executives. This update shows there has been an increasing companywide emphasis on and appreciation for the value of strategic management activities. It also provides evidence that practicing managers have given increasing attention to the need for frequent and widespread involvement in the formulation and implementation phases of the strategic management process. Finally, it indicates that, as managers and their firms gain knowledge, experience, skill, and understanding in how to design and manage their planning activities, they become better able to avoid the potential negative consequences of instituting a vigorous strategic management process.

Summary

Strategic management is the set of decisions and actions that result in the formulation and implementation of plans designed to achieve a company's objectives. Because it involves long-term, future-oriented, complex decision making and requires considerable resources, top-management participation is essential.

Strategic management is a three-tier process involving corporate-, business-, and functional-level planners, and support personnel. At each progressively lower level, strategic activities were shown to be more specific, narrow, short-term, and action oriented, with lower risks but fewer opportunities for dramatic impact.

The strategic management model presented in this chapter will serve as the structure for understanding and integrating all the major phases of strategy formulation and implementation. The chapter provided a summary account of these phases, each of which is given extensive individual attention in subsequent chapters.

The chapter stressed that the strategic management process centers on the belief that a firm's mission can be best achieved through a systematic and comprehensive assessment of both its internal capabilities and its external environment. Subsequent evaluation of the firm's opportunities leads, in turn, to the choice of long-term objectives and grand strategies and, ultimately, to annual objectives and operating strategies, which must be implemented, monitored, and controlled.

Key Terms

adaptive mode, *p. 8*	functional tactics, *p. 13*	short-term objectives, *p. 13*
company mission, *p. 11*	generic strategies, *p. 12*	stakeholders, *p. 14*
continuous improvement, *p. 14*	grand strategies, *p. 12*	strategic control, *p. 14*
dynamic, *p. 15*	long-term objectives, *p. 12*	strategic management, *p. 3*
entrepreneurial mode, *p. 8*	planning mode, *p. 8*	strategy, *p. 3*
feedback, *p. 15*	policies, *p. 13*	tactics, *p. 13*
formality, *p. 7*	process, *p. 14*	

Questions for Discussion

1. Find a recent copy of *Business Week* and read the "Corporate Strategies" section. Was the main decision discussed strategic? At what level in the organization was the key decision made?
2. In what ways do you think the subject matter in this strategic management–business policy course will differ from that of previous courses you have taken?
3. After graduation, you are not likely to move directly to a top-level management position. In fact, few members of your class will ever reach the top-management level. Why, then, is it important for all business majors to study the field of strategic management?

4. Do you expect outstanding performance in this course to require a great deal of memorization? Why or why not?
5. You undoubtedly have read about individuals who seemingly have given singled-handed direction to their corporations. Is a participative strategic management approach likely to stifle or suppress the contributions of such individuals?
6. Think about the courses you have taken in functional areas, such as marketing, finance, production, personnel, and accounting. What is the importance of each of these areas to the strategic planning process?
7. Discuss with practicing business managers the strategic management models used in their firms. What are the similarities and differences between these models and the one in the text?
8. In what ways do you believe the strategic planning approach of not-for-profit organizations would differ from that of profit-oriented organizations?
9. How do you explain the success of firms that do not use a formal strategic planning process?
10. Think about your postgraduation job search as a strategic decision. How would the strategic management model be helpful to you in identifying and securing the most promising position?

Chapter 1 Discussion Case

Carlyle Changes Its Stripes

BusinessWeek

1 In the two decades since private equity firms first stormed the business world, they've been called a lot of things, from raiders to barbarians. But only one firm has been tagged in the popular imagination with warmongering, treason, and acting as cold-eyed architects of government conspiracies. The broadsides got to be more than David M. Rubenstein, William E. Conway Jr., and Daniel A. D'Aniello, founders of Washington's Carlyle Group, could take. "It was nauseating," Rubenstein says.

2 Carlyle, founded 20 years ago in the shadow of Washington's power centers, long went about its business far from the public eye. Its ranks were larded with the politically connected, including former Presidents, Cabinet members, even former British Prime Minister John Major. It used its partners' collective relationships to build a lucrative business buying, transforming, and selling companies—particularly defense companies that did business with governments.

3 Carlyle might have continued happily in that niche except for the confluence of three events. First there were the terrorist attacks of September 11, 2001. In the aftermath, conspiracy theorists seized on Carlyle's huge profits, intense secrecy, and close dealings with wealthy Saudi investors. The scrutiny reached a crescendo in Michael Moore's documentary *Fahrenheit 9/11,* which made Carlyle seem like the sort of company image-conscious investors like public pension funds might choose to avoid. The second factor was the tsunami of

capital that has been sloshing around the globe for five years, providing almost limitless funding for the kind of dealmaking that is Carlyle's specialty. All that liquidity has brought with it immense opportunity as well as stiff new competition. Finally, there's the succession issue. Carlyle's baby boomer founders can see retirement around the corner. And they badly want the firm, their legacy, to outlast them.

4 At this make-or-break juncture, Carlyle's founders, billionaires all, decided to refashion their firm radically—to transform it into something more ambitious, more diverse, and more lasting.

5 Stage I of what some have dubbed the Great Experiment was largely cosmetic. The founders asked members of the bin Laden family to take back their money. They sat down with George H. W. Bush and John Major and discussed, improbable though it might seem, how the two were no longer wanted as senior advisers because they hurt the firm's image. Out went former Reagan Defense Secretary Frank C. Carlucci as chairman. In came highly regarded former chairman and CEO of IBM, Louis V. Gerstner Jr., along with former Securities and Exchange Commission Chairman Arthur Levitt, former General Electric Vice Chairman David Calhoun, and former Time Inc. Editor-in-Chief Norman Pearlstine, among others, to underscore Carlyle's commitment to portfolio diversification and upright corporate citizenship. Carlyle also pared back its defense holdings dramatically.

6   Stage II went much further and, indeed, might come to redefine the very nature of private equity. While other major buyout firms raise a few massive funds that hunt big prey—companies they can take private, rejigger financially, and, eventually, sell off or take public again—Carlyle has spread its money among no fewer than 48 funds around the world. Whereas the other giant firms—Blackstone Group, Kohlberg Kravis Roberts, and Texas Pacific Group—manage just 14, 7, and 6 funds, respectively, according to Thomson Financial, Carlyle launched a mind-boggling 11 in 2005 and 11 more in 2006.

7   More important, Carlyle now deals in a broad swath of alternative assets that include venture capital, real estate, collateralized debt obligations, and other investing exotica, which now make up a third of its assets. Rubenstein expects that percentage to grow to half by 2012. By getting into so many different areas, Carlyle seeks to exploit lucrative opportunities now and gain flexibility later when the booming buyout market slumps. The risk lies in getting it right. Having never managed such disparate assets before, Carlyle is on a steep learning curve. And it will be competing with traders and managers who have seen every kind of market—up, down, sideways.

8   Carlyle's radical makeover has turned the firm into the biggest fund-raising juggernaut the private equity world has ever seen. By the end of this year it expects to have an unprecedented $85 billion in investor commitments under management, up sixfold from 2001 and more than any other firm expects. Rubenstein sees the total swelling to as much as $300 billion by 2012. This year alone, Carlyle plans to raise a record $34 billion. Thanks to the surging debt markets, which are pumping up leveraged buyouts, that easily translates into more than $200 billion in purchasing power, enough for Carlyle to take out, say, Yahoo!, Caterpillar, and FedEx and still have $100 billion left over. "People probably look at them with a bit of envy," says Joncarlo Mark, a senior portfolio manager at California Public Employees' Retirement System (CalPERS), which owns 5.5 percent of the firm. Texas Pacific co-founder David Bonderman considers Conway, Carlyle's chief investment officer, "one of the best in our business."

9   So what, exactly, is Carlyle? Part buyout shop, part investment bank, part asset-management firm, it has set out on a course all its own. "There are going to be some major financial institutions that emerge from the phenomenal growth [in private equity] of the last years," says Colin Blaydon, director of the Center for Private Equity & Entrepreneurship at Dartmouth's Tuck School of Business. "Carlyle is very deliberately moving in that direction. It looks a bit like the mid-'80s, when a handful of big, multiline investment-banking firms emerged as the bulge bracket."

10   Make no mistake—Carlyle is already massive. It owns nearly 200 companies that generate a combined $68 billion in revenue and employ 200,000 people. Last year it bought a new company approximately once every three days and sold one almost once a week—all while dabbling in increasingly esoteric investments.

11   Such feats might qualify Rubenstein for Master of the Universe status, but his New York office certainly doesn't announce it. Bespectacled and tightly wound, Rubenstein, 57, sits behind a dark mahogany desk so spare it's hard to believe he ever uses it. And the place has none of the typical trappings of the private equity elite. No photographs of Rubenstein with famous people (although he knows plenty). No artwork. No "love me" collages of degrees and awards. "[Carlyle] is a serious money-management business," says Rubenstein, "and we have to operate it that way if it's to have duration beyond the founders." Besides, he says, his austere offices in Washington and New York serve as reminders that he could lose everything at any moment. "I don't have things on the walls because I might have to take them down," he says. Rubenstein is ascetic by nature. He shuns red meat, avoids alcohol and desserts, and limits his business attire to navy pin-striped suits.

12   Rubenstein doesn't have much time to gaze at the walls anyway. With money flowing in so fast and opportunities increasing exponentially, the firm's expansion is creating problems buyout shops have never had to deal with before.

13   Coping with the hypergrowth is Stage III of the Great Experiment. Carlyle has overhauled its management structure, decentralizing decision making in a way that would shock the typical larger-than-life buyout baron. Now, instead of relying on the founders to bless every deal, it sprinkles investment committees around the firm, each made up of managers from different funds and backgrounds. Before memos reach THE TOP, they have to make it through each fund's committee. If a big deal in, say, Japan, looks tempting, the Japan fund might solicit money from bigger Carlyle funds, which perform their own due diligence. This is management more along the lines of a professionally run, shareholder-owned corporation than a private partnership where the founders' dictates, wise or not, carry the force of law. In the annals of business, it's the juncture at which many a hot boutique has failed. Rubenstein says big private equity firms, including his own, will one day be publicly held.

14   The new setup allows Carlyle's founders, known inside the firm as "DBD" for David-Bill-Daniel, to concentrate on what they do best. Rubenstein travels the globe 260 days a year to raise funds. The fiery Conway, 57, scrambles to put the money to work. D'Aniello, 60, is chief operating officer and, in many ways, the glue of the operation. Underneath DBD and Chairman Gerstner, a web of investment managers runs money while seasoned executives not only manage companies but beat the bushes looking for deals. Carlyle estimates that at any one time it has headhunters conducting 10 to 15 searches for high-level talent. When Carlyle and its partners landed Calhoun, they were willing to pay him $100 million. Carlyle has promoted 50 of its people to the level of partner—a path that typically takes 12 years. Below them sit associates, who earn about $150,000 to start.

15   Central to Carlyle's Great Experiment is old-fashioned risk management. The more diverse the assets, say finance textbooks, the better the risk-adjusted returns. Carlyle has long been known as one of the most risk-averse of the major firms. Its main U.S. buyout fund has lost money on only 4 percent of its investments, making it one of the most consistent performers in an industry that typically sees losses on 10 to 15 percent of its positions, according to Hamilton Lane, an institutional money-management and advisory firm. Thus far, Carlyle's aversion to risk hasn't come at the expense of returns. Quite the opposite: Since its founding in 1987 it has generated annualized after-fee returns of 26 percent, compared with the industry average in the mid-teens. But already, DBD is telling investors they shouldn't expect private equity returns of 30 percent a year to continue.

16   Carlyle's longtime focus on small and midmarket deals—less than $1 billion—has also set it apart from the other megafirms. In buyouts, KKR and Blackstone concentrate on the biggest acquisitions, while Texas Pacific Group is known for doing difficult deals that other firms won't touch. Carlyle's specialty is turning small deals into big successes. Even its most ardent former skeptic praises the approach. Stephen L. Norris, one of the firm's original five founders, split in 1995 in a bitter fight over Carlyle's direction. "I was wrong," Norris says flatly. "David is a billionaire, and I'm not." (The other original partner, Greg A. Rosenbaum, left during the first year.)

17   But overheated debt markets have changed Carlyle's formula, at least for now. When interest rates plunged earlier in the decade, deal financing got much cheaper, and Carlyle took full advantage, making successively bigger purchases. Founder Conway acknowledges the worry. "Our business right now is being propelled by the rocket fuel of cheap debt," he says. "Rocket fuel is explosive, and you have to be careful how you handle it." Daniel F. Akerson, co-head of the firm's U.S. buyout fund, says one bank last year offered to give Carlyle twice the financing it needed for an acquisition. "That's when you say to yourself: Wow.' That's the craziness of it."

RED FLAGS

18   Such easy access to capital now can set up big trouble later on. To paraphrase Alan Greenspan, the worst of deals are made at the best of times. Right now almost all dealmakers look like geniuses. But history tells us that when the cycle turns, many who are riding the current wave of hope and euphoria will be washed out to sea. If interest rates rise, opportunities to refinance debt will disappear. Cash flows will shrivel. There will be bankruptcies.

19   Carlyle has a longer and more lustrous record than most firms, but there's no doubt it's getting increasingly audacious in its financial footwork. In June, along with partners Clayton, Dubilier & Rice and Merrill Lynch, it collected an unprecedented $1 billion dividend from rental-car company Hertz just six months after taking it private for $15 billion—and

then promptly took it public again, a lightning-quick flip in buyout land. Carlyle estimates it has already earned back 54 percent of its $765 million investment and points out that it and its partners still own 71 percent of the company and are managing it for the long term.

20   Conway makes no apologies for returning money to investors—institutions, pension funds, and wealthy individuals—as quickly as possible. He's paid to spot opportunities and seize them. For example, in 2002, Carlyle beat a pack of other firms to buy the Dex Media Yellow Pages Division from struggling Qwest Communications International for $7 billion with partner Welsh, Carson, Anderson & Stowe. Then the largest buyout since RJR Nabisco, the deal was beset by regulatory hurdles and was ultimately carried out in two stages. (Carlyle made 2.6 times its investment when it took Dex public in 2004 and exited last year.)

21   When Stephen A. Schwarzman, CEO of Blackstone Group, called Rubenstein last August to gauge his interest in Austin (Texas)–based Freescale Semiconductor, Carlyle's Great Experiment was put to the test. Schwarzman gave Carlyle only a few weeks to decide. So 40 investment professionals from the firm's U.S., Asian, Japanese, and European buyout funds got to work. They probed Freescale's ability to service its clients worldwide, researched its management team, and wrestled with the risks involved in the company's valuation, which had more than doubled in two years. Buyouts of tech companies, with their high capital expenditures and boom-and-bust product cycles, have been rare. Ultimately, the group decided the deal was worth the risk, and Carlyle bid alongside Blackstone.

22   Such moves have raised red flags among regulators. Carlyle is one of several firms that received letters from the U.S. Department of Justice last fall asking for information on club deals. And the firm's sprawling portfolio is beginning to raise eyebrows, too. On January 25, 2007, the Federal Trade Commission told Carlyle it could complete a $27.5 billion buyout of energy-distribution holding company Kinder Morgan Inc. only if it agrees to give up operational control of another company it owns. Carlyle has gotten so big and so diverse that it's actually raising antitrust concerns—a first for a buyout firm.

23   Back in 1987 no one would have imagined that Carlyle's founders would one day count themselves among the private equity aristocracy. Rubenstein was an unhappy lawyer whose main calling card was a stint as a domestic policy adviser in the Carter Administration. Conway had dealt with junk-bond czar Michael R. Milken as treasurer and chief financial officer of MCI Communications but had little experience buying companies. D'Aniello's expertise was handling hotel financings at Marriott Corp. "People laughed at us," Rubenstein recalls.

24   With a bankroll of just $5 million, Carlyle struggled. It began by marketing Alaskan tax write-offs to corporations—hardly the stuff of Wall Street or Washington folklore. Its first attempt at a buyout turned into a painful learning experience. Carlyle hit up one of its founding investors, the

Mellon family of Pittsburgh, for money to buy the restaurant chain Chi-Chi's. Then the group made a pilgrimage to Milken to get the rest of the money. They lost the auction to a company called Foodmaker and learned afterward that Milken had financed each of the four bidders. "It was stunning to us," recalls D'Aniello of his introduction to the buyout business. Milken was not available for comment.

25   Their fortunes turned when they wooed former Defense Secretary Carlucci to the firm in 1989. He delivered a sweet deal in his first year—a defense think tank called BDM International that was involved in large projects like manned space stations and, eventually, the deployment of Operation Desert Shield. "All these little jewels were coming available from larger companies that were looking to [pare their holdings to] find their core competencies," recalls D'Aniello. Carlyle was able to sell BDM in 1997 and make its investors 10.5 times their initial stake. The firm went on to become a force in the defense industry: Carlyle was one of the nation's 15 biggest defense contractors from 1998 to 2003, according to the Pentagon.

26   By 2005, thanks to the diversification strategy, it wasn't even among the top 100 defense contractors. Today, investment professionals in New York, Washington, Los Angeles, and London buy and sell loans, stocks, bonds, and other securities. Their largest holdings are in secured bank loans. But on the 42nd floor of Carlyle's New York office, some now trade in the securities of deeply distressed companies—the kind that Carlyle's buyout business once refused to touch.

ACROSS THE GLOBE

27   The seeds of that business were sown in 2002, when debt was getting cheaper and Managing Director Michael J. Zupon convinced DBD that there were profitable opportunities in distressed companies. He had taken a position in the bonds of an aerospace company at less than 50 cents on the dollar, and the company's executives pitched him on buying preferred stock. Keenly aware of Carlyle's expertise in aerospace, Zupon consulted with one of the firm's senior dealmakers in the sector. The two decided that Carlyle's high-yield fund and its U.S. buyout fund should buy the $15 million stake. Its value soared to $45 million in 18 months. "That was the catalyst," Zupon says. The business has since expanded into buying companies outright. One of the group's first purchases was titanium-component maker Stellex Aerostructures Inc., which Carlyle had once considered acquiring. The distressed team bought it after it emerged from bankruptcy in 2004. Two years later it sold for 6.3 times what Carlyle paid.

28   At the other end of the investing spectrum, a group of 50 people spread out in Washington, San Francisco, Mumbai, Beijing, Shanghai, Hong Kong, and London are looking to put $3.6 billion to work in venture and other deals. "We're seeing a set of opportunities with strong growth attributes but

which just don't lend themselves to the traditional leveraged-buyout approach," explains Brooke B. Coburn, who co-heads Carlyle's American venture fund. Most of the group's investments are in small businesses and fledgling divisions carved from companies. For example, the U.S. venture group paid $44 million for the English-as-a-second-language instruction division of publicly traded Laureate Education Inc. in 2005. Carlyle's venture team saw a chance to expand dramatically. The company's revenues have surged 70 percent, to more than $120 million.

29   Increasingly, Carlyle is also backing entrepreneurs who have little more than a patent. One investment is with a group that patented the idea for an advanced liposuction machine. In theory it damages fat cells with ultrasound waves so they can be secreted naturally, eliminating the need for surgery. "We've been in [that investment] for five to six years, and [the company] has no revenue at this point," says Coburn. Carlyle has invested $6.7 million.

30   In China, Carlyle's venture fund focuses on consumer-oriented investments like Ctrip.com, the Chinese version of Travelocity. Carlyle invested $8 million, took it public, and reaped $117 million. In India, Carlyle is backing technology, including a company called Claris Lifesciences Ltd., which makes low-cost medicines and hospital-care products.

31   Carlyle may soon become even more far-flung. Its recent hiring of a team of traders from hedge fund Amaranth Advisors, which lost $6 billion last year on bad natural gas bets, has prompted speculation that Carlyle is preparing to launch a hedge fund. There's also talk that the firm may start new buyout funds focusing on emerging markets. On January 28, 2007, Carlyle announced the hiring of a dealmaker in Cairo to oversee investments in Egypt and North Africa. Citing SEC restrictions, the firm declined to comment on potential new funds.

32   Investors like the new, diversified approach. "The remarkable thing about the firm [is that] a lot of their funds have done exceptionally well," says CalPERS' Mark. "But you [also] have the safety net of the broader organization."

33   The biggest question facing Carlyle is whether it can maintain the discipline and top-notch performance it has been known for through this period of hypergrowth. The tension between Rubenstein rushing out new funds and Conway racing to find the financial expertise to keep up is palpable. Good investment professionals "don't grow on trees," Conway complains. "You talk to a headhunter who says: 'I know 50 of those people.' Then you hire the headhunter and . . . the 50 becomes 3."

34   With so much money flowing in, finding and keeping talent has become an obsession. D'Aniello, who oversees Carlyle's real estate and energy investments, has been moonlighting as the firm's management guru. He has hired human resources staff to attract top people, implemented 360-degree performance reviews, started succession planning, instituted Carlyle's annual management retreat, and spearheaded

an initiative called "One Carlyle," designed to encourage teamwork across borders and silos. What could be more corporate-sounding?

35   "We don't want isolationists," D'Aniello says of the employees he's trying to attract to sustain his firm long into the future. "We also don't want crybabies. And we don't want mercenaries—people who are here to put a notch on their own gun. We want people to help us build a cannon."

Source: Reprinted with special permission from Emily Thornton, "Carlyle Changes Its Stripes," *BusinessWeek,* February 12, 2007. Copyright © 2007 The McGraw-Hill Companies.

DISCUSSION QUESTIONS

1. What do you believe are the keys to success in the venture capital industry?
2. What do you believe are the keys to success in the private equity industry?
3. How would Carlyle define its business strategy?
4. What current conditions in Carlyle's external environment favor its success?
5. What are the keys to Carlyle's future strategic success given its impressive and stiffer competition?

Part Two

Strategy Formulation

Strategy formulation guides executives in defining the business their firm is in, the ends it seeks, and the means it will use to accomplish those ends. The approach of strategy formulation is an improvement over that of traditional long-range planning. As discussed in the next eight chapters—about developing a firm's competitive plan of action—strategy formulation combines a future-oriented perspective with concern for the firm's internal and external environments.

The strategy formulation process begins with definition of the company mission, as discussed in Chapter 2. In this chapter, the purpose of business is defined to reflect the values of a wide variety of interested parties. In Chapter 3 social responsibility is discussed as a critical consideration for a company's strategic decision makers because the mission statement must express how the company intends to contribute to the societies that sustain it. Central to the idea that companies should be operated in socially responsible ways is the belief that managers will behave in an ethical manner. Management ethics are discussed in this chapter with special attention to the utilitarian, moral rights, and social justice approaches.

Chapter 4 deals with the principal factors in a firm's external environment that strategic managers must assess so they can anticipate and take advantage of future business conditions. It emphasizes the importance to a firm's planning activities of factors in the firm's remote, industry, and operating environments.

Chapter 5 describes the key differences in strategic planning among domestic, multinational, and global firms. It gives special attention to the new vision that a firm must communicate when it multinationalizes.

Chapter 6 shows how firms evaluate their company's strengths and weaknesses to produce an internal analysis. Strategic managers use such profiles to target competitive advantages they can emphasize and competitive disadvantages they should correct or minimize.

Chapter 7 examines the types of long-range objectives strategic managers set and specifies the qualities these objectives must have to provide a basis for direction and evaluation. The chapter also examines the generic and grand strategies that firms use to achieve long-range objectives.

Comprehensive approaches to the evaluation of strategic opportunities and to the final strategic decision are the focus of Chapter 8. The chapter shows how a firm's strategic options can be compared in a way that allows selection of the best available option. It also discusses how a company can create competitive advantages for each of its businesses.

Chapter 9 extends the attention on strategic analysis and choice by showing how managers can build value in multibusiness companies.

Chapter Two

Company Mission

After reading and studying this chapter, you should be able to

1. Describe a company mission and explain its value.

2. Explain why it is important for the mission statement to include the company's basic product or service, its primary markets, and its principal technology.

3. Explain which goal of a company is most important: survival, profitability, or growth.

4. Discuss the importance of company philosophy, public image, and company self-concept to stockholders.

5. Give examples of the newest trends in mission statement components: customer emphasis, quality, and company vision.

6. Describe the role of a company's board of directors.

7. Explain agency theory and its value in helping a board of directors improve corporate governance.

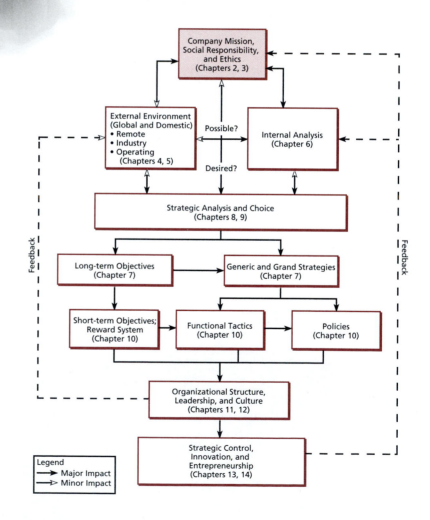

Mission Statement of Nicor Inc.

PREAMBLE

We, the management of Nicor Inc., here set forth our belief as to the purpose for which the company is established and the principles under which it should operate. We pledge our effort to the accomplishment of these purposes within these principles.

BASIC PURPOSE

The basic purpose of Nicor Inc. is to perpetuate an investor-owned company engaging in various phases of the energy business, striving for balance among those phases so as to render needed satisfactory products and services and earn optimum, long-range profits.

WHAT WE DO

The principal business of the company, through its utility subsidiary, is the provision of energy through a pipe system to meet the needs of ultimate consumers. To accomplish its basic purpose, and to ensure its strength, the company will engage in other energy-related activities, directly or through subsidiaries or in participation with other persons, corporations, firms, or entities.

All activities of the company shall be consistent with its responsibilities to investors, customers, employees, and the public and its concern for the optimum development and utilization of natural resources and for environmental needs.

WHERE WE DO IT

The company's operations shall be primarily in the United States, but no self-imposed or regulatory geographical limitations are placed upon the acquisition, development, processing, transportation, or storage of energy resources, or upon other energy-related ventures in which the company may engage. The company will engage in such activities in any location where, after careful review, it has determined that such activity is in the best interest of its stockholders.

Utility service will be offered in the territory of the company's utility subsidiary to the best of its ability, in accordance with the requirements of regulatory agencies and pursuant to the subsidiary's purposes and principles.

Source: Nicor Inc., http://www.nicor.com/

WHAT IS A COMPANY MISSION?

company mission
The unique purpose that sets a company apart from others of its type and identifies the scope of its operations in product, market, and technology terms.

Whether a firm is developing a new business or reformulating direction for an ongoing business, it must determine the basic goals and philosophies that will shape its strategic posture. This fundamental purpose that sets a firm apart from other firms of its type and identifies the scope of its operations in product and market terms is defined as the company mission. As discussed in Chapter 1, the **company mission** is a broadly framed but enduring statement of a firm's intent. It embodies the business philosophy of the firm's strategic decision makers, implies the image the firm seeks to project, reflects the firm's self-concept, and indicates the firm's principal product or service areas and the primary customer needs the firm will attempt to satisfy. In short, it describes the firm's product, market, and technological areas of emphasis, and it does so in a way that reflects the values and priorities of the firm's strategic decision makers. An excellent example is the company mission statement of Nicor Inc., shown in Exhibit 2.1, Strategy in Action.

The Need for an Explicit Mission

No external body requires that the company mission be defined, and the process of defining it is time-consuming and tedious. Moreover, it contains broadly outlined or implied objectives and strategies rather than specific directives. Characteristically, it is a statement, not of measurable targets but of attitude, outlook, and orientation.

The mission statement is a message designed to be inclusive of the expectations of all stakeholders for the company's performance over the long run. The executives and board who prepare the mission statement attempt to provide a unifying purpose for the company that will provide a basis for strategic objective setting and decision making. In general terms, the mission statement addresses the following questions:

Why is this firm in business?

What are our economic goals?

What is our operating philosophy in terms of quality, company image, and self-concept?

What are our core competencies and competitive advantages?

What customers do and can we serve?

How do we view our responsibilities to stockholders, employees, communities, environment, social issues, and competitors?

FORMULATING A MISSION

The process of defining the company mission for a specific business can perhaps be best understood by thinking about the business at its inception. The typical business begins with the beliefs, desires, and aspirations of a single entrepreneur. Such an owner-manager's sense of mission usually is based on the following fundamental beliefs:

1. The product or service of the business can provide benefits at least equal to its price.

2. The product or service can satisfy a customer need of specific market segments that is currently not being met adequately.

3. The technology that is to be used in production will provide a cost- and quality-competitive product or service.

4. With hard work and the support of others, the business can not only survive but also grow and be profitable.

5. The management philosophy of the business will result in a favorable public image and will provide financial and psychological rewards for those who are willing to invest their labor and money in helping the business to succeed.

6. The entrepreneur's self-concept of the business can be communicated to and adopted by employees and stockholders.

As the business grows or is forced by competitive pressures to alter its product, market, or technology, redefining the company mission may be necessary. If so, the revised mission statement will contain the same components as the original. It will state the basic type of product or service to be offered, the primary markets or customer groups to be served; the technology to be used in production or delivery; the firm's fundamental concern for survival through growth and profitability; the firm's managerial philosophy; the public image the firm seeks; and the self-concept those affiliated with the firm should have of it. This chapter will discuss in detail these components. The examples shown in Exhibit 2.2, Strategy in Action, provide insights into how some major corporations handle them.

Basic Product or Service; Primary Market; Principal Technology

Three indispensable components of the mission statement are specification of the basic product or service, specification of the primary market, and specification of the principal technology for production or delivery. These components are discussed under one heading because only in combination do they describe the company's business activity. A good example of the three components is to be found in the business plan of ITT Barton,

Identifying Mission Statement Components: A Compilation of Excerpts from Actual Corporate Mission Statements

1. Customer-market	We believe our first responsibility is to the doctors, nurses, and patients, to mothers and all others who use our products and services. (Johnson & Johnson)
	To anticipate and meet market needs of farmers, ranchers, and rural communities within North America. (CENEX)
2. Product-service	AMAX's principal products are molybdenum, coal, iron ore, copper, lead, zinc, petroleum and natural gas, potash, phosphates, nickel, tungsten, silver, gold, and magnesium. (AMAX)
3. Geographic domain	We are dedicated to total success of Corning Glass Works as a worldwide competitor. (Corning Glass)
4. Technology	Control Data is in the business of applying microelectronics and computer technology in two general areas: computer-related hardware and computing-enhancing services, which include computation, information, education, and finance. (Control Data)
	The common technology in these areas relates to discrete particle coatings. (NASHUA)
5. Concern for survival	In this respect, the company will conduct its operation prudently, and will provide the profits and growth which will assure Hoover's ultimate success. (Hoover Universal)
6. Philosophy	We are committed to improve health care throughout the world. (Baxter Travenol)
	We believe human development to be the worthiest of the goals of civilization and independence to be the superior condition for nurturing growth in the capabilities of people. (Sun Company)
7. Self-concept	Hoover Universal is a diversified, multi-industry corporation with strong manufacturing capabilities, entrepreneurial policies, and individual business unit autonomy. (Hoover Universal)
8. Concern for public image	We are responsible to the communities in which we live and work and to the world community as well. (Johnson & Johnson)
	Also, we must be responsive to the broader concerns of the public, including especially the general desire for improvement in the quality of life, equal opportunity for all, and the constructive use of natural resources. (Sun Company)

a division of ITT. Under the heading of business mission and area served, the following information is presented:

> The unit's mission is to serve industry and government with quality instruments used for the primary measurement, analysis, and local control of fluid flow, level, pressure, temperature, and fluid properties. This instrumentation includes flow meters, electronic readouts, indicators, recorders, switches, liquid level systems, analytical instruments such as titrators, integrators, controllers, transmitters, and various instruments for the measurement of fluid properties (density, viscosity, gravity) used for processing variable sensing, data collecting, control, and transmission. The unit's mission includes fundamental loop-closing control and display devices, when economically justified, but excludes broadline central control room instrumentation, systems design, and turnkey responsibility.
>
> Markets served include instrumentation for oil and gas production, gas transportation, chemical and petrochemical processing, cryogenics, power generation, aerospace, government, and marine, as well as other instrument and equipment manufacturers.

In only 129 words, this segment of the mission statement clearly indicates to all readers—from company employees to casual observers—the basic products, primary markets, and principal technologies of ITT Barton.

Often the most referenced public statement of a company's selected products and markets appears in "silver bullet" form in the mission statement; for example, "Dayton-Hudson Corporation is a diversified retailing company whose business is to serve the American consumer through the retailing of fashion-oriented quality merchandise." Such an abstract of company direction is particularly helpful to outsiders who value condensed overviews.

Company Goals: Survival; Growth; Profitability

Three economic goals guide the strategic direction of almost every business organization. Whether or not the mission statement explicitly states these goals, it reflects the firm's intention to secure *survival* through *growth* and *profitability.*

A firm that is unable to survive will be incapable of satisfying the aims of any of its stakeholders. Unfortunately, the goal of survival, like the goals of growth and profitability, often is taken for granted to such an extent that it is neglected as a principal criterion in strategic decision making. When this happens, the firm may focus on short-term aims at the expense of the long run. Concerns for expediency, a quick fix, or a bargain may displace the assessment of long-term impact. Too often, the result is near-term economic failure owing to a lack of resource synergy and sound business practice. For example, Consolidated Foods, maker of Shasta soft drinks and L'eggs hosiery, sought growth through the acquisition of bargain businesses. However, the erratic sales patterns of its diverse holdings forced it to divest itself of more than four dozen companies. This process cost Consolidated Foods millions of dollars and hampered its growth.

Profitability is the mainstay goal of a business organization. No matter how profit is measured or defined, profit over the long term is the clearest indication of a firm's ability to satisfy the principal claims and desires of employees and stockholders. The key phrase here is "over the long term." Obviously, basing decisions on a short-term concern for profitability would lead to a strategic myopia. Overlooking the enduring concerns of customers, suppliers, creditors, ecologists, and regulatory agents may produce profit in the short term, but, over time, the financial consequences are likely to be detrimental.

The following excerpt from the Hewlett-Packard statement of mission ably expresses the importance of an orientation toward long-term profit:

> To achieve sufficient profit to finance our company growth and to provide the resources we need to achieve our other corporate objectives.
>
> In our economic system, the profit we generate from our operation is the ultimate source of the funds we need to prosper and grow. It is the one absolutely essential measure of our corporate performance over the long term. Only if we continue to meet our profit objective can we achieve our other corporate objectives.

A firm's growth is tied inextricably to its survival and profitability. In this context, the meaning of growth must be broadly defined. Although product impact market studies (PIMS) have shown that growth in market share is correlated with profitability, other important forms of growth do exist. Growth in the number of markets served, in the variety of products offered, and in the technologies that are used to provide goods or services frequently lead to improvements in a firm's competitive ability. Growth means change, and proactive change is essential in a dynamic business environment.

AOL's strategy provides an example. In 2003, some analysts believed that AOL Time Warner should change to a survival strategy because of the amount of debt that it was carrying. They believed that AOL should try to reduce debt and regain some market share that it had lost over the previous year. AOL did decide to reduce its $7 billion debt by the end of 2004, but not simply to survive. AOL was trying to position itself for the acquisition of either Adelphia or Cablevision. AOL felt that if it could acquire one of these two companies or possibly both, it could increase its footprint in the market. AOL believed that growth for its company would have to come from the cable TV market and that the only way to grow was to serve more markets. Luckily, AOL's top competitor, Comcast, was in the same debt position as AOL and could not immediately preempt the acquisitions.

Hewlett-Packard's mission statement provides another excellent example of corporate regard for growth:

> Objective: To let our growth be limited only by our profits and our ability to develop and produce technical products that satisfy real customer needs.
>
> We do not believe that large size is important for its own sake; however, for at least two basic reasons, continuous growth is essential for us to achieve our other objectives.
>
> In the first place, we serve a rapidly growing and expanding segment of our technological society. To remain static would be to lose ground. We cannot maintain a position of strength and leadership in our field without growth.
>
> In the second place, growth is important in order to attract and hold high-caliber people. These individuals will align their future only with a company that offers them considerable opportunity for personal progress. Opportunities are greater and more challenging in a growing company.

The issue of growth raises a concern about the definition of the company mission. How can a firm's product, market, and technology be specified sufficiently to provide direction without precluding the exercise of unanticipated strategic options? How can a firm so define its mission that it can consider opportunistic diversification while maintaining the parameters that guide its growth decision? Perhaps such questions are best addressed when a firm's mission statement outlines the conditions under which the firm might depart from ongoing operations. General Electric Company's extensive global mission provided the foundation for its GE Appliances (GEA) in Louisville, Kentucky. GEA did not see consumer preferences in the world market becoming Americanized. Instead, its expansion goals allowed for flexibility in examining the unique characteristics of individual foreign markets and tailoring strategies to fit them.

The growth philosophy of Dayton-Hudson also embodies this approach:

> The stability and quality of the corporation's financial performance will be developed through the profitable execution of our existing businesses, as well as through the acquisition or development of new businesses. Our growth priorities, in order, are as follows:
>
> 1. Development of the profitable market preeminence of existing companies in existing markets through new store development or new strategies within existing stores.
> 2. Expansion of our companies to feasible new markets.
> 3. Acquisition of other retailing companies that are strategically and financially compatible with Dayton-Hudson.
> 4. Internal development of new retailing strategies.

Capital allocations to fund the expansion of existing Dayton-Hudson operating companies will be based on each company's return on investment (ROI), in relationship to its ROI objective and its consistency in earnings growth and on the ability of its management to perform up to the forecasts contained in its capital requests. Expansion via acquisition or new venture will occur when the opportunity promises an acceptable rate of long-term growth and profitability, an acceptable degree of risk, and compatibility with Dayton-Hudson's long-term strategy.

Keith Rattie, the CEO of Questar, is a top strategist who has been consistent in using his company's mission to guide its growth. Read Exhibit 2.3, Top Strategist, to learn how he helps create success by designing and executing strategies that are consistent with long-term business goals.

Questar traces its roots to a natural gas discovery in Wyoming back in 1922. Today, the Salt Lake City outfit is one of the nation's top-performing energy companies. The reason for its success? Focus. Under CEO Keith Rattie, the company has rapidly added new natural gas reserves at low cost by staying close to its Rocky Mountain beginnings. Questar combs over old fields at greater depths than ever by using the latest drilling technologies. Its biggest natural gas field, Pinedale, is still just 150 miles from that 1922 strike in southeastern Wyoming. The company reaps most of its revenue from exploration, but it also owns gas pipelines and a natural gas utility serving more than 800,000 customers in Utah. Revenue from those other businesses provide a nice cushion to help offset the ebb and flow of natural gas prices—and keep Questar's earnings and dividends flowing.

Source: Reprinted with special permission from "The *BusinessWeek* 50—The Best Performers," *BusinessWeek*, March 26, 2007. Copyright © 2007 The McGraw-Hill Companies.

Company Philosophy

company creed
A company's statement of its philosophy.

The statement of a company's philosophy, often called the **company creed,** usually accompanies or appears within the mission statement. It reflects or specifies the basic beliefs, values, aspirations, and philosophical priorities to which strategic decision makers are committed in managing the company. Fortunately, the philosophies vary little from one firm to another. Owners and managers implicitly accept a general, unwritten, yet pervasive code of behavior that governs business actions and permits them to be largely self-regulated. Unfortunately, statements of company philosophy are often so similar and so platitudinous that they read more like public relations handouts than the commitment to values they are meant to be.

Saturn's statement of philosophy, presented in Exhibit 2.4, Strategy in Action, indicates the company's clearly defined initiatives for satisfying the needs of its customers, employees, suppliers, and dealers.

Despite the similarity of these statements, the intentions of the strategic managers in developing them do not warrant cynicism. Company executives attempt to provide a distinctive and accurate picture of the firm's managerial outlook. One such statement of company philosophy is that of AIM Private Asset Management, Inc. As Exhibit 2.5, Strategy in Action, shows, AIM's board of directors and executives have established especially clear directions for company decision making and action based on growth.

As seen in Exhibit 2.6, Global Strategy in Action, the philosophy of Nissan Motor Manufacturing is expressed by the company's People Principles and Key Corporate Principles. These principles form the basis of the way the company operates on a daily basis. They address the principal concepts used in meeting the company's established goals. Nissan

Saturn's Statement of Philosophy

We, the Saturn Team, in concert with the UAW and General Motors, believe that meeting the needs of customers, Saturn members, suppliers, dealers, and neighbors is fundamental to fulfilling our mission.

To meet our customer's needs . . .

- our products and services must be world leaders in value and satisfaction.

To meet our members' needs, we . . .

- will create a sense of belonging in an environment of mutual trust, respect, and dignity;
- believe that all people want to be involved in decisions that affect them, care about their jobs and each other, take pride in themselves and in their contributions, and want to share in the success of their efforts;
- will develop the tools, training, and education for each member, recognizing individual skills and knowledge;
- believe that creative, motivated, responsible team members who understand that change is critical to success are Saturn's most important asset.

To meet our suppliers' and dealers' needs, we . . .

- will strive to create real partnerships with them;
- will be open and fair in our dealings, reflecting trust, respect, and their importance to Saturn;
- want dealers and suppliers to feel ownerships in Saturn's mission and philosophy as their own.

To meet the needs of our neighbors, the communities in which we live and operate, we . . .

- will be good citizens, protect the environment, and conserve natural resources;
- will seek to cooperate with government at all levels and strive to be sensitive, open, and candid in all our public statements.

Source: Saturn Corp., http://www.saturn.com

focuses on the distinction between the role of the individual and the corporation. In this way, employees can link their productivity and success to the productivity and success of the company. Given these principles, the company is able to concentrate on the issues most important to its survival, growth, and profitability.

Exhibit 2.7, Strategy in Action, provides an example of how General Motors uses a statement of company philosophy to clarify its environmental principles.

Public Image

Both present and potential customers attribute certain qualities to particular businesses. Gerber and Johnson & Johnson make safe products; Cross Pen makes high-quality writing instruments; Étienne Aigner makes stylish but affordable leather products; Corvettes are power machines; and Izod Lacoste stands for the preppy look. Thus, mission statements should reflect the public's expectations, because this makes achievement of the firm's goals more likely. Gerber's mission statement should not open the possibility for diversification into pesticides, and Cross Pen's should not open the possibility for diversification into $0.59 brand-name disposables.

On the other hand, a negative public image often prompts firms to reemphasize the beneficial aspects of their mission. For example, in response to what it saw as a disturbing trend in public opinion, Dow Chemical undertook an aggressive promotional campaign to

Growth Philosophy at AIM Private Asset Management Inc.

AIM's growth philosophy focuses on earnings—a tangible measure of a company's growth. Because stock prices can gyrate widely on rumors, we use earnings to weed out "high-flying" speculative stocks.

In selecting investments, we look for:
- Quality earnings growth—because we believe earnings drive stock prices.
- Positive earnings momentum—stocks with greater positive momentum will rise above the crowd.

Our growth philosophy adheres to four basic rules:
- Remain fully invested.
- Focus on individual companies rather than industries, sectors or countries.
- Strive to find the best earnings growth.
- Maintain a strong sell discipline.

Why growth philosophy?
- Investment decisions are based on facts, not guesses or big-picture economic forecasts.
- Earnings—not emotions—dictate when we should buy and sell.
- AIM's investment managers have followed the same earnings-driven philosophy for decades.
- This approach has proven itself in domestic and foreign markets.

Source: AIM Private Asset Management Inc., http://sma.aiminvestments .com/

fortify its credibility, particularly among "employees and those who live and work in [their] plant communities." Dow described its approach in its annual report:

> All around the world today, Dow people are speaking up. People who care deeply about their company, what it stands for, and how it is viewed by others. People who are immensely proud of their company's performance, yet realistic enough to realize it is the public's perception of that performance that counts in the long run.

Firms seldom address the question of their public image in an intermittent fashion. Although public agitation often stimulates greater attention to this question, firms are concerned about their public image even in the absence of such agitation. The following excerpt from the mission statement of Intel Corporation is an example of this attitude:

> We are sensitive to our *image with our customers and the business community*. Commitments to customers are considered sacred, and we are upset with ourselves when we do not meet our commitments. We strive to demonstrate to the business world on a continuing basis that we are credible in describing the state of the corporation, and that we are well organized and in complete control of all things that determine the numbers.

Exhibit 2.8, Strategy in Action, presents a marketing translation of the essence of the mission statements of six high-end shoe companies. The impressive feature of the exhibit is that it shows dramatically how closely competing firms can incorporate subtle, yet meaningful, differences into their mission statements.

Company Self-Concept

A major determinant of a firm's success is the extent to which the firm can relate functionally to its external environment. To achieve its proper place in a competitive situation, the firm realistically must evaluate its competitive strengths and weaknesses. This idea—that the firm must know itself—is the essence of the company self-concept. The idea is not commonly integrated into theories of strategic management; its importance for individuals has been recognized since ancient times.

Principles of Nissan Motor Manufacturing (UK) Ltd.

People Principles **(All other objectives can only be achieved by people)**	
Selection	Hire the highest caliber people; look for technical capabilities and emphasize attitude.
Responsibility	Maximize the responsibility; staff by devolving decision making.
Teamwork	Recognize and encourage individual contributions, with everyone working toward the same objectives.
Flexibility	Expand the role of the individual: multiskilled, no job description, generic job titles.
Kaizen	Continuously seek 100.1 percent improvements; give "ownership of change."
Communications	"Every day, face to face."
Training	Establish individual "continuous development programs."
Supervisors	Regard as "the professionals at managing the production process"; give them much responsibility normally assumed by individual departments; make them the genuine leaders of their teams.
Single status	Treat everyone as a "first class" citizen; eliminate all illogical differences.
Trade unionism	Establish single union agreement with AEU emphasizing the common objective for a successful enterprise.
Key Corporate Principles	
Quality	Building profitably the highest quality car sold in Europe.
Customers	Achieve target of no. 1 customer satisfaction in Europe.
Volume	Always achieve required volume.
New products	Deliver on time, at required quality, within cost.
Suppliers	Establish long-term relationship with single-source suppliers; aim for zero defects and just-in-time delivery; apply Nissan principles to suppliers.
Production	Use "most appropriate" technology; develop predictable "best method" of doing job; build in quality.
Engineering	Design "quality" and "ease of working" into the product and facilities; establish "simultaneous engineering" to reduce development time.

Source: Nissan Motor Co. Ltd., http://www.nissanmotors.com/

Both individuals and firms have a crucial need to know themselves. The ability of either to survive in a dynamic and highly competitive environment would be severely limited if they did not understand their impact on others or of others on them.

In some senses, then, firms take on personalities of their own. Much behavior in firms is organizationally based; that is, a firm acts on its members in other ways than their individual interactions. Thus, firms are entities whose personality transcends the personalities of their members. As such, they can set decision-making parameters based on aims different and distinct from the aims of their members. These organizational considerations have pervasive effects.

Ordinarily, descriptions of the company self-concept per se do not appear in mission statements. Yet such statements often provide strong impressions of the company self-concept. For example, ARCO's environment, health, and safety (EHS) managers were adamant about

General Motors Environmental Principles

As a responsible corporate citizen, General Motors is dedicated to protecting human health, natural resources, and the global environment. This dedication reaches further than compliance with the law to encompass the integration of sound environmental practices into our business decisions.

The following environmental principles provide guidance to General Motors personnel worldwide in the conduct of their daily business practices:

1. We are committed to actions to restore and preserve the environment.

2. We are committed to reducing waste and pollutants, conserving resources, and recycling materials at every stage of the product life cycle.

3. We will continue to participate actively in educating the public regarding environmental conservation.

4. We will continue to pursue vigorously the development and implementation of technologies for minimizing pollutant emissions.

5. We will continue to work with all governmental entities for the development of technically sound and financially responsible environmental laws and regulations.

6. We will continually assess the impact of our plants and products on the environment and the communities in which we live and operate with a goal of continuous improvement.

Source: General Motors Corporation, http://www.gm.com/

emphasizing the company's position on safety and environmental performance as a part of the mission statement. The challenges facing the ARCO EHS managers included dealing with concerned environmental groups and a public that has become environmentally aware. They hoped to motivate employees toward safer behavior while reducing emissions and waste. They saw this as a reflection of the company's positive self-image.

The following excerpts from the Intel Corporation mission statement describe the corporate persona that its top management seeks to foster:

Management is self-critical. The leaders must be capable of recognizing and accepting their mistakes and learning from them.

Open (constructive) confrontation is encouraged at all levels of the corporation and is viewed as a method of problem solving and conflict resolution.

Decision by consensus is the rule. Decisions once made are supported. Position in the organization is not the basis for quality of ideas.

A highly communicative, open management is part of the style.

Management must be ethical. Managing by telling the truth and treating all employees equitably has established credibility that is ethical.

We strive to provide an opportunity for rapid development.

Intel is a results-oriented company. The focus is on substance versus form, quality versus quantity.

We believe in the principle that hard work, high productivity is something to be proud of.

The concept of assumed responsibility is accepted. (If a task needs to be done, assume you have the responsibility to get it done.)

Commitments are long term. If career problems occur at some point, reassignment is a better alternative than termination.

We desire to have all employees involved and participative in their relationship with Intel.

Newest Trends in Mission Components

Recently, three issues have become so prominent in the strategic planning for organizations that they are increasingly becoming integral parts in the development and revisions

Mission Statements for the High-End Shoe Industry

ALLEN-EDMONDS

Allen-Edmonds provides high-quality shoes for the affluent consumer who appreciates a well-made, finely crafted, stylish dress shoe.

BALLY

Bally shoes set you apart. They are the perfect shoe to complement your lifestyle. Bally shoes project an image of European style and elegance that ensures one is not just dressed, but well dressed.

BOSTONIAN

Bostonian shoes are for those successful individuals who are well-traveled, on the "go" and want a stylish dress shoe that can keep up with their variety of needs and activities. With Bostonian, you know you will always be well dressed whatever the situation.

COLE-HAHN

Cole-Hahn offers a line of contemporary shoes for the man who wants to go his own way. They are shoes for the urban, upscale, stylish man who wants to project an image of being one step ahead.

FLORSHEIM

Florsheim shoes are the affordable classic men's dress shoes for those who want to experience the comfort and style of a solid dress shoe.

JOHNSTON & MURPHY

Johnston & Murphy is the quintessential business shoe for those affluent individuals who know and demand the best.

Source: "Thinking on Your Feet, the Johnston & Murphy Guerrilla Marketing Competition" (Johnston & Murphy, a GENESCO Company).

of mission statements: sensitivity to consumer wants, concern for quality, and statements of company vision.

Customers

"The customer is our top priority" is a slogan that would be claimed by the majority of businesses in the United States and abroad. For companies including Caterpillar Tractor, General Electric, and Johnson & Johnson this means analyzing consumer needs before as well as after a sale. The bonus plan at Xerox allows for a 40 percent annual bonus, based on high customer reviews of the service that they receive, and a 20 percent penalty if the feedback is especially bad. For these firms and many others, the overriding concern for the company has become consumer satisfaction.

In addition many U.S. firms maintain extensive product safety programs to help ensure consumer satisfaction. RCA, Sears, and 3M boast of such programs. Other firms including Calgon Corporation, Amoco, Mobil Oil, Whirlpool, and Zenith provide toll-free telephone lines to answer customer concerns and complaints.

The focus on customer satisfaction is demonstrated by retailer JCPenney in this excerpt from its statement of philosophy: "The Penney Idea is (1) To serve the public as nearly as we can to its complete satisfaction; (2) To expect for the service we render a fair remuneration, and not all the profit the traffic will bear; (3) To do all in our power to pack the customer's dollar full of value, quality, and satisfaction."

A focus on customer satisfaction causes managers to realize the importance of providing quality customer service. Strong customer service initiatives have led some firms to gain competitive advantages in the marketplace. Hence, many corporations have made the customer service initiative a key component of their corporate mission.

Quality

"Quality is job one!" is a rallying point not only for Ford Motor Corporation but for many resurging U.S. businesses as well. Two U.S. management experts fostered a worldwide

Visions of Quality

CADILLAC

The Mission of the Cadillac Motor Company is to engineer, produce, and market the world's finest automobiles known for uncompromised levels of distinctiveness, comfort, convenience, and refined performance. Through its people, who are its strength, Cadillac will continuously improve the quality of its products and services to meet or exceed customer expectations and succeed as a profitable business.

MOTOROLA

Dedication to quality is a way of life at our company, so much so that it goes far beyond rhetorical slogans. Our ongoing program is one of continued improvement reaches out for change, refinement, and even revolution in our pursuit of quality excellence.

It is the objective of Motorola Inc. to produce and provide products and services of the highest quality. In its activities, Motorola will pursue goals aimed at the achievement of quality excellence. These results will be derived from the dedicated efforts of each employee in conjunction with supportive participation from management at all levels of the corporation.

ZYTEC

Zytec is a company that competes on value; is market driven; provides superior quality and service; builds strong relationship with its customers; and provides technical excellence in its products.

emphasis on quality in manufacturing. W. Edwards Deming and J. M. Juran's messages were first embraced by Japanese managers, whose quality consciousness led to global dominance in several industries including automobile, TV, audio equipment, and electronic components manufacturing. Deming summarizes his approach in 14 now well-known points:

1. Create constancy of purpose.
2. Adopt the new philosophy.
3. Cease dependence on mass inspection to achieve quality.
4. End the practice of awarding business on price tag alone. Instead, minimize total cost, often accomplished by working with a single supplier.
5. Improve constantly the system of production and service.
6. Institute training on the job.
7. Institute leadership.
8. Drive out fear.
9. Break down barriers between departments.
10. Eliminate slogans, exhortations, and numerical targets.
11. Eliminate work standards (quotas) and management by objective.
12. Remove barriers that rob workers, engineers, and managers of their right to pride of workmanship.
13. Institute a vigorous program of education and self-improvement.
14. Put everyone in the company to work to accomplish the transformation.

Firms in the United States responded aggressively. The new philosophy is that quality should be the norm. For example, Motorola's production goal is 60 or fewer defects per every billion components that it manufactures.

Exhibit 2.9, Strategy in Action, presents the integration of the quality initiative into the mission statements of three corporations. The emphasis on quality has received added emphasis in many corporate philosophies since the Congress created the Malcolm Baldrige

Examples of Vision Statements

ALLIANCE CORPORATE VISION
Alliance is the most innovative and feature rich ACH processing platform available to client originators today and will remain on the cutting edge for electronic funds transfer services.

AMD CORPORATE VISION
A connected global population.

CUTCO CORPORATE VISION
To become the largest, most respected and widely recognized cutlery company in the world.

FEDERAL EXPRESS CORPORATE VISION
Our vision is to change the way we all connect with each other in the New Network Economy.

FIRSTENERGY CORPORATE VISION
FirstEnergy will be a leading regional energy provider, recognized for operational excellence and service; the choice for long-term growth, investment, value and financial strength; and a company committed to safety and driven by the leadership, skills, diversity, and character of its employees.

FORD MOTOR COMPANY CORPORATE VISION
Ford Motor Company's vision is to become the world's leading consumer company for automotive products and services.

GENERAL ELECTRIC CORPORATE VISION
We bring good things to life.

MAGNA CORPORATE VISION
Magna's corporate vision is to provide world class services that help maximize the customers ROI (Return on Investment) and promote teamwork and creativity. The company strongly believes in the corporate philosophy of fulfilling its commitments to its customers.

MICROSOFT CORPORATE VISION
Microsoft's vision is to enable people and businesses throughout the world to realize their full potential.

Quality Award. Each year up to two Baldrige Awards can be given in three categories of a company's operations: manufacturing, services, and small businesses.

Vision Statement

vision statement
A statement that presents a firm's strategic intent designed to focus the energies and resources of the company on achieving a desirable future.

Whereas the mission statement expresses an answer to the question "What business are we in?" a company **vision statement** is sometimes developed to express the aspirations of the executive leadership. A vision statement presents the firm's strategic intent that focuses the energies and resources of the company on achieving a desirable future. However, in actual practice, the mission and vision statement are frequently combined into a single statement. When they are separated, the vision statement is often a single sentence, designed to be memorable. For examples, see Exhibit 2.10, Strategy in Action.

An Exemplary Mission Statement

When BB&T merged with Southern Bank, the board of directors and officers undertook the creation of a comprehensive mission statement that was designed to include most of the topics that we discussed in this chapter. In 2003, the company updated its statement and mailed the resulting booklet to its shareholders and other interested parties. The foreword to the document expresses the greatest values of such a public pronouncement and was signed by BB&T's chairman and CEO, John A. Allison:

> In a rapidly changing and unpredictable world, individuals and organizations need a clear set of fundamental principles to guide their actions. At BB&T we know the content of our business will, and should, experience constant change. Change is necessary for progress. However, the context, our fundamental principles, is unchanging because these principles are based on basic truths.

BB&T is a mission-driven organization with a clearly defined set of values. We encourage our employees to have a strong sense of purpose, a high level of self-esteem and the capacity to think clearly and logically.

We believe that competitive advantage is largely in the minds of our employees as represented by their capacity to turn rational ideas into action towards the accomplishment of our mission.

The Chapter 2 Appendix presents BB&T's vision, mission, and purpose statement in its entirety. It also includes detailed expressions of the company's values and views on the role of emotions, management style, the management concept, attributes of an outstanding employee, the importance of positive attitude, obligations to its employees, virtues of an outstanding credit culture, achieving the company goal, the nature of a "world standard" revenue-driven sales organization, the nature of a "world standard" client service community bank, the company's commitment to education and learning, and its passions.

BOARDS OF DIRECTORS

Who is responsible for determining the firm's mission? Who is responsible for acquiring and allocating resources so the firm can thoughtfully develop and implement a strategic plan? Who is responsible for monitoring the firm's success in the competitive marketplace to determine whether that plan was well designed and activated? The answer to all of these questions is strategic decision makers. Most organizations have multiple levels of strategic decision makers; typically, the larger the firm, the more levels it will have. The strategic managers at the highest level are responsible for decisions that affect the entire firm, commit the firm and its resources for the longest periods, and declare the firm's sense of values. In other words, this group of strategic managers is responsible for overseeing the creation and accomplishment of the company mission. The term that describes the group is **board of directors**.

board of directors
The group of stock-holder representatives and strategic managers responsible for over-seeing the creation and accomplishment of the company mission.

In overseeing the management of a firm, the board of directors operates as the representatives of the firm's stockholders. Elected by the stockholders, the board has these major responsibilities:

1. To establish and update the company mission.
2. To elect the company's top officers, the foremost of whom is the CEO.
3. To establish the compensation levels of the top officers, including their salaries and bonuses.
4. To determine the amount and timing of the dividends paid to stockholders.
5. To set broad company policy on such matters as labor–management relations, product or service lines of business, and employee benefit packages.
6. To set company objectives and to authorize managers to implement the long-term strategies that the top officers and the board have found agreeable.
7. To mandate company compliance with legal and ethical dictates.

In the current business environment, boards of directors are accepting the challenge of shareholders and other stakeholders to become active in establishing the strategic initiatives of the companies that they serve.

This chapter considers the board of directors because the board's greatest impact on the behavior of a firm results from its determination of the company mission. The philosophy espoused in the mission statement sets the tone by which the firm and all of its employees will be judged. As logical extensions of the mission statement, the firm's objectives and strategies embody the board's view of proper business demeanor. Through its appointment

Hello, You Must Be Going

When Catherine West arrived at JCPenney Co.'s Plano (Texas) offices in June 2006 as the new chief operating officer, she brought a gold-plated record. Penney CEO Myron E. Ullman called her a "world-class" executive. He was so confident she had what it would take to succeed that he gave her a contract guaranteeing a $10 million payment when she left the retailer, even in the remote event that she took off in less than a year.

That's just what happened. By December 28, 2006, Ullman felt no holiday goodwill toward West. She was terminated "due to her failure to satisfy performance objectives," primarily "gaining an understanding of the company's operations," Penney reported.

At Wal-Mart Stores Inc., two marketing managers and the head of global procurement left, all in under 12 months. Home Depot Inc. lost its head of marketing and merchandising, Tom Taylor, in similarly short order. Gap Inc. said good-bye to veteran Liz Claiborne Inc. manager Denise Johnston after only 9 months in her role heading up Gap Adult. Software maker Adobe Systems Inc. and retailer Sears Holdings Corp. both lost chief financial officers within 6 months. And Ford Motor Co. continued to crank through executives, among them Chief Operations Officer Anne Stevens, who lasted 11 months in that role.

The brutal reality is that executives have less time than ever to prove their worth. Tough global competition, more diligent regulators, increasingly engaged boards of directors, and demanding investors have combined to create an environment in which a new hire has to show results almost from Day One. In 2006, there were 28,058 executive turnovers, including board members and executives from CEO down to vice-president, a 68 percent increase over 2005, according to Liberum Research's analysis of North American public companies.

When a company ejects a high-profile hire in under a year, the problem is usually not one of ability but of style. The person clashes with the CEO, inspires resentment in co-workers, or pushes for too much change too quickly.

The new high-pressure climate reaches to every member of a company's top management. At large companies, chief financial officers are turning over at a rate of 22 percent a year, according to Russell Reynolds Associates, because CFOs are under pressure in the regime of Sarbanes-Oxley, but also because they are the face of the company to Wall Street.

But if there's one job that is most firmly in the danger zone at present, it's the chief of marketing, a spot with a dangerous combination of lofty goals and quickly measured returns. So while the typical CEO today has a five-year tenure, search firm Spencer Stuart has found the chief marketing officer has only 23 months in the job.

Source: Reprinted with special permission from Nanette Byrnes and David Kiley, "Hello, You Must Be Going," *BusinessWeek*, February 12, 2007. Copyright © 2007 The McGraw-Hill Companies.

of top executives and its decisions about their compensation, the board reveals its priorities for organizational achievement.

Evidence of the high level of involvement of the board of directors in providing active direction for their businesses is the increasing rate of CEO replacement. Exhibit 2.11, Strategy in Action, provides an interesting discussion on the short tenure that CEOs frequently experience.

AGENCY THEORY

Whenever there is a separation of the owners (principals) and the managers (agents) of a firm, the potential exists for the wishes of the owners to be ignored. This fact, and the recognition that agents are expensive, established the basis for a set of complex but helpful ideas known as **agency theory.** Whenever owners (or managers) delegate decision-making authority to others, an agency relationship exists between the two parties. Agency relationships, such as those between stockholders and managers, can be very effective as

agency theory
A set of ideas on organizational control based on the belief that the separation of the ownership from management creates the potential for the wishes of owners to be ignored.

long as managers make investment decisions in ways that are consistent with stockholders' interests. However, when the interests of managers diverge from those of owners, then managers' decisions are more likely to reflect the managers' preferences than the owners' preferences.

In general, owners seek stock value maximization. When managers hold important blocks of company stock, they too prefer strategies that result in stock appreciation. However, when managers better resemble "hired hands" than owner-partners, they often prefer strategies that increase their personal payoffs rather than those of shareholders. Such behavior can result in decreased stock performance (as when high executive bonuses reduce corporate earnings) and in strategic decisions that point the firm in the direction of outcomes that are suboptimal from a stockholder's perspective.

If, as agency theory argues, self-interested managers act in ways that increase their own welfare at the expense of the gain of corporate stockholders, then owners who delegate decision-making authority to their agents will incur both the loss of potential gain that would have resulted from owner-optimal strategies and/or the costs of monitoring and control systems that are designed to minimize the consequences of such self-centered management decisions. In combination, the cost of agency problems and the cost of actions taken to minimize agency problems are called **agency costs.** These costs can often be identified by their direct benefit for the agents and their negative present value. Agency costs are found when there are differing self-interests between shareholders and managers, superiors and subordinates, or managers of competing departments or branch offices.

agency costs
The cost of agency problems and the cost of actions taken to minimize them.

How Agency Problems Occur

Because owners have access to only a relatively small portion of the information that is available to executives about the performance of the firm and cannot afford to monitor every executive decision or action, executives are often free to pursue their own interests. This condition is known as the **moral hazard problem.** It is also called shirking to suggest "self-interest combined with smile."

moral hazard problem
An agency problem that occurs because owners have limited access to company information, making executives free to pursue their own interests.

As a result of moral hazards, executives may design strategies that provide the greatest possible benefits for themselves, with the welfare of the organization being given only secondary consideration. For example, executives may presell products at year-end to trigger their annual bonuses even though the deep discounts that they must offer will threaten the price stability of their products for the upcoming year. Similarly, unchecked executives may advance their own self-interests by slacking on the job, altering forecasts to maximize their performance bonuses; unrealistically assessing acquisition targets' outlooks in order to increase the probability of increasing organizational size through their acquisition; or manipulating personnel records to keep or acquire key company personnel.

adverse selection
An agency problem caused by the limited ability of stockholders to precisely determine the competencies and priorities of executives at the time they are hired.

The second major reason that agency costs are incurred is known as **adverse selection.** This refers to the limited ability that stockholders have to precisely determine the competencies and priorities of executives at the time that they are hired. Because principals cannot initially verify an executive's appropriateness as an agent of the owners, unanticipated problems of nonoverlapping priorities between owners and agents are likely to occur.

The most popular solution to moral dilemma and adverse selection problems is for owners to attempt to more closely align their own best interests with those of their agents through the use of executive bonus plans.[1] Foremost among these approaches are stock option plans, which enable executives to benefit directly from the appreciation of the company's stock just as other stockholders do. In most instances, executive bonus plans are unabashed attempts to align the interests of owners and executives and to thereby induce

---

[1] An in-depth discussion of executive bonus compensation is provided in Chapter 10.

executives to support strategies that increase stockholder wealth. While such schemes are unlikely to eliminate self-interest as a major criterion in executive decision making, they help to reduce the costs associated with moral dilemmas and adverse selections.

Problems That Can Result from Agency

From a strategic management perspective there are five different kinds of problems that can arise because of the agency relationship between corporate stockholders and their company's executives:

1. Executives pursue growth in company size rather than in earnings. Shareholders generally want to maximize earnings, because earnings growth yields stock appreciation. However, because managers are typically more heavily compensated for increases in firm size than for earnings growth, they may recommend strategies that yield company growth such as mergers and acquisitions.

In addition, managers' stature in the business community is commonly associated with company size. Managers gain prominence by directing the growth of an organization, and they benefit in the forms of career advancement and job mobility that are associated with increases in company size.

Finally, executives need an enlarging set of advancement opportunities for subordinates whom they wish to motivate with nonfinancial inducements. Acquisitions can provide the needed positions.

2. Executives attempt to diversify their corporate risk. Whereas stockholders can vary their investment risks through management of their individual stock portfolios, managers' careers and stock incentives are tied to the performance of a single corporation, albeit the one that employs them. Consequently, executives are tempted to diversify their corporation's operation, businesses, and product lines to moderate the risk incurred in any single venture. While this approach serves the executives' personal agendas, it compromises the "pure play" quality of their firm as an investment. In other words, diversifying a corporation reduces the beta associated with the firm's return, which is an undesirable outcome for many stockholders.

3. Executives avoid risk. Even when, or perhaps especially when, executives are willing to restrict the diversification of their companies, they are tempted to minimize the risk that they face. Executives are often fired for failure, but rarely for mediocre corporate performance. Therefore, executives may avoid desirable levels of risk if they anticipate little reward and opt for conservative strategies that minimize the risk of company failure. If they do, executives will rarely support plans for innovation, diversification, and rapid growth.

However, from an investor's perspective, risk taking is desirable when it is systematic. In other words, when investors can reasonably expect that their company will generate higher long-term returns from assuming greater risk, they may wish to pursue the greater payoff, especially when the company is positioned to perform better than its competitors that face the same nominal risks. Obviously, the agency relationship creates a problem—should executives prioritize their job security or the company's financial returns to stockholders?

4. Managers act to optimize their personal payoffs. If executives can gain more from an annual performance bonus by achieving objective 1 than from stock appreciation resulting from the achievement of objective 2, then owners must anticipate that the executives will target objective 1 as their priority, even though objective 2 is clearly in the best interest of the shareholders. Similarly, executives may pursue a range of expensive perquisites that have a net negative effect on shareholder returns. Elegant corner offices, corporate jets, large staffs, golf club memberships, extravagant retirement programs, and limousines for executive benefit are rarely good investments for stockholders.

5. Executives act to protect their status. When their companies expand, executives want to ensure that their knowledge, experience, and skills remain relevant and central to the strategic direction of the corporation. They favor doing more of what they already do well. In contrast, investors may prefer revolutionary advancement to incremental improvement. For example, when confronted with Amazon.com, competitor Barnes & Noble initiated a joint venture Web site with Bertelsmann. In addition, Barnes & Noble used vertical integration with the nation's largest book distributor, which supplies 60 percent of Amazon's books. This type of revolutionary strategy is most likely to occur when executives are given assurances that they will not make themselves obsolete within the changing company that they create.

Solutions to the Agency Problem

In addition to defining an agent's responsibilities in a contract and including elements like bonus incentives that help align executives' and owners' interests, principals can take several other actions to minimize agency problems. The first is for the owners to pay executives a premium for their service. This premium helps executives to see their loyalty to the stockholders as the key to achieving their personal financial targets.

A second solution to agency problems is for executives to receive backloaded compensation. This means that executives are paid a handsome premium for superior future performance. Strategic actions taken in year one, which are to have an impact in year three, become the basis for executive bonuses in year three. This lag time between action and bonus more realistically rewards executives for the consequences of their decision making, ties the executive to the company for the long term, and properly focuses strategic management activities on the future.

Finally, creating teams of executives across different units of a corporation can help to focus performance measures on organizational rather than personal goals. Through the use of executive teams, owner interests often receive the priority that they deserve.

Summary

Defining the company mission is one of the most often slighted tasks in strategic management. Emphasizing the operational aspects of long-range management activities comes much more easily for most executives. But the critical role of the mission statement repeatedly is demonstrated by failing firms whose short-run actions have been at odds with their long-run purposes.

The principal value of the mission statement is its specification of the firm's ultimate aims. A firm gains a heightened sense of purpose when its board of directors and its top executives address these issues: "What business are we in?" "What customers do we serve?" "Why does this organization exist?" However, the potential contribution of the company mission can be undermined if platitudes or ambiguous generalizations are accepted in response to these questions. It is not enough to say that Lever Brothers is in the business of "making anything that cleans anything" or that Polaroid is committed to businesses that deal with "the interaction of light and matter." Only if a firm clearly articulates its long-term intentions can its goals serve as a basis for shared expectations, planning, and performance evaluation.

A mission statement that is developed from this perspective provides managers with a unity of direction transcending individual, parochial, and temporary needs. It promotes a sense of shared expectations among all levels and generations of employees. It consolidates values over time and across individuals and interest groups. It projects a sense of worth and intent that can be identified and assimilated by outside stakeholders, that is, customers, suppliers, competitors, local committees, and the general public. Finally, it asserts the firm's commitment to responsible action in symbiosis with the preservation and protection of the essential claims of insider stakeholders' survival, growth, and profitability.

Key Terms

adverse selection, *p. 40*	board of directors, *p. 38*	moral hazard problem, *p. 40*
agency costs, *p. 40*	company creed, *p. 30*	vision statement, *p. 37*
agency theory, *p. 40*	company mission, *p. 25*	

Questions for Discussion

1. Reread Nicor Inc.'s mission statement in Exhibit 2.1, Strategy in Action. List five insights into Nicor that you feel you gained from knowing its mission.
2. Locate the mission statement of a company not mentioned in the chapter. Where did you find it? Was it presented as a consolidated statement, or were you forced to assemble it yourself from various publications of the firm? How many of the mission statement elements outlined in this chapter were discussed or revealed in the statement you found?
3. Prepare a two-page typewritten mission statement for your school of business or for a firm selected by your instructor.
4. List five potentially vulnerable areas of a firm without a stated company mission.
5. Mission statements are often criticized for being lists of platitudes. What can strategic managers do to prevent their statements from appearing to be simple statements of obvious truths?
6. What evidence do you see that mission statements are valuable?
7. How can a mission statement be an enduring statement of values and simultaneously provide a basis of competitive advantage?
8. If the goal of survival refers to ability to maintain a specific legal form, what are the comparative advantages of sole proprietorships, partnerships, and corporations?
9. In the 1990s many Nasdaq firms favored growth over profitability; in the 2000s the goal of profitability is displacing growth. How might each preference be explained?
10. Do you agree that a mission statement provides substantive guidance while a vision statement provides inspirational guidance? Explain.

Chapter 2 Discussion Case

BusinessWeek

Anger over CEO Pay Has Put Directors on the Hot Seat

1 A new era for directors dawned with the passage of the Sarbanes-Oxley Act of 2002. Then board members were hit with the frightening prospect of real financial liability in a smattering of lawsuits that followed the corporate crime wave. Now the heat on directors is growing more intense. Their reputations are increasingly at risk when the companies they watch over are tainted by scandal. Their judgment is being questioned by activist shareholders outraged by sky-high pay packages. And investors and regulators are subjecting their actions to higher scrutiny. Long gone are the days when a director could get away with a quick rubber-stamp of a CEO's plans.

2 The old rules of civility that discouraged directors from asking managers tough or embarrassing questions are eroding. At the same time, board members are being forced to devote more time and energy to many of their most important duties: setting CEO compensation, overseeing the auditing of financial statements, and, when needed, investigating crises. That's the good news. The bad news is they are so busy delving into the minutiae of compliance that they don't have nearly as much time to advise corporate chieftains on strategy. Many board candidates no longer find the job attractive.

3 The hottest issue for boards is executive compensation. For the first time ever, companies are required to disclose a complete tally of everything they have promised to pay their executives, including such until now hidden or difficult-to-find items as severance, deferred pay, accumulated pension benefits, and perks worth more than $10,000. They will also have to provide an explanation of how and why they've chosen to pay executives as they do. The numbers are likely to be eye-popping. Michael S. Melbinger, a top compensation lawyer in Chicago, thinks that when all the proxies are filed, there could be 50 companies or more with CEO pay packages worth $150 million-plus.

4   And this is, believe it or not, coming as just as big a surprise to many directors as it will be to investors. Up to now, most directors have never seen a tally for the total pay they've promised to executives. "Pay was all compartmentalized: Boards would approve a salary, a certain amount for a bonus, or a certain amount if he got fired, but no one ever added it all up," says Fred Whittlesey, the head of pay consultants Compensation Venture Group.

5   It's not just compensation committee members who find the world changing. Audit committees used to meet only twice a year: once when it was time to take the audit in and once more to ratify it. Dick Swanson, chair of the audit committees of two NASDAQ-traded companies, says he now holds 8 to 12 meetings a year for each committee. In addition, he spends many more hours keeping up on what all the other board committees are doing, especially focusing on any risk—financial, operational, or otherwise—that the company may run. "It's not like the old days when you could join a board for the twice-a-year dinners," says Swanson.

PLAYBOOK: BEST-PRACTICE IDEAS

6   The New Rules for Directors

Pay

7   Companies will disclose full details of CEO payouts for the first time in their 2007 SEC filings. Activist investors are already drawing up hit lists of companies where CEO paychecks are out of step with performance.

Know the Math

8   Before OK'ing any financial package, directors must make sure they can explain the numbers. They need to adopt the mindset of an activist investor and ask, What's the harshest criticism someone could make about this package?

Strategy

9   Boards have been so focused on compliance that duties like strategy and leadership oversight too often get short shrift. Only 59 percent of directors in a recent study rated their board favorably on setting strategy.

Make It a Priority

10   To avoid spending too much time on compliance issues, strategy has to move up to the beginning of the meeting. Annual one-, two- or three-day offsite meetings on strategy alone are becoming standard for good boards.

Financials

11   Although 95 percent of directors in the recent study said they were doing a good job of monitoring financials, the number of earnings restatements hit a new high in 2006, after breaking records in 2004 and 2005.

Put in the Time

12   Even nonfinancial board members need to monitor the numbers and keep a close eye on cash flows. Audit committee members: prepare to spend 300 hours a year on committee responsibilities.

Crisis Management

13   Some 120 companies are under scrutiny for options backdating, and the 100 largest companies have replaced 56 CEOs in the past five years, nearly double the terminations in the prior five years.

Dig In

14   The increased scrutiny on boards means that a perfunctory review will not suffice if a scandal strikes. Directors can no longer afford to defer to management in a crisis. They must roll up their sleeves and move into watchdog mode.

DISCUSSION QUESTIONS

1. What influence do you believe shareholders have over a company's board of directors?
2. What is an appropriate compensation package for a CEO?
3. What relationship do you see between a company's board of directors and the development of the business strategy?
4. Do you believe that a company's board of directors can change the ethical standards in a business? How can they do it?
5. Would you like to serve on a company's board of directors? What do you think that you could accomplish? What do you believe would be fair compensation to you for your contribution and personal liability?

Chapter 2 Appendix

BB&T Vision, Mission, and Purpose

BB&T Vision

To create the best financial institution possible: *"The Best of The Best."*

BB&T Mission

To make the world a better place to live by: helping our clients achieve economic success and financial security; creating a place where our employees can learn, grow and be fulfilled in their work; making the communities in which we work better places to be; and thereby: optimizing the long-term return to our shareholders, while providing a safe and sound investment.

BB&T Purpose

Our ultimate purpose is to create superior long-term economic rewards for our shareholders.

This purpose is defined by the free market and is as it should be. Our shareholders provide the capital that is necessary to make our business possible. They take the risk if the business is unsuccessful. They have the right to receive economic rewards for the risk which they have undertaken.

However, our purpose, to create superior long-term economic rewards for our shareholders, can only be accomplished by providing excellent service to our clients, as our clients are our source of revenues.

To have excellent client relations, we must have outstanding employees to serve our clients. To attract and retain outstanding employees, we must reward them financially and create an environment where they can learn and grow.

Our economic results are significantly impacted by the success of our communities. The community's "quality of life" impacts its ability to attract industry for growth.

Therefore, we manage our business in a long-term context, as an integrated whole, with the ultimate objective of rewarding the shareholders for their investment, while realizing that the cause of this result is quality client service. Excellent service will be delivered by motivated employees working as an integrated team. These results will be impacted by our capacity to contribute to the growth and well-being of the communities we serve.

Values

"Excellence is an art won by training and habituation. We are what we repeatedly do. Excellence then is not an act, but a habit."—Aristotle

The great Greek philosophers saw values as guides to excellence in thinking and action. In this context, values are standards which we strive to achieve. Values are practical habits that enable us as individuals to live, be successful and achieve happiness. For BB&T, our values enable us to achieve our mission and corporate purpose.

To be useful, values must be consciously held and be consistent (noncontradictory). Many people have conflicting values which prevent them from acting with clarity and self-confidence.

There are 10 primary values at BB&T. These values are consistent with one another and are integrated. To fully act on one of these values, you must also act consistently with the other values. Our focus on values grows from our belief that ideas matter and that an individual's character is of critical significance.

Values are important at BB&T!

1. Reality (Fact-Based)

What is, is. If we want to be better, we must act within the context of reality (the facts). Businesses and individuals often make serious mistakes by making decisions based on what they "wish was so," or based on theories which are disconnected from reality. The foundation for quality decision making is a careful understanding of the facts.

There is a fundamental difference between the laws of nature (reality), which are immutable, and the man-made. The law of gravity is the law of gravity. The existence of the law of gravity does not mean man can not create an airplane. However, an airplane must be created within the context of the law of gravity. At BB&T, we believe in being "reality grounded."

2. Reason (Objectivity)

Mankind has a specific means of survival, which is his ability to think, i.e., his capacity to reason logically from the facts of reality as presented to his five senses. A lion has claws to hunt. A deer has swiftness to avoid the hunter. Man has his ability to think. There is only one "natural resource"—the human mind.

Clear thinking is not automatic. It requires intellectual discipline and begins with sound premises based on observed facts. You must be able to draw general conclusions in a rational manner from specific examples (induction) and be able to apply general principles to the solution of specific problems (deduction). You must be able to think in an integrated way, thereby avoiding logical contradictions.

We cannot all be geniuses, but each of us can develop the mental habits which ensure that when making decisions we carefully examine the facts and think logically without contradiction in deriving a conclusion. We must learn to think in terms of what is essential, i.e., about what is important. Our goal is to objectively make the best decision to accomplish our purpose.

Rational thinking is a learned skill which requires mental focus and a fundamental commitment to consistently improving the clarity of our mental processes. At BB&T, we are looking for people who are committed to constantly improving their ability to reason.

3. Independent Thinking
All employees are challenged to use their individual minds to their optimum to make rational decisions. In this context, each of us is *responsible* for what we do and who we are. In addition, creativity is strongly encouraged and only possible with independent thought.

We learn a great deal from each other. Teamwork is important at BB&T (as will be discussed later). However, each of us thinks alone. Our minds are not physically connected. In this regard, each of us must be willing to make an independent judgment of the facts based on our capacity to think logically. Just because the "crowd" says it is so, does not make it so.

In this context, each of us is responsible for our own actions. Each of us is responsible for our personal success or failure; that is, it is not the bank's fault if someone does not achieve his objectives.

All human progress by definition is based on creativity, because creativity is the source of positive change. Creativity is only possible to an independent thinker. Creativity is not about just doing something different. It is about doing something better. To be better, the new method/process must be judged by its impact on the whole organization, and as to whether it contributes to the accomplishment of our mission.

There is an infinite opportunity for each of us to do whatever we do better. A significant aspect of the self-fulfillment which work can provide comes from creative thought and action.

4. Productivity
We are committed to being producers of wealth and well-being by taking the actions necessary to accomplish our mission. The tangible evidence of our productivity is that we have rationally allocated capital through our lending and investment process, and that we have provided needed services to our clients in an efficient manner resulting in superior profitability.

Profitability is a measure of the differences in the economic value of the products/services we produce and the cost of producing these products/services. In a long-term context and in a free market, the bigger the profit, the better. This is true not only from our shareholders' perspective (which would be enough justification), but also in terms of the impact of our work on society as a whole. Healthy profits represent productive work. At BB&T we are looking for people who want to create, to produce, and who are thereby committed to turning their thoughts into actions that improve economic well-being.

5. Honesty
Being honest is simply being consistent with reality. To be dishonest is to be in conflict with reality, which is therefore self-defeating. A primary reason that individuals fail is because they become disconnected from reality, pretending that facts are other than they are.

To be honest does not require that we know everything. Knowledge is always contextual and man is not omniscient. However, we must be responsible for saying what we mean and meaning what we say.

6. Integrity
Because we have developed our principles logically, based on reality, we will always act consistently with our principles. Regardless of the short-term benefits, acting inconsistently with our principles is to our long-term detriment. We do not, therefore, believe in compromising our principles in any situation.

Principles provide carefully thought-out concepts which will lead to our long-term success and happiness. Violating our principles will always lead to failure. BB&T is an organization of the highest integrity.

7. Justice (Fairness)
Individuals should be evaluated and rewarded objectively (for better or worse) based on their contributions toward accomplishing our mission and adherence to our values. Those who contribute the most should receive the most.

The single most significant way in which employees evaluate their managers is in determining whether the manager is just. Employees become extremely unhappy (and rightly so) when they perceive that a person who is not contributing is overrewarded or a strong contributor is underrewarded.

If we do not reward those who contribute the most, they will leave and our organization will be less successful. Even more important, if there is no reward for superior performance, the average person will not be motivated to maximize his productivity.

We must evaluate whether the food we eat is healthy, the clothes we wear attractive, the car we drive functional, etc., and we must also evaluate whether relationships with other people are good for us or not.

In evaluating other people, it is critical that we judge based on essentials. At BB&T we do not discriminate based on nonessentials such as race, sex, nationality, etc. We do discriminate based on competency, performance and character. We consciously reject egalitarianism and collectivism. Individuals must be judged individually based on their personal merits, not their membership in any group.

8. Pride
Pride is the psychological reward we earn from living by our values, that is, from being just, honest, having integrity, being an independent thinker, being productive and rational.

Aristotle believed that "earned" pride (not arrogance) was the highest of virtues, because it presupposed all the others. Striving for earned pride simply reinforces the importance of having high moral values.

Each of us must perform our work in a manner as to be able to be justly proud of what we have accomplished. BB&T must be the kind of organization with which each employee and client can be proud to be associated.

9. Self-Esteem (Self-Motivation)

We expect our employees to earn positive self-esteem from doing their work well. We expect and want our employees to act in their rational, long-term self-interest. We want employees who have strong personal goals and who expect to be able to accomplish their goals within the context of our mission.

A necessary attribute for self-esteem is self-motivation. We have a strong work ethic. We believe that you receive from your work in proportion to how much you contribute. If you do not want to work hard, work somewhere else.

While there are many trade-offs in the content of life, you need to be clear that BB&T is the best place, all things considered, for you to work to accomplish your long-term goals. When you know this, you can be more productive and happy.

10. Teamwork/Mutual Supportiveness

While independent thought and strong personal goals are critically important, our work is accomplished within teams. Each of us must consistently act to achieve the agreed-upon objectives of the team, with respect for our fellow employees, while acting in a mutually supportive manner.

Our work at BB&T is so complex that it requires an integrated effort among many people to accomplish important tasks. While we are looking for self-motivated and independent thinking individuals, these individuals must recognize that almost nothing at BB&T can be accomplished without the help of their team members. One of the responsibilities of leadership in our organization is to ensure that each individual is rewarded based on their contribution to the success of the total team. We need outstanding individuals working together to create an outstanding team.

Our values are held consciously and are logically consistent. To fully execute on any one value, you must act consistently with all 10 values. At BB&T values are practical and important.

The Role of Emotions

Often people believe that making logical decisions means that we should be unemotional and that emotions are thereby unimportant. In fact, emotions are important. However, the real issue is how rational are our emotions. Emotions are mental habits which are often developed as children. Emotions give us automatic responses to people and events; these responses can either be very useful or destructive indicators. Emotions as such are not means of decision or of knowledge; the issue is: How were your emotions formed? The real question is, Are we happy when we should be happy, and unhappy when we should be unhappy, or are we unhappy when we should be happy?

Emotions are learned behaviors. The goal is to "train up" our emotions so that our emotions objectively reinforce the best decisions and behaviors toward our long-term success and happiness. Just because someone is unemotional does not mean that they are logical.

Concepts That Describe BB&T

1. Client-Driven

"World class" client service organization.
Our clients are our partners.
Our goal is to create win/win relationships.
"You can tell we want your business."
"It is easy to do business with BB&T."
"Respect the individual, value the relationship."

We will absolutely never, ever, take advantage of anyone, nor do we want to do business with those who would take advantage of us. Our clients are long-term partners and should be treated accordingly. One of the attributes of partnerships is that both partners must keep their agreements. We keep our agreements. When our partners fail to keep their agreements, they are terminating the partnership.

There are an infinite number of opportunities where we can get better together, where we can help our clients achieve their financial goals and where our client will enable us to make a profit in doing so.

2. Quality Oriented

Quality must be built into the process.

In every aspect of our business we want to execute and deliver quality. It is easier and less expensive to do things correctly than to fix what has been done incorrectly.

3. Efficient

"Waste not, want not."
Design efficiency into the system.

4. Growing Both Our Business and Our People

Grow or die.
Life requires constant, focused thought and actions towards one's goals.

5. Continuous Improvement

Everything can be done better.
Fundamental commitment to innovation.
Every employee should constantly use their reasoning ability to do whatever they do better every day. All managers of systems/processes should constantly search for better methods to solve problems and serve the client.

6. Objective Decision Making

Fact-based and rational.

BB&T Management Style

Participative
Team Oriented
Fact-Based
Rational
Objective

Our management process, by intention, is designed to be participative and team oriented. We work hard to create consensus. When people are involved in the decision process, better information is available to make decisions. The participant's understanding of the decision is greater and, therefore, execution is better.

However, there is a risk in participative decision making: the decision process can become a popularity contest. Therefore, our decision process is disciplined. Our decisions will be made based on the facts using reason. The best objective decision will be the one which is enacted.

Therefore, it does not matter whom you know, who your friends are, etc.; it matters whether you can offer the best objective solution to accomplishing the goal or solving the problem at hand.

BB&T Management Concept

Hire excellent people
Train them well
Give them an appropriate level of authority and responsibility
Expect a high level of achievement
Reward their performance

Our concept is to operate a highly autonomous, entrepreneurial organization. In order to execute this concept, we must have extremely competent individuals who are "masters" of BB&T's philosophy and who are "masters" in their field of technical expertise.

By having individuals who are "masters" in their field, we can afford to have less costly control systems and be more responsive in meeting the needs of our clients.

Attributes of an Outstanding BB&T Employee

Purpose
Rationality
Self-esteem

Consistent with our values, successful individuals at BB&T have a sense of purpose for their lives; that is, they believe that their lives matter and that they can accomplish something meaningful through their work. We are looking for people who are rational and have a high level of personal self-esteem. People with a strong personal self-esteem get along better with others, because they are at peace with themselves.

BB&T Positive Attitude

Since we build on the facts of reality and our ability to reason, we are capable of achieving both success and happiness.

We do not believe that "realism" means pessimism. On the contrary, precisely because our goals are based on and consistent with reality, we fully expect to accomplish them.

BB&T'S Obligations to Its Employees

We will do our best to:

Compensate employees fairly in relation to internal equity and market-comparable pay practices—performance-based compensation.

Provide a comprehensive and market-competitive benefit program.

Create a place where employees can learn and grow—to become more productive workers and better people.

Train employees so they are competent to do the work asked of them. (Never ask anyone to do anything they are not trained to do.)

Evaluate and recognize performance objectively, fairly and consistently based on the individual's contribution to the accomplishment of our mission and adherence to our values.

Treat each employee as an individual with dignity and respect.

Virtues of an Outstanding Credit Culture

Just as individuals need a set of values (virtues) to guide their actions, systems should be designed to have a set of attributes which optimize their performance towards our goals. In this regard, our credit culture has seven fundamental virtues:

1. Provides fundamental insight to help clients achieve their economic goals and solve their financial problems: We are in the high-quality financial advice business.
2. Responsive: The client deserves an answer as quickly as possible, even when the answer is no.
3. Flexible (Creative): We are committed to finding better ways to meet the client's financial needs.
4. Reliable: Our clients are selected as long-term partners and treated accordingly. BB&T must continue to earn the right to be known as the most reliable bank.
5. Manages risk within agreed-upon limits: Clients do not want to fail financially, and the bank does not want a bad loan.
6. Ensures an appropriate economic return to the bank for risk taken: The higher the risk, the higher the return. The lower the risk, the lower the return. This is an expression of justice.
7. Creates a "premium" for service delivery: The concept is to provide superior value to the client through outstanding service quality. A rational client will fairly compensate us when we provide sound financial advice, are responsive, creative and reliable, because these attributes are of economic value to the client.

Strategic Objectives

Create a high performance financial institution that can survive and prosper in a rapidly changing, highly competitive, globally integrated environment.

Achieving Our Goal

The key to maximizing our probability of being both independent and prosperous over the long term is to create a superior earnings per share (EPS) growth rate without sacrificing the fundamental quality and long-term competitiveness of our business and without taking unreasonable risk.

While being fundamentally efficient is critical, the "easy" way to rapid EPS growth is to artificially cut cost. However, not investing for the future is long-term suicide, as it destroys our capability to compete.

The intelligent process to achieve superior EPS growth is to grow revenues by providing (and selling) superior quality service while systematically enhancing our margins, improving our efficiency, expanding our profitable product offerings and creating more effective distribution channels.

The "World Standard" Revenue-Driven Sales Organization

At BB&T, selling is about identifying our clients' legitimate financial needs and finding a way to help the client achieve economic goals by providing the right products and services.

Effective selling requires a disciplined approach in which the BB&T employee asks the client about financial goals and problems and has a complete understanding of how our products can help the client achieve objectives and solve financial problems.

It also requires exceptional execution by support staffs and product managers, since service and sales are fundamentally connected and creativity is required in product design and development.

"World Standard" Client Service Community Banks

BB&T operates as a series of "Community Banks." The "Community Bank" concept is the foundation for local decision making and the basis for responsive, reliable and empathetic client service.

By putting decision making closer to the client, all local factors can be considered, and we can ensure that the client is being treated as an individual.

To operate in this decentralized decision-making fashion, we must have highly trained employees who understand BB&T's philosophy and are "masters" of their areas of responsibility.

Commitment to Education/Learning

Competitive advantage is in the minds of our employees. We are committed to making substantial investments in employee education to create a "knowledge-based learning organization" founded on the premise that knowledge (understanding), properly applied, is the source of superior performance.

We believe in systematized learning founded on Aristotle's concept that "excellence is an art won by training and habituation." We attempt to train our employees with the best knowledge/methods in their fields and to habituate those behaviors through consistent management reinforcement. The goal is for each employee to be a "master" of his or her role, whether it be a computer operator, teller, lender, financial consultant or any other job responsibility.

Our Passions

To create the best financial institution possible.

To consistently provide the client with better value through rational innovation and productivity improvement.

At BB&T we have two powerful passions. Our fundamental passion is our Vision: To Create The Best Financial Institution Possible—The "World Standard"—The "Best of the Best." We believe that the best can be objectively evaluated by rational performance standards in relation to the accomplishment of our mission.

To be the best of the best, we must constantly find ways to deliver better value to our clients in a highly profitable manner. This requires us to keep our minds focused at all times on innovative ways to enhance our productivity.

Chapter **Three**

Corporate Social Responsibility and Business Ethics

After reading and studying this chapter, you should be able to

1. Understand the importance of the stakeholder approach to social responsibility.

2. Explain the continuum of social responsibility and the effect of various options on company profitability.

3. Describe a social audit and explain its importance.

4. Discuss the effect of the Sarbanes-Oxley Act of 2002 on the ethical conduct of business.

5. Compare the advantages of collaborative social initiatives with alternative approaches to CSR.

6. Explain the five principles of collaborative social initiatives.

7. Compare the merits of different approaches to business ethics.

8. Explain the relevance of business ethics to strategic management practice.

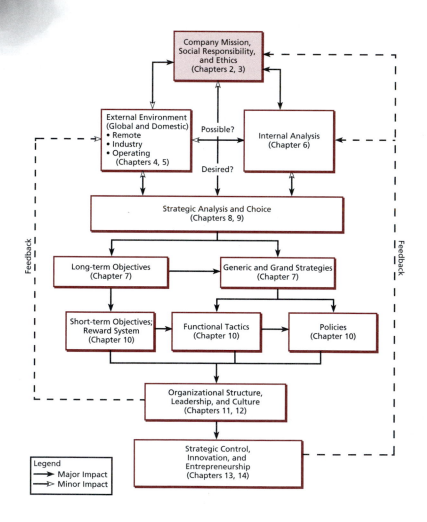

THE STAKEHOLDER APPROACH TO SOCIAL RESPONSIBILITY

In defining or redefining the company mission, strategic managers must recognize the legitimate rights of the firm's claimants. These include not only stockholders and employees but also outsiders affected by the firm's actions. Such outsiders commonly include customers, suppliers, governments, unions, competitors, local communities, and the general public. Each of these interest groups has justifiable reasons for expecting (and often for demanding) that the firm satisfy their claims in a responsible manner. In general, stockholders claim appropriate returns on their investment; employees seek broadly defined job satisfactions; customers want what they pay for; suppliers seek dependable buyers; governments want adherence to legislation; unions seek benefits for their members; competitors want fair competition; local communities want the firm to be a responsible citizen; and the general public expects the firm's existence to improve the quality of life.

According to a survey of 2,361 directors in 291 of the largest southeastern U.S. companies,

1. Directors perceived the existence of distinct stakeholder groups.
2. Directors have high stakeholder orientations.
3. Directors view some stakeholders differently, depending on their occupation (CEO directors versus non-CEO directors) and type (inside versus outside directors).

The study also found that the perceived stakeholders were, in the order of their importance, customers and government, stockholders, employees, and society. The results clearly indicated that boards of directors no longer believe that the stockholder is the only constituency to whom they are responsible.

However, when a firm attempts to incorporate the interests of these groups into its mission statement, broad generalizations are insufficient. These steps need to be taken:

1. Identification of the stakeholders.
2. Understanding the stakeholders' specific claims vis-à-vis the firm.
3. Reconciliation of these claims and assignment of priorities to them.
4. Coordination of the claims with other elements of the company mission.

Identification   The left-hand column of Exhibit 3.1 lists the commonly encountered stakeholder groups, to which the executive officer group often is added. Obviously, though, every business faces a slightly different set of stakeholder groups, which vary in number, size, influence, and importance. In defining the company, strategic managers must identify all of the stakeholder groups and weigh their relative rights and their relative ability to affect the firm's success.

Understanding   The concerns of the principal stakeholder groups tend to center on the general claims listed in the right-hand column of Exhibit 3.1. However, strategic decision makers should understand the specific demands of each group. They then will be better able to initiate actions that satisfy these demands.

Reconciliation and Priorities   Unfortunately, the claims of various stakeholder groups often conflict. For example, the claims of governments and the general public tend to limit profitability, which is the central claim of most creditors and stockholders. Thus, claims must be reconciled in a mission statement that resolves the competing, conflicting, and contradicting claims of stakeholders. For objectives and strategies to be internally consistent and precisely focused, the statement must display a single-minded, though multidimensional, approach to the firm's aims.

EXHIBIT 3.1

A Stakeholder View of Company Responsibility

Stakeholder	Nature of the Claim
Stockholders	Participation in distribution of profits, additional stock offerings, assets on liquidation; vote of stock; inspection of company books; transfer of stock; election of board of directors; and such additional rights as have been established in the contract with the corporation.
Creditors	Legal proportion of interest payments due and return of principal from the investment. Security of pledged assets; relative priority in event of liquidation. Management and owner prerogatives if certain conditions exist with the company (such as default of interest payments).
Employees	Economic, social, and psychological satisfaction in the place of employment. Freedom from arbitrary and capricious behavior on the part of company officials. Share in fringe benefits, freedom to join union and participate in collective bargaining, individual freedom in offering up their services through an employment contract. Adequate working conditions.
Customers	Service provided with the product; technical data to use the product; suitable warranties; spare parts to support the product during use; R&D leading to product improvement; facilitation of credit.
Suppliers	Continuing source of business; timely consummation of trade credit obligations; professional relationship in contracting for, purchasing, and receiving goods and services.
Governments	Taxes (income, property, and so on); adherence to the letter and intent of public policy dealing with the requirements of fair and free competition; discharge of legal obligations of business-people (and business organizations); adherence to antitrust laws.
Unions	Recognition as the negotiating agent for employees. Opportunity to perpetuate the union as a participant in the business organization.
Competitors	Observation of the norms for competitive conduct established by society and the industry. Business statesmanship on the part of peers.
Local communities	Place of productive and healthful employment in the community. Participation of company officials in community affairs, provision of regular employment, fair play, reasonable portion of purchases made in the local community, interest in and support of local government, support of cultural and charitable projects.
The general public	Participation in and contribution to society as a whole; creative communications between governmental and business units designed for reciprocal understanding; assumption of fair proportion of the burden of government and society. Fair price for products and advancement of the state-of-the-art technology that the product line involves.

Source: William R. King and David I. Cleland, *Strategic Planning and Policy,* © 1978, by Litton Educational Publishing, Inc., p. 153.

There are hundreds, if not thousands, of claims on any firm—high wages, pure air, job security, product quality, community service, taxes, occupational health and safety regulations, equal employment opportunity regulations, product variety, wide markets, career opportunities, company growth, investment security, high ROI, and many, many more. Although most, perhaps all, of these claims may be desirable ends, they cannot be pursued with equal emphasis. They must be assigned priorities in accordance with the relative emphasis that the firm will give them. That emphasis is reflected in the criteria that the firm uses in its strategic decision making; in the firm's allocation of its human, financial, and physical resources; and in the firm's long-term objectives and strategies.

Coordination with Other Elements The demands of stakeholder groups constitute only one principal set of inputs to the company mission. The other principal sets are the managerial operating philosophy and the determinants of the product-market offering. Those determinants constitute a reality test that the accepted claims must pass. The key question is, How can the firm satisfy its claimants and at the same time optimize its economic success in the marketplace?

The Dynamics of Social Responsibility

As indicated in Exhibit 3.2, the various stakeholders of a firm can be divided into inside stakeholders and outside stakeholders. The insiders are the individuals or groups that are stockholders or employees of the firm. The outsiders are all the other individuals or groups that the firm's actions affect. The extremely large and often amorphous set of outsiders makes the general claim that the firm be socially responsible.

Perhaps the thorniest issues faced in defining a company mission are those that pertain to social responsibility. Corporate social responsibility is the idea that a business has a duty to serve society in general as well as the financial interests of its stockholders. The stakeholder approach offers the clearest perspective on such issues. Broadly stated, outsiders often demand that insiders' claims be subordinated to the greater good of the society; that is, to the greater good of outsiders. They believe that such issues as pollution, the disposal of solid and liquid wastes, and the conservation of natural resources should be principal considerations in strategic decision making. Also broadly stated, insiders tend to believe that the competing claims of outsiders should be balanced against one another in a way that protects the company mission. For example, they tend to believe that the need of consumers for a product should be balanced against the water pollution resulting from its production if the firm cannot eliminate that pollution entirely and still remain profitable. Some insiders also argue that the claims of society, as expressed in government regulation, provide tax money that can be used to eliminate water pollution and the like if the general public wants this to be done.

EXHIBIT 3.2
Inputs to the Development of the Company Mission

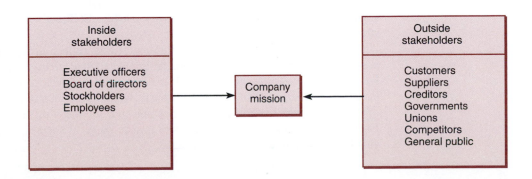

Beyond the Green Corporation

BusinessWeek

Under conventional notions of how to run a conglomerate like Unilever, CEO Patrick Cescau should wake up each morning with a laserlike focus: how to sell more soap and shampoo than Procter & Gamble Co. But ask Cescau about the $52 billion Dutch-British giant's biggest strategic challenges for the twenty-first century, and the conversation roams from water-deprived villages in Africa to the planet's warming climate.

The world is Unilever's laboratory. In Brazil, the company operates a free community laundry in a Sao Paulo slum, provides financing to help tomato growers convert to eco-friendly "drip" irrigation, and recycles 17 tons of waste annually at a toothpaste factory. Unilever funds a floating hospital that offers free medical care in Bangladesh, a nation with just 20 doctors for every 10,000 people. In Ghana, it teaches palm oil producers to reuse plant waste while providing potable water to deprived communities. In India, Unilever staff help thousands of women in remote villages start micro-enterprises. And responding to green activists, the company discloses how much carbon dioxide and hazardous waste its factories spew out around the world.

As Cescau sees it, helping such nations wrestle with poverty, water scarcity, and the effects of climate change is vital to staying competitive in coming decades. Some 40 percent of the company's sales and most of its growth now take place in developing nations. Unilever food products account for roughly 10 percent of the world's crops of tea and 30 percent of all spinach. It is also one of the world's biggest buyers of fish. As environmental regulations grow tighter around the world, Unilever must invest in green technologies or its leadership in packaged foods, soaps, and other goods could be imperiled. "You can't ignore the impact your company has on the community and environment," Cescau says. CEOs used to frame thoughts like these in the context of moral responsibility, he adds. But now, "it's also about growth and innovation. In the future, it will be the only way to do business."

The accompanying table on page 55 lists corporations and the actions that they have taken to be judged as having made important contributions to social initiatives.

Source: Reprinted with special permission from Pete Engardino, with Kerry Capell in London, John Carey in Washington, Kenji Hall in Tokyo, "Beyond the Green Corporation," *BusinessWeek*, January 29, 2007. Copyright © 2007 The McGraw-Hill Companies.

The issues are numerous, complex, and contingent on specific situations. Thus, rigid rules of business conduct cannot deal with them. Each firm *regardless of size* must decide how to meet its perceived social responsibility. While large, well-capitalized companies may have easy access to environmental consultants, this is not an affordable strategy for smaller companies. However, the experience of many small businesses demonstrates that it is feasible to accomplish significant pollution prevention and waste reduction without big expenditures and without hiring consultants. Once a problem area has been identified, a company's line employees frequently can develop a solution. Other important pollution prevention strategies include changing the materials used or redesigning how operations are bid out. Making pollution prevention a social responsibility can be beneficial to smaller companies. Publicly traded firms also can benefit directly from socially responsible strategies.

Different approaches adopted by different firms reflect differences in competitive position, industry, country, environmental and ecological pressures, and a host of other factors. In other words, they will reflect both situational factors and differing priorities in the acknowledgment of claims. Obviously, winning the loyalty of the growing legions of consumers will require new strategies and new alliances in the twenty-first century. Exhibit 3.3, Strategy in Action, discusses a wide range of socially responsible actions in which corporations are currently engaged.

Who's Doing Well by Doing Good

Automobiles

Toyota
The maker of the top-selling Prius hybrid leads in developing efficient gas-electric vehicles.

Renault
Integrates sustainability throughout organization; has fuel-efficient cars and factories.

Volkswagen
A market leader in small cars and clean diesel technologies.

Computers and Peripherals

Hewlett-Packard
Rates high on ecological standards and digital tech for the poor.

Toshiba
At forefront of developing eco-efficient products, such as fuel cells for notebook PC batteries.

Dell
Among the first U.S. PC makers to take hardware back from consumers and recycle it for free.

Health Care

Fresenius Medical Care
Discloses costs of its patient treatment in terms of energy and water use and waste generated.

IMS Health
Places unusual emphasis on environmental issues in its global health consulting work.

Quest Diagnostics
Has diversity program promoting businesses owned by minorities, women, and veterans.

Oil and Gas

Royal Dutch Shell
Since Nigerian human rights woes in 1990s, leads in community relations; invests in wind and solar.

Norsk Hydro
Cut greenhouse gas emissions 32 percent since 1990; strong in assessing social, environmental impact.

Suncor Energy
Ties with aboriginals help it deal with social and ecological issues in Canada's far north.

Retail

Marks & Spencer
Buys local product to cut transit costs and fuel use; good wages and benefits help retain staff.

Home retail group
High overall corporate responsibility standards have led to strong consumer and staff loyalty.

Aeon
Environmental accounting has saved $5.6 million; good employee policies in China and Southeast Asia.

Communications Equipment

Nokia
Makes phones for handicapped and low-income consumers; a leader in phasing out toxic materials.

Ericsson
Eco-friendly initiatives include wind- and fuel-cell-powered telecom systems in Nigerian villages.

Motorola
Good disclosure of environmental data; takes back used equipment in Mexico, United States, and Europe.

Financial Services

ABN Amro
Involved in carbon-emissions trading; finances everything from micro-enterprises to biomass fuels.

HSBC
Lending guidelines for forestry, freshwater, and chemical sectors factor in social, ecological risks.

Ing
Weighs sustainability in project finance; helps developing nations improve financial institutions.

Household Durables

Philips Electronics
Top innovator of energy-saving appliances, lighting, and medical gear and goods for developing world.

Sony
Is ahead on green issues and ensuring quality, safety, and labor standards of global suppliers.

Matsushita Electric
State-of-the-art green products; eliminated 96 percent of the most toxic substances in its global operations.

Pharmaceuticals

Roche
Committed to improving access to medicine in poor nations; invests in drug research for Third World.

Novo Nordisk
Spearheads efforts in diseases like leprosy and bird flu and is a leading player in lower-cost generics.

Glaxo-Smithkline
One of few pharmas to devote R&D to malaria and TB; first to offer AIDS drugs at cost.

Utilities

FPL
Largest U.S. solar generator; has 40 percent of wind-power capacity; strong shareholder relations.

Iberdrola
Since Scottish Power takeover, renewable energy accounts for 17 percent of capacity; wants that to grow.

Scottish & Southern
Aggressively discloses environmental risk, including air pollution and climate change.

Occidental Petroleum faces issues of corporate social responsibility in addressing the needs of the many stakeholders involved in the firm's oil exploration in developing countries. Many parties that have potential to be affected by the company's endeavors, including local inhabitants and government, environmental groups, and institutional investors.

Despite differences in their approaches, most American firms now try to assure outsiders that they attempt to conduct business in a socially responsible manner. Many firms, including Abt Associates, Dow Chemical, Eastern Gas and Fuel Associates, ExxonMobil, and the Bank of America, conduct and publish annual social audits. Such audits attempt to evaluate a firm from the perspective of social responsibility. Private consultants often conduct them for the firm and offer minimally biased evaluations on what are inherently highly subjective issues.

TYPES OF SOCIAL RESPONSIBILITY

To better understand the nature and range of social responsibilities for which they must plan, strategic managers can consider four types of social commitment: economic, legal, ethical, and discretionary social responsibilities.

economic responsibilities
The duty of managers, as agents of the company owners, to maximize stockholder wealth.

Economic responsibilities are the most basic social responsibilities of business. As we have noted, some economists see these as the only legitimate social responsibility of business. Living up to their economic responsibilities requires managers to maximize profits whenever possible. The essential responsibility of business is assumed to be providing goods and services to society at a reasonable cost. In discharging that economic responsibility, the company also emerges as socially responsible by providing productive jobs for its workforce, and tax payments for its local, state, and federal governments.

legal responsibilities
The firm's obligations to comply with the laws that regulate business activities.

Legal responsibilities reflect the firm's obligations to comply with the laws that regulate business activities. The consumer and environmental movements focused increased public attention on the need for social responsibility in business by lobbying for laws that govern business in the areas of pollution control and consumer safety. The intent of consumer legislation has been to correct the "balance of power" between buyers and sellers in the marketplace. Among the most important laws are the Federal Fair Packaging and Labeling Act that regulates labeling procedures for business, the Truth in Lending Act that regulates the extension of credit to individuals, and the Consumer Product Safety Act that protects consumers against unreasonable risks of injury in the use of consumer products.

The environmental movement has had a similar effect on the regulation of business. This movement achieved stricter enforcement of existing environmental protections and it spurred the passage of new, more comprehensive laws such as the National Environmental Policy Act, which is devoted to preserving the United States' ecological balance and making environmental protection a federal policy goal. It requires environmental impact studies whenever new construction may threaten an existing ecosystem, and it established the Council on Environmental Quality to guide business development. Another product of the environmental movement was the creation of the federal Environmental Protection Agency, which interprets and administers the environmental protection policies of the U.S. government.

Clearly, these legal responsibilities are supplemental to the requirement that businesses and their employees comply fully with the general civil and criminal laws that apply to all individuals and institutions in the country. Yet, strangely, individual failures to adhere to the law have recently produced some of the greatest scandals in the history of American free enterprise. Exhibit 3.4, Strategy in Action, presents an overview of seven of these cases that involved executives from Adelphia Communications, Arthur Andersen, Global Crossing, ImClone Systems, Merrill Lynch, WorldCom, and Xerox.

An Overview of Corporate Scandals*

ADELPHIA COMMUNICATIONS

On July 24, 2002, John Rigas, the 77-year-old founder of the country's sixth largest cable television operator was arrested, along with two of his sons, and accused of looting the now-bankrupt company. Several other former Adelphia executives were also arrested. The Securities and Exchange Commission (SEC) brought a civil suit against the company for allegedly fraudulently excluding billions of dollars in liabilities from its financial statements, falsifying statistics, inflating its earnings to meet Wall Street's expectations, and concealing "rampant self-dealing by the Rigas family." The family, which founded Adelphia in 1952, gave up control of the firm in May, and on June 25 the company filed for bankruptcy protection. The company was delisted by NASDAQ in June 2002.

ARTHUR ANDERSEN

On June 15, 2002, a Texas jury found the accounting firm guilty of obstructing justice for its role in shredding financial documents related to its former client Enron. Andersen, founded in 1913, had already been largely destroyed after admitting that it sped up the shredding of Enron documents following the launch of an SEC investigation. Andersen fired David Duncan, who led its Houston office, saying he was responsible for shredding the Enron documents. Duncan admitted to obstruction of justice, turned state's evidence, and testified on behalf of the government.

GLOBAL CROSSING

The SEC and the Federal Bureau of Investigation (FBI) are probing the five-year-old telecom company Global Crossing regarding alleged swaps of network capacity with other telecommunications firms to inflate revenue. The company ran into trouble by betting that it could borrow billions of dollars to build a fiber-optic infrastructure that would be in strong demand by corporations. Because others made the same bet, there was a glut of fiber optics and prices plunged, leaving Global Crossing with massive debts. It filed for bankruptcy on January 28, 2002. Chairman Gary Winnick, who founded Global Crossing in 1997, cashed out $734 million in stock before the company collapsed. Global Crossing was delisted from the New York Stock Exchange (NYSE) in January 2002.

IMCLONE SYSTEMS

The biotech firm is being investigated by a congressional committee that is seeking to find out if ImClone correctly informed investors that the Food and Drug Administration (FDA) had declined to accept for review its key experimental cancer drug, Erbitux. Former CEO Samuel Waksal pled guilty in June 2003 to insider trading charges related to Erbitux and was sentenced to seven years in prison. Also, federal investigators filed charges against home decorating diva Martha Stewart for using insider information on the cancer drug when she sold 4,000 ImClone shares one day before the FDA initially said it would reject the drug.

MERRILL LYNCH

On May 21, 2002, Merrill Lynch agreed to pay $100 million to settle New York Attorney General Eliot Spitzer's charges that the nation's largest securities firm knowingly peddled Internet stocks to investors to generate lucrative investment banking fees. Internal memos written by Merrill's feted Internet analyst Henry Blodgett revealed that company analysts thought little of the Web stocks that they urged investors to buy. Merrill agreed to strengthen firewalls between its research and investment-banking divisions, ensuring advice given to investors is not influenced by efforts to win underwriting fees.

WORLDCOM

The nation's second largest telecom company filed for the nation's biggest ever bankruptcy on July 21, 2002. WorldCom's demise accelerated on June 25, 2002, when it admitted it hid $3.85 billion in expenses, allowing it to post net income of $1.38 billion in 2001, instead of a loss. The company fired its CFO Scott Sullivan and on June 28 began cutting 17,000 jobs, more than 20 percent of its workforce. CEO Bernie Ebbers resigned in April amid questions about $408 million of personal loans he received from the company to cover losses he incurred in buying its shares. WorldCom was delisted from NASDAQ in July 2002.

XEROX

Xerox said on June 28, 2002, that it would restate five years of financial results to reclassify more than $6 billion in revenues. In April, the company settled SEC charges that it used "accounting tricks" to defraud investors, agreeing to pay a $10 million fine. The firm admitted no wrongdoing. Xerox manufactures imaging products, such as copiers, printers, fax machines, and scanners.

* This section was derived in its entirety from "A Guide to Corporate Scandals," MSNBC, www.msnbc.com/news/corpscandal front.

ethical responsibilities
The strategic managers' notion of right and proper business behavior.

Ethical responsibilities reflect the company's notion of right and proper business behavior. Ethical responsibilities are obligations that transcend legal requirements. Firms are expected, but not required, to behave ethically. Some actions that are legal might be considered unethical. For example, the manufacture and distribution of cigarettes is legal. But in light of the often-lethal consequences of smoking, many consider the continued sale of cigarettes to be unethical. The topic of management ethics receives additional attention later in this chapter.

discretionary responsibilities
Responsibilities voluntarily assumed by a business, such as public relations, good citizenship, and full corporate responsibility.

Discretionary responsibilities are those that are voluntarily assumed by a business organization. They include public relations activities, good citizenship, and full corporate social responsibility. Through public relations activities, managers attempt to enhance the image of their companies, products, and services by supporting worthy causes. This form of discretionary responsibility has a self-serving dimension. Companies that adopt the good citizenship approach actively support ongoing charities, public service advertising campaigns, or issues in the public interest. A commitment to full corporate responsibility requires strategic managers to attack social problems with the same zeal in which they attack business problems. For example, teams in the National Football League provide time off for players and other employees afflicted with drug or alcohol addictions who agree to enter rehabilitation programs.

It is important to remember that the categories on the continuum of social responsibility overlap, creating gray areas where societal expectations on organizational behavior are difficult to categorize. In considering the overlaps among various demands for social responsibility, however, managers should keep in mind that in the view of the general public, economic and legal responsibilities are required, ethical responsibility is expected, and discretionary responsibility is desired.

Corporate Social Responsibility and Profitability
CSR and the Bottom Line

corporate social responsibility
The idea that business has a duty to serve society in general as well as the financial interest of stockholders.

The goal of every firm is to maintain viability through long-run profitability. Until all costs and benefits are accounted for, however, profits may not be claimed. In the case of **corporate social responsibility** (CSR), costs and benefits are both economic and social. While economic costs and benefits are easily quantifiable, social costs and benefits are not. Managers therefore risk subordinating social consequences to other performance results that can be more straightforwardly measured.

The dynamic between CSR and success (profit) is complex. While one concept is clearly not mutually exclusive of the other, it is also clear that neither is a prerequisite of the other. Rather than viewing these two concepts as competing, it may be better to view CSR as a component in the decision-making process of business that must determine, among other objectives, how to maximize profits.

Attempts to undertake a cost-benefit analysis of CSR have not been very successful. The process is complicated by several factors. First, some CSR activities incur no dollar costs at all. For example, Second Harvest, the largest nongovernment, charitable food distributor in the nation, accepts donations from food manufacturers and food retailers of surplus food that would otherwise be thrown out due to overruns, warehouse damage, or labeling errors. In 10 years, Second Harvest has distributed more than 2 billion pounds of food. Gifts in Kind America is an organization that enables companies to reduce unsold or obsolete inventory by matching a corporation's donated products with a charity's or other nonprofit organization's needs. In addition, a tax break is realized by the company. In the past, corporate donations have included 130,000 pairs of shoes from Nike, 10,000 pairs of gloves from Aris Isotoner, and 480 computer systems from Apple Computer.

In addition, philanthropic activities of a corporation, which have been a traditional mainstay of CSR, are undertaken at a discounted cost to the firm since they are often tax deductible. The benefits of corporate philanthropy can be enormous as is shown by the many national social welfare causes that have been spurred by corporate giving. While such acts of benevolence often help establish a general perception of the involved companies within society, some philanthropic acts bring specific credit to the firm.

Second, socially responsible behavior does not come at a prohibitive cost. One needs only to look at the problems of A. H. Robbins Company (Dalkon Shield), Beech-Nut Corporation (apple juice), Drexel Burnham (insider trading), and Exxon *(Valdez)* for stark answers on the "cost" of social responsibility (or its absence) in the business environment.

Third, socially responsible practices may create savings and, as a result, increase profits. SET Laboratories uses popcorn to ship software rather than polystyrene peanuts. It is environmentally safer and costs 60 percent less to use. Corporations that offer part-time and adjustable work schedules have realized that this can lead to reduced absenteeism, greater productivity and increased morale. DuPont opted for more flexible schedules for its employees after a survey revealed 50 percent of women and 25 percent of men considered working for another employer with more flexibility for family concerns.

Proponents argue that CSR costs are more than offset in the long run by an improved company image and increased community goodwill. These intangible assets can prove valuable in a crisis, as Johnson & Johnson discovered with the Tylenol cyanide scare in 1982. Because it had established a solid reputation as a socially responsible company before the incident, the public readily accepted the company's assurances of public safety. Consequently, financial damage to Johnson & Johnson was minimized, despite the company's $100 million voluntary recall of potentially tainted capsules. CSR may also head off new regulation, preventing increased compliance costs. It may even attract investors who are themselves socially responsible. Proponents believe that for these reasons, socially responsible behavior increases the financial value of the firm in the long run. The mission statement of Johnson & Johnson is provided as Exhibit 3.5, Strategy in Action.

Performance To explore the relationship between socially responsible behavior and financial performance, an important question must first be answered: How do managers measure the financial effect of corporate social performance?

Critics of CSR believe that companies that behave in a socially responsible manner, and portfolios comprising these companies' securities, should perform more poorly financially than those that do not. The costs of CSR outweigh the benefits for individual firms, they suggest. In addition, traditional portfolio theory holds that investors minimize risk and maximize return by being able to choose from an infinite universe of investment opportunities. Portfolios based on social criteria should suffer, critics argue, because they are by definition restrictive in nature. This restriction should increase portfolio risk and reduce portfolio return.

CSR Today

CSR has become a priority with American business. In addition to a commonsense belief that companies should be able to "do well by doing good," at least three broad trends are driving businesses to adopt CSR frameworks: the resurgence of environmentalism, increasing buyer power, and the globalization of business.

The Resurgence of Environmentalism In March 1989, the Exxon *Valdez* ran aground in Prince William Sound, spilling 11 million gallons of oil, polluting miles of ocean and shore, and helping to revive worldwide concern for the ecological environment. Six months after the *Valdez* incident, the Coalition for Environmentally Responsible Economies (CERES) was formed to establish new goals for environmentally responsible corporate behavior.

Mission Statement: Johnson & Johnson

"We believe our first responsibility is to the doctors, nurses and patients, to mothers and fathers and all others who use our products and services. In meeting their needs everything we do must be of high quality. We must constantly strive to reduce our costs in order to maintain reasonable prices. Customers' orders must be serviced promptly and accurately. Our suppliers and distributors must have an opportunity to make a fair profit.

"We are responsible to our employees, the men and women who work with us throughout the world. Everyone must be considered as an individual. We must respect their dignity and recognize their merit. They must have a sense of security in their jobs. Compensation must be fair and adequate, and working conditions clean, orderly and safe. Employees must feel free to make suggestions and complaints. There must be equal opportunity for employment, development and advancement for those qualified. We must provide competent management, and their actions must be just and ethical.

"We are responsible to the communities in which we live and work and to the world community as well. We must be good citizens—support good works and charities and bear our fair share of taxes. We must encourage civic improvements and better health and education. We must maintain in good order the property we are privileged to use, protecting the environment and natural resources.

"Our final responsibility is to our stockholders. Business must make a sound profit. We must experiment with new ideas. Research must be carried on, innovative programs developed and mistakes paid for. New equipment must be purchased, new facilities provided and new products launched. Reserves must be created to provide for adverse times. When we operate according to these principles, the stockholders should realize a fair return."

Source: Johnson & Johnson, http://www.jnsj.com

The group drafted the CERES Principles to "establish an environmental ethic with criteria by which investors and others can assess the environmental performance of companies. Companies that sign these Principles pledge to go voluntarily beyond the requirements of the law."

The most prevalent forms of environmentalism are efforts to preserve natural resources and eliminating environmental pollution, often referred to as the concern for "greening." Exhibit 3.6, Strategy in Action, provides cutting-edge methods by which Bank of America is helping promote environmentalism in the construction of its new office building in New York City.

Increasing Buyer Power The rise of the consumer movement has meant that buyers—consumers and investors—are increasingly flexing their economic muscle. Consumers are becoming more interested in buying products from socially responsible companies. Organizations such as the Council on Economic Priorities (CEP) help consumers make more informed buying decisions through such publications as *Shopping for a Better World,* which provides social performance information on 191 companies making more than 2,000 consumer products. CEP also sponsors the annual Corporate Conscience Awards, which recognize socially responsible companies. One example of consumer power at work is the effective outcry over the deaths of dolphins in tuna fishermen's nets.

Investors represent a second type of influential consumer. There has been a dramatic increase in the number of people interested in supporting socially responsible companies through their investments. Membership in the Social Investment Forum, a trade association serving social investing professionals, has been growing at a rate of about 50 percent annually. As baby boomers achieve their own financial success, the social investing movement has continued its rapid growth.

Bank of America Tower: The World's Greenest Skyscraper

BusinessWeek

The world's greenest skyscraper is set to open in 2008 near Times Square. The $1.3 billion building will be New York's second tallest. The energy-efficient design of the Bank of America (BoA) building has several unique features.

- **Water from sky and earth.** Not a drop of rain that falls on BoA Tower is sent down the drain. Rather, it's collected, routed to flush toilets, used to irrigate the green roof, and to run the air conditioning (AC) system. The tower also harvests water from condensation that drips from AC systems, which in turn are cooled by groundwater that seeps in from the bedrock before being added to the rainwater tank. All this promises to save enough fresh water to supply 125 homes per year.

- **Daylight savings.** Sunlight helps students learn and workers focus. It will also help cut BoA Tower's lighting energy needs by 25 percent. Floor-to-ceiling windows, 9.5 feet tall, are made of low iron glass manufactured by PPG Industries and assembled by Permasteelisa. This lets in more visible light than normal glass, yet still insulates well. Inside, sensors control ceiling lights, turning them down when daylight is plentiful or rooms are empty.

- **Chill factor.** Heat rises. That simple force lets BoA Tower virtually do away with costly, overhead chilled-air ducts and fans. Instead, cool air is pumped into a void under raised floors. As it warms, the air rises to ceiling vents, pulling more chilled air up from below. Since this works passively, under low pressure, the AC can be set to 65°F, rather than 55°F. And eliminating miles of moist ductwork—where pathogens can play—helps improve overall building health.

- **Aired out.** Clean, oxygen-rich air delivers big productivity gains, too. BoA Tower draws in air 10 floors up or higher—far above the stew of tailpipe emissions. Filters catch 95 percent of particulate matter, allergens, ozone, and other compounds that can cause illness. Oxygen sensors trigger injections of fresh air into crowed spaces to help prevent "meeting room coma." When the used air is vented from the building, it's still cleaner than the outside atmosphere.

- **Homemade juice.** A super-efficient power plant, running on clean-burning natural gas, nearly trebles the tower's overall energy efficiency. By reusing waste heat and eliminating losses caused when electricity is shipped via power lines over long distances, the turbine meets four-fifths of the tower's peak needs. The setup wastes just 23 percent of the energy from the fuel source, far better than the 70 percent lost at a conventional grid-connected building.

- **No parking.** In gridlocked New York, a project this big would normally have hundreds of basement parking spots. BoA Tower has practically none. Instead, the tower enhances midtown's network of public transport. New pedestrian tunnels connect the tower to 17 subway lines and commuter rails. With secure bike storage and shower access, bicycling is an option, too. And if a car is a must, BoA uses OZOcar, New York's first hybrid-only fleet of liveries

- **Ice storage.** The twenty-first century's most advanced skyscraper takes a lesson from Victorian-era ice houses that collected lake ice in winter to use in summer. In the tower's basement, 44 squat cylindrical ice tanks will make ice at night, when power is cheaper, to help cool the AC system during the day. The trick cuts by 50 percent the energy needed to run the tower's AC on the hottest days, enough savings to pay for itself in three to five years. Made by CALMAC Manufacturing, the ice promises to cut pollution, too. When demand for power spikes on hot summer days, utilities fire up their least efficient, most polluting plants. BoA Tower won't need to tap much of his dirty power.

- **Waterless urinals.** For male tenants, at least, the tower's most noticeable water-savings trick may be Falcon Waterfree's flushless urinals. Made of an antibacterial, superslick material, these fixtures will save 3 million gallons of water a year. They funnel urine into a tank filled with a liquid that floats on top, like oil on water. Urine settles to the bottom and drains out to sewers.

While social investing wields relatively low power as an individual private act (selling one's shares of ExxonMobil does not affect the company), it can be very powerful as a collective public act. When investors vote their shares in behalf of pro-CSR issues, companies may be pressured to change their social behavior. The South African divestiture movement is one example of how effective this pressure can be.

The Vermont National Bank has added a Socially Responsible Banking Fund to its product line. Investors can designate any of their interest-bearing accounts with a $500 minimum balance to be used by the fund. This fund then lends these monies for purposes such as low-income housing, the environment, education, farming, or small business development. Although it has had a "humble" beginning of approximately 800 people investing about $11 million, the bank has attracted out-of-state depositors and is growing faster than expected.

Social investors comprise both individuals and institutions. Much of the impetus for social investing originated with religious organizations that wanted their investments to mirror their beliefs. At present, the ranks of social investors have expanded to include educational institutions and large pension funds.

Large-scale social investing can be broken down into the two broad areas of guideline portfolio investing and shareholder activism. Guideline portfolio investing is the largest and fastest-growing segment of social investing. Individual and institutional guideline portfolio investors use ethical guidelines as screens to identify possible investments in stocks, bonds, and mutual funds. The investment instruments that survive the social screens are then layered over the investor's financial screens to create the investor's universe of possible investments.

Screens may be negative (e.g., excluding all tobacco companies) or they may combine negative and positive elements (e.g., eliminating companies with bad labor records while seeking out companies with good ones). Most investors rely on screens created by investment firms such as Kinder, Lydenberg Domini & Co. or by industry groups such as the Council on Economic Priorities. In addition to ecology, employee relations, and community development, corporations may be screened on their association with "sin" products (alcohol, tobacco, gambling), defense/weapons production, and nuclear power.

In contrast to guideline portfolio investors, who passively indicate their approval or disapproval of a company's social behavior by simply including or excluding it from their portfolios, shareholder activists seek to directly influence corporate social behavior. Shareholder activists invest in a corporation hoping to improve specific aspects of the company's social performance, typically by seeking a dialogue with upper management. If this and successive actions fail to achieve the desired results, shareholder activists may introduce proxy resolutions to be voted upon at the corporation's annual meeting. The goal of these resolutions is to achieve change by gaining public exposure for the issue at hand. While the number of shareholder activists is relatively small, they are by no means small in achievement: shareholder activists, led by such groups as the Interfaith Center on Corporate Responsibility, were the driving force behind the South African divestiture movement. Currently, there are more than 35 socially screened mutual funds available in the United States alone.

The Globalization of Business Management issues, including CSR, have become more complex as companies increasingly transcend national borders: It is difficult enough to come to a consensus on what constitutes socially responsible behavior within one culture, let alone determine common ethical values across cultures. In addition to different cultural views, the high barriers facing international CSR include differing corporate disclosure practices, inconsistent financial data and reporting methods, and the lack of CSR research organizations within countries. Despite these problems, CSR is growing abroad. The United Kingdom has 30 ethical mutual funds and Canada offers 6 socially responsible funds.

One of the most contentious social responsibility issues confronting multinational firms pertains to human rights. For example, many U.S. firms reduce their costs either by relying on foreign manufactured goods or by outsourcing their manufacturing to foreign manufacturers. These foreign manufacturers, often Chinese, offer low pricing because they pay very low wages by U.S. standards, even though they are extremely competitive by Chinese pay rates.

Helping Big Brother in China Go High Tech

BusinessWeek

Cisco, Oracle, and other U.S. companies are supplying China's police with software and gear that can be used to keep tabs on criminals and dissidents.

Google, Yahoo!, and Microsoft endured a wave of public disapproval in 2006 over their compliance with Chinese censorship of their Web sites. But another striking form of tech commerce with China is taking place below the radar of the U.S. public: major American manufacturers are rushing to supply China's police with the latest information technology.

Oracle Corp. has sold software to the Chinese Ministry of Public Security, which oversees both criminal and ideological investigations. The ministry uses the software to manage digital identity cards that are replacing the paper ID that Chinese citizens must carry. Meanwhile, regional Chinese police departments are modernizing their computer networks with routers and switches purchased from Cisco Systems Inc. And Motorola Inc. has sold the Chinese authorities handheld devices that will allow street cops to tap into the sorts of sophisticated data repositories that EMC Corp. markets to the Ministry of Public Security. "It's a booming market," says Simon Zhou, the top executive in Beijing for EMC, which is based in Hopkinton, Mass. "We can expect big revenue from public security" agencies in China.

The scramble to sell technology to Chinese law enforcers seems, for starters, to be at odds with the intent of an American export law enacted after the massacre of hundreds of pro-democracy demonstrators in Tiananmen Square in 1989. The Tiananmen sanctions prohibited the export "of any crime control or detection instruments or equipment" to China. "We wanted to undermine the effectiveness of the police in rounding up, imprisoning, and torturing political dissidents, not only those involved in the Tiananmen Square movement, but for years to come," explains Representative Tom Lantos (D–CA), who helped draft the law. Despite the improvement of its image on the world stage, China still has a dismal human rights record. The U.S. State Department says that the Communist government is holding at least 260,000 people in ideological "reeducation" camps.

The upshot is that "manufacturers of handcuffs aren't allowed to sell their products to China's police, but Cisco and other companies are selling Chinese authorities much more useful technology," Harry Wu, a former Chinese political prisoner living in the United States, told a House subcommittee on human rights in February 2006. His testimony was eclipsed by the panel's heavily covered excoriation of Google, Yahoo!, and Microsoft for their agreement to block parts of their Chinese Web sites as a condition of operating in the country.

Source: Reprinted with special permission from Bruce Einhorn and Ben Elgin, "Helping Big Brother Go High Tech," *BusinessWeek*, September 18, 2006. Copyright © 2006 The McGraw-Hill Companies.

While Chinese workers are happy to earn manufacturer wages and U.S. customers are pleased by the lower prices charged for foreign manufactured goods, others are unhappy. They believe that such U.S. firms are failing to satisfy their social responsibilities. Some U.S. workers and their unions argue that jobs in the United States are being eliminated or devalued by foreign competition. Some human rights advocates argue that the working conditions and living standards of foreign workers are so substandard when compared with U.S. standards that they verge on inhumane. A troubling twist on American corporations' role in the human rights debate about conditions in China arises from the sale of software to the Chinese government. Developed by Cisco, Oracle, and other U.S. companies, the software is used by China's police to monitor the activities of individuals that the Chinese government labels as criminals and dissidents. A fuller discussion of this issue appears in Exhibit 3.7, Strategy in Action.

SARBANES-OXLEY ACT OF 2002

Following a string of wrongdoings by corporate executives in 2000 to 2002, and the subsequent failures of their firms, Washington lawmakers proposed more than 50 policies to reassure investors. None of the resulting bills were able to pass both houses of Congress until the Banking Committee Chairman Paul Sarbanes (D–MD) proposed legislation to

Sarbanes-Oxley Act of 2002

The following outline presents the major elements of the Sarbanes-Oxley Act of 2002.

CORPORATE RESPONSIBILITY

- The CEO and CFO of each company are required to submit a report, based on their knowledge, to the SEC certifying the company's financial statements are fair representations of the financial condition without false statements or omissions.

- The CEO and CFO must reimburse the company for any bonuses or equity-based incentives received for the last 12-month period if the company is required to restate its financial statements due to material noncompliance with any financial reporting requirement that resulted from misconduct.

- Directors and executive officers are prohibited from trading a company's 401(k) plan, profit sharing plan, or retirement plan during any blackout period. The plan administrators are required to notify the plan participants and beneficiaries with notice of all blackout periods, reasons for the blackout period, and a statement that the participant or beneficiary should evaluate their investment even though they are unable to direct or diversify their accounts during the blackout.

- No company may make, extend, modify, or renew any personal loans to its executives or directors. Limited exceptions are for loans made in the course of the company's business, on market terms, for home improvement and home loans, consumer credit, or extension of credit.

INCREASED DISCLOSURE

- Each annual and quarterly financial report filed with the SEC must disclose all material off-balance-sheet transactions, arrangements, and obligations that may affect the current or future financial condition of the company or its operations.

- Companies must present pro forma financial information with the SEC in a manner that is not misleading and must be reconciled with the company's financial condition and with generally accepted accounting principles (GAAP).

- Each company is required to disclose whether they have adopted a code of ethics for its senior financial officers. If not, the company must explain the reasons. Any change or waiver of the code of ethics must be disclosed.

- Each annual report must contain a statement of management's responsibility for establishing and maintaining an internal control structure and procedures for financial reporting. The report must also include an assessment of the effectiveness of the internal control procedures.

- The Form 4 will be provided within two business days after the execution date of the trading of a company's securities by directors and executive officers. The SEC may extend this deadline if it determines the two-day period is not feasible.

- The company must disclose information concerning changes in financial conditions or operations "on a rapid and current basis," in plain English.

The SEC must review the financial statements of each reporting company no less than once every three years.

AUDIT COMMITTEES

- The audit committee must be composed entirely of independent directors. Committee members are not permitted to accept any fees from the company, cannot control 5 percent or more of the voting of

---

Sarbanes-Oxley Act of 2002

Law that revised and strengthened auditing and accounting standards.

establish new auditing and accounting standards. The bill was called the Public Company Accounting Reform and Investor Protection Act of 2002. Later the name was changed to the **Sarbanes-Oxley Act of 2002.**

On July 30, 2002, President George Bush signed the Sarbanes-Oxley Act into law. This revolutionary act applies to public companies with securities registered under Section 12 of the Securities Act of 1934 and those required to file reports under Section 15(d) of the Exchange Act. Sarbanes-Oxley includes required certifications for financial statements, new corporate regulations, disclosure requirements, and penalties for failure to comply. More details on the Act are provided in Exhibit 3.8, Strategy in Action.

the company, nor be an officer, director, partner, or employee of the company.

- The audit committee must have the authority to engage the outside auditing firm.
- The audit committee must establish procedures for the treatment of complaints regarding accounting controls or auditing matters. They are responsible for employee complaints concerning questionable accounting and auditing.
- The audit committee must disclose whether at least one of the committee members is a "financial expert." If not, the committee must explain why not.

NEW CRIMES AND INCREASED CRIMINAL PENALTIES

- Tampering with records with intent to impede or influence any federal investigation or bankruptcy will be punishable by a fine and/or prison sentence up to 20 years.
- Failure by an accountant to maintain all auditing papers for five years after the end of the fiscal period will be punishable by a fine and/or up to 10-year prison sentence.
- Knowingly executing, or attempting to execute, a scheme to defraud investors will be punishable by a fine and/or prison sentence of up to 25 years.
- Willfully certifying a report that does not comply with the law can be punishable with a fine up to $5,000,000 and/or a prison sentence up to 20 years.

NEW CIVIL CAUSE OF ACTION AND INCREASED ENFORCEMENT POWERS

- Protection will be provided to whistle-blowers who provide information or assist in an investigation by law enforcement, congressional committee, or employee supervisor.
- Bankruptcy cannot be used to avoid liability from securities laws violations.
- Investors are able to file a civil action for fraud up to two years after discovery of the facts and five years after the occurrence of fraud.
- The SEC can receive a restraining order prohibiting payments to insiders during an investigation.
- The SEC can prevent individuals from holding an officer's or director's position in a public company as a result of violation of the securities law.

AUDITOR INDEPENDENCE

- All audit services must be preapproved by the audit committee and must be disclosed to investors.
- The lead audit or reviewing audit partner from the auditing accounting firm must change at least once every five fiscal years.
- The registered accounting firms must report to the audit committee all accounting policies and practices used, alternative uses of the financial information within GAAP that has been discussed with management, and written communications between the accounting firm and management.
- An auditing firm is prohibited from auditing a company if the company's CEO or CFO was employed by the auditing firm within the past year.

A Public Company Accounting Oversight Board is established by the SEC to oversee the audits of public companies. The Board will register public accounting firms, establish audit standards, inspect registered accounting firms, and discipline violators of the rules. No person can take part in an audit if not employed by a registered public accounting firm.

The Sarbanes-Oxley Act states that the CEO and CFO must certify every report containing the company's financial statements. The certification acknowledges that the CEO or CFO (chief financial officer) has reviewed the report. As part of the review, the officer must attest that the information does not include untrue statements or necessary omitted information. Furthermore, based on the officer's knowledge, the report is a reliable source of the company's financial condition and result of operations for the period represented. The certification also makes the officers responsible for establishing and maintaining internal controls such that they are aware of any material information relating to the company. The officers must also evaluate the effectiveness of the internal controls within 90 days of the release of the report and present their conclusions of the effectiveness of the controls.

Also, the officers must disclose any fraudulent material, deficiencies in the reporting of the financial reports, or problems with the internal control to the company's auditors and auditing committee. Finally, the officers must indicate any changes to the internal controls or factors that could affect them.

The Sarbanes-Oxley Act includes provisions restricting the corporate control of executives, accounting firms, auditing committees, and attorneys. With regard to executives, the Act bans personal loans. A company can no longer directly or indirectly issue, extend, or maintain a personal loan to any director or executive officer. Executive officers and directors are not permitted to purchase, sell, acquire, or transfer any equity security during any pension fund blackout period. Executives are required to notify fund participants of any blackout period and the reasons for the blackout period. The SEC will provide the company's executives with a code of ethics for the company to adopt. Failure to meet the code must be disclosed to the SEC.

The Act limits some and issues new duties of the registered public accounting firms that conduct the audits of the financial statements. Accounting firms are prohibited from performing bookkeeping or other accounting services related to the financial statements, designing or implementing financial systems, appraising, internal auditing, brokering banking services, or providing legal services unrelated to the audit. All critical accounting policies and alternative treatments of financial information within generally accepted accounting principles (GAAP), and written communication between the accounting firm and the company's management must be reported to the audit committee.

The Act defines the composition of the audit committee and specifies its responsibilities. The members of the audit committee must be members of the company's board of directors. At least one member of the committee should be classified as a "financial expert." The audit committee is directly responsible for the work of any accounting firm employed by the company, and the accounting firm must report directly to the audit committee. The audit committee must create procedures for employee complaints or concerns over accounting or auditing matters. Upon discovery of unlawful acts by the company, the audit committee must report and be supervised in its investigation by a Public Company Accounting Oversight Board.

The Act includes rules for attorney conduct. If a company's attorneys find evidence of securities violations, they are required to report the matter to the chief legal counsel or CEO. If there is not an appropriate response, the attorneys must report the information to the audit committee or the board of directors.

Other sections of the Sarbanes-Oxley Act stipulate disclosure periods for financial operations and reporting. Relevant information relating to changes in the financial condition or operations of a company must be immediately reported in plain English. Off-balance-sheet transactions, correcting adjustments, and pro-forma information must be presented in the annual and quarterly financial reports. The information must not contain any untrue statements, must not omit material facts, and must meet GAAP standards.

Stricter penalties have been issued for violations of the Sarbanes-Oxley Act. If a company must restate its financial statements due to noncompliance, the CEO and CFO must relinquish any bonus or incentive-based compensation or realized profits from the sale of securities during the 12-month period following the filing with the SEC. Other securities fraud, such as destruction or falsification of records, results in fines and prison sentences up to 25 years.

The New Corporate Governance Structure

A major consequence of the 2000–2002 accounting scandals was the Sarbanes-Oxley Act of 2002, and a major consequence of Sarbanes-Oxley has been the restructuring of the governance structure of American corporations. The most significant change in the restructuring

The New Corporate Governance Structure

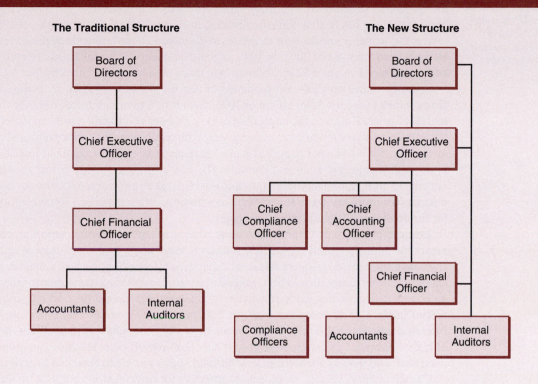

is the heightened role of corporate internal auditors, as depicted in Exhibit 3.9, Strategy in Action. Auditors have traditionally been viewed as performing a necessary but perfunctory function, namely to probe corporate financial records for unintentional or illicit misrepresentations. Although a majority of U.S. corporations have longstanding traditions of reporting that their auditors operated independently of CFO approval and that they had direct access to the board, in practice, the auditors' work usually traveled through the organization's hierarchical chain of command.

In the past, internal auditors reviewed financial reports generated by other corporate accountants. The auditors considered professional accounting and financial practices, as well as relevant aspects of corporate law, and then presented their findings to the chief financial officer (CFO). Historically, the CFO reviewed the audits and determined the financial data and information that was to be presented to top management, directors, and investors of the company.

However, because Sarbanes-Oxley requires that CEOs and audit committees sign off on financial results, auditors now routinely deal directly with top corporate officials, as shown in the new structure in Exhibit 3.9, Strategy in Action. Approximately 75 percent of senior corporate auditors now report directly to the Board of Directors' audit committee. Additionally, to eliminate the potential for accounting problems, companies are establishing direct lines of communication between top managers and the board and auditors that inform the CFO but that are not dependent on CFO approval or authorization.

The new structure also provides the CEO information provided directly by the company's chief compliance and chief accounting officers. Consequently, the CFO, who is responsible for ultimately approving all company payments, is not empowered to be the sole provider of data for financial evaluations by the CEO and board.

Privatization as a Response to Sarbanes-Oxley

privatization
A restructuring in which the ownership structure of a publicly traded corporation is converted into a privately held company.

A trend in financial restructuring that supports internal growth is **privatization**, in which the ownership structure of a publicly traded corporation is converted into a privately held company. There has been a dramatic upswing in the number of privatizations, due largely to negative manager and investor responses to the increased government regulation required by Sarbanes-Oxley Act of 2002. In 2006, a record number of 322 publicly traded companies with a combined value of $215.4 billion were taken private in the United States.

Some privatization deals are prompted by the huge funds attracted by private equity firms, which exceeded $280 billion in 2006, that allow a premium to be paid over the current stock price. However, the motivation in most cases of privatization is that privately held firms are not subject to the costs of complying with regulations for public companies stemming from the Sarbanes-Oxley legislation. Sarbanes-Oxley legislates that outside firms must audit a company's internal controls. The cost of hiring outside firms, maintaining systems to meet compliance standards, and establishing an audit committee on the board of directors to ensure that these activities are monitored is estimated to be $500,000 on average for the 16,000 publicly reporting companies.

Because of Sarbanes-Oxley, much more time is needed to manage reporting requirements for publicly traded companies. Managers must attest to the accuracy of quarterly financials and provide frequent releases of specified information, such as same-day notification of insider trades. In addition, general counsels are spending much more of their time on compliance activities, with 36 percent of companies incurring the cost and complication of hiring a chief compliance officer. Litigation costs have also risen because of the increased personal liability of board members and key executives, especially in the form of higher insurance premiums. The cost of directors' and officers' insurance premiums has risen nearly 40 percent for companies with solid sheets and clean financial histories.

Certain industry sectors are especially attractive for privatization strategies. In the technology sector, firms that were posting double-digit growth throughout most of the 1980s and 1990s are now having trouble growing their maturing businesses. Although Applied Materials, Dell, EMC, Intel, and Hewlett-Packard have considerable cash flow, equity investors have little interest in these slower-growing companies, cutting off a favorite source of equity funding and making them attractive privatization candidates.

Another active sector for privatization is real estate. In the first half of 2007, the stock prices for real estate investment trusts (REITs) were below the net asset value of their underlying real estate portfolios. This meant that investors believed that REITs were worth less as a company than the total value of their properties, creating an opportunity for investors to acquire the portfolio at a discount.

In the maturing technology sector, where slowing growth is lowering the price to earning multiples, executives look to other sources of funding outside of equity financing. Privatization offers a good alternative because it allows managers to avoid the distractions of short-term technical investors and traders, who react especially strongly to any unanticipated performance variation.

Exhibit 3.10, Strategy in Action provides an example of the role of private equity in the strategic activities of a company. Samsonite Corporation was taken private with the expressed intention of repositioning it as a public firm once its competitiveness had been reestablished.

CSR's Effect on the Mission Statement

The mission statement not only identifies what product or service a company produces, how it produces it, and what market it serves, it also embodies what the company believes. As such, it is essential that the mission statement recognize the legitimate claims of its external

Sleek. Stylish. Samsonite?

BusinessWeek

Marcello Bottoli had a gilded career as the chief executive of Louis Vuitton when, three years ago, he left to run Samsonite Corp. It was a move from one of the world's great luxury brands to a company that had been mistreated by its private investors, was still recovering from a sharp drop in business after September 11, 2001, and had, in fact, come dangerously close to declaring bankruptcy for the second time in a decade.

And Bottoli's plan is obvious; even he says so. He wants Samsonite to find its place in the expanding world of accessible luxury.

Since it was founded by Jesse Shwayder almost 100 years ago in Denver, Samsonite has been a near-complete reflection of the best and worst inclinations of the business world. Now Samsonite is in the hands of new private-equity investors (Ares Management, Bain Capital, and the Ontario Teachers' Pension Plan), who brought in Bottoli and gave him a piece of the business (management owns 10 percent of the company).

The owners, ready to cash out, want to take the company public again, perhaps this spring. This time, though, they would like Samsonite to be traded on the London Stock Exchange. That would make it among the first U.S. companies to have its primary listing outside the country. "But," says Bottoli, "we stick to and are proud of our American heritage."

Bottoli, who is 45, also hopes to give Samsonite a modern sensibility and fashion edge. To that end, he has brought in designers such as Alexander McQueen, the haute couture celebrity, to create signature lines of Black Label luggage. Bottoli hired the company's first creative director, who has gone back to the archives to create a vintage collection. The company is starting to sell leather shoes (they've been available in Italy for years), wallets, and stationery. Bottoli has doubled the amount Samsonite spends on marketing and persuaded inveterate traveler and showman Richard Branson to appear on the company's behalf.

Bottoli, like many chief executives brought into companies best by problems, had to determine how thoroughly to upend the status quo, staff included. Frank Steed, a former president of Samsonite USA and now a licensee for the company, says: "People there are trying to move along as fast as Marcello wants." Sales for the first nine months of 2006 were $784.4 million, 9.3 percent higher than the previous year's.

Source: Reprinted with special permission from Susan Berfield, "Sleek. Stylish. Samsonite?: The Brand Has Been Kicked Around for Years: Now Marcello Bottoli Wants to Take It Upscale," *BusinessWeek*, February 26, 2007. Copyright © 2007 The McGraw-Hill Companies.

stakeholders, which may include creditors, customers, suppliers, government, unions, competitors, local communities, and elements of the general public. This stakeholder approach has become widely accepted by U.S. business. For example, a survey of directors in 291 of the largest southeastern U.S. companies found that directors had high stakeholder orientations. Customers, government, stockholders, employees, and society, in that order, were the stakeholders these directors perceived as most important.

In developing mission statements, managers must identify all stakeholder groups and weigh their relative rights and abilities to affect the firm's success. Some companies are proactive in their approach to CSR, making it an integral part of their raison d'être (e.g., Ben & Jerry's ice cream); others are reactive, adopting socially responsible behavior only when they must (e.g., Exxon after the *Valdez* incident).

Social Audit

social audit

An attempt to measure a company's actual social performance against its social objectives.

A **social audit** attempts to measure a company's actual social performance against the social objectives it has set for itself. A social audit may be conducted by the company itself. However, one conducted by an outside consultant who will impose minimal biases may prove more beneficial to the firm. As with a financial audit, an outside auditor brings credibility to the evaluation. This credibility is essential if management is to take the results seriously and if the general public is to believe the company's public relations pronouncements.

Careful, accurate monitoring and evaluation of a company's CSR actions are important not only because the company wants to be sure it is implementing CSR policy as planned but also because CSR actions by their nature are open to intense public scrutiny. To make sure it is making good on its CSR promises, a company may conduct a social audit of its performance.

Once the social audit is complete, it may be distributed internally or both internally and externally, depending on the firm's goals and situation. Some firms include a section in their annual report devoted to social responsibility activities; others publish a separate periodic report on their social responsiveness. Companies publishing separate social audits include General Motors, Bank of America, Atlantic Richfield, Control Data, and Aetna Life and Casualty Company. Nearly all *Fortune* 500 corporations disclose social performance information in their annual reports.

Large firms are not the only companies employing the social audit. Boutique ice cream maker Ben & Jerry's, a CSR pioneer, publishes a social audit in its annual report. The audit, conducted by an outside consultant, scores company performance in such areas as employee benefits, plant safety, ecology, community involvement, and customer service. The report is published unedited.

The social audit may be used for more than simply monitoring and evaluating firm social performance. Managers also use social audits to scan the external environment, determine firm vulnerabilities, and institutionalize CSR within the firm. In addition, companies themselves are not the only ones who conduct social audits; public interest groups and the media watch companies who claim to be socially responsible very closely to see if they practice what they preach. These organizations include consumer groups and socially responsible investing firms that construct their own guidelines for evaluating companies. An excellent example of a company that worked with an environmental interest group to turn opposition into collaboration is shown in the case of the private equity takeover of a major Texas utility company, as described in Exhibit 3.11, Strategy in Action.

The Body Shop learned what can happen when a company's behavior falls short of its espoused mission and objectives. The 20-year-old manufacturer and retailer of naturally based hair and skin products had cultivated a socially responsible corporate image based on a reputation for socially responsible behavior. In late 1994, however, *Business Ethics* magazine published an exposé claiming that the company did not "walk the talk." It accused The Body Shop of using nonrenewable petrochemicals in its products, recycling far less than it claimed, using ingredients tested on animals, and making threats against investigative journalists. The Body Shop's contradictions were noteworthy because Anita Roddick, the company's founder, made CSR a centerpiece of the company's strategy.[1]

MANAGEMENT ETHICS

The Nature of Ethics in Business

ethics
The moral principles that reflect society's beliefs about the actions of an individual or group that are right and wrong.

Central to the belief that companies should be operated in a socially responsive way for the benefit of all stakeholders is the belief that managers will behave in an ethical manner. The term **ethics** refers to the moral principles that reflect society's beliefs about the actions of an individual or a group that are right and wrong. Of course, the values of one individual, group, or society may be at odds with the values of another individual, group, or society. Ethical standards, therefore, reflect not a universally accepted code, but rather the end product of a process of defining and clarifying the nature and content of human interaction.

[1] Jon Entine, "Shattered Image," *Business Ethics* 8, no. 5 (September/October 1994), pp. 23–28.

Hugging the Tree-Huggers

BusinessWeek

When William K. Reilly was plotting the private equity takeover of Texas Utility TXU Corp., he foresaw one potential dealbreaker. Says Reilly, "We decided the walk-away issue for us was not getting environmentalists' support." So Reilly called Fred Krupp, president of Environmental Defense, whose Texas attorney, James D. Marston, had been waging an all-out war on TXU's plans to build 11 coal-fired power plants. Krupp told Marston to hop on a plane to San Francisco for a top-secret meeting with Reilly's team.

The ensuing negotiations were often tense. After a marathon 17 hours, Reilly ended up giving Marston a big chunk of what he wanted: commitments by the new TXU owners to ax 8 of the 11 proposed plants and to join the call for mandatory national carbon emissions curbs. Meanwhile, the corporate raiders got exactly what they craved: public praise from Environmental Defense and the Natural Resources Defense Council (NRDC) for the deal.

The TXU takeover is a sign of a remarkable evolution in the dynamic between corporate executives and activists. Once fractious and antagonistic, it has moved toward accommodation and even mutual dependence. Companies increasingly seek a "green" imprimatur, while enviros view changes in how business operates as key to protecting the planet.

Examples of this new relationship are everywhere. Wal-Mart Stores Inc. turned to Conservation International to help shape ambitious goals to cut energy use, switch to renewable power, and sell millions of efficient fluorescent bulbs. When the CEOs of 10 major U.S. corporations converged on Washington on January 22, 2007, and issued a call for mandatory carbon emissions limits, sitting with them at the table were Fred Krupp and the president of the NRDC.

Source: Reprinted with special permission from John Carey, "Hugging the Tree-Huggers: Why So Many Companies are Suddenly Linking Up With Eco Groups. Hint: Smart Business," *BusinessWeek*, March 12, 2007. Copyright © 2007 The McGraw-Hill Companies.

SATISFYING CORPORATE SOCIAL RESPONSIBILITY

Corporate social responsibility has become a vital part of the business conversation. The issue is not whether companies will engage in socially responsible activities, but how. For most companies, the challenge is how best to achieve the maximum social benefit from a given amount of resources available for social projects. Research points to five principles that underscore better outcomes for society and for corporate participants.[2]

In 1999, William Ford Jr. angered Ford Motor Co. executives and investors when he wrote that "there are very real conflicts between Ford's current business practices, consumer choices, and emerging views of (environmental) sustainability." In his company citizenship report, the grandson of Henry Ford, then the automaker's nonexecutive chairman, even appeared to endorse a Sierra Club statement declaring that "the gas-guzzling SUV is a rolling monument to environmental destruction."

Bill Ford has had to moderate his strongest environmental beliefs since assuming the company's CEO position in October 2001, just after the Firestone tire scandal. Nevertheless, while he has strived to improve Ford's financial performance and restore trust among its diverse stakeholders, he remains strongly committed to corporate responsibility and environmental protection. In his words, "A good company delivers excellent products and services, and a great company does all that and strives to make the world a better place."[3] Today, Ford is a leader in producing vehicles that run on alternative sources of fuel, and

[2] This section was excerpted from J. A. Pearce II and J. Doh, "Enhancing Corporate Responsibility through Skillful Collaboration," *Sloan Management Review* 46, no. 3 (2005), pp. 30–39.

[3] "Ford Motor Company Encourages Elementary School Students to Support America's National Parks," www.ford.com/en/company/nationalParks.htm.

it is performing as well as or better than its major North American rivals, all of whom are involved in intense global competition. The new CEO is successfully pursuing a strategy that is showing improved financial performance, increased confidence in the brand, and clear evidence that the car company is committed to contributing more broadly to society. Among Ford's more notable outreach efforts are an innovative HIV/AIDS initiative in South Africa that is now expanding to India, China, and Thailand; a partnership with the U.S. National Parks Foundation to provide environmentally friendly transportation for park visitors; and significant support for the Clean Air Initiative for Asian Cities.

Ford's actions are emblematic of the corporate social responsibility initiatives of many leading companies today. Corporate-supported social initiatives are now a given. For some time now, many *Fortune* 500 corporations have had senior manager titles dedicated to helping their organizations "give back" more effectively. CSR is now almost universally embraced by top managers as an integral component of their executive roles, whether motivated by self-interest, altruism, strategic advantage, or political gain. Their outreach is usually plain to see on the companies' corporate Web sites. CSR is high on the agenda at major executive gatherings such as the World Economic Forum. It is very much in evidence during times of tragedy—as seen in the corporate responses to the Asian tsunami of December 2004—and it is the subject of many conferences, workshops, newsletters, and more. "Consultancies have sprung up to advise companies on how to do corporate social responsibility and how to let it be known that they are doing it," noted *The Economist* in a survey on CSR in 2005.

Executives face conflicting pressures to contribute to social responsibility while honoring their duties to maximize shareholder value. These days they face many belligerent critics who challenge the idea of a single-minded focus on profits—witness the often violent antiglobalization protests in recent years. They also face skeptics who contend that CSR initiatives are chiefly a convenient marketing gloss. However, the reality is that most executives are eager to improve their CSR effectiveness. The issue is not whether companies will engage in socially responsible activities, but how. For most companies, the challenge is how best to achieve the maximum social benefit from a given amount of resources available for social projects.

Studies of dozens of social responsibility initiatives at major corporations show that senior managers struggle to find the right balance between "low-engagement" solutions such as charitable gift-giving and "high-commitment" solutions that run the risk of diverting attention from the company's core mission. In this section, we will see that collaborative social initiatives (CSIs)—a form of engagement in which companies provide ongoing and sustained commitments to a social project or issue—provide the best combination of social and strategic impact.

Jean-Pierre Garnier, CEO of GlaxoSmithKline, believes that the economic and CSR goals of a company are best met by pursuing them simultaneously. Exhibit 3.12, Top Strategist describes some of his corporation's recent strategic successes.

The Core of the CSR Debate

The proper role of CSR—the actions of a company to benefit society beyond the requirement of the law and the direct interests of shareholders—has generated a century's worth of philosophically and economically intriguing debates. Since steel baron Andrew Carnegie published *The Gospel of Wealth* in 1899, the argument that businesses are the trustees of societal property that should be managed for the public good has been seen as one end of a continuum with, at the other end, the belief that profit maximization is management's only legitimate goal. The CSR debates had been largely confined to the background for most of the twentieth century, making the news after an oil spill or when a consumer product caused harm, or when ethics scandals reopened the question of business's fundamental purpose.

Top Strategist
Jean-Pierre Garnier, CEO of GlaxoSmithKline

Exhibit 3.12

When Jean-Pierre Garnier took over as CEO of GlaxoSmith-Kline in 2000, the company's reputation on corporate social responsibility was at its nadir. As part of a coalition of 39 pharmaceutical companies, the drugmaker was suing Nelson Mandela's South African government for voiding patents on prescription drugs. Mandela's top priority was giving desperately sick patients access to HIV treatments, and GSK—the world's largest supplier—was standing in the way. "It was a public relations disaster," Garnier concedes.

The experience convinced Garnier that GSK should lead the crusade to improve access to medicine. In 2001, GSK became the first major drugmaker to sell its AIDS medicines at cost in 100 countries worldwide. In fact, GSK sells 90 percent of its vaccines, in volume terms, at not-for-profit prices to customers in the developing world. In 2005, it set a new paradigm in the vaccine industry. It chose Mexico over other, wealthier nations as the launch pad for Rotarix, a new vaccine against gastrointestinal rotavirus. "We wanted to get the vaccine to the children who needed it most," Garnier explains.

Creating medicines for the Third World while still posting a profit required fancy financial footwork. GSK has formed 14 different partnerships with the World Health Organization and other nongovernmental bodies, and with philanthropies such as the Bill & Melinda Gates Foundation. A collaboration with the Gates Foundation led to a vaccine that provides a minimum of 18 months of protection against malaria.

Garnier says efforts such as these give the company several advantages over its rivals. Top scientists are drawn to GSK because they want their research to make a difference. Doing good, and being admired for it, also boosts general morale at the company, he says. "This creates a more aligned and engaged workforce, which helps us outperform our competitors."

Source: Reprinted with special permission from Kerry Capell, 2007. "GlaxoSmithKline: Getting AIDS Drugs to More Sick People," *BusinessWeek*, January 29, 2007. Copyright © 2007 The McGraw-Hill Companies.

The debates surfaced in more positive ways in the last 30 years as new businesses set up shop with altruism very much in mind and on display. Firms such as ice cream maker Ben & Jerry's argued that CSR and profits do not clash; their stance was that doing good led to making good money, too. That line of thinking has gained popularity as more executives have come to understand the value of their companies' reputations with customers—and with investors and employees. But only recently have business leaders begun to get a clearer understanding of the appropriate role of CSR and its effect on financial performance.

In the past, research on the financial effect of CSR produced inconsistent findings, with some studies reporting a positive relationship, others a negative one, and others no relationship at all. Since the mid-1990s, improvements in theory, research designs, data, and analysis have produced empirical research with more consistent results.[4] Importantly, a recent meta-analysis (a methodological technique that aggregates findings of multiple

[4] J. J. Griffin and J. F. Mahon, "The Corporate Social Performance and Corporate Financial Performance Debate: Twenty-Five Years of Incomparable Research," *Business and Society* 36 (1997), pp. 5–31; R. M. Roman, S. Hayibor, and B. R. Agle, "The Relationship between Social and Financial Performance: Repainting a Portrait," *Business and Society* 38 (1999), pp. 109–125; and J. D. Margolis and J. P. Walsh, "Misery Loves Companies: Rethinking Social Initiatives by Business," *Administrative Science Quarterly* 48 (2003), pp. 268–305.

Exhibit 3.13
**Continuum of
Corporate Social
Responsibility
Commitments**

studies) of more than 10 studies found that on balance, positive relationships can be expected from CSR initiatives but that the primary vehicle for achieving superior financial performance from social responsibility is via reputation effects.[5]

There is no shortage of options with which businesses can advance their CSR goals. The greater challenge is finding the right balance. Philanthropy without active engagement—cash donations, for instance—has been criticized as narrow, self-serving, and often motivated to improve the corporation's reputation and keep nongovernmental organization (NGO) critics and other naysayers at bay.[6] However, redirecting the company toward a socially responsible mission, while seemingly attractive, may have the unintended consequences of diverting both managers and employees from their core mission. Exhibit 3.13 presents a simple illustration of the range of options available to corporations as they consider their CSR commitments.

What managers need is a model that they can use to guide them in selecting social initiatives and through which they can exploit their companies' core competencies for the maximum positive impact. As a starting point, research confirms that a business must determine the social causes that it will support and why and then decide how its support should be organized.[7] According to one perspective, businesses have three basic support options: donations of cash or material, usually to a nongovernmental or nonprofit agency; creation of a functional operation within the company to assist external charitable efforts; and development of a collaboration approach, whereby a company joins with an organization that has particular expertise in managing the way benefits are derived from corporate support.[8]

Mutual Advantages of Collaborative Social Initiatives

The term *social initiative* describes initiatives that take a collaborative approach. Research on alliances and networks among companies in competitive commercial environments tells us that each partner benefits when the other brings resources, capabilities, or other assets that it cannot easily attain on its own. These *combinative capabilities* allow the company to acquire and synthesize resources and build new applications from those resources, generating innovative responses to rapidly evolving environments.

It is no different with collaborative social initiatives. While neither companies nor nonprofits are well-equipped to handle escalating social or environmental problems, each participant has the potential to contribute valuable material resources, services, or individuals' voluntary time, talents, energies, and organizational knowledge. Those cumulative offerings are vastly superior to cash-only donations, which are a minimalist solution to

[5] M. Orlitzky, F. L. Schmidt, and S. L. Rynes, "Corporate Social and Financial Performance: A Meta-Analysis," *Organization Studies* 24, no. 3 (2003), pp. 403–441.

[6] B. Husted, "Governance Choices for Corporate Social Responsibility: To Contribute, Collaborate or Internalize?" *Long Range Planning* 36, no. 5 (2003), pp. 481–498.

[7] N. C. Smith. "Corporate Social Responsibility: Whether or How?" *California Management Review* 45, no. 4 (2003), pp. 52–76.

[8] Husted, "Governance Choices for Corporate Social Responsibility."

the challenges of social responsibility. Social initiatives involve ongoing information and operational exchanges among participants and are especially attractive because of their potential benefits for both the corporate and not-for-profit partners.

There is strong evidence to show that CSR activities increasingly confer benefits beyond enhanced reputation. For some participants, they can be a tool to attract, retain, and develop managerial talent. The PricewaterhouseCoopers (PwC) Project Ulysses is a leadership development program that sends small teams of PwC partners to developing countries to apply their expertise to complex social and economic challenges. The cross-cultural PwC teams collaborate with NGOs, community-based organizations, and intergovernmental agencies, working pro bono in eight-week assignments in communities struggling with the effects of poverty, conflict, and environmental degradation. The Ulysses program was designed in part to respond to a growing challenge confronting professional services companies: identifying and training up-and-coming leaders who can find nontraditional answers to intractable problems.

All 24 Ulysses graduates still work at PwC; most say they have a stronger commitment to the firm because of the commitment it made to them and because they now have a different view of PwC's values. For PwC, the Ulysses program provides a tangible message to its primary stakeholders that the company is committed to making a difference in the world. According to Brian McCann, the first U.S.-based partner to participate in Ulysses, "This is a real differentiator—not just in relation to our competitors, but to all global organizations."

Five Principles of Successful Collaborative Social Initiatives

There are five principles that are central to successful CSIs, as shown in Exhibit 3.14, Strategy in Action. When CSR initiatives include most or all of these elements, companies can indeed maximize the effects of their social contributions while advancing broader strategic goals. While most CSIs will not achieve complete success with all five elements, some progress with each is requisite for success. Here are the five principles, along with examples of companies that have adhered to them well:

1. Identify a Long-Term Durable Mission

Companies make the greatest social contribution when they identify an important, long-standing policy challenge and they participate in its solution over the long term. Veteran *Wall Street Journal* reporter and author Ron Alsop argues that companies that are interested in contributing to corporate responsibility and thus burnishing their reputations should "own the issue."[9] Companies that step up to tackle problems that are clearly important to society's welfare and that require substantial resources are signaling to internal and external constituencies that the initiative is deserving of the company's investment.

Among the more obvious examples of social challenges that will demand attention for years to come are hunger, inadequate housing, ill health, substandard education, and degradation of the environment. While a company's long-term commitment to any one of those problems embeds that issue in the fabric of the company, it is more important that the company can develop competencies that allow it to become better at its social activities yet be able to keep investing in those outputs. It is also important to identify limited-scope projects and shorter-term milestones that can be accomplished through direct contributions by the company. Solving global hunger is a worthy goal, but it is too large for any individual company to make much of a dent.

Avon Products Inc., the seller of beauty and related products, offers a fine example of a long-term commitment to a pervasive and longstanding problem. In 1992, the company's Avon Foundation—a public charity established in 1955 to improve the lives of women and

[9] R. Alsop, *The 18 Immutable Laws of Corporate Reputation* (New York: Free Press, 2004).

Five Principles of Successful Corporate Social Responsibility Collaboration

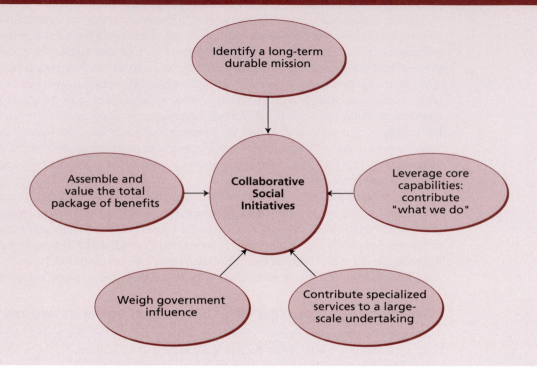

their families—launched its Breast Cancer Crusade in the United Kingdom. The program has expanded to 50 countries. Funds are raised through a variety of programs, product sales, and special events, including the Avon Walk for Breast Cancer series. The company distinguishes itself from other corporations that fund a single institution or scientific investigator because it operates as part of a collaborative, supporting a national network of research, medical, social service, and community-based organizations, each of which makes its own unique contribution to helping patients or advancing breast cancer research. The Crusade has awarded more than $300 million to breast cancer research and care organizations worldwide. In its first 10 years, The Avon Walks program raised more than $250 million for research, awareness, detection, and treatment.

Another example of a powerful CSI is found in IBM Corp.'s Reinventing Education initiative. Since 1994, IBM works with nonprofit school partners throughout the world to develop and implement innovative technology solutions designed to solve some of education's toughest problems: from coping with shrinking budgets and increasing parental involvement to moving to team teaching and developing new lesson plans. This initiative responds to a nearly universal agreement that education—especially education of young girls and women—provides the essential foundation for addressing a range of social and economic challenges in developing countries. Overcoming the existing educational deficit requires a long-term commitment to achieve school reform, such as methods for measuring learning.

One element of the Reinventing Education initiative is a Web-based "Change Toolkit" developed by IBM and Harvard Business School professor Rosabeth Moss Kanter, with sponsorship from the Council of Chief State School Officers, the National Association of Secondary School Principals, and the National Association of Elementary School Principals. The program has been lauded as a compelling model to systemic school reform.

The Home Depot has identified housing as its principal CSI. In 2002, the company set up its Home Depot Foundation with the primary mission of building "affordable, efficient, and healthy homes." Thirty million Americans face some sort of challenge in securing dependable housing, including living in substandard or overcrowded housing; lacking hot water, electricity, toilet, or bathtub/shower; or simply paying too high a percentage of their income on housing. Hence, Home Depot's long-term commitment in this area is unassailable. Its Foundation works closely with Home Depot suppliers and with a variety of nonprofits, placing a strong emphasis on local volunteer efforts.

2. Contribute "What We Do"

Companies maximize the benefits of their corporate contributions when they leverage core capabilities and contribute products and services that are based on expertise used in or generated by their normal operations. Such contributions create a mutually beneficial relationship between the partners; the social-purpose initiatives receive the maximum gains while the company minimizes costs and diversions. It is not essential that these services be synonymous with those of the company's business, but they should build upon some aspect of its strategic competencies.

The issue was aired at the recent World Economic Forum gathering in Davos, Switzerland. "We see corporate social responsibility as part and parcel of doing business, part of our core skills," said Antony Burgmans, chairman of consumer-products giant Unilever NV. "The major value for Unilever is the corporate reputation it helps create."

The thinking is similar at IBM, where, as part of its Reinventing Education initiative, the company contributes financial resources, researchers, educational consultants, and technology to each site to find new ways for technology to spur and support fundamental school restructuring and broad-based systemic change to raise student achievement. In effect, IBM leverages its technological and systems expertise, and its experience providing systems solutions to educational clients, to meet a broader educational challenge. Says Stanley Litow, vice president of Corporate Community Relations at IBM: "IBM believes that a strong community is a key to a company's success . . . To this end, a key focus of our work has been on raising the quality of public education and bridging the digital divide."[10] IBM gains significant goodwill and brand identity with important target markets, in some ways repeating Apple Computer Inc.'s successful strategy in the 1980s under which it donated computers to schools as a way to gain recognition.

There are many comparable initiatives on the procurement side. Retailers such as Starbucks Coffee Company now source much of their bean supply directly from producers, thereby ensuring that those farmers receive fair compensation without being exploited by powerful middlemen. Many retail supermarkets have followed with their own versions of the "fair trade" model.

3. Contribute Specialized Services to a Large-Scale Undertaking

Companies have the greatest social impact when they make specialized contributions to large-scale cooperative efforts. Those that contribute to initiatives in which other private, public, or nonprofit organizations are also active have an effect that goes beyond their limited contributions. Although it is tempting for a company to identify a specific cause that will be associated only with its own contributions, such a strategy is likely to be viewed as a "pet project" and not as a contribution to a larger problem where a range of players have important interests.

A good example is The AES Corp.'s carbon offset program. AES, headquartered in Arlington, Virginia, is one of the world's largest independent power producers, with 30,000 employees and generation and distribution businesses in 27 countries. Some years ago, the company

[10] "Reinventing Education," www.ibm.com/ibm/ibmgives/grant/education/programs/reinventing/re_school_reform.shtml.

recognized that it could make a contribution to the battle against global warming—a significant environmental threat with serious consequences such as habitat and species depletion, drought, and water scarcity. AES developed a program that offsets carbon emissions, creating carbon "sinks," a practical and effective means of combating this global problem.

Research has concluded that planting and preserving trees (technically "forest enhancement") provides the most practical and effective way to address the CO_2 emissions problem. Trees absorb CO_2 as they grow and convert it to carbon that is locked up (sequestered) in biomass as long as they live. AES leaders believed that if their company could contribute to increasing the standing stock of trees, the additional trees might be able to absorb enough CO_2 to offset the emissions from an AES cogeneration plant. This approach became one of the many mitigation measures now accepted in the global climate change treaty—the Kyoto Protocol—as a means of achieving legally binding emissions reduction targets.

For its part, packaged-foods giant ConAgra Foods Inc. helps to fight hunger in partnership with America's Second Harvest, an organization that leads the food recovery effort in the United States. Set up as the nationwide clearinghouse for handling the donations of prepared and perishable foods, ConAgra's coordination efforts enable smaller, local programs to share resources, making the food donation and distribution process more effective. In October 1999, ConAgra joined with food bank network America's Second Harvest in a specific initiative, the Feeding Children Better program, distributing food to 50,000 local charitable agencies, which, in turn, operate more than 94,000 food programs.

4. Weigh Government's Influence

Government support for corporate participation in CSIs—or at least its willingness to remove barriers—can have an important positive influence. Tax incentives, liability protection, and other forms of direct and indirect support for businesses all help to foster business participation and contribute to the success of CSIs.

For instance, in the United States, ConAgra's food recovery initiatives can deduct the cost (but not market value) of the donated products plus one half of the product's profit margin; the value of this deduction is capped at twice the cost of the product. To encourage further participation of businesses in such food recovery programs, America's Second Harvest generated a series of recommendations for the U.S. government. The recommendations seek to improve the tax benefits associated with food donation, including a proposal that tax deductions be set at the fair market value of donations. Tax deductions provide economic enticement for companies to consider participation, as Boston Market, KFC, and Kraft Foods have publicly acknowledged. Donating food also allows companies to identify the amount of food wasted because it is tracked for tax purposes.

Similar efforts are being applied to reforms that will ease businesses' concerns about their liability from contributing to social enterprises. The Bill Emerson Good Samaritan Food Donation Act, enacted in 1996, protects businesses from liability for food donations except in the case of gross negligence. Building on this federal U.S. act, all 50 states and the District of Columbia have enacted "good Samaritan" laws to protect donors except in cases evidencing negligence. Many companies and nonprofits would like to see more comprehensive tort reform to support their efforts.

Government endorsements are invaluable too. The Home Depot's partnership with Habitat for Humanity is actively supported by the U.S. Department of Housing and Urban Development (HUD). This support takes the form of formal endorsement, logistical facilitation, and implicit acknowledgement that the partnership's initiatives complement HUD's own efforts. Home Depot is assured that the agency will not burden the program with red tape. In the case of AES's efforts in the area of global warming, organizations such as the World Bank, the Global Environmental Facility, and the UN Environment and Development Program endorse and encourage offsets via grants, loans, and scientific research.

5. Assemble and Value the Total Package of Benefits

Companies gain the greatest benefits from their social contributions when they put a price on the total benefit package. The valuation should include both the social contributions delivered and the reputation effects that solidify or enhance the company's position among its constituencies. Positive reputation—by consumers, suppliers, employees, regulators, interest groups, and other stakeholders—is driven by genuine commitment rather than episodic or sporadic interest; consumers and other stakeholders see through nominal commitments designed simply to garner short-term positive goodwill. "The public can smell if [a CSR effort] is not legitimate," said Shelly Lazarus, chairman and CEO of advertising agency Ogilvy & Mather USA. Hence, social initiatives that reflect the five principles discussed here can generate significant reputation benefits for participating companies.

AES's commitment to carbon offsets has won it several awards and generates favorable consideration from international financial institutions such as the World Bank, International Finance Corporation, and Inter-American Development Bank, as well as from governments, insurers, and NGOs. In the consumer products sector, Avon receives extensive media recognition from the advertising and marketing of cancer walks, nationwide special events including a gala fund-raising concert, and an awards ceremony. Avon has become so closely associated with the breast cancer cause that many consumers now identify the company's commitment—and the trademark pink ribbon—as easily as its traditional door-to-door marketing and distribution systems.

While difficult to quantify precisely, the potential value of the pink ribbon campaign, and the brand awareness associated with it, generates economic benefits for Avon in the form of goodwill and overall reputation. Avon's strategy of focusing on a cause that women care about, leveraging its contributions, and partnering with respected NGOs has enabled it to gain trust and credibility in the marketplace. "There needs to be a correlation between the cause and the company," said Susan Heany, director for corporate social responsibility at Avon. "The linkage between corporate giving and the corporate product creates brand recognition. Both buyers and sellers want to achieve the same goal: improving women's health care worldwide."[11]

Assembling the Components

A range of corporate initiatives lend themselves to the CSI model because they share most of the five key attributes we have described here: they have long-term objectives, they are sufficiently large to allow a company to specialize in its contributions, they provide many opportunities for the company to contribute from its current activities or products, they enjoy government support, and they provide a package of benefits that adds value to the company. Exhibit 3.15, Strategy in Action, summarizes five very successful CSI programs and their performance against each of the five principles.

Of the five principles, the most important by far is the second one. Companies must apply what they do best in their normal commercial operations to their social responsibility undertakings. This tenet is consistent with research that argues that social activities most closely related to the company's core mission are most efficiently administered through internalization or collaboration. It is applicable far beyond the examples in this chapter; to waste management companies and recycling programs, for instance, or to publishing companies and after-school educational initiatives, or pharmaceutical companies and local immunization and health education programs.

---

[11] "Corporate Social Responsibility in Practice Casebook," *The Catalyst Consortium,* July 2002, p. 8. Available at www.rhcatalyst.org.

Strategy in Action

Exhibit 3.15

Five Successful Collaborative Social Initiatives

Program	Pursue a Long-Term, Durable Mission	Contribute "What We Do"	Contribute Specialized Resources to a Large Scale Undertaking	Weigh Government Influence	Assemble and Value Total Package of Benefits
ConAgra Foods' Feeding Children Better	Individuals needing food from charity in the United States grew to more than 23 million in 2001. In the United Kingdom, the total was 4 million people in 2003.	ConAgra uses its electronic inventory control systems and refrigerated trucks to assist America's food rescue programs.	ConAgra fights child hunger in America by assembling a powerful partnership with America's Second Harvest, Brandeis University's Center on Hunger and Poverty, and the Ad Council.	The Bill Emerson Good Samaritan Food Donation Act protects businesses from liability for food donations.	ConAgra's brand-sponsored support of food rescue programs sustains its image as provider of "the largest corporate initiative dedicated solely to fighting child hunger in America."
Avon's Breast Cancer Crusade	Breast cancer is the second-leading cause of death in women in the United States and the most common cancer among women.	Avon's commitment to being "the company for women" is shown by their 550,000 sales representatives who sell Crusade "pink ribbon" items.	Avon distinguishes itself by supporting a national network of research, medical, social service, and local organizations to advance cancer research.	Government agencies often match individual contributions; local governments provide logistical support for fundraising walks.	Avon receives media recognition from the advertising and marketing of cancer walks and nationwide special events, including a gala fundraising concert and awards ceremony.
IBM's Reinventing Education	Education in developing countries requires a long-term commitment to school reform, such as methods for measuring learning.	IBM uses its leading researchers, educational consultants, and technology to spur and support fundamental school restructuring.	IBM monitors the program with rigorous, independent evaluations from the Center for Children & Technology in conjunction with the Harvard Business School.	IBM teams with the U.S. Department of Education and the U.K. Department of Education and Employment on many reinvention projects.	IBM views a commitment to education as a strategic business investment. By investing in its future workforce and its customers, IBM feels that it promotes its own success.
Home Depot's In Your Community	30 million Americans face housing problems, such as overcrowding, no hot water, no electricity, and no toilet, bathtub, or shower.	Home Depot offers help with the construction of homes, plus donations and volunteers to help provide affordable housing for low-income families.	More than 1,500 Home Depot stores have Team Depot volunteer programs to support Habitat for Humanity, Rebuilding Together, and KaBOOM with the help of its 315,000 company associates.	Home Depot's partnership with Habitat for Humanity is actively supported by the U.S. Department of Housing and Urban Development.	Home Depot's volunteer programs and "how-to" clinics "invite the community into their stores." Hundreds of thousands of potential customers participate each year.
AES's Carbon Offsets Program	Global warming is an environmental threat. Carbon offsets or "sinks" are one proven, effective means of combating this problem.	AES is a leading international power producer with extensive knowledge of developing countries and their resources, including the dangers from cogeneration plants.	AES has teamed with the World Resources Institute, Nature Conservancy, and CARE to find and evaluate appropriate forestry-based offset projects.	The Environmental Protection Agency, European environmental organizations, U.N. Development Program, and other agencies support carbon offsets.	AES has committed $12 million to carbon offset projects to offset 67 million tons of carbon emitted over the next 40 years—the equivalent of the emissions from a 1,000-MW coal facility over its lifetime.

The Limits of CSR Strategies

Some companies such as Ben & Jerry's have embedded social responsibility and sustainability commitments deeply in their core strategies. Research suggests that such single-minded devotion to CSR may be unrealistic for larger, more established corporations. For example, some analysts have suggested that the intense focus on social responsibility goals by the management team at Levi Strauss & Co. may have diverted the company from its core operational challenges, accelerating the company's closure of all of its North American manufacturing operations.

Larger companies must move beyond the easy options of charitable donations but also steer clear of overreaching commitments. This is not to suggest that companies should not think big—research shows that projects can be broad in scale and scope and still succeed. Rather, it suggests that companies need to view their commitments to corporate responsibility as one important part of their overall strategy but not let the commitment obscure their broad strategic business goals. By starting with a well-defined CSR strategy and developing the collaborative initiatives that support that strategy by meeting the five criteria we have identified, companies and their leaders can make important contributions to the common good while advancing their broader financial and market objectives.

CSR strategies can also run afoul of the skeptics, and the speed with which information can be disseminated via the Web—and accumulated in Web logs—makes this an issue with serious ramifications for reputation management. Nike has been a lightning rod for CSR activists for its alleged tolerance of hostile and dangerous working conditions in its many factories and subcontractors around the world. Despite the considerable efforts the company has made to respond to its critics, it has consistently been on the defensive in trying to redeem its reputation.

Touching on this issue at the World Economic Forum, Unilever chief Antony Burgmans noted the importance of "making people who matter in society aware of what you do." His point was amplified by Starbucks CEO Orin Smith, who invited the authors of an NGO report critical of Starbucks' sourcing strategies to the company's offices and showed them the books. "In many instances we ended up partnering with them," he said.

The Future of CSR

CSR is firmly and irreversibly part of the corporate fabric. Managed properly, CSR programs can confer significant benefits to participants in terms of corporate reputation; in terms of hiring, motivation, and retention; and as a means of building and cementing valuable partnerships. And of course, the benefits extend well beyond the boundaries of the participating organizations, enriching the lives of many disadvantaged communities and individuals and pushing back on problems that threaten future generations, other species, and precious natural resources.

That is the positive perspective. The more prickly aspect of CSR is that for all of their resources and capabilities, corporations will face growing demands for social responsibility contributions far beyond simple cash or in-kind donations. Aggressive protesters will keep the issues hot, employees will continue to have their say, and shareholders will pass judgment with their investments—and their votes.

The challenge for management, then, is to know how to meet the company's obligations to all stakeholders without compromising the basic need to earn a fair return for its owners. As research shows, a collaborative approach is the foundation for the most effective CSR initiatives. By then adhering to the five key principles outlined in this section, business leaders can maintain ongoing commitments to carefully chosen initiatives that can have positive and tangible effects on social problems while meeting their obligations to shareholders, employees, and the broader communities in which they operate.

Enron: Running on Empty

BusinessWeek

The fall of mighty Enron Corp. (ENE)—once one of the most valuable companies in America—was a collapse of mind-boggling proportions. In 2001, Enron had $101 billion in revenues, a stock-market capitalization of $63 billion, and a chairman who was a high-profile confidant of President Bush. Yet in a sickeningly swift spiral, the powerful energy trading company tumbled to the brink of bankruptcy in late November 2001—the victim of a botched expansion attempt, an accounting scandal, and the overweening ambition of its once widely admired top executives.

The end came quickly because Enron had overextended itself—and because investors and customers lost faith in its secretive and complex financial maneuvers. With legions of traders working out of a Houston skyscraper, the company put together trades so exotic that they mystified many Wall Street veterans. Under Chairman Kenneth L. Lay—who pressed the administration to embrace a controversial policy of electricity deregulation—and former CEO Jeffrey K. Skilling, Enron had become largely a trading operation, dubbed by some the Goldman, Sachs & Co. of the energy business.

Enron's success depended on maintaining the trust of customers that it would make good on its dealings in the market. But that trust evaporated as it shocked the market with changes to its nearly incomprehensible financial statements. "If you are running a trading operation, you have to be like Caesar's wife, beyond reproach."

The fall of Enron—to 61 cents a share on November 28, 2001—wiped out more than 99 percent of its stock-market value. Banks that lent billions to Enron will have to fight for a share in bankruptcy court. Enron's biggest lenders are J. P. Morgan Chase & Co. and Citigroup, which together have an estimated $1.6 billion in exposure. Of that, $900 million is unsecured. Other losers: Enron's customers, who traded everything from electricity, gas, and metals to telecom bandwidth, credit insurance, and weather derivatives.

Already the once-arrogant Enron has become vulture meat. In addition to clamoring creditors, it faces class actions by shareholders and employees, whose pensions were heavily invested in Enron stock. That raises questions about how much value is left in the company, which will probably be dismembered and sold off in parts.

Who's to blame? Perhaps the biggest culprit was arrogance, which has caused Enron to be compared to past self-proclaimed masters of the universe such as Drexel Burnham Lambert Inc. in the 1980s and Long-Term Capital Management in the 1990s. Many fingers are pointing at Skilling, the longtime Enron financial engineer who took over as CEO in February and Lay and Andrew S. Fastow, who was ousted as chief financial officer on October 24, 2001. Fastow put together several partnerships that were intended to streamline Enron's balance sheet by taking on certain assets and liabilities. That created a conflict of interest for Fastow, who made over $30 million from his partnerships.

The most poignant aspect of Enron's failure is the damage to its own employees. "People have had their total savings disappear," says William Miller, business manager of the International Brotherhood of Electrical Workers union local in Portland, Oregon, which represents employees of Enron's Portland General Electric Co. subsidiary. "Some lives have been pretty well destroyed." Enron flew high, but when it fell, it fell hard.

Source: Reprinted with special permission from Peter Coy, Emily Thornton, Stephanie Anderson Forest, and Christopher Palmeri, "Enron: Running on Empty," *BusinessWeek*, December 10, 2001. Copyright © 2001 The McGraw-Hill Companies.

Unfortunately, the public's perception of the ethics of corporate executives in America is near its all-time low. A major cause is a spate of corporate scandals prompted by self-serving, and often criminal, executive action that resulted in the loss of stakeholder investments and employee jobs. The most notorious of these cases was the failure of the Enron Corporation, as described in Exhibit 3.16, Strategy in Action. The obvious goal of every company is to avoid scandal through a combination of high moral and ethical standards and careful monitoring to assure that those standards are maintained. However, when problems arise, the management task of restoring the credibility of the company becomes paramount.

External stakeholders are not the only critics of the current state of business ethics. Exhibit 3.17, Strategy in Action, presents the findings of a major survey of human resource managers in which they indicate that strategic managers have much work to do to establish high ethical standards in their organizations.

HR Professionals Believe Ethical Conduct Not Rewarded in Business

A major survey indicates that nearly half of human resources (HR) professionals believe ethical conduct is not rewarded in business today. Over the past five years, HR professionals have felt increasingly more pressure to compromise their organizations' ethical standards; however, they also indicate personally observing fewer cases of misconduct.

The Society for Human Resource Management (SHRM) and the Ethics Resource Center (ERC) jointly conducted the 2003 Business Ethics Survey, with 462 respondents. The survey results show the following:

- 79 percent of respondent organizations have written ethics standards.
- 49 percent say that ethical conduct is not rewarded in business today.

- 35 percent of HR professionals often or occasionally personally observed ethics misconduct in the last year.
- 24 percent of HR professionals feel pressured to compromise ethics standards. In comparison, 13 percent indicated they felt pressured in 1997.
- The top five reasons HR professionals compromise an organization's ethical standards are the need to follow the boss's directives (49 percent); meeting overly aggressive business/financial objectives (48 percent); helping the organization survive (40 percent); meeting schedule pressures (35 percent); and wanting to be a team player (27 percent).

Source: Society for Human Resource Management, www.shrm.org/press.

Even when groups agree on what constitutes human welfare in a given case, the means they choose to achieve this welfare may differ. Therefore, ethics also involve acting to attain human goals. For example, many people would agree that health is a value worth seeking—that is, health enhances human welfare. But what if the means deemed necessary to attain this value for some include the denial or risk of health for others, as is commonly an issue faced by pharmaceutical manufacturers? During production of some drugs, employees are sometimes subjected to great risk of personal injury and infection. For example, if contacted or inhaled, the mercury used in making thermometers and blood pressure equipment can cause heavy metal poisoning. If inhaled, ethylene oxide used to sterilize medical equipment before it is shipped to doctors can cause fetal abnormalities and miscarriages. Even penicillin, if inhaled during its manufacturing process, can cause acute anaphylaxis or shock. Thus, although the goal of customer health might be widely accepted, the means (involving jeopardy to production employees) may not be.

The spotlight on business ethics is a widespread phenomenon. For example, a 2004 survey by the Institute of Business Ethics helps to clarify how companies use their codes of ethics.[12] It found that more than 90 percent of Financial Times Stock Exchange (FTSE) companies in the United Kingdom have an explicit commitment to doing business ethically in the form of a code of ethical conduct. The respondents also reported that 26 percent of boards of directors are taking direct responsibility for the ethical programs of companies, up from 16 percent in 2001. The main reasons for having a code of ethics were to provide guidance to staff (38 percent) and to reduce legal liability (33 percent). Many of the managers (41 percent) also reported that they had used their code in disciplinary procedures in the last three years, usually on safety, security, and environmental ethical issues.

Approaches to Questions of Ethics

Managers report that the most critical quality of ethical decision making is consistency. Thus, they often try to adopt a philosophical approach that can provide the basis for the

[12] Accessed in 2005 from http://www.ibe.org.uk/ExecSumm.pdf.

consistency they seek. There are three fundamental ethical approaches for executives to consider: the utilitarian approach, the moral rights approach, and the social justice approach.

utilitarian approach
Judging the appropriateness of a particular action based on a goal to provide the greatest good for the greatest number of people.

Managers who adopt the **utilitarian approach** judge the effects of a particular action on the people directly involved, in terms of what provides the greatest good for the greatest number of people. The utilitarian approach focuses on actions, rather than on the motives behind the actions. Potentially positive results are weighed against potentially negative results. If the former outweigh the latter, the manager taking the utilitarian approach is likely to proceed with the action. That some people might be adversely affected by the action is accepted as inevitable. For example, the Council on Environmental Quality conducts cost-benefit analyses when selecting air pollution standards under the Clean Air Act, thereby acknowledging that some pollution must be accepted.

moral rights approach
Judging the appropriateness of a particular action based on a goal to maintain the fundamental rights and privileges of individuals and groups.

Managers who subscribe to the **moral rights approach** judge whether decisions and actions are in keeping with the maintenance of fundamental individual and group rights and privileges. The moral rights approach (also referred to as deontology) includes the rights of human beings to life and safety, a standard of truthfulness, privacy, freedom to express one's conscience, freedom of speech, and private property.

social justice approach
Judging the appropriateness of a particular action based on equity, fairness, and impartiality in the distribution of rewards and costs among individuals and groups.

Managers who take the **social justice approach** judge how consistent actions are with equity, fairness, and impartiality in the distribution of rewards and costs among individuals and groups. These ideas stem from two principles known as the liberty principle and the difference principle. The *liberty principle* states that individuals have certain basic liberties compatible with similar liberties of other people. The *difference principle* holds that social and economic inequities must be addressed to achieve a more equitable distribution of goods and services.

In addition to these defining principles, three implementing principles are essential to the social justice approach. According to the *distributive-justice principle,* individuals should not be treated differently on the basis of arbitrary characteristics, such as race, sex, religion or national origin. This familiar principle is embodied in the Civil Rights Act. The *fairness principle* means that employees must be expected to engage in cooperative activities according to the rules of the company, assuming that the company rules are deemed fair. The most obvious example is that, in order to further the mutual interests of the company, themselves, and other workers, employees must accept limits on their freedom to be absent from work. The *natural-duty principle* points up a number of general obligations, including the duty to help others who are in need or danger, the duty not to cause unnecessary suffering, and the duty to comply with the just rules of an institution.

CODES OF BUSINESS ETHICS

To help ensure consistency in the application of ethical standards, an increasing number of professional associations and businesses are establishing codes of ethical conduct. Associations of chemists, funeral directors, law enforcement agents, migration agents, hockey players, Internet providers, librarians, military arms sellers, philatelists, physicians, and psychologists all have such codes. So do companies such as Amazon.com, Colgate, Honeywell, New York Times, Nokia, PricewaterhouseCoopers, Sony Group, and Riggs Bank.

Nike faces the problems of a large global corporation in enforcing a code of conduct. Nike's products are manufactured in factories owned and operated by other companies. Nike's supply chain includes more than 660,000 contract manufacturing workers in more than 900 factories in more than 50 countries, including the United States. The workers are predominantly women, ages 19 to 25. The geographic dispersion of its manufacturing facilities is driven by many factors including pricing, quality, factory capacity, and quota allocations.

With such cultural, societal, and economic diversity, the ethics challenge for Nike is to "do business with contract factories that consistently demonstrate compliance with

Nike Code of Conduct

Nike, Inc. was founded on a handshake. Implicit in that act was the determination that we would build our business with all of our partners based on trust, teamwork, honesty, and mutual respect. We expect all of our business partners to operate on the same principles.

At the core of the Nike corporate ethic is the belief that we are a company comprised of many different kinds of people, appreciating individual diversity, and dedicated to equal opportunity for each individual.

Nike designs, manufactures, and markets products for sports and fitness consumers. At every step in that process, we are driven to do not only what is required by law, but what is expected of a leader. We expect our business partners to do the same. Nike partners with contractors who share our commitment to best practices and continuous improvement in:

1. Management practices that respect the rights of all employees, including the right to free association and collective bargaining.
2. Minimizing our impact on the environment.
3. Providing a safe and healthy workplace.
4. Promoting the health and well-being of all employees.

Contractors must recognize the dignity of each employee, and the right to a workplace free of harassment, abuse or corporal punishment. Decisions on hiring, salary, benefits, advancement, termination, or retirement must be based solely on the employee's ability to do the job. There shall be no discrimination based on race, creed, gender, marital or maternity status, religious or political beliefs, age, or sexual orientation.

Wherever Nike operates around the globe, we are guided by this Code of Conduct, and we bind our contractors to these principles. Contractors must post this Code in all major workspaces, translated into the language of the employee, and must train employees on their rights and obligations as defined by this Code and applicable local laws.

While these principles establish the spirit of our partnerships, we also bind our partners to specific standards of conduct. The core standards are set forth below.

FORCED LABOR
The contractor does not use forced labor in any form—prison, indentured, bonded, or otherwise.

CHILD LABOR
The contractor does not employ any person below the age of 18 to produce footwear. The contractor does not employ any person below the age of 16 to produce apparel, accessories, or equipment. If at the time Nike production begins, the contractor employs people of the legal working age who are at least 15, that employment may continue, but the contractor will not hire any person going forward who is younger than the Nike or legal age limit, whichever is higher.

To further ensure these age standards are complied with, the contractor does not use any form of homework for Nike production.

COMPENSATION
The contractor provides each employee at least the minimum wage, or the prevailing industry wage, whichever is higher; provides each employee a clear, written accounting for every pay period; and does not deduct from employee pay for disciplinary infractions.

BENEFITS
The contractor provides each employee all legally mandated benefits.

HOURS OF WORK/OVERTIME
The contractor complies with legally mandated work hours; uses overtime only when each employee is fully compensated according to local law; informs each employee at the time of hiring if mandatory overtime is a condition of employment; and, on a regularly scheduled basis, provides one day off in seven, and requires no more than 60 hours of work per week on a regularly scheduled basis, or complies with local limits if they are lower.

ENVIRONMENT, SAFETY AND HEALTH (ES&H)
The contractor has written environmental, safety, and health policies and standards and implements a system to minimize negative impacts on the environment, reduce work-related injury and illness, and promote the general health of employees.

DOCUMENTATION AND INSPECTION
The contractor maintains on file all documentation needed to demonstrate compliance with this Code of Conduct and required laws, agrees to make these documents available for Nike or its designated monitor, and agrees to submit to inspections with or without prior notice.

Source: www.nike.com/nikebiz, 2007.

standards we set and that operate in an ethical and lawful manner." To help in this process, Nike has developed its own code of ethics, which it calls a Code of Conduct. It is a set of ethical principles intended to guide management decision making. Nike's code is presented in Exhibit 3.18, Strategy in Action.

Major Trends in Codes of Ethics

The increased interest in codifying business ethics has led to both the proliferation of formal statements by companies and to their prominence among business documents. Not long ago, codes of ethics that existed were usually found solely in employee handbooks. The new trend is for them to also be prominently displayed on corporate Web sites, in annual reports, and next to Title VII posters on bulletin boards.

A second trend is that companies are adding enforcement measures to their codes, including policies that are designed to guide employees on what to do if they see violations occur and sanctions that will be applied, including consequences on their employment and civil and criminal charges. As a consequence, businesses are increasingly requiring all employees to sign the ethics statement as a way to acknowledge that they have read and understood their obligations. In part this requirement reflects the impact of the Sarbanes-Oxley rule that CEOs and CFOs certify the accuracy of company financials. Executives want employees at all levels to recognize their own obligations to pass accurate information up the chain of command.

The third trend is increased attention by companies in improving employees' training in understanding their obligations under the company's code of ethics. The objective is to emphasize the consideration of ethics during the decision-making process. Training, and subsequent monitoring of actual work behavior, is also aided by computer software that identifies possible code violations, which managers can then investigate in detail.

Summary

Given the amount of time that people spend working, it is reasonable that they should try to shape the organizations in which they work. Inanimate organizations are often blamed for setting the legal, ethical, and moral tones in the workplace when, in reality, people determine how people behave. Just as individuals try to shape their neighborhoods, schools, political and social organizations, and religious institutions, employees need to help determine the major issues of corporate social responsibility and business ethics.

Strategic decisions, indeed all decisions, involve trade-offs. We choose one thing over another. We pursue one goal while subordinating another. On the topic of corporate social responsibility, individual employees must work to achieve the outcomes that they want. By volunteering for certain community welfare options they choose to improve that option's chances of being beneficial. Business ethics present a parallel opportunity. By choosing proper behaviors, employees help to build an organization that can be respected and economically viable in the long run.

Often, the concern is expressed that business activities tend to be illegal or unethical and that the failure of individuals to follow the pattern will leave them at a competitive disadvantage. Such claims, often prompted by high-profile examples, are absurd. Rare but much publicized criminal activities mask the meaningful reality that business conduct is as honest and honorable as any other activity in our lives. The people who are involved are the same, with the same values, ideals, and aspirations.

In this chapter, we have studied corporate social responsibility to understand it and to learn how our businesses can occasionally use some of their resources to make differential, positive impacts on our society. We also looked at business ethics to gain an appreciation for the importance of maintaining and promoting social values in the workplace.

Key Terms

corporate social
responsibility, *p. 58*
discretionary
responsibilities, *p. 58*
economic
responsibilities, *p. 56*

ethical responsibilities, *p. 58*
ethics, *p. 70*
legal responsibilities, *p. 56*
moral rights approach, *p. 84*
privatization, *p. 68*

Sarbanes-Oxley Act of
2002, *p. 64*
social audit, *p. 69*
social justice approach, *p. 84*
utilitarian approach, *p. 84*

**Questions for
Discussion**

1. Define the term *social responsibility.* Find an example of a company action that was legal but not socially responsible. Defend your example on the basis of your definition.
2. Name five potentially valuable indicators of a firm's social responsibility and describe how company performance in each could be measured.
3. Do you think a business organization in today's society benefits by defining a socially responsible role for itself? Why or why not?
4. Which of the three basic philosophies of social responsibility would you find most appealing as the chief executive of a large corporation? Explain.
5. Do you think society's expectations for corporate social responsibility will change in the next decade? Explain.
6. How much should social responsibility be considered in evaluating an organization's overall performance?
7. Is it necessary that an action be voluntary to be termed socially responsible? Explain.
8. Do you think an organization should adhere to different philosophies of corporate responsibility when confronted with different issues, or should its philosophy always remain the same? Explain.
9. Describe yourself as a stakeholder in a company. What kind of stakeholder role do you play now? What kind of stakeholder roles do you expect to play in the future?
10. What sets the affirmative philosophy apart from the stakeholder philosophy of social responsibility? In what areas do the two philosophies overlap?
11. Cite examples of both ethical and unethical behavior drawn from your knowledge of current business events.
12. How would you describe the contemporary state of business ethics?
13. How can business self-interest also serve social interests?

Chapter 3 Discussion Case

The Poverty Business

BusinessWeek

1 Roxanne Tsosie decided in late 2005 to pull her life together. She was 28 years old and still lived in her mother's two-room apartment in a poor neighborhood in southeast Albuquerque known as the War Zone. She survived mostly on food stamps and welfare. The Tsosies are Navajo, and Roxanne's mother wanted to move back to a reservation in western New Mexico where the family has a dilapidated house lacking electricity and running water. Roxanne, unmarried and with four children of her own, could make out her future, and she didn't like what she saw.

2 With only a high school diploma, her employment options were limited. She landed a job as a home health care aide for the elderly and infirm. It paid $15,000 a year and required

that she have a car to make her rounds of Albuquerque and its rambling desert suburbs. A friend told her about a used-car place called J. D. Byrider Systems Inc.

3 The bright orange car lot stands out amid a jumble of payday lenders, pawn shops, and rent-to-own electronics stores on Central Avenue in the War Zone. Signs in Spanish along the street promise *Financiamos a Todos*—Financing for All. On the same day she walked into Byrider, Tsosie drove off, jubilant, in a 1999 Saturn subcompact she bought entirely on credit. "I was starting to think I could actually get things I wanted," she says.

4 In recent years, a range of businesses have made financing more readily available to even the riskiest of borrowers. Greater access to credit has put cars, computers, credit cards,

and even homes within reach for many more of the working poor. But this remaking of the marketplace for low-income consumers has a dark side: innovative and zealous firms have lured unsophisticated shoppers by the hundreds of thousands into a thicket of debt from which many never emerge.

5   Federal Reserve data show that in relative terms, that debt is getting expensive. In 1989 households earning $30,000 or less a year paid an average annual interest rate on auto loans that was 16.8 percent higher than what households earning more than $90,000 a year paid. By 2004 the discrepancy had soared to 56.1 percent. Roughly the same thing happened with mortgage loans: a leap from a 6.4 percent gap to one of 25.5 percent. "It's not only that the poor are paying more; the poor are paying a lot more," says Sheila C. Bair, chairman of the Federal Deposit Insurance Corp.

6   Once, substantial businesses had little interest in chasing customers of the sort who frequent the storefronts surrounding the Byrider dealership in Albuquerque. Why bother grabbing for the few dollars in a broke man's pocket? Now there's reason.

7   Armed with the latest technology for assessing credit risks—some of it so fine-tuned it picks up spending on cigarettes—ambitious corporations like Byrider see profits in those thin wallets. The liquidity lapping over all parts of the financial world also has enabled the dramatic expansion of lending to the working poor. Byrider, with financing from Bank of America Corp. (BAC) and others, boasts 130 dealerships in 30 states. At company headquarters in Carmel, Indiana, a profusion of colored pins decorates wall maps, marking the 372 additional franchises it aims to open from California to Florida. CompuCredit Corp., based in Atlanta, aggressively promotes credit cards to low-wage earners with a history of not paying their bills on time. And BlueHippo Funding, a self-described "direct response merchandise lender," has retooled the rent-to-own model to sell PCs and plasma TVs.

8   The recent furor over subprime mortgage loans fits into this broader story about the proliferation of subprime credit. In some instances, marketers essentially use products as the bait to hook less-well-off shoppers on expensive loans. "It's the finance business," explains Russ Darrow Jr., a Byrider franchisee in Milwaukee. "Cars happen to be the commodity that we sell." In another variation, tax-preparation services offer instant refunds, skimming off hefty fees. Attorneys general in several states say these techniques at times have violated consumer-protection laws.

9   Some economists applaud how the spread of credit to the tougher parts of town has raised home and auto-ownership rates. But others warn that in the long run the development could slow upward mobility. Wages for the working poor have been stagnant for three decades. Meanwhile, their spending has consistently and significantly exceeded their income since the mid-1980s. They are making up the difference by borrowing more. From 1989 through 2004, the total amount owed by households earning $30,000 or less a year has grown 247 percent to $691 billion, according to the most recent Federal Reserve data available.

10   "Having access to credit should be helping low-income individuals," says Nouriel Roubini, an economics professor at New York University's Stern School of Business. "But instead of becoming an opportunity for upward social and economic mobility, it becomes a debt trap for many trying to move up."

11   Happy as she was with the Saturn (GM) she bought in December 2005, Roxanne Tsosie soon ran into trouble paying off the loan on it. The car had 103,000 miles on the odometer. She agreed to a purchase price of $7,992, borrowing the full amount at a sky-high 24.9 percent. Based on her conversation with the Byrider salesman, she thought she had signed up for $150 monthly installments. The paperwork indicated she owed that amount every other week. She soon realized she couldn't manage the payments. Dejected, she agreed to give the car back, having already paid $900. "It kind of knocked me down," Tsosie says. "I felt I'd never get anywhere."

12   The abortive purchase meant Byrider could dust off and resell the Saturn. Nearly half of Byrider sales in Albuquerque do not result in final payoff, and many vehicles are repossessed, says David Brotherton, managing partner of the dealership. A former factory worker, he says he sympathizes with customers who barely get by. "Many of these people are locked in perpetual cycle of debt," he says. "It's all motivated by self-interest, of course, but we do want to help credit-challenged people get to the finish line."

13   Byrider dealers say they can generally figure out which customers will pay back their loans. Salesmen, many of whom come from positions at banks and other lending companies, use proprietary software called Automated Risk Evaluator (ARE) to assess customers' financial vital signs, ranging from credit scores from major credit agencies to amounts spent on alimony and cigarettes.

14   Unlike traditional dealers, Byrider doesn't post prices—which average $10,200 at company-owned showrooms—directly on its cars. Salesmen, after consulting ARE, calculate the maximum that a person can afford to pay, and only then set the total price, down payment, and interest rate. Byrider calls this process fair and accurate; critics call it "opportunity pricing."

15   So how did Byrider figure that Tsosie had $300 a month left over from her small salary for car payments? Barely a step up from destitution, she now lives in her own cramped apartment in a dingy two-story adobe-style building. Decorated with an old bow and arrow and sepia-tinted photographs of Navajo chiefs, the apartment is also home to her new husband, Joey A. Garcia, a grocery-store stocker earning $25,000 a year, his two children from a previous marriage, and two of Tsosie's kids. She and Garcia are paying off several other high-interest loans, including one for his used car and another for the $880 wedding ring he bought her this year.

16   Asked by *BusinessWeek* to review Tsosie's file, Byrider's Brotherton raises his eyebrows, taps his keyboard, and studies

the screen for a few minutes, "We probably should have spent more time explaining the terms to her," he says. Pausing, he adds that given Tsosie's finances, she should never have received a 24.9 percent loan for nearly $8,000.

17   That still leaves her $900 in Byrider's till. "No excuses; I apologize," Brotherton says. He promises to return the money (and later does). In most transactions, of course, there's no reporter on the scene asking questions.

18   A quarter century ago, Byrider's founder, the late James F. Devoe, saw before most people the untapped profits in selling expensive, highly financed products to marginal customers. "The light went on that there was a huge market of people with subprime and unconventional credit being turned down," says Devoe's 38-year-old son, James Jr., who is now chief executive.

19   The formula produces profits. Last year, net income on used cars sold by outlets Byrider owns averaged $828 apiece. That compared with only $223 for used cars sold as a sideline by new-car dealers, and a $31 loss for the typical new car, according to the National Automobile Dealers Assn. Nationwide, Byrider dealerships reported sales last year of $700 million, up 7 percent from 2005.

20   "Good Cars for People Who Need Credit," the company declares in its sunny advertising, but some law enforcers say Byrider's inventive sales techniques are unfair. Joel Cruz-Esparza, director of consumer protection in the New Mexico Attorney General's Office from 2002 to 2006, says he received numerous complaints from buyers about Byrider. His office contacted the dealer, but he never went to court. "They're taking advantage of people, but it's not illegal," he says.

21   Officials elsewhere disagree. Attorneys general in Kentucky and Ohio have alleged in recent civil suits that opportunity pricing misleads customers. Without admitting liability, Byrider and several franchises settled the suits in 2005 and 2006, agreeing to inform buyers of "maximum retail prices." Dealers now post prices somewhere on their premises, though still not on cars. Doing so would put them "at a competitive disadvantage," says CEO Devoe. Sales reps flip through charts telling customers they have the right to know prices. Even so, Devoe says, buyers "talk to us about the price of the car less than 10 percent of the time."

22   Tsosie recently purchased a 2001 Pontiac from another dealer. She's straining to make the $277 monthly payment on a 14.9 percent loan.

23   Nobody, poor or rich, is compelled to pay a high price for a used car, a credit card, or anything else. Some see the debate ending there. "The only feasible way to run a capitalist society is to allow companies to maximize their profits," says Tyler Cowen, an economist at George Mason University in Fairfax, Virginia. "That will sometimes include allowing them to sell things to people that will sometimes make them worse off."

24   Others worry, however, that the widening income gap between the wealthy and the less fortunate is being exacerbated by the spread of high-interest, high-fee financing. "People are being encouraged to live beyond their means by companies that are preying on low-income consumers," says Jacob S. Hacker, a political scientist at Yale.

25   Higher rates aren't deterring low-income borrowers. Payday lenders, which provide expensive cash advances due on the customer's next payday, have multiplied from 300 in the early 1990s to more than 25,000. Savvy financiers are rolling up payday businesses and pawn shops to form large chains. The stocks of five of these companies now trade publicly on the New York Stock Exchange (NYX) and NASDAQ (NDAQ). The investment bank Stephens Inc. estimates that the volume of "alternative financial services" provided by these sorts of businesses totals more than $250 billion a year.

26   Mainstream financial institutions are helping to fuel this explosion in subprime lending to the working poor. Wells Fargo & Co. (WFC) and U.S. Bancorp (USB) now offer their own versions of payday loans, charging $2 for every $20 borrowed. Based on a 30-day repayment period, that's an annual interest rate of 120 percent. (Wells Fargo says the loans are designed for emergencies not long-term financial needs.) Bank of America's revolving credit line to Byrider provides up to $110 million. Merrill Lynch & Co. (MER) works with CompuCredit to package credit-card receivables as securities, which are bought by hedge funds and other big investors.

27   Once, major banks and companies avoided the poor side of town. "The mentality was: low income means low revenue, so let's not locate there," says Matt Fellowes, a researcher at the Brookings Institution in Washington, D.C. Now, he says, a growing number of sizable corporations are realizing that viewed in the aggregate, the working poor are a choice target. Income for the 40 million U.S. households earning $30,000 or less totaled $650 billion in 2004, according to Federal Reserve data.

28   John T. Hewitt a pioneer in the tax-software industry, recognized the opportunity. The founder of Jackson Hewitt Tax Service Inc. (JTX) says that as his company grew in the 1980s, "we focused on the low-hanging fruit: the less affluent people who wanted their money quick."

29   In the 1990s, Jackson Hewitt franchises blanketed lower-income neighborhoods around the country. They soaked up fees not just by preparing returns but also by loaning money to taxpayers too impatient or too desperate to wait for the government to send them their checks. During this period, Congress expanded the Earned-Income Tax Credit, a program that guarantees refunds to the working poor. Jackson Hewitt and rival tax-prep firms inserted themselves into this wealth-transfer system and became "the new welfare office," observes Kathryn Edin, a visiting professor at Harvard University's John F. Kennedy School of Government. Today, recipients of the tax credit are Jackson Hewitt's prime customers.

30   "Money Now," as Jackson Hewitt markets its refund-anticipation loans, comes at a steep price. Lakissisha M. Thomas learned that the hard way. For years, Thomas, 29, has bounced between government assistance and low-paying jobs catering to the wealthy of Hilton Head Island, South Carolina. She worked most recently as a cahier at a jewelry store, earning $8.50 an hour, until she was laid off in April. The single mother lives with her five children in a dimly lit four-bedroom apartment in a public project a few hundred yards from the manicured entrance of Indigo Run, a resort where homes sell for more than $1 million.

31   Thomas finances much of what she buys, but admits she usually doesn't understand the terms. "What do you call it—interest?" she asks, sounding confused. Two years ago she borrowed $400 for and food from Advance America Cash Advance Centers Inc. (AEA), a payday chain. She renewed the loan every two weeks until last November, paying more than $2,500 in fees.

32   This January, eager for a $4,351 earned-income credit, she took out a refund-anticipation loan from Jackson Hewitt. She used the money to pay overdue rent and utility bills, she says. "I thought it would help me get back on my feet."

33   A public housing administrator who reviews tenants' tax returns pointed out to Thomas that Jackson Hewitt had pared $453, or 10.4 percent in tax-prep fees and interest from Thomas' anticipated refund. Only then did she discover that various services for low-income consumers prepare taxes for free and promise returns in as little as a week. "Why should I pay somebody else, some big company, when I could go to the free service?" she asks.

34   The lack of sophistication of borrowers like Thomas helps ensure that the Money Now loan and similar offerings remain big sellers. "I don't know whether I was more bothered by the ignorance of the customers or by the company taking advantage of the ignorance of the customers," says Kehinde Powell, who worked during 2005 as a preparer at a Jackson Hewitt office in Columbus, Ohio. She changed jobs voluntarily.

35   State and federal law enforcers lately have objected to some of Jackson Hewitt's practices. In a settlement in January of a suit brought by the California Attorney General's Office, the company, which is based in Parsippany, New Jersey, agreed to pay $5 million, including $4 million in consumer restitution. The state alleged Jackson Hewitt had pressured customers to take out expensive loans rather than encourage them to wait a week or two to get refunds for free. The company denied liability. In a separate series of suits filed in April, the U.S. Justice Department alleged that more than 125 Jackson Hewitt outlets in Chicago, Atlanta, Detroit, and the Raleigh-Durham (North Carolina) area had defrauded the Treasury by seeking undeserved refunds.

36   Jackson Hewitt stressed that the federal suits targeted a single franchisee. The company announced an internal investigation and stopped selling one type of refund-anticipation loan, known as a preseason loan. The bulk of refund loans are unaffected. More broadly, the company said in a written statement prepared for *BusinessWeek* that customers are "made aware of all options available," including direct electronic filing with the IRS. Refund loan applicants, the company said, receive "a variety of both verbal and written disclosures" that include cost comparisons. Jackson Hewitt added that it provides a valuable service for people who "have a need for quick access to funds to meet a timely expense." The two

franchises that served Thomas declined to comment or didn't return calls.

37   Vincent Humphries, 61, has watched the evolution of low-end lending with a rueful eye. Raised in Detroit and now living in Atlanta, he never got past high school. He started work in the early 1960s at Ford Motor Co.'s hulking Rouge plant outside Detroit for a little over $2 an hour. Later he did construction, rarely earning more than $25,000 a year while supporting five children from two marriages. A masonry business he financed on credit cards collapsed. None of his children have attended college, and all hold what he calls "dead-end jobs."

38   Over the years he has "paid through the nose" for used cars, furniture, and appliances, he says. He has borrowed from short-term, high-interest lenders and once worked as a deliveryman for a rent-to-own store in Atlanta that allowed buyers to pay for televisions over time but ended up charging much more than a conventional retailer. "You would have paid for it three times," he says. As for himself, he adds: "I've had plenty of accounts that have gone into collection. I hope I can pay them before I die." His biggest debts now are medical bills related to a heart condition. He lives on $875 a month from Social Security.

39   Around the time his heath problems ended his work as a bricklayer eight years ago, Humphries picked up a new hobby, computer programming. The shelves of the tidy two-room apartment where he lives alone, in a high-rise on Atlanta's crime-ridden South Side, are crammed with books on programming languages Java, C++, and HTML. He spends most days at his PC on a wooden desk nestled in the corner.

40   When his computer broke down in 2005, Humphries fretted that he would never be able to afford a new one. A solution appeared one night in a TV ad for a company with a catchy name. BlueHippo offered "top-of-the-line" PCs, no credit check necessary. He telephoned the next day.

41   He remembers the woman on the other end describing the computer in vague terms, but she was emphatic about getting his checking account information. She said BlueHippo would debit the account for $124, and Humphries then would owe 17 payments of $71.98 every other week. At the time, $800 would have bought a faster computer at Circuit City Stores (CC), but he didn't have the cash.

42   It wasn't until a week after placing his order that he realized that BlueHippo's terms meant he would pay $1,347.66 over nine months, Humphries says. He called to cancel. The company told him that would take as many as 10 days, he says. When he called again, a week later a customer-service representative said cancellation would take an additional 15 days. "I sensed then that I had my hand in the lion's mouth," Humphries says. During his next call, a phone rep told him BlueHippo had a no-refund policy. He would lose his $124, even though he had never received a computer.

43   Humphries takes some responsibility for this frustrating encounter. "I should have done my homework" before ordering, he says. But he also believes he was "strong armed" out of

$124. He was angry enough to send a detailed complaint to the attorney general of Maryland, where BlueHippo is based. That led to his becoming a lead plaintiff in a private class action pending in California against the company. The suit alleges that scores of customers were similarly duped. Blue-Hippo denies the allegation and says it treats all customers fairly.

44   The attorneys general of New York and West Virginia are investigating the company, and the Illinois attorney general has filed a consumer-protection suit in that state. In response to a Freedom of information Act request by *BusinessWeek*, the Federal Trade Commission says it has accumulated 8,000 pages of consumer complaints about BlueHippo. The FTC is investigating whether the company has engaged in deceptive practices.

45   Chief Executive Joseph K. Rensin started BlueHippo four years ago at the same Baltimore address where he had operated a company called Creditrust Corp. Creditrust, which bought other companies' bad customer debts, enjoyed some success but ultimately slid into Chapter 11 bankruptcy proceedings. In 2005, Rensin and his insurer agreed to pay $7.5 million to settle shareholder allegations that he made misleading statements in an attempt to inflate Creditrust's stock. Rensin and the company denied acting improperly.

46   Rensin established himself anew with BlueHippo, whose cartoon mascot adorns a sign in the lobby of its Baltimore building. Most of the 200 employees inside answer phones. Call-center training materials reviewed by *BusinessWeek* refer to BlueHippo's prime prospects as families, "typically $25k/yr income & less" who "have had trouble getting credit."

47   BlueHippo sells well-known brands such as Apple Inc. (AAPL) computers and Sony Corp. (SNE) televisions. Gateway Inc. (GTW) became a major supplier in December 2003. "We've clearly been aware of their business model from the get-go," says Gateway spokesman David Hallisey. More recently, Gateway became troubled by customer complaints and decided earlier this year to sever ties with BlueHippo. Given its knowledge all along about BlueHippo's methods, why did the separation occur only this year? Hallisey explains: "We're publicly traded and trying to make a profit, so that's a consideration."

48   Three former workers say BlueHippo typically tries to commit consumers to regular electronic debits, then, as in the Humphries case, stalls when they cancel orders or ask about receiving shipment. Many customers give up, according to these employees. Refusing refunds, the company keeps whatever money it receives, whether or not it ships a computer, the trio of form her employees say. "We knew we were misleading people. They weren't getting their computers," says Quinn Smith, a former call-center salesman who says he was fired last December after complaining about these practices. Smith has provided information to the plaintiffs in the California class action but isn't party to the suit.

49   Rensin declined to comment. In a written statement, the company denied any impropriety. It said it ships purchases when promised, though it acknowledged that consumers who can purchase products outright "are better off" doing so, rather than using its "hybrid" layaway and installment financing. The company confirmed that it refuses refunds but said customers may "use any funds paid to purchase other items form BlueHippo." It added that its prices are relatively high because of the "added risk of dealing with customers who have poor credit." In contrast to its training materials, the company said its typical customer earns more than $40,000 a year.

50   A few months after his BlueHippo experience, Humphries did buy a new computer. He borrowed $400 from a friend and bought a General Quality PC from Fry's Electronics, a retail chain. The loan covered the purchase of a 17-inch flat-screen monitor, a DVD burner, and a desktop computer with a 40-gigabyte hard drive. Humphries tightened his belt and paid his friend back in $100 installments over four months, interest-free.

51   Just like everyone else, the working poor find their mailboxes stuffed with "pre-approved" credit card offers. Luisa and Rose Ajuria have trouble saying no. The Ajuria sisters live in a brown-brick bungalow on Chicago's financially pressed South Side. They care for a niece named Caroline and five cats. Neither sister studied past high school or married. "Momma said I wasn't college material," says Luisa, 57. She and Rose, 54, lived most of their lives under the strict supervision of their father, Manuel, who died in 1993. A Mexican immigrant and former sheet-metal press operator, he dutifully paid all the bills. Every week, Lusia handed him her paycheck from Warshawsky & Co., an auto-parts seller where she worked as a supervisor.

52   The sisters now manage their finances themselves—by their own admission, badly. Their father had paid off the $60,000 mortgage. But twice in the past six years, Luisa refinanced the cluttered bungalow, using the money to pay bills and repair aging fixtures in two bathrooms and the kitchen of the 75-year-old house. Now there's a new $140,000 mortgage, with Wells Fargo charging 8 percent interest. The $1,130 monthly payments eat up more than half of Luisa's paycheck from her current job as a secretary at the IRS. If she also made full payments on a $9,000 home-equity line of credit from HSBC Finance Corp. (HBC) and a half-dozen credit-card accounts, they would consume the rest. In total, Luisa owes creditors $169,585. "I don't read things. I just sign them," she says.

53   The debt has forced the Ajurias to consider selling their house and moving to an apartment. But it hasn't stopped companies from offering more credit. Last year, Rose received a come-on for a Tribute MasterCard. She was surprised a company would offer her credit, since she brings in only about $7,500 a year in disability benefits and wages as a part-time worker at an adult day care center. She signed up for the card.

54   Caroline, the 32-year-old niece, who is agoraphobic and rarely leaves the house, quickly ran up $1,268 in charges on the Tribute card, shopping online for Christmas and birthday gifts. Of her newest card, Rose says: "I regret this one. Truly, I do."

55   Terms of the Tribute MasterCard are a world away from the money-back and frequent-flier offers familiar to more prosperous cardholders. Marketed by Atlanta-based CompuCredit, a giant in the subprime card business, Tribute MasterCard offers no such fringe benefits. Rose Ajuria's card carries an interest rate of 28 percent, compared with about 10 percent on a typical card. Since she's paying only a nominal $10 a month, the debt her niece incurred is growing swiftly. "I think we've painted ourselves into a corner," Rose says. Many Tribute MasterCard customers pay a lower 20 percent interest, but CompuCredit typically charges them a $150 annual fee, a separate $6 monthly fee, and a one-time payment of $20 required before using the card.

56   This is the sort of choppy water where many of CompuCredit's customers paddle—and where the company manages to find profits. CompuCredit was co-founded 11 years ago by David G. Hanna, scion of a family that made a fortune in debt collection. Its 55-member analytics team has devised models to assess more than 200 categories of customer data, from the duration of past credit-card accounts to the number of bad debts. The algorithms apparently work: last year CompuCredit reported earnings of $107 million on $1.3 billion in revenue.

57   Whether the company will make money on Rose Ajuria's account is uncertain at this point. CompuCredit says that customers offered the Tribute MasterCard at 28 percent generally have middling credit histories and that it is willing to work with those who have trouble paying their bills.

58   Executives say the company clearly discloses interest rates and imposes fees up front so consumers won't be surprised later. But in February 2007, CompuCredit disclosed that the FTC and the FDIC had launched separate civil investigations into the marketing of one of its other credit cards. The company denies any wrongdoing. As a goodwill gesture, it says it has stopped charging late fees and interest on accounts more than 90 days past due.

59   On its Web sites and in its marketing brochures, CompuCredit says it helps customers "rebuild credit" by reporting all of their loan payments to credit bureaus, unlike traditional payday lenders. Not that altruism drives the operation, says co-founder Hanna. "We're not going to chase somebody where we can't make money."

60   Even for those who climb above the lowest rungs of the economic ladder, a legacy of debt can threaten to undercut progress. Connie McBride, a 44-year-old computer programmer who lives near Tacoma, Washington, grew up in foster homes and has led an adult life notably lacking in stability. She has held decent jobs but sometimes has subsisted on food stamps. She earns $47,000 a year as a freelance programmer, working from the weather-beaten aluminum trailer she rents for $590 a month. Wind whistles through small holes in the walls, and she keeps warm in the winter by feeding a wood-fired stove on a cracked cement foundation.

61   McBride showed an early aptitude for math and received a GED at age 16. In the late 1980s, she studied computer science at Washington State University, sometimes arriving for class with her three young children. "Taking those classes, given my life, I felt this was the only way out," she says.

62   She graduated in 1992, owing $45,000 on student loans. That debt became her main financial burden, she says. The 9.5 percent interest rate isn't particularly steep, but she tended to view the payments as less pressing than putting food on the table or paying rent. Late fees piled up. Today she owes $159,991, up from $117,000 only 18 months ago. When dunning notices arrive, she tosses them in the stove.

63   Personal bankruptcy proceedings in 2003 dissolved dozens of McBride's liabilities. But by law her debt to student lender SLM Corp. (SLM), better known as Sallie Mae, wasn't affected. Every month, $450 is garnisheed from her wages, reducing her take-home pay to $1,338. The garnishment doesn't even cover interest and penalties, let alone the principal. Says McBride: "There's no way this thing will ever be paid off."

64   New obligations are piling up. She pays $385 a month on a 21 percent car loan. And now she's buying baby supplies. McBride says her adult son can't deal with his four-month-old daughter, who has medical problems. McBride can't bear the thought of her granddaughter going to a foster home. So she is postponing nonessential expenditures such as fixing a badly chipped front tooth.

65   McBride acknowledges her mistakes. "My life is full of bad decisions," she says. But if she had started out with the funds for college, she wonders whether she would at least be able to afford an apartment and a trip to the dentist. "If you have money to begin with, you don't have these issues or these kinds of bills," she says. "You don't have to worry about the rent or pay double for a car."

Source: Reprinted with special permission from Brian Grow and Keith Epstein, "The Poverty Business: Inside U.S. Companies' Audacious Drive to Extract More Profits from the Nation's Working Poor," *BusinessWeek Online*, May 11, 2007. Copyright © 2007 The McGraw-Hill Companies.

DISCUSSION QUESTIONS

1. What is the responsibility of for-profit companies to attempt to help customers like Roxanne Tsosie see the dangers of indebtedness?

2. Assuming that Byrider is acting legally, is it acting ethically?

3. Under what conditions must customers take responsibility for their decisions?

4. Do you believe that customers who are poor credit risks deserve to be charged higher interest rates? If you say yes, are you not taking advantage of customers who can least afford to pay extra for the things that they buy?

5. Do you believe that every consumer pays hidden or unanticipated charges for the things that they buy? High interest rates on unpaid balances? Annual membership fees? Service charges? Are such charges ethical? Do you want to work for companies that make such charges?

Chapter Four

The External Environment

After reading and studying this chapter, you should be able to

1. Describe the three tiers of environmental factors that affect the performance of a firm.

2. List and explain the five factors in the remote environment.

3. Give examples of the economic, social, political, technological, and ecological influences on a business.

4. Explain the five forces model of industry analysis and give examples of each force.

5. Give examples of the influences of entry barriers, supplier power, buyer power, substitute availability, and competitive rivalry on a business.

6. List and explain the five factors in the operating environment.

7. Give examples of the influences of competitors, creditors, customers, labor, and direct suppliers on a business.

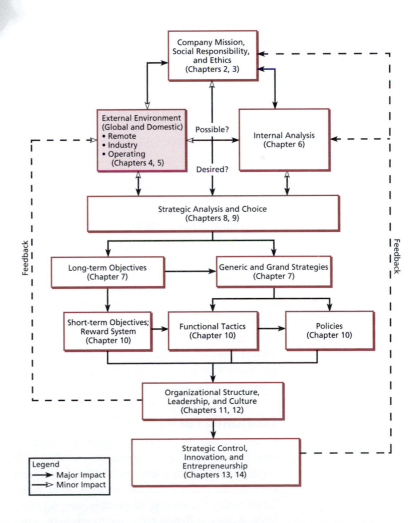

Company Mission, Social Responsibility, and Ethics (Chapters 2, 3)

External Environment (Global and Domestic)
• Remote
• Industry
• Operating
(Chapters 4, 5)

Possible?

Internal Analysis (Chapter 6)

Desired?

Strategic Analysis and Choice (Chapters 8, 9)

Long-term Objectives (Chapter 7)

Generic and Grand Strategies (Chapter 7)

Short-term Objectives; Reward System (Chapter 10)

Functional Tactics (Chapter 10)

Policies (Chapter 10)

Organizational Structure, Leadership, and Culture (Chapters 11, 12)

Strategic Control, Innovation, and Entrepreneurship (Chapters 13, 14)

Feedback

Feedback

Legend
→ Major Impact
⇢ Minor Impact

EXHIBIT 4.1
The Firm's External Environment

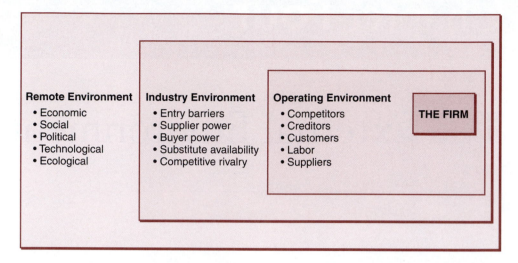

Remote Environment
- Economic
- Social
- Political
- Technological
- Ecological

Industry Environment
- Entry barriers
- Supplier power
- Buyer power
- Substitute availability
- Competitive rivalry

Operating Environment
- Competitors
- Creditors
- Customers
- Labor
- Suppliers

THE FIRM

THE FIRM'S EXTERNAL ENVIRONMENT

external environment
The factors beyond the control of the firm that influence its choice of direction and action, organizational structure, and internal processes.

A host of external factors influence a firm's choice of direction and action and, ultimately, its organizational structure and internal processes. These factors, which constitute the **external environment,** can be divided into three interrelated subcategories: factors in the remote environment, factors in the industry environment, and factors in the operating environment. This chapter describes the complex necessities involved in formulating strategies that optimize a firm's market opportunities. Exhibit 4.1 suggests the interrelationship between the firm and its remote, its industry, and its operating environments. In combination, these factors form the basis of the opportunities and threats that a firm faces in its competitive environment.

REMOTE ENVIRONMENT

remote environment
Economic, social, political, technological, and ecological factors that originate beyond, and usually irrespective of, any single firm's operating situation.

The **remote environment** comprises factors that originate beyond, and usually irrespective of, any single firm's operating situation: (1) economic, (2) social, (3) political, (4) technological, and (5) ecological factors. That environment presents firms with opportunities, threats, and constraints, but rarely does a single firm exert any meaningful reciprocal influence. For example, when the economy slows and construction starts to decrease, an individual contractor is likely to suffer a decline in business, but that contractor's efforts in stimulating local construction activities would be unable to reverse the overall decrease in construction starts. The trade agreements that resulted from improved relations between the United States and China and the United States and Russia are examples of political factors that impact individual firms. The agreements provided individual U.S. manufacturers with opportunities to broaden their international operations.

Economic Factors

Economic factors concern the nature and direction of the economy in which a firm operates. Because consumption patterns are affected by the relative affluence of various market segments, each firm must consider economic trends in the segments that affect its industry. On both the national and international level, managers must consider the general availability of credit, the level of disposable income, and the propensity of people to spend. Prime interest rates, inflation rates, and trends in the growth of the gross national product are other economic factors they should monitor.

Top Strategist
Harold Messmer, CEO of Robert Half International

**Exhibit
4.2**

Robert Half CEO Harold Messmer has been around long enough to know how to ride a wave. And he has surfed the tightening of labor markets like an old pro. The jobless rate for professionals has been low, especially in the company's sweet spot: placing accountants, marketing specialists, attorneys, and programmers. Messmer excels by targeting small and midsize companies. Smaller clients are less likely to seek discounts and don't mind paying a higher price for top-caliber personnel. In 2006, most of its units grew 20 percent or more, and the one that places permanent accountants saw revenue jump 53 percent. Messmer also has pushed deeper into the international arena, breaking ground in both Germany and Spain, where the market for temporary staffing is less developed than in the United States. And he set up his temp business for the first time in Asia by taking advantage of existing office space in Robert Half units already operating there.

Source: Reprinted with special permission from The *BusinessWeek* 50—The Best Performers, *BusinessWeek*, March 26, 2007. Copyright © 2007 The McGraw-Hill Companies.

For example, in 2003, the depressed economy hit Crown Cork & Seal Co. especially hard because it had $2 billion in debt due in the year and no way to raise the money to pay it. The down market had caused its stock price to be too low to raise cash as it normally would. Therefore, Crown Cork managers turned to issuing bonds to refinance its debt. With the slow market, investors were taking advantage of such bonds because they could safely gain higher returns over stocks. Not only were investors getting a deal, but Crown Cork and other companies were seeing the lowest interest rates on bonds in years and by issuing bonds could reorganize their balance sheets.

Closely monitoring the economic conditions that affect growth in the financial services industry has been a key to the success of Robert Half International. Its CEO adjusts the company's business strategy to maximize opportunities that arise during changing employment cycles, as described in, Exhibit 4.2, Top Strategist.

The emergence of new international power brokers has changed the focus of economic environmental forecasting. Among the most prominent of these power brokers are the European Economic Community (EEC, or Common Market), the Organization of Petroleum Exporting Countries (OPEC), and coalitions of developing countries.

The EEC, whose members include most of the West European countries, eliminated quotas and established a tariff-free trade area for industrial products among its members. By fostering intra-European economic cooperation, it has helped its member countries compete more effectively in non-European international markets.

Social Factors

The social factors that affect a firm involve the beliefs, values, attitudes, opinions, and lifestyles of persons in the firm's external environment, as developed from cultural, ecological, demographic, religious, educational, and ethnic conditioning. As social attitudes change, so

Tapping a Market That Is Hot, Hot, Hot

BusinessWeek

When National City Corp. bank decided to roll out 78 new branches in Chicago two years ago, it went in knowing its market. With Hispanics expected to account for virtually all of the city's population growth over the next decade, the bank hired dozens of Spanish-speaking staffers and printed thousands of glossy pamphlets, hawking savings accounts to new immigrants and explaining the benefits of IRAs to more established Latinos. This year, the nation's 10th-largest bank will double its Hispanic marketing budget, targeting middle-class Latinos with direct mail offering mortgage financing and money-market accounts, all written *en español*.

The growing economic clout of the Hispanic community is well known. So what's driving the banking push? For starters, it's the fact that relatively few Latinos have any kind of banking accounts. Fully 56 percent of the nation's 40 million Hispanics have never held a bank account, according to market researcher Simmons Inc.

That's a rich vein for banks to tap. With Hispanics' wealth and population rising three times faster than the U.S. average, the FDIC [Federal Deposit Insurance Corporation] predicts that they will account for more than 50 percent of U.S. retail banking growth over the next decade. That amounts to more than $200 billion in new business, since U.S. retail banking revenues are projected to increase 44 percent, to $963 billion over the decade, according to Economy.com.

At Bank of America, Spanish-language advertising brought in 1 million new checking accounts from Hispanics last year—fully 25 percent of the new accounts opened. And Banco Popular, a fast-growing bank based in Puerto Rico, now sends trucks that are outfitted with teller booths to U.S. construction sites so Latino laborers can deposit their checks directly into banking accounts. Wherever Latinos live and work, banks are not far behind.

Source: Reprinted with special permission from Brian Grow, "Tapping a Market That Is Hot, Hot, Hot," *BusinessWeek,* January 17, 2005. Copyright © 2005 The McGraw-Hill Companies.

too does the demand for various types of clothing, books, leisure activities, and so on. Like other forces in the remote external environment, social forces are dynamic, with constant change resulting from the efforts of individuals to satisfy their desires and needs by controlling and adapting to environmental factors. Teresa Iglesias-Soloman hopes to benefit from social changes with *Niños,* a children's catalog written in both English and Spanish. The catalog features books, videos, and Spanish cultural offerings for English-speaking children who want to learn Spanish and for Spanish-speaking children who want to learn English. *Niños'* target market includes middle- to upper-income Hispanic parents, consumers, educators, bilingual schools, libraries, and purchasing agents. Iglesias-Solomon has reason to be optimistic about the future of *Niños,* because the Hispanic population is growing five times faster than the general U.S. population and ranks as the nation's largest minority.

The increasing awareness of the market power of Hispanics in the U.S. has reached almost every business sector. Exhibit 4.3, Strategy in Action, provides a few of the details that drive many businesses' interest in attracting Hispanics as customers.

One of the most profound social changes in recent years has been the entry of large numbers of women into the labor market. This has not only affected the hiring and compensation policies and the resource capabilities of their employers; it has also created or greatly expanded the demand for a wide range of products and services necessitated by their absence from the home. Firms that anticipated or reacted quickly to this social change offered such products and services as convenience foods, microwave ovens, and day care centers.

A second profound social change has been the accelerating interest of consumers and employees in quality-of-life issues. Evidence of this change is seen in recent contract negotiations. In addition to the traditional demand for increased salaries, workers demand such benefits as sabbaticals, flexible hours or four-day workweeks, lump-sum vacation plans, and opportunities for advanced training.

A third profound social change has been the shift in the age distribution of the population. Changing social values and a growing acceptance of improved birth control methods are expected to raise the mean age of the U.S. population, which was 27.9 in 1970, and 34.9 in the year 2000. This trend will have an increasingly unfavorable effect on most producers of predominantly youth-oriented goods and will necessitate a shift in their long-range marketing strategies. Producers of hair and skin care preparations already have begun to adjust their research and development to reflect anticipated changes in demand.

A consequence of the changing age distribution of the population has been a sharp increase in the demands made by a growing number of senior citizens. Constrained by fixed incomes, these citizens have demanded that arbitrary and rigid policies on retirement age be modified and have successfully lobbied for tax exemptions and increases in Social Security benefits. Such changes have significantly altered the opportunity-risk equations of many firms—often to the benefit of firms that anticipated the changes.

Cutting across these issues is concern for individual health. The fast-food industry has been the target of a great deal of public concern. A great deal of popular press attention has been directed toward Americans' concern over the relationship between obesity and health. As documented by the hit movie *Supersize Me,* McDonald's was caught in the middle of this new social concern because its menu consisted principally of high-calorie, artery-clogging foods. Health experts blamed the fast-food industry for the rise in obesity, claiming that companies like McDonald's created an environment that encouraged overeating and discouraged physical activity. Specifically, McDonald's was charged with taking advantage of the fact that kids and adults were watching more TV, by targeting certain program slots to increase sales.

McDonald's responded aggressively and successfully. The company's strategists soon established McDonald's Corp. as an innovator in healthy food options. By 2005, the world's largest fast-food chain launched a new promotional campaign touting healthy lifestyles, including fruit and milk in Happy Meals, activity programs in schools, and a new partnership with the International Olympic Committee. At the time of the announcement, McDonald's was enjoying its longest ever period of same-store sales growth in 25 years, with 24 consecutive months of improved global sales resulting from new healthy menu options, later hours, and better customer service, such as cashless payment options. McDonald's healthy options included a fruit and walnut salad, Paul Newman's brand lowfat Italian dressing, and premium chicken sandwiches in the United States and chicken flatbread and fruit smoothies in Europe.

Translating social change into forecasts of business effects is a difficult process, at best. Nevertheless, informed estimates of the impact of such alterations as geographic shifts in populations and changing work values, ethical standards, and religious orientation can only help a strategizing firm in its attempts to prosper.

Political Factors

The direction and stability of political factors are a major consideration for managers on formulating company strategy. Political factors define the legal and regulatory parameters within which firms must operate. Political constraints are placed on firms through fair-trade decisions, antitrust laws, tax programs, minimum wage legislation, pollution and pricing policies, administrative jawboning, and many other actions aimed at protecting employees, consumers, the general public, and the environment. Because such laws and regulations are most commonly restrictive, they tend to reduce the potential profits of firms. However, some political actions are designed to benefit and protect firms. Such actions include patent laws, government subsidies, and product research grants. Thus, political factors either may limit or benefit the firms they influence. For example, in a pair of surprising decisions in 2003, the Federal Communications Commission (FCC) ruled that local phone companies had to continue to lease their lines to the long-distance carriers at what the locals said was below cost. At the same time, the FCC ruled that the local companies were not required to lease their broadband lines to the national carriers. These decisions were good and bad for the local companies because, although they would lose money by leasing to the long-distance carriers, they could regain some of that loss with their broadband services that did not have to be leased.

The decisions did not mean that the local carriers had to remove existing lines and replace them with broadband lines. Instead, the local carriers would have to run two networks to areas where they want to incorporate broadband because the long-distance carriers had a right to the conventional lines as ruled in the decision. These regulations caused the local carriers to alter their strategies. For example, they often chose to reduce capital investments on new broadband lines because they had to maintain old lines as well. The reduction in capital investments was used to offset the losses they incurred in subsidizing their current lines to the long-distance carriers.

The direction and stability of political factors are a major consideration when evaluating the remote environment. Consider piracy. Microsoft's performance in the Chinese market is greatly affected by the lack of legal enforcement of piracy and also by the policies of the Chinese government. Likewise, the government's actions in support of its competitor, Linux, have limited Microsoft's ability to penetrate the Chinese market.

Political activity also has a significant impact on two governmental functions that influence the remote environment of firms: the supplier function and the customer function.

Supplier Function

Government decisions regarding the accessibility of private businesses to government-owned natural resources and national stockpiles of agricultural products will affect profoundly the viability of the strategies of some firms.

Customer Function

Government demand for products and services can create, sustain, enhance, or eliminate many market opportunities. For example, the Kennedy administration's emphasis on landing a man on the moon spawned a demand for thousands of new products; the Carter administration's emphasis on developing synthetic fuels created a demand for new skills, technologies, and products; the Reagan administration's strategic defense initiative (the "Star Wars" defense) sharply accelerated the development of laser technologies; Clinton's federal block grants to the states for welfare reform led to office rental and lease opportunities; and the war against terrorism during the Bush administration created enormous investment in aviation.

Technological Factors

The fourth set of factors in the remote environment involves technological change. To avoid obsolescence and promote innovation, a firm must be aware of technological changes that might influence its industry. Creative technological adaptations can suggest possibilities for new products or for improvements in existing products or in manufacturing and marketing techniques.

technological forecasting
The quasi-science of anticipating environmental and competitive changes and estimating their importance to an organization's operations.

A technological breakthrough can have a sudden and dramatic effect on a firm's environment. It may spawn sophisticated new markets and products or significantly shorten the anticipated life of a manufacturing facility. Thus, all firms, and most particularly those in turbulent growth industries, must strive for an understanding both of the existing technological advances and the probable future advances that can affect their products and services. This quasi-science of attempting to foresee advancements and estimate their impact on an organization's operations is known as **technological forecasting.**

Technological forecasting can help protect and improve the profitability of firms in growing industries. It alerts strategic managers to both impending challenges and promising opportunities. As examples: (1) Advances in xerography were a key to Xerox's success but caused major difficulties for carbon paper manufacturers, and (2) the perfection of transistors changed the nature of competition in the radio and television industry, helping such giants as RCA while seriously weakening smaller firms whose resource commitments required that they continue to base their products on vacuum tubes.

The key to beneficial forecasting of technological advancement lies in accurately predicting future technological capabilities and their probable impacts. A comprehensive analysis of the effect of technological change involves study of the expected effect of new technologies on the remote environment, on the competitive business situation, and on the business-society interface. In recent years, forecasting in the last area has warranted particular attention. For example, as a consequence of increased concern over the environment, firms must carefully investigate the probable effect of technological advances on quality-of-life factors, such as ecology and public safety.

For example, by combining the powers of Internet technologies with the capability of downloading music in a digital format, Bertelsmann has found a creative technological adaptation for distributing music online to millions of consumers whenever or wherever they might be. Bertelsmann, AOL Time Warner, and EMI formed a joint venture called Musicnet. The ease and wide availability of Internet technologies is increasing the marketplace for online e-tailers. Bertelsmann's response to the shifts in technological factors enables it to distribute music more rapidly through Musicnet to a growing consumer base.

Ecological Factors

ecology
The relationships among human beings and other living things and the air, soil, and water that supports them.

pollution
Threats to life-supporting ecology caused principally by human activities in an industrial society.

The most prominent factor in the remote environment is often the reciprocal relationship between business and the ecology. The term **ecology** refers to the relationships among human beings and other living things and the air, soil, and water that support them. Threats to our life-supporting ecology caused principally by human activities in an industrial society are commonly referred to as **pollution.** Specific concerns include global warming, loss of habitat and biodiversity, as well as air, water, and land pollution.

The global climate has been changing for ages; however, it is now evident that humanity's activities are accelerating this tremendously. A change in atmospheric radiation, due in part to ozone depletion, causes global warming. Solar radiation that is normally absorbed into the atmosphere reaches the earth's surface, heating the soil, water, and air.

Another area of great importance is the loss of habitat and biodiversity. Ecologists agree that the extinction of important flora and fauna is occurring at a rapid rate and, if this pace is continued, could constitute a global extinction on the scale of those found in fossil records. The earth's life-forms depend on a well-functioning ecosystem. In addition, immeasurable advances in disease treatment can be attributed to research involving substances found in plants. As species become extinct, the life support system is irreparably harmed. The primary cause of extinction on this scale is a disturbance of natural habitat. For example, current data suggest that the earth's primary tropical forests, a prime source of oxygen and potential plant "cure," could be destroyed in only five decades.

Air pollution is created by dust particles and gaseous discharges that contaminate the air. Acid rain, or rain contaminated by sulfur dioxide, which can destroy aquatic and plant life, is believed to result from coal-burning factories in 70 percent of all cases. A health-threatening "thermal blanket" is created when the atmosphere traps carbon dioxide emitted from smokestacks in factories burning fossil fuels. This "greenhouse effect" can have disastrous consequences, making the climate unpredictable and raising temperatures.

Water pollution occurs principally when industrial toxic wastes are dumped or leak into the nation's waterways. Because fewer than 50 percent of all municipal sewer systems are in compliance with Environmental Protection Agency requirements for water safety, contaminated waters represent a substantial present threat to public welfare. Efforts to keep from contaminating the water supply are a major challenge to even the most conscientious of manufacturing firms.

Land pollution is caused by the need to dispose of ever-increasing amounts of waste. Routine, everyday packaging is a major contributor to this problem. Land pollution is more dauntingly caused by the disposal of industrial toxic wastes in underground sites. With approximately 90 percent of the annual U.S. output of 500 million metric tons of hazardous industrial wastes being placed in underground dumps, it is evident that land pollution and its resulting endangerment of the ecology have become a major item on the political agenda.

As a major contributor to ecological pollution, business now is being held responsible for eliminating the toxic by-products of its current manufacturing processes and for cleaning up the environmental damage that it did previously. Increasingly, managers are being required by the government or are being expected by the public to incorporate ecological concerns into their decision making. For example, between 1975 and 1992, 3M cut its pollution in half by reformulating products, modifying processes, redesigning production equipment, and recycling by-products. Similarly, steel companies and public utilities have invested billions of dollars in costlier but cleaner-burning fuels and pollution control equipment. The automobile industry has been required to install expensive emission controls in cars. The gasoline industry has been forced to formulate new low-lead and no-lead products. And thousands of companies have found it necessary to direct their R&D resources into the search for ecologically superior products, such as Sears's phosphate-free laundry detergent and Pepsi-Cola's biodegradable plastic soft-drink bottle.

Environmental legislation impacts corporate strategies worldwide. Many companies fear the consequences of highly restrictive and costly environmental regulations. However, some manufacturers view these new controls as an opportunity, capturing markets with products that help customers satisfy their own regulatory standards. Other manufacturers contend that the costs of environmental spending inhibit the growth and productivity of their operations.

Despite cleanup efforts to date, the job of protecting the ecology will continue to be a top strategic priority—usually because corporate stockholders and executives choose it, increasingly because the public and the government require it. As evidenced by Exhibit 4.4, the government has made numerous interventions into the conduct of business for the purpose of bettering the ecology.

Benefits of Eco-Efficiency

Many of the world's largest corporations are realizing that business activities must no longer ignore environmental concerns. Every activity is linked to thousands of other transactions and their environmental impact; therefore, corporate environmental responsibility must be taken seriously and environmental policy must be implemented to ensure a comprehensive organizational strategy. Because of increases in government regulations and consumer environmental concerns, the implementation of environmental policy has become a point of competitive advantage. Therefore, the rational goal of business should be to limit its impact on the environment, thus ensuring long-run benefits to both the firm and society. To neglect this responsibility is to ensure the demise of both the firm and our ecosystem.

Responding to this need, General Electric unveiled plans in 2005 to double its research funds for technologies that reduce energy use, pollution, and emissions tied to global warming. GE said it would focus even more on solar and wind power as well as other environmental technologies it is involved with, such as diesel-electric locomotives, lower emission aircraft engines, more efficient lighting, and water purification. The company's "ecomagination" plans for 2010 include investing $1.5 billion annually in cleaner technologies research, up from $700 million in 2004; and doubling revenues to $20 billion from environmentally friendly products and services.

EXHIBIT 4.4
Federal Ecological Legislation

National Environmental Policy Act, 1969 Established Environmental Protection Agency; consolidated federal environmental activities under it. Established Council on Environmental Quality to advise president on environmental policy and to review environmental impact statements.

Air Pollution:

Clean Air Act, 1963 Authorized assistance to state and local governments in formulating control programs. Authorized limited federal action in correcting specific pollution problems.
Clean Air Act, Amendments (Motor Vehicle Air Pollution Control Act), 1965 Authorized federal standards for auto exhaust emission. Standards first set for 1968 models.
Air Quality Act, 1967 Authorized federal government to establish air quality control regions and to set maximum permissible pollution levels. Required states and localities to carry out approved control programs or else give way to federal controls.
Clean Air Act Amendments, 1970 Authorized EPA to establish nationwide air pollution standards and to limit the discharge of six principal pollutants into the lower atmosphere. Authorized citizens to take legal action to require EPA to implement its standards against undiscovered offenders.
Clean Air Act Amendments, 1977 Postponed auto emission requirements. Required use of scrubbers in new coal-fired power plants. Directed EPA to establish a system to prevent deterioration of air quality in clean areas.

Solid Waste Pollution:

Solid Waste Disposal Act, 1965 Authorized research and assistance to state and local control programs.
Resource Recovery Act, 1970 Subsidized construction of pilot recycling plants; authorized development of nationwide control programs.
Resource Conservation and Recovery Act, 1976 Directed EPA to regulate hazardous waste management, from generation through disposal.
Surface Mining and Reclamation Act, 1976 Controlled strip mining and restoration of reclaimed land.

Water Pollution:

Refuse Act, 1899 Prohibited dumping of debris into navigable waters without a permit. Extended by court decision to industrial discharges.
Federal Water Pollution Control Act, 1956 Authorized grants to states for water pollution control. Gave federal government limited authority to correct specific pollution problems.
Water Quality Act, 1965 Provided for adoption of water quality standards by states, subject to federal approval.
Water Quality Improvement Act, 1970 Provided for federal cleanup of oil spills. Strengthened federal authority over water pollution control.
Federal Water Pollution Control Act Amendments, 1972 Authorized EPA to set water quality and effluent standards; provided for enforcement and research.
Safe Drinking Water Act, 1974 Set standards for drinking water quality.
Clean Water Act, 1977 Ordered control of toxic pollutants by 1984 with best available technology economically feasible.

eco-efficiency
Company actions that produce more useful goods and services while continuously reducing resource consumption and pollution.

    Stephen Schmidheiny, chairman of the Business Council for Sustainable Development, has coined the term **eco-efficiency** to describe corporations that produce more-useful goods and services while continuously reducing resource consumption and pollution. He cites a number of reasons for corporations to implement environmental policy: customers demand cleaner products, environmental regulations are increasingly more stringent, employees prefer to work for environmentally conscious firms, and financing is more readily available for eco-efficient firms. In addition, the government provides incentives for environmentally responsible companies.

Setting priorities, developing corporate standards, controlling property acquisition and use to preserve habitats, implementing energy-conserving activities, and redesigning products (e.g., minimizing packaging) are a number of measures the firm can implement to enhance an eco-efficient strategy. One of the most important steps a firm can take in achieving a competitive position with regard to the eco-efficient strategy is to fully capitalize on technological developments as a method of gaining efficiency.

There are four key characteristics of eco-efficient corporations:

- Eco-efficient firms are proactive, not reactive. Policy is initiated and promoted by business because it is in their own interests and the interest of their customers, not because it is imposed by one or more external forces.
- Eco-efficiency is designed in, not added on. This characteristic implies that the optimization of eco-efficiency requires every business effort regarding the product and process to internalize the strategy.
- Flexibility is imperative for eco-efficient strategy implementation. Continuous attention must be paid to technological innovation and market evolution.
- Eco-efficiency is encompassing, not insular. In the modern global business environment, efforts must cross not only industrial sectors but national and cultural boundaries as well.

International Environment

Monitoring the international environment, perhaps better thought of as the international dimension of the global environment, involves assessing each nondomestic market on the same factors that are used in a domestic assessment. While the importance of factors will differ, the same set of considerations can be used for each country. For example, Exhibit 4.5, Global Strategy in Action, lists economic, political, legal, and social factors used to assess international environments. However, there is one complication to this process, namely, that the interplay among international markets must be considered. For example, in recent years, conflicts in the Middle East have made collaborative business strategies among firms in traditionally antagonistic countries especially difficult to implement.

INDUSTRY ENVIRONMENT

industry environment
The general conditions for competition that influence all businesses that provide similar products and services.

Harvard professor Michael E. Porter propelled the concept of **industry environment** into the foreground of strategic thought and business planning. The cornerstone of his work first appeared in the *Harvard Business Review,* in which Porter explains the five forces that shape competition in an industry. His well-defined analytic framework helps strategic managers to link remote factors to their effects on a firm's operating environment.

With the special permission of Professor Porter and the *Harvard Business Review,* we present in this section of the chapter the major portion of his seminal article on the industry environment and its impact on strategic management.[1]

HOW COMPETITIVE FORCES SHAPE STRATEGY

The essence of strategy formulation is coping with competition. Yet it is easy to view competition too narrowly and too pessimistically. While we sometimes hear executives complaining to the contrary, intense competition in an industry is neither coincidence nor bad luck.

[1] M. E. Porter, "How Competitive Forces Shape Strategy," *Harvard Business Review,* March–April 1979, pp. 137–45. Copyright © 1979 by the Harvard Business School Publishing Corporation; all rights reserved.

Used to Assess the International Environment

ECONOMIC ENVIRONMENT

Level of economic development

Population

Gross national product

Per capita income

Literacy level

Social infrastructure

Natural resources

Climate

Membership in regional economic blocs (EU, NAFTA, LAFTA)

Monetary and fiscal policies

Wage and salary levels

Nature of competition

Currency convertibility

Inflation

Taxation system

Interest rates

LEGAL ENVIRONMENT

Legal tradition

Effectiveness of legal system

Treaties with foreign nations

Patent trademark laws

Laws affecting business firms

POLITICAL SYSTEM

Form of government

Political ideology

Stability of government

Strength of opposition parties and groups

Social unrest

Political strife and insurgency

Governmental attitude towards foreign firms

Foreign policy

CULTURAL ENVIRONMENT

Customs, norms, values, beliefs

Language

Attitudes

Motivations

Social institutions

Status symbols

Religious beliefs

Source: Arvind V. Phatak, *International Management* (Cincinnati, OH: South-Western College Publishing, 1997), p. 6. Reprinted with permission of the author.

Moreover, in the fight for market share, competition is not manifested only in the other players. Rather, competition in an industry is rooted in its underlying economics, and competitive forces exist that go well beyond the established combatants in a particular industry. Customers, suppliers, potential entrants, and substitute products are all competitors that may be more or less prominent or active depending on the industry.

The state of competition in an industry depends on five basic forces, which are diagrammed in Exhibit 4.6. The collective strength of these forces determines the ultimate profit potential of an industry. It ranges from intense in industries like tires, metal cans, and steel, where no company earns spectacular returns on investment, to mild in industries like oil-field services and equipment, soft drinks, and toiletries, where there is room for quite high returns.

In the economists' "perfectly competitive" industry, jockeying for position is unbridled and entry to the industry very easy. This kind of industry structure, of course, offers the worst prospect for long-run profitability. The weaker the forces collectively, however, the greater the opportunity for superior performance.

Whatever their collective strength, the corporate strategist's goal is to find a position in the industry where his or her company can best defend itself against these forces or can influence them in its favor. The collective strength of the forces may be painfully apparent to all the antagonists; but to cope with them, the strategist must delve below the surface and analyze the sources of competition. For example, what makes the industry vulnerable to entry? What determines the bargaining power of suppliers?

EXHIBIT 4.6   **Forces Driving Industry Competition**

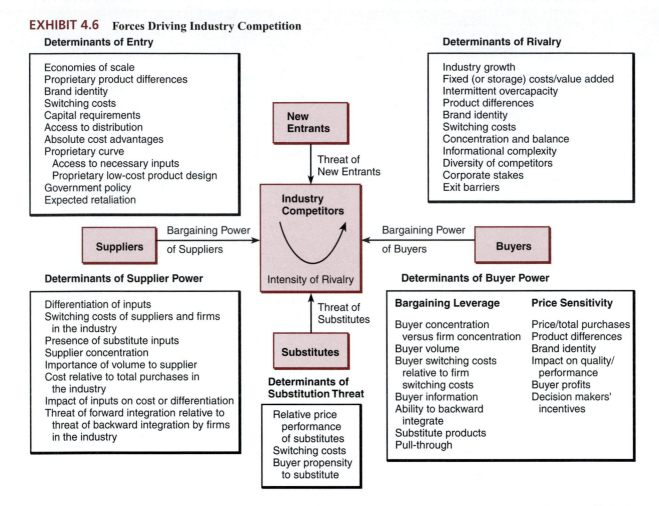

Determinants of Entry

Economies of scale
Proprietary product differences
Brand identity
Switching costs
Capital requirements
Access to distribution
Absolute cost advantages
Proprietary curve
  Access to necessary inputs
  Proprietary low-cost product design
Government policy
Expected retaliation

Determinants of Rivalry

Industry growth
Fixed (or storage) costs/value added
Intermittent overcapacity
Product differences
Brand identity
Switching costs
Concentration and balance
Informational complexity
Diversity of competitors
Corporate stakes
Exit barriers

New Entrants

Threat of New Entrants

Industry Competitors

Bargaining Power of Suppliers

Suppliers

Bargaining Power of Buyers

Buyers

Intensity of Rivalry

Threat of Substitutes

Substitutes

Determinants of Supplier Power

Differentiation of inputs
Switching costs of suppliers and firms
  in the industry
Presence of substitute inputs
Supplier concentration
Importance of volume to supplier
Cost relative to total purchases in
  the industry
Impact of inputs on cost or differentiation
Threat of forward integration relative to
  threat of backward integration by firms
  in the industry

Determinants of Substitution Threat

Relative price
  performance
  of substitutes
Switching costs
Buyer propensity
  to substitute

Determinants of Buyer Power

Bargaining Leverage	Price Sensitivity
Buyer concentration versus firm concentration	Price/total purchases
Buyer volume	Product differences
Buyer switching costs relative to firm switching costs	Brand identity
Buyer information	Impact on quality/ performance
Ability to backward integrate	Buyer profits
Substitute products	Decision makers' incentives
Pull-through	

Source: Reprinted by permission of *Harvard Business Review*, Exhibit from "How Competitive Forces Shape Strategy," by M.E. Porter, March—April 1979. Copyright © 1979 by the Harvard Business School Publishing Corporation; all rights reserved.

Knowledge of these underlying sources of competitive pressure provides the groundwork for a strategic agenda of action. They highlight the critical strengths and weaknesses of the company, animate the positioning of the company in its industry, clarify the areas where strategic changes may yield the greatest payoff, and highlight the places where industry trends promise to hold the greatest significance as either opportunities or threats.

Understanding these sources also proves to be of help in considering areas for diversification.

CONTENDING FORCES

The strongest competitive force or forces determine the profitability of an industry and so are of greatest importance in strategy formulation. For example, even a company with a strong position in an industry unthreatened by potential entrants will earn low returns if it faces a superior or a lower-cost substitute product—as the leading manufacturers of vacuum tubes and coffee percolators have learned to their sorrow. In such a situation, coping with the substitute product becomes the number one strategic priority.

Different forces take on prominence, of course, in shaping competition in each industry. In the ocean-going tanker industry, the key force is probably the buyers (the major oil companies),

Kodak's Moment of Truth

BusinessWeek

Antonio M. Perez left the consumer inkjet printer business after he lost out to Carly Fiorina for the top slot at Hewlett-Packard. But it has never been far from his mind. That's why, a few weeks after he joined a struggling Eastman Kodak Co. as president, he was peering into a microscope in a lab on Kodak's sprawling Rochester (New York) campus. Ever since then, Perez and Kodak have been working on a top-secret plan, code-named Goya, to make a big entrance into the consumer inkjet printer business.

The Kodak printers are designed, first and foremost, to print high-quality photos: the ink is formulated so prints will stay vibrant for 100 years rather than 15. Most impressive of all, replacement ink cartridges will cost half of what consumers are used to paying. The new printers arrived in stores in March 2007, priced at $149 to $299. Black ink cartridges cost $9.99, color $14.99. If consumers buy Kodak's economical Photo Value Pack, which combines paper and ink, the cost per print is about 10 cents, versus 24 cents for HP's comparable package.

If Kodak pulls this off—and that's a big if, considering the forces it's up against—it could pose a huge challenge to the $50 billion printer industry. Those companies now rely on a razor-and-blades strategy, often discounting machines and making most of their profits on replacement cartridges. In particular, Kodak's strategy is an assault on the profit engine of industry leader HP. Printing supplied 60 percent of HP's $6.56 billion in operating earnings in 2006.

Perez predicts the inkjet printers will become a multibillion-dollar product line. He'd better be right. Kodak has struggled for years to find a replacement for its rapidly declining photo-film business. If he doesn't show growth soon, investors could bail out.

Analysts who have seen Kodak's printers have come away impressed. "The print quality is really good. They're at least as good as everybody else," says Larry Jamieson, director of industry-watcher Lyra Research Inc.

But Perez and Kodak are challenging a giant competitor that has a 33 percent worldwide market share and a sterling reputation among PC and digital-camera users. HP not only gets prime merchandising spots for its printers and ink in stores, but also gets to display its printers in the computer sections, because it bundles printers with its PCs. "HP has a lot of customer loyalty. They build a great product. The printers don't break," says analyst Alyson Frasco of market researcher Interactive Data Corp.

while in tires it is powerful OEM buyers coupled with tough competitors. In the steel industry the key forces are foreign competitors and substitute materials.

Every industry has an underlying structure, or a set of fundamental economic and technical characteristics, that gives rise to these competitive forces. The strategist, wanting to position his or her company to cope best with its industry environment or to influence that environment in the company's favor, must learn what makes the environment tick.

This view of competition pertains equally to industries dealing in services and to those selling products. To avoid monotony, I refer to both products and services as *products*. The same general principles apply to all types of business.

A few characteristics are critical to the strength of each competitive force. They will be discussed in this section.

Threat of Entry

New entrants to an industry bring new capacity, the desire to gain market share, and often substantial resources. Kodak's entry into the consumer inkjet printer business, described in Exhibit 4.7, Strategy in Action, presented a classic threat to the competitive dynamics in the industry. Similarly, companies diversifying through acquisition into the industry from other markets often leverage their resources to cause a shake-up, as Philip Morris did with Miller beer.

The seriousness of the threat of entry depends on the barriers present and on the reaction from existing competitors that the entrant can expect. If barriers to entry are high and a newcomer can expect sharp retaliation from the entrenched competitors, he or she obviously will not pose a serious threat of entering.

There are six major sources of barriers to entry:

Economies of Scale

These economies deter entry by forcing the aspirant either to come in on a large scale or to accept a cost disadvantage. Scale economies in production, research, marketing, and service are probably the key barriers to entry in the mainframe computer industry, as Xerox and GE sadly discovered. **Economies of scale** also can act as hurdles in distribution, utilization of the sales force, financing, and nearly any other part of a business.

Economies of scale refer to the savings that companies within an industry achieve due to increased volume. Simply put, when the volume of production increases, the long-range average cost of a unit produced will decline.

Economies of scale result from technological and nontechnological sources. The technological sources of these economies are higher levels of mechanization or automation and a greater modernization of plant and facilities The nontechnological sources include better managerial coordination of production functions and processes, long-term contractual agreements with suppliers, and enhanced employee performance arising from specialization.

Economies of scale are an important determinant of the intensity of competition in an industry. Firms that enjoy such economies can charge lower prices than their competitors. They also can create barriers to entry by reducing their prices temporarily, or permanently, to deter new firms from entering the industry.

Product Differentiation

Product differentiation, or brand identification, creates a barrier by forcing entrants to spend heavily to overcome customer loyalty. Advertising, customer service, being first in the industry, and product differences are among the factors fostering brand identification. It is perhaps the most important entry barrier in soft drinks, over-the-counter drugs, cosmetics, investment banking, and public accounting. To create high fences around their business, brewers couple brand identification with economies of scale in production, distribution, and marketing.

Capital Requirements

The need to invest large financial resources to compete creates a barrier to entry, particularly if the capital is required for unrecoverable expenditures in upfront advertising or R&D. Capital is necessary not only for fixed facilities but also for customer credit, inventories, and absorbing start-up losses. While major corporations have the financial resources to invade almost any industry, the huge capital requirements in certain fields, such as computer manufacturing and mineral extraction, limit the pool of likely entrants.

Cost Disadvantages Independent of Size

Entrenched companies may have cost advantages not available to potential rivals, no matter what their size and attainable economies of scale. These advantages can stem from the effects of the learning curve (and of its first cousin, the experience curve), proprietary technology, access to the best raw materials sources, assets purchased at preinflation prices, government subsidies, or favorable locations. Sometimes cost advantages are enforceable

---

economies of scale
The savings that companies achieve because of increased volume.

product differentiation
The extent to which customers perceive differences among products and services.

The Experience Curve as an Entry Barrier

In recent years, the experience curve has become widely discussed as a key element of industry structure. According to this concept, unit costs in many manufacturing industries (some dogmatic adherents say in all manufacturing industries) as well as in some service industries decline with "experience," or a particular company's cumulative volume of production. (The experience curve, which encompasses many factors, is a broader concept than the better-known learning curve, which refers to the efficiency achieved over time by workers through much repetition.)

The causes of the decline in unit costs are a combination of elements, including economies of scale, the learning curve for labor, and capital-labor substitution. The cost decline creates a barrier to entry because new competitors with no "experience" face higher costs than established ones, particularly the producer with the largest market share, and have difficulty catching up with the entrenched competitors.

Adherents of the experience curve concept stress the importance of achieving market leadership to maximize this barrier to entry, and they recommend aggressive action to achieve it, such as price cutting in anticipation of falling costs in order to build volume. For the combatant that cannot achieve a healthy market share, the prescription is usually, "Get out."

Is the experience curve an entry barrier on which strategies should be built? The answer is, not in every industry. In fact, in some industries, building a strategy on the experience curve can be potentially disastrous.

That costs decline with experience in some industries is not news to corporate executives. The significance of the experience curve for strategy depends on what factors are causing the decline.

A new entrant may well be more efficient than the more experienced competitors: if it has built the newest plant, it will face no disadvantage in having to catch up. The strategic prescription, "You must have the largest, most efficient plant," is a lot different from "You must produce the greatest cumulative output of the item to get your costs down."

Whether a drop in costs with cumulative (not absolute) volume erects an entry barrier also depends on the sources of the decline. If costs go down because of technical advances known generally in the industry or because of the development of improved equipment that can be copied or purchased from equipment suppliers, the experience curve is not an entry barrier at all—in fact, new or less-experienced competitors may actually enjoy a cost advantage over the leaders. Free of the legacy of heavy past investments, the newcomer or less-experienced competitor can purchase or copy the newest and lowest cost equipment and technology.

If, however, experience can be kept proprietary, the leaders will maintain a cost advantage. But new entrants may require less experience to reduce their costs than the leaders needed. All this suggests that the experience curve can be a shaky entry barrier on which to build a strategy.

legally, as they are through patents. (For analysis of the much-discussed experience curve as a barrier to entry, see Exhibit 4.8, Strategy in Action.)

Access to Distribution Channels

The new boy or girl on the block must, of course, secure distribution of his or her product or service. A new food product, for example, must displace others from the supermarket shelf via price breaks, promotions, intense selling efforts, or some other means. The more limited the wholesale or retail channels are and the more that existing competitors have these tied up, obviously the tougher that entry into the industry will be. Sometimes this barrier is so high that, to surmount it, a new contestant must create its own distribution channels, as Timex did in the watch industry.

Government Policy

The government can limit or even foreclose entry to industries, with such controls as license requirements, limits on access to raw materials, and tax incentives. Regulated industries like trucking, liquor retailing, and freight forwarding are noticeable examples; more subtle government restrictions operate in fields like ski-area development and coal mining. The government also can play a major indirect role by affecting entry barriers through such controls as air and water pollution standards and safety regulations.

The potential rival's expectations about the reaction of existing competitors also will influence its decision on whether to enter. The company is likely to have second thoughts if incumbents have previously lashed out at new entrants, or if

> The incumbents possess substantial resources to fight back, including excess cash and unused borrowing power, productive capacity, or clout with distribution channels and customers.

> The incumbents seem likely to cut prices because of a desire to keep market shares or because of industrywide excess capacity.

> Industry growth is slow, affecting its ability to absorb the new arrival and probably causing the financial performance of all the parties involved to decline.

Powerful Suppliers

Suppliers can exert bargaining power on participants in an industry by raising prices or reducing the quality of purchased goods and services. Powerful suppliers, thereby, can squeeze profitability out of an industry unable to recover cost increases in its own prices. By raising their prices, soft-drink concentrate producers have contributed to the erosion of profitability of bottling companies because the bottlers—facing intense competition from powdered mixes, fruit drinks, and other beverages—have limited freedom to raise their prices accordingly.

The power of each important supplier (or buyer) group depends on a number of characteristics of its market situation and on the relative importance of its sales or purchases to the industry compared with its overall business.

A *supplier* group is powerful if

1. It is dominated by a few companies and is more concentrated than the industry it sells.

2. Its product is unique or at least differentiated, or if it has built-up switching costs. Switching costs are fixed costs that buyers face in changing suppliers. These arise because, among other things, a buyer's product specifications tie it to particular suppliers, it has invested heavily in specialized ancillary equipment or in learning how to operate a supplier's equipment (as in computer software), or its production lines are connected to the supplier's manufacturing facilities (as in some manufacturing of beverage containers).

3. It is not obliged to contend with other products for sale to the industry. For instance, the competition between the steel companies and the aluminum companies to sell to the can industry checks the power of each supplier.

4. It poses a credible threat of integrating forward into the industry's business. This provides a check against the industry's ability to improve the terms on which it purchases.

5. The industry is not an important customer of the supplier group. If the industry is an important customer, suppliers' fortunes will be tied closely to the industry, and they will want to protect the industry through reasonable pricing and assistance in activities like R&D and lobbying.

Powerful Buyers

Customers likewise can force down prices, demand higher quality or more service, and play competitors off against each other—all at the expense of industry profits.

A *buyer* group is powerful if

1. It is concentrated or purchases in large volumes. Large-volume buyers are particularly potent forces if heavy fixed costs characterize the industry—as they do in metal containers,

corn refining, and bulk chemicals, for example—which raise the stakes to keep capacity filled.

2. The products it purchases from the industry are standard or undifferentiated. The buyers, sure that they always can find alternative suppliers, may play one company against another, as they do in aluminum extrusion.

3. The products it purchases from the industry form a component of its product and represent a significant fraction of its cost. The buyers are likely to shop for a favorable price and purchase selectively. Where the product sold by the industry in question is a small fraction of buyers' costs, buyers are usually much less price sensitive.

4. It earns low profits, which create great incentive to lower its purchasing costs. Highly profitable buyers, however, are generally less price sensitive (i.e., of course, if the item does not represent a large fraction of their costs).

5. The industry's product is unimportant to the quality of the buyers' products or services. Where the quality of the buyers' products is very much affected by the industry's product, buyers are generally less price sensitive. Industries in which this situation exists include oil field equipment, where a malfunction can lead to large losses, and enclosures for electronic medical and test instruments, where the quality of the enclosure can influence the user's impression about the quality of the equipment inside.

6. The industry's product does not save the buyer money. Where the industry's product or service can pay for itself many times over, the buyer is rarely price sensitive; rather, he or she is interested in quality. This is true in services like investment banking and public accounting, where errors in judgment can be costly and embarrassing, and in businesses like the mapping of oil wells, where an accurate survey can save thousands of dollars in drilling costs.

7. The buyers pose a credible threat of integrating backward to make the industry's product. The Big Three auto producers and major buyers of cars often have used the threat of self-manufacture as a bargaining lever. But sometimes an industry so engenders a threat to buyers that its members may integrate forward.

Most of these sources of buyer power can be attributed to consumers as a group as well as to industrial and commercial buyers; only a modification of the frame of reference is necessary. Consumers tend to be more price sensitive if they are purchasing products that are undifferentiated, expensive relative to their incomes, and of a sort where quality is not particularly important.

The buying power of retailers is determined by the same rules, with one important addition. Retailers can gain significant bargaining power over manufacturers when they can influence consumers' purchasing decisions, as they do in audio components, jewelry, appliances, sporting goods, and other goods.

Substitute Products

By placing a ceiling on the prices it can charge, substitute products or services limit the potential of an industry. Unless it can upgrade the quality of the product or differentiate it somehow (as via marketing), the industry will suffer in earnings and possibly in growth.

Manifestly, the more attractive the price-performance trade-off offered by substitute products, the firmer the lid placed on the industry's profit potential. Sugar producers confronted with the large-scale commercialization of high-fructose corn syrup, a sugar substitute, learned this lesson.

Substitutes not only limit profits in normal times but also reduce the bonanza an industry can reap in boom times. The producers of fiberglass insulation enjoyed unprecedented demand as a result of high energy costs and severe winter weather. But the industry's ability to raise prices was tempered by the plethora of insulation substitutes, including cellulose, rock wool, and Styrofoam. These substitutes are bound to become an even stronger force once the current round of plant additions by fiberglass insulation producers has boosted capacity enough to meet demand (and then some).

Substitute products that deserve the most attention strategically are those that *(a)* are subject to trends improving their price-performance trade-off with the industry's product or *(b)* are produced by industries earning high profits. Substitutes often come rapidly into play if some development increases competition in their industries and causes price reduction or performance improvement.

Jockeying for Position

Rivalry among existing competitors takes the familiar form of jockeying for position—using tactics like price competition, product introduction, and advertising slug fests. This type of intense rivalry is related to the presence of a number of factors:

1. Competitors are numerous or are roughly equal in size and power. In many U.S. industries in recent years, foreign contenders, of course, have become part of the competitive picture.

2. Industry growth is slow, precipitating fights for market share that involve expansion-minded members.

3. The product or service lacks differentiation or switching costs, which lock in buyers and protect one combatant from raids on its customers by another.

4. Fixed costs are high or the product is perishable, creating strong temptation to cut prices. Many basic materials businesses, like paper and aluminum, suffer from this problem when demand slackens.

5. Capacity normally is augmented in large increments. Such additions, as in the chlorine and vinyl chloride businesses, disrupt the industry's supply–demand balance and often lead to periods of overcapacity and price cutting.

6. Exit barriers are high. Exit barriers, like very specialized assets or management's loyalty to a particular business, keep companies competing even though they may be earning low or even negative returns on investment. Excess capacity remains functioning, and the profitability of the healthy competitors suffers as the sick ones hang on. If the entire industry suffers from overcapacity, it may seek government help—particularly if foreign competition is present.

7. The rivals are diverse in strategies, origins, and "personalities." They have different ideas about how to compete and continually run head-on into each other in the process.

As an industry matures, its growth rate changes, resulting in declining profits and (often) a shakeout. In the booming recreational vehicle industry of the early 1970s, nearly every producer did well; but slow growth since then has eliminated the high returns, except for the strongest members, not to mention many of the weaker companies. The same profit story has been played out in industry after industry—snowmobiles, aerosol packaging, and sports equipment are just a few examples. Exhibit 4.9, Strategy in Action, describes some of the competitive dynamics in the flat-panel television industry and details several strategic responses of the companies involved.

An acquisition can introduce a very different personality to an industry, as has been the case with Black & Decker's takeover of McCullough, the producer of chain saws. Technological innovation can boost the level of fixed costs in the production process, as it did in the shift from batch to continuous-line photo finishing.

While a company must live with many of these factors—because they are built into the industry economics—it may have some latitude for improving matters through strategic shifts. For example, it may try to raise buyers' switching costs or increase product

Flat Panels, Thin Margins

BusinessWeek

Like just about everyone else checking out the flat-panel TVs at Best Buy in Manhattan, graphic designer Roy Gantt came in coveting a Philips, Sony, or Panasonic. But after seeing the price tags, he figured a Westinghouse might be a better buy. At $800, the Westinghouse 32-inch set seems like a steal compared with $950 to $1,400 for better-known brands.

Thanks to the likes of Westinghouse, which undercut the prices of premier brands by 20 percent to 40 percent, LCDs are no longer a luxury item. Nearly one-third of the 30 million TVs sold in North America in 2006 had LCDs, and in 2007 they accounted for half of all TV sales. The average 27-inch LCD set now retails for less than $650, compared with $1,000 in early 2006, says iSuppli, while 40-inch models have plunged to about $1,600, down from $3,000 during the same period.

For many in the industry, though, the competition is brutal. Prices for LCD sets are falling so rapidly that retailers who place orders too far in advance risk getting stuck with expensive inventory. Circuit City Stores Inc. cited plummeting prices in its February 8, 2007, announcement that it will shutter nearly 70 outlets. The Asian companies that make the LCD panels that go into the TVs are getting slammed, too. Korea's LG.Philips LCD Co. attributed a $186 million loss in the fourth quarter to the 40 percent drop in display prices last year. With panel prices falling 20 percent in 2007, the world's dozen or so makers of displays are scrambling to sell at almost any price just to generate the cash to survive.

Chalk it up to the new dynamics of TV manufacturing in the age of globalization. The wide availability of standardized digital components from Asian suppliers has ushered in virtual manufacturers such as Westinghouse Digital, Vizio, and Syntax-Brillian. With annual sales of $650 million and just 120 employees, Westinghouse Digital typifies the model.

Westinghouse rival Vizio Inc. is even more spartan. The brand didn't exist three years ago, but now it's no. 6 overall in LCD sets, iSupply says, with 7 percent of the North American market. Vizio has a mere 55 full-time employees, but saw sales of $700 million last year. The private company claims its overhead costs are just 0.7 percent of sales, compared with 10 to 20 percent for big, diversified electronics conglomerates, and that it gets by on profit margins of just 2 percent.

With LCD prices falling by 3 to 5 percent a month, Vizio's biggest challenge is making sure it doesn't pay too much for orders placed months in advance. The company negotiates flexible terms with suppliers and manages to keep only two weeks of inventory on hand by constantly monitoring retailers' shelves. That's a big challenge given that Vizio says it has enough orders from retailers to sell nearly 3 million TVs this year, which would triple its revenues.

Source: Reprinted with special permission from Pete Engardio, "Flat Panels, Thin Margins: Rugged Competition from Smaller Brands Has Made the TV Sets Cheaper Than Ever," *BusinessWeek*, February 26, 2007. Copyright © 2007 The McGraw-Hill Companies.

differentiation. A focus on selling efforts in the fastest growing segments of the industry or on market areas with the lowest fixed costs can reduce the impact of industry rivalry. If it is feasible, a company can try to avoid confrontation with competitors having high exit barriers and, thus, can sidestep involvement in bitter price cutting.

INDUSTRY ANALYSIS AND COMPETITIVE ANALYSIS

Designing viable strategies for a firm requires a thorough understanding of the firm's industry and competition. The firm's executives need to address four questions: (1) What are the boundaries of the industry? (2) What is the structure of the industry? (3) Which firms are our competitors? (4) What are the major determinants of competition? The answers to these questions provide a basis for thinking about the appropriate strategies that are open to the firm.

Industry Boundaries

An **industry** is a collection of firms that offer similar products or services. By "similar products," we mean products that customers perceive to be substitutable for one another. Consider, for example, the brands of personal computers (PCs) that are now being marketed. The firms that produce these PCs, such as Hewlett-Packard, IBM, Apple, and Dell, form the nucleus of the microcomputer industry.

Suppose a firm competes in the microcomputer industry. Where do the boundaries of this industry begin and end? Does the industry include desktops? Laptops? These are the kinds of questions that executives face in defining industry boundaries.

Why is a definition of industry boundaries important? First, it helps executives determine the arena in which their firm is competing. A firm competing in the microcomputer industry participates in an environment very different from that of the broader electronics business. The microcomputer industry comprises several related product families, including personal computers, inexpensive computers for home use, and workstations. The unifying characteristic of these product families is the use of a central processing unit (CPU) in a microchip. On the other hand, the electronics industry is far more extensive; it includes computers, radios, supercomputers, superconductors, and many other products.

The microcomputer and electronics industries differ in their volume of sales, their scope (some would consider microcomputers a segment of the electronics industry), their rate of growth, and their competitive makeup. The dominant issues faced by the two industries also are different. Witness, for example, the raging public debate being waged on the future of the "high-definition TV." U.S. policy makers are attempting to ensure domestic control of that segment of the electronics industry. They also are considering ways to stimulate "cutting-edge" research in superconductivity. These efforts are likely to spur innovation and stimulate progress in the electronics industry.

Second, a definition of industry boundaries focuses attention on the firm's competitors. Defining industry boundaries enables the firm to identify its competitors and producers of substitute products. This is critically important to the firm's design of its competitive strategy.

Third, a definition of industry boundaries helps executives determine key factors for success. Survival in the premier segment of the microcomputer industry requires skills that are considerably different from those required in the lower end of the industry. Firms that compete in the premier segment need to be on the cutting edge of technological development and to provide extensive customer support and education. On the other hand, firms that compete in the lower end need to excel in imitating the products introduced by the premier segment, to focus on customer convenience, and to maintain operational efficiency that permits them to charge the lowest market price. Defining industry boundaries enables executives to ask these questions: Do we have the skills it takes to succeed here? If not, what must we do to develop these skills?

Finally, a definition of industry boundaries gives executives another basis on which to evaluate their firm's goals. Executives use that definition to forecast demand for their firm's products and services. Armed with that forecast, they can determine whether those goals are realistic.

Problems in Defining Industry Boundaries

Defining industry boundaries requires both caution and imagination. Caution is necessary because there are no precise rules for this task and because a poor definition will lead to poor planning. Imagination is necessary because industries are dynamic—in every industry, important changes are under way in such key factors as competition, technology, and consumer demand.

Defining industry boundaries is a very difficult task. The difficulty stems from three sources:

1. The evolution of industries over time creates new opportunities and threats. Compare the financial services industry as we know it today with that of the 1990s, and then try to imagine how different the industry will be in the year 2020.

2. Industrial evolution creates industries within industries. The electronics industry of the 1960s has been transformed into many "industries"—TV sets, transistor radios, micro and macrocomputers, supercomputers, superconductors, and so on. Such transformation allows some firms to specialize and others to compete in different, related industries.

3. Industries are becoming global in scope. Consider the civilian aircraft manufacturing industry. For nearly three decades, U.S. firms dominated world production in that industry. But small and large competitors were challenging their dominance by 1990. At that time, Airbus Industries (a consortium of European firms) and Brazilian, Korean, and Japanese firms were actively competing in the industry.

Developing a Realistic Industry Definition

Given the difficulties just outlined, how do executives draw accurate boundaries for an industry? The starting point is a definition of the industry in global terms; that is, in terms that consider the industry's international components as well as its domestic components.

Having developed a preliminary concept of the industry (e.g., computers), executives flesh out its current components. This can be done by defining its product segments. Executives need to select the scope of their firm's potential market from among these related but distinct areas.

To understand the makeup of the industry, executives adopt a longitudinal perspective. They examine the emergence and evolution of product families. Why did these product families arise? How and why did they change? The answers to such questions provide executives with clues about the factors that drive competition in the industry.

Executives also examine the companies that offer different product families, the overlapping or distinctiveness of customer segments, and the rate of substitutability among product families.

To realistically define their industry, executives need to examine five issues:

1. Which part of the industry corresponds to our firm's goals?
2. What are the key ingredients of success in that part of the industry?
3. Does our firm have the skills needed to compete in that part of the industry? If not, can we build those skills?
4. Will the skills enable us to seize emerging opportunities and deal with future threats?
5. Is our definition of the industry flexible enough to allow necessary adjustments to our business concept as the industry grows?

Industry Structure

structural attributes
The enduring characteristics that give an industry its distinctive character.

Defining an industry's boundaries is incomplete without an understanding of its structural attributes. **Structural attributes** are the enduring characteristics that give an industry its distinctive character. Consider the cable television and financial services industries. Both industries are competitive, and both are important for our quality of life. But these industries have very different requirements for success. To succeed in the cable television industry, firms require vertical integration, which helps them lower their operating costs and ensures their access to quality programs; technological innovation, to enlarge the scope of their services and deliver them in new ways; and extensive marketing, using appropriate segmentation techniques to locate potentially viable niches. To succeed in the financial services industry, firms need to meet very different requirements, among which are extensive orientation of customers and an extensive capital base.

How can we explain such variations among industries? The answer lies in examining the four variables that industry comprises: (1) concentration, (2) economies of scale (discussed earlier), (3) product differentiation, and (4) barriers to entry.

Concentration

concentration
The extent to which industry sales are dominated by a few firms.

Concentration refers to the extent to which industry sales are dominated by only a few firms. In a highly concentrated industry (i.e., an industry whose sales are dominated by a handful of companies), the intensity of competition declines over time. High concentration serves as a barrier to entry into an industry because it enables the firms that hold large market shares to achieve significant economies of scale (e.g., savings in production costs due to increased production quantities) and, thus, to lower their prices to stymie attempts of new firms to enter the market.

The U.S. aircraft manufacturing industry is highly concentrated. Its concentration ratio—the percent of market share held by the top four firms in the industry—is 67 percent. Competition in the industry has not been vigorous. Firms in the industry have been able to deter entry through proprietary technologies and the formation of strategic alliances (e.g., joint ventures).

Product Differentiation

This variable refers to the extent to which customers perceive products or services offered by firms in the industry as different.

The differentiation of products can be real or perceived. The differentiation between Apple's Macintosh and IBM's PS/2 Personal Computer was a prime example of real differentiation. These products differed significantly in their technology and performance. Similarly, the civilian aircraft models produced by Boeing differed markedly from those produced by Airbus. The differences resulted from the use of different design principles and different construction technologies. For example, the newer Airbus planes followed the principle of "fly by wire," whereas Boeing planes utilized the laws of hydraulics. Thus, in Boeing planes, wings were activated by mechanical handling of different parts of the plane, whereas in the Airbus planes, this was done almost automatically.

Perceived differentiation results from the way in which firms position their products and from their success in persuading customers that their products differ significantly from competing products. Marketing strategies provide the vehicles through which this is done. Witness, for example, the extensive advertising campaigns of the automakers, each of which attempts to convey an image of distinctiveness. BMW ads highlight the excellent engineering of the BMW and its symbolic value as a sign of achievement. Some automakers focus on roominess and durability, which are desirable attributes for the family segment of the automobile market.

Real and perceived differentiations often intensify competition among existing firms. On the other hand, successful differentiation poses a competitive disadvantage for firms that attempt to enter an industry.

Barriers to Entry

barriers to entry
The conditions that a firm must satisfy to enter an industry.

Barriers to entry are the obstacles that a firm must overcome to enter an industry. The barriers can be tangible or intangible. The tangible barriers include capital requirements, technological know-how, resources, and the laws regulating entry into an industry. The intangible barriers include the reputation of existing firms, the loyalty of consumers to existing brands, and access to the managerial skills required for successful operation in an industry.

Entry barriers both increase and reflect the level of concentration, economies of scale, and product differentiation in an industry, and such increases make it more difficult for new firms to enter the industry. Therefore, when high barriers exist in an industry, competition in that industry declines over time.

In summary, analysis of concentration, economies of scale, product differentiation, and barriers to entry in an industry enable a firm's executives to understand the forces that determine competition in an industry and set the stage for identifying the firm's competitors and how they position themselves in the marketplace.

Industry regulations are a key element of industry structure and can constitute a significant barrier to entry for corporations. Escalating regulatory standards costs have been a serious concern for corporations for years. As legislative bodies continue their stronghold on corporate activities, businesses feel the impact on their bottom line. In-house counsel departments have been perhaps the most significant additions to corporate structure in the past decade. Legal fees have skyrocketed and managers have learned the hard way about the importance of adhering to regulatory standards.

Competitive Analysis

How to Identify Competitors

In identifying their firm's current and potential competitors, executives consider several important variables:

1. How do other firms define the scope of their market? The more similar the definitions of firms, the more likely the firms will view each other as competitors.

2. How similar are the benefits the customers derive from the products and services that other firms offer? The more similar the benefits of products or services, the higher the level of substitutability between them. High substitutability levels force firms to compete fiercely for customers.

3. How committed are other firms to the industry? Although this question may appear to be far removed from the identification of competitors, it is in fact one of the most important questions that competitive analysis must address, because it sheds light on the long-term intentions and goals. To size up the commitment of potential competitors to the industry, reliable intelligence data are needed. Such data may relate to potential resource commitments (e.g., planned facility expansions).

Common Mistakes in Identifying Competitors

Identifying competitors is a milestone in the development of strategy. But it is a process laden with uncertainty and risk, a process in which executives sometimes make costly mistakes. Examples of these mistakes are:

1. Overemphasizing current and known competitors while giving inadequate attention to potential entrants.

2. Overemphasizing large competitors while ignoring small competitors.

3. Overlooking potential international competitors.

4. Assuming that competitors will continue to behave in the same way they have behaved in the past.

5. Misreading signals that may indicate a shift in the focus of competitors or a refinement of their present strategies or tactics.

6. Overemphasizing competitors' financial resources, market position, and strategies while ignoring their intangible assets, such as a top management team.

7. Assuming that all of the firms in the industry are subject to the same constraints or are open to the same opportunities.

8. Believing that the purpose of strategy is to outsmart the competition, rather than to satisfy customer needs and expectations.

OPERATING ENVIRONMENT

operating environment
Factors in the immediate competitive situation that affect a firm's success in acquiring needed resources.

The **operating environment**, also called the *competitive* or *task environment,* comprises factors in the competitive situation that affect a firm's success in acquiring needed resources or in profitably marketing its goods and services. Among the most important of these factors are the firm's competitive position, the composition of its customers, its reputation among suppliers and creditors, and its ability to attract capable employees. The operating environment is typically much more subject to the firm's influence or control than the remote environment. Thus, firms can be much more proactive (as opposed to reactive) in dealing with the operating environment than in dealing with the remote environment.

Competitive Position

Assessing its competitive position improves a firm's chances of designing strategies that optimize its environmental opportunities. Development of competitor profiles enables a firm to more accurately forecast both its short- and long-term growth and its profit potentials. Although the exact criteria used in constructing a competitor's profile are largely determined by situational factors, the following criteria are often included:

1. Market share.
2. Breadth of product line.
3. Effectiveness of sales distribution.
4. Proprietary and key account advantages.
5. Price competitiveness.
6. Advertising and promotion effectiveness.
7. Location and age of facility.
8. Capacity and productivity.
9. Experience.
10. Raw materials costs.
11. Financial position.
12. Relative product quality.
13. R&D advantages position.
14. Caliber of personnel.
15. General images.
16. Customer profile.
17. Patents and copyrights.
18. Union relations.
19. Technological position.
20. Community reputation.

Once appropriate criteria have been selected, they are weighted to reflect their importance to a firm's success. Then the competitor being evaluated is rated on the criteria, the ratings are multiplied by the weight, and the weighted scores are summed to yield a numerical profile of the competitor, as shown in Exhibit 4.10.

This type of competitor profile is limited by the subjectivity of its criteria selection, weighting, and evaluation approaches. Nevertheless, the process of developing such profiles is of considerable help to a firm in defining its perception of its competitive position. Moreover, comparing the firm's profile with those of its competitors can aid its managers in identifying factors that might make the competitors vulnerable to the strategies the firm might choose to implement.

Customer Profiles

Perhaps the most vulnerable result of analyzing the operating environment is the understanding of a firm's customers that this provides. Developing a profile of a firm's present and prospective customers improves the ability of its managers to plan strategic operations,

EXHIBIT 4.10
Competitor Profile

Key Success Factors	Weight	Rating*	Weighted Score
Market share	0.30	4	1.20
Price competitiveness	0.20	3	0.60
Facilities location	0.20	5	1.00
Raw materials costs	0.10	3	0.30
Caliber of personnel	0.20	1	0.20
	1.00†		3.30

*The rating scale suggested is as follows: very strong competitive position (5 points), strong (4), average (3), weak (2), very weak (1).
†The total of the weights must always equal 1.00.

to anticipate changes in the size of markets, and to reallocate resources so as to support forecast shifts in demand patterns. The traditional approach to segmenting customers is based on customer profiles constructed from geographic, demographic, psychographic, and buyer behavior information.

Enterprising companies have quickly learned the importance of identifying target segments. In recent years, market research has increased tremendously as companies realize the benefits of demographic and psychographic segmentation. Research by American Express (AMEX) showed that competitors were stealing a prime segment of the company's business, affluent business travelers. AMEX's competing companies, including Visa and Mastercard, began offering high-spending business travelers frequent flier programs and other rewards including discounts on new cars. In turn, AMEX began to invest heavily in rewards programs, while also focusing on its strongest capabilities, assets, and competitive advantage. Unlike most credit card companies, AMEX cannot rely on charging interest to make money because its customers pay in full each month. Therefore, the company charges higher transaction fees to its merchants. In this way, increases in spending by AMEX customers who pay off their balances each month are more profitable to AMEX than to competing credit card companies.

Assessing consumer behavior is a key element in the process of satisfying your target market needs. Many firms lose market share as a result of assumptions made about target segments. Market research and industry surveys can help to reduce a firm's chances of relying on illusive assumptions. Firms most vulnerable are those that have had success with one or more products in the marketplace and as a result try to base consumer behavior on past data and trends.

Geographic
It is important to define the geographic area from which customers do or could come. Almost every product or service has some quality that makes it variably attractive to buyers from different locations. Obviously, a Wisconsin manufacturer of snow skis should think twice about investing in a wholesale distribution center in South Carolina. On the other hand, advertising in the *Milwaukee Journal-Sentinel* could significantly expand the geographically defined customer market of a major Myrtle Beach hotel in South Carolina.

Demographic
Demographic variables most commonly are used to differentiate groups of present or potential customers. Demographic information (e.g., information on sex, age, marital status, income, and occupation) is comparatively easy to collect, quantify, and use in strategic forecasting, and such information is the minimum basis for a customer profile.

Psychographic
Personality and lifestyle variables often are better predictors of customer purchasing behavior than geographic or demographic variables. In such situations, a psychographic

study is an important component of the customer profile. Advertising campaigns by soft-drink producers—Pepsi-Cola ("the Pepsi generation"), Coca-Cola ("the real thing"), and 7UP ("America's turning 7UP")—reflect strategic management's attention to the psychographic characteristics of their largest customer segment—physically active, group-oriented non-professionals.

Buyer Behavior

Buyer behavior data also can be a component of the customer profile. Such data are used to explain or predict some aspect of customer behavior with regard to a product or service. Information on buyer behavior (e.g., usage rate, benefits sought, and brand loyalty) can provide significant aid in the design of more accurate and profitable strategies.

Suppliers

Dependable relationships between a firm and its suppliers are essential to the firm's long-term survival and growth. A firm regularly relies on its suppliers for financial support, services, materials, and equipment. In addition, it occasionally is forced to make special requests for such favors as quick delivery, liberal credit terms, or broken-lot orders. Particularly at such times, it is essential for a firm to have had an ongoing relationship with its suppliers.

In the assessment of a firm's relationships with its suppliers, several factors, other than the strength of that relationship, should be considered. With regard to its competitive position with its suppliers, the firm should address the following questions:

Are the suppliers' prices competitive? Do the suppliers offer attractive quantity discounts?

How costly are their shipping charges? Are the suppliers competitive in terms of production standards?

In terms of deficiency rates, are the suppliers' abilities, reputations, and services competitive?

Are the suppliers reciprocally dependent on the firm?

Creditors

Because the quantity, quality, price, and accessibility of financial, human, and material resources are rarely ideal, assessment of suppliers and creditors is critical to an accurate evaluation of a firm's operating environment. With regard to its competitive position with its creditors, among the most important questions that the firm should address are the following:

Do the creditors fairly value and willingly accept the firm's stock as collateral?

Do the creditors perceive the firm as having an acceptable record of past payment?

A strong working capital position? Little or no leverage?

Are the creditors' loan terms compatible with the firm's profitability objectives?

Are the creditors able to extend the necessary lines of credit?

The answers to these and related questions help a firm forecast the availability of the resources it will need to implement and sustain its competitive strategies.

Human Resources: Nature of the Labor Market

A firm's ability to attract and hold capable employees is essential to its success. However, a firm's personnel recruitment and selection alternatives often are influenced by the nature of its operating environment. A firm's access to needed personnel is affected primarily by four factors: the firm's reputation as an employer, local employment rates, the ready availability of people with the needed skills, and its relationship with labor unions.

Reputation

A firm's reputation within its operating environment is a major element of its ability to satisfy its personnel needs. A firm is more likely to attract and retain valuable employees if it is seen as permanent in the community, competitive in its compensation package, and concerned with the welfare of its employees, and if it is respected for its product or service and appreciated for its overall contribution to the general welfare.

Employment Rates

The readily available supply of skilled and experienced personnel may vary considerably with the stage of a community's growth. A new manufacturing firm would find it far more difficult to obtain skilled employees in a vigorous industrialized community than in an economically depressed community in which similar firms had recently cut back operations.

Availability

The skills of some people are so specialized that relocation may be necessary to secure the jobs and the compensation that those skills commonly command. People with such skills include oil drillers, chefs, technical specialists, and industry executives. A firm that seeks to hire such a person is said to have broad labor market boundaries; that is, the geographic area within which the firm might reasonably expect to attract qualified candidates is quite large. On the other hand, people with more common skills are less likely to relocate from a considerable distance to achieve modest economic or career advancements. Thus, the labor market boundaries are fairly limited for such occupational groups as unskilled laborers, clerical personnel, and retail clerks.

Many manufacturers in the United States attempt to minimize the labor cost disadvantage they face in competing with overseas producers by outsourcing to lower-cost foreign locations or by hiring immigrant workers. Similarly, companies in construction and other labor-intensive industries try to provide themselves with a cost advantage by hiring temporary, often migrant, workers. An example of the sophistication of such worker location efforts is described in Exhibit 4.11, Strategy in Action.

Labor Unions

Approximately 12 percent of all workers in the United States belong to a labor union; the percentages are higher in Japan and western Europe at about 25 and 40 percent, respectively, and extremely low in developing nations. Unions represent the workers in their negotiations with employers through the process of collective bargaining. When managers' relationships with their employees are complicated by the involvement of a union, the company's ability to manage and motivate the people that it needs can be compromised.

EMPHASIS ON ENVIRONMENTAL FACTORS

This chapter has described the remote, industry, and operating environments as encompassing five components each. While that description is generally accurate, it may give the false impression that the components are easily identified, mutually exclusive, and equally applicable in all situations. In fact, the forces in the external environment are so dynamic and interactive that the impact of any single element cannot be wholly disassociated from the effect of other elements. For example, are increases in OPEC oil prices the result of economic, political, social, or technological changes? Or are a manufacturer's surprisingly good relations with suppliers a result of competitors', customers', or creditors' activities or

Strategy in Action

Exhibit 4.11

Click for Foreign Labor:
Companies Are Using Online Middlemen to Find Legal Workers

BusinessWeek

When she could not find enough workers for the construction firm owned by her son Thomas, Ann Carroll decided to go online. After typing in such search terms as "construction laborer" and "Mexican workers," she landed on the Web site for Labormex Foreign Labor Solutions. Within days she had a quote: $100 each for 11 Mexican workers and $1,340 to cover the visas. In October, Carroll Construction Co.'s recruits began laying sewer pipes in Ocean Springs, Mississippi, where the company is located. "I don't know what we would've done if we didn't go this route," says Carroll. "We're very happy with the workers."

Amid a federal crackdown on illegal immigration—including the December 2006 arrest of 1,282 Swift & Co. meatpacking workers—and a roiling political debate over expanding guest-worker programs, companies are turning to online middlemen to find legitimate foreign laborers. Job sites such as Monster. com and CareerBuilder.com have been helping companies scour the globe for white-collar talent since the late 1990s. Now unskilled workers, too, are a few clicks away, a boon for such chronically labor-starved industries as construction, agriculture, and catering.

Labormex was founded in 2002 by Seymour Taylor, an entrepreneur descended from a family of American settlers in Mexico. Business took off when he set up a Web site about a year ago and began advertising on Yahoo! and Google. The site boasts of "hardworking people acclimated to tough physical labor and who have worked under severe warm-weather conditions"— guys like Andreas Alcala Martinez, 29, who works for Carroll Construction. "Little money, but not hard work," says Martinez. He makes $9 an hour and arrived on an H-2B visa, of which the United States. issues 66,000 annually for low-skilled work. He can work for Carroll for 10 months, with the option of renewal.

Next to the big job sites, Labormex is a minnow. Taylor says he placed about 200 people in 2006 and expects to triple that in 2007. But the company, which has offices in New York and Monterrey, Mexico, has reeled in big clients, including Super 8 Motels and the Sonic Drive-Ins fast-food chain.

The U.S. Department of Labor lists hundreds of officially sanctioned recruiting agencies on its Web site. The online recruiters are already providing ammunition for immigration critics. "They're getting employers addicted to a supply of cheap labor and lowering incentives for them to look for domestic workers," says Jessica M. Vaughn, a senior policy analyst at the Center for Immigration Studies, which opposes expanding guest-worker programs. But with many Americans unwilling to mow lawns, build houses, and wait tables, many companies see online recruiters as a necessary way to tap a labor pool that is increasingly global.

Source: Reprinted with special permission from Moira Herbst, "Click for Foreign Labor," *BusinessWeek,* January 15, 2007. Copyright © 2007 The McGraw-Hill Companies.

of the supplier's own activities? The answer to both questions is probably that a number of forces in the external environment have combined to create the situation. Such is the case in most studies of the environment.

Strategic managers are frequently frustrated in their attempts to anticipate the environment's changing influences. Different external elements affect different strategies at different times and with varying strengths. The only certainty is that the effect of the remote and operating environments will be uncertain until a strategy is implemented. This leads many managers, particularly in less powerful or smaller firms to minimize long-term planning, which requires a commitment of resources. Instead, they favor allowing managers to adapt to new pressures from the environment. While such a decision has considerable merit for many firms, there is an associated trade-off, namely that absence of a strong resource and psychological commitment to a proactive strategy effectively bars a firm from assuming a leadership role in its competitive environment.

There is yet another difficulty in assessing the probable impact of remote, industry, and operating environments on the effectiveness of alternative strategies. Assessment of this kind involves collecting information that can be analyzed to disclose predictable effects.

EXHIBIT 4.12
Strategic Forecasting Issues

Key Issues in the Remote Environment Economy

What are the probable future directions of the economies in the firm's regional, national, and international market? What changes in economic growth, inflation, interest rates, capital availability, credit availability, and consumer purchasing power can be expected? What income differences can be expected between the wealthy upper middle class, the working class, and the underclass in various regions? What shifts in relative demand for different categories of goods and services can be expected?

Society and demographics

What effects will changes in social values and attitudes regarding childbearing, marriage, lifestyle, work, ethics, sex roles, racial equality, education, retirement, pollution, and energy have on the firm's development? What effects will population changes have on major social and political expectations—at home and abroad? What constraints or opportunities will develop? What pressure groups will increase in power?

Ecology

What natural or pollution-caused disasters threaten the firm's employees, customers, or facilities? How rigorously will existing environment legislature be enforced? What new federal, state, and local laws will affect the firm, and in what ways?

Politics

What changes in government policy can be expected with regard to industry cooperation, antitrust activities, foreign trade, taxation, depreciation, environmental protection, deregulation, defense, foreign trade barriers, and other important parameters? What success will a new administration have in achieving its stated goals? What effect will that success have on the firm? Will specific international climates be hostile or favorable? Is there a tendency toward instability, corruption, or violence? What is the level of political risk in each foreign market? What other political or legal constraints or supports can be expected in international business (e.g., trade barriers, equity requirements, nationalism, patent protection)?

Technology

What is the current state of the art? How will it change? What pertinent new products or services are likely to become technically feasible in the foreseeable future? What future impact can be expected from technological breakthroughs in related product areas? How will those breakthroughs interface with the other remote considerations, such as economic issues, social values, public safety, regulations, and court interpretations?

Key Issues in the Industry Environment

New entrants

Will new technologies or market demands enable competitors to minimize the impact of traditional economies of scale in the industry? Will consumers accept our claims of product or service differentiation? Will potential new entrants be able to match the capital requirements that currently exist? How permanent are the cost disadvantages (independent of size) in our industry? Will conditions change so that all competitors have equal access to marketing channels? Is government policy toward competition in our industry likely to change?

Bargaining power of suppliers

How stable are the size and composition of our supplier group? Are any suppliers likely to attempt forward integration into our business level? How dependent will our suppliers be in the future? Are substitute suppliers likely to become available? Could we become our own supplier?

EXHIBIT 4.12
(continued)

Substitute products or services

Are new substitutes likely? Will they be price competitive? Could we fight off substitutes by price competition? By advertising to sharpen product differentiation? What actions could we take to reduce the potential for having alternative products seen as legitimate substitutes?

Bargaining power of buyers

Can we break free of overcommitment to a few large buyers? How would our buyers react to attempts by us to differentiate our products? What possibilities exist that our buyers might vertically integrate backward? Should we consider forward integration? How can we make the value of our components greater in the products of our buyers?

Rivalry among existing firms

Are major competitors likely to undo the established balance of power in our industry? Is growth in our industry slowing such that competition will become fiercer? What excess capacity exists in our industry? How capable are our major competitors of withstanding intensified price competition? How unique are the objectives and strategies of our major competitors?

Key Issues in the Operating Environment

Competitive position

What strategic moves are expected by existing rivals—inside and outside the United States? What competitive advantage is necessary in selected foreign markets? What will be our competitors' priorities and ability to change? Is the behavior of our competitors predictable?

Customer profiles and market changes

What will our customer regard as needed value? Is marketing research done, or do managers talk to each other to discover what the customer wants? Which customer needs are not being met by existing products? Why? Are R&D activities under way to develop means for fulfilling these needs? What is the status of these activities? What marketing and distribution channels should we use? What do demographic and population changes portend for the size and sales potential of our market? What new market segments or products might develop as a result of these changes? What will be the buying power of our customer groups?

Supplier relationships

What is the likelihood of major cost increases because of dwindling supplies of a needed natural resource? Will sources of supply, especially of energy, be reliable? Are there reasons to expect major changes in the cost or availability of inputs as a result of money, people, or subassembly problems? Which suppliers can be expected to respond to emergency requests?

Creditors

What lines of credit are available to help finance our growth? What changes may occur in our creditworthiness? Are creditors likely to feel comfortable with our strategic plan and performance? What is the stock market likely to feel about our firm? What flexibility would our creditors show toward us during a downturn? Do we have sufficient cash reserves to protect our creditors and our credit rating?

Labor market

Are potential employees with desired skills and abilities available in the geographic areas in which our facilities are located? Are colleges and vocational/technical schools that can aid in meeting our training needs located near our plant or store sites? Are labor relations in our industry conducive to meeting our expanding needs for employees? Are workers whose skills we need shifting toward or away from the geographic location of our facilities?

Except in rare instances, however, it is virtually impossible for any single firm to anticipate the consequences of a change in the environment; for example, what is the precise effect on alternative strategies of a 2 percent increase in the national inflation rate, a 1 percent decrease in statewide unemployment, or the entry of a new competitor in a regional market?

Still, assessing the potential impact of changes in the external environment offers a real advantage. It enables decision makers to narrow the range of the available options and to eliminate options that are clearly inconsistent with the forecast opportunities. Environmental assessment seldom identifies the best strategy, but it generally leads to the elimination of all but the most promising options.

Exhibit 4.12 provides a set of key strategic forecasting issues for each level of environmental assessment—remote, industry, and operating. While the issues that are presented are not inclusive of all of the questions that are important, they provide an excellent set of questions with which to begin. Chapter 4 Appendix, Sources for Environmental Forecasting, is provided to help identify valuable sources of data and information from which answers and subsequent forecasts can be constructed. It lists governmental and private marketplace intelligence that can be used by a firm to gain a foothold in undertaking a strategic assessment of any level of the competitive environment.

Summary

A firm's external environment consists of three interrelated sets of factors that play a principal role in determining the opportunities, threats, and constraints that the firm faces. The remote environment comprises factors originating beyond, and usually irrespective of, any single firm's operating situation—economic, social, political, technological, and ecological factors. Factors that more directly influence a firm's prospects originate in the environment of its industry, including entry barriers, competitor rivalry, the availability of substitutes, and the bargaining power of buyers and suppliers. The operating environment comprises factors that influence a firm's immediate competitive situation—competitive position, customer profiles, suppliers, creditors, and the labor market. These three sets of factors provide many of the challenges that a particular firm faces in its attempts to attract or acquire needed resources and to profitably market its goods and services. Environmental assessment is more complicated for multinational corporations (MNCs) than for domestic firms because multinationals must evaluate several environments simultaneously.

Thus, the design of business strategies is based on the conviction that a firm able to anticipate future business conditions will improve its performance and profitability. Despite the uncertainty and dynamic nature of the business environment, an assessment process that narrows, even if it does not precisely define, future expectations is of substantial value to strategic managers.

Key Terms

barriers to entry, *p. 114*
concentration, *p. 114*
eco-efficiency, *p. 101*
ecology, *p. 99*
economies of scale, *p. 106*

external environment, *p. 94*
industry, *p. 112*
industry environment, *p. 102*
operating environment, *p. 116*
pollution, *p. 99*

product differentiation, *p. 106*
remote environment, *p. 94*
structural attributes, *p. 113*
technological
forecasting, *p. 98*

Questions for Discussion

1. Briefly describe two important recent changes in the remote environment of U.S. business in each of the following areas:
   a. Economic.
   b. Social.
   c. Political.
   d. Technological.
   e. Ecological.

2. Describe two major environmental changes that you expect to have a major impact on the whole-sale food industry in the next 10 years.

3. Develop a competitor profile for your college and for the college geographically closest to yours. Next, prepare a brief strategic plan to improve the competitive position of the weaker of the two colleges.

4. Assume the invention of a competitively priced synthetic fuel that could supply 25 percent of U.S. energy needs within 20 years. In what major ways might this change the external environment of U.S. business?

5. With your instructor's help, identify a local firm that has enjoyed great growth in recent years. To what degree and in what ways do you think this firm's success resulted from taking advantage of favorable conditions in its remote, industry, and operating environments?

6. Choose a specific industry and, relying solely on your impressions, evaluate the impact of the five forces that drive competition in that industry.

7. Choose an industry in which you would like to compete. Use the five-forces method of analysis to explain why you find that industry attractive.

8. Many firms neglect industry analysis. When does this hurt them? When does it not?

9. The model below depicts industry analysis as a funnel that focuses on remote-factor analysis to better understand the impact of factors in the operating environment. Do you find this model satisfactory? If not, how would you improve it?

10. Who in a firm should be responsible for industry analysis? Assume that the firm does not have a strategic planning department.

Chapter 4 Discussion Case

Siemens' Culture Clash

BusinessWeek

1 If things had turned out a little differently, Siemens Chief Executive Klaus Kleinfeld might already be on his way to executive stardom, like his role model Jack Welch. Just two years after Kleinfeld took over the Munich electronics and engineering behemoth, Siemens is on track to hit its aggressive internal earnings targets for the first time since 2000. In fact, it is expanding both sales and profits faster than Welch's former fiefdom, General Electric Co. What's more, the company has a larger presence than GE in rapid-growth markets such as India.

2 But instead of literary agents breaking down his door in pursuit of a tome of management wisdom, Kleinfeld has angry employees demonstrating outside his window. He has gotten little applause for boosting 2006 sales by 16 percent and profits by 35 percent, and he faces questions about a bribery scandal that has sapped his authority even though he is not personally implicated.

3 Transforming Siemens was never going to be easy. With branches in 190 countries and $114 billion in sales last year, the company has long been respected for its engineering prowess but derided for its sluggishness. And Germany Inc., with its long-standing tradition of labor harmony and powerful workers' councils, is highly resistant to the kind of change Kleinfeld has tried to implement. That's one reason Siemens lags seriously in overall profits, with a margin of 3.5 percent compared with 12.6 percent for GE. Kleinfeld concedes that some people doubt Siemens can change its ways, but he counters: "It took less time than we originally planned to get that growth momentum started."

4 Against the odds, in just two years Kleinfeld has managed a mighty restructuring. He has quoted the management precepts of Welch and has drawn on the GE playbook to realign Siemens as the world's leading provider of such infrastructure as airports, power plants, and medical equipment. He has

pushed Siemens' 475,000 employees to make decisions faster and focus as much on customers as on technology. He spun off underperforming telecommunications-gear businesses and simplified the company's structure. And when one group of managers failed to deliver, he broke up an entire division.

RESPECT AND RESENTMENT

5 Although restructuring has dominated his tenure, Kleinfeld isn't just a cost-cutter. If you want to make his eyes light up, say "megatrends." The 49-year-old believes Siemens is perfectly positioned to profit from huge global shifts in population and wealth, and he spent $8.6 billion last year on acquisitions in areas such as medical diagnostics and wind power. As people in the developing world get richer, he says, Siemens will supply CT and MRI scanners to diagnose their ills. It will build switching systems and engines for their trains and subways. And it will sell them water-purification equipment, power plants, and machines to run mines and factories. Barely a day goes by without Siemens announcing orders to modernize a steel mill in Russia, build a cement plant in Yemen, or set up a desalination operation in Pakistan. Says Kleinfeld: "This company is solving the biggest issues this planet has."

6 Investors have warmed to Kleinfeld's vision. Siemens shares have risen 26 percent in the two years since he took over versus 6 percent for GE. But his tactics have made him a target for German resentment of globalization and the perceived heartlessness of U.S.-style management methods. When, in an attempt at openness, Kleinfeld invited workers to respond to his blog, they did—in spades. "I used to feel good in the Siemens family," one employee wrote. "But there's not much of that feeling left."

7 More alarming, Siemens is the target of an expanding investigation by Munich prosecutors. In the probe of alleged bribes to foreign officials to win telecommunications contracts, authorities briefly jailed a former member of Siemens' executive board and many lower-ranking managers. Siemens admits that as much as $546 million may have been misused. Kleinfeld, who was stationed in the United States during much of the time the alleged misconduct took place, has not been identified as a target of the investigation and has taken measures to prevent future scandals. He has hired a former senior German prosecutor to serve as compliance officer and retained an outside law firm to conduct an independent inquiry. Munich prosecutors say Siemens is cooperating in the bribery probe. That hasn't stopped some shareholder activists from criticizing Kleinfeld's handling of the crisis, and he is sure to come under fire when the company holds its annual meeting in Munich on January 25, 2007. Shareholder groups have already filed motions to withhold approval of the Siemens management board, normally a formality in Germany.

8 The pressure is apt to grow. Siemens says it expects the U.S. Securities & Exchange Commission to investigate, potentially exposing the company to hundreds of millions of dollars in fines. But unless new and far more damaging revelations arise, Kleinfeld is unlikely to be forced out. Still, the crisis has become a distraction. "Yes, it is taking part of my time," says Kleinfeld, who has offloaded some responsibilities to other members of the management board as a result.

9 If Kleinfeld is worried, though, he isn't showing it. A few weeks after Munich prosecutors seized documents from 30 Siemens locations—including his office—Kleinfeld seems relaxed and self-assured. Never mind that in a waiting room a few feet from his door, headlines on a stack of newspapers arrayed neatly on a table blare the latest news on the scandal. He yawns occasionally, the only sign of fatigue.

10 Provided Kleinfeld weathers all the turbulence, he still has the potential to emerge as one of Europe's most dynamic chief executives. With an eye to his German critics, Kleinfeld these days deflects comparisons to Welch. But it's hard not to see some of the former GE chief's energy and competitive spirit—not to mention impatience—in Kleinfeld. He rises before dawn to jog and often barrages subordinates with phone calls and e-mails late into the night. "If you turn off your phone, he calls your wife," says one manager who counts himself a Kleinfeld admirer. Siemens executives know that an e-mail ending with the word bitte ("please") means get it done now—or else. "I wonder when that guy sleeps," says Hermann Requardt, Siemens' chief of research and development.

HAPPY IN THE HEARTLAND

11 Kleinfeld downplays the influence of his three years in the United States, a stint ordinary Germans view as a blot on his résumé. There's no question, though, that he counts those years among his best. "I liked it over there," says Kleinfeld, who served as CEO of Siemens' U.S. operations in 2002 and 2003. "Wherever I went, I made friends." And to this day, Kleinfeld's style is decidedly less German-centric than that of his predecessor, Heinrich von Pierer. Von Pierer played tennis with the Chancellor. Kleinfeld runs the New York Marathon. Von Pierer served on a half-dozen boards of German companies. Kleinfeld does so for Citigroup, Alcoa, and the New York Metropolitan Opera. Von Pierer speaks English well but prefers German. Kleinfeld is totally fluent in English.

12 His affection for the United States comes naturally, perhaps because Kleinfeld personifies the American ideal of the self-made man. He was 10 when his father died, and by the age of 12 he was working in a supermarket and taking on other part-time jobs to help make ends meet. Later, while working full-time at Siemens, he completed his doctoral work on corporate communications strategy, which was published as a book.

13 Today, Kleinfeld is as comfortable hobnobbing with global leaders as he is chatting with entry-level employees.

September 2006 found him speaking about climate change at the Clinton Global Initiative in New York, then meeting workers in a nearby suburb.

14 He also knows how to enjoy himself. In December 2006, Kleinfeld danced the night away at a Christmas party for U.S. employees at New York's B.B. King Blues Club. He even plays a decent blues harmonica, though never in public.

15 One of Kleinfeld's problems is that few inside Siemens can match his energy. The Old Guard tend to grumble that Kleinfeld is too impatient and demanding. Soon after taking office in January 2005, he vowed that Siemens would finally achieve ambitious profit-margin goals established in 2000 for each unit. The targets range from 6 percent for auto parts to 13 percent for the top-performing medical-equipment division. Kleinfeld staked his job on the company hitting those numbers by April 2007—which now looks likely, analysts say. His message: everyone, including the boss, is accountable. "We commit to something, and we deliver," Kleinfeld says. "That is the culture we want to form."

16 Communicating that culture change across such a sprawling enterprise is a massive challenge. The company's 11 main business units operate almost as separate entities, with their own boards and distinct corporate cultures, making it hard for directives from the top to filter down to the troops. One executive says Kleinfeld's biggest impact so far has been increased pressure to speak English throughout the company—hardly an earth-shattering reform. And while Siemens excels at technological breakthroughs, such as mobile phones with built-in music players, they have often failed because of poor marketing and a lack of focus on the consumers who use the products. So how do you persuade Siemens' vaunted engineers to pay more attention to customers? Kleinfeld declared that he would personally visit Siemens' 100 biggest clients in his first 100 days in office. He wound up meeting more than 300 of them.

17 Kleinfeld isn't shy about administering harsh medicine when he feels it's needed. That's something new at the 159-year-old company. At the end of 2005, it became clear that the Logistics & Assembly Systems Division, which made products such as sorting equipment used by the U.S. Postal Service, would deliver only a 2 percent profit margin. Most unpardonable in Kleinfeld's eyes was that the unit's managers waited too long to alert him to the problem. So Kleinfeld transferred the most profitable parts of the division, such as baggage-handling systems for airports, to other parts of Siemens. The rest was sold. Within weeks, an entire Siemens division with $1.9 billion in annual sales was vaporized. Around Siemens, there was a collective gasp.

TOSSING OUT TELECOM

18 He has been equally tough on some sacred pieces of the Siemens empire. Founder Werner von Siemens made his name laying intercontinental telegraph lines in the mid-1800s, but that didn't stop Kleinfeld from getting rid of communications businesses. He paid Taiwan's BenQ Corp. to take the money-losing mobile-phone division off his hands at a total cost to Siemens of $1.4 billion. And he put most of Siemens' telecommunications-equipment business into a joint venture run by Finland's Nokia Corp. But the Nokia deal has been delayed until questions about the bribery scandal are cleared up. In September 2006, BenQ declared the German handset unit insolvent. Although Kleinfeld insists he thought it had a future under BenQ, workers have charged that he should have foreseen the disaster. In the face of pressure from labor leaders and German politicians, Siemens ultimately coughed up $46 million to aid workers who lost their jobs.

19 Some Siemens watchers say Kleinfeld has become more cautious following the bribery investigation and the uproar over his restructuring moves. Those controversies clearly rob him of political capital, and plenty of people both inside and outside Siemens would surely love to see Kleinfeld fail. Says a consultant who has worked closely with Siemens: "Some people are betting that he doesn't survive and that they can go on in the normal way."

20 Kleinfeld, though, has no plans to give up, and he is pressing to reshape the "normal" ways in which the giant company operates even as the investigations continue. Says Kleinfeld: "We are fitter than ever."

Source: Reprinted with special permission from Jack Ewing, "Siemens' Culture Clash," *BusinessWeek*, January 29, 2007. Copyright © 2007 The McGraw-Hill Companies.

DISCUSSION QUESTIONS

1. What are the industry forces that dominate Siemens' industries?

2. What are the different types of responsibility that Kleinfeld shoulders in his job as CEO? Do you consider them to be strategic responsibilities?

3. Do you think that the level of strategic turbulence and restructuring that Kleinfeld faces is common in business? Do you believe that Kleinfeld helps to create this turmoil?

4. How do you see the U.S. and German business environments as different?

5. To what degree do you believe Kleinfeld must simply react to his environments as opposed to "creating" them?

Chapter 4 Appendix

Sources for Environmental Forecasting

Remote and Industry Environments

A. Economic considerations:
1. *Predicasts* (most complete and up-to-date review of forecasts)
2. National Bureau of Economic Research
3. *Handbook of Basic Economic Statistics*
4. *Statistical Abstract of the United States* (also includes industrial, social, and political statistics)
5. Publications by Department of Commerce agencies:
   a. Office of Business Economics (e.g., *Survey of Business*)
   b. Bureau of Economic Analysis (e.g., *Business Conditions Digest*)
   c. Bureau of the Census (e.g., *Survey of Manufacturers* and various reports on population, housing, and industries)
   d. Business and Defense Services Administration (e.g., *United States Industrial Outlook*)
6. Securities and Exchange Commission (various quarterly reports on plant and equipment, financial reports, working capital of corporations)
7. The Conference Board
8. *Survey of Buying Power*
9. *Marketing Economic Guide*
10. *Industrial Arts Index*
11. U.S. and national chambers of commerce
12. American Manufacturers Association
13. *Federal Reserve Bulletin*
14. *Economic Indicators,* annual report
15. *Kiplinger Newsletter*
16. International economic sources:
   a. *Worldcasts*
   b. Master key index for business international publications
   c. Department of Commerce
      (1) Overseas business reports
      (2) Industry and Trade Administration
      (3) Bureau of the Census—*Guide to Foreign Trade Statistics*
17. *Business Periodicals Index*

B. Social considerations:
1. Public opinion polls
2. Surveys such as *Social Indicators and Social Reporting,* the annals of the American Academy of Political and Social Sciences
3. Current controls: Social and behavioral sciences
4. Abstract services and indexes for articles in sociological, psychological, and political journals

5. Indexes for *The Wall Street Journal, New York Times,* and other newspapers
6. Bureau of the Census reports on population, housing, manufacturers, selected services, construction, retail trade, wholesale trade, and enterprise statistics
7. Various reports from such groups as the Brookings Institution and the Ford Foundation
8. World Bank Atlas (population growth and GNP data)
9. World Bank–World Development Report

C. Political considerations:
1. *Public Affairs Information Services Bulletin*
2. CIS Index (Congressional Information Index)
3. Business periodicals
4. Funk & Scott (regulations by product breakdown)
5. Weekly compilation of presidential documents
6. *Monthly Catalog of Government Publications*
7. *Federal Register* (daily announcements of pending regulations)
8. *Code of Federal Regulations* (final listing of regulations)
9. Business International Master Key Index (regulations, tariffs)
10. Various state publications
11. Various information services (Bureau of National Affairs, Commerce Clearing House, Prentice Hall)

D. Technological considerations:
1. *Applied Science and Technology Index*
2. *Statistical Abstract of the United States*
3. Scientific and Technical Information Service
4. University reports, congressional reports
5. Department of Defense and military purchasing publishers
6. Trade journals and industrial reports
7. Industry contacts, professional meetings
8. Computer-assisted information searches
9. National Science Foundation annual report
10. *Research and Development Directory* patent records

E. Industry considerations:
1. *Concentration Ratios in Manufacturing* (Bureau of the Census)
2. *Input-Output Survey* (productivity ratios)
3. *Monthly Labor Review* (productivity ratios)
4. *Quarterly Failure Report* (Dun & Bradstreet)
5. *Federal Reserve Bulletin* (capacity utilization)

6. *Report on Industrial Concentration and Product Diversification in the 1,000 Largest Manufacturing Companies* (Federal Trade Commission)
7. Industry trade publications
8. Bureau of Economic Analysis, Department of Commerce (specialization ratios)

Industry and Operating Environments

A. Competition and supplier considerations:
   1. Target Group Index
   2. U.S. Industrial Outlook
   3. Robert Morris annual statement studies
   4. Troy, Leo *Almanac of Business & Industrial Financial Ratios*
   5. *Census of Enterprise Statistics*
   6. Securities and Exchange Commission (10-K reports)
   7. Annual reports of specific companies
   8. *Fortune 500 Directory, The Wall Street Journal, Barron's, Forbes, Dun's Review*
   9. Investment services and directories: Moody's, Dun & Bradstreet, Standard & Poor's, Starch Marketing, Funk & Scott Index
   10. Trade association surveys
   11. Industry surveys
   12. Market research surveys
   13. *Country Business Patterns*
   14. *Country and City Data Book*
   15. Industry contacts, professional meetings, salespeople
   16. *NFIB Quarterly Economic Report for Small Business*

B. Customer profile:
   1. *Statistical Abstract of the United States,* first source of statistics
   2. *Statistical Sources* by Paul Wasserman (a subject guide to data—both domestic and international)
   3. *American Statistics Index* (Congressional Information Service Guide to statistical publications of U.S. government—monthly)
   4. Office of the Department of Commerce:
      a. Bureau of the Census reports on population, housing, and industries
      b. *U.S. Census of Manufacturers* (statistics by industry, area, and products)
      c. *Survey of Current Business* (analysis of business trends, especially February and July issues)

5. Market research studies (*A Basic Bibliography on Market Review,* compiled by Robert Ferber et al., American Marketing Association)
6. *Current Sources of Marketing Information: A Bibliography of Primary Marketing Data* by Gunther & Goldstein, AMA
7. *Guide to Consumer Markets,* The Conference Board (provides statistical information with demographic, social, and economic data—annual)
8. *Survey of Buying Power*
9. *Predicasts* (abstracts of publishing forecasts of all industries, detailed products, and end-use data)
10. *Predicasts Basebook* (historical data from 1960 to present, covering subjects ranging from population and GNP to specific products and services; series are coded by Standard Industrial Classifications)
11. *Market Guide* (individual market surveys of over 1,500 U.S. and Canadian cities; includes population, location, trade areas, banks, principal industries, colleges and universities, department and chain stores, newspapers, retail outlets, and sales)
12. *Country and City Data Book* (includes bank deposits, birth and death rates, business firms, education, employment, income of families, manufacturers, population, savings, and wholesale and retail trade)
13. *Yearbook of International Trade Statistics* (UN)
14. *Yearbook of National Accounts Statistics* (UN)
15. *Statistical Yearbook* (UN—covers population, national income, agricultural and industrial production, energy, external trade, and transport)
16. *Statistics of (Continents): Sources for Market Research* (includes separate books on Africa, America, Europe)

C. Key natural resources:
   1. *Minerals Yearbook, Geological Survey* (Bureau of Mines, Department of the Interior)
   2. *Agricultural Abstract* (Department of Agriculture)
   3. Statistics of electric utilities and gas pipeline companies (Federal Power Commission)
   4. Publications of various institutions: American Petroleum Institute, Atomic Energy Commission, Coal Mining Institute of America, American Steel Institute, and Brookings Institution

Chapter **Five**

The Global Environment

After reading and studying this chapter, you should be able to

1. Explain the importance of a company's decision to globalize.

2. Describe the four main strategic orientations of global firms.

3. Understand the complexity of the global environment and the control problems that are faced by global firms.

4. Discuss major issues in global strategic planning, including the differences for multinational and global firms.

5. Describe the market requirements and product characteristics in global competition.

6. Evaluate the competitive strategies for firms in foreign markets, including niche market exporting, licensing and contract manufacturing, franchising, joint ventures, foreign branching, private equity, and wholly owned subsidiaries.

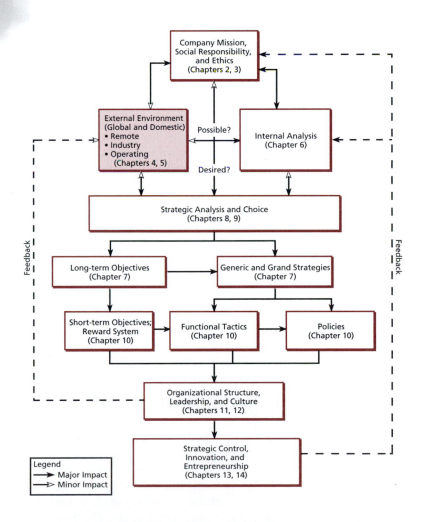

GLOBALIZATION

globalization
The strategy of
approaching worldwide
markets with standard-
ized products.

Special complications confront a firm involved in the globalization of its operations. **Globalization** refers to the strategy of approaching worldwide markets with standardized products. Such markets are most commonly created by end consumers that prefer lower-priced, standardized products over higher-priced, customized products and by global corporations that use their worldwide operations to compete in local markets. Global corporations headquartered in one country with subsidiaries in other countries experience difficulties that are understandably associated with operating in several distinctly different competitive arenas.

Awareness of the strategic opportunities faced by global corporations and of the threats posed to them is important to planners in almost every domestic U.S. industry. Among corporations headquartered in the United States that receive more than 50 percent of their annual profits from foreign operations are Citicorp, Coca-Cola, ExxonMobil, Gillette, IBM, Otis Elevator, and Texas Instruments. In fact, the 100 largest U.S. globals earn an average of 37 percent of their operating profits abroad. Equally impressive is the effect of foreign-based globals that operate in the United States. Their "direct foreign investment" in the United States now exceeds $90 billion, with Japanese, German, and French firms leading the way.

Understanding the myriad and sometimes subtle nuances of competing in global markets or against global corporations is rapidly becoming a required competence of strategic managers. For example, experts in the advertising community contend that Korean companies only recently recognized the importance of making their names known abroad. In the 1980s, there was very little advertising of Korean brands, and the country had very few recognizable brands abroad. Korean companies tended to emphasize sales and production more than marketing. The opening of the Korean advertising market in the 1990s indicated that Korean firms had acquired a new appreciation for the strategic competencies that are needed to compete globally and created an influx of global firms like Saatchi and Saatchi, J. W. Thompson, Ogilvy and Mather, and Bozell. Many of them established joint ventures or partnerships with Korean agencies. An excellent example of such a strategic approach to globalization by Philip Morris's KGFI is described in Exhibit 5.1, Global Strategy in Action. The opportunities for corporate growth often seem brightest in global markets. Exhibit 5.2 reports on the growth in national shares of the world's outputs and growth in national economies to the year 2020. While the United States had a commanding lead in the size of its economy in 1992, it was caught by China in the year 2000 and will be far surpassed by 2020. Overall, in less than 20 years, rich industrial countries will be overshadowed by developing countries in their produced share of the world's output.

Because the growth in the number of global firms continues to overshadow other changes in the competitive environment, this section will focus on the nature, outlook, and operations of global corporations.

DEVELOPMENT OF A GLOBAL CORPORATION

The evolution of a global corporation often entails progressively involved strategy levels. The first level, which often entails export-import activity, has minimal effect on the existing management orientation or on existing product lines. The second level, which can involve foreign licensing and technology transfer, requires little change in management or operation. The third level typically is characterized by direct investment in overseas operations, including manufacturing plants. This level requires large capital outlays and the development of global management skills. Although the domestic operations of a firm at this level

The Globalization of Philip Morris's KGFI

Outside of its core Western markets, Kraft General Foods International's (KGFI) food products have a growing presence in one of the most dynamic business environments in the world—the Asia-Pacific region. Its operations there are expanding rapidly, often aided by links with local manufacturers and distributors.

Japan and Korea are important examples. In both countries, local alliances can be crucial to market entry and success. Realizing this fact in the early 1970s, General Foods established joint ventures in both Japan and Korea. These joint ventures, combined with Kraft General Foods International's (KGFI) stand-alone operations, generate more than $1 billion in revenues. In the aggregate, their combined food operations in Japan and Korea are larger than many *Fortune* 500 companies.

Whereas soluble coffee accounts for just over 25 percent of the coffee consumed in U.S. homes, it fills more than 70 percent of the cups consumed in the homes of convenience-minded Japan. Additionally, Japan is the origin of a unique form of packaged coffee—liquid—and a unique channel of distribution—vending machines. Japanese consumers have purchased packaged liquid coffee for years, and it amounts to a $5 billion category. Some 2 million vending machines dispense 9 billion cans of liquid coffee annually—an average of 75 cans per person.

Japan offers a culturally unique distribution channel for coffee products—the gift-set market. Many Japanese exchange specially packaged food or beverage assortments at least twice a year to commemorate holidays as well as special personal or business occasions. The gift-set business has helped Maxim products reinforce their quality image; it also will be a launching pad and support vehicle for Carte Noire coffees.

Outside the Ajinomoto General Foods joint venture, KGFI is developing a freestanding food business under the name Kraft Japan. It is building a cheese business with imported Philadelphia Brand cream cheese,

the leading cream cheese in the Tokyo metropolitan market, as well as locally manufactured and licensed Kraft Milk Farm cheese slices. The cheese market is expected to grow approximately 5 percent per year. This is a rapid growth rate for a large food category. In addition to cheese, KGFI also imports Oscar Mayer prepared meats and Jacobs Suchard chocolates.

KGFI's joint venture in Korea, Doug Suh Foods Corporation, is one of the top 10 food companies in the country. Doug Suh manufactures coffees and cereals and has its own distribution network. One of Doug Suh's other businesses in Korea, Post Cereals, is also a strong number two, with a 42 percent category share.

Korea's $400 million coffee market is the fastest-growing major coffee market in the world, expanding at an average annual rate of 14 percent. Growing with the market, Maxim and Maxwell soluble coffees, in both traditional "agglomerate" and freeze-dried forms, account for more than 70 percent of the country's soluble coffee sales. The strength of these brands also brings the company a strong number one position in coffee mix, a mixture of soluble coffee, creamer, and sugar. In addition, its Frima brand leads the market in the nondairy creamer segment.

Beyond Japan and Korea, KGFI is targeting many other countries for geographic expansion. In Indonesia, for instance, KGFI has established a rapidly growing cheese business through a licensee and introduced other KGFI products. In Taiwan, the joint venture company, PremierFoods Corporation, holds a 34 percent share of the soluble coffee market and is aggressively developing a Kraft cheese and Jacobs Suchard import business. KGFI Philippines, a wholly owned subsidiary, has a leading position in the cheese and powdered soft-drink markets in its country. In the People's Republic of China, the company produces and markets Maxwell House coffees and Tang powdered soft drinks through two successful and rapidly growing joint ventures.

continue to dominate its policy, such a firm is commonly categorized as a true multinational corporation (MNC). The most involved strategy level is characterized by a substantial increase in foreign investment, with foreign assets comprising a significant portion of total assets. At this level, the firm begins to emerge as a global enterprise with global approaches to production, sales, finance, and control.

To get a more complete understanding of the many elements of a multinational environment that need to be considered by strategic planners, study Appendix 5-A. It contains lists of important competitive issues that will help you to see the complexity of the multinational landscape and to better appreciate the complicated and sophisticated nature of strategic planning.

EXHIBIT 5.2   **Projected Economic Growth**

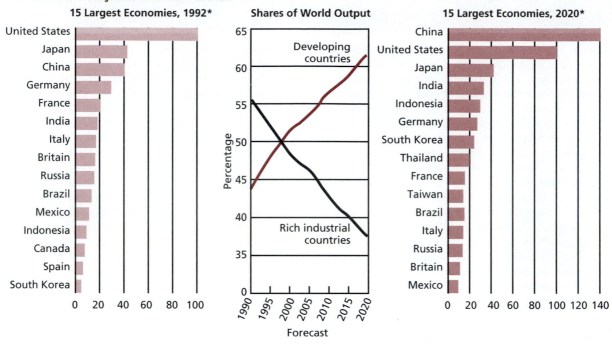

Source: World Bank, *Global Economic Prospects and the Developing Countries.*

Some firms downplay their global nature (to never appear distracted from their domestic operations), whereas others highlight it. For example, General Electric's formal statement of mission and business philosophy includes the following commitment:

> To carry out a diversified, growing, and profitable worldwide manufacturing business in electrical apparatus, appliances, and supplies, and in related materials, products, systems, and services for industry, commerce, agriculture, government, the community, and the home.

A similar global orientation is evident at IBM, which operates in 125 countries, conducts business in 30 languages and more than 100 currencies, and has 23 major manufacturing facilities in 14 countries.

WHY FIRMS GLOBALIZE

The technological advantage once enjoyed by the United States has declined dramatically during the past 30 years. In the late 1950s, more than 80 percent of the world's major technological innovations were first introduced in the United States. By 1990, the figure had declined to less than 50 percent. In contrast, France is making impressive advances in electric traction, nuclear power, and aviation. Germany leads in chemicals and pharmaceuticals, precision and heavy machinery, heavy electrical goods, metallurgy, and surface transport equipment. Japan leads in optics, solid-state physics, engineering, chemistry, and process metallurgy. Eastern Europe and the former Soviet Union, the so-called COMECON (Council for Mutual Economic Assistance) countries, generate 30 percent of annual worldwide patent applications. However, the United States has regained some of its lost technological advantage. Through globalization, U.S. firms often can reap benefits from industries and technologies developed abroad. Even a relatively small service firm that possesses a distinct competitive advantage can capitalize on large overseas operations.

Diebold Inc. once operated solely in the United States, selling automated teller machines (ATMs), bank vaults, and security systems to financial institutions. However, with the U.S. market saturated, Diebold needed to expand internationally to continue its growth. The firm's globalization efforts led to both the development of new technologies in emerging markets and opportunistic entry into entirely new industries that significantly improved Diebold's sales.

In many situations, global development makes sense as a competitive weapon. Direct penetration of foreign markets can drain vital cash flows from a foreign competitor's domestic operations. The resulting lost opportunities, reduced income, and limited production can impair the competitor's ability to invade U.S. markets. A case in point is IBM's move to establish a position of strength in the Japanese mainframe computer industry before two key competitors, Fiyitsue and Hitachi, could dominate it. Once IBM had achieved a substantial share of the Japanese market, it worked to deny its Japanese competitors the vital cash and production experience they needed to invade the U.S. market.

Firms that operate principally in the domestic environment have an important decision to make with regard to their globalization: Should they act before being forced to do so by competitive pressures or after? Should they (1) be proactive by entering global markets in advance of other firms and thereby enjoy the first-mover advantages often accruing to risk-taker firms that introduce new products or services or (2) be reactive by taking the more conservative approach and following other companies into global markets once customer demand has been proven and the high costs of new-product or new-service introductions have been absorbed by competitors? Although the answers to these questions are determined by the specifics of the company and the context, the issues raised in Exhibit 5.3 are helpful to strategic decision makers faced with the dilemma.

Strategic Orientations of Global Firms

Multinational corporations typically display one of four orientations toward their overseas activities. They have a certain set of beliefs about how the management of foreign operations should be handled. A company with an **ethnocentric orientation** believes that the values and priorities of the parent organization should guide the strategic decision making of all its operations. If a corporation has a **polycentric orientation,** then the culture of the country in which a strategy is to be implemented is allowed to dominate the decision-making process. In contrast, a **regiocentric orientation** exists when the parent attempts to blend its own predispositions with those of the region under consideration, thereby arriving at a region-sensitive compromise. Finally, a corporation with a **geocentric orientation** adopts a global systems approach to strategic decision making, thereby emphasizing global integration.

American firms often adopt a regiocentric orientation for pursing strategies in Europe. U.S. e-tailers have attempted to blend their own corporate structure and expertise with that of European corporations. For example, Amazon has been able to leverage its experience in the United States while developing regionally and culturally specific strategies overseas. By purchasing European franchises that have had regional success, E*Trade is pursuing a foreign strategy in which they insert their European units into corporate structure. This strategy requires the combination and use of culturally different management styles and involves major challenges for upper management.

Exhibit 5.4 shows the effects of each of the four orientations on key activities of the firm. It is clear from the figure that the strategic orientation of a global firm plays a major role in determining the locus of control and corporate priorities of the firm's decision makers.

ethnocentric orientation
When the values and priorities of the parent organization guide the strategic decision making of all its international operations.

polycentric orientation
When the culture of the country in which the strategy is to be implemented is allowed to dominate a company's international decision-making process.

regiocentric orientation
When a parent company blends its own predisposition with those of its international units to develop region-sensitive strategies.

geocentric orientation
When an international firm adopts a systems approach to strategic decision making that emphasizes global integration.

EXHIBIT 5.3

Reasons for Going Global

Proactive	
Advantage/Opportunity	**Explanation of Action**
Additional resources	Various inputs—including natural resources, technologies, skilled personnel, and materials—may be obtained more readily outside the home country.
Lowered costs	Various costs—including labor, materials, transportation, and financing—may be lower outside the home country.
Incentives	Various incentives may be available from the host government or the home government to encourage foreign investment in specific locations.
New, expanded markets	New and different markets may be available outside the home country; excess resources—including management, skills, machinery, and money—can be utilized in foreign locations.
Exploitation of firm-specific advantages	Technologies, brands, and recognized names can all provide opportunities in foreign locations.
Taxes	Differing corporate tax rates and tax systems in different locations provide opportunities for companies to maximize their after-tax worldwide profits.
Economies of scale	National markets may be too small to support efficient production, while sales from several combined allow for larger-scale production.
Synergy	Operations in more than one national environment provide opportunities to combine benefits from one location with another, which is impossible without both of them.
Power and prestige	The image of being international may increase a company's power and prestige and improve its domestic sales and relations with various stakeholder groups.
Protect home market through offense in competitor's home	A strong offense in a competitor's market can put pressure on the competitor that results in a pull-back from foreign activities to protect itself at home.

Reactive	
Outside Occurrence	**Explanation of Reaction**
Trade barriers	Tariffs, quotas, buy-local policies, and other restrictive trade practices can make exports to foreign markets less attractive; local operations in foreign locations thus become attractive.
International customers	If a company's customer base becomes international, and the company wants to continue to serve it, then local operations in foreign locations may be necessary.
International competition	If a company's competitors become international, and the company wants to remain competitive, foreign operations may be necessary.
Regulations	Regulations and restrictions imposed by the home government may increase the cost of operating at home; it may be possible to avoid these costs by establishing foreign operations.
Chance	Chance occurrence results in a company deciding to enter foreign locations.

EXHIBIT 5.4 **Orientation of a Global Firm**

	Orientation of the Firm			
	Ethnocentric	**Polycentric**	**Regiocentric**	**Geocentric**
Mission	Profitability (viability)	Public acceptance (legitimacy)	Profitability and public acceptance (viability and legitimacy)	Same as regiocentric
Governance	Top-down	Bottom-up (each subsidiary decides on local objectives)	Mutually negotiated between region and its subsidiaries	Mutually negotiated at all levels of the corporation
Strategy	Global integration	National responsiveness	Regional integration and national responsiveness	Global integration and national responsiveness
Structure	Hierarchical product divisions	Hierarchical area divisions, with autonomous national units	Product and regional organization tied through a matrix	A network of organizations (including some competitors)
Culture Technology Marketing	Home country Mass production Product development determined by the needs of home country	Host country Batch production Local product development based on local needs	Regional Flexible manufacturing Standardize within region but not across regions	Global Flexible manufacturing Global product, with local variations
Finance	Repatriation of profits to home country	Retention of profits in host country	Redistribution within region	Redistribution globally
Personnel practices	People of home country developed for key positions in the world	People of local nationality developed for key positions in their own country	Regional people developed for key positions anywhere in the region	Global personnel development and placement

Source: Reprinted from *Columbia Journal of World Business*, Summer 1985, Balaji S. Chakravarthy and Howard V. Perlmutter. "Strategic Planning for a Global Business," p. 506. Copyright © 1985 with permission from Elsevier.

AT THE START OF GLOBALIZATION

External and internal assessments are conducted before a firm enters global markets. For example, Japanese investors conduct extensive assessments and analyses before selecting a U.S. site for a Japanese-owned firm. They prefer states with strong markets, low unionization rates, and low taxes. In addition, Japanese manufacturing plants prefer counties characterized by manufacturing conglomeration; low unemployment and poverty rates; and concentrations of educated, productive workers.

External assessment involves careful examination of critical features of the global environment, particular attention being paid to the status of the host nations in such areas as economic progress, political control, and nationalism. Expansion of industrial facilities, favorable balances of payments, and improvements in technological capabilities over the past decade are gauges of the host nation's economic progress. Political status can be gauged by the host nation's power in and impact on global affairs.

Internal assessment involves identification of the basic strengths of a firm's operations. These strengths are particularly important in global operations, because they are often the characteristics of a firm that the host nation values most and, thus, offer significant

Global Strategy in Action

Exhibit 5.5

Checklist of Factors to Consider in Choosing a Foreign Manufacturing Site

The following considerations were drawn from an 88-point checklist developed by Business International Corporation.

Economic Factors:
1. Size of GNP and projected rate of growth
2. Foreign exchange position
3. Size of market for the firm's products; rate of growth

Political Factors:
4. Form and stability of government
5. Attitude toward private and foreign investment by government, customers, and competition
6. Degree of antiforeign discrimination

Geographic Factors:
7. Proximity of site to export markets
8. Availability of local raw materials
9. Availability of power, water, gas

Labor Factors:
10. Availability of managerial, technical, and office personnel able to speak the language of the parent company
11. Degree of skill and discipline at all levels
12. Degree and nature of labor voice in management

Tax Factors:
13. Tax-rate trends
14. Joint tax treaties with home country and others
15. Availability of tariff protection

Capital Source Factors:
16. Cost of local borrowing
17. Modern banking systems
18. Government credit aids to new businesses

Business Factors:
19. State of marketing and distribution system
20. Normal profit margins in the firm's industry
21. Competitive situation in the firm's industry: do cartels exist?

bargaining leverage. The firm's resource strengths and global capabilities must be analyzed. The resources that should be analyzed include, in particular, technical and managerial skills, capital, labor, and raw materials. The global capabilities that should be analyzed include the firm's product delivery and financial management systems.

A firm that gives serious consideration to internal and external assessment is Business International Corporation, which recommends that seven broad categories of factors be considered. As shown in Exhibit 5.5, Global Strategy in Action, these categories include economic, political, geographic, labor, tax, capital source, and business factors.

COMPLEXITY OF THE GLOBAL ENVIRONMENT

By 2003, Coke was finally achieving a goal that it had set a decade earlier when it went to India. That goal was to take the market away from Pepsi and local beverage companies. However, when it arrived, Coke found that the Indian market was extremely complex and smaller than it had estimated. Coke also encountered cultural problems, in part because the chief of Coke India was an expatriate. The key to overcoming this cultural problem was promoting an Indian to operations chief. Coke also changed its marketing strategy by pushing their "Thums Up" products, a local brand owned by Coke. Then, they began to focus their efforts on creating new products for rural areas and lowering the prices of their existing products to increase sales. Once Coke had new products in the market, they focused on a new advertising campaign to better relate to Indian consumers.

A Milestone for Human Rights

BusinessWeek

In the mid-1990s, reports emerged out of Burma that villagers in the remote Yadana region had been forced by the military to clear jungle for the construction of a $1.2 billion natural gas pipeline. The allegations were horrendous: to round up workers for the project, the Burmese military had resorted to torture, rape, and murder to enslave villagers, even throwing one woman's baby in a fire after killing her husband. Before long, U.S. human rights groups had filed suit against Unocal Corp., based in El Segundo, California, one of the four pipeline partners, on behalf of 15 unnamed Burmese villagers.

Now, after years of courtroom sparring, Unocal has quietly agreed to settle the suits, one filed in California state court and another in the U.S. District Court in Los Angeles. Insiders say that Unocal will pay about $30 million in damages to settle the cases. The award will include money for the 15 plaintiffs and for a fund to improve living conditions, health care, and education in the pipeline region.

The settlement may mark a milestone in human rights advocates' struggle to use U.S. courts to force American multinationals to protect their workers against abuse by repressive regimes. The Unocal case "shows that corporations have both direct and indirect human rights responsibilities," says Susan Aaronson, director of globalization studies at the Kennan Institute, a Washington think tank.

Unocal is the first of a series of U.S. multinationals to face allegations that they acquiesced in or benefited from human rights violations, committed mostly by authoritarian governments. Other defendants include ExxonMobil, Coca-Cola, Drummond, Occidental Petroleum, and Del Monte Foods. The companies are all fighting the suits.

Source: Reprinted with special permission from Paul Magnusson, "A Milestone for Human Rights," *BusinessWeek*, January 24, 2005. Copyright © 2005 The McGraw-Hill Companies.

Coke's experience highlights the fact that global strategic planning is more complex than purely domestic planning. There are at least five factors that contribute to this increase in complexity:

1. Globals face multiple political, economic, legal, social, and cultural environments as well as various rates of changes within each of them. Occasionally, foreign governments work in concert with their militaries to advance economic aims even at the expense of human rights. International firms must resist the temptation to benefit financially from such immoral opportunities. Specifics of just one abusive situation are presented in Exhibit 5.6, Strategy in Action.

2. Interactions between the national and foreign environments are complex, because of national sovereignty issues and widely differing economic and social conditions.

3. Geographic separation, cultural and national differences, and variations in business practices all tend to make communication and control efforts between headquarters and the overseas affiliates difficult.

4. Globals face extreme competition, because of differences in industry structures within countries.

5. Globals are restricted in their selection of competitive strategies by various regional blocs and economic integrations, such as the European Economic Community, the European Free Trade Area, and the Latin American Free Trade Area.

CONTROL PROBLEMS OF THE GLOBAL FIRM

An inherent complicating factor for many global firms is that their financial policies typically are designed to further the goals of the parent company and pay minimal attention to

Top Strategist
Francisco D'Souza, CEO of Cognizant Technology Solutions

Exhibit
5.7

Even in the fast-growing outsourcing industry, Cognizant is a standout. Propelled by the increased outsourcing of health care data processing and by a growing number of European clients, Cognizant's 2006 sales jumped 61 percent. Its bread and butter, though, remains managing financial and information-tech services for U.S. clients; companies such as Wells Fargo, Citigroup, and Aetna account for 86 percent of its sales. To keep growth humming, CEO Francisco D'Souza plans to hew to the company's policy of investing aggressively in operations and staff, adding 16,000 workers, mostly in India and China. And he plans to spend $200 million on more office space and infrastructure in India, where Cognizant has 70 percent of its operations. The outlay comes at the cost of margins lower than Indian rivals Wipro and Infosys Technologies, but so far these bets have paid off in growth.

Source: Reprinted with special permission from The *BusinessWeek* 50—The Best Performers, *BusinessWeek*, March 26, 2007. Copyright © 2007 The McGraw-Hill Companies.

the goals of the host countries. This built-in bias creates conflict between the different parts of the global firm, between the whole firm and its home and host countries, and between the home country and host country themselves. The conflict is accentuated by the use of various schemes to shift earnings from one country to another in order to avoid taxes, minimize risk, or achieve other objectives.

Moreover, different financial environments make normal standards of company behavior concerning the disposition of earnings, sources of finance, and the structure of capital more problematic. Thus, it becomes increasingly difficult to measure the performance of international divisions.

In addition, important differences in measurement and control systems often exist. Fundamental to the concept of planning is a well-conceived, future-oriented approach to decision making that is based on accepted procedures and methods of analysis. Consistent approaches to planning throughout a firm are needed for effective review and evaluation by corporate headquarters. In the global firm, planning is complicated by differences in national attitudes toward work measurement, and by differences in government requirements about disclosure of information.

Although such problems are an aspect of the global environment, rather than a consequence of poor management, they are often most effectively reduced through increased attention to strategic planning. Such planning will aid in coordinating and integrating the firm's direction, objectives, and policies around the world. It enables the firm to anticipate and prepare for change. It facilitates the creation of programs to deal with worldwide development. Finally, it helps the management of overseas affiliates become more actively involved in setting goals and in developing means to more effectively utilize the firm's total resources. A strategic manager who shares this view is Francisco D'Souza, the CEO of Cognizant Technology Solutions. Some of his company's recent global strategic initiatives are discussed in Exhibit 5.7, Top Strategist.

An example of the need for coordination in global ventures and evidence that firms can successfully plan for global collaboration (e.g., through rationalized production) is the Ford Escort (Europe), the best-selling automobile in the world, which has a component manufacturing network that consists of plants in 15 countries.

GLOBAL STRATEGIC PLANNING

It should be evident from the previous sections that the strategic decisions of a firm competing in the global marketplace become increasingly complex. In such a firm, managers cannot view global operations as a set of independent decisions. These managers are faced with trade-off decisions in which multiple products, country environments, resource sourcing options, corporate and subsidiary capabilities, and strategic options must be considered.

A recent trend toward increased activism of stakeholders has added to the complexity of strategic planning for the global firm. **Stakeholder activism** refers to demands placed on the global firm by the foreign environments in which it operates, principally by foreign governments. This section provides a basic framework for the analysis of strategic decisions in this complex setting.

stakeholder activism
Demands placed on a global firm by the stakeholders in the environments in which it operates.

Multidomestic Industries and Global Industries
Multidomestic Industries
International industries can be ranked along a continuum that ranges from multidomestic to global.

multidomestic industry
An industry in which competition is segmented from country to country.

A **multidomestic industry** is one in which competition is essentially segmented from country to country. Thus, even if global corporations are in the industry, competition in one country is independent of competition in other countries. Examples of such industries include retailing, insurance, and consumer finance.

In a multidomestic industry, a global corporation's subsidiaries should be managed as distinct entities; that is, each subsidiary should be rather autonomous, having the authority to make independent decisions in response to local market conditions. Thus, the global strategy of such an industry is the sum of the strategies developed by subsidiaries operating in different countries. The primary difference between a domestic firm and a global firm competing in a multidomestic industry is that the latter makes decisions related to the countries in which it competes and to how it conducts business abroad.

Factors that increase the degree to which an industry is multidomestic include[1]

- The need for customized products to meet the tastes or preferences of local customers.
- Fragmentation of the industry, with many competitors in each national market.
- A lack of economies of scale in the functional activities of firms in the industry.
- Distribution channels unique to each country.
- A low technological dependence of subsidiaries on R&D provided by the global firm.

An interesting example of a multidomestic strategy is the one designed by Renault-Nissan for the low-cost automobile industry. As described in Exhibit 5.8, Strategy in Action, Renault's strategy involves designing cars to fit the budgets of buyers in different countries, rather than being restricted to the production of cars that meet the safety and emission standards of countries in Western Europe and the United States or by their consumer preferences for technological advancements and stylish appointments.

[1] Y. Doz and C. K. Prahalad, "Patterns of Strategic Control within Multinational Corporations," *Journal of International Business Studies,* Fall 1984, pp. 55–72.

Strategy in Action

The Race to Build Really Cheap Cars

BusinessWeek

How cheap is cheap? Renault-Nissan Chief Executive Carlos Ghosn is betting that for autos, the magic number is under $3,000. At a plant-opening ceremony in India in 2007, he was already talking up the industry's next challenge: a future model that would sport a sticker price as low as $2,500—about 40 percent less than the least expensive subcompact currently on the market.

Renault already has a runaway hit with its bare-bones Logan sedan. The automaker began offering the roomy Logan in Europe for just $7,200 in 2004—some 40 percent less than rival sedans—and has since sold 450,000 of the cars in 51 countries. A $3,000 car for Asian markets, built in low-cost India with a local partner, is the next logical step.

That realization is now dawning on the industry's giants. When Tata made its vow to build a $2,500 car, many Western auto executives ridiculed the project, dubbing it a four-wheel bicycle. They aren't laughing anymore. Tata's model is a real car with four doors, a 33-horsepower engine, and a top speed of around 80 mph. The automaker claims it will even pass a crash test. The key is India's low-cost engineers and their prodigious ability to trim needless spending to the bone, a skill developed by years of selling to the bottom of the pyramid.

By 2012, the market for vehicles priced under $10,000 is likely to reach 18 million cars, or a fifth of world auto sales, according to Roland Berger Strategy Consultants. That's up from 12 million in 2007.

Car manufacturers, of course, have always sought to cut costs and pack more value into each new-model generation to stay competitive. But now, emerging markets like India offer cheap engineering, inexpensive parts-sourcing, and low-cost manufacturing. For its new car, for example, Tata should be able to slash the cost of the engine to about $700, or 50 percent lower than a Western-developed equivalent, says one consultant close to the company.

To make a success of the Logan, Renault manufactured in low-cost Romania. It developed a design that reduced the total number of parts and made assembly a cinch. It stripped out sophisticated electronics, dispensed with high-tech curved windshields, and even saved $3 per vehicle by using identical rear-view mirrors on each side. The biggest breakthrough: Renault was able to eliminate expensive prototypes and the pricey tooling involved in building them, an innovation that saved the French car company $40 million.

The majority of low-cost cars will range from $5,000 to $10,000, depending on size and features. Analysts say adding equipment required for safety and emissions control in Western markets would automatically bring the price of a cheap Chinese or Indian car up to $6,000 to $7,000.

Source: Reprinted with special permission from Gail Edmondson, "The Race to Build Really Cheap Cars," *BusinessWeek*, April 23, 2007. Copyright © 2007 The McGraw-Hill Companies.

Global Industries

global industry
An industry in which competition crosses national borders on a worldwide basis.

A **global industry** is one in which competition crosses national borders. In fact, it occurs on a worldwide basis. In a global industry, a firm's strategic moves in one country can be significantly affected by its competitive position in another country. The very rapidly expanding list of global industries includes commercial aircraft, automobiles, mainframe computers, and electronic consumer equipment. Many authorities are convinced that almost all product-oriented industries soon will be global. As a result, strategic management planning must be global for at least six reasons:

1. *The increased scope of the global management task.* Growth in the size and complexity of global firms made management virtually impossible without a coordinated plan of action detailing what is expected of whom during a given period. The common practice of management by exception is impossible without such a plan.

2. *The increased globalization of firms.* Three aspects of global business make global planning necessary: (*a*) differences among the environmental forces in different countries, (*b*) greater distances, and (*c*) the interrelationships of global operations.

3. *The information explosion.* It has been estimated that the world's stock of knowledge is doubling every 10 years. Without the aid of a formal plan, executives can no longer know all that they must know to solve the complex problems they face. A global planning process provides an ordered means for assembling, analyzing, and distilling the information required for sound decisions.

4. *The increase in global competition.* Because of the rapid increase in global competition, firms must constantly adjust to changing conditions or lose markets to competitors. The increase in global competition also spurs managements to search for methods of increasing efficiency and economy.

5. *The rapid development of technology.* Rapid technological development has shortened product life cycles. Strategic management planning is necessary to ensure the replacement of products that are moving into the maturity stage, with fewer sales and declining profits. Planning gives management greater control of all aspects of new-product introduction.

6. *Strategic management planning breeds managerial confidence.* Like the motorist with a road map, managers with a plan for reaching their objectives know where they are going. Such a plan breeds confidence, because it spells out every step along the way and assigns responsibility for every task. The plan simplifies the managerial job.

A firm in a global industry must maximize its capabilities through a worldwide strategy. Such a strategy necessitates a high degree of centralized decision making in corporate headquarters so as to permit trade-off decisions across subsidiaries.

Among the factors that make for the creation of a global industry are

- Economies of scale in the functional activities of firms in the industry.
- A high level of R&D expenditures on products that require more than one market to recover development costs.
- The presence in the industry of predominantly global firms that expect consistency of products and services across markets.
- The presence of homogeneous product needs across markets, which reduces the requirement of customizing the product for each market. The presence of a small group of global competitors.
- A low level of trade regulation and of regulation regarding foreign direction investment.[2]

Six factors that drive the success of global companies are listed in Exhibit 5.9, Strategy in Action. They address key aspects of globalizing a business's operations and provide a framework within which companies can effectively pursue the global marketplace.

The Global Challenge

Although industries can be characterized as global or multidomestic, few "pure" cases of either type exist. A global firm competing in a global industry must be responsive, to some degree, to local market conditions. Similarly, a global firm competing in a multidomestic industry cannot totally ignore opportunities to utilize intracorporate resources in competitive positioning. Thus, each global firm must decide which of its corporate functional activities should be performed where and what degree of coordination should exist among them.

[2] G. Harveland and C. K. Prahalad, "Managing Strategic Responsibility in the MNC," *Strategic Management Journal,* October–December 1983, pp. 341–51.

Factors That Drive Global Companies

1. Global Management Team

Possesses global vision and culture.

Includes foreign nationals.

Leaves management of subsidiaries to foreign nationals.

Frequently travels internationally.

Has cross-cultural training.

2. Global Strategy

Implement strategy as opposed to independent country strategies.

Develop significant cross-country alliances.

Select country targets strategically rather than opportunistically.

Perform business functions where most efficient—no home-country bias.

Emphasize participation in the triad—North America, Europe, and Japan.

3. Global Operations and Products

Use common core operating processes worldwide to ensure quantity and uniformity.

Product globally to obtain best cost and market advantage.

4. Global Technology and R&D

Design global products but take regional differences into account.

Manage development work centrally but carry out globally.

Do not duplicate R&D and product development; gain economies of scale.

5. Global Financing

Finance globally to obtain lowest cost.

Hedge when necessary to protect currency risk.

Price in local currencies.

List shares on foreign exchanges.

6. Global Marketing

Market global products but provide regional discretion if economies of scale are not affected.

Develop global brands.

Use core global marketing practices and themes.

Simultaneously introduce new global products worldwide.

Source: Reprinted from *Business Horizons*, Volume 37, Robert N. Lussier, Robert W. Baeder and Joel Corman, "Measuring Global Practices: Global Strategic Planning through Company Situational Analysis," p. 57. Copyright © 1994, with permission from Elsevier.

Location and Coordination of Functional Activities

Typical functional activities of a firm include purchases of input resources, operations, research and development, marketing and sales, and after-sales service. A multinational corporation has a wide range of possible location options for each of these activities and must decide which sets of activities will be performed in how many and which locations. A multinational corporation may have each location perform each activity, or it may center an activity in one location to serve the organization worldwide. For example, research and development centered in one facility may serve the entire organization.

A multinational corporation also must determine the degree to which functional activities are to be coordinated across locations. Such coordination can be extremely low, allowing each location to perform each activity autonomously, or extremely high, tightly linking the functional activities of different locations. Coca-Cola tightly links its R&D and marketing functions worldwide to offer a standardized brand name, concentrate formula, market positioning, and advertising theme. However, its operations function is more autonomous, with the artificial sweetener and packaging differing across locations.

Location and Coordination Issues

Exhibit 5.10 presents some of the issues related to the critical dimensions of location and coordination in multinational strategic planning. It also shows the functional activities that

EXHIBIT 5.10
Location and Coordination Issues of Functional Activities

Functional Activity	Location Issues	Coordination Issues
Operations	Location of production facilities for components.	Networking of international plants.
Marketing	Product line selection. Country (market) selection.	Commonality of brand name worldwide. Coordination of sales to multinational accounts. Similarity of channels and product positioning worldwide. Coordination of pricing in different countries
Service	Location of service organization.	Similarity of service standards and procedures worldwide.
Research and development	Number and location of R&D centers.	Interchange among dispersed R&D centers. Developing products responsive to market needs in many countries. Sequence of product introductions around the world.
Purchasing	Location of the purchasing function.	Managing suppliers located in different countries. Transferring market knowledge. Coordinating purchases of common items.

Source: From Michael E. Porter, "Changing Patterns of International Competition," *California Management Review,* Winter 1986. Copyright © 1986, by The Regents of the University of California. Reprinted from the California Management review, Vol. 28, No. 2. By permission of The Regents.

the firm performs with regard to each of these dimensions. For example, in connection with the service function, a firm must decide where to perform after-sale service and whether to standardize such service.

How a particular firm should address location and coordination issues depends on the nature of its industry and on the type of international strategy that the firm is pursuing. As discussed earlier, an industry can be ranked along a continuum that ranges between multidomestic at one extreme and global at the other. Little coordination of functional activities across countries may be necessary in a multidomestic industry, since competition occurs within each country in such an industry. However, as its industry becomes increasingly global, a firm must begin to coordinate an increasing number of functional activities to effectively compete across countries.

Going global impacts every aspect of a company's operations and structure. As firms redefine themselves as global competitors, workforces are becoming increasingly diversified. The most significant challenge for firms, therefore, is the ability to adjust to a workforce of varied cultures and lifestyles and the capacity to incorporate cultural differences to the benefit of the company's mission.

Market Requirements and Product Characteristics

Businesses have discovered that being successful in foreign markets often demands much more than simply shipping their well-received domestic products overseas. Firms must

Rate of Change of Product

Fast

Maintain differentiation	**Operate an ever-changing "global warehouse"**	
Computer chips	Consumer	Watch cases
Automotive electronics	electronics	Dolls
Color film	Automobiles	
Pharmaceutical	Trucks	
Chemicals		
Telecommunications		
Network equipment	Toothpaste	Industrial
	Shampoo	machinery

Standardized in All Markets ——————————————— **Customized Market-by-Market**

Minimize Delivered Cost	**Practice**	Toilets
Steel	**Opportunistic**	Chocolate
Petrochemicals (e.g.,	**Niche**	bars
polyethylene)	**Exploration**	
Cola beverages		
Fabric for		
men's shirts		

Slow

Source: Lawrence H. Wortzel, *1989 International Business Book* (Strategic Direction Publishers, 1989).

assess two key dimensions of customer demand: customers' acceptance of standardized products and the rate of product innovation desired. As shown in Exhibit 5.11, Global Strategy in Action, all markets can be arrayed along a continuum from markets in which products are standardized to markets in which products must be customized for customers from market to market. Standardized products in all markets include color film and petrochemicals, while dolls and toilets are good examples of customized products.

Similarly, products can be arrayed along a continuum from products that are not subject to frequent product innovations to products that are often upgraded. Products with a fast rate of change include computer chips and industrial machinery, while steel and chocolate bars are products that fit in the slow rate of change category.

Exhibit 5.11 shows that the two dimensions can be combined to enable companies to simultaneously assess both customer need for product standardization and rate of product innovation. The examples listed demonstrate the usefulness of the model in helping firms to determine the degree of customization that they must be willing to accept to become engaged in transnational operations.

International Strategy Options

Exhibit 5.12, Global Strategy in Action, presents the basic multinational strategy options that have been derived from a consideration of the location and coordination dimensions. Low coordination and geographic dispersion of functional activities are implied if a firm is operating in a multidomestic industry and has chosen a country-centered strategy. This allows each subsidiary to closely monitor the local market conditions it faces and to respond freely to these conditions.

High coordination and geographic concentration of functional activities result from the choice of a pure global strategy. Although some functional activities, such as after-sale

		Geographically Dispersed	Geographically Concentrated
Coordination of Activities	**High**	High foreign investment with extensive coordination among subsidiaries	Global strategy
	Low	Country-centered strategy by multinationals with a number of domestic firms operating in only one country	Export-based strategy with decentralized marketing

Location of Activities

Source: From Michael E. Porter, "Changing Patterns of International Competition," *California Management Review,* Winter 1986. Copyright © 1986, by The Regents of the University of California. Reprinted from the *California Management Review,* Vol. 28, No. 2. By permission of The Regents.

service, may need to be located in each market, tight control of those activities is necessary to ensure standardized performance worldwide. For example, IBM expects the same high level of marketing support and service for all of its customers, regardless of their location.

Two other strategy options are shown in Exhibit 5.12. High foreign investment with extensive coordination among subsidiaries would describe the choice of remaining at a particular growth stage, such as that of an exporter. An export-based strategy with decentralized marketing would describe the choice of moving toward globalization, which a multinational firm might make.

COMPETITIVE STRATEGIES FOR FIRMS IN FOREIGN MARKETS

Strategies for firms that are attempting to move toward globalization can be categorized by the degree of complexity of each foreign market being considered and by the diversity in a company's product line (see Exhibit 5.13, Global Strategy in Action). *Complexity* refers to the number of critical success factors that are required to prosper in a given competitive arena. When a firm must consider many such factors, the requirements of success increase in complexity. *Diversity,* the second variable, refers to the breadth of a firm's business lines. When a company offers many product lines, diversity is high.

Together, the complexity and diversity dimensions form a continuum of possible strategic choices. Combining these two dimensions highlights many possible actions.

Niche Market Exporting

The primary niche market approach for the company that wants to export is to modify select product performance or measurement characteristics to meet special foreign demands.

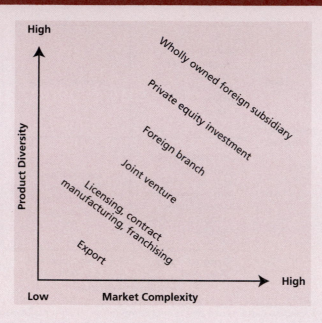

Combining product criteria from both the U.S. and the foreign markets can be slow and tedious. There are, however, a number of expansion techniques that provide the U.S. firm with the know-how to exploit opportunities in the new environment. For example, copying product innovations in countries where patent protection is not emphasized and utilizing nonequity contractual arrangements with a foreign partner can assist in rapid product innovation. N. V. Philips and various Japanese competitors, such as Sony and Matsushita, now are working together for common global product standards within their markets. Siemens, with a centralized R&D in electronics, also has been very successful with this approach.

The Taiwanese company, Gigabyte, researched the U.S. market and found that a sizable number of computer buyers wanted a PC that could complete the basic tasks provided by domestic desktops, but that would be considerably smaller. Gigabyte decided to serve this niche market by exporting their mini-PCs into the United States with a price tag of $200 to $300. This price was considerably less than the closest U.S. manufacturer, Dell, whose minicomputer was still larger and cost $766.

Exporting usually requires minimal capital investment. The organization maintains its quality control standards over production processes and finished goods inventory, and risk to the survival of the firm is typically minimal. Additionally, the U.S. Commerce Department through its Export Now Program and related government agencies lowers the risks to smaller companies by providing export information and marketing advice.

Licensing and Contract Manufacturing

Establishing a contractual arrangement is the next step for U.S. companies that want to venture beyond exporting but are not ready for an equity position on foreign soil. Licensing involves the transfer of some industrial property right from the U.S. licensor to a motivated licensee. Most tend to be patents, trademarks, or technical know-how that are granted to the licensee for a specified time in return for a royalty and for avoiding tariffs or import quotas. Bell South and U.S. West, with various marketing and service competitive advantages valuable to Europe, have extended a number of licenses to create personal computer networks in the United Kingdom.

Another licensing strategy open to U.S. firms is to contract the manufacturing of its product line to a foreign company to exploit local comparative advantages in technology, materials, or labor.

U.S. firms that use either licensing option will benefit from lowering the risk of entry into the foreign markets. Clearly, alliances of this type are not for everyone. They are used best in companies large enough to have a combination of international strategic activities and for firms with standardized products in narrow margin industries.

Two major problems exist with licensing. One is the possibility that the foreign partner will gain the experience and evolve into a major competitor after the contract expires. The experience of some U.S. electronics firms with Japanese companies shows that licensees gain the potential to become powerful rivals. The other potential problem stems from the control that the licensor forfeits on production, marketing, and general distribution of its products. This loss of control minimizes a company's degrees of freedom as it reevaluates its future options.

Franchising

A special form of licensing is franchising, which allows the franchisee to sell a highly publicized product or service, using the parent's brand name or trademark, carefully developed procedures, and marketing strategies. In exchange, the franchisee pays a fee to the parent company, typically based on the volume of sales of the franchisor in its defined market area. The franchise is operated by the local investor who must adhere to the strict policies of the parent.

Franchising is so popular that an estimated 500 U.S. businesses now franchise to over 50,000 local owners in foreign countries. Among the most active franchisees are Avis, Burger King, Canada Dry, Coca-Cola, Hilton, Kentucky Fried Chicken, Manpower, Marriott, Midas, Muzak, Pepsi, and ServiceMaster. However, the acknowledged global champion of franchising is McDonald's, which has 70 percent of its company-owned stores as franchisees in foreign nations.

Joint Ventures

As the multinational strategies of U.S. firms mature, most will include some form of joint venture (JV) with a target nation firm. AT&T followed this option in its strategy to produce its own personal computer by entering into several joint ventures with European producers to acquire the required technology and position itself for European expansion. Because JVs begin with a mutually agreeable pooling of capital, production or marketing equipment, patents, trademarks, or management expertise, they offer more permanent cooperative relationships than export or contract manufacturing.

Compared with full ownership of the foreign entity, JVs provide a variety of benefits to each partner. U.S. firms without the managerial or financial assets to make a profitable independent impact on the integrated foreign markets can share management tasks and cash requirements often at exchange rates that favor the dollar. The coordination of manufacturing and marketing allows ready access to new markets, intelligence data, and reciprocal flows of technical information.

For example, Siemens, the German electronics firm, has a wide range of strategic alliances throughout Europe to share technology and research developments. For years, Siemens grew by acquisitions, but now, to support its horizontal expansion objectives,

Wrapping the Globe in Tortillas

BusinessWeek

Tortillas are a hot topic in Mexico these days. Since December 2006, prices for the staple disks of corn have shot up 67 percent, spurring the government to impose price controls on both finished tortillas and the flour used to make them. In theory, that should be devastating for a company such as Gruma, Mexico's leading flour producer. But that's not so. While Gruma's earnings in Mexico will likely take a hit due to the controls, it is the world's no. 1 tortilla maker, and more than two-thirds of its $3 billion-plus in sales this year will come from outside its home country.

That's because Gruma has spent years building a global market for its quintessentially Mexican comestibles. In September 2006, Gruma opened a new factory in Shanghai that will churn out tens of millions of tortillas annually for KFC restaurants and other customers in China. All told, the company now produces tortillas and chips in 89 factories from Australia to Britain.

But Gruma's global expansion is now speeding up, thanks to CEO Jairo Senise. After getting the top job last year, he took a month-long trip with stops in cities from Manila to Moscow, sampling food in local markets with an eye toward producing tortillas that might fit the local fare. "We're able to think globally but respect the tastes and preferences of each country where we operate," Senise says.

The Shanghai plant is a key part of Gruma's global expansion. The company built the facility at the request of KFC, which had been importing frozen Gruma tortillas from California for the chicken wrap sandwiches it offers in more than 1,800 restaurants in China.

The company's international operations seem to be running more smoothly than those at home. That's because of the price controls, which the government introduced on January 18, 2007, after the cost of imported corn soared. Gruma, which supplies 75 percent of Mexico's corn flour for tortillas, had to agree to keep a lid on its prices. As a result, Merrill Lynch & Co. predicts Gruma will earn $111 million on $3.1 billion in sales in 2007, versus estimated profits of $145 million and revenues of $2.85 billion in 2006.

Senise is now eyeing opportunities in South Africa, Morocco, Egypt, and India. And he'd like to move into industrial tortilla production at home, where mom-and-pop tortillerias dominate the market and Gruma mainly sells flour. That could be tough. Today, Gruma makes tortillas only in a few cities, and Mexico's anti-monopoly watchdog may not allow it to expand.

Source: Reprinted with special permission from Geri Smith, "Wrapping the Globe in Tortillas," *BusinessWeek*, February 26, 2007. Copyright © 2007 The McGraw-Hill Companies.

it is engaged in joint ventures with companies like Groupe Bull of France, International Computers of Britain, General Electric Company of Britain, IBM, Intel, Philips, and Rolm. Another example is Airbus Industries, which produces wide-body passenger planes for the world market as a direct result of JVs among many companies in Britain, France, Spain, and Germany.

JVs speed up the efforts of U.S. firms to integrate into the political, corporate, and cultural infrastructure of the foreign environment, often with a lower financial commitment than acquiring a foreign subsidiary. General Electric's (GE) 3 percent share in the European lighting market was very weak and below expectations. Significant increases in competition throughout many of their American markets by the European giant, Philips Lighting, forced GE to retaliate by expanding in Europe. GE's first strategy was an attempted joint venture with the Siemens lighting subsidiary, Osram, and with the British electronics firm, Thorn EMI. Negotiations failed over control issues. When recent events in Eastern Europe opened the opportunity for a JV with the Hungarian lighting manufacturer, Tungsram, which was receiving 70 percent of revenues from the West, GE capitalized on it.

Although joint ventures can address many of the requirements of complex markets and diverse product lines, U.S. firms considering either equity- or non-equity-based JVs face many challenges. For example, making full use of the native firm's comparative advantage

Russians Have Driven a Ford Lately

BusinessWeek

In 2006, New York Motors, on a commercial strip in southwest Moscow, sold more Fords than any other dealership in the world. All told, salesmen in the crowded showroom moved 10,060 vehicles, helping Ford race past rivals Hyundai, Toyota, and Chevrolet to become the top-selling auto nameplate in Russia.

The brand's success in Russia stands in striking contrast to Ford Motor Co.'s flagging fortunes elsewhere. The automaker clocked a global loss of $12.7 billion in 2006, but sales of Ford-branded vehicles in Russia soared 92 percent, to 115,985 cars and trucks, for some $2 billion in revenues. That's partly due to Russia's thriving economy, which has stoked strong demand for foreign models. In 2006, foreign brands outsold domestic nameplates for the first time, topping 1 million—a 65 percent increase from 2005 and 20 times the level in 2000, according to the Association of European Businesses in Moscow.

In 1999, Ford made a big bet on Russia, spending $150 million on a plant near St. Petersburg—the country's first foreign-owned auto factory. The facility opened in 2002, and in 2006 production climbed to 62,400 Focus sedans, hatchbacks, and wagons.

Competition is heating up as rivals copy Ford's strategy of local production. Volkswagen, Toyota, Nissan, GM, and Fiat have all announced plans to build plants in Russia.

Still, local production has helped Ford keep prices down. Although about 80 percent of the parts used in the Focus are imported, the company sells the cars for as little as $13,000, or about $3,000 less than similarly equipped imports, which are subject to a 25 percent duty. While that's not exactly pocket change in Russia, it's low enough for a growing number of middle-class consumers. Sure, the cheapest Focus is nearly $4,000 more than a Russian-made Lada or low-cost foreign cars such as the Renault Logan and Daewoo Nexia.

Source: Reprinted with special permission from Jason Bush, "They've Driven a Ford Lately: Russians Are Snapping Up Its Locally Made Models in Record Numbers," *BusinessWeek*, February 26, 2007. Copyright © 2007 The McGraw-Hill Companies.

may involve managerial relationships where no single authority exists to make strategic decisions or solve conflicts. Additionally, dealing with host-company management requires the disclosure of proprietary information and the potential loss of control over production and marketing quality standards. Addressing such challenges with well-defined covenants agreeable to all parties is difficult. Equally important is the compatibility of partners and their enduring commitments to mutually supportive goals. Without this compatibility and commitment, a joint venture is critically endangered.

Foreign Branching

A foreign branch is an extension of the company in its foreign market—a separately located strategic business unit directly responsible for fulfilling the operational duties assigned to it by corporate management, including sales, customer service, and physical distribution. Host countries may require that the branch be "domesticated," that is, have some local managers in middle and upper-level positions. The branch most likely will be outside any U.S. legal jurisdiction, liabilities may not be restricted to the assets of the given branch, and business licenses for operations may be of short duration, requiring the company to renew them during changing business regulations. Gruma, Mexico's leading flour producer and the world's leading tortillas manufacturer has manufacturing branches in 89 foreign countries. The story of Gruma's success is presented in Exhibit 5.14, Strategy in Action.

Equity Investment

Small and medium-size enterprises with strong growth potential frequently have the need for additional funds to be able to grow further before deciding to trade their stock publicly

private equity
Money from private
sources that is invested
by a venture capital or
private equity company
in start-ups and other
risky—but potentially
very profitable—small
and medium-size
enterprises.

in the marketplace. These firms often enlist the support of a venture capital firm or **private equity** company that invests its shareholders' money in start-ups and other risky but potentially very profitable small and medium-size enterprises. In exchange for a private equity stake, which is sometimes a majority or controlling position, the Venture Capital (VC) or private equity company provides investment capital and a range of business services, including management expertise.

Wholly Owned Subsidiaries

Wholly owned foreign subsidiaries are considered by companies that are willing and able to make the highest investment commitment to the foreign market. These companies insist on full ownership for reasons of control and managerial efficiency. Policy decisions about local product lines, expansion, profits, and dividends typically remain with the U.S. senior managers. An excellent example of a wholly owned subsidiary is the manufacturing and sales organization of Ford Motor in Russia, as described in Exhibit 5.15, Strategy in Action.

Fully owned subsidiaries can be started either from scratch or by acquiring established firms in the host country. U.S. firms can benefit significantly if the acquired company has complementary product lines or an established distribution or service network.

U.S. firms seeking to improve their competitive postures through a foreign subsidiary face a number of risks to their normal mode of operations. First, if the high capital investment is to be rewarded, managers must attain extensive knowledge of the market, the host nation's language, and its business culture. Second, the host country expects both a long-term commitment from the U.S. enterprise and a portion of their nationals to be employed in positions of management or operations. Fortunately, hiring or training foreign managers for leadership positions is commonly a good policy, because they are close to both the market and contacts. This is especially important for smaller firms when markets are regional. Third, changing standards mandated by foreign regulations may eliminate a company's protected market niche. Product design and worker protection liabilities also may extend back to the home office.

The strategies shown in Exhibit 5.13 are not exhaustive. For example, a firm may engage in any number of joint ventures while maintaining an export business. Additionally, there are a number of other strategies that a firm should consider before deciding on its long-term approach to foreign markets. These will be discussed in detail in Chapter 6 under the topic of grand strategies. However, the strategies discussed in this chapter provide the most popular starting points for planning the globalization of a firm.

Summary

To understand the strategic planning options available to a corporation, its managers need to recognize that different types of industry-based competition exist. Specifically, they must identify the position of their industry along the global versus multidomestic continuum and then consider the implications of that position for their firm.

The differences between global and multidomestic industries about the location and coordination of functional corporate activities necessitate differences in strategic emphasis. As an industry becomes global, managers of firms within that industry must increase the coordination and concentration of functional activities.

The Appendix at the end of this chapter lists many components of the environment with which global corporations must contend. This list is useful in understanding the issues that confront global corporations and in evaluating the thoroughness of global corporation strategies.

As a starting point for global expansion, the firm's mission statement needs to be reviewed and revised. As global operations fundamentally alter the direction and strategic capabilities of a firm, its mission statement, if originally developed from a domestic perspective, must be globalized.

The globalized mission statement provides the firm with a unity of direction that transcends the divergent perspectives of geographically dispersed managers. It provides a basis for strategic decisions in situations where strategic alternatives may appear to conflict. It promotes corporate values and commitments that extend beyond single cultures and satisfies the demands of the firm's internal and external claimants in different countries. Finally, it ensures the survival of the global corporation by asserting the global corporation's legitimacy with respect to support coalitions in a variety of operating environments.

Movement of a firm toward globalization often follows a systematic pattern of development. Commonly, businesses begin their foreign nation involvements progressively through niche market exporting, license-contract manufacturing, franchising, joint ventures, foreign branching, and foreign subsidiaries.

Key Terms

ethnocentric orientation, *p. 133*
geocentric orientation, *p. 133*
global industry, *p. 140*

globalization, *p. 130*
multidomestic industry, *p. 139*
polycentric orientation, *p. 133*

private equity, *p. 150*
regiocentric orientation, *p. 133*
stakeholder activism, *p. 139*

Questions for Discussion

1. How does environmental analysis at the domestic level differ from global analysis?
2. Which factors complicate environmental analysis at the global level? Which factors are making such analysis easier?
3. Do you agree with the suggestion that soon all industries will need to evaluate global environments?
4. Which industries operate almost devoid of global competition? Which inherent immunities do they enjoy?
5. Explain when and why it is important for a company to globalize.
6. Describe the four main strategic orientations of global firms.
7. Explain the control problems that are faced by global firms.
8. Describe the differences between multinational and global firms.
9. Describe the market requirements and product characteristics in global competition.
10. Evaluate the competitive strategies for firms in foreign markets:
    a. Niche market exporting
    b. Licensing and contract manufacturing
    c. Franchising
    d. Joint ventures
    e. Foreign branching
    f. Private equity investment
    g. Wholly owned subsidiaries

Chapter 5 Discussion Case

China Mobile's Hot Signal

BusinessWeek

1 Dagoucun feels like the kind of place that progress missed entirely in its sweep through China. Nestled at 10,000 feet in the pine-studded foothills of the Tibetan plateau, the village is little more than a few dozen stone houses and a Buddhist shrine. Getting there from the nearest big city, Chengdu, takes five hours by car, much of it on a muddy, rutted road.

2 But given the electronic trills emanating from the fields of barley, potatoes, and corn, it's clear that the twenty-first century has finally made it to Dagoucun. Last year, the village got cell-phone service, dramatically transforming the way its residents live and work. With better information about crop prices delivered to their phones, farmers have started planting more marketable crops such as Chinese cabbage and herbs for traditional medicines. And they no longer have to truck their produce to distant cities in hopes of finding buyers. "Before, we had to travel 20 kilometers to make a phone call," says village chief Xie Sufang, a 65-year-old mother of seven. "Now we contact the buyers, and they come to us."

3 The company responsible for bringing change to this rural outpost: China Mobile Ltd. Since it was spun off from fixed-line operator China Telecom Corp. in 2000, China Mobile has grown into the world's biggest cellular carrier. The company is signing up nearly 5 million new customers a month and recently topped the 300 million mark—more than the entire population of the United States. In 2006, revenues grew 21 percent, to $37.8 billion, and net income 23 percent, to $8.7 billion, estimates Deutsche Bank. And its Hong Kong–traded shares more than doubled in the past year, giving China Mobile a market capitalization of $198 billion and making it the most valuable cellular carrier on earth. The company also has global ambitions: on January 22, 2007, it announced it was buying 89 percent of Paktel Ltd., Pakistan's fifth-largest cellular carrier.

4 China Mobile built its early success on urban China. Problem is, just about everyone in mainland cities who can afford cellular service already has it. Mobile-phone penetration in Beijing, Shanghai, and Shenzhen is approaching 100 percent. So to keep growing, China Mobile is plunging ever deeper into the interior, building cell towers from the deserts of Inner Mongolia to the mountains of Tibet. In rural China, home to 700 million, just over 1 in 10 people has a cell phone. "It is a market with huge potential," says China Mobile Chairman Wang Jianzhou.

5 China Mobile's torrid growth hasn't escaped the attention of Western companies seeking to tap the potential of China, both urban and rural. The carrier has inked agreements with Vodafone Group, News Corp., Viacom's MTV Networks, and the National Basketball Association. Last summer, China Mobile launched a music-download service called M.Music in partnership with Sony bmg, Universal Music Group, emi,

and Warner Music. And on January, 4, 2007, Google Inc. announced that its search engine would be featured on China Mobile's Monternet mobile phone portal.

6 What's behind the flurry of deals? "We want to make the cell phone into a new medium," says Wang. The company is aggressively pushing extras such as ringtones and music downloads. Demand for such services is expected to surge with the launch of third-generation (3G) mobile technology in time for the Beijing Olympics in 2008. Beijing telecom consultancy BDA China estimates revenues from such services will jump from $10.4 billion last year to $28.6 billion by 2010. Wang believes his company's continued dominance of China's cell-phone market will depend on the news, entertainment, and music it can beam to subscribers. So in June, China Mobile plunked down $166 million for a 19.9 percent stake in Phoenix Satellite Television Holdings, the mainland's most popular cable news and entertainment channel.

7 China Mobile is also turning its sights overseas. Its $284 million purchase of Paktel, likely to conclude in late February, 2007, will be the company's first overseas acquisition, though early last year it bought Hong Kong's No. 4 mobile company, People's Telephone, with 1.1 million subscribers. Last summer, China Mobile made a $5 billion-plus play for Luxembourg's Millicom International Cellular—Paktel's parent—which has mobile networks in Africa and Latin America as well as Asia. But negotiations broke down due to concerns about the big price tag, analysts say. While Wang declined to comment on the collapse of the Millicom talks, he says China Mobile is interested in acquisitions in other developing countries: "We are familiar with emerging markets. Their experiences may be very similar to ours."

8 Wang has plenty to keep him busy at home as the government turns up the competitive heat on the cell-phone industry. Until now, China Mobile has had to contend with just one rival: China Unicom Ltd. Like China Mobile, Unicom is listed in Hong Kong and is state-controlled. With 143 million subscribers, though, Unicom is a distant no. 2, which some attribute to the complications it faces in maintaining a network that uses two mobile standards. China Mobile, by contrast, can operate more efficiently using a single technology, the gsm standard developed in Europe. Sometime this year, Beijing is expected to award 3G licenses to both current carriers and also possibly to two new rivals, most likely China's state-owned fixed-line operators, China Netcom Group and China Telecom.

PROFIT PUSH

9 China's leadership could complicate life for Wang & Co. in other ways, too. In an effort to boost its international prestige,

Beijing is pushing the development of a homegrown 3G standard not used elsewhere. China Mobile, China Netcom, and China Telecom are all currently running trials of the new technology. But analysts expect China Mobile to win the dubious honor of leading the rollout, which could be a costly distraction that will almost certainly be more complex than introducing one of the 3G standards already deployed in other countries. Being forced to build a network using China's technology "definitely is a liability," says Zhang Dongming, director of research at consultancy BDA.

10 Even with a smooth rollout of 3G, China Mobile could have a tough time keeping revenue and earnings growing at double-digit rates. As it pushes ever deeper into the interior, the company faces the same dilemma as the likes of Procter & Gamble Co. and General Motors Corp.: how to win new customers without sacrificing profit margins. Incomes in rural China average just over $400 per year, or less than one-third what city dwellers earn. To drum up business in places such as Dagoucun, China Mobile is cutting prices, and the amount of money it gets from each subscriber has declined modestly in the past year, to about $11. "The key is to maintain profitability even while penetrating rural areas," says Steve Zhang, CEO of Beijing's AsiaInfo Holdings Inc., a telecom software and services company that works with China Mobile.

11 Wang insists he's not jeopardizing earnings. One reason, he says, is that China Mobile runs a much leaner operation in the countryside. It has largely dispensed with stores and is instead relying on village chiefs such as Xie to persuade neighbors to buy handsets and prepaid cards. China Mobile offers cell-phone plans tailored for farmers that include information such as crop prices and tips on duck breeding delivered via text message, the Internet, and a call-in phone service. The plan costs a nominal 25 cents a month, but users must pay extra to place calls and send text messages. Since its launch in October, 2006, the service has been rolled out to 12 provinces in western China and is expected to go nationwide later this year. "Our main purpose now is to provide farmers with information that benefits them," says Qin Dabin, vice general manager of China Mobile's operations in the western city of Chongqing. Although it will take some time before the initiative turns a profit, Qin says it's helping to attract subscribers.

12 China Mobile isn't abandoning cities, either. Far from it. The company has an upscale service called Go-Tone for businesspeople. The $6.40 basic monthly fee (phone and message charges are extra) includes reduced membership rates at golf courses and access to VIP waiting rooms at many Chinese airports. And a $2-a-month plan called M-Zone is aimed at music-mad teenagers and twentysomethings. China Mobile puts on special events for M-Zone members, such as appearances by the likes of Chinese-American pop star Pan Weibo.

13 Meanwhile, back in the mountains of Sichuan, villagers are figuring out more ways to wring money from their new phones. Cabbages from Dagoucun now travel all the way to the southern cities of Guangzhou and Shenzhen as it's easier to reach buyers across the country. Villagers have sold a rare caterpillar fungus—prized in Asia for its antiviral attributes—to customers in Singapore who were contacted via cell phone. And residents are building a three-story lodge for mountain climbers and anglers in a bid to transform their remote village into a flourishing center for ecotourism. "With our mobile phones, potential tourists can contact us and learn more about our village," says village chief Xie. "We can increase our incomes in many ways."

Telecom Titans: The World's Biggest Cellular Companies

Operator	Subscriber Accounts (millions)	Average Revenue per User
China Mobile	300	$11.19
China Unicom	143	6.80
Cingular	60	49.76
Verizon Wireless	59	50.59
Sprint USA	54	52.25

Source: Reprinted with special permission from Dexter Roberts, "China Mobile's Hot Signal: It's Already the World's Biggest Cellular Carrier. Now It's Planning to Get Even Bigger," *BusinessWeek*, February 2007. Copyright © 2007 The McGraw-Hill Companies.

DISCUSSION QUESTIONS

1. How do you believe that the mobile phone industry in China differs form the one in the United States?
2. Do you think that the investment opportunity in China's mobile phone industry is attractive?
3. What difficulties do you expect China's mobile phone industry to encounter as it tries to expand?
4. Can you detect any patterns or rules of development from the China mobile phone industry that could be applied to the development of the mobile phone industry in other countries?
5. Do you agree that "globalization is the strategy of approaching worldwide markets with standardized products?" Are mobile phones an example?

Chapter 5 Appendix

Components of the Multinational Environment

Multinational firms must operate within an environment that has numerous components. These components include the following:

1. Government, laws, regulations, and policies of home country (United States, for example)
   a. Monetary and fiscal policies and their effect on price trends, interest rates, economic growth, and stability
   b. Balance-of-payments policies
   c. Mandatory controls on direct investment
   d. Interest equalization tax and other policies
   e. Commercial policies, especially tariffs, quantitative import restrictions, and voluntary import controls
   f. Export controls and other restrictions on trade
   g. Tax policies and their impact on overseas business
   h. Antitrust regulations, their administration, and their impact on international business
   i. Investment guarantees, investment surveys, and other programs to encourage private investments in less-developed countries
   j. Export-import and government export expansion programs
   k. Other changes in government policy that affect international business

2. Key political and legal parameters in foreign countries and their projection
   a. Type of political and economic system, political philosophy, national ideology
   b. Major political parties, their philosophies, and their policies
   c. Stability of the government
      (1) Changes in political parties
      (2) Changes in governments
   d. Assessment of nationalism and its possible impact on political environment and legislation
   e. Assessment of political vulnerability
      (1) Possibilities of expropriation
      (2) Unfavorable and discriminatory national legislation and tax laws
      (3) Labor laws and problems
   f. Favorable political aspects
      (1) Tax and other concessions to encourage foreign investments
      (2) Credit and other guarantees
   g. Differences in legal system and commercial law
   h. Jurisdiction in legal disputes
   i. Antitrust laws and rules of competition
   j. Arbitration clauses and their enforcement
   k. Protection of patents, trademarks, brand names, and other industrial property rights

3. Key economic parameters and their projection
   a. Population and its distribution by age groups, density, annual percentage increase, percentage of working age, percentage of total in agriculture, and percentage in urban centers
   b. Level of economic development and industrialization
   c. Gross national product, gross domestic product, or national income in real terms and also on a per capita basis in recent years and projections over future planning period
   d. Distribution of personal income
   e. Measures of price stability and inflation, wholesale price index, consumer price index, other price indexes
   f. Supply of labor, wage rates
   g. Balance-of-payments equilibrium or disequilibrium, level of international monetary reserves, and balance-of-payments policies
   h. Trends in exchange rates, currency stability, evaluation of possibility of depreciation of currency
   i. Tariffs, quantitative restrictions, export controls, border taxes, exchange controls, state trading, and other entry barriers to foreign trade
   j. Monetary, fiscal, and tax policies
   k. Exchange controls and other restrictions on capital movements, repatriation of capital, and remission of earnings

4. Business system and structure
   a. Prevailing business philosophy: mixed capitalism, planned economy, state socialism
   b. Major types of industry and economic activities
   c. Numbers, size, and types of firms, including legal forms of business
   d. Organization: proprietorships, partnerships, limited companies, corporations, cooperatives, state enterprises
   e. Local ownership patterns: public and privately held corporations, family-owned enterprises
   f. Domestic and foreign patterns of ownership in major industries
   g. Business managers available: their education, training, experience, career patterns, attitudes, and reputations
   h. Business associations and chambers of commerce and their influence
   i. Business codes, both formal and informal
   j. Marketing institutions: distributors, agents, wholesalers, retailers, advertising agencies, advertising media, marketing research, and other consultants

> *k.* Financial and other business institutions: commercial and investment banks, other financial institutions, capital markets, money markets, foreign exchange dealers, insurance firms, engineering companies
>
> *l.* Managerial processes and practices with respect to planning, administration, operations, accounting, budgeting, and control

5. Social and cultural parameters and their projections

   a. Literacy and educational levels

   b. Business, economic, technical, and other specialized education available

   c. Language and cultural characteristics

   d. Class structure and mobility

   e. Religious, racial, and national characteristics

   f. Degree of urbanization and rural-urban shifts

   g. Strength of nationalistic sentiment

   h. Rate of social change

   i. Impact of nationalism on social and institutional change

Chapter **Six**

Internal Analysis

After reading and studying this chapter, you should be able to

1. Understand how to conduct a SWOT analysis, and be able to summarize its limitations.

2. Understand value chain analysis and how to use it to disaggregate a firm's activities and determine which are most critical to generating competitive advantage.

3. Understand the resource-based view of a firm and how to use it to disaggregate a firm's activities and resources to determine which resources are best used to build competitive advantage.

4. Apply four different perspectives for making meaningful comparisons to assess a firm's internal strengths and weaknesses.

5. Refamiliarize yourself with ratio analysis and basic techniques of financial analysis to assist you in doing internal analysis to identify a firm's strengths and weaknesses.

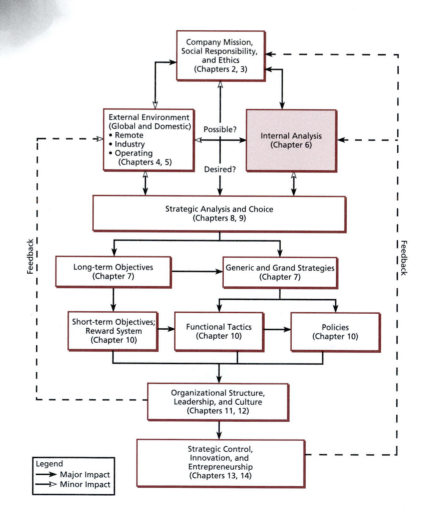

The late R. David Thomas was once ridiculed by many restaurant industry veterans and analysts as he set about building "yet another" hamburger chain named after his young daughter, Wendy. While they thought the name was fine, critics argued that North America was already saturated with hamburger outlets such as McDonald's, Burger King, Hardees, Dairy Queen, White Castle, and others. Yet, as things turned out, Wendy's became the fastest growing restaurant chain in the history of the world, having replaced Burger King as the second largest chain. Cisco, the global leader in networking equipment and switching devices linking wired and wireless computer systems worldwide, twice entered and tried to dominate the home-networking market. It failed each time, wasting more than $250 million in the process. Finally, just a few years ago, it acquired Link-Sys, the market leader, with the promise it would never try to bring Link-Sys into the normal Cisco company structure for fear of destroying the extraordinary success Link-Sys had achieved—not the least of which was vanquishing the much more powerful and wealthy Cisco twice in the last decade. Apple Computer was being written off in the increasingly competitive personal computer industry when it introduced, to a lukewarm reception, its new iPod device and iTunes service. Written off by many as a cute fad, that modest start pioneered a vast new global industry—much like Apple's original personal computer did three decades earlier.

Common to each of these diverse settings were insightful managers and business leaders who based their firm's pursuit of market opportunities not only on the existence of external opportunities but also on a very sound awareness of their firm's competitive advantages arising from the firm's internal resources, capabilities, and skills. A *sound, realistic aware-ness and appreciation of their firm's internally generated advantages* brought Wendy's, Apple, and Link-Sys immense success while its absence brought much the opposite to Cisco's home-networking ventures and to the competitors and critics of R. David Thomas and Steven Jobs. This chapter, then, focuses on how managers identify the key resources and capabilities around which to build successful strategies.

Managers often do this subjectively, based on intuition and "gut feel." Years of seasoned industry experience positions managers to make sound subjective judgments. But just as often, or more often, this may not be the case. In fast-changing environments, reliance on past experiences can cause management myopia—or a tendency to accept the status quo and disregard signals that change is needed. And with managers new to strategic decision making, subjective decisions are particularly suspect. A lack of experience is easily replaced by emotion, narrow functional expertise, and the opinions of others, thus creating the foundation on which newer managers build strategic recommendations. So it is that new managers' subjective assessments often come back to haunt them.

John W. Henry broke the most fabled curse in sports when his Boston Red Sox won their first World Championship since 1918. Most sports analysts, sports business managers, and regular fans (if they are honest now) would have bet a small fortune, based on their own subjective assessment, that there was no way the Boston Red Sox, having already lost three games, would win four straight games to beat the New York Yankees and then go on to win the World Series. That subjective assessment or "feel" would have led them to believe there were just too many reasons to bet the Red Sox could pull it out. At the same time, a seasoned global futures market trader, John W. Henry, relied on applying his systematic global futures market approach to baseball player selection along with selected other resources and capa-bilities unique to the Boston area and situation in his bet that the Red Sox could win it all. His very systematic approach to internal analysis of the Boston Red Sox sports enterprise and the leveraging of his/their strengths led to the World Series championship and perhaps many more, as described in Exhibit 6.1, Top Strategist.

Managers often start their internal analysis with questions like, How well is the current strategy working? What is our current situation? Or what are our strengths and weaknesses? The chapter begins with a review of a long-standing, traditional approach managers have

**John W. Henry, CEO of the Boston
Red Sox, and Slugger David Ortiz**

John W. Henry long ago earned his fortune—and a reputation as one of the nation's premier players in the global futures markets. But in 2004 and 2007, Henry may have achieved immortality by leading the Boston Red Sox to their first two World Championships since 1918, reversing the most fabled curse in sports. This triumph was due to more than inspired play of a team that rallied from 0–3 in the American League Championship Series to beat the New York Yankees.

Henry set the stage for victory by applying the same statistical acumen that made him a fortune in the futures market. He also boosted revenue by making the most of Fenway park, the oldest stadium in Major League Baseball, by squeezing in more seats and then charging the highest prices for home games, all of which sold out. At the same time, they started broadcasting home games in high definition on their 80 percent–owned cable sports network, New England Sports Network—helping it routinely win in regional prime-time ratings.

All of this turned the Red Sox into baseball's second-most-lucrative franchise and gave it the financial muscle to take on the Yankees, who consistently open every season with a league-leading record payroll. The Sox are now consistently second in payroll, thanks to Henry.

Henry—a numbers genius, whose proprietary futures-trading system consistently produces double-digit returns—closed the gap with sabermetrics. That's a system for mining baseball stats to find undervalued players while avoiding long contracts for aging stars—such as pitcher Pedro Martinez—whose performance is likely to decline. Henry built baseball's most effective team but won't settle for one championship. After ending an 86-year drought, he's aiming for a dynasty.

Sources: Reprinted with special permission from "Who Needs Johnny Damon," *BusinessWeek,* March 20, 2006; and "John Henry: Boston Red Sox," *BusinessWeek,* January 10, 2005, p. 61. Copyright © 2006 The McGraw-Hill Companies.

frequently used to answer these questions, SWOT analysis. This approach is a logical framework intended to help managers thoughtfully consider their company's internal capabilities and use the results to shape strategic options. Its value and continued use is found in its simplicity. At the same time, SWOT analysis has limitations that have led strategists to seek more comprehensive frameworks for conducting internal analysis.

Value chain analysis is one such framework. Value chain analysis views a firm as a "chain" or sequential process of value-creating activities. The sum of all of these activities represents the "value" the firm exists to provide its customers. So undertaking an internal analysis that breaks down the firm into these distinct value activities allows for a detailed, interrelated evaluation of a firm's internal strengths and weaknesses that improves upon what strategists can create using only SWOT analysis.

The resource-based view (RBV) of a firm is another important framework for conducting internal analysis. This approach improves upon SWOT analysis by examining a variety of different yet specific types of resources and capabilities any firm possesses and then evaluating the degree to which they become the basis for sustained competitive advantage based on industry and competitive considerations. In so doing, it provides a disciplined approach to internal analysis.

Common to all the approaches to internal analysis is the use of meaningful standards for comparison in internal analysis. We conclude this chapter by examining how managers use past performance, comparison with competitors or other "benchmarks," industry norms, and traditional financial analysis to make meaningful comparisons.

SWOT ANALYSIS: A TRADITIONAL APPROACH TO INTERNAL ANALYSIS

SWOT analysis
SWOT is an acronym for the internal Strengths and Weaknesses of a firm, and the environmental Opportunities and Threats facing that firm. SWOT analysis is a technique through which managers create a quick overview of a company's strategic situation.

SWOT is an acronym for the internal **S**trengths and **W**eaknesses of a firm and the environmental **O**pportunities and **T**hreats facing that firm. **SWOT analysis** is a historically popular technique through which managers create a quick overview of a company's strategic situation. It is based on the assumption that an effective strategy derives from a sound "fit" between a firm's internal resources (strengths and weaknesses) and its external situation (opportunities and threats). A good fit maximizes a firm's strengths and opportunities and minimizes its weaknesses and threats. Accurately applied, this simple assumption has sound, insightful implications for the design of a successful strategy.

Environmental and industry analysis in Chapters 3 and 4 provides the information needed to identify opportunities and threats in a firm's environment, the first fundamental focus in SWOT analysis.

Opportunities

opportunity
A major favorable situation in a firm's environment.

An **opportunity** is a major favorable situation in a firm's environment. Key trends are one source of opportunities. Identification of a previously overlooked market segment, changes in competitive or regulatory circumstances, technological changes, and improved buyer or supplier relationships could represent opportunities for the firm. Sustained, growing interest in organic foods has created an opportunity that is a critical factor shaping strategic decisions at groceries and restaurants worldwide.

Threats

threat
A major unfavorable situation in a firm's environment.

A **threat** is a major unfavorable situation in a firm's environment. Threats are key impediments to the firm's current or desired position. The entrance of new competitors, slow market growth, increased bargaining power of key buyers or suppliers, technological changes, and new or revised regulations could represent threats to a firm's success.

Large national residential home builders have seen rising interest rates start to slow demand for single-family housing developments nationwide. These same residential home builders have had to face an increasing threat of rapidly accelerating energy and materials costs brought on both by their collective, fast-paced development activities, further exacerbated by the exploding demand for these same building supplies in the Chinese marketplace. So these large national home builders had to craft strategies built around these major threats to survive and eventually grow.

Once managers agree on key opportunities and threats facing their firm, they have a frame of reference or context from which to evaluate their firm's ability to take advantage of opportunities and minimize the effect of key threats. And vice versa: Once managers agree on their firm's core strengths and weaknesses, they can logically move to consider opportunities that best leverage their firm's strengths while minimizing the effect certain weaknesses may present until remedied.

Strengths

strength
A resource advantage relative to competitors and the needs of the markets a firm serves or expects to serve.

A **strength** is a resource or capability controlled by or available to a firm that gives it an advantage relative to its competitors in meeting the needs of the customers it serves.

Strengths arise from the resources and competencies available to the firm. Southland Log Homes' southeastern plant locations (Virginia, South Carolina, and Mississippi) provide both transportation and raw material cost advantages along with ideal proximity to the United States' most rapidly growing second-home markets. Southland has leveraged these strengths to take advantage of the moderate interest rates and rapidly growing baby boomer second-home demand trend to become the largest log home company in North America.

Weaknesses

weakness
A limitation or deficiency in one or more resources or competencies relative to competitors that impedes a firm's effective performance.

A **weakness** is a limitation or deficiency in one or more of a firm's resources or capabilities relative to its competitors that create a disadvantage in effectively meeting customer needs. Limited financial capacity was a weakness recognized by Southwest Airlines, which charted a selective route expansion strategy to build the best profit record in a deregulated airline industry.

Using SWOT Analysis in Strategic Analysis

The most common use of SWOT analysis is as a logical framework guiding discussion and reflection about a firm's situation and basic alternatives. This often takes place as a series of managerial group discussions. What one manager sees as an opportunity, another may see as a potential threat. Likewise, a strength to one manager may be a weakness to another. The SWOT framework provides an organized basis for insightful discussion and information sharing, which may improve the quality of choices and decisions managers subsequently make. Consider what initial discussions among Apple Computer's management team might have been that led to the decision to pursue the rapid development and introduction of the iPod. A brief SWOT analysis of their situation might have identified:

Strengths

Sizable miniature storage expertise

User-friendly engineering skill

Reputation and image with youthful consumers

Brand name

Web-savvy organization and people

Jobs's Pixar experience

Weaknesses

Economies of scale versus computer rivals

Maturing computer markets

Limited financial resources

Limited music industry expertise

Opportunities

Confused online music situation

Emerging file-sharing restrictions

Few core computer-related opportunities

Digitalization of movies and music

Threats

Growing global computer companies

Major computer competitors

EXHIBIT 6.2
SWOT Analysis
Diagram

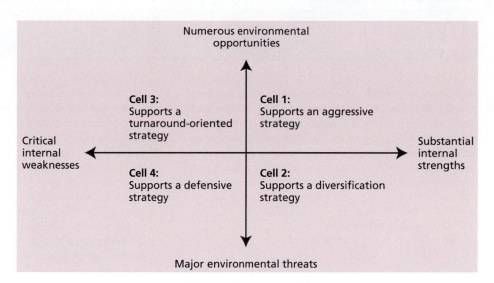

It is logical to envision Apple managers' discussions evolving to a consensus that the combination of Apple's storage and digitalization strengths along with their strong brand franchise with "hip" consumers, when combined with the opportunity potentially arising out of the need for a simple way to legally buy and download music on the Web would be the basis for a compelling strategy for Apple to become a first mover in the emerging downloadable music industry.

Exhibit 6.2 illustrates how SWOT analysis might take managerial planning discussions into a slightly more structured approach to aid strategic analysis. The objective is identification of one of four distinct patterns in the match between a firm's internal resources and external situation. Cell 1 is the most favorable situation; the firm faces several environmental opportunities and has numerous strengths that encourage pursuit of those opportunities. This situation suggests growth-oriented strategies to exploit the favorable match. Our example of Apple Computer's intensive market development strategy in the online music services and the iPod is the result of a favorable match of its strong technical expertise, early entry, and reputation resources with an opportunity for impressive market growth as millions of people sought a legally viable, convenient way to obtain, download, store, and use their own customized music choices.

Sun Microsystems applied SWOT analysis, creating an advertisement responding to the Hewlett-Packard (HP) board of directors' ongoing search for a new CEO after their dismissal of celebrity CEO Carly Fiorina. The ad shows Sun Microsystems attempting a Cell 1 strategic response pursuing a key opportunity made available by the uncertainty for HP corporate clients during this time (see Exhibit 6.3, Strategy in Action). In the ad, as you can see, Sun simply attempts to state—in very direct terms—what it believes its strengths might be for interested and frustrated HP clients (and, subtly, IBM's customers) in the face of this opportunity created for Sun by HP's strategic confusion.

Cell 4 is the least favorable situation, with the firm facing major environmental threats from a weak resource position. This situation clearly calls for strategies that reduce or redirect involvement in the products or markets examined by means of SWOT analysis. Texas Instruments offers a good example of a cell 4 firm. It was a sprawling maker of chips, calculators, laptop PCs, military electronics, and engineering software on a sickening slide toward oblivion just 10 years ago. Its young CEO, Tom Engibous, reinvigorated the ailing electronics giant and turned it into one of the hottest plays in semiconductors by betting the company on an emerging class of chips known

Sun Microsystems Uses a SWOT Analysis to Target Frustrated HP Customers in 2005

BusinessWeek

Hewlett-Packard celebrity CEO Carly Fiorina was dismissed by the HP board, five years after her hard-fought decision to merge Compaq and HP failed to produce the payoffs she predicted. Sun Microsystems placed the following ad in *The Wall Street Journal* and other business periodicals, aimed at disgruntled HP and Compaq business customers (a SWOT opportunity) and highlighting key strengths at Sun Microsystems:

To: HP Customers
From: Sun Microsystems Inc.
Subject: Time for one last change?
Cc: IBM

Odds are, you're an HP customer because you believed in the HP way. You believed in the DEC strategy. The Compaq strategy. The PA-RISC/HP-UX strategy. The Tru64 strategy. The Itanium strategy. But time after time, you've been disappointed.

We at Sun have taken a different tack: there's enough change in the world. Focus. Innovate. Grow customers 1 by 1. And stay consistent to your mission, even when the pundits and competitors say otherwise.

We've had a consistent vision for 24 years: The Network is the Computer™. More true today than 10 years ago.

We've had a consistent vision of how the network should be programmed: Java™. More true today than 10 years ago.

We've had a consistent vision of how operating systems should be built: to military-grade security, carrier-grade scale, and open to the world: Solaris™ 10. More true today than 10 years ago.

We've had a consistent view that servers and storage should be: built to scale, built to last, built with best-in-class innovation. That's why SPARC® is the #1 64-bit microprocessor out there, and our AMD Opteron™ processor-based systems now claim seven new performance world records, and we've got the most compelling storage product in the industry (the Sun StorEdge™ 6920). More true today than 10 years ago.

We've had a consistent view that innovation matters—from Linux and the open source world, to Microsoft interoperability. More true today than 10 years ago.

And most of all, we've had a consistent view that simplicity is our single biggest competitive advantage. $1/cpu-hr is a simpler grid offering than forcing customers to buy consultants "on demand." More true today than 10 years ago.

So if you'd like to experience a partner driven to focus while you try to drive change–versus the opposite–call us. (800) SUN-0404. Or go to www.sun.com/welcome_2_Sun to learn about our special HP migration programs.

Sources: Reprinted with special permission from "Sun's Rebound," *BusinessWeek Online*, September 13, 2006; and "A New Dawn for Sun Microsystems," *BusinessWeek*, May 9, 2005. Copyright © 2006 The McGraw-Hill Companies.

as digital signal processors (DSPs). The chips crunch vast streams of data for an array of digital gadgets, including modems and cellular phones. Engibous shed billions of dollars worth of assets to focus on DSPs, which he calls "the most important silicon technology of the next decade." TI now commands half of the $8 billion global market for the most advanced DSPs, and it is the No. 1 chip supplier to the digital wireless phone market.

In cell 2, a firm that has identified several key strengths faces an unfavorable environment. In this situation, strategies would seek to redeploy those strong resources and competencies to build long-term opportunities in more opportunistic product markets. IBM, a dominant manufacturer of mainframes, servers, and PCs worldwide, has nurtured many strengths in computer-related and software-related markets for many years. Increasingly, however, it has had to address major threats that include product commoditization, pricing pressures, accelerated pace of innovation, and the like. IBM's decision to sell its PC business to the Chinese firm Lenovo and focus instead on continued development of ISSC, better known now as IBM Global Services, has allowed IBM to build a long-term opportunity in the (hopefully) more profitable, growing markets of the next decade. In the past 10 years, Global

Services has become the fastest-growing division of the company, its largest employer, and the keystone of IBM's strategic future. The group does everything from running a customer's IT (information technology) department to consulting on legacy system upgrades to building custom supply-chain management applications. As IBM's hardware divisions struggle against price wars and commoditization and its software units fight to gain share beyond mainframes, it is Global Services that drives the company's growth.

A firm in cell 3 faces impressive market opportunity but is constrained by weak internal resources. The focus of strategy for such a firm is eliminating the internal weaknesses so as to more effectively pursue the market opportunity. Microsoft has big problems with computer viruses. Alleviating such problems, or weaknesses, is driving massive changes in how Microsoft writes software—to make it more secure before it reaches the market rather than fix it later with patches. Microsoft is also shaking up the security software industry by acquiring several smaller companies to accelerate its own efforts to create specialized software that detects, finds, and removes malicious code.[1]

Limitations of SWOT Analysis

SWOT analysis has been a framework of choice among many managers for a long time because of its simplicity and its portrayal of the essence of sound strategy formulation— matching a firm's opportunities and threats with its strengths and weaknesses. But SWOT analysis is a broad conceptual approach, making it susceptible to some key limitations.

1. A SWOT analysis can overemphasize internal strengths and downplay external threats. Strategists in every company have to remain vigilant against building strategies around what the firm does well now (its strengths) without due consideration of the external environment's impact on those strengths. Apple's success with the iPod and its iTunes downloadable music Web site provides a good example of strategists who placed a major emphasis on external considerations—the legal requirements for downloading and subsequently using individual songs, what music to make available, and the evolution of the use of the Web to download music—as a guide to shaping Apple's eventual strategy. What would Apple's success have been like if its strategy had been built substantially with a focus on its technology in making the iPod device and offering it in the consumer marketplace—without bothering with the development and creation of iTunes?

2. A SWOT analysis can be static and can risk ignoring changing circumstances. A frequent admonition about the downfall of planning processes says that plans are one-time events to be completed, typed, and relegated to their spot on a manager's shelf while s/he goes about the actual work of the firm. So it is not surprising that critics of SWOT analysis, with good reason, warn that it is a one-time view of a changing, or moving, situation. Major U.S. airlines pursued strategies built around strengths that were suddenly much less important when airline deregulation took place. Likewise, those airlines built huge competitive advantages around "hub and spoke" systems for bringing small-town flyers to key hubs to be redistributed to flights elsewhere and yet allow for centralized maintenance and economies of scale. The change brought about by discount airlines that "cherry-picked" key routes, and eventual outsourcing of routine maintenance to Latin America and the Caribbean, did great harm to those strategies. Bottom line: SWOT analysis, along with most planning techniques, must avoid being static and ignoring change.

3. A SWOT analysis can overemphasize a single strength or element of strategy. Dell Computer's long-dominant strength based on a highly automated, Internet, or phone-based direct sales model gave Dell, according to chairman and founder Michael Dell, "a competitive advantage [strength] as wide as the Grand Canyon." He viewed it as being

---

[1] "Aiming to Fix Flaws, Microsoft Buys Another Antivirus Firm," *The Wall Street Journal,* February 9, 2005, p. B1.

prohibitively expensive for any rival to copy this source of strength. Unfortunately for Dell shareholders, Dell's reliance on that "key" strength proved to be an oversimplified basis around which to sustain the company's strategy for continued dominance and growth in the global PC industry. HP's size alone, with its reemphasis on printing and technical skills, and Lenovo's home base in the fast-growing Asian market seemingly have overcome Dell's dominance in the global PC industry.

4. A strength is not necessarily a source of competitive advantage. Cisco Systems Inc. has been a dominant player in providing switching equipment and other key networking infrastructure items around which the global computer communications system has been able to proliferate. It has substantial financial, technological, and branding expertise. Cisco Systems twice attempted to use its vast strengths in these areas as the basis to enter and remain in the market for home computer networks and wireless home-networking devices. It failed both times and lost hundreds of millions of dollars in the process. It possesses several compelling strengths, but none were sources of sustainable competitive advantage in the home-computer-networking industry. After leaving that industry for several years, it recently chose to reenter it by acquiring Link-Sys, an early pioneer in that industry. Cisco management acknowledged that it was doing so precisely because it did not possess those sources of competitive advantage and that, furthermore, it would avoid any interference with that business lest it disrupt the advantage around which Link-Sys's success has been built.

In summary, SWOT analysis is a longtime, traditional approach to internal analysis among many strategists. It offers a generalized effort to examine internal capabilities in light of external factors, most notably key opportunities and threats. It has limitations that must be considered if SWOT analysis is to be the basis for any firm's strategic decision-making process. Another approach to internal analysis that emerged, in part, to add more rigor and depth in the identification of competitive advantages around which a firm might build a successful strategy is value chain analysis. We examine it next.

VALUE CHAIN ANALYSIS

value chain
A perspective in which business is seen as a chain of activities that transforms inputs into outputs that customers value.

The term **value chain** describes a way of looking at a business as a chain of activities that transform inputs into outputs that customers value. Customer value derives from three basic sources: activities that differentiate the product, activities that lower its cost, and activities that meet the customer's need quickly. **Value chain analysis** (VCA) attempts to understand how a business creates customer value by examining the contributions of different activities within the business to that value.

value chain analysis
An analysis that attempts to understand how a business creates customer value by examining the contributions of different activities within the business to that value.

VCA takes a process point of view: It divides (sometimes called disaggregates) the business into sets of activities that occur *within the business,* starting with the inputs a firm receives and finishing with the firm's products (or services) and after-sales service to customers. VCA attempts to look at its costs across the series of activities the business performs to determine where low-cost advantages or cost disadvantages exist. It looks at the attributes of each of these different activities to determine in what ways each activity that occurs between purchasing inputs and after-sales service helps differentiate the company's products and services. Proponents of VCA believe it allows managers to better identify their firm's competitive advantages by looking at the business as a process—a chain of activities—of what actually happens in the business rather than simply looking at it based on arbitrary organizational dividing lines or historical accounting protocol.

Exhibit 6.4 shows a typical value chain framework. It divides activities within the firm into two broad categories: primary activities and support activities. **Primary activities** (sometimes called *line functions*) are those involved in the physical creation of the product, marketing and transfer to the buyer, and after-sale support. **Support activities** (sometimes

EXHIBIT 6.4
The Value Chain

Source: Based on Michael
Porter. *On Competition*, 1998.
Harvard Business School Press.

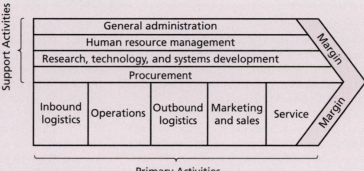

The Value Chain

Support Activities

| General administration |
| Human resource management |
| Research, technology, and systems development |
| Procurement |

| Inbound logistics | Operations | Outbound logistics | Marketing and sales | Service |

Margin

Primary Activities

primary activities
The activities in a firm
of those involved in the
physical creation of the
product, marketing and
transfer to the buyer,
and after-sale support.

Primary Activities

- **Inbound logistics**—Activities, costs, and assets associated with obtaining fuel, energy, raw materials, parts components, merchandise, and consumable items from vendors; receiving, storing, and disseminating inputs from suppliers; inspection; and inventory management.
- **Operations**—Activities, costs, and assets associated with converting inputs into final product form (production, assembly, packaging, equipment maintenance, facilities, operations, quality assurance, environmental protection).
- **Outbound logistics**—Activities, costs, and assets dealing with physically distributing the product to buyers (finished goods warehousing, order processing, order picking and packing, shipping, delivery vehicle operations).
- **Marketing and sales**—Activities, costs, and assets related to sales force efforts, advertising and promotion, market research and planning, and dealer/distributor support.
- **Service**—Activities, costs, and assets associated with providing assistance to buyers, such as installation, spare parts delivery, maintenance and repair, technical assistance, buyer inquiries, and complaints.

support activities
The activities in a firm
that assist the firm as
a whole by providing
infrastructure or inputs
that allow the primary
activities to take place
on an ongoing basis.

Support Activities

- **General administration**—Activities, costs, and assets relating to general management, accounting and finance, legal and regulatory affairs, safety and security, management information systems, and other "overhead" functions.
- **Human resources management**—Activities, costs, and assets associated with the recruitment, hiring, training, development, and compensation of all types of personnel; labor relations activities; development of knowledge-based skills.
- **Research, technology, and systems development**—Activities, costs, and assets relating to product R&D, process R&D, process design improvement, equipment design, computer software development, telecommunications systems, computer-assisted design and engineering, new database capabilities, and development of computerized support systems.
- **Procurement**—Activities, costs, and assets associated with purchasing and providing raw materials, supplies, services, and outsourcing necessary to support the firm and its activities. Sometimes this activity is assigned as part of a firm's inbound logistic purchasing activities.

Value Chain Analysis "Morphs" Federal Express into an Information Company

BusinessWeek

Founder Fred Smith and executives running companies controlled by FedEx sought a monumental shift in the FedEx mission. They accelerated plans to focus on information systems that track and coordinate packages. They sought to "morph" from being a transportation company into an information company.

FedEx had one of the most heavily used Web sites on the Internet. Company management claimed to have 1,500 in-house programmers writing more software code than almost any other nonsoftware company. To complement package delivery, FedEx designs and operates high-tech warehouses and distribution systems for big manufacturers and retailers around the world. For almost two decades, FedEx steadily invested massive amounts to develop software and create a giant digital network. FedEx has built corporate technology campuses around the world, and its electronic systems are directly linked via the Internet or otherwise to millions of customers worldwide. That system allows FedEx to track packages on an hourly basis, and it also allows FedEx to predict future flows of goods and then rapidly refigure the information and logistical network to handle those flows.

"Moving an item from point A to point B is no longer a big deal," says James Barksdale, early architect of

FedEx's information strategies. "Having the information about that item, and where it is, and the best way to use it . . . That is value. The companies that will be big winners will be the ones who can best maximize the value of these information systems." Where FedEx's value has long been built on giant airplanes and big trucks, founder Smith envisioned a time when it will be built on information, computers, and the allure of the FedEx brand name. These days FedEx is a linchpin of the just-in-time deliveries revolution—its planes and trucks serve as mobile warehouses—that has helped companies around the globe cut costs and boost their productivity. FedEx's logistics info services now contribute the lion's share—92 percent—of FedEx's annual revenue. FedEx's value chain has shrunk in areas involved with inbound and outbound operations—taking off and landing on the tarmac—and expanded in areas involved with zapping around the pristine and pilot-free world of cyberspace to manage a client's supply chain and its distribution network.

Sources: Reprinted with special permission from "FedEx Delivers a Boost," *BusinessWeek,* November 7, 2006; and Dean Foust, "Fred Smith on the Birth of FedEx," *BusinessWeek,* September 20, 2004. Copyright © 2006 The McGraw-Hill Companies.

called *staff* or *overhead functions*) assist the firm as a whole by providing infrastructure or inputs that allow the primary activities to take place on an ongoing basis. The value chain includes a profit margin because a markup above the cost of providing a firm's value-adding activities is normally part of the price paid by the buyer—creating value that exceeds cost so as to generate a return for the effort.[2]

Judgment is required across individual firms and different industries because what may be seen as a support activity in one firm or industry may be a primary activity in another. Computer operations might typically be seen as infrastructure support, for example, but may be seen as a primary activity in airlines, newspapers, or banks. Exhibit 6.5, Strategy in Action, describes how Federal Express reconceptualized its company using a value chain analysis that ultimately saw its information support become its primary activity and source of customer value.

Conducting a Value Chain Analysis

Identify Activities

The initial step in value chain analysis is to divide a company's operations into specific activities or business processes, usually grouping them similarly to the primary and support activity categories shown earlier in Exhibit 6.4. Within each category, a firm typically performs a number of discrete activities that may be key to the firm's success. Service

---

[2] Different "value chain" or value activities may become the focus of value chain analysis. For example, companies using Hammer's *Reengineering the Corporation* might use (1) order procurement, (2) order fulfillment, (3) customer service, (4) product design, and (5) strategic planning plus support activities.

EXHIBIT 6.6   **The Difference between Traditional Cost Accounting and Activity-Based Cost Accounting**

Traditional Cost Accounting in a Purchasing Department		Activity-Based Cost Accounting in the Same Purchasing Department for Its "Procurement" Activities	
Wages and salaries	$175,000	Evaluate supplier capabilities	$ 67,875
Employee benefits	57,500	Process purchase orders	41,050
Supplies	3,250	Expedite supplier deliveries	11,750
Travel	1,200	Expedite internal processing	7,920
Depreciation	8,500	Check quality of items purchased	47,150
Other fixed charges	62,000	Check incoming deliveries against	
Miscellaneous operating expenses	12,625	purchase orders	24,225
	$320,075	Resolve problems	55,000
		Internal administration	65,105
			$320,075

activities, for example, may include such discrete activities as installation, repair, parts distribution, and upgrading—any of which could be a major source of competitive advantage or disadvantage. The manager's challenge at this point is to be very detailed attempting to "disaggregate" what actually goes on into numerous distinct, analyzable activities rather than settling for a broad, general categorization.

Allocate Costs

The next step is to attempt to attach costs to each discrete activity. Each activity in the value chain incurs costs and ties up time and assets. Value chain analysis requires managers to assign costs and assets to each activity, thereby providing a very different way of viewing costs than traditional cost accounting methods would produce. Exhibit 6.6 helps illustrate this distinction. Both approaches in Exhibit 6.6 tell us that the purchasing department (procurement activities) cost $320,075. The traditional method lets us see that payroll expenses are 73 percent [($175 + $57.5)/$320] of our costs with "other fixed charges" the second largest cost, 19 percent [$62/$320] of the total procurement costs. VCA proponents would argue that the benefit of this information is limited. Their argument might be the following:

> With this information we could compare our procurement costs to key competitors, budgets, or industry averages and conclude that we are better, worse, or equal. We could then ascertain that our "people" costs and "other fixed charges" cost are advantages, disadvantages, or "in line" with competitors. Managers could then argue to cut people, add people, or debate fixed overhead charges. However, they would get lost in what is really a budgetary debate without ever examining what it is those people do in accomplishing the procurement function, what value that provides, and how cost effective each activity is.

VCA proponents hold that the activity-based VCA approach would provide a more meaningful analysis of the procurement function's costs and consequent value added. The activity-based side of Exhibit 6.6 shows that approximately 21 percent of the procurement cost or value added involves evaluating supplier capabilities. A rather sizable cost, 20 percent, involves internal administration, with an additional 17 percent spent resolving problems and almost 15 percent spent on quality control efforts. VCA advocates see this information as being much more useful than traditional cost accounting information, especially when compared with the cost information of key competitors or other "benchmark" companies. VCA supporters assert the following argument that the benefit of this activity-based information is substantial:

> Rather than analyzing just "people" and "other charges," we are now looking at meaningful categorizations of the work that procurement actually does. We see, for example, that a key value-added activity (and cost) involves "evaluating supplier capabilities." The amount spent on "internal administration" and "resolving problems" seems high and may indicate a weakness or area for improvement if the other activities' costs are in line and outcomes favorable. The bottom line is that this approach lets us look at what we actually "do" in the business—the specific activities—to create customer value, and that in turn allows more specific internal analysis than traditional, accounting-based cost categories.

Recognizing the Difficulty in Activity-Based Cost Accounting

It is important to note that existing financial management and accounting systems in many firms are not set up to easily provide activity-based cost breakdowns. Likewise, in virtually all firms, the information requirements to support activity-based cost accounting can create redundant work because of the financial reporting requirements that may force firms to retain the traditional approach for financial statement purposes. The time and energy to change to an activity-based approach can be formidable and still typically involve arbitrary cost allocation decisions—trying to allocate selected asset or people costs across multiple activities in which they are involved. Challenges dealing with a cost-based use of VCA have not deterred use of the framework to identify sources of differentiation. Indeed, conducting a VCA to analyze competitive advantages that differentiate the firm is compatible with the resource-based view's examination of intangible assets and capabilities as sources of distinctive competence.

Identify the Activities That Differentiate the Firm

Scrutinizing a firm's value chain may not only reveal cost advantages or disadvantages, it may also bring attention to several sources of differentiation advantage relative to competitors. Google considers its Internet-based search algorithms (activities) to be far superior to any competitor's. Google knows it has a cost advantage because of the time and expense replicating this activity would take. But Google considers it an even more important source of value to the customer because of the importance customers place on this activity, which differentiates Google from many would-be competitors. Likewise, Federal Express, as we noted in Exhibit 6.5, considers its information management skills to have become the core competence and essence of the company because of the value these skills allow FedEx to provide its customers and the importance they in turn place on such skills. Exhibit 6.7 suggests some factors for assessing primary and support activities' differentiation and contribution.

Examine the Value Chain

Once the value chain has been documented, managers need to identify the activities that are critical to buyer satisfaction and market success. It is those activities that deserve major scrutiny in an internal analysis. Three considerations are essential at this stage in the value chain analysis. First, the company's basic mission needs to influence managers' choice of activities to be examined in detail. If the company is focused on being a low-cost provider, then management attention to lower costs should be very visible, and missions built around commitment to differentiation should find managers spending more on activities that are differentiation cornerstones. Retailer Wal-Mart focuses intensely on costs related to inbound logistics, advertising, and loyalty to build its competitive advantage (see Exhibit 6.10, page 176), while Nordstrom builds its distinct position in retailing by emphasizing sales and support activities on which they spend twice the retail industry average.

Second, the nature of value chains and the relative importance of the activities within them vary by industry. Lodging firms like Holiday Inn have major costs and concerns that

EXHIBIT 6.7 **Possible Factors for Assessing Sources of Differentiation in Primary and Support Activities**

Support Activities

General Administration
- Capability to identify new-product market opportunities and potential environmental threats
- Quality of the strategic planning system to achieve corporate objectives
- Coordination and integration of all value chain activities among organizational subunits
- Ability to obtain relatively low-cost funds for capital expenditures and working capital
- Level of information systems support in making strategic and routine decisions
- Timely and accurate management information on general and competitive environments
- Relationships with public policymakers and interest groups
- Public image and corporate citizenship

Human Resource Management
- Effectiveness of procedures for recruiting, training, and promoting all levels of employees
- Appropriateness of reward systems for motivating and challenging employees
- A work environment that minimizes absenteeism and keeps turnover at desirable levels
- Relations with trade unions
- Active participation by managers and technical personnel in professional organizations
- Levels of employee motivation and job satisfaction

Technology Development
- Success of research and development activities in leading to product and process innovations
- Quality of working relationships between R&D personnel and other departments
- Timeliness of technology development activities in meeting critical deadlines
- Quality of laboratories and other facilities
- Qualification and experience of laboratory technicians and scientists
- Ability of work environment to encourage creativity and innovation

Procurement
- Development of alternate sources for inputs to minimize dependence on a single supplier
- Procurement of raw materials (1) on a timely basis, (2) at lowest possible cost, (3) at acceptable levels of quality
- Procedures for procurement of plant, machinery, and buildings
- Development of criteria for lease-versus-purchase decisions
- Good, long-term relationships with reliable suppliers

Profit Margin

Inbound Logistics	Operations	Outbound Logistics	Marketing and Sales	Service
▪ Soundness of material and inventory control systems ▪ Efficiency of raw material warehousing activities	▪ Productivity of equipment compared to that of key competitors ▪ Appropriate automation of production processes ▪ Effectiveness of production control systems to improve quality and reduce costs ▪ Efficiency of plant layout and work-flow design	▪ Timeliness and efficiency of delivery of finished goods and services ▪ Efficiency of finished goods warehousing activities	▪ Effectiveness of market research to identify customer segments and needs ▪ Innovation in sales promotion and advertising ▪ Evaluation of alternate distribution channels ▪ Motivation and competence of sales force ▪ Development of an image of quality and a favorable reputation ▪ Extent of brand loyalty among customers ▪ Extent of market dominance within the market segment or overall market	▪ Means to solicit customer input for product improvements ▪ Promptness of attention to customer complaints ▪ Appropriateness of warranty and guarantee policies ▪ Quality of customer education and training ▪ Ability to provide replacement parts and repair services

Profit Margin

Primary Activities

Source: Based on Michael Porter, *On Competition,* 1998, Harvard Business School Press.

involve operational activities—it provides its service instantaneously at each location—and marketing activities, while having minimal concern for outbound logistics. Yet for a distributor, such as the food distributor PYA, inbound and outbound logistics are the most critical area. Major retailers like Wal-Mart have built value advantages focusing on purchasing and inbound logistics, while the most successful personal computer companies have built via sales, outbound logistics, and service through the mail-order process.

Third, the relative importance of value activities can vary by a company's position in a broader value system that includes the value chains of its upstream suppliers and downstream customers or partners involved in providing products or services to end users. A producer of roofing shingles depends heavily on the downstream activities of wholesale distributors and building supply retailers to reach roofing contractors and do-it-yourselfers. Maytag manufactures its own appliances, sells them through independent distributors, and provides warranty service to the buyer. Sears outsources the manufacture of its appliances while it promotes its brand name—Kenmore—and handles all sales and service.

As these examples suggest, it is important that managers take into account their level of vertical integration when comparing their cost structure for activities on their value chain to those of key competitors. Comparing a fully integrated rival with a partially integrated one requires adjusting for the scope of activities performed to achieve meaningful comparison. It also suggests the need for examining costs associated with activities provided by upstream or downstream companies; these activities ultimately determine comparable, final costs to end users. Said another way, one company's comparative cost disadvantage (or advantage) may emanate more from activities undertaken by upstream or downstream "partners" than from activities under the direct control of that company—therefore suggesting less of a relative advantage or disadvantage within the company's direct value chain.

RESOURCE-BASED VIEW OF THE FIRM

Toyota versus GM is a competitive situation virtually all of us recognize. Stock analysts look at the two and conclude that Toyota is the clear leader. They cite Toyota's superiority in tangible assets (newer factories worldwide, R&D facilities, computerization, cash, etc.) and intangible assets (reputation, brand name awareness, quality-control culture, global business system, etc.). They also mention that Toyota leads GM in several capabilities to make use of these assets effectively—managing distribution globally, influencing labor and supplier relations, managing franchise relations, marketing savvy, and speed of decision making to take quick advantage of changing global conditions are just a few that are frequently mentioned. The combination of capabilities and assets, most analysts conclude, creates several competencies that give Toyota key competitive advantages over GM that are durable and not easily imitated.

resource-based view
A method of analyzing and identifying a firm's strategic advantages based on examining its distinct combination of assets, skills, capabilities, and intangibles as an organization.

The Toyota–GM situation provides a useful illustration for understanding several concepts central to the **resource-based view** (RBV) of the firm. The RBV is a method of analyzing and identifying a firm's strategic advantages based on examining its distinct combination of assets, skills, capabilities, and intangibles as an organization. The RBV's underlying premise is that firms differ in fundamental ways because each firm possesses a unique "bundle" of resources—tangible and intangible assets and organizational capabilities to make use of those assets. Each firm develops competencies from these resources, and, when developed especially well, these become the source of the firm's competitive advantages. Toyota's decision to enter global markets locally and regularly invest in or build newer factory locations in those global markets has given Toyota a competitive advantage analysts estimate GM has lost and will take at least 20 years or longer, if ever, to match. Toyota's strategy for the last 15 years was based in part on the identification of these resources and the development of them into a distinctive competence—a sustained competitive advantage.

Core Competencies

core competence
A capability or skill that a firm emphasizes and excels in doing while in pursuit of its overall mission.

Executives charting the strategy of their business have more recently concentrated their thinking on the notion of a "core competence." A **core competence** is a capability or skill that a firm emphasizes and excels in doing while in pursuit of its overall mission. Core competencies that differ from those found in competing firms would be considered *distinctive competencies*. Apple's competencies in pulling together available technologies and others' software and combining this with their own product design skills and new-product introduction prowess result in an innovation competence that is different and distinct from any firm against which Apple competes. Toyota's pervasive organizationwide pursuit of quality; Wendy's systemwide emphasis on and ability to provide fresh meat daily; and the University of Phoenix's ability to provide comprehensive educational options for working adults worldwide are all examples of competencies that are unique to these firms and distinctive when compared to their competitors.

Distinctive competencies that are identified and nurtured throughout the firm, allowing it to execute effectively so as to provide products or services to customers that are superior to competitor's offerings, become the basis for a lasting *competitive advantage*. Executives, enthusiastic about the notion that their job as strategists was to identify and leverage core competencies into distinctive ones that create sustainable competitive advantage, encountered difficulty applying the concept because of the generality of its level of analysis. The RBV emerged as a way to make the core competency notion and thought process more focused and measurable—creating a very important, and more meaningful, tool for internal analysis. Let's look at the basic concepts underlying the RBV.

Three Basic Resources: Tangible Assets, Intangible Assets, and Organizational Capabilities

tangible assets
The most easily identified assets, often found on a firm's balance sheet. They include production facilities, raw materials, financial resources, real estate, and computers.

The RBV's ability to create a more focused, measurable approach to internal analysis starts with its delineation of three basic types of resources, some of which may become the building blocks for distinctive competencies. These resources are defined below and illustrated in Exhibit 6.8.

Tangible assets are the easiest "resources" to identify and are often found on a firm's balance sheet. They include production facilities, raw materials, financial resources, real estate, and computers. Tangible assets are the physical and financial means a company uses to provide value to its customers.

intangible assets
A firm's assets that you cannot touch or see but that are very often critical in creating competitive advantage: brand names, company reputation, organizational morale, technical knowledge, patents and trademarks, and accumulated experience within an organization.

Intangible assets are "resources" such as brand names, company reputation, organizational morale, technical knowledge, patents and trademarks, and accumulated experience within an organization. While they are not assets that you can touch or see, they are very often critical in creating competitive advantage.

organizational capabilities
Skills (the ability and ways of combining assets, people, and processes) that a company uses to transform inputs into outputs.

Organizational capabilities are not specific "inputs" like tangible or intangible assets; rather, they are the skills—the ability and ways of combining assets, people, and processes—that a company uses to transform inputs into outputs. Apple pioneered and has subsequently leveraged its iPod and iTunes success into a major leadership position in digitalized music, entertainment, and communication on a global basis for individual consumers. Microsoft and others have attempted to copy Dell, but remain far behind Apple's diverse organizational capabilities. Apple has subsequently revolutionized its own iPod, using it to automate and customize a whole new level of entertainment capability that combines assets, people and processes throughout and beyond the Apple organization. Finely developed capabilities, such as Apple's Internet-based, customer-friendly iPod/iTunes

EXHIBIT 6.8

Examples of Different "Resources"

Source: From R.M. Grant, *Contemporary Strategy Analysis,* Blackwell Publishing, 2001, p. 140. Reprinted with permission of Wiley-Blackwell.

Tangible Assets	Intangible Assets	Organizational Capabilities
Hampton Inn's reservation system	Budweiser's brand name	Travelocity's customer service P&G's management training program
Toyota Motor Company's cash reserves	Apple's reputation	Wal-Mart's purchasing and inbound logistics
Georgia Pacific's land holdings	Nike's advertising with LeBron James	Google's product-development processes
FedEx's plane fleet	Katie Couric as CBS's *Evening News* anchor	Coke's global distribution coordination
Coca-Cola's Coke formula	eBay's management team Goldman Sach's culture	3M's innovation process

Classifying and Assessing the Firm's Resources

Resource	Relevant Characteristics	Key Indicators
Tangible Resources		
Financial resources	The firm's borrowing capacity and its internal funds generation determine its resilience and capacity for investment.	• Debt/equity ratio • Operating cash flow/free cash flow • Credit rating
Physical resources	Physical resources constrain the firm's set of production possibilities and impact its cost position. Key characteristics include • The size, location, technical sophistication, and flexibility of plant and equipment • Location and alternative uses for land and buildings • Reserves of raw materials	• Market values of fixed assets • Vintage of capital equipment • Scale of plants • Flexibility of fixed assets
Intangible Resources		
Technological resources	Intellectual property: patent portfolio, copyright, trade secrets Resources for innovation: research facilities, technical and scientific employees	• Number and significance of patents • Revenue from licensing patents and copyrights • R&D staff as a percent of total employment • Number and location of research facilities
Reputation	Reputation with customers through the ownership of brands and trademarks; established relationships with customers; the reputation of the firm's products and services for quality and reliability. The reputation of the company with suppliers (including component suppliers, banks and financiers, employees and potential employees), with government and government agencies, and with the community.	• Brand recognition • Brand equity • Percent of repeat buying • Objective measures of comparative product performance (e.g., Consumers' Association ratings, J. D. Power ratings) • Surveys of corporate reputation (e.g., *BusinessWeek*)

system, can be a source of sustained competitive advantage. They enable a firm to take the same input factors as rivals (such as Microsoft, HP, or Dell) and convert them into products and services, either with greater efficiency in the process or greater quality in the output, or both.

What Makes a Resource Valuable?

Once managers identify their firm's tangible assets, intangible assets, and organizational capabilities, the RBV applies a set of guidelines to determine which of those resources represent strengths or weaknesses—which resources generate core competencies that are sources of sustained competitive advantage. These RBV guidelines derive from the idea that resources are more valuable when they

1. Are *critical to* being able to *meet a customer's need* better than other alternatives.
2. Are *scarce*—few others if any possess that resource or skill to the degree you do.
3. *Drive* a key portion of overall *profits,* in a manner controlled by your firm.
4. Are *durable* or sustainable over time.

Before proceeding to explain each basis for making resources valuable, we suggest that you keep in mind a simple, useful idea: Resources are most valuable when they meet all four of these guidelines. We will return to this point after we explain each guideline more thoroughly.

RBV Guideline 1: Is the resource or skill critical to fulfilling a customer's need better than that of the firm's competitors?

Two restaurants offer similar food, at similar prices, but one has a location much more convenient to downtown offices than the other. The tangible asset, location, helps fulfill daytime workers' lunch-eating needs better than its competitor, resulting in greater profitability and sales volume for the conveniently located restaurant. Wal-Mart redefined discount retailing and outperformed the industry in profitability by 4.5 percent of sales—a 200 percent improvement. Four resources—store locations, brand recognition, employee loyalty, and sophisticated inbound logistics—allowed Wal-Mart to fulfill customer needs much better and more cost effectively than Kmart and other discount retailers (see Exhibit 6.10, page 176). In both of these examples, *it is important to recognize that only resources that contributed to competitive superiority were valuable.* At the same time, other resources such as the restaurant's menu and specific products or parking space at Wal-Mart were essential to doing business but contributed little to competitive advantage because they did not help fulfill customer needs better than those of the firm's key competitors.

RBV Guideline 2: Is the resource scarce? Is it in short supply or not easily substituted for or imitated?

Short Supply   When a resource is scarce, it is more valuable. When a firm possesses a resource and few if any others do, and it is central to fulfilling customers' needs, then it can become the basis of a competitive advantage for the firm. Literal physical scarcity is perhaps the most obvious way a resource might meet this guideline. Very limited natural resources, a unique location, skills that are truly rare—all represent obvious types of scarce resource situations.

Availability of Substitutes   We discussed the threat of substitute products in Chapter 3 as part of the five forces model for examining industry profitability. This basic idea can be taken further and used to gauge the scarcity-based value of particular resources. Whole Foods has been an exciting growth company for several years, focused exclusively on selling wholesome, organic food. The basic idea was to offer food grown organically, without pesticides or manipulation, in a convenient grocery atmosphere. Investors were excited about this concept because of the processed, nonorganic foods offered by virtually every existing grocery chain. Unfortunately for their more recent investors, substitutes for Whole Foods's offerings are becoming easily available from several grocery chains and regional organic chains. Publix, Harris-Teeter, and even Wal-Mart are easily adapting their grocery operations to offer organic fare. With little change to their existing facilities and operational resources, these companies are quickly creating alternatives to Whole Foods's offerings if not offering some of the same items, cheaper. So some worry about the long-term impact on Whole Foods. Investors have seen the value of their Whole Foods's stock decline as substitute resources and capabilities are readily created by existing and new entrants into the organic grocery sectors.

Imitation   A resource that competitors can readily copy can only generate temporary value. It is "scarce" for only a short time. It cannot generate a long-term competitive advantage. When Wendy's first emerged, it was the only major hamburger chain with a drive-through window. This unique organizational capability was part of a "bundle" of resources that allowed Wendy's to provide unique value to its target customers: young adults seeking convenient food service. But once this resource, or organizational capability, proved valuable to fast-food customers, every fast-food chain copied the feature. Then Wendy's continued success was built on other resources that generated other distinctive competencies.

The scarcity that comes with an absence of imitation seldom lasts forever, as the Wendy's example illustrates. Competitors will match or better any resource as soon as they can. It should be obvious, then, that the firm's ability to forestall this eventuality is very important. So how does a firm create resource scarcity by making resources hard to imitate? The RBV identifies four characteristics, called **isolating mechanisms,** that make resources difficult to imitate:

isolating mechanisms
Characteristics that make resources difficult to imitate. In the RBV context these are physically unique resources, path-dependent resources, causal ambiguity, and economic deterrence.

• *Physically unique resources* are virtually impossible to imitate. A one-of-a-kind real estate location, mineral rights, and patents are examples of resources that cannot be imitated. Disney's Mickey Mouse copyright or Winter Park, Colorado's Iron Horse resort possess physical uniqueness. While many strategists claim that resources are physically unique, this is seldom true. Rather, other characteristics are typically what make most resources difficult to imitate.

• *"Path-dependent" resources* are very difficult to imitate because of the difficult "path" another firm must follow to create the resource. These are resources that cannot be instantaneously acquired but rather must be created over time in a manner that is frequently very expensive and always difficult to accelerate. When Michael Dell once said that "Anyone who tries to go direct now will find it very difficult—like trying to jump over the Grand Canyon," he was asserting that Dell's system of selling customized PCs direct via the Internet and Dell's unmatched customer service is, in effect, a path-dependent organizational capability. It would take any competitor years to develop the expertise, infrastructure, reputation, and capabilities necessary to compete effectively with Dell, which HP eventually accomplished after 10 years and considerable effort. Coca-Cola's brand name, Gerber Baby Food's reputation for quality, and Steinway's expertise in piano manufacture would take competitors many years and millions of dollars to match. Consumers' many years of experience drinking Coke or using Gerber or playing a Steinway would also need to be matched.

• *Causal ambiguity* is a third way resources can be very difficult to imitate. This refers to situations in which it is difficult for competitors to understand exactly how a firm has created the advantage it enjoys. Competitors can't figure out exactly what the uniquely valuable resource is or how resources are combined to create the competitive advantage. Causally ambiguous resources are often organizational capabilities that arise from

EXHIBIT 6.9
Resource Imitation

Source: From David J. Collins and Cynthia A. Montgomery, *Corporate Strategy: A Resource-Based Approach,* McGraw-Hill/Irwin, 2005, p. 39. Copyright © 2005 The McGraw-Hill Companies, Inc. Reprinted with permission.

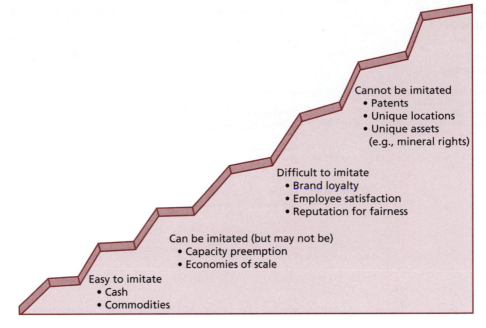

subtle combinations of tangible and intangible assets and culture, processes, and organizational attributes the firm possesses. Southwest Airlines has regularly faced competition from major and regional airlines, with some like United and Continental eschewing their traditional approach and attempting to compete by using their own version of the Southwest approach—same planes, routes, gate procedures, number of attendants, and so on. They have yet to succeed. The most difficult thing to replicate is Southwest's "personality," or culture of fun, family, and frugal yet focused services and attitude. Just how that works is hard for United and Continental to figure out.

• *Economic deterrence* is a fourth source of inimitability. This usually involves large capital investments in capacity to provide products or services in a given market that are scale sensitive. It occurs when a competitor understands the resources that provide a competitive advantage and may even have the capacity to imitate, but chooses not to because of the limited market size that realistically would not support two players the size of the first mover.

While we may be inclined to think of the ability to imitate a resource as a yes-or-no situation, imitation is more accurately measured on a continuum that reflects difficulty and time. Exhibit 6.9 illustrates such a continuum. Some resources may have multiple imitation deterrents. For example, 3M's reputation for innovativeness may involve path dependencies and causal ambiguity.

RBV Guideline 3: Appropriability: Who actually gets the profit created by a resource?

Warren Buffett is known worldwide as one of the most successful investors of the last 25 years. One of his legendary investments was the Walt Disney Company, which he once said he liked "because the Mouse does not have an agent."[3] What he was really saying was that Disney owned the Mickey Mouse copyright, and all profits from that valuable resource went directly to Disney. Other competitors in the "entertainment" industry generated similar profits from their competing offerings, for example, movies, but they often "captured" substantially less of those profits because of the amounts that had to be paid to well-known

[3] *The Harbus,* March 25, 1996, p. 12.

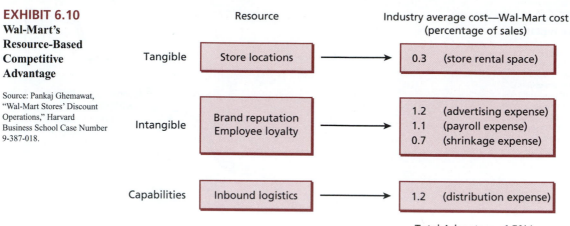

EXHIBIT 6.10
Wal-Mart's Resource-Based Competitive Advantage

Source: Pankaj Ghemawat, "Wal-Mart Stores' Discount Operations," Harvard Business School Case Number 9-387-018.

* Wal-Mart's cost advantage as a percent of sales. Each percentage point advantage is worth well over $500 million in net income to Wal-Mart.

actors or directors or other entertainment contributors seen as the real creators of the movie's value.

Disney's eventual acquisition of Pixar illustrates just the opposite situation for the home of the Mouse. Pixar's expertise in digital animation had proven key to the impressive success of several major animation films released by Disney in the past several years. While Disney apparently thought its name and distribution clout justified its sizable share of the profits this five-year joint venture generated, Steve Jobs and his Pixar team felt otherwise. Pixar's assessment was that their capabilities were key drivers of the huge profits by *Ants* and *Finding Nemo,* leading them not to renew their Disney partnership. Pixar's unmatched digitalization animation expertise quickly "appropriated" the profits generated by this key competitive advantage, and Disney Studios struggled to catch up. Disney eventually solved the dilemma by acquiring Pixar at a handsome premium. The movie *Cars* soon followed.[4]

Sports teams, investment services, and consulting businesses are other examples of companies that generate sizable profits based on resources (e.g., key people, skills, contacts) that are not inextricably linked to the company and therefore do not allow the company to easily capture the profits. Superstar sports players can move from one team to another or command excessively high salaries, and this circumstance could arise in other personal services business situations. It could also occur when one firm joint ventures with another, sharing resources and capabilities and the profits that result. Sometimes restaurants or lodging facilities that are franchisees of a national organization are frustrated by the fees they pay the franchisor each month and decide to leave the organization and go "independent." They often find, to their dismay, that the business declines significantly. The value of the franchise name, reservation system, and brand recognition is critical in generating the profits of the business.

Wal-Mart's success in appropriating profits associated with five key resources or capabilities (see Exhibit 6.10) has, for many years, meant an additional 4.5 cents out of every sales dollar more than its average competitor accrues to Wal-Mart (Wal-Mart "appropriates it") and that money in turn flows to its bottom line. The discount retailing industry is extremely competitive, and this historically allowed Wal-Mart's profitability to reach two to three times the industry average—a sizable competitive advantage for Wal-Mart that was durable and largely under Wal-Mart's control (for the past 20 years). Interestingly, as you will see later in Exhibit 6.13 (page 181), competitors like Target and Kroger have worked intently over the past 10 years to reduce Wal-Mart's intangible and capabilities resource

[4] "Disney Buys Pixar," *Money.CNN.com,* January 1, 2006.

advantages in a way that is beginning to create a new resource-based source of competitive advantage for them.

RBV Guideline 4: Durability: How rapidly will the resource depreciate?

The slower a resource depreciates, the more valuable it is. Tangible assets, such as commodities or capital, can have their depletion measured. Intangible resources, such as brand names or organizational capabilities, present a much more difficult depreciation challenge. The Coca-Cola brand has continued to appreciate, whereas technical know-how in various computer technologies depreciates rapidly. In the increasingly hypercompetitive global economy of the twenty-first century, distinctive competencies and competitive advantages can fade quickly, making the notion of durability a critical test of the value of key resources and capabilities. Some believe that this reality makes well-articulated visions and associated cultures within organizations potentially the most important contributor to long-term survival.[5]

Using the Resource-Based View in Internal Analysis

To use the RBV in internal analysis, a firm must first identify and evaluate its resources to find those that provide the basis for future competitive advantage. This process involves defining the various resources the firm possesses and examining them based on the preceding discussion to gauge which resources truly have strategic value. It is usually helpful in this undertaking to

• *Disaggregate resources*—break them down into more specific competencies—rather than stay with broad categorizations. Saying that Domino's Pizza has better marketing skills than Pizza Hut conveys little information. But dividing that into subcategories such as advertising that, in turn, can be divided into national advertising, local promotions, and coupons allows for a more measurable assessment. Exhibit 6.11 provides a useful illustration of this at the United Kingdom's largest full-service restaurant operator—Whitbread's Restaurant.

• *Utilize a functional perspective.* Looking at different functional areas of the firm, disaggregating tangible and intangible assets as well as organizational capabilities that are present, can begin to uncover important value-building resources and activities that deserve further analysis. Appendix 6A lists a variety of functional area resources and activities that deserve consideration.

• *Look at organizational processes* and combinations of resources and not only at isolated assets or capabilities. While disaggregation is critical, you must also take a creative, gestalt look at what competencies the firm possesses or has the potential to possess that might generate competitive advantage.

• *Use the value chain approach* to uncover organizational capabilities, activities, and processes that are valuable potential sources of competitive advantage.

Once the resources are identified, managers apply the four RBV guidelines for uncovering "valuable" resources. The objective for managers at this point is to identify resources and capabilities that are valuable for most if not all of the reasons our guidelines suggest a resource can be valuable.

If a resource creates the ability to meet a unique customer need, it has value. But if it is not scarce, or if it is easily imitated, it would be unwise to build a firm's strategy on that resource or capability unless that strategy included plans to build scarcity or inimitability into it. If a resource provided the basis for meeting a unique need, was scarce, was not

[5] James C. Collins, *Good to Great: Why Some Companies Make the Leap . . . and Others Don't* (New York: HarperCollins, 2001).

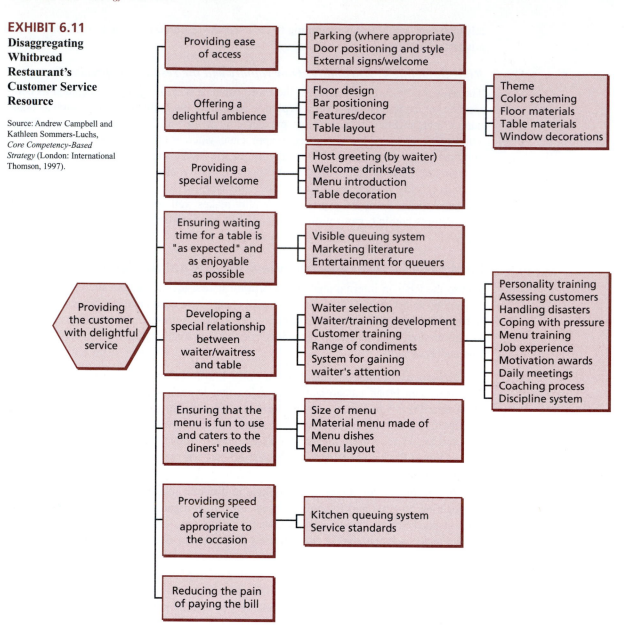

EXHIBIT 6.11

Disaggregating Whitbread Restaurant's Customer Service Resource

Source: Andrew Campbell and Kathleen Sommers-Luchs, *Core Competency-Based Strategy* (London: International Thomson, 1997).

easily imitated, and was easily sustainable over time, managers would be attracted to build a strategy on it more than likely. Our example of Pixar's relationship with Disney earlier in this chapter would seem to suggest this was Pixar's position early in its joint venture with Disney. Yet even with all of those sources confirming a very high value in its digital animation expertise and intellectual property resources, Pixar was not "appropriating" the share of the animation movie profits that were attributable to those resources. Pixar was fortunate: it had the choice not to renew its five-year contract with Disney, and so it did. That eventually led Disney to pay a premium price to acquire Pixar, to regain the strategic value of Pixar's unique resources.

The key point here is that applying RBV analysis should focus on identifying resources that contain all sources of value identified in our four guidelines. Consider the diagram in

EXHIBIT 6.12

Applying the Resource-Based View to Identify the Best Sources of Competitive Advantage

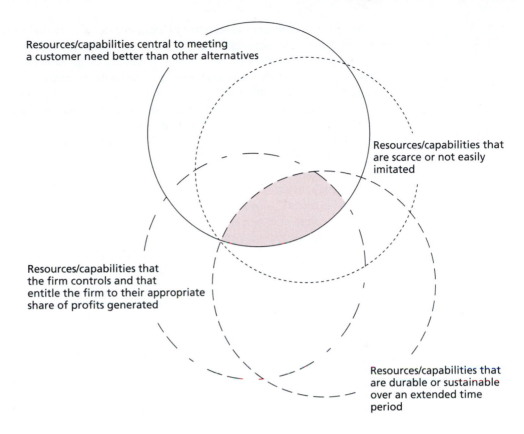

Resources/capabilities central to meeting a customer need better than other alternatives

Resources/capabilities that are scarce or not easily imitated

Resources/capabilities that the firm controls and that entitle the firm to their appropriate share of profits generated

Resources/capabilities that are durable or sustainable over an extended time period

Exhibit 6.12. Each circle in that diagram represents one way resources have value. The area where all circles intersect or overlap would represent resources that derive value in all four ways. Such resources are the ones managers applying the RBV should seek to identify. They are powerful sources around which to build competitive advantage and craft successful strategies. And resources that possess some but not all sources of value become points of emphasis by a management team able to identify ways to build the missing source of value into that resource over time much like Pixar did in its relationship with Disney.

By using RBV, value chain analysis, and SWOT analysis, firms are virtually certain to improve the quality of internal analysis undertaken to help craft a company's competitive strategy. Central to the success of each technique is the strategists' ability to make meaningful comparisons. The next section examines how meaningful comparisons can be made.

INTERNAL ANALYSIS: MAKING MEANINGFUL COMPARISONS

Managers need objective standards to use when examining internal resources and value-building activities. Whether applying the SWOT approach, VCA, or the RBV, strategists rely on three basic perspectives to evaluate how their firms stack up on internal capabilities. These three perspectives are discussed in this section.

Comparison with Past Performance

Strategists use the firm's historical experience as a basis for evaluating internal factors. Managers are most familiar with the internal capabilities and problems of their firms because they have been immersed in the financial, marketing, production, and R&D activities. Not surprisingly, a manager's assessment of whether a certain internal factor—such as production facilities, sales organization, financial capacity, control systems, or key personnel—is a strength or a weakness will be strongly influenced by his or her experience in connection with that factor. In the capital-intensive package delivery industry, for example, operating margin is a strategic internal factor affecting a firm's flexibility to add capacity. UPS managers view UPS's declining operating margins (down from 16 percent to 13.9 percent in 2007) as a potential weakness, limiting its flexibility to aggressively continue to expand its overnight air fleet. FedEx managers view its considerably lower 2007 operating margin of 9.3 percent as a growing strength because it has almost doubled from its 5.0 percent level five years earlier.

Although historical experience can provide a relevant evaluation framework, strategists must avoid tunnel vision in making use of it. NEC, Japan's IBM, initially dominated Japan's PC market with a 70 percent market share by using a proprietary hardware system, much higher screen resolution, powerful distribution channels, and a large software library from third-party vendors. Far from worried, Hajime Ikeda, manager of NEC's planning division at the time, was quoted as saying, "We don't hear complaints from our users." Soon, IBM, Apple, and HP filled the shelves in Japan's famous consumer electronics district, Akihabara. Hiroki Kamata, president of a Japanese computer research firm, reported that Japan's PC market, worth more than $35 billion, saw Apple, Dell, IBM, and HP with more market share than NEC because of better technology, software, and the restrictions created by NEC's proprietary technology. As NEC eventually learned, using only historical experience as a basis for identifying strengths and weaknesses can prove dangerously inaccurate.

Benchmarking: Comparison with Competitors

A major focus in determining a firm's resources and competencies is comparison with existing (and potential) competitors. Firms in the same industry often have different marketing skills, financial resources, operating facilities and locations, technical know-how, brand images, levels of integration, managerial talent, and so on. These different internal resources can become relative strengths (or weaknesses) depending on the strategy a firm chooses. In choosing a strategy, managers should compare the firm's key internal capabilities with those of its rivals, thereby isolating its key strengths and weaknesses.

In the U.S. home appliance industry, for example, Sears and General Electric have been major rivals. Sears's principal strength is its retail network. For GE, distribution—through independent franchised dealers—has traditionally been a relative weakness. GE's possession of the financial resources needed to support modernized mass production has enabled it to maintain both cost and technological advantages over its rivals, particularly Sears. This major strength for GE is a relative weakness for Sears, which depends solely on subcontracting to produce its Kenmore appliances. On the other hand, maintenance and repair service are important in the appliance industry. Historically, Sears has had strength in this area because it maintains fully staffed service components and spreads the costs of components over numerous departments at each retail location. GE, on the other hand, has had to depend on regional service centers and on local contracting with independent service firms by its independent local dealers. Among the internal factors that Sears and GE must consider in developing a strategy are distribution networks, technological capabilities, operating costs, and service facilities. For example, GE's major move creating alliances with Home Depot and Lowe's to sell appliances has been a major factor in turning what has been a relative weakness into what now appears to be a major strength. Managers in both Sears and GE have built successful strategies, yet those strategies are quite different. Benchmarking each other, they have identified ways to build on relative strengths while avoiding dependence on capabilities at which the other firm excels.

Wal-Mart's Midlife Crisis: Falling Behind Its Rivals in Key Success Factors

For nearly five decades, Wal-Mart's signature "everyday low prices" and their enabler—low costs—defined not only its business model but also the distinctive personality of this proud, insular company that emerged from the Ozarks backwoods to dominate retailing. Over the past year and a half, though, Wal-Mart's growth formula has stopped working. In 2006 its U.S. division eked out a 1.9 percent gain in same-store sales—its worst performance ever—and this year has begun no better. By this key measure, such competitors as Target, Costco, Kroger, Safeway, Walgreen's, CVS, and Best Buy now are all growing two to five times faster than Wal-Mart.

One can argue that the deceleration of Wal-Mart's organic growth is a function of the aging of its outlets, given that same-store sales rates slow as stores mature. Outlets five years or older accounted for 17 percent of all U.S. Supercenters in 2000 and 44 percent in 2006, and will top 60 percent in 2010. Meanwhile, the underlying economics of expansion have turned against Wal-Mart, even as it relies increasingly on store-building to compensate for sagging same-store sales. On balance, the new Supercenters are just not pulling in enough sales to offset fully the sharply escalating costs of building them.

Part of the problem is that many new stores are located so close to existing ones that Wal-Mart ends up competing with itself. All in all, the retailer's pretax return on fixed assets, which includes things such as computers and trucks as well as stores, has plunged 40 percent since 2000. Wal-Mart disclosed a year and a half ago that same-store sales were rising 10 times, or 1,000 percent, faster at the 800 best-managed outlets than at the 800 worst-run ones. Equally shocking was its admission that 25 percent of its stores failed to meet minimum expectations of cleanliness, product availability, checkout times, and so on.

Over the past decade, top competitors in most every retailing specialty have succeeded in narrowing their cost gap with Wal-Mart by restructuring their operations. They eliminated jobs, remodeled stores, and replaced warehouses, investing heavily in new technology to tie it all together. Unionized supermarkets even managed to chip away at Wal-Mart's nonunion-labor cost advantage, signaling their resolve by taking a long strike in Southern California in 2003–2004. The end result: rival chains gradually were able to bring their prices down closer to Wal-Mart's and again make good money.

Consider the return to form of Kroger Co., the largest and oldest U.S. supermarket chain. Cincinnati-based Kroger competes against more Wal-Mart Supercenters—1,000 at last count—than any other grocer. Which is why until recently the only real interest Wall Street took in the old-line giant was measuring it for a coffin. Today, though, a rejuvenated Kroger is gaining share faster in the 32 markets where it competes with Wal-Mart than in the 12 where it does not.

A recent Bank of America survey of three such markets—Atlanta, Houston, and Nashville—found that Kroger's prices were 7.5 percent higher on average than Wal-Mart's, compared with 20 to 25 percent five years ago. This margin is thin enough to allow Kroger to again bring to bear such "core competencies" as service, quality, and convenience, says BofA's Scott A. Mushkin, who recently switched his Kroger rating to buy from sell. "We're saying the game has changed, and it looks like it has changed substantially in Kroger's favor," he says.

benchmarking
Evaluating the sustainability of advantages against key competitors. Comparing the way a company performs a specific activity with a competitor or other company doing the same thing.

Benchmarking, or comparing the way "our" company performs a specific activity with a competitor or other company doing the same thing, has become a central concern of managers in quality commitment companies worldwide. Particularly as the value chain framework has taken hold in structuring internal analysis, managers seek to systematically benchmark the costs and results of the smallest value activities against relevant competitors or other useful standards because it has proven to be an effective way to continuously improve that activity. The ultimate objective in benchmarking is to identify the "best practices" in performing an activity and to learn how lower costs, fewer defects, or other outcomes linked to excellence are achieved. Companies committed to benchmarking attempt to isolate and identify where their costs or outcomes are out of line with what the best practices of a particular activity experience (competitors and noncompetitors) and then attempt to change their activities to achieve the new best practices standard. General Electric sends managers to benchmark FedEx's customer service practices, seeking to compare and improve on its own practices within a diverse set of businesses none of which compete directly with FedEx. It earlier did the same thing with Motorola, leading it to embrace Motorola's Six Sigma program for quality control and continuous improvement.

Comparison with Success Factors in the Industry

Industry analysis (see Chapter 4) involves identifying the factors associated with successful participation in a given industry. As was true for the evaluation methods discussed earlier, the key determinants of success in an industry may be used to identify a firm's internal strengths and weaknesses. By scrutinizing industry competitors as well as customer needs, vertical industry structure, channels of distribution, costs, barriers to entry, availability of substitutes, and suppliers, a strategist seeks to determine whether a firm's current internal capabilities represent strengths or weaknesses in new competitive arenas. The discussion in Chapter 4 provides a useful framework—five industry forces—against which to examine a firm's potential strengths and weaknesses. General Cinema Corporation, the largest U.S. movie theater operator, determined that its internal skills in marketing, site analysis, creative financing, and management of geographically dispersed operations were key strengths relative to major success factors in the soft-drink bottling industry. This assessment proved accurate. Within 10 years after it entered the soft-drink bottling industry, General Cinema became the largest franchised bottler of soft drinks in the United States, handling Pepsi, 7UP, Dr Pepper, and Sunkist. Exhibit 6.13, Strategy in Action, describes the dilemma facing once-mighty Wal-Mart as it falls precipitously behind key rivals on two critical success factors in discount retailing: same-store sales growth and age/quality of 60 percent of its U.S. stores. These two critical success factors drive and indicate the relative health of large discount retail firms. Firms with solid same-store sales growth indicate wise choices in location, attractiveness of their stores, and the merchandise inside them. Likewise, aging and probably substandard store facilities are typically not as efficient as newer ones, nor are they as inviting to shoppers. So Wal-Mart, Target, and other discount retailers conduct internal analyses in part by comparing themselves on these two (and surely others) critical success factors to interpret their strength or weakness relative to factors that drive industry success.

product life cycle (PLC)

A concept that describes a product's sales, profitability, and competencies that are key drivers of the success of that product as it moves through a sequence of stages from development, introduction to growth, maturity, decline, and eventual removal from a market.

Product Life Cycle

Product life cycle (PLC) is one way to identify success factors against which executives can evaluate their firm's competencies relative to its key product or products. The **product life cycle** is a concept that describes a product's sales, profitability, and competencies that are key drivers of the success of that product as it moves through a sequence of stages from development, introduction to growth, maturity, decline, and eventual removal from a market. Exhibit 6.14 illustrates the "typical" product life cycle.

EXHIBIT 6.14
Illustration of the Product Life Cycle

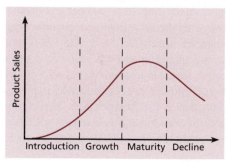

Core competencies associated with success are thought to vary across different stages of the product life cycle. Those competencies might include the following:

Introduction Stage

During this stage the firm needs competence in building product awareness and market development along with the resources to support initial losses:

- Ability to create product awareness.
- Good channel relationships in ways to get the product introduced quickly, gaining a first-mover advantage.
- Premium pricing to "skim" profitability if few competitors exist.
- Solid relationships with and access to trend-setting early adopters.
- Financial resources to absorb an initial cash drain and lack of profitability.

Growth

During this stage market growth accelerates rapidly, with the firm seeking to build brand awareness and establish/increase market share:

- Brand awareness and ability to build brand.
- Advertising skills and resources to back them.
- Product features that differentiate versus increased competitive offerings.
- Establishing and stabilizing market shares.
- Access to multiple distribution channels.
- Ability to add additional features.

Maturity

This stage sees growth in sales slow significantly, along with increased competition and similar product offerings leading the firm to need competencies that allow it to defend its market share while maximizing profit:

- Sustained brand awareness.
- Ability to differentiate products and features.
- Resources to initiate or sustain price wars.
- Operating advantages to improve slimming margins.
- Judgment to know whether to stay in or exit saturated market segments.

Decline

At this point the product and its competitors start to experience declining sales and increased pressure on margins. Competencies needed are:

- Ability to withstand intense price-cutting.
- Brand strength to allow reduced marketing.
- Cost cutting capacity and slack to allow it.
- Good supplier relationships to gain cost concessions.
- Innovation skills to create new products or "re-create" existing ones.

The PLC is an interesting concept or framework against which executives might gauge the strength of relevant competencies. Caution is necessary in its use beyond that purpose, however. In reality, very few products follow exactly the cycle portrayed in the PLC model. The length in each stage can vary, the length and nature of the PLC for any particular product can vary dramatically, and it is not easy to tell exactly what stage a product might be in at any given time. Not all products go through each stage. Some, for example, go from introduction to decline. And movement from one stage to the next can be accelerated by strategies or tactics executives emphasize. For example, price-cutting can accelerate the movement from maturity to decline.

Product life cycles can describe a single product, a category of products, or an industry segment. Applying the basic idea to an industry segment (category of products) rather than a specific product has been a more beneficial adaptation of the PLC concept, providing executives with a conceptual tool to aid them in strategic analysis and choice in the context of the evolution of an industry segment in which their firm competes. So we will examine the concept of stages of evolution of an industry segment or category of products as a tool of strategic analysis and choice in Chapter 8.

Summary

This chapter looked at several ways managers achieve greater objectivity and rigor as they analyze their company's internal resources and capabilities. Managers often start their internal analysis with questions like, How well is the current strategy working? What is our current situation? What are our strengths and weaknesses? SWOT analysis is a traditional approach that has been in use for decades to help structure managers' pursuit of answers to these questions. A logical approach still used by many managers today, SWOT analysis has limitations linked to the depth of its analysis and the risk of overlooking key considerations.

Two techniques for internal analysis have emerged that overcome some of the limitations of SWOT analysis, offering more comprehensive approaches that can help managers identify and assess their firm's internal resources and capabilities in a more systematic, objective, and measurable manner. Value chain analysis has managers look at and disaggregate their business as a chain of activities that occur in a sequential manner to create the products or services they sell. The value chain approach breaks down the firm's activities into primary and support categories of activities, then breaks these down further into specific types of activities with the objective to disaggregate activity into as many meaningful subdivisions as possible. Once done, managers attempt to attribute costs to each. Doing this gives managers very distinct ways of isolating the things they do well and not so well, and it isolates activities that are truly key in meeting customer needs—true potential sources of competitive advantage.

The third approach covered in this chapter was the resource-based view (RBV). RBV is based on the premise that firms build competitive advantage based on the unique resources, skills, and capabilities they control or develop, which can become the basis of unique, sustainable competitive advantages that allow them to craft successful competitive strategies. The RBV provides a useful conceptual frame to first inventory a firm's potential competitive advantages among its tangible assets, intangible assets, and its organizational capabilities. Once inventoried, the RBV provides four fundamental guidelines that managers can use to "value" these resources and capabilities. Those with major value, defined as ones that are valuable for several reasons, become the bases for building strategies linked to sustainable competitive advantages.

Finally, this chapter covered three ways objectivity and realism are enhanced when managers use meaningful standards for comparison regardless of the particular analytical framework they employ in internal analysis. This chapter is followed by two appendixes. The first provides a useful inventory of the types of activities in different functional areas of a firm that can be sources of competitive advantage. The second appendix covers traditional financial analysis to serve as a refresher and reminder about this basic internal analysis tool.

When matched with management's environmental analyses and mission priorities, the process of internal analysis provides the critical foundation for strategy formulation. Armed with an accurate, thorough, and timely internal analysis, managers are in a better position to formulate effective strategies. The next chapter describes basic strategy alternatives that any firm may consider.

Key Terms

benchmarking, *p. 181*
core competence, *p. 171*
intangible assets, *p. 171*
isolating mechanisms, *p. 174*
opportunity, *p. 159*
organizational capabilities, *p. 171*

primary activities, *p. 165*
product life cycle (PLC), *p. 182*
resource-based view, *p. 170*
strength, *p. 159*
SWOT analysis, *p. 159*
support activities, *p. 165*

tangible assets, *p. 171*
threat, *p. 159*
value chain, *p. 164*
value chain analysis, *p. 164*
weakness, *p. 160*

Questions for Discussion

1. Describe SWOT analysis as a way to guide internal analysis. How does this approach reflect the basic strategic management process?
2. What are potential weaknesses of SWOT analysis?
3. Describe the difference between primary and support activities using value chain analysis.
4. How is VCA different from SWOT analysis?
5. What is the resource-based view? Give examples of three different types of resources.
6. What are three ways resources become more valuable? Provide an example of each.
7. Explain how you might use VCA, RBV, and SWOT analysis to get a better sense of what might be a firm's key building blocks for a successful strategy.
8. Attempt to apply SWOT, VCA, and RBV to yourself and your career aspirations. What are your major strengths and weaknesses? How might you use your knowledge of these strengths and weaknesses to develop your future career plans?

Chapter 6 Discussion Case

Apple's Blueprint for Genius

BusinessWeek

DESIGNED BY APPLE IN CALIFORNIA

1   The words are printed in such small type on the back of Apple's tiny iPod Nano MP3 player that you have to squint to read them. But they speak volumes about why Apple is standing so far out from the crowd these days. At a time when rivals are outsourcing as much design as possible to cut costs, Apple remains at its core a product company—one that would never give up control of how those products are created.

2   In this age of commodity tech products, design, after all, is what makes Apple Apple. This focus is apparent to anyone who has used one of its trailblazing products. While the Silicon Valley pioneer sells only a few dozen models, compared to the hundreds offered by many of its rivals, many of those "designed in California" products are startling departures from the norm—and they often set the directions for the rest of the industry. Examples abound, from the iPhone to Apple TV to the iPod, the Airport Extreme, or the simple smallness of the new Mac mini PC.

3   What's the secret? The precise details are almost impossible to get, because Apple treats its product-development processes like state secrets—going so far as to string black drapes around the production lines at the factories of the contract manufacturers it hires to assemble its products. In one case, says a source who once worked on an Apple project, the outfit even insisted that its wares be built only on the midnight shift, when fewer prying eyes might be around.

INSANELY GREAT

4   But the general themes are clear. Most CEOs are focused on achieving their financial and operational goals, and on executing a strategy. But Apple's Steve Jobs believes his company's ultimate advantage comes from its ability to make unique, or as he calls them, "insanely great" products. Introducing the iPhone in 2007, Jobs simply said, "We reinvented the phone."

5   Jobs's entire company is focused on that task. That means while rival computer, phone, and digital media product makers increasingly rely on so-called outsourced design manufacturers (ODMs) for key design decisions, Jobs keeps most of those tasks in-house. Sure, he relies on ODMs to manufacture his products, but the big decisions on Apple products are made in Silicon Valley.

6   Jobs himself is a crucial part of the formula. He's unique among big-time hardware CEOs for his hands-on involvement in the design process. Even product-design experts marvel at the power of the Jobs factor.

FIRST, AN IDEA

7   "I've been thinking hard about the Apple product-development process since I left," says design guru Donald Norman, co-founder of the design consultants Nielsen Norman Group, who left Apple in 1997. "If you follow my [guidelines], it will guarantee good design. But Steve Jobs doesn't want good design. He wants great design, and my method will never give you that. That takes a rare leader, who can bring both the cohesion and commitment and style. And Steve has it."

8   Many executives believe that outsourcing design allows them to lower the salaries they must pay and lets them have engineers working on the products across all time zones. Jobs thinks that's short-sighted. He argues that the cost-savings aren't worth what you give up in terms of teamwork, communication, and the ability to get groups of people working together to bring a new idea to life. Indeed, with top-notch mechanical, electrical, software, and industrial designers all housed at Apple's Infinite Loop campus in Cupertino, Calif., the company's design capability is more vertically integrated than almost any other tech outfit.

9   Typically, a new Apple product starts with a big idea for an unmet customer need. For the original iPod, it was for an MP3 player that, unlike earlier models, could hold and easily manage your entire music collection. Then, Apple's product architects and industrial designers figure out what that product should look like and what features it should have—and, importantly, not have. "Apple has a much more holistic view of product design," says David Carey, president of design consulting firm Portelligent. "Good product design starts from the outside, and works its way inside."

HALF MEASURE

10   Already, that's different from the process by which the bulk of tech products are made. Increasingly, tech companies meet with ODMs to see what designs they have cooked up. Then, the ODMs are asked to tweak those basic blueprints to add a few features and to match the look and feel of the company's other products.

11   That's where the "design" input might end for most companies. But since it's almost always trying to create one-of-a-kind products, Apple has to ask its own engineers to do the critical electrical and mechanical work to bring products to life.

12   In the iPod Shuffle, for example, designers cut a circuit card in two and stacked the pieces, bunk-bed style, to make use of the empty air space created by the height of the battery in the device. "They realized they could erase the height penalty [of the battery] to help them win the battle of the bulge," says Carey, whose company did a detailed engineering analysis of the iPod Nano.

SCREW-FREE

13   Even more important, Apple's products are designed to run a particular set of programs or services. By contrast, a Dell or HP device must be ready for whatever new features Microsoft comes out with or whatever Windows program a customer opts to install.

14   But Apple makes much of its own software, from the MAS OSX operating system to applications such as iPhoto and iTunes. "That's Apple's trump card," says one Apple rival. "The ODMs just don't have the world-class industrial design, the style, or the ability to make easy-to-use software—or the ability to integrate it all. They may some day, but they don't have it now."

15   Of course, Apple also sets itself apart by designing machines that are also little works of art—even if it means making life difficult for manufacturers contracted to build those designs. During a trip to visit ODMs in Asia, one executive told securities analyst Jim Grossman of Thrivent Investment Management about Steve Jobs's insistence that no screws be visible on the laptop his company was manufacturing for Apple. The executive said his company had no idea how to handle the job and had to invent a new tooling process for the job. "They had to learn new ways to do things just to meet Apple's design," says Grossman.

TOUGH CUSTOMER

16   That's not to say Apple is completely bucking the outsourcing trend. All its products are manufactured by ODMs in Asia. Just as it buys chips and disk drives from other suppliers, sources say Apple lets ODMs take some role in garden-variety engineering work—but not much. "This is an issue for Apple, because the A-team engineers [at the ODMs] don't like working with Apple. It's like when you were a kid, all your dad let you do was hold the flashlight, rather than let you try to fix the car yourself," says an executive at a rival MP3 maker.

17   In fairness, Apple's reliance on a smaller number of products than its rivals and go-it-alone design means it's always a dud or two from disaster. But at the moment, it's proving that "made in Cupertino" is a trademark for success.

VOICES OF INNOVATION

An Interview with Steve Jobs, Chairman and CEO of Apple

BusinessWeek: What can we learn from Apple's struggle to innovate during the decade before your return in 1997?

Steve Jobs: "You need a very product-oriented culture. Apple had a monopoly on the graphical user interface for almost 10 years. How are monopolies lost? Some very good product people invent some very good products, and the company achieves a monopoly. [But] what's the point of focusing on making the product even better when the only company you can take business from is yourself? So a different group of people starts to move up. And who usually ends up running the show?

The sales guy. Then one day the monopoly expires, for whatever reason . . . but by then, the best product people have left or they are no longer listened to. And so the company goes through this tumultuous time, and it either survives or it doesn't.

BusinessWeek: How do you systematize innovation?

Steve Jobs: You don't. You hire good people who will challenge each other every day to make the best products possible. That's why you don't see any big posters on the walls around here, stating our mission statement. Our corporate culture is simple.

BusinessWeek: So the key is to have good people with a passion for excellence.

Steve Jobs: When I got back, Apple had forgotten who we were. Remember that "Think Different" ad campaign we ran? It was certainly for customers, but it was even more for Apple. That ad was to remind us of who our heroes are and who we are. Companies sometimes do forget. Fortunately, we woke up. And Apple is doing the best work in its history.

DISCUSSION QUESTIONS

1. Apply the three internal analysis frameworks—SWOT analysis, value chain analysis, and the resource-based view—as a way to explain and evaluate aspects of Apple's internal environment highlighted in the Chapter Case about Apple and the interview with Steve Jobs.

   a. What are Apple's strengths and weaknesses, opportunities and threats?

   b. Roughly what would Apple's value chain look like, and how might it differ from other companies mentioned in this case?

   c. What are Apple's key resources and capabilities? Which are most valuable? Why?

2. Which is the most meaningful type of comparison you make use of in conducting each approach to internal analysis at Apple?

3. Which approach to internal analysis works best in your internal analysis of the aspects about Apple covered in this case? Why?

4. In your opinion, would it be best to use that approach (your answer to question 3) alone or to use it along with the other two approaches if you were a manager responsible for conducting an internal analysis of your company as part of its strategic management process?

Sources: Reprinted with special permission from "The Future of Apple," *BusinessWeek*, January 10, 2007, "Apple's Blueprint for Genius," *BusinessWeek Online Extra*, March 23, 2005; and "Steven Jobs on Apple Innovation," *BusinessWeek*, October 4, 2005. Copyright © 2007 The McGraw-Hill Companies.

Chapter 6 Appendix A

Key Resources across Functional Areas

MARKETING

Firm's products-services: breadth of product line
Concentration of sales in a few products or to a few customers
Ability to gather needed information about markets
Market share or submarket shares
Product-service mix and expansion potential: life cycle of key products; profit-sales balance in product-service
Channels of distribution: number, coverage, and control
Effective sales organization: knowledge of customer needs
Internet usage; Web presence
Product-service image, reputation, and quality
Imaginativeness, efficiency, and effectiveness of sales promotion and advertising
Pricing strategy and pricing flexibility
Procedures for digesting market feedback and developing new products, services, or markets
After-sale service and follow-up
Goodwill—brand loyalty

FINANCIAL AND ACCOUNTING

Ability to raise short-term capital
Ability to raise long-term capital; debt-equity
Corporate-level resources (multibusiness firm)
Cost of capital relative to that of industry and competitors
Tax considerations
Relations with owners, investors, and stockholders
Leverage position; capacity to utilize alternative financial strategies, such as lease or sale and leaseback
Cost of entry and barriers to entry
Price-earnings ratio
Working capital; flexibility of capital structure
Effective cost control; ability to reduce cost
Financial size
Efficiency and effectiveness of accounting system for cost, budget, and profit planning

PRODUCTION, OPERATIONS, TECHNICAL

Raw materials' cost and availability, supplier relationships
Inventory control systems; inventory turnover
Location of facilities; layout and utilization of facilities
Economies of scale
Technical efficiency of facilities and utilization of capacity
Effectiveness of subcontracting use
Degree of vertical integration; value added and profit margin
Efficiency and cost-benefit of equipment

Effectiveness of operation control procedures: design, scheduling, purchasing, quality control, and efficiency
Costs and technological competencies relative to those of industry and competitors
Research and development—technology—innovation
Patents, trademarks, and similar legal protection

PERSONNEL

Management personnel
Employees' skill and morale
Labor relations costs compared with those of industry and competitors
Efficiency and effectiveness of personnel policies
Effectiveness of incentives used to motivate performance
Ability to level peaks and valleys of employment
Employee turnover and absenteeism
Specialized skills
Experience

QUALITY MANAGEMENT

Relationship with suppliers, customers
Internal practices to enhance quality of products and services
Procedures for monitoring quality

INFORMATION SYSTEMS

Timeliness and accuracy of information about sales, operations, cash, and suppliers
Relevance of information for tactical decisions
Information to manage quality issues: customer service
Ability of people to use the information that is provided
Linkages to suppliers and customers

ORGANIZATION AND GENERAL MANAGEMENT

Organizational structure
Firm's image and prestige
Firm's record in achieving objectives
Organization of communication system
Overall organizational control system (effectiveness and utilization)
Organizational climate; organizational culture
Use of systematic procedures and techniques in decision making
Top-management skill, capabilities, and interest
Strategic planning system
Intraorganizational synergy (multibusiness firms)

Chapter 6 Appendix B

Using Financial Analysis

One of the most important tools for assessing the strength of an organization within its industry is financial analysis. Managers, investors, and creditors all employ some form of this analysis as the beginning point for their financial decision making. Investors use financial analyses in making decisions about whether to buy or sell stock, and creditors use them in deciding whether or not to lend. They provide managers with a measurement of how the company is doing in comparison with its performance in past years and with the performance of competitors in the industry.

Although financial analysis is useful for decision making, some weaknesses should be noted. Any picture that it provides of the company is based on past data. Although trends may be noteworthy, this picture should not automatically be assumed to be applicable to the future. In addition, the analysis is only as good as the accounting procedures that have provided the information. When making comparisons between companies, one should keep in mind the variability of accounting procedures from firm to firm.

There are four basic groups of financial ratios: liquidity, leverage, activity, and profitability.

Depicted in Exhibit 6.B1 are the specific ratios calculated for each of the basic groups. Liquidity and leverage ratios represent an assessment of the risk of the firm. Activity and profitability ratios are measures of the return generated by the assets of the firm. The interaction between certain groups of ratios is indicated by arrows.

Typically, two common financial statements are used in financial analyses: the balance sheet and the income statement. Exhibit 6.B2 is a balance sheet and Exhibit 6.B3 an income statement for the ABC Company. These statements will be used to illustrate the financial analyses.

LIQUIDITY RATIOS

Liquidity ratios are used as indicators of a firm's ability to meet its short-term obligations. These obligations include any current liabilities, including currently maturing long-term debt. Current assets move through a normal cash cycle of inventories—sales—accounts receivable—cash. The firm then uses cash to pay off or reduce its current liabilities. The best-known liquidity ratio is the current ratio: current assets divided by current liabilities. For the ABC Company, the current ratio is calculated as follows:

$$\frac{\text{Current assets}}{\text{Current liabilities}} = \frac{\$4,125,000}{\$2,512,500} = 1.64 \ (2011)$$

$$= \frac{\$3,618,000}{\$2,242,250} = 1.161 \ (2010)$$

Most analysts suggest a current ratio of 2 to 3. A large current ratio is not necessarily a good sign; it may mean that an organization is not making the most efficient use of its assets. The optimum current ratio will vary from industry to industry, with the more volatile industries requiring higher ratios.

Because slow-moving or obsolescent inventories could overstate a firm's ability to meet short-term demands, the quick ratio is sometimes preferred to assess a firm's liquidity. The quick ratio is current assets minus inventories, divided by current liabilities. The quick ratio for the ABC Company is calculated as follows:

$$\frac{\text{Current assets} - \text{Inventories}}{\text{Current liabilities}} = \frac{\$1,950,000}{\$2,512,500} = 0.78 \ (2011)$$

$$= \frac{\$1,618,000}{\$2,242,250} = 0.72 \ (2010)$$

A quick ratio of approximately 1 would be typical for American industries. Although there is less variability in the quick ratio than in the current ratio, stable industries would be able to operate safely with a lower ratio.

LEVERAGE RATIOS

Leverage ratios identify the source of a firm's capital—owners or outside creditors. The term *leverage* refers to the fact that using capital with a fixed interest charge will "amplify" either profits or losses in relation to the equity of holders of common stock. The most commonly used ratio is total debt divided by total assets. Total debt includes current liabilities and long-term liabilities. This ratio is a measure of the percentage of total funds provided by debt. A total debt–total assets ratio higher than 0.5 is usually considered safe only for firms in stable industries.

$$\frac{\text{Total debt}}{\text{Total assets}} = \frac{\$3,862,500}{\$7,105,000} = 0.54 \ (2011)$$

$$= \frac{\$3,667,250}{\$6,393,000} = 0.57 \ (2010)$$

The ratio of long-term debt to equity is a measure of the extent to which sources of long-term financing are provided by creditors. It is computed by dividing long-term debt by the stockholders' equity:

$$\frac{\text{Long-term debt}}{\text{Equity}} = \frac{\$1,350,000}{\$3,242,500} = 0.42 \ (2011)$$

$$= \frac{\$1,425,000}{\$2,725,750} = 0.52 \ (2010)$$

EXHIBIT 6.B1   Financial Ratios

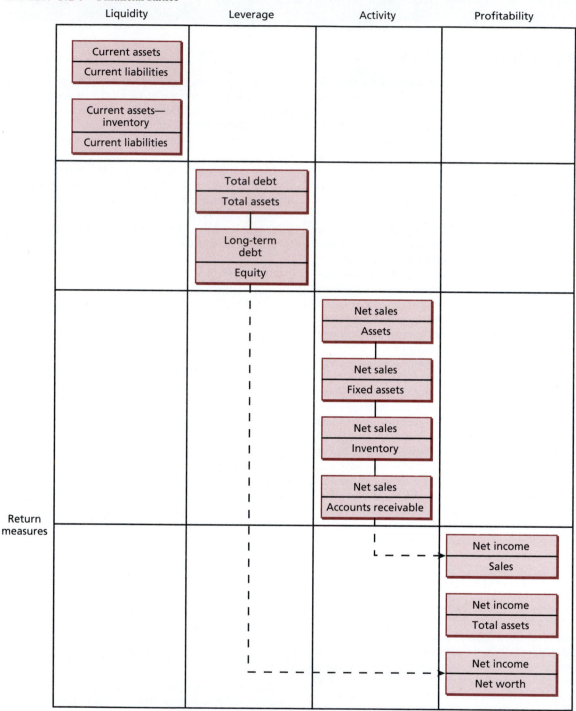

EXHIBIT 6.B2   ABC Company Balance Sheet as of December 31, 2010, and 2011

		2011		2010
Assets				
Current assets:				
Cash		$ 140,000		$ 115,00
Accounts receivable		1,760,000		1,440,000
Inventory		2,175,000		2,000,000
Prepaid expenses		50,000		63,000
Total current assets		4,125,000		3,618,000
Fixed assets:				
Long-term receivable		1,255,000		1,090,000
Property and plant	$2,037,000		$2,015,000	
Less: Accumulated depreciation	862,000		860,000	
Net property and plant		1,175,000		1,155,000
Other fixed assets		550,000		530,000
Total fixed assets		2,980,000		2,775,000
Total assets		$7,105,000		$6,393,000
Liabilities and Stockholders' Equity				
Current liabilities:				
Accounts payable		$1,325,000		$1,225,000
Bank loans payable		475,000		550,000
Accrued federal taxes		675,000		425,000
Current maturities (long-term debt)		17,500		26,000
Dividends payable		20,000		16,250
Total current liabilities		2,512,500		2,242,250
Long-term liabilities		1,350,000		1,425,000
Total liabilities		3,862,000		3,667,250
Stockholders' equity:				
Common stock				
(104,046 shares outstanding in 2005;				
101,204 shares outstanding in 2004)		44,500		43,300
Additional paid-in-capital		568,000		372,450
Retained earnings		2,630,000		2,310,000
Total stockholders' equity		3,242,500		2,725,750
Total liabilities and stockholders' equity		$7,105,000		$6,393,000

EXHIBIT 6.B3   ABC Company Income Statement for the years ending December 31, 2010, and 2011

		2011		2010
Net sales		$8,250,000		$8,000,000
Cost of goods sold	$5,100,000		$5,000,000	
Administrative expenses	1,750,000		1,680,000	
Other expenses	420,000		390,000	
Total		7,270,000		7,070,000
Earnings before interest and taxes		980,000		930,000
Less: Interest expense		210,000		210,000
Earnings before taxes		770,000		720,000
Less: Federal income taxes		360,000		325,000
Earnings after taxes (net income)		$ 410,000		$ 395,000
Common stock cash dividends		$ 90,000		$ 84,000
Addition to retained earnings		$ 320,000		$ 311,000
Earnings per common share		$ 3.940		$ 3.90
Dividends per common share		$ 0.865		$ 0.83

ACTIVITY RATIOS

Activity ratios indicate how effectively a firm is using its resources. By comparing revenues with the resources used to generate them, it is possible to establish an efficiency of operation. The asset turnover ratio indicates how efficiently management is employing total assets. Asset turnover is calculated by dividing sales by total assets. For the ABC Company, asset turnover is calculated as follows:

$$\text{Asset turnover} = \frac{\text{Sales}}{\text{Total assets}} = \frac{\$8,250,000}{\$7,105,000} = 1.16 \, (2011)$$

$$= \frac{\$8,000,0000}{\$6,393,000} = 1.25 \, (2010)$$

The ratio of sales to fixed assets is a measure of the turnover on plant and equipment. It is calculated by dividing sales by net fixed assets.

$$\frac{\text{Fixed asset}}{\text{turnover}} = \frac{\text{Sales}}{\text{Net fixed assets}} = \frac{\$8,250,000}{\$2,980,000} = 2.77 \, (2011)$$

$$= \frac{\$8,000,000}{\$2,775,000} = 2.88 \, (2010)$$

Industry figures for asset turnover will vary with capital-intensive industries, and those requiring large inventories will have much smaller ratios.

Another activity ratio is inventory turnover, estimated by dividing sales by average inventory. The norm for U.S. industries is 9, but whether the ratio for a particular firm is higher or lower normally depends on the product sold. Small, inexpensive items usually turn over at a much higher rate than larger, expensive ones. Because inventories normally are carried at cost, it would be more accurate to use the cost of goods sold in place of sales in the numerator of this ratio. Established compilers of industry ratios, such as Dun & Bradstreet, however, use the ratio of sales to inventory.

$$\frac{\text{Inventory}}{\text{turnover}} = \frac{\text{Sales}}{\text{Inventory}} = \frac{\$8,250,000}{\$2,175,000} = 3.79 \, (2011)$$

$$= \frac{\$8,000,000}{\$2,000,000} = 4.00 \, (2010)$$

The accounts receivable turnover is a measure of the average collection period on sales. If the average number of days varies widely from the industry norm, it may be an indication of poor management. A too-low ratio could indicate the loss of sales because of a too-restrictive credit policy. If the ratio is too high, too much capital is being tied up in accounts receivable, and management may be increasing the chance of bad debts. Because of varying industry credit policies, a comparison for the firm over time or within an industry is the only useful analysis. Because information on credit sales for other firms generally is unavailable, total sales must be used. Because not all firms have the same percentage of credit sales, there is only approximate comparability among firms:

$$\frac{\text{Accounts}}{\text{receivable}} = \frac{\text{Sales}}{\text{Accounts receivable}} = \frac{\$8,250,000}{\$1,760,000} = 4.69 \, (2011)$$

$$= \frac{\$8,000,000}{\$1,440,000} = 5.56 \, (2010)$$

$$\text{Average collection period} = \frac{360}{\text{Accounts receivable turnover}}$$

$$= \frac{360}{4.69} = 77 \text{ days} \, (2011)$$

$$= \frac{360}{5.56} = 65 \text{ days} \, (2010)$$

PROFITABILITY RATIOS

Profitability is the net result of a large number of policies and decisions chosen by an organization's management. Profitability ratios indicate how effectively the total firm is being managed. The profit margin for a firm is calculated by dividing net earnings by sales. This ratio is often called *return on sales* (ROS). There is wide variation among industries, but the average for U.S. firms is approximately 5 percent.

$$\frac{\text{Net earnings}}{\text{Sales}} = \frac{\$410,000}{\$8,250,000} = 0.0497 \, (2011)$$

$$= \frac{\$395,000}{\$8,000,000} = 0.0494 \, (2010)$$

A second useful ratio for evaluating profitability is the *return on investment*—or ROI, as it is frequently called—found by dividing net earnings by total assets. The ABC Company's ROI is calculated as follows:

$$\frac{\text{Net earnings}}{\text{Total assets}} = \frac{\$410,000}{\$7,105,000} = 0.0577 \, (2011)$$

$$= \frac{\$395,000}{\$6,393,000} = 0.0618 \, (2010)$$

The ratio of net earnings to net worth is a measure of the rate of return or profitability of the stockholders' investment. It is calculated by dividing net earnings by net worth, the common stock equity and retained earnings account. ABC Company's *return on net worth* or *return on equity,* also called ROE, is calculated as follows:

$$\frac{\text{Net earnings}}{\text{Net worth}} = \frac{\$410,000}{\$3,242,500} = 0.1264 \, (2011)$$

$$= \frac{\$395,000}{\$2,725,750} = 0.1449 \, (2010)$$

It is often difficult to determine causes for lack of profitability. The Du Pont system of financial analysis provides

EXHIBIT 6.B4 **Du Pont's Financial Analysis**

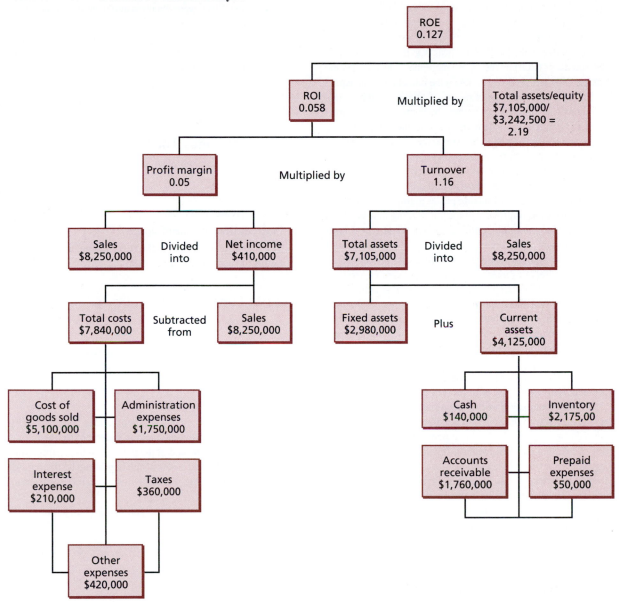

management with clues to the lack of success of a firm. This financial tool brings together activity, profitability, and leverage measures and shows how these ratios interact to determine the overall profitability of the firm. A depiction of the system is set forth in Exhibit 6.B4.

The right side of the exhibit develops the turnover ratio. This section breaks down total assets into current assets (cash, marketable securities, accounts receivable, and inventories) and fixed assets. Sales divided by these total assets gives the turnover on assets.

The left side of the exhibit develops the profit margin on sales. The individual expense items plus income taxes are subtracted from sales to produce net profits after taxes. Net profits divided by sales gives the profit margin on sales. When the asset turnover ratio on the right side of Exhibit 6.B4 is multiplied by the profit margin on sales developed on the left side of the exhibit, the product is the return on assets (ROI) for the firm. This can be shown by the following formula:

$$\frac{\text{Sales}}{\text{Total assets}} \times \frac{\text{Net earnings}}{\text{Sales}} = \frac{\text{Net earnings}}{\text{Total assets}} = \text{ROI}$$

The last step in the Du Pont analysis is to multiply the rate of return on assets (ROI) by the equity multiplier, which is the ratio of assets to common equity, to obtain the rate of return on equity (ROE). This percentage rate of return, of course, could be calculated directly by dividing net income by common equity. However, the Du Pont analysis demonstrates how the return on assets and the use of debt interact to determine the return on equity.

The Du Pont system can be used to analyze and improve the performance of a firm. On the left, or profit, side of the exhibit, attempts to increase profits and sales could be investigated. The possibilities of raising prices to improve profits (or lowering prices to improve volume) or seeking new products or markets, for example, could be studied. Cost accountants and production engineers could investigate ways to reduce costs. On the right, or turnover, side, financial officers could analyze the effect of reducing investment in various assets as well as the effect of using alternative financial structures.

There are two basic approaches to using financial ratios. One approach is to evaluate the corporation's performance over several years. Financial ratios are computed for different years, and then an assessment is made about whether there has been an improvement or deterioration over time. Financial ratios also can be computed for projected, pro forma, statements and compared with present and past ratios.

The other approach is to evaluate a firm's financial condition and compare it with the financial conditions of similar firms or with industry averages in the same period. Such a comparison gives insight into the firm's relative financial condition and performance. Financial ratios for industries are provided by Robert Morris Associates, Dun & Bradstreet, Prentice Hall, and various trade association publications. (Associations and their addresses are listed in the *Encyclopedia of Associations* and in the *Directory of National Trade Associations.*) Information about individual firms is available through *Moody's Manual,* Standard & Poor's manuals and surveys, annual reports to stockholders, and the major brokerage houses.

To the extent possible, accounting data from different companies must be so standardized that companies can be compared or so a specific company can be compared with an industry average. It is important to read any footnotes of financial statements, because various accounting or management practices can have an effect on the financial picture of the company. For example, firms using sale-leaseback methods may have leverage pictures quite different from what is shown as debts or assets on the balance sheet.

ANALYSIS OF THE SOURCES AND USES OF FUNDS

The purpose of this analysis is to determine how the company is using its financial resources from year to year. By comparing balance sheets from one year to the next, we can determine how funds were obtained and how these funds were employed during the year.

To prepare a statement of the sources and uses of funds, it is necessary to (1) classify balance sheet changes that increase and decrease cash, (2) classify from the income statement those factors that increase or decrease cash, and (3) consolidate this information on a sources and uses of funds statement form.

Sources of Funds That Increase Cash

1. A net decrease in any other asset than a depreciable fixed asset.
2. A gross decrease in a depreciable fixed asset.
3. A net increase in any liability.
4. Proceeds from the sale of stock.
5. The operation of the company (net income, and depreciation if the company is profitable).

Uses of Funds

1. A net increase in any other asset than a depreciable fixed asset.
2. A gross increase in depreciable fixed assets.
3. A net decrease in any liability.
4. A retirement or purchase of stock.
5. Payment of cash dividends.

We compute gross changes to depreciable fixed assets by adding depreciation from the income statement for the period to net fixed assets at the end of the period and then subtracting from the total net fixed assets at the beginning of the period. The residual represents the change in depreciable fixed assets for the period.

For the ABC Company, the following change would be calculated:

Net property and plant (2011)	$1,175,000
Depreciation for 2011	+ 80,000
	$1,255,000
Net property and plant (2010)	−1,155,000
	$ 100,000

To avoid double counting, the change in retained earnings is not shown directly in the funds statement. When the funds statement is prepared, this account is replaced by the earnings after taxes, or net income, as a source of funds, and dividends paid during the year as a use of funds. The difference between net income and the change in the retained earnings account will equal the amount of dividends paid during the year. The accompanying sources and uses of funds statement was prepared for the ABC Company.

A funds analysis is useful for determining trends in working-capital positions and for demonstrating how the firm has acquired and employed its funds during some period.

ABC Company Sources and Uses of Funds Statement for 2011

Sources		Uses	
Prepaid expenses	$ 13,000	Cash	$ 25,000
Accounts payable	100,000	Accounts receivable	320,000
Accrued federal taxes	250,000	Inventory	175,000
Dividends payable	3,750	Long-term receivables	165,000
Common stock	1,200	Property and plant	100,000
Additional paid-in capital	195,000	Other fixed assets	20,000
Earnings after taxes (net income)	410,000	Bank loans payable	75,000
Depreciation	80,000	Current maturities of long-term debt	8,500
Total sources	$1,053,500	Long-term liabilities	75,000
		Dividends paid	90,000
		Total uses	$1,053,500

Conclusion

It is recommended that you prepare a chart, such as that shown in Exhibit 6.B5, so you can develop a useful portrayal of these financial analyses. The chart allows a display of the ratios over time. The "Trend" column could be used to indicate your evaluation of the ratios over time (e.g., "favorable," "neutral," or "unfavorable"). The "Industry Average" column could include recent industry averages on these ratios or those of key competitors. These would provide information to aid interpretation of the analyses. The "Interpretation" column could be used to describe your interpretation of the ratios for this firm. Overall, this chart gives a basic display of the ratios that provides a convenient format for examining the firm's financial condition.

Finally, Exhibit 6.B6 is included to provide a quick reference summary of the calculations and meanings of the ratios discussed earlier.

EXHIBIT 6.B5   **A Summary of the Financial Position of a Firm**

Ratios and Working Capital	2007	2008	2009	2010	2011	Trend	Industry Average	Interpretation
Liquidity: Current								
Quick								
Leverage: Debt-assets								
Debt-equity								
Activity: Asset turnover								
Fixed asset ratio								
Inventory turnover								
Accounts receivable turnover								
Average collection period								
Profitability: ROS								
ROI								
ROE								
Working-capital position								

EXHIBIT 6.B6 **A Summary of Key Financial Ratios**

Ratio	Calculation	Meaning
Liquidity Ratios:		
Current ratio	$\dfrac{\text{Current assets}}{\text{Current liabilities}}$	The extent to which a firm can meet its short-term obligations.
Quick ratio	$\dfrac{\text{Current assets} - \text{Inventory}}{\text{Current liabilities}}$	The extent to which a firm can meet its short-term obligations without relying on the sale of inventories.
Leverage Ratios:		
Debt-to-total-assets ratio	$\dfrac{\text{Total debt}}{\text{Total assets}}$	The percentage of total funds that are provided by creditors.
Debt-to-equity ratio	$\dfrac{\text{Total debt}}{\text{Total stockholders' equity}}$	The percentage of total funds provided by creditors versus the percentage provided by owners.
Long-term-debt-to-equity ratio	$\dfrac{\text{Long-term debt}}{\text{Total stockholders' equity}}$	The balance between debt and equity in a firm's long-term capital structure.
Times-interest-earned ratio	$\dfrac{\text{Profits before interest and taxes}}{\text{Total interest charges}}$	The extent to which earnings can decline without the firm becoming unable to meet its annual interest costs.
Activity Ratios:		
Inventory turnover	$\dfrac{\text{Sales}}{\text{Inventory of finished goods}}$	Whether a firm holds excessive stocks of inventories and whether a firm is selling its inventories slowly compared to the industry average.
Fixed assets turnover	$\dfrac{\text{Sales}}{\text{Fixed assets}}$	Sales productivity and plant equipment utilization.
Total assets turnover	$\dfrac{\text{Sales}}{\text{Total assets}}$	Whether a firm is generating a sufficient volume of business for the size of its assets investment.
Accounts receivable turnover	$\dfrac{\text{Annual credit sales}}{\text{Account receivable}}$	In percentage terms, the average length of time it takes a firm to collect on credit sales.
Average collection period	$\dfrac{\text{Account receivable}}{\text{Total sales}/365 \text{ days}}$	In days, the average length of time it takes a firm to collect on credit sales.
Profitability Ratios:		
Gross profit margin	$\dfrac{\text{Sales} - \text{Cost of goods sold}}{\text{Sales}}$	The total margin available to cover operating expenses and yield a profit.
Operating profit margin	$\dfrac{\text{Earning before interest and taxes (EBIT)}}{\text{Sales}}$	Profitability without concern for taxes and interest.
Net profit margin	$\dfrac{\text{Net income}}{\text{Sales}}$	After-tax profits per dollar of sales.
Return on total assets (ROA)	$\dfrac{\text{Net income}}{\text{Total assets}}$	After-tax profits per dollar of assets; this ratio is also called *return on investment* (ROI).

EXHIBIT 6.B6 *(continued)*

Ratio	Calculation	Meaning
Return on stockholders' equity (ROE)	$\dfrac{\text{Net income}}{\text{Total Stockholders' equity}}$	After-tax profits per dollar of stock-holders investment in the firm.
Earnings per share (EPS)	$\dfrac{\text{Net income}}{\substack{\text{Number of shares of common stock} \\ \text{outstanding}}}$	Earnings available to the owners of common stock.
Growth Ratios:		
Sales	Annual percentage growth in total sales	Firm's growth rate in sales.
Income	Annual percentage growth in profits	Firm's growth rate in profits.
Earnings per share	Annual percentage growth in EPS	Firm's growth rate in EPS.
Dividends per share	Annual percentage growth in dividends per share	Firm's growth rate in dividends per share.
Price-earnings ratio	$\dfrac{\text{Market price per share}}{\text{Earnings per share}}$	Faster-growing and less risky firms tend to have higher price-earnings ratios.

Chapter Seven

Long-Term Objectives and Strategies

After reading and studying this chapter, you should be able to

1. Discuss seven different topics for long-term corporate objectives.

2. Describe the five qualities of long-term corporate objectives that make them especially useful to strategic managers.

3. Explain the generic strategies of low-cost leadership, differentiation, and focus.

4. Discuss the importance of the value disciplines.

5. List, describe, evaluate, and give examples of the 15 grand strategies that decision makers use as building blocks in forming their company's competitive plan.

6. Understand the creation of sets of long-term objectives and grand strategies options.

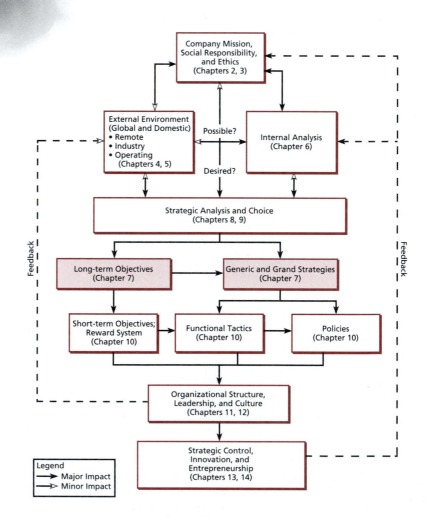

The company mission was described in Chapter 2 as encompassing the broad aims of the firm. The most specific statement of aims presented in that chapter appeared as the goals of the firm. However, these goals, which commonly dealt with profitability, growth, and survival, were stated without specific targets or time frames. They were always to be pursued but could never be fully attained. They gave a general sense of direction but were not intended to provide specific benchmarks for evaluating the firm's progress in achieving its aims. Providing such benchmarks is the function of objectives.[1]

The first part of this chapter will focus on long-term objectives. These are statements of the results a firm seeks to achieve over a specified period, typically three to five years. The second part will focus on the formulation of grand strategies. In combination, these two components of long-term planning provide a comprehensive general approach in guiding major actions designed to accomplish the firm's long-term objectives.

The chapter has two major aims: (1) to discuss in detail the concept of long-term objectives, the topics they cover, and the qualities they should exhibit; and (2) to discuss the concept of grand strategies and to describe the 15 principal grand strategy options that are available to firms singly or in combination, including three newly popularized options that are being used to provide the basis for global competitiveness.

LONG-TERM OBJECTIVES

Strategic managers recognize that short-run profit maximization is rarely the best approach to achieving sustained corporate growth and profitability. An often repeated adage states that if impoverished people are given food, they will eat it and remain impoverished; however, if they are given seeds and tools and shown how to grow crops, they will be able to improve their condition permanently. A parallel choice confronts strategic decision makers:

1. Should they eat the seeds to improve the near-term profit picture and make large dividend payments through cost-saving measures such as laying off workers during periods of slack demand, selling off inventories, or cutting back on research and development?

2. Or should they sow the seeds in the effort to reap long-term rewards by reinvesting profits in growth opportunities, committing resources to employee training, or increasing advertising expenditures?

For most strategic managers, the solution is clear—distribute a small amount of profit now but sow most of it to increase the likelihood of a long-term supply. This is the most frequently used rationale in selecting objectives.

To achieve long-term prosperity, strategic planners commonly establish long-term objectives in seven areas:

Profitability   The ability of any firm to operate in the long run depends on attaining an acceptable level of profits. Strategically managed firms characteristically have a profit objective, usually expressed in earnings per share or return on equity.

Productivity   Strategic managers constantly try to increase the productivity of their systems. Firms that can improve the input-output relationship normally increase profitability. Thus, firms almost always state an objective for productivity. Commonly used productivity objectives are the number of items produced or the number of services rendered per unit of input. However, productivity objectives sometimes are stated in terms of desired cost decreases. For example, objectives may be set for reducing defective items, customer

---

[1] The terms *goals* and *objectives* are each used to convey a special meaning, with goals being the less specific and more encompassing concept. Most authors follow this usage; however, some use the two words interchangeably, while others reverse the usage.

complaints leading to litigation, or overtime. Achieving such objectives increases profitability if unit output is maintained.

Competitive Position One measure of corporate success is relative dominance in the marketplace. Larger firms commonly establish an objective in terms of competitive position, often using total sales or market share as measures of their competitive position. An objective with regard to competitive position may indicate a firm's long-term priorities. For example, Gulf Oil set a five-year objective of moving from third to second place as a producer of high-density polypropylene. Total sales were the measure.

Employee Development Employees value education and training, in part because they lead to increased compensation and job security. Providing such opportunities often increases productivity and decreases turnover. Therefore, strategic decision makers frequently include an employee development objective in their long-range plans. For example, PPG has declared an objective of developing highly skilled and flexible employees and, thus, providing steady employment for a reduced number of workers.

Employee Relations Whether or not they are bound by union contracts, firms actively seek good employee relations. In fact, proactive steps in anticipation of employee needs and expectations are characteristic of strategic managers. Strategic managers believe that productivity is linked to employee loyalty and to appreciation of managers' interest in employee welfare. They, therefore, set objectives to improve employee relations. Among the outgrowths of such objectives are safety programs, worker representation on management committees, and employee stock option plans.

Technological Leadership Firms must decide whether to lead or follow in the marketplace. Either approach can be successful, but each requires a different strategic posture. Therefore, many firms state an objective with regard to technological leadership. For example, Caterpillar Tractor Company established its early reputation and dominant position in its industry by being in the forefront of technological innovation in the manufacture of large earthmovers. E-commerce technology officers will have more of a strategic role in the management hierarchy of the future, demonstrating that the Internet has become an integral aspect of corporate long-term objective setting. In offering an e-technology manager higher-level responsibilities, a firm is pursuing a leadership position in terms of innovation in computer networks and systems. Officers of e-commerce technology at GE and Delta Air have shown their ability to increase profits by driving down transaction-related costs with Web-based technologies that seamlessly integrate their firms' supply chains. These technologies have the potential to "lock in" certain suppliers and customers and heighten competitive position through supply chain efficiency.

Public Responsibility Managers recognize their responsibilities to their customers and to society at large. In fact, many firms seek to exceed government requirements. They work not only to develop reputations for fairly priced products and services but also to establish themselves as responsible corporate citizens. For example, they may establish objectives for charitable and educational contributions, minority training, public or political activity, community welfare, or urban revitalization. In an attempt to exhibit their public responsibility in the United States, Japanese companies, such as Toyota, Hitachi, and Matsushita, contribute more than $500 million annually to American educational projects, charities, and nonprofit organizations.

Qualities of Long-Term Objectives

What distinguishes a good objective from a bad one? What qualities of an objective improve its chances of being attained? These questions are best answered in relation to five criteria that should be used in preparing long-term objectives: flexible, measurable over time, motivating, suitable, and understandable.

Flexible   Objectives should be adaptable to unforeseen or extraordinary changes in the firm's competitive or environmental forecasts. Unfortunately, such flexibility usually is increased at the expense of specificity. One way of providing flexibility while minimizing its negative effects is to allow for adjustments in the level, rather than in the nature, of objectives. For example, the personnel department objective of providing managerial development training for 15 supervisors per year over the next five-year period might be adjusted by changing the number of people to be trained. In contrast, changing the personnel department's objective of "assisting production supervisors in reducing job-related injuries by 10 percent per year" after three months had gone by would understandably create dissatisfaction.

Measurable   Objectives must clearly and concretely state what will be achieved and when it will be achieved. Thus, objectives should be measurable over time. For example, the objective of "substantially improving our return on investment" would be better stated as "increasing the return on investment on our line of paper products by a minimum of 1 percent a year and a total of 5 percent over the next three years."

Motivating   People are most productive when objectives are set at a motivating level—one high enough to challenge but not so high as to frustrate or so low as to be easily attained. The problem is that individuals and groups differ in their perceptions of what is high enough. A broad objective that challenges one group frustrates another and minimally interests a third. One valuable recommendation is that objectives be tailored to specific groups. Developing such objectives requires time and effort, but objectives of this kind are more likely to motivate.

Objectives must also be achievable. This is easier said than done. Turbulence in the remote and operating environments affects a firm's internal operations, creating uncertainty and limiting the accuracy of the objectives set by strategic management. To illustrate, the rapidly declining U.S. economy in 2000–2003 made objective setting extremely difficult, particularly in such areas as sales projections. Motorola provides a good example of well-constructed company objectives. Motorola saw its market share of the mobile telephone market shrink from 26 to 14 percent between 1996 and 2001, while its main rival Nokia captured all of Motorola's lost share and more. As a key part of a plan to recapture its market position, Motorola's CEO challenged his company with the following long-term objectives:

1. Cut sales, marketing, and administrative expenses from $2.4 billion to $1.6 billion in the next fiscal year.
2. Increase gross markings from 20 to 27 percent by 2002.
3. Reduce the number of Motorola telephone styles by 84 percent to 20 and the number of silicon components by 82 percent to 100 by 2003.

Suitable   Objectives must be suited to the broad aims of the firm, which are expressed in its mission statement. Each objective should be a step toward the attainment of overall goals. In fact, objectives that are inconsistent with the company mission can subvert the firm's aims. For example, if the mission is growth oriented, the objective of reducing the debt-to-equity ratio to 1.00 would probably be unsuitable and counterproductive.

Understandable   Strategic managers at all levels must understand what is to be achieved. They also must understand the major criteria by which their performance will be evaluated. Thus, objectives must be so stated that they are as understandable to the recipient as they are to the giver. Consider the misunderstandings that might arise over the objective of "increasing the productivity of the credit card department by 20 percent within two years." What does this objective mean? Increase the number of outstanding cards? Increase the use of outstanding cards? Increase the employee workload? Make productivity gains each year? Or hope that the new computer-assisted system, which should improve productivity, is approved by year 2? As this simple example illustrates, objectives must be clear, meaningful, and unambiguous.

The Balanced Scorecard

balanced scorecard
A set of four measures directly linked to a company's strategy: financial performance, customer knowledge, internal business processes, and learning and growth.

The **balanced scorecard** is a set of measures that are directly linked to the company's strategy. Developed by Robert S. Kaplan and David P. Norton, it directs a company to link its own long-term strategy with tangible goals and actions. The scorecard allows managers to evaluate the company from four perspectives: financial performance, customer knowledge, internal business processes, and learning and growth.

The balanced scorecard, as shown in Exhibit 7.1, contains a concise definition of the company's vision and strategy. Surrounding the vision and strategy are four additional boxes; each box contains the objectives, measures, targets, and initiatives for one of the four perspectives:

- The box at the top of Exhibit 7.1 represents the financial perspective and answers the question "To succeed financially, how should we appear to our shareholders?"
- The box to the right represents the internal business process perspective and addresses the question "To satisfy our shareholders and customers, what business processes must we excel at?"

Exhibit 7.1   The Balanced Scorecard

The balanced scorecard provides a framework to translate a strategy into operational terms

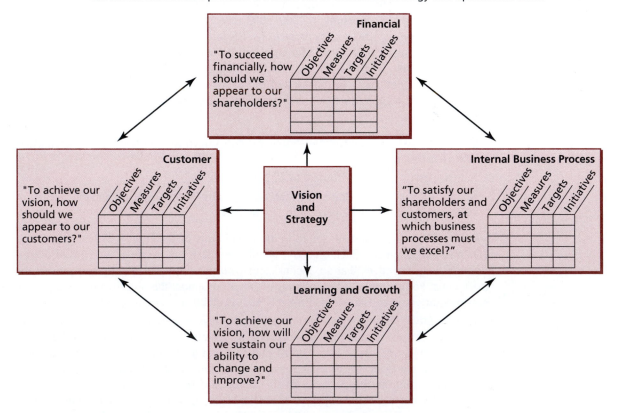

- The learning and growth box at the bottom of Exhibit 7.1 answers the question "To achieve our vision, how will we sustain our ability to change and improve?"
- The box at the left reflects the customer perspective and responds to the question "To achieve our vision, how should we appear to our customers?"

All of the boxes are connected by arrows to illustrate that the objectives and measures of the four perspectives are linked by cause-and-effect relationships that lead to the successful implementation of the strategy. Achieving one perspective's targets should lead to desired improvements in the next perspective, and so on, until the company's performance increases overall.

A properly constructed scorecard is balanced between short- and long-term measures, financial and nonfinancial measures, and internal and external performance perspectives.

The balanced scorecard is a management system that can be used as the central organizing framework for key managerial processes. Chemical Bank, Mobil Corporation's US Marketing and Refining Division, and CIGNA Property and Casualty Insurance have used the Balanced Scorecard approach to assist in individual and team goal setting, compensation, resource allocation, budgeting and planning, and strategic feedback and learning.

GENERIC STRATEGIES

Many planning experts believe that the general philosophy of doing business declared by the firm in the mission statement must be translated into a holistic statement of the firm's strategic orientation before it can be further defined in terms of a specific long-term strategy. In other words, a long-term or grand strategy must be based on a core idea about how the firm can best compete in the marketplace.

generic strategy
A core idea about how a firm can best compete in the marketplace.

The popular term for this core idea is **generic strategy.** From a scheme developed by Michael Porter, many planners believe that any long-term strategy should derive from a firm's attempt to seek a competitive advantage based on one of three generic strategies:

1. Striving for overall *low-cost leadership* in the industry.
2. Striving to create and market unique products for varied customer groups through *differentiation.*
3. Striving to have special appeal to one or more groups of consumer or industrial buyers, *focusing* on their cost or differentiation concerns.

Advocates of generic strategies believe that each of these options can produce above average returns for a firm in an industry. However, they are successful for very different reasons.

Low-Cost Leadership

Low-cost leaders depend on some fairly unique capabilities to achieve and sustain their low-cost position. Examples of such capabilities are having secured suppliers of scarce raw materials, being in a dominant market share position, or having a high degree of capitalization. Low-cost producers usually excel at cost reductions and efficiencies. They maximize economies of scale, implement cost-cutting technologies, stress reductions in overhead and in administrative expenses, and use volume sales techniques to propel themselves up the earning curve. The commonly accepted requirements for successful implementation of the low-cost and the other two generic strategies are overviewed in Exhibit 7.2.

A low-cost leader is able to use its cost advantage to charge lower prices or to enjoy higher profit margins. By so doing, the firm effectively can defend itself in price wars, attack competitors on price to gain market share, or, if already dominant in the industry,

EXHIBIT 7.2
Requirements for Generic Competitive Strategies

Source: Adapted with the permission of The Free Press, a division of Simon & Schuster Adult Publishing Group, from *Competitive Strategy: Techniques for Analyzing Industries and Competitors* by Michael E. Porter. Copyright © 1980, 1998 by The Free Press. All rights reserved.

Generic Strategy	Commonly Required Skills and Resources	Common Organizational Requirements
Overall cost leadership	Sustained capital investment and access to capital. Process engineering skills. Intense supervision of labor. Products designed for ease in manufacture. Low-cost distribution system.	Tight cost control. Frequent, detailed control reports. Structured organization and responsibilities. Incentives based on meeting strict quantitative targets.
Differentiation	Strong marketing abilities. Product engineering. Creative flare. Strong capability in basic research. Corporate reputation for quality or technological leadership. Long tradition in the industry or unique combination of skills drawn from other businesses. Strong cooperation from channels.	Strong coordination among functions in R&D, product development, and marketing. Subjective measurement and incentives instead of quantitative measures. Amenities to attract highly skilled labor, scientists, or creative people.
Focus	Combination of the above policies directed at the particular strategic target.	Combination of the above policies directed at the regular strategic target.

simply benefit from exceptional returns. As an extreme case, it has been argued that National Can Company, a corporation in an essentially stagnant industry, is able to generate attractive and improving profits by being the low-cost producer.

In the wake of the tremendous successes of such low-cost leaders as Wal-Mart and Target, only a rare few companies can ignore the mandate to reduce cost. Yet, doing so without compromising the key attributes of a company's products or services is a difficult challenge. One company that has succeeded in its efforts to become a low-cost leader while maintaining quality standards is Nucor. The company's Top Strategist, Daniel Dimicco, is profiled in Exhibit 7.3.

Differentiation

Strategies dependent on differentiation are designed to appeal to customers with a special sensitivity for a particular product attribute. By stressing the attribute above other product qualities, the firm attempts to build customer loyalty. Often such loyalty translates into a firm's ability to charge a premium price for its product. Cross-brand pens, Brooks Brothers suits, Porsche automobiles, and Chivas Regal Scotch whiskey are all examples.

The product attribute also can be the marketing channels through which it is delivered, its image for excellence, the features it includes, and the service network that supports it. As a result of the importance of these attributes, competitors often face "perceptual" barriers to entry when customers of a successfully differentiated firm fail to see largely identical products as being interchangeable. For example, General Motors hopes that customers will accept "only genuine GM replacement parts."

Because advertising plays a major role in a company's development and differentiation of it brand, many strategists use celebrity spokespeople to represent their companies. These spokespeople, most often actors, models, and athletes, help give the company's products and services a popular, successful, trendy, modern, cache. An example of such a celebrity

Top Strategist
Daniel Dimicco, CEO of Nucor

**Exhibit
7.3**

Nucor has long been known as the best operator in the steel business and is especially famous for its enlightened workforce relations and commitment to new technologies. It pays line workers according to their productivity and listens to, and implements, their ideas to make the process better. Responsibility is pushed as close to the front line as possible. For most of its history, Nucor only grew organically, but under CEO Daniel Dimicco the com-

pany has found it's often cheaper to buy than build. Now executives export the Nucor way to a series of acquired plants: in the past year, it has bought Connecticut Steel, Harris Steel Group, and the assets of Verco Manufacturing. Acquisitions such as Verco, a maker of steel floors and roof decks, help broaden Nucor's product line and support its migration into higher-margin products.

Source: Reprinted with special permission from "The *BusinessWeek* 50—The Best Performers," *BusinessWeek*, March 26, 2007. Copyright © 2007 The McGraw-Hill Companies.

endorser is Dwyane Wade of the Miami Heat, who is discussed in Exhibit 7.4, Strategy in Action.

Focus

A focus strategy, whether anchored in a low-cost base or a differentiation base, attempts to attend to the needs of a particular market segment. Likely segments are those that are ignored by marketing appeals to easily accessible markets, to the "typical" customer, or to customers with common applications for the product. A firm pursuing a focus strategy is willing to service isolated geographic areas; to satisfy the needs of customers with special financing, inventory, or servicing problems; or to tailor the product to the somewhat unique demands of the small- to medium-sized customer. The focusing firms profit from their willingness to serve otherwise ignored or underappreciated customer segments. The classic example is cable television. An entire industry was born because of a willingness of cable firms to serve isolated rural locations that were ignored by traditional television services. Brick producers that typically service a radius of less than 100 miles and commuter airlines that serve regional geographic areas are other examples of industries where a focus strategy frequently yields above-average industry profits.

A well-known brand that is enjoying tremendous success with a focus strategy is the automobile manufacturer Lamborghini. Its financial turnaround, which is based on controlled growth, is described in Exhibit 7.5, Strategy in Action.

While each of the generic strategies enables a firm to maximize certain competitive advantages, each one also exposes the firm to a number of competitive risks. For example, a low-cost leader fears a new low-cost technology that is being developed by a competitor; a differentiating firm fears imitators; and a focused firm fears invasion by a firm that largely targets customers. As Exhibit 7.6 suggests, each generic strategy presents the firm with a number of risks.

Practice is over at American Airlines Arena, and Dwyane Wade takes a minute to explain how he's putting his touch on a new mobile phone. The All-Star guard for the Miami Heat and a self-proclaimed budding businessman is helping wireless carrier T-Mobile USA Inc. design a limited-edition Sidekick, the texting device/cell phone beloved by 20-somethings.

Wade is changing the marketing landscape in ways other phenoms can learn from. He isn't simply endorsing products, he's partnering with major brands to design items other than sports equipment and apparel. On February 17, 2007, the weekend of the NBA All-Star Game, the D Wade Sidekick—the T-Mobile device he co-designed—was introduced with much fanfare.

Team Wade, led by agent Henry Thomas, aims to transform its young client into one of the top 10 brands in sports. The idea, says marketing strategist Andrew Stroth of Chicago's CSMG Sports Ltd., is to create a global brand that transcends sports. "Forget his peers in the NBA," he says. "We want people to think of Dwyane Wade the same way they think of [David] Beckham, Jordan, and Tiger."

Wade's original Converse contract was worth $500,000 a year. But after Wade showed his mettle in the 2005 playoffs, the Converse contract was renegotiated to about $10 million a year. As part of the deal, Converse agreed to make not only Wade basketball shoes but also casual and active attire. He'll receive incentives based on the success

of these breakout categories, says Ric Wilson, sports marketing chief at Converse. "Converse is backed by the Nike engine, and it gives us the opportunity to reinvent Converse with Wade as the face."

But the most innovative aspect of the Wade branding campaign may be its Web strategy—which was born from a moment of serendipity in the sky. Team Wade had already launched a Web site but knew they needed to leverage the Internet more effectively to engage his young fans. On October, 17, 2006, on a flight from New York to Chicago, Stroth sat next to a Google executive. They agreed the two camps should meet. The next week, in Chicago, Google reps preached moving beyond "independent sites" such as Wade's. Those sites, along with charity appearances, TV ads, and video games, make for an "episodic" relationship between the athlete and fans. But digital media allow for brands to be built daily or hourly—what Google calls "dialogue" marketing.

So Team Wade gave Google the go-ahead to develop a plan that would make Dwyanewade.com an integral part of fans' daily digital lives. The goal? A fully interactive site built by Google with Google Search functions embedded. Fans would get a customized mix of e-mail, sports news feeds, flash games, and promotional messages.

Source: Reprinted with special permission from Roger O. Crockett, "Building a Megabrand Named Dwyane," *BusinessWeek,* February 12, 2007. Copyright © 2007 The McGraw-Hill Companies.

THE VALUE DISCIPLINES

International management consultants Michael Treacy and Fred Wiersema propose an alternative approach to generic strategy that they call the value disciplines.[2] They believe that strategies must center on delivering superior customer value through one of three value disciplines: operational excellence, customer intimacy, or product leadership.

Operational excellence refers to providing customers with convenient and reliable products or services at competitive prices. Customer intimacy involves offerings tailored to match the demands of identified niches. Product leadership, the third discipline, involves offering customers leading-edge products and services that make rivals' goods obsolete.

Companies that specialize in one of these disciplines, while simultaneously meeting industry standards in the other two, gain a sustainable lead in their markets. This lead is derived from the firm's focus on one discipline, aligning all aspects of operations with it. Having decided on the value that must be conveyed to customers, firms understand more clearly what must be done to attain the desired results. After transforming their

[2] The ideas and examples in this section are drawn from Michael Treacy and Fred Wiersema, "Customer Intimacy and Other Value Disciplines," *Harvard Business Review* 71, no. 1 (1993), pp. 84–94.

A Burst of Speed at Lamborghini

BusinessWeek

After years of restructuring, the sports car maker is finally a serious rival to Ferrari.

Lamborghini has long held mythic sway over car aficionados. Its exotic flying-saucer design, its horse-power on steroids, and its deafening engines have been a powerful draw for fans such as comedian Jay Leno and actor Jamie Foxx. But for years, Lamborghini suffered from financial woes and quality problems. The Italian super-sports-car maker went through six owners in 16 years and spent 1978–1981 in bankruptcy. So for most of Lamborghini's 44-year history, it has been a mere speck in Ferrari's rearview mirror, selling just about 250 cars a year at $274,000 for a Gallardo Spyder and $354,000 for a Murcielago roadster.

Now an infusion of German cash is helping Lamborghini burn rubber. In 1998, automaker Audi bought the company. After spending some $500 million revamping production and developing models, Lamborghini has the scale to mount a real challenge to Ferrari. In 2006, Lamborghini says it sold more than 2,000 cars, and sales in the U.S. shot up 48 percent in the first 10 months alone. The company today has about 100 showrooms worldwide, up from only 45 in 1998, although Ferrari still has roughly twice as many dealers.

Besieged with orders, Lamborghini's factory in Sant'Agata Bolognese, near Modena, is running full tilt, turning out 10 cars daily. That's brisk, considering it takes a worker an entire day just to cut and hand-stitch one leather seat. Still, it's not fast enough for all the Lamborghini lovers getting in line. Both the 640-hp Murcielago and the 520-hp Gallardo have one-year waiting lists.

With sales finally soaring, Lamborghini is on a stronger financial footing, too. Cost-cutting helped boost 2006 operating margins to nearly 4 percent, up from 1.8 percent in 2005, Morgan Stanley estimates. The brokerage predicts pretax profit could more than double in 2007, to $14 million, as revenues increase 30 percent to $400 million. That's still small compared with Ferrari's expected 2006 sales of $1.9 billion and 5,400 cars. But by tapping into Audi's engineering expertise, purchasing power, and supplier relationships, Lamborghini could eventually match Ferrari's sales—and surpass its 12 percent operating margin.

To preserve its super-luxury image, Lamborghini will take a page from Ferrari and pursue profits over growth. In 2007, it expects to expand sales less than 10 percent. "We are a niche of a niche," says chief executive Stephan Winkelmann. The former Fiat executive wants to boost earnings with limited-edition models packed with pricey options. Another untapped vein for Lamborghini is clothing and other gear emblazoned with its raging-bull logo. The company is starting to license merchandise, a business that generates some $200 million a year each for Ferrari and Porsche.

Source: Reprinted with special permission from Gail Edmondson, "A Burst of Speed at Lamborghini," *BusinessWeek*, January 15, 2007. Copyright © 2007 The McGraw-Hill Companies.

organizations to focus on one discipline, companies can concentrate on smaller adjustments to produce incremental value. To match this advantage, less focused companies require larger changes than the tweaking that discipline leaders need.

Operational Excellence

Operational excellence is a specific strategic approach to the production and delivery of products and services. A company that follows this strategy attempts to lead its industry in price and convenience by pursuing a focus on lean and efficient operations. Companies that employ operational excellence work to minimize costs by reducing overhead, eliminating intermediate production steps, reducing transaction costs, and optimizing business processes across functional and organizational boundaries. The focus is on delivering products or services to customers at competitive prices with minimal inconvenience. Exhibit 7.7, Strategy in Action, provides an example of successful operational excellence in the personal computer (PC) industry.

Operational excellence is also the strategic focus of General Electric's large appliance business. Historically, the distribution strategy for large appliances was based on

EXHIBIT 7.6
Risks of the Generic Strategies

Risks of Cost Leadership	Risks of Differentiation	Risks of Focus
Cost of leadership is not sustained: • Competitors imitate. • Technology changes. • Other bases for cost leadership erode.	Differentiation is not sustained: • Competitors imitate. • Bases for differentiation become less important to buyers.	The focus strategy is imitated. The target segment becomes structurally unattractive: • Structure erodes. • Demand disappears.
Proximity in differentiation is lost.	Cost proximity is lost.	Broadly targeted competitors overwhelm the segment: • The segment's differences from other segments narrow. • The advantages of a broad line increase.
Cost focusers achieve even lower cost in segments.	Differentiation focusers achieve even greater differentiation in segments.	New focusers subsegment the industry.

requiring that dealers maintain large inventories. Price breaks for dealers were based on order quantities. However, as the marketplace became more competitive, principally as a result of competition for multibrand dealers like Sears, GE recognized the need to adjust its production and distribution plans.

The GE system addresses the delivery of products. As a step toward organizational excellence, GE created a computer-based logistics system to replace its in-store inventories model. Retailers use this software to access a 24-hour online order processing system that guarantees GE's best price. This system allows dealers to better meet customer needs, with instantaneous access to a warehouse of goods and accurate shipping and production information. GE benefits from the deal as well. Efficiency is increased since manufacturing now occurs in response to customer sales. Additionally, warehousing and distribution systems have been streamlined to create the capability of delivering to 90 percent of destinations in the continental United States within one business day.

Firms that implement the strategy of operational excellence typically restructure their delivery processes to focus on efficiency and reliability, and use state-of-the art information systems that emphasize integration and low-cost transactions.

Customer Intimacy

Companies that implement a strategy of customer intimacy continually tailor and shape products and services to fit an increasingly refined definition of the customer. Companies excelling in customer intimacy combine detailed customer knowledge with operational flexibility. They respond quickly to almost any need, from customizing a product to fulfilling special requests to create customer loyalty.

Customer-intimate companies are willing to spend money now to build customer loyalty for the long term, considering each customer's lifetime value to the company, not the profit of any single transaction. Consequently, employees in customer-intimate companies go to great lengths to ensure customer satisfaction with low regard for initial cost.

Home Depot implements the discipline of customer intimacy. Home Depot clerks spend the necessary time with customers to determine the product that best suits their needs,

A Racer Called Acer

BusinessWeek

It's a good thing Gianfranco Lanci likes coffee. He shuttles between his home in Milan and job in Taiwan as president of computer maker Acer Inc. "You cannot waste time, since you spend so much time already on the plane," says Lanci, 52. "The coffee," he adds, "also helps."

Acer seems to be on a caffeine kick of its own. Americans who know the brand likely recall it hit the big time in the 1990s, then quickly fell into obscurity. While Acer remains weak in the United States, globally it's no. 4 in PCs overall, behind Hewlett-Packard, Dell, and Lenovo. In 2006, Acer boosted its share by 1.2 percentage points, to 5.9 percent, according to IDC Corp. That puts Acer just behind Lenovo, which rose to no. 3 when it bought IBM PC division two years ago. Lenovo is "successful in China, [but] we are growing everywhere," says Acer CEO J. T. Wang.

The battle to overtake Lenovo is about more than just bragging rights. The PC industry has shrunk to a handful of players, and more consolidation is likely. For Acer, getting bigger is "a survival issue," says Kevin Chang, an analyst in Taipei with Credit Suisse Group. "You need to be a top-three player to make a sustainable profit." Acer had sales of $11.1 billion in 2006 and profits of $338 million, estimates Credit Suisse.

Acer has been gaining ground thanks to low-cost machines and unconventional distribution. It shuns direct sales, instead selling only through distributors and outsourcing all production to factories in China. Acer has also been the driving force in price wars that have taken a toll on former no. 1 Dell Inc. Although Acer has some premium offerings, such as its Ferrari line of sleek machines in red racing stripes, it typically underprices competitors by 5 to 10 percent. Even so, Acer usually offers retailers a bigger chunk of the selling price than rivals do.

The strategy is working: Sales have more than doubled since 2003, although it has cut Acer's profit margin to about 2 percent, or less than half that of HP or Dell.

To keep the momentum going, Acer must expand beyond its stronghold in Europe. There, it's the market leader in laptops and no. 3 overall, thanks to Lanci. Now Acer is taking the fight directly to China, where it is no. 9. In 2005, Acer revamped its operation on the mainland, halving head count to 200 and outsourcing distribution.

Acer also hopes to improve its position in the United States, where it has just 1.8 percent of the market. Acer has raised its profile with U.S. consumers over the past two years through deals to sell its wares at Wal-Mart, CompUSA, and Circuit City—which could ultimately pay off with big companies, says U.S. sales chief Mark Hill.

because the company's business strategy is built around selling information and service in addition to home-repair and improvement items. Consequently, consumers concerned solely with price fall outside Home Depot's core market.

Companies engaged in customer intimacy understand the difference between the profitability of a single transaction and the profitability of a lifetime relationship with a single customer. The company's profitability depends in part on its maintaining a system that differentiates quickly and accurately the degree of service that customers require and the revenues their patronage is likely to generate. Firms using this approach recognize that not every customer is equally profitable. For example, a financial services company installed a telephone-computer system capable of recognizing individual clients by their telephone numbers when they call. The system routes customers with large accounts and frequent transactions to their own senior account representative. Other customers may be routed to a trainee or junior representative. In any case, the customer's file appears on the representative's screen before the phone is answered.

The new system allows the firm to segment its services with great efficiency. If the company has clients who are interested in trading in a particular financial instrument, it can group them under the one account representative who specializes in that instrument.

This saves the firm the expense of training every representative in every facet of financial services. Additionally, the company can direct certain value-added services or products to a specific group of clients that would have interest in them.

Businesses that select a customer intimacy strategy have decided to stress flexibility and responsiveness. They collect and analyze data from many sources. Their organizational structure emphasizes empowerment of employees close to customers. Additionally, hiring and training programs stress the creative decision-making skills required to meet individual customer needs. Management systems recognize and utilize such concepts as customer lifetime value, and norms among employees are consistent with a "have it your way" mind set.

Product Leadership

Companies that pursue the discipline of product leadership strive to produce a continuous stream of state-of-the-art products and services. Three challenges must be met to attain that goal. Creativity is the first challenge. Creativity is recognizing and embracing ideas usually originating outside the company. Second, innovative companies must commercialize ideas quickly. Thus, their business and management processes need to be engineered for speed. Product leaders relentlessly pursue new solutions to problems. Finally, firms utilizing this discipline prefer to release their own improvements rather than wait for competitors to enter. Consequently, product leaders do not stop for self-congratulation; they focus on continual improvement.

For example, Johnson & Johnson's organizational design brings good ideas in, develops them quickly, and looks for ways to improve them. In 1983, the president of J&J's Vistakon Inc., a maker of specialty contact lenses, received a tip concerning an ophthalmologist who had conceived of a method to manufacture disposable contact lenses inexpensively. Vistakon's president received this tip from a J&J employee from a different subsidiary whom he had never met. Rather than dismiss the tip, the executives purchased the rights to the technology, assembled a management team to oversee the product's development team to oversee the product's development, and built a state-of-the-art facility in Florida to manufacture disposable contact lenses called Acuvue. Vistakon and its parent, J&J, were willing to incur high manufacturing and inventory costs before a single lens was sold. A high-speed production facility helped give Vistakon a six-month head start over the competition that, taken off guard, never caught up.

Like other product leaders, J&J creates and maintains an environment that encourages employees to share ideas. Additionally, product leaders continually scan the environment for new-product or service possibilities and rush to capitalize them. Product leaders also avoid bureaucracy because it slows commercialization of their ideas. In a product leadership company, a wrong decision often is less damaging than one made late. As a result, managers make decisions quickly, their companies encouraging them to decide today and implement tomorrow. Product leaders continually look for new methods to shorten their cycle times.

The strength of product leaders lies in reacting to situations as they occur. Shorter reaction times serve as an advantage in dealings with the unknown. For example, when competitors challenged the safety of Acuvue lenses, the firm responded quickly and distributed data combating the charges to eye care professionals. This reaction created goodwill in the marketplace.

Product leaders act as their own competition. These firms continually make the products and services they have created obsolete. Product leaders believe that if they do not develop a successor, a competitor will. So, although Acuvue is successful in the marketplace, Vistakon continues to investigate new material that will extend the wearability of contact lenses and technologies that will make current lenses obsolete. J&J and other innovators recognize that the long-run profitability of an existing product or service is less important to the company's future than maintaining its product leadership edge and momentum.

GRAND STRATEGIES

grand strategy
A master long-term plan that provides basic direction for major actions directed toward achieving long-term business objectives.

While the need for firms to develop generic strategies remains an unresolved debate, designers of planning systems agree about the critical role of grand strategies. **Grand strategies,** often called master or business strategies, provide basic direction for strategic actions. They are the basis of coordinated and sustained efforts directed toward achieving long-term business objectives.

The purpose of this section is twofold: (1) to list, describe, and discuss 15 grand strategies that strategic managers should consider and (2) to present approaches to the selection of an optimal grand strategy from the available alternatives.

Grand strategies indicate the time period over which long-range objectives are to be achieved. Thus, a grand strategy can be defined as a comprehensive general approach that guides a firm's major actions.

The 15 principal grand strategies are concentrated growth, market development, product development, innovation, horizontal integration, vertical integration, concentric diversification, conglomerate diversification, turnaround, divestiture, liquidation, bankruptcy, joint ventures, strategic alliances, and consortia. Any one of these strategies could serve as the basis for achieving the major long-term objectives of a single firm. But a firm involved with multiple industries, businesses, product lines, or customer groups—as many firms are—usually combines several grand strategies. For clarity, however, each of the principal grand strategies is described independently in this section, with examples to indicate some of its relative strengths and weaknesses.

Concentrated Growth

concentrated growth
A grand strategy in which a firm directs its resources to the profitable growth of a single product, in a single market, with a single dominant technology.

Many of the firms that fell victim to merger mania were once mistakenly convinced that the best way to achieve their objectives was to pursue unrelated diversification in the search for financial opportunity and synergy. By rejecting that "conventional wisdom," such firms as Martin-Marietta, KFC, Compaq, Avon, Hyatt Legal Services, and Tenant have demonstrated the advantages of what is increasingly proving to be sound business strategy. A firm that has enjoyed special success through a strategic emphasis on increasing market share through concentration is Chemlawn. With headquarters in Columbus, Ohio, Chemlawn is the North American leader in professional lawn care. Like others in the lawn care industry, Chemlawn is experiencing a steadily declining customer base. Market analysis shows that the decline is fueled by negative environmental publicity, perceptions of poor customer service, and concern about the price versus the value of the company's services, given the wide array of do-it-yourself alternatives. Chemlawn's approach to increasing market share hinges on addressing quality, price, and value issues; discontinuing products that the public or environmental authorities perceive as unsafe; and improving the quality of its workforce.

These firms are just a few of the majority of businesses worldwide firms that pursue a concentrated growth strategy by focusing on a dominant product-and-market combination. **Concentrated growth** is the strategy of the firm that directs its resources to the profitable growth of a dominant product, in a dominant market, with a dominant technology. The main rationale for this approach, sometimes called a market penetration strategy, is that by thoroughly developing and exploiting its expertise in a narrowly defined competitive arena, the company achieves superiority over competitors that try to master a greater number of product and market combinations.

Rationale for Superior Performance

Concentrated growth strategies lead to enhanced performance. The ability to assess market needs, knowledge of buyer behavior, customer price sensitivity, and effectiveness of promotion are characteristics of a concentrated growth strategy. Such core capabilities are a more important determinant of competitive market success than are the environmental forces faced by the firm. The high success rates of new products also are tied to avoiding situations that require undeveloped skills, such as serving new customers and markets, acquiring new technology, building new channels, developing new promotional abilities, and facing new competition.

A major misconception about the concentrated growth strategy is that the firm practicing it will settle for little or no growth. This is certainly not true for a firm that correctly utilizes the strategy. A firm employing concentrated growth grows by building on its competencies, and it achieves a competitive edge by concentrating in the product-market segment it knows best. A firm employing this strategy is aiming for the growth that results from increased productivity, better coverage of its actual product-market segment, and more efficient use of its technology.

Conditions That Favor Concentrated Growth

Specific conditions in the firm's environment are favorable to the concentrated growth strategy. The first is a condition in which the firm's industry is resistant to major technological advancements. This is usually the case in the late growth and maturity stages of the product life cycle and in product markets where product demand is stable and industry barriers, such as capitalization, are high. Machinery for the paper manufacturing industry, in which the basic technology has not changed for more than a century, is a good example.

An especially favorable condition is one in which the firm's targeted markets are not product saturated. Markets with competitive gaps leave the firm with alternatives for growth, other than taking market share away from competitors. The successful introduction of traveler services by Allstate and Amoco demonstrates that even an organization as entrenched and powerful as the AAA could not build a defensible presence in all segments of the automobile club market.

A third condition that favors concentrated growth exists when the firm's product markets are sufficiently distinctive to dissuade competitors in adjacent product markets from trying to invade the firm's segment. John Deere scrapped its plans for growth in the construction machinery business when mighty Caterpillar threatened to enter Deere's mainstay, the farm machinery business, in retaliation. Rather than risk a costly price war on its own turf, Deere scrapped these plans.

A fourth favorable condition exists when the firm's inputs are stable in price and quantity and are available in the amounts and at the times needed. Maryland-based Giant Foods is able to concentrate in the grocery business largely due to its stable long-term arrangements with suppliers of its private-label products. Most of these suppliers are makers of the national brands that compete against the Giant labels. With a high market share and aggressive retail distribution, Giant controls the access of these brands to the consumer. Consequently, its suppliers have considerable incentive to honor verbal agreements, called bookings, in which they commit themselves for a one-year period with regard to the price, quality, and timing of their shipments to Giant.

The pursuit of concentrated growth also is favored by a stable market—a market without the seasonal or cyclical swings that would encourage a firm to diversify. Night Owl Security, the District of Columbia market leader in home security services, commits its customers to initial four-year contracts. In a city where affluent consumers tend to be quite transient, the length of this relationship is remarkable. Night Owl's concentrated growth strategy has been reinforced by its success in getting subsequent owners of its customers' homes to extend and renew the security service contracts. In a similar way, Lands' End reinforced its growth strategy by asking customers for names and addresses of friends and relatives living overseas who would like to receive Lands' End catalogs.

A firm also can grow while concentrating, if it enjoys competitive advantages based on efficient production or distribution channels. These advantages enable the firm to formulate advantageous pricing policies. More efficient production methods and better handling of distribution also enable the firm to achieve greater economies of scale or, in conjunction with marketing, result in a product that is differentiated in the mind of the consumer. Graniteville Company, a large South Carolina textile manufacturer, enjoyed decades of growth and profitability by adopting a "follower" tactic as part of its concentrated growth strategy. By producing fabrics only after market demand had been well established, and by featuring products that reflected its expertise in adopting manufacturing innovations and in maintaining highly efficient long production runs, Graniteville prospered through concentrated growth.

Finally, the success of market generalists creates conditions favorable to concentrated growth. When generalists succeed by using universal appeals, they avoid making special appeals to particular groups of customers. The net result is that many small pockets are left open in the markets dominated by generalists, and that specialists emerge and thrive in these pockets. For example, hardware store chains, such as Home Depot, focus primarily on routine household repair problems and offer solutions that can be easily sold on a self-service, do-it-yourself basis. This approach leaves gaps at both the "semiprofessional" and "neophyte" ends of the market—in terms of the purchaser's skill at household repairs and the extent to which available merchandise matches the requirements of individual homeowners.

Risk and Rewards of Concentrated Growth

Under stable conditions, concentrated growth poses lower risk than any other grand strategy; but, in a changing environment, a firm committed to concentrated growth faces high risks. The greatest risk is that concentrating in a single product market makes a firm particularly vulnerable to changes in that segment. Slowed growth in the segment would jeopardize the firm because its investment, competitive edge, and technology are deeply entrenched in a specific offering. It is difficult for the firm to attempt sudden changes if its product is threatened by near-term obsolescence, a faltering market, new substitutes, or changes in technology or customer needs. For example, the manufacturers of IBM clones faced such a problem when IBM adopted the OS/2 operating system for its personal computer line. That change made existing clones out of date.

The concentrating firm's entrenchment in a specific industry makes it particularly susceptible to changes in the economic environment of that industry. For example, Mack Truck, the second-largest truck maker in America, lost $20 million as a result of an 18-month slump in the truck industry.

Entrenchment in a specific product market tends to make a concentrating firm more adept than competitors at detecting new trends. However, any failure of such a firm to properly forecast major changes in its industry can result in extraordinary losses. Numerous makers of inexpensive digital watches were forced to declare bankruptcy because they failed to anticipate the competition posed by Swatch, Guess, and other trendy watches that emerged from the fashion industry.

A firm pursuing a concentrated growth strategy is vulnerable also to the high opportunity costs that result from remaining in a specific product market and ignoring other options that could employ the firm's resources more profitably. Overcommitment to a specific technology and product market can hinder a firm's ability to enter a new or growing product market that offers more attractive cost-benefit trade-offs. Had Apple Computers maintained its policy of making equipment that did not interface with IBM equipment, it would have missed out on what have proved to be its most profitable strategic options.

Concentrated Growth Is Often the Most Viable Option

Examples abound of firms that have enjoyed exceptional returns on the concentrated growth strategy. Such firms as McDonald's, Goodyear, and Apple Computers have used firsthand knowledge and deep involvement with specific product segments to become powerful competitors in their markets. The strategy is associated even more often with successful smaller firms that have steadily and doggedly improved their market position.

The limited additional resources necessary to implement concentrated growth, coupled with the limited risk involved, also make this strategy desirable for a firm with limited funds. For example, through a carefully devised concentrated growth strategy, medium-sized John Deere & Company was able to become a major force in the agricultural machinery business even when competing with such firms as Ford Motor Company. While other firms were trying to exit or diversify from the farm machinery business, Deere spent $2 billion in upgrading its machinery, boosting its efficiency, and engaging in a program to strengthen its dealership system. This concentrated growth strategy enabled it to become the leader in the farm machinery business despite the fact that Ford was more than 10 times its size.

The firm that chooses a concentrated growth strategy directs its resources to the profitable growth of a narrowly defined product and market, focusing on a dominant technology. Firms that remain within their chosen product market are able to extract the most from their technology and market knowledge and, thus, are able to minimize the risk associated with unrelated diversification. The success of a concentration strategy is founded on the firm's use of superior insights into its technology, product, and customer to obtain a sustainable competitive advantage. Superior performance on these aspects of corporate strategy has been shown to have a substantial positive effect on market success.

A grand strategy of concentrated growth allows for a considerable range of action. Broadly speaking, the firm can attempt to capture a larger market share by increasing the usage rates of present customers, by attracting competitors' customers, or by selling to nonusers. In turn, each of these options suggests more specific options, some of which are listed in the top section of Exhibit 7.8.

When strategic managers forecast that their current products and their markets will not provide the basis for achieving the company mission, they have two options that involve moderate costs and risk: market development and product development.

Market Development

market development
A grand strategy of marketing present products, often with only cosmetic modification, to customers in related marketing areas.

Market development commonly ranks second only to concentration as the least costly and least risky of the 15 grand strategies. It consists of marketing present products, often with only cosmetic modifications, to customers in related market areas by adding channels of distribution or by changing the content of advertising or promotion. Several specific market development approaches are listed in Exhibit 7.8. Thus, as suggested by the figure, firms that open branch offices in new cities, states, or countries are practicing market development. Likewise, firms are practicing market development if they switch from advertising in trade publications to advertising in newspapers or if they add jobbers to supplement their mail-order sales efforts.

Market development allows firms to leverage some of their traditional strengths by identifying new uses for existing products and new demographically, psychographically, or geographically defined markets. Frequently, changes in media selection, promotional appeals, and distribution signal the implementation of this strategy. Du Pont used market development when it found a new application for Kevlar, an organic material that police,

EXHIBIT 7.8

Specific Options under the Grand Strategies of Concentration, Market Development, and Product Development

Source: Adapted from Philip Kotler and Kevin Keller, *Marketing Management,* 12th ed., 2006. Reprinted by permission of Pearson Education, Upper Saddle River, NJ.

Concentration (increasing use of present products in present markets):

1. Increasing present customers' rate of use:
   a. Increasing the size of purchase.
   b. Increasing the rate of product obsolescence.
   c. Advertising other uses.
   d. Giving price incentives for increased use.
2. Attracting competitors' customers:
   a. Establishing sharper brand differentiation.
   b. Increasing promotional effort.
   c. Initiating price cuts.
3. Attracting nonusers to buy the product:
   a. Inducing trial use through sampling, price incentives, and so on.
   b. Pricing up or down.
   c. Advertising new uses.

Market development (selling present products in new markets):

1. Opening additional geographic markets:
   a. Regional expansion.
   b. National expansion.
   c. International expansion.
2. Attracting other market segments:
   a. Developing product versions to appeal to other segments.
   b. Entering other channels of distribution.
   c. Advertising in other media.

Product development (developing new products for present markets):

1. Developing new-product features:
   a. Adapt (to other ideas, developments).
   b. Modify (change color, motion, sound, odor, form, shape).
   c. Magnify (stronger, longer, thicker, extra value).
   d. Minify (smaller, shorter, lighter).
   e. Substitute (other ingredients, process, power).
   f. Rearrange (other patterns, layout, sequence, components).
   g. Reverse (inside out).
   h. Combine (blend, alloy, assortment, ensemble; combine units, purposes, appeals, ideas).
2. Developing quality variations.
3. Developing additional models and sizes (product proliferation).

security, and military personnel had used primarily for bulletproofing. Kevlar now is being used to refit and maintain wooden-hulled boats, since it is lighter and stronger than glass fibers and has 11 times the strength of steel.

The medical industry provides other examples of new markets for existing products. The National Institutes of Health's report of a study showing that the use of aspirin may lower the incidence of heart attacks was expected to boost sales in the $2.2 billion analgesic market. It was predicted that the expansion of this market would lower the market share of nonaspirin brands, such as industry leaders Tylenol and Advil. Product extensions currently planned include Bayer Calendar Pack, 28-day packaging to fit the once-a-day prescription for the prevention of a second heart attack.

Another example is Cheesebrough-Ponds, a major producer of health and beauty aids, which decided several years ago to expand its market by repacking its Vaseline Petroleum Jelly in pocket-size squeeze tubes as Vaseline "Lip Therapy." The corporation decided to place a strategic emphasis on market development, because it knew from market studies that its petroleum-jelly customers already were using the product to prevent chapped lips. Company leaders reasoned that their market could be expanded significantly if the product were repackaged to fit conveniently in consumers' pockets and purses.

Product Development

product development
A grand strategy that involves the substantial modification of existing products that can be marketed to current customers.

Product development involves the substantial modification of existing products or the creation of new but related products that can be marketed to current customers through established channels. The product development strategy often is adopted either to prolong the life cycle of current products or to take advantage of a favorite reputation or brand name. The idea is to attract satisfied customers to new products as a result of their positive experience with the firm's initial offering. The bottom section in Exhibit 7.8 lists some of the options available to firms undertaking product development. A revised edition of a college textbook, a new car style, and a second formula of shampoo for oily hair are examples of the product development strategy.

Similarly, Pepsi changed its strategy on beverage products by creating new products to follow the industry movement away from mass branding. This new movement was designed to attract a younger, hipper customer segment. Pepsi's new products include a version of Mountain Dew, called Code Red, and new Pepsi brands, called Pepsi Twist and Pepsi Blue.

The product development strategy is based on the penetration of existing markets by incorporating product modifications into existing items or by developing new products with a clear connection to the existing product line. The telecommunications industry provides an example of product extension based on product modification. To increase its estimated 8 to 10 percent share of the $5 to $6 billion corporate user market, MCI Communication Corporation extended its direct-dial service to 146 countries, the same as those serviced by AT&T, at lower average rates than those of AT&T. MCI's addition of 79 countries to its network underscores its belief in this market, which it expects to grow 15 to 20 percent annually. Another example of expansions linked to existing lines is Gerber's decision to engage in general merchandise marketing. Gerber's recent introduction included 52 items that ranged from feeding accessories to toys and children's wear. Likewise, Nabisco Brands seeks competitive advantage by placing its strategic emphasis on product development. With headquarters in Parsippany, New Jersey, the company is one of three operating units of RJR Nabisco. It is the leading producer of biscuits, confections, snacks, shredded cereals, and processed fruits and vegetables. To maintain its position as leader, Nabisco pursues a strategy of developing and introducing new products and expanding its existing product line. Spoon Size Shredded Wheat and Ritz Bits crackers are two examples of new products that are variations on existing products.

The development of new products is so critical to companies in many industries that a cottage industry has sprung up to help provide them. To read about one of the firms that specialize in idea creation, see Exhibit 7.9, Strategy in Action.

Innovation

innovation
A grand strategy that seeks to reap the premium margins associated with creation and customer acceptance of a new product or service.

In many industries, it has become increasingly risky not to innovate. Both consumer and industrial markets have come to expect periodic changes and improvements in the products offered. As a result, some firms find it profitable to make **innovation** their grand strategy. They seek to reap the initially high profits associated with customer acceptance of a new or greatly improved product. Then, rather than face stiffening competition as the basis of profitability shifts from innovation to production or marketing competence, they search for other original or novel ideas. The underlying rationale of the grand strategy of innovation is to create a new product life cycle and thereby make similar existing products obsolete. Thus, this strategy differs from the product development strategy of extending an existing

Strategy in Action

Exhibit 7.9

Inside a White-Hot Idea Factory

BusinessWeek

Some big names are turning to upstart Fahrenheit 212 to dream up new products.

For several years, spirits giant Diageo rode high on the popularity of its Smirnoff Ice beverage. Then consumers got bored, and the party was over. Try as it might, the no. 1 global liquor company couldn't reignite sales of Ice—a crucial part of its Smirnoff brand. So Diageo turned to Fahrenheit 212, a tiny New York outfit that promises to help clients dream up hit products and services. Fahrenheit listened, then disappeared.

The firm reemerged with some startling advice: forget the Smirnoff Ice brand for now. Instead, Diageo should use its malt technology to create wildly different Smirnoff drinks. Among Fahrenheit's 10 or so fully realized products: Smirnoff Raw Tea, which appeared in August, and Smirnoff Source, an alcoholic water expected to launch this spring.

Fahrenheit 212 specializes in a new approach to product development. With little to no inside knowledge of its clients, the company dives into their problems and within months cooks up a portfolio of products it thinks will solve them. One part management consultant, one part advertising agency, and one part design house, Fahrenheit 212 attempts to deliver ready-to-go answers, including everything from an analysis of each potential market down to the design and packaging of the product itself. As companies seek to maximize efficiency by outsourcing just about everything, Fahrenheit 212 promises to serve up something most chief executives dream about: new products created from existing assets that will earn sizable revenue from untapped markets.

Spun off from advertising agency Saatchi & Saatchi in November 2006, Fahrenheit 212 expects to generate only about $8 million in revenues in 2007. But it has signed up an impressive roster of clients. It won't disclose specifics, but Fahrenheit has come up with new applications for Samsung's LCD panels, cooked up new products for Hershey as the company moves beyond candy, and is helping NBC Universal identify new sources of revenue in the digital world.

Clients think of the firm as a way to make long-shot bets without having to use their own research and development resources. "Samsung is a lean organization. We can't afford to have people coming up with ideas that don't work," says chief marketing officer Gregory Lee. "The people at Fahrenheit are very helpful because they are working on ideas that can fail—it allows you to experiment a bit." What's more, Fahrenheit ties much of its compensation to the success of the product, making it an even safer bet.

Source: Reprinted with special permission from Burt Helm, "Inside a White-Hot Idea Factory," *BusinessWeek*, January 15, 2007. Copyright © 2007 The McGraw-Hill Companies.

product's life cycle. For example, Intel, a leader in the semiconductor industry, pursues expansion through a strategic emphasis on innovation. With headquarters in California, the company is a designer and manufacturer of semiconductor components and related computers, of microcomputer systems, and of software. Its Pentium microprocessor gives a desktop computer the capability of a mainframe. Exhibit 7.10, Strategy in Action, makes an important point. Companies under pressure to innovate often supplement their own R&D efforts by partnering with other firms in their industry that have complementary needs.

While most growth-oriented firms appreciate the need to be innovative, a few firms use it as their fundamental way of relating to their markets. An outstanding example is Polaroid, which heavily promotes each of its new cameras until competitors are able to match its technological innovation; by this time, Polaroid normally is prepared to introduce a dramatically new or improved product. For example, it introduced consumers in quick succession to the Swinger, the SX-70, the One Step, and the Sun Camera 660.

Few innovative ideas prove profitable because the research, development, and premarketing costs of converting a promising idea into a profitable product are extremely high. A study by the Booz Allen & Hamilton management research department provides some understanding of the risks. As shown in Exhibit 7.11, Booz Allen & Hamilton found that less than 2 percent of the innovative projects initially considered by 51 companies

The Power of the Pipeline for Bristol-Myers Squibb

BusinessWeek

As interim CEO James M. Cornelius tries to steady Bristol's wobbly finances—the New York drug maker, Bristol-Myers Squibb just recorded its first quarterly loss since 1995—the one part of the company he's barely touching is Dr. Elliot Sigal's. Bristol has launched eight new drugs since Sigal became head of development in 2002, has three cancer drugs in late-stage development, and has more than a dozen compounds in its pipeline to treat diseases ranging from diabetes to depression. With many growth-starved Big Pharma companies desperate for new potential blockbusters, and a verdict due soon in the Plavix trial, a Bristol acquisition, predicts Morgan Stanley analyst Jami Rubin, "is not a question of if. It's a question of when."

Sigal has turned around Bristol's unproductive research labs using a combination of hard and soft incentives. He has fine-tuned a compensation plan that ties scientists' bonuses to the drugs they discover, awarding the highest premiums to the compounds that reach late-stage clinical trials. Sigal keeps his troops motivated by introducing them to patients who have been treated with Bristol's drugs, most recently bringing in a cancer patient who has benefited from Bristol's new product, Sprycel.

Another way Sigal has managed to pump up Bristol's pipeline is through what he calls the globalization of the research process. While developing Sprycel, for example, the company recruited 911 trial patients in 33 countries. Because the drug treats a rare form of leukemia, it would have taken several months to find enough patients just in the United States.

Bristol has also become more selective in choosing its partners, seeking deals that will fill holes in its strategy of developing drugs to address large, unmet medical needs without stretching its resources too thin. In January 2007, Bristol structured a smart deal with London-based drug giant AstraZeneca PLC to develop two diabetes drugs.

Investors and potential acquirers will be watching closely for the verdict in the Plavix patent trial. Bristol is expected to prevail and regain its exclusive hold on the market until 2011. But the damage has already been done: Bristol's generic rival, Weston (Ontario)-based Apotex Inc., flooded distribution channels with six months' worth of its version of Plavix before a judge ordered it to stop selling the drug last August.

The Plavix debacle only underscores the urgency of Sigal's quest to generate a variety of new drug candidates that will mitigate the risk of future patent losses.

Source: Reprinted with special permission from Arlene Weintraub, "The Power of the Pipeline: Bristol-Myers Squibb is Beset with Troubles, But Its New-Drug Potential Makes It a Target," *BusinessWeek*, February 26, 2007. Copyright © 2007 The McGraw-Hill Companies.

eventually reached the marketplace. Specifically, out of every 58 new product ideas, only 12 pass an initial screening test that finds them compatible with the firm's mission and long-term objectives, only 7 remain after an evaluation of their potential, and only 3 survive development attempts. Of the three survivors, two appear to have profit potential after test marketing and only one is commercially successful.

Horizontal Integration

horizontal integration
A grand strategy based on growth through the acquisition of similar firms operating at the same stage of the production-marketing chain.

When a firm's long-term strategy is based on growth through the acquisition of one or more similar firms operating at the same stage of the production-marketing chain, its grand strategy is called **horizontal integration**. Such acquisitions eliminate competitors and provide the acquiring firm with access to new markets. One example is Warner-Lambert's acquisition of Parke Davis, which reduced competition in the ethical drugs field for Chilcott Laboratories, a firm that Warner-Lambert previously had acquired. Another example is the long-range acquisition pattern of White Consolidated Industries, which expanded in the refrigerator and freezer market through a grand strategy of horizontal integration, by acquiring Kelvinator Appliance, the Refrigerator Products Division of Bendix Westinghouse Automotive Air Brake, and Frigidaire Appliance from General Motors.

Exhibit 7.11
**Decay of New
Product Ideas
(51 Companies)**

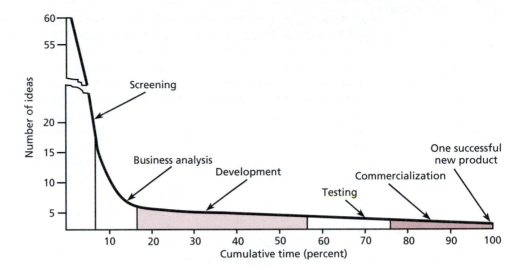

Nike's acquisition in the dress shoes business and N. V. Homes's purchase of Ryan Homes have vividly exemplified the success that horizontal integration strategies can bring.

The attractions of a horizontal acquisition strategy are many and varied.[3] However every benefit provides the parent firm with critical resources that it needs to improve overall profitability. For example, the acquiring firm that uses a horizontal acquisition can quickly expand its operations geographically, increase its market share, improve its production capabilities and economies of scale, gain control of knowledge-based resources, broaden its product line, and increase its efficient use of capital. An added attraction of horizontal acquisition is that these benefits are achieved with only moderately increased risk, because the success of the expansion is principally dependent on proven abilities.

A horizontal merger can provide the firm with an opportunity to offer its customers a broader product line. This motivation has sparked a series of acquisitions in the security software industry. Because Entrust purchased Business Signatures, the consolidated company is able to offer banks a full suite of antifraud products. Similarly, Verisign's acquisitions of m-Qube and Snapcentric, enabled Verisign to expand its cross-marketing options by offering password-generating software, transaction monitoring software, and identity protection. RSA Security's horizontal acquisitions started with the purchase of PassMark, which reduced competitors in the authentication software space. RSA Security then acquired Cyota to provide its customers with both transaction monitoring and authentication software. As a final example, Symantec bought both Veritas Software and WholeSecurity to provide its customers of storage with additional features, such as antivirus software.

The motivation to gain market share has prompted the financial industry to feature horizontal merger strategies. The acquisition of First Coastal Bank by Citizens Business Bank provided new bases of operation in Los Angeles and Manhattan for Citizen Business Bank. The merger of Raincross Credit Union with Visterra Credit Union enabled these credit unions to achieve the size to justify the expansion of services their customers were demanding.

Some horizontal mergers are motivated by the opportunity to combine resources as a means to improve operational efficiency. In the energy industry, for example, there were eight announced horizontal acquisitions with a combined value of $64 billion between January 2004 and January 2007. In each case, increased operational efficiencies resulted

---

[3] This section was drawn from John A. Pearce II and D. Keith Robbins, "Strategic Transformation as the Essential Last Step in the Process of Business Turnaround," *Business Horizons* 50, no. 5 (2008).

from the elimination of duplicated costs. In 2005, Duke Energy acquired Cinergy Corp. for $14.1 billion. The friendly takeover worked well because Duke's Energy North America division was a great match with Cinergy's energy trading operation and provided economies of scale and scope. The combined company lowered costs by an estimated $400 million per year by using a broad platform to serve both electricity and natural gas customers.[4]

A second example of an efficiency-driven merger is one between Constellation and FPL, which saves between $1.5 and $2.1 billion by eliminating overlapping operations.[5] Another example is the acquisition of Green Mountain Power by Gaz Metro, a subsidiary of Northern New England Energy Power for $187 million. The merger was prompted by Green Mountain Power's expiring supplier contracts that threatened it with high costs of going to suppliers who were out of its geographic region—but within the region of Gaz Metro. The horizontal acquisition enabled Green Mountain Power to avail itself of Gaz Metro's suppliers.

Deutsche Telekom's growth strategy was horizontal acquisition. Deutsche Telekom was a dominant player in the European wireless services market, but without a presence in the fast-growing U.S. market in 2000. To correct this limitation, Deutsche Telekom horizontally integrated by purchasing the American firm Voice-Stream Wireless, a company that was growing faster than most domestic rivals and that owned spectrum licenses providing access to 220 million potential customers.

Vertical Integration

vertical integration
A grand strategy based on the acquisition of firms that supply the acquiring firm with inputs or new customers for its outputs.

When a firm's grand strategy is to acquire firms that supply it with inputs (such as raw materials) or are customers for its outputs (such as warehousers for finished products), **vertical integration** is involved. To illustrate, if a shirt manufacturer acquires a textile producer—by purchasing its common stock, buying its assets, or exchanging ownership interests—the strategy is vertical integration. In this case, it is *backward* vertical integration, because the acquired firm operates at an earlier stage of the production-marketing process. If the shirt manufacturer had merged with a clothing store, it would have been *forward* vertical integration—the acquisition of a firm nearer to the ultimate consumer.

Amoco emerged as North America's leader in natural gas reserves and products as a result of its acquisition of Dome Petroleum. This backward integration by Amoco was made in support of its downstream businesses in refining and in gas stations, whose profits made the acquisition possible.

Exhibit 7.12 depicts both horizontal and vertical integration. The principal attractions of a horizontal integration grand strategy are readily apparent. The acquiring firm is able to greatly expand its operations, thereby achieving greater market share, improving economies of scale, and increasing the efficiency of capital use. In addition, these benefits are achieved with only moderately increased risk, because the success of the expansion is principally dependent on proven abilities.

The reasons for choosing a vertical integration grand strategy are more varied and sometimes less obvious. The main reason for backward integration is the desire to increase the dependability of the supply or quality of the raw materials used as production inputs. That desire is particularly great when the number of suppliers is small and the number of competitors is large. In this situation, the vertically integrating firm can better control its costs and, thereby, improve the profit margin of the expanded production-marketing system. Forward integration is a preferred grand strategy if great advantages accrue to stable production. A firm can increase the predictability of demand for its output through forward integration; that is, through ownership of the next stage of its production-marketing chain.

---

[4] G. Terzo, "Duke and Cinergy Spur Utility M&A, "*The Investment Dealer's Digest IDD,* January 16, 2006, p. 1.
[5] J. Fontana, "A New Wave of Consolidation in the Utility Industry," *Electric Light and Power,* 84, no. 4 (July/August 2006), pp. 36–38.

Exhibit 7.12
Vertical and Horizontal Integrations

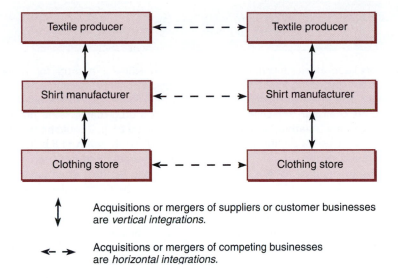

Acquisitions or mergers of suppliers or customer businesses are *vertical integrations.*

Acquisitions or mergers of competing businesses are *horizontal integrations.*

Some increased risks are associated with both types of integration. For horizontally integrated firms, the risks stem from increased commitment to one type of business. For vertically integrated firms, the risks result from the firm's expansion into areas requiring strategic managers to broaden the base of their competencies and to assume additional responsibilities.

Concentric Diversification

concentric diversification
A grand strategy that involves the operation of a second business that benefits from access to the first firm's core competencies.

Concentric diversification involves the acquisition of businesses that are related to the acquiring firm in terms of technology, markets, or products. With this grand strategy, the selected new businesses possess a high degree of compatibility with the firm's current businesses. The ideal concentric diversification occurs when the combined company profits increase the strengths and opportunities and decrease the weaknesses and exposure to risk. Thus, the acquiring firm searches for new businesses whose products, markets, distribution channels, technologies, and resource requirements are similar to but not identical with its own, whose acquisition results in synergies but not complete interdependence.

Abbott Laboratories pursues an aggressive concentric growth strategy. As described in Exhibit 7.13, Strategy in Action, Abbott seeks to acquire a wide range of businesses that have some important connection to its basic business. In recent years, this strategy has led the company to acquire pharmaceuticals, a diagnostic business, and a medical device manufacturer.

Conglomerate Diversification

conglomerate diversification
A grand strategy that involves the acquisition of a business because it presents the most promising investment opportunity available.

Occasionally a firm, particularly a very large one, plans to acquire a business because it represents the most promising investment opportunity available. This grand strategy is commonly known as **conglomerate diversification**. The principal concern, and often the sole concern, of the acquiring firm is the profit pattern of the venture. Unlike concentric diversification, conglomerate diversification gives little concern to creating product-market synergy with existing businesses. What such conglomerate diversifiers as ITT, Textron, American Brands, Litton, U.S. Industries, Fuqua, and I. C. Industries seek is financial synergy. For example, they may seek a balance in their portfolios between current businesses with cyclical sales and acquired businesses with countercyclical sales, between high-cash/low-opportunity and low-cash/high-opportunity businesses, or between debt-free and highly leveraged businesses.

Diagnosis: Shrewd Moves

Over nine months, Abbott Laboratories has dished out $10.1 billion for acquisitions, including $3.7 billion for cholesterol drug specialists Kos Pharmaceuticals Inc. In 2006, many analysts figured, chairman and chief executive Miles D. White would take a breather to allow the company to absorb its newest assets or lighten its $7 billion debt load. They figured wrong.

Just a month after closing the deal for Kos, Abbott was set to announce on January 18, 2007, that it was selling about two-thirds of its $4 billion diagnostics business to General Electric Co. for $8.1 billion in cash. While emphasizing that he's not going to rush into doing deals, White says he'll likely use the money to buy more medical products outfits to help boost overall sales and profits by at least 10 percent a year into the next decade. When it comes to acquisitions, White says, "you can never afford to rest."

White, 51, has been wheeling and dealing almost since the day in 1999 that he was promoted to CEO, after earlier heading Abbott's diagnostics operations. He began with a bang, paying $7.2 billion in cash for the Knoll Pharmaceuticals Co. subsidiary of Germany's BASF in 2001. Among other deals, White bought TheraSense Inc., an Alameda (California) maker of devices that monitor blood glucose, for $1.2 billion in cash in 2004.

While many big drug companies have come to rue their growth-by-acquisition strategies, analysts say Abbott has done well. The Knoll purchase, for example,

yielded Humira, a drug for rheumatoid arthritis that topped $2 billion in sales in 2006. And a $4.1 billion takeover of Guidant Corp.'s stent operations in early 2006 gave Abbott a drug-coated stent, branded Xience. If it passes final clinical trials, it could hit the U.S. market by year-end; it's projected to reach $1.5 billion in sales in 2008. Abbott hasn't overpaid and has been adroit in integrating personnel and facilities, often putting managers of acquired entities in charge of similar Abbott units.

White's dealmaking has lifted Abbott's top and bottom lines. In 2006, Abbott earned $3.8 billion on sales of $22.5 billion, with gross margins nearing 59 percent, says Glenn J. Novarro of Banc of America Securities in New York. That's up roughly 10 percent annually from $2.4 billion in net income on $13.2 billion in sales in 1999, when gross margins were 54.5 percent, and puts Abbott ahead of Merck, Bristol-Myers Squibb, and Eli Lilly in sales and earnings growth.

Abbott has a 20-person business development team that works full-time with chiefs of Abbott units to find and evaluate deals. "We make sure we're up-to-date on our homework so that if we want to get into a new segment, we can," White says. "We won't be doing nothing."

Source: Reprinted with special permission from Michael Arndt, "Diagnosis: Shrewd Moves," *BusinessWeek,* January 29, 2007. Copyright © 2007 The McGraw-Hill Companies.

The principal difference between the two types of diversification is that concentric diversification emphasizes some commonality in markets, products, or technology, whereas conglomerate diversification is based principally on profit considerations.

Several of the grand strategies discussed above, including concentric and conglomerate diversification and horizontal and vertical integration, often involve the purchase or acquisition of one firm by another. It is important to know that the majority of such acquisitions fail to produce the desired results for the companies involved. Exhibit 7.14, Strategy in Action, provides seven guidelines that can improve a company's chances of a successful acquisition.

Motivation for Diversification

Grand strategies involving either concentric or conglomerate diversification represent distinctive departures from a firm's existing base of operations, typically the acquisition or internal generation (spin-off) of a separate business with synergistic possibilities counterbalancing the strengths and weaknesses of the two businesses. For example, Head Ski sought to diversify into summer sporting goods and clothing to offset the seasonality of its "snow" business. Additionally, diversifications occasionally are undertaken as unrelated

Seven Deadly Sins of Strategy Acquisition

1. The wrong target.

The first step to avoid such a mistake is for the acquirer and its financial advisors to determine the strategic goals and identify the mission. The product of this strategic review will be specifically identified criteria for the target.

The second step required to identify the right target is to design and carry out an effective due diligence process to ascertain whether the target indeed has the identified set of qualities selected in the strategic review.

2. The wrong price.

The key to avoiding this problem lies in the acquirer's valuation model. The model will incorporate assumptions concerning industry trends and growth patterns developed in the strategic review.

3. The wrong structure.

The two principal aspects of the acquisition process that can prevent this problem are a comprehensive regulatory compliance review and tax and legal analysis.

4. The lost deal.

The letter of intent must spell out not only the price to be paid but also many of the relational aspects that will make the strategic acquisition successful. Although an acquirer may justifiably focus on expenses, indemnification, and other logical concerns in the letter of intent, relationship and operational concerns are also important.

5. Management difficulties.

The remedy for this problem must be extracted from the initial strategic review. The management compensation structure must be designed with legal and business advisors to help achieve those goals. The financial rewards to management must depend upon the financial and strategic success of the combined entity.

6. The closing crisis.

Closing crises may stem from unavoidable changed conditions, but most often they result from poor communication. Negotiators sometimes believe that problems swept under the table maintain a deal's momentum and ultimately allow for its consummation. They are sometimes right—and often wrong. Charting a course through an acquisition requires carefully developed skills for every kind of professional—business, accounting, and legal.

7. The operating transition crisis.

Even the best conceived and executed acquisition will prevent significant transition and postclosing operation issues. Strategic goals cannot be achieved by quick asset sales or other accelerated exit strategies. Management time and energy must be spent to ensure that the benefits identified in the strategic review are achieved.

Source: From Academy of Management Review by D.A. Tanner. Copyright © 1991 by Academy of Management. Reproduced with permission of Academy of Management via Copyright Clearance Center.

investments, because of their high profit potential and their otherwise minimal resource demands.

Regardless of the approach taken, the motivations of the acquiring firms are the same:

- Increase the firm's stock value. In the past, mergers often have led to increases in the stock price or the price-earnings ratio.
- Increase the growth rate of the firm.
- Make an investment that represents better use of funds than plowing them into internal growth.
- Improve the stability of earnings and sales by acquiring firms whose earnings and sales complement the firm's peaks and valleys.
- Balance or fill out the product line.
- Diversify the product line when the life cycle of current products has peaked.
- Acquire a needed resource quickly (e.g., high-quality technology or highly innovative management).

- Achieve tax savings by purchasing a firm whose tax losses will offset current or future earnings.
- Increase efficiency and profitability, especially if there is synergy between the acquiring firm and the acquired firm.[6]

Turnaround

turnaround
A grand strategy of cost reduction and asset reduction by a company to survive and recover from declining profits.

For any one of a large number of reasons, a firm can find itself with declining profits. Among these reasons are economic recessions, production inefficiencies, and innovative breakthroughs by competitors. In many cases, strategic managers believe that such a firm can survive and eventually recover if a concerted effort is made over a period of a few years to fortify its distinctive competencies. This grand strategy is known as **turnaround.** It typically is begun through one of two forms of retrenchment, employed singly or in combination:

1. *Cost reduction.* Examples include decreasing the workforce through employee attrition, leasing rather than purchasing equipment, extending the life of machinery, eliminating elaborate promotional activities, laying off employees, dropping items from a production line, and discontinuing low-margin customers.
2. *Asset reduction.* Examples include the sale of land, buildings, and equipment not essential to the basic activity of the firm and the elimination of "perks," such as the company airplane and executives' cars.

Interestingly, the turnaround most commonly associated with this approach is in management positions. In a study of 58 large firms, researchers Shendel, Patton, and Riggs found that turnaround almost always was associated with changes in top management.[7] Bringing in new managers was believed to introduce needed new perspectives on the firm's situation, to raise employee morale, and to facilitate drastic actions, such as deep budgetary cuts in established programs.

Strategic management research provides evidence that the firms that have used a *turnaround strategy* have successfully confronted decline. The research findings have been assimilated and used as the building blocks for a model of the turnaround process shown in Exhibit 7.15, Strategy in Action.

The model begins with a depiction of external and internal factors as causes of a firm's performance downturn. When these factors continue to detrimentally impact the firm, its financial health is threatened. Unchecked decline places the firm in a turnaround situation.

A *turnaround situation* represents absolute and relative-to-industry declining performance of a sufficient magnitude to warrant explicit turnaround actions. Turnaround situations may be the result of years of gradual slowdown or months of sharp decline. In either case, the recovery phase of the turnaround process is likely to be more successful in accomplishing turnaround when it is preceded by planned retrenchment that results in the achievement of near-term financial stabilization. For a declining firm, stabilizing operations and restoring profitability almost always entail strict cost reduction followed by a shrinking back to those segments of the business that have the best prospects of attractive profit margins. The need for retrenchment was reflected in unemployment figures during the 2000–2003 recession. More layoffs of American workers were announced in 2001 than in any of the previous eight

[6] Godfrey Devlin and Mark Bleackley, "Strategic Alliances—Guidelines for Success," *Long Range Planning,* October 1988, pp. 18–23.

[7] Other forms of joint ventures (such as leasing, contract manufacturing, and management contracting) offer valuable support strategies. They are not included in the categorization, however, because they seldom are employed as grand strategies.

A Model of the Turnaround Process

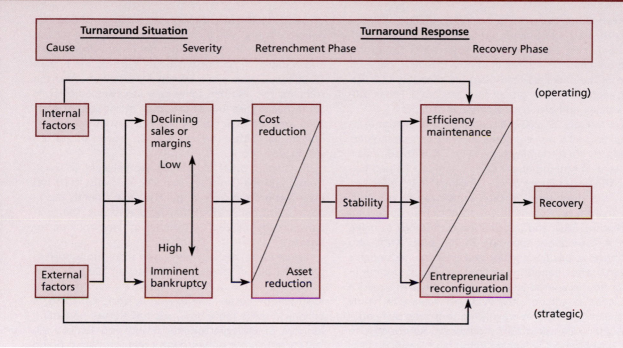

years when U.S. companies announced nearly 2 million layoffs as the economy sunk into its first recession in a decade.

The immediacy of the resulting threat to company survival posed by the turnaround situation is known as *situation severity.* Severity is the governing factor in estimating the speed with which the retrenchment response will be formulated and activated. When severity is low, a firm has some financial cushion. Stability may be achieved through cost retrenchment alone. When turnaround situation severity is high, a firm must immediately stabilize the decline or bankruptcy is imminent. Cost reductions must be supplemented with more drastic asset reduction measures. Assets targeted for divestiture are those determined to be underproductive. In contrast, more productive resources are protected from cuts and represent critical elements of the future core business plan of the company (i.e., the intended recovery response).

Turnaround responses among successful firms typically include two stages of strategic activities: retrenchment and the recovery response. *Retrenchment* consists of cost-cutting and asset-reducing activities. The primary objective of the retrenchment phase is to stabilize the firm's financial condition. Situation severity has been associated with retrenchment responses among successful turnaround firms. Firms in danger of bankruptcy or failure (i.e., severe situations) attempt to halt decline through cost and asset reductions. Firms in less severe situations have achieved stability merely through cost retrenchment. However, in either case, for firms facing declining financial performance, the key to successful turnaround rests in the effective and efficient management of the retrenchment process.

The primary causes of the turnaround situation have been associated with the second phase of the turnaround process, the *recovery response.* For firms that declined primarily

It Just Got Hotter in Kraft's Kitchen

BusinessWeek

As Kraft Foods Inc. used to remind consumers, America spells cheese k-r-a-f-t. Lately, those letters have been spelling something else: frustration. Since Altria Group Inc. spun off a minority interest in Kraft in mid-2001, the stock price of the packaged-food giant has risen just 12.6 percent, lagging its peer group, the Standard & Poor's 500-stock index, and even bank certificates of deposit.

On January 31, 2007, Altria said it will distribute its remaining 88.6 percent stake in Kraft to shareholders on March 30. Altria may have been OK with an underachiever; if nothing else, Kraft's steadiness helped balance the uncertainties of Altria's cigarette business.

In the short term, in fact, Kraft's results may suffer. Analysts say Rosenfeld will have to hike outlays on marketing, R&D, and information technology to make up for inadequate spending in the past. Kraft also will have to pay 4.9 percent more for raw ingredients in 2007, after benefiting from a small cost decline in 2006, figures analyst Edgar Roesch of Banc of America Securities. In addition, the overnight release of nearly 1.5 billion Kraft shares is expected to swamp demand.

Higher expenses in 2007 should keep returns close to flat. David Nelson, an analyst with Credit Suisse, predicts Kraft will net $3.1 billion, or $1.90 a share, in 2007 on sales of $35.1 billion. Nelson's target price for Kraft stock over the next 12 months: $31 a share, the same price it opened at in its initial public offering 5½ years ago.

Kraft has a lot going for it, of course. The Northfield (Illinois) company is the nation's biggest maker of packaged foods and second worldwide only to Nestlé of Switzerland. Look through the kitchens of 200 U.S. households and you'll find a Kraft product in all but one of them. Its brands include Oscar Mayer, Post, and Nabisco. A half-dozen boast sales of more than $1 billion a year, while 50 top $100 million. And the company has also had some new successes. Sales of its South Beach Diet line of products, introduced in early 2005, rose to $350 million last year, estimates analyst Roesch. Its California Pizza Kitchen frozen pizzas are selling well, too.

Problem is, other old brands like Velveeta, Maxwell House, and Jell-O are sinking. Like its rivals, Kraft has extended product lines to get the most from its blockbusters. But the strategy may be played out. The company already markets 14 varieties of Oreo cookies, for instance.

Under Altria, management used acquisitions, such as the $18.9 billion takeover of Nabisco in 2000, to overcome slow internal growth. Rosenfeld says that now Kraft will be better able to use its stock, worth $57.8 billion, to make more buys. She has started unloading noncore or underperforming brands; on January 23, 2007, Kraft sold it slow-growth Cream of Wheat brand for $200 million. Others sales could include Oscar Mayer, Planters nuts, and Grey Poupon mustard.

Source: Reprinted with special permission from Michael Arndt, "It Just Got Hotter in Kraft's Kitchen," *BusinessWeek*, February 12, 2007. Copyright © 2007 The McGraw-Hill Companies.

as a result of external problems, turnaround most often has been achieved through creative new entrepreneurial strategies. For firms that declined primarily as a result of internal problems, turnaround has been most frequently achieved through efficiency strategies. *Recovery* is achieved when economic measures indicate that the firm has regained its predownturn levels of performance.

Divestiture

divestiture strategy
A grand strategy that involves the sale of a firm or a major unit of a firm as a going concern.

A **divestiture strategy** involves the sale of a firm or a major component of a firm. Sara Lee Corp. (SLE) provides a good example. It sells everything from Wonderbras and Kiwi shoe polish to Endust furniture polish and Chock Full o'Nuts coffee. The company used a conglomerate diversification strategy to build Sara Lee into a huge portfolio of disparate brands. A new president, C. Steven McMillan, faced stagnant revenues and earnings. So he consolidated, streamlined, and focused the company on its core categories—food, underwear, and household products. He divested 15 businesses, including Coach leather goods, which together equaled more than 20 percent of the company's revenue, and laid off 13,200 employees, nearly 10 percent of the workforce. McMillan used the cash from asset sales to snap up brands that enhanced Sara Lee's clout in key categories, like the $2.8 billion purchase of St. Louis–based breadmaker Earthgrains Co. to quadruple Sara Lee's bakery operations. In another case of divestitures, Kraft Foods found that it could improve its overall operations by selling some of its best-known brands, as discussed in Exhibit 7.16, Strategy in Action.

When retrenchment fails to accomplish the desired turnaround, as in the Goodyear situation, or when a nonintegrated business activity achieves an unusually high market value, strategic managers often decide to sell the firm. However, because the intent is to find a buyer willing to pay a premium above the value of a going concern's fixed assets, the term *marketing for sale* is often more appropriate. Prospective buyers must be convinced that because of their skills and resources or because of the firm's synergy with their existing businesses, they will be able to profit from the acquisition.

Corning undertook a turnaround that followed retrenchment with divestitures. In 2001, Corning found itself in a declining market for its core product of fiber-optic cable. The company needed to develop a strategy that would allow it to turn around its falling sales and begin to grow once more. It began with retrenchment. Corning laid off 12,000 workers in 2001 and another 4,000 in 2002. Corning also began the divestiture of its noncore assets, such as its nontelecom businesses and its money-losing photonics operation, to stabilize its financial situation so that it could begin its recovery.

The reasons for divestiture vary. They often arise because of partial mismatches between the acquired firm and the parent corporation. Some of the mismatched parts cannot be integrated into the corporation's mainstream activities and, thus, must be spun off. A second reason is corporate financial needs. Sometimes the cash flow or financial stability of the corporation as a whole can be greatly improved if businesses with high market value can be sacrificed. The result can be a balancing of equity with long-term risks or of long-term debt payments to optimize the cost of capital. A third, less frequent reason for divestiture is government antitrust action when a firm is believed to monopolize or unfairly dominate a particular market.

Although examples of the divestiture grand strategy are numerous, CBS Inc. provides an outstanding example. In a two-year period, the once diverse entertainment and publishing giant sold its Records Division to Sony, its magazine publishing business to Diamandis Communications, its book publishing operations to Harcourt Brace Jovanovich, and its music publishing operations to SBK Entertainment World. Other firms that have pursued this type of grand strategy include Esmark, which divested Swift & Company, and White Motors, which divested White Farm.

Liquidation

liquidation
A grand strategy that involves the sale of the assets of the business for their salvage value.

When **liquidation** is the grand strategy, the firm typically is sold in parts, only occasionally as a whole—but for its tangible asset value and not as a going concern. In selecting liquidation, the owners and strategic managers of a firm are admitting failure and recognize that this action is likely to result in great hardships to themselves and their employees. For these reasons, liquidation usually is seen as the least attractive of the grand strategies. As a long-term strategy, however, it minimizes the losses of all the firm's stockholders. Faced with bankruptcy, the liquidating firm usually tries to develop a planned and orderly system that will result in the greatest possible return and cash conversion as the firm slowly relinquishes its market share.

Planned liquidation can be worthwhile. For example, Columbia Corporation, a $130 million diversified firm, liquidated its assets for more cash per share than the market value of its stock.

Bankruptcy

bankruptcy
When a company is unable to pay its debts as they become due, or has more debts than assets.

Business failures are playing an increasingly important role in the American economy. In an average week, more than 300 companies fail and file for **bankruptcy**. More than 75 percent of these financially desperate firms file for a *liquidation bankruptcy*—they agree to a complete distribution of their assets to creditors, most of whom receive a small fraction of the amount they are owed. Liquidation is what the layperson views as bankruptcy: the business cannot pay its debts, so it must close its doors. Investors lose their money, employees lose their jobs, and managers lose their credibility. In owner-managed firms, company and personal bankruptcy commonly go hand in hand.

The other 25 percent of these firms refuse to surrender until one final option is exhausted. Choosing a strategy to recapture its viability, such a company asks the courts for a *reorganization bankruptcy*. The firm attempts to persuade its creditors to temporarily freeze their claims while it undertakes to reorganize and rebuild the company's operations more profitably. The appeal of a reorganization bankruptcy is based on the company's ability to convince creditors that it can succeed in the marketplace by implementing a new strategic plan, and that when the plan produces profits, the firm will be able to repay its creditors, perhaps in full. In other words, the company offers its creditors a carefully designed alternative to forcing an immediate, but fractional, repayment of its financial obligations. The option of reorganization bankruptcy offers maximum repayment of debt at some specified future time if a new strategic plan is successful.

The Bankruptcy Situation

Imagine that your firm's financial reports have shown an unabated decline in revenue for seven quarters. Expenses have increased rapidly, and it is becoming difficult, and at times not possible, to pay bills as they become due. Suppliers are concerned about shipping goods without first receiving payment, and some have refused to ship without advanced payment in cash. Customers are requiring assurances that future orders will be delivered and some are beginning to buy from competitors. Employees are listening seriously to rumors of financial problems and a higher than normal number have accepted other employment. What can be done? What strategy can be initiated to protect the company and resolve the financial problems in the short term?

Chapter 7: The Harshest Resolution

If the judgment of the owners of a business is that its decline cannot be reversed, and the business cannot be sold as a going concern, then the alternative that is in the best interest of all may be a liquidation bankruptcy, also known as Chapter 7 of the Bankruptcy Code. The court appoints a trustee, who collects the property of the company, reduces it to cash, and distributes the proceeds proportionally to creditors on a pro rata basis as expeditiously as possible. Because all assets are sold to pay outstanding debt, a liquidation bankruptcy terminates a business. This type of filing is critically important to sole proprietors or partnerships. Their owners are personally liable for all business debts not covered by the sale of the business assets unless they can secure a Chapter 7 bankruptcy, which will allow them to cancel any debt in excess of exempt assets. Although they will be left with little personal property, the liquidated debtor is discharged from paying the remaining debt.

The shareholders of corporations are not liable for corporate debt and any debt existing after corporate assets are liquidated is absorbed by creditors. Corporate shareholders may simply terminate operations and walk away without liability to remaining creditors. However, filing a Chapter 7 proceeding will provide for an orderly and fair distribution of assets to creditors and thereby may reduce the negative impact of the business failure.

Chapter 11: A Conditional Second Chance

A proactive alternative for the endangered company is reorganization bankruptcy. Chosen for the right reasons, and implemented in the right way, reorganization bankruptcy can provide a financially, strategically, and ethically sound basis on which to advance the interests of all of the firm's stakeholders.

A thorough and objective analysis of the company may support the idea of its continuing operations if excessive debt can be reduced and new strategic initiatives can be undertaken. If the realistic possibility of long-term survival exists, a reorganization under Chapter 11 of the Bankruptcy Code can provide the opportunity. Reorganization allows a business debtor to restructure its debts and, with the agreement of creditors and approval of the court, to continue as a viable business. Creditors involved in Chapter 11 actions often receive less than the total debt due to them but far more than would be available from liquidation.

A Chapter 11 bankruptcy can provide time and protection to the debtor firm (which we will call the *Company*) to reorganize and use future earnings to pay creditors. The Company may restructure debts, close unprofitable divisions or stores, renegotiate labor contracts, reduce its workforce, or propose other actions that could create a profitable business. If the plan is accepted by creditors, the Company will be given another chance to avoid liquidation and emerge from the bankruptcy proceedings rehabilitated.

Seeking Protection of the Bankruptcy Court

If creditors file lawsuits or schedule judicial sales to enforce liens, the Company will need to seek the protection of the Bankruptcy Court. Filing a bankruptcy petition will invoke the protection of the court to provide sufficient time to work out a reorganization that was not achievable voluntarily. If reorganization is not possible, a Chapter 7 proceeding will allow for the fair and orderly dissolution of the business.

If a Chapter 11 proceeding is the required course of action, the Company must determine what the reorganized business will look like, if such a structure can be achieved, and how it will be accomplished while maintaining operations during the bankruptcy proceeding. Will sufficient cash be available to pay for the proceedings and reorganization? Will customers continue to do business with the Company or seek other more secure businesses with which to deal? Will key personnel stay on or look for more secure employment? Which operations should be discontinued or reduced?

Emerging from Bankruptcy

Bankruptcy is only the first step toward recovery for a firm. Many questions should be answered: How did the business get to the point at which the extreme action of bankruptcy was necessary? Were warning signs overlooked? Was the competitive environment understood? Did pride or fear prevent objective analysis? Did the business have the people and resources to succeed? Was the strategic plan well designed and implemented? Did financial problems result from unforeseen and unforeseeable problems or from bad management decisions?

Commitments to "try harder," "listen more carefully to the customer," and "be more efficient" are important but insufficient grounds to inspire stakeholder confidence. A recovery strategy must be developed to delineate how the company will compete more successfully in the future.

An assessment of the bankruptcy situation requires executives to consider the causes of the Company's decline and the severity of the problem it now faces. Investors must decide whether the management team that governed the company's operations during the downturn can return the firm to a position of success. Creditors must believe that the company's managers have learned how to prevent a recurrence of the observed and similar problems. Alternatively, they must have faith that the company's competencies can be sufficiently augmented by key substitutions to the management team, with strong support in decision making from a board of directors and consultants, to restore the firm's competitive strength.

The 12 grand strategies discussed earlier, used singly and much more often in combinations, represent the traditional alternatives used by firms in the United States. Recently, three new grand types have gained in popularity (thus totaling the 15 grand strategies we said we would discuss); all fit under the broad category of corporate combinations. Although they do not fit the criterion by which executives retain a high degree of control over their operations, these grand strategies deserve special attention and consideration especially by companies that operate in global, dynamic, and technologically driven industries. These three newly popularized grand strategies are joint ventures, strategic alliances, and consortia.

Joint Ventures

joint venture
A grand strategy in which companies create a co-owned business that operates for their mutual benefit.

Occasionally two or more capable firms lack a necessary component for success in a particular competitive environment. For example, no single petroleum firm controlled sufficient resources to construct the Alaskan pipeline. Nor was any single firm capable of processing and marketing all of the oil that would flow through the pipeline. The solution was a set of **joint ventures**, which are commercial companies (children) created and operated for the benefit of the co-owners (parents). These cooperative arrangements provided both the funds needed to build the pipeline and the processing and marketing capacities needed to profitably handle the oil flow.

The particular form of joint ventures discussed above is *joint ownership.* In recent years, it has become increasingly appealing for domestic firms to join foreign firms by means of this form. For example, Diamond-Star Motors is the result of a joint venture between a U.S. company, Chrysler Corporation, and Japan's Mitsubishi Motors corporation. Located in Normal, Illinois, Diamond-Star was launched because it offered Chrysler and Mitsubishi a chance to expand on their long-standing relationship in which subcompact cars (as well as Mitsubishi engines and other automotive parts) are imported to the United States and sold under the Dodge and Plymouth names.

The joint venture extends the supplier-consumer relationship and has strategic advantages for both partners. For Chrysler, it presents an opportunity to produce a high-quality car using expertise brought to the venture by Mitsubishi. It also gives Chrysler the chance to try new production techniques and to realize efficiencies by using the workforce that was not included under Chrysler's collective bargaining agreement with the United Auto Workers. The agreement offers Mitsubishi the opportunity to produce cars for sale in the United States without being subjected to the tariffs and restrictions placed on Japanese imports.

As a second example, Bethlehem Steel acquired an interest in a Brazilian mining venture to secure a raw material source. The stimulus for this joint ownership venture was grand strategy, but such is not always the case. Certain countries virtually mandate that foreign firms entering their markets do so on a joint ownership basis. India and Mexico are good examples. The rationale of these countries is that joint ventures minimize the threat of foreign domination and enhance the skills, employment, growth, and profits of local firms.

It should be noted that strategic managers understandably are wary of joint ventures. Admittedly, joint ventures present new opportunities with risks that can be shared. On the other hand, joint ventures often limit the discretion, control, and profit potential of partners, while demanding managerial attention and other resources that might be directed toward the firm's mainstream activities. Nevertheless, increasing globalization in many industries may require greater consideration of the joint venture approach, if historically national firms are to remain viable.

Collaborative Growth in China through Joint Ventures[8]

A prime example of the value of joint ventures is seen in their use by foreign businesses that seek to do business in China. Until very recently, China enthusiastically invited foreign

[8] This section was drawn from Pearce II and Robbins, "Strategic Transformation as the Essential Last Step in the Process of Business Turnaround."

investment to help in the development of its economy. However, in the early 2000s, China increased its regulations on foreign investment to moderate its economic growth and to ensure that Chinese businesses would not be at a competitive disadvantage when competing for domestic markets. The new restrictions require local companies to retain control of Chinese trademarks and brands, prevent foreign investors from buying property that is not for their own use, limit the size of foreign-owned retail chains, and restrict foreign investment in selected industries.[9] With these increasing regulations, investment in China through joint ventures with Chinese companies has become a prominent strategy for foreign investors who hope to circumvent some of the limitations on their strategies, therefore more fully capitalizing on China's economic growth.

In China, a host country partner can greatly facilitate the acceptance of a foreign investor and help minimize the costs of doing business in an unknown nation. Typically, the foreign partner contributes financing and technology, while the Chinese partner provides the land, physical facilities, workers, local connections, and knowledge of the country.[10] In a wholly owned venture, the foreign company is forced to acquire the land, build the workspace, and hire and train the employees, all of which are especially expensive propositions in a country in which the foreign company lacks guanxi.[11] Additionally, because China restricts direct foreign investment in the life insurance, energy, construction of transportation facilities, higher education, and health care industries, asset or equity joint ventures are sometimes the only option for foreign firms.

Foreign partners in equity joint ventures benefit from speed of entry to the Chinese market, tax incentives, motivational and competitive advantages of a mutual long-term commitment, and access to the resources of its Chinese partner. In 2006, two large joint ventures in the media industry were created when Canada's AGA Resources partnered with Beijing Tangde International Film and Culture Co and when the United States' Sequoia Capital formed a joint venture with Hunan Greatdreams Cartoon Media.[12] Joint ventures in China's asset management industry include the 2006 partnerships between Italy's Banca Lombarda, the United States' Lord Abbett, and Chinese companies.

Similar opportunities exist for international joint ventures in the construction and operation of oil refineries, in the building of the nation's railroad transportation system, and in the development of specific geographic areas. In special economic zones, foreign firms operate businesses with Chinese joint venture partners. The foreign companies receive tax incentives in the form of rates that are lower than the standard 30 percent corporate tax rate. For example, in the Shanghai Pudong New Area, a 15 percent tax rate applies.[13]

The number of international joint ventures is increasing because of China's admission to the World Trade Organization (WTO). Under the conditions of its membership, China is expanding the list of industries that permit foreign investment.[14] As of 2007, for example, foreign investors that participate with Chinese partners in joint ventures are permitted to hold an increased share of JVs in several major industries: banks (up to 20 percent), investment funds (33 percent), life insurance (50 percent), and telecommunications (25 percent).

[9] E. Kurtenbach, "China Raising Stakes for Foreign Investment," *Philadelphia Inquirer*, September 24, 2006.

[10] Ying Qui, "Problems of Managing Joint Ventures in China's Interior: Evidence from Shaanxi," *Advanced Management Journal* 70, no. 3 (2005), pp. 46–57.

[11] J. A. Pearce II and R. B. Robinson Jr., "Cultivating Guanxi as a Corporate Foreign-Investor Strategy," *Business Horizons* 43, no. 1 (2000), pp. 31–38.

[12] Andrew Bagnell, "China Business," *China Business Review* 33, no. 5 (2006), pp. 88–92.

[13] N. P. Chopey, "China Still Beckons Petrochemical Investments," *Chemical Engineering* 133, no. 8 (2006) pp. 19–23.

[14] "China's WTO Scorecard: Selected Year-Three Service Commitments," *The US-China Business Council* (2005), pp. 1–2.

Yahoo!'s Unlikely Amigos

BusinessWeek

Evidently the newspapers are going to try to partner their way out of it. In this case, "it" is whatever disadvantages the medium faces in the online world. And sliding revenues, reported by major newspaper companies in the last half of 2006. And those companies' steep stock price declines. A nine-company consortium representing more than 215 U.S. dailies has already signed on with Yahoo!—itself no stranger to share price slippage of late—to partner with Yahoo! HotJobs in an online classifieds venture. This consortium, including the likes of E. W. Scripps (which is mulling what it may do with its newspapers), Hearst Newspapers, and MediaNews Group, is in a 90-day exclusive negotiating period with the online giant over at least five key areas to broaden the partnership. And the three companies behind the online help-wanted classifieds site careerbuilder.com—Gannett, McClatchy, and Tribune—are discussing an alliance to create an online ad network.

Both groups welcome other partners, but the Yahoo! partnership has had better luck in scoring them so far. Morris Communications and Media General have signed on since the HotJobs deal was announced. New York Times Co. and the newspaper division of Advance Publications (which also owns the glossy magazine world's Conde Nast Publications) are discussing joining up as well, say executives familiar with the matter.

The Yahoo! partnership has a weakness for wacky monikers. The online giant and its "Nine Amigos" have assigned at least five "tiger teams" to explore relationships with Yahoo!. Among them: extending distribution of Amigos news stories with Yahoo! including spotlighting them in search results; turning over Amigos site-search engines to Yahoo! and creating co-branded search toolbars; finding ways to integrate Yahoo!'s local search with newspapers' data; having newspaper sales staffs sell Yahoo! ads to local advertisers and having Yahoo! staff sell national ads for the Amigos sites; and allowing the Amigos Web sites to use Yahoo!'s ad technology.

You can argue that newspapers are dealing with a sworn enemy here, but the reality is more nuanced. The big online players have a horrible record in tailoring products to local markets.

Yahoo! seeks a fix appropriate to its content-centric ways. The world's no. 1 portal is betting that, like Microsoft, it can't do local by itself. It's also betting there is huge upside in the local space for the kinds of display ads in which it still outshines Google. And it's a nod to the reality that advertisers remain more comfortable having their ads around tamer and more traditional media rather than, say, user-generated videos. As for the newspapers, nuances aside, they are dealing with the kind of company—online, and measuring profit by the billion—that they once feared. But these days, they fear reality more.

Source: Reprinted with special permission from Jon Fine, "Yahoo!'s Unlikely Amigos," *BusinessWeek*, January 29, 2007. Copyright © 2007 The McGraw-Hill Companies.

Strategic Alliances

strategic alliances
Contractual partnerships because the companies involved do not take an equity position in one another

Strategic alliances are distinguishable from joint ventures because the companies involved do not take an equity position in one another. In many instances, strategic alliances are *partnerships* that exist for a defined period during which partners contribute their skills and expertise to a cooperative project. For example, one partner provides manufacturing capabilities while a second partner provides marketing expertise. In other situations, a strategic alliance can enable similar companies to combine their capabilities to counter the threats of a much larger or new type of competitor. Exhibit 7.17, Strategy in Action, provides an example of a strategic alliance that provides "strength in numbers."

Strategic alliances are sometimes undertaken because the partners want to develop in-house capabilities to supplant the partner when the contractual arrangement between them reaches its termination date. Such relationships are tricky because, in a sense, the partners are attempting to "steal" each other's know-how. Exhibit 7.18, Global Strategy in Action, lists some important questions about their learning intentions that prospective partners should ask themselves before entering into a strategic alliance.

In other instances, strategic alliances are synonymous with *licensing agreements*. Licensing involves the transfer of some industrial property right from the U.S. licensor to a motivated licensee in a foreign country. Most tend to be patents, trademarks, or technical

Global Strategy in Action

Key Issues in Strategic Alliance Learning

Objective	Major Questions
1. Assess and value partner knowledge.	• What were the strategic objectives in forming the alliance? • What are the core competencies of our alliance partner? • What specific knowledge does the partner have that could enhance our competitive strategy?
2. Determine knowledge accessibility.	• How have key alliance responsibilities been allocated to the partners? • Which partner controls key managerial responsibilities? • Does the alliance agreement specify restrictions on our access to the alliance operations?
3. Evaluate knowledge tacitness and ease of transfer.	• Is our learning objective focused on explicit operational knowledge? • Where in the alliance does the knowledge reside? • What are we trying to learn and how can we use the knowledge?
4. Establish knowledge connections between the alliance and the partner.	• Are parent managers in regular contact with senior alliance managers? • Has the alliance been incorporated into parent strategic plans? • What is the level of trust between parent and alliance managers?
5. Draw on existing knowledge to facilitate learning.	• In the learning process, have efforts been made to involve managers with prior experience in either/both alliance management and partner ties? • Are experiences with other alliances being used as the basis for managing the current alliance?
6. Ensure that partner and alliance managerial cultures are in alignment.	• Is the alliance viewed as a threat or an asset by parent managers? • In the parent, is there agreement on the strategic rationale for the alliance? • In the alliance, do managers understand the importance of the parent's learning objective?

Source: From *Academy of Management Executive* by Andrew C. Inkpen. Copyright © 1998 by Academy of Management. Reproduced with permission of Academy of Management via Copyright Clearance Center.

know-how that are granted to the licensee for a specified time in return for a royalty and for avoiding tariffs or import quotas. Bell South and U.S. West, with various marketing and service competitive advantages valuable to Europe, have extended a number of licenses to create personal computers networks in the United Kingdom. Another example of licensing is discussed in Exhibit 7.19, Strategy in Action, which describes UTEK Corporation's successful strategy for licensing discoveries resulting from research efforts at universities.

Another licensing strategy is to contract the manufacturing of its product line to a foreign company to exploit local comparative advantages in technology, materials, or labor. MIPS Computer Systems has licensed Digital Equipment Corporation, Texas Instruments, Cypress Semiconductor, and Bipolar Integrated Technology in the United States and Fujitsu, NEC, and Kubota in Japan to market computers based on its designs in the partner's country.

A Matchmaker for Inventors

BusinessWeek

For George E. Inglett, a researcher with the U.S. Department of Agriculture, the eureka moment came in 1995. Searching for a use for oat hulls, he shoveled a couple of pounds into a high-speed centrifuge in his lab in Peoria, Illinois. What emerged was a white gel with no taste or calories. Adding it to food cut the fat and calories dramatically but the gel had no impact on taste or texture. Inglett had discovered nutrition's Holy Grail: an all-natural fat substitute.

Inglett's discovery might have been for naught without UTEK Corp., which ultimately found a small company to commercialize his product: ZTrim in Mundelein, Illinois. UTEK, a technology matchmaker with an unusual business model, gives researchers like Inglett an outlet for their ideas, and it gives companies like ZTrim a way to outsource innovation by providing access to a database of more than 35,000 discoveries that would otherwise go unnoticed.

For university and government researchers struggling to license their discoveries, UTEK can make all the difference. Many universities have technology-transfer offices that are understaffed and underfunded. And many risk-averse companies are unwilling to take a flyer on an interesting idea with uncertain commercial potential. The result: only about 30 percent of the 18,000 discoveries made by university and government researchers each year ever see the light of day as commercial products.

North Carolina A&T State University's experience is instructive. When a researcher there stumbled on a way to detect microscopic cracks in an airplane fuselage, the discovery, while promising, turned out to be nearly impossible to sell. The technology-transfer office spent two years scouring North America and Europe for a buyer.

Then UTEK showed up, with Material Technologies Inc. in tow. Unlike other technology-transfer companies, which license technologies they've acquired or charge fees to broker deals, UTEK pays the research lab for licensing rights to its discovery. It then sells those rights to the client company for shares of stock, which UTEK agrees to hold for one year. UTEK might pay $500,000 for the discovery and receive stock worth $2.5 million. A lot can happen in a year—UTEK's stake in ZTrim, for example, ballooned to $6 million.

UTEK has had more hits than misses, including deals involving technologies for fertilizer production, pollution monitoring, even land mine detection. Since 2003 the number of tech-transfer deals UTEK has brokered has quadrupled, despite robust competition, which includes 10 publicly traded tech-transfer companies. UTEK, which went public in 2000, now holds equity stakes in 55 companies, for a portfolio valued at $60 million. And each year it adds several thousand discoveries to its database.

Service and franchise-based firms—including Anheuser-Busch, Avis, Coca-Cola, Hilton, Hyatt, Holiday Inns, Kentucky Fried Chicken, McDonald's, and Pepsi—have long engaged in licensing arrangements with foreign distributors as a way to enter new markets with standardized products that can benefit from marketing economies.

Outsourcing is a basic approach to strategic alliances that enables firms to gain a competitive advantage. Significant changes within many segments of American business continue to encourage the use of outsourcing practices. Within the health care arena, an industry survey recorded 67 percent of hospitals using provider outsourcing for at least one department within their organization. Services such as information systems, reimbursement, and risk and physician practice management are outsourced by 51 percent of the hospitals that use outsourcing.

Another successful application of outsourcing is found in human resources. A survey of human resource executives revealed 85 percent have personal experience leading an outsourcing effort within their organization. In addition, it was found that two-thirds of pension departments have outsourced at least one human resource function. Within customer service and sales departments, outsourcing increases productivity in such areas as product information, sales and order taking, sample fulfillment, and complaint handling. For an interesting example of the use of outsourcing to save money in the retail sector, see Exhibit 7.20, Strategy in Action.

What Happens to That Scarf You Really Hated?

BusinessWeek

Shoppers, on average, return about 6 percent of everything they buy. That proportion spikes in January to nearly 10 percent. This used to be a sore point for retailers. Rather than try to make sense of a hodgepodge of generally used, sometimes broken goods with packaging shredded or instructions missing, stores tended just to write the lot off as a loss. But over the past decade, an opportunistic industry has sprung up to give the reject pile a new lease on life.

Most big-box retailers—Sears, Target, Best Buy, Kohl's, and many others—now outsource the handling of returns to companies that specialize in so-called reverse logistics. These third parties' job, basically, is to pick up a store's returns and figure out what to do with them—restock an item, sell it somewhere else, like in Peru or at a flea market, or throw it in the trash.

For retailers, it's a way to squeeze money from what previously was a cost center, because they get a cut of any eventual sales. Genco, the biggest such service provider, charges stores a management fee to collect and sort the products at its 33 return centers. If it's able to sell a returned item to a secondary market, the proceeds are split with the retailer. Newgistics, an Austin (Texas) company, handles returns specifically for online sales—where return rates can surge up to 20 percent—for Amazon.com, J. Crew, and Nordstrom, among others, charging by package. Other companies, such as Liquidity Services, don't charge a fee, only taking a cut from auctions of the goods.

The best gift you can give a returns processor is to bring back something for no other reason than you just changed your mind. If that item gets back to a Genco center, for example, the manufacturer may give the retailer a credit for the return (free money). Then Genco will send the defect-free, originally wrapped product back to the retailer to be sold again (more money).

Pittsburgh-based, privately held Genco helped develop this niche in 1993 when, as a $34 million-a-year company, it started handling returns for Wal-Mart Stores Inc. By 2006, Genco had $570 million in revenue. Now it does logistics work for more than 100 clients.

The trick for logistics companies is to find other places for returned merchandise. Much of what Genco sells goes to closeout retailers or dollar stores. If something is defective, it goes back to the manufacturer, or if that's not possible, Genco will try to fix it. It even puts products up on eBay. Each retailer has its own restrictions about its returned goods' eventual home. About 40 percent of Genco's $1 billion in turnover comes from goods it sells in secondary markets overseas. Some retailers require Genco to scrub the product of logos; some just want the highest bid.

Source: Reprinted with special permission from Brian Hindo, "What Happens to that Scarf You Really Hated?" *BusinessWeek*, January 15, 2007. Copyright © 2007 The McGraw-Hill Companies.

Consortia, *Keiretsus*, and *Chaebols*

consortia
Large interlocking relationships between businesses of an industry.

keiretsus
A Japanese consortia of businesses that is coordinated by a large trading company to gain a strategic advantage.

chaebol
A Korean consortia financed through government banking groups to gain a strategic advantage.

Consortia are defined as large interlocking relationships between businesses of an industry. In Japan such consortia are known as *keiretsus;* in South Korea as *chaebols.*

In Europe, consortia projects are increasing in number and in success rates. Examples include the Junior Engineers' and Scientists' Summer Institute, which underwrites cooperative learning and research; the European Strategic Program for Research and Development in Information Technologies, which seeks to enhance European competitiveness in fields related to computer electronics and component manufacturing; and EUREKA, which is a joint program involving scientists and engineers from several European countries to coordinate joint research projects.

A Japanese *keiretsu* is an undertaking involving up to 50 different firms that are joined around a large trading company or bank and are coordinated through interlocking directories and stock exchanges. It is designed to use industry coordination to minimize risks of competition, in part through cost sharing and increased economies of scale. Examples include Sumitomo, Mitsubishi, Mitsui, and Sanwa.

A South Korean chaebol resembles a consortium or keiretsu except that they are typically financed through government banking groups and are largely run by professional managers trained by participating firms expressly for the job.

A Profile of Strategic Choice Options

	Six Strategic Choice Options					
	1	**2**	**3**	**4**	**5**	**6**
Interactive opportunities	West Coast markets present little competition		Current markets sensitive to price competition		Current industry product lines offer too narrow a range of markets	
Appropriate long-range objectives (limited sample): Average 5-year ROI.	15%	19%	13%	17%	23%	15%
Company sales by year 5.	+ 50%	+ 40%	+ 20%	+ 0%	+ 35%	+ 25%
Risk of negative profits.	.30	.25	.10	.15	.20	.05
Grand strategies	Horizontal integration	Market development	Concentration	Selective retrenchment	Product development	Concentration

SELECTION OF LONG-TERM OBJECTIVES AND GRAND STRATEGY SETS

At first glance, the strategic management model, which provides the framework for study throughout this book, seems to suggest that strategic choice decision making leads to the sequential selection of long-term objectives and grand strategies. In fact, however, strategic choice is the simultaneous selection of long-range objectives and grand strategies. When strategic planners study their opportunities, they try to determine which are most likely to result in achieving various long-range objectives. Almost simultaneously, they try to forecast whether an available grand strategy can take advantage of preferred opportunities so the tentative objectives can be met. In essence, then, three distinct but highly interdependent choices are being made at one time. Several triads, or sets, of possible decisions are usually considered.

A simplified example of this process is shown in Exhibit 7.21, Strategy in Action. In this example, the firm has determined that six strategic choice options are available. These options stem from three interactive opportunities (e.g., West Coast markets that present little competition). Because each of these interactive opportunities can be approached through different grand strategies—for options 1 and 2, the grand strategies are horizontal integration and market development—each offers the potential for achieving long-range objectives to varying degrees. Thus, a firm rarely can make a strategic choice only on the basis of its preferred opportunities, long-range objectives, or grand strategy. Instead, these three elements must be considered simultaneously, because only in combination do they constitute a strategic choice.

In an actual decision situation, the strategic choice would be complicated by a wider variety of interactive opportunities, feasible company objectives, promising grand strategy options, and evaluative criteria. Nevertheless, Exhibit 7.21 does partially reflect the nature and complexity of the process by which long-term objectives and grand strategies are selected.

In the next chapter, the strategic choice process will be fully explained. However, knowledge of long-term objectives and grand strategies is essential to understanding that process.

SEQUENCE OF OBJECTIVES AND STRATEGY SELECTION

The selection of long-range objectives and grand strategies involves simultaneous, rather than sequential, decisions. While it is true that objectives are needed to prevent the firm's direction and progress from being determined by random forces, it is equally true that objectives can be achieved only if strategies are implemented. In fact, long-term objectives and grand strategies are so interdependent that some business consultants do not distinguish between them. Long-term objectives and grand strategies are still combined under the heading of company strategy in most of the popular business literature and in the thinking of most practicing executives.

However, the distinction has merit. Objectives indicate what strategic managers want but provide few insights about how they will be achieved. Conversely, strategies indicate what types of actions will be taken but do not define what ends will be pursued or what criteria will serve as constraints in refining the strategic plan.

Does it matter whether strategic decisions are made to achieve objectives or to satisfy constraints? No, because constraints are themselves objectives. The constraint of increased inventory capacity is a desire (an objective), not a certainty. Likewise, the constraint of an increase in the sales force does not ensure that the increase will be achieved, given such factors as other company priorities, labor market conditions, and the firm's profit performance.

DESIGNING A PROFITABLE BUSINESS MODEL

business model
A clear understanding of how the firm will generate profits and the strategic actions it must take to succeed over the long term.

The process of combining long-term objectives and grand strategies produces a **business model**. Creating an effective model requires a clear understanding of how the firm will generate profits and the strategic action it must take to succeed over the long term.

Adrian Slywotzky and David Morrison identified 22 business models—designs that generate profits in a unique way.[15] They present these models as examples, believing that others do or can exist. The authors also believe that in some instances profitability depends on the interplay of two or more business models. Their study demonstrates that the mechanisms of profitability can be very different but that a focus on the customer is the key to the effectiveness of each model.

Slywotzky and Morrison suggest that the two most productive questions asked of executives are these:

1. What is our business model?
2. How do we make a profit?

The classic strategy rule suggested, "Gain market share and profits will follow." This approach once worked for some industries. However, because of competitive turbulence

---

[15] This section is excerpted from A. J. Slywotzky, D. J. Morrison, and B. Andelman, *The Profit Zone; How Strategic Business Design Will Lead You To Tomorrow's Profits* (New York: Times Books, 1997).

caused by globalization and rapid technological advancements, the once-popular belief in a strong correlation between market share and profitability has collapsed in many industries.

How can businesses earn sustainable profits? The answer is found by analyzing the following questions: Where will the firm make a profit in this industry? How should the business model be designed so that the firm will be profitable? Slywotzky and Morrison describe the following profitability business models as ways to answer those questions.

1. *Customer development customer solutions profit model.* Companies that use this business model make money by finding ways to improve their customers' economics and investing in ways for customers to improve their processes.

2. *Product pyramid profit model.* This model is effective in markets where customers have strong preferences for product characteristics, including variety, style, color, and price. By offering a number of variations, companies can build so-called product pyramids. At the base are low-priced, high-volume products, and at the top are high-priced, low-volume products. Profit is concentrated at the top of the pyramid, but the base is the strategic firewall (i.e., a strong, low-priced brand that deters competitor entry), thereby protecting the margins at the top. Consumer goods companies and automobile companies use this model.

3. *Multicomponent system profit model.* Some businesses are characterized by a production/marketing system that consists of components that generate substantially different levels of profitability. In hotels, for example, there is a substantial difference between the profitability of room rentals and that of bar operations. In such instances, it often is useful to maximize the use of the highest-profit components to maximize the profitability of the whole system.

4. *Switchboard profit model.* Some markets function by connecting multiple sellers to multiple buyers. The switchboard profit model creates a high-value intermediary that concentrates these multiple communication pathways through one point or "switchboard" and thereby reduces costs for both parties in exchange for a fee. As volume increases, so too do profits.

5. *Time profit model.* Sometimes, speed is the key to profitability. This business model takes advantage of first-mover advantage. To sustain this model, constant innovation is essential.

6. *Blockbuster profit model.* In some industries, profitability is driven by a few great product successes. This business model is representative of movie studios, pharmaceutical firms, and software companies, which have high R&D and launch costs and finite product cycles. In this type of environment, it pays to concentrate resource investments in a few projects rather than to take positions in a variety of products.

7. *Profit multiplier model.* This business model reaps gains, repeatedly, from the same product, character, trademark capability, or service. Think of the value that Michael Jordan Inc. creates with the image of the great basketball legend. This model can be a powerful engine for businesses with strong consumer brands.

8. *Entrepreneurial profit model.* Small can be beautiful. This business model stresses that diseconomies of scale can exist in companies. They attack companies that have become comfortable with their profit levels with formal, bureaucratic systems that are remote from customers. As their expenses grow and customer relevance declines, such companies are vulnerable to entrepreneurs who are in direct contact with their customers.

Where Dell Went Wrong

BusinessWeek

At Dell, how it all began is never forgotten. Even on January 31, 2007, as founder Michael S. Dell returned to the role of CEO after 18 months of bad news and faltering financials, the press release trumpeted how, 23 years ago, Dell launched what would become a $56 billion business with just $1,000 and a simple idea.

Like many long-forgotten former champions, Dell succumbed to complacency in the belief that its business model would always keep it far ahead of the pack. While Dell broadened its product line, it never dealt with the vast improvement in the competition or used its lead in direct sales and the cash generated to invest in new business lines, talent, or innovation that could provide another competitive edge. "Dell is a text-book example of single-formula growth: 'We make PCs cheap. This is what we do, and we do it a lot,'" says Jim Mackey, managing director at the Billion Dollar Growth Network. "You can grow very fast when you're on a single formula, but when you get to a certain point, you don't have the ability to create new growth."

"When it's all you can do to keep up with the growth your current business model is providing, you just don't feel that urgency," says Harvard Business School professor Clayton Christensen. "It's hard to get worried." He visited Dell's Round Rock (Texas) offices in 1998 and again in 2000, and warned Dell and then-CEO Kevin Rollins that they needed to focus on growth five to eight years out, on the model that would augment their built-to-order machines. Instead, Dell pushed its model into new types of hardware, such as storage, printers, and TVs, in the hopes of making easy profits by selling products made by other companies.

Hubris crept in. In 1999, Dell bought a start-up called ConvergeNet, which had a sophisticated storage product that turned out to be not ready for prime time. Dubbing rival EMC Corp. the "Excessive Margin Company," Dell seemed to expect storage to follow the same pattern PCs had, moving from pricey, feature-laden models into a standards-based commodity. Dell underestimated the competition and is an also-ran in the segment. By 2005, PC rivals, particularly HP, which has taken the market-share lead from Dell, had closed the efficiency gap and were enjoying resurgent sales at retail stores.

Dell's loyalty to its business model could make it difficult to recapture growth. Dell has suggested a new offensive to enlarge its computer services business, which so far has focused largely on repair and upgrading of Dell's hardware. Dell has struggled to find other growth areas large enough to matter. After a promising start in printers, moving quickly to no. 3, the most recent quarterly data from research firm IDC shows Dell's market share at 3.6 percent, down from 6.2 percent the previous year. Its once-promising move into networking gear has fizzled, and its share in the storage systems market is flat compared with a year ago.

9. *Specialization profit model.* This business model stresses growth through sequenced specialization. Consulting companies have used this design successfully.

10. *Installed base profit model.* A company that pursues this model profits because its established user base subsequently buys the company's brand of consumables or follow-on products. Installed base profits provide a protected annuity stream. Examples include razors and blades, software and upgrades, copiers and toner cartridges, and cameras and film.

11. *De facto standard profit model.* A variant of the installed base profit model, this model is appropriate when the installed base model becomes the de facto standard that governs competitive behavior in the industry.

Exhibit 7.22, Strategy in Action, discusses the business model of Dell. Once praised as innovative, it is now criticized as overly narrow, blind to opportunities, and insufficiently ambitious.

Summary

Before we learn how strategic decisions are made, it is important to understand the two principal components of any strategic choice; namely, long-term objectives and the grand strategy. The purpose of this chapter was to convey that understanding.

Long-term objectives were defined as the results a firm seeks to achieve over a specified period, typically five years. Seven common long-term objectives were discussed: profitability, productivity, competitive position, employee development, employee relations, technological leadership, and public responsibility. These, or any other long-term objectives, should be flexible, measurable over time, motivating, suitable, and understandable.

Grand strategies were defined as comprehensive approaches guiding the major actions designed to achieve long-term objectives. Fifteen grand strategy options were discussed: concentrated growth, market development, product development, innovation, horizontal integration, vertical integration, concentric diversification, conglomerate diversification, turnaround, divestiture, liquidation, bankruptcy, joint ventures, strategic alliances, and consortia.

Key Terms

balanced scorecard, *p. 202*
bankruptcy, *p. 227*
business model, *p. 237*
chaebol, *p. 235*
concentrated growth, *p. 211*
concentric diversification, *p. 221*
conglomerate diversification, *p. 221*

consortia, *p. 235*
divestiture strategy, *p. 226*
generic strategy, *p. 203*
grand strategy, *p. 211*
horizontal integration, *p. 218*
innovation, *p. 216*
joint venture, *p. 230*

keiretsus, *p. 235*
liquidation, *p. 227*
market development, *p. 214*
product development, *p. 216*
strategic alliances, *p. 232*
turnaround strategy, *p. 224*
vertical integration, *p. 220*

Questions for Discussion

1. Identify firms in the business community nearest to your college or university that you believe are using each of the 15 grand strategies discussed in this chapter.
2. Identify firms in your business community that appear to rely principally on 1 of the 15 grand strategies. What kind of information did you use to classify the firms?
3. Write a long-term objective for your school of business that exhibits the seven qualities of long-term objectives described in this chapter.
4. Distinguish between the following pairs of grand strategies:

   a. Horizontal and vertical integration.
   b. Conglomerate and concentric diversification.
   c. Product development and innovation.
   d. Joint venture and strategic alliance.

5. Rank each of the 15 grand strategy options discussed in this chapter on the following three scales:

   High   Low
   _____
                   Cost

   High   Low
   _____
               Risk of failure

   High   Low
   _____
        Potential for exceptional growth

6. Identify firms that use the eight specific options shown in Exhibit 7.8 under the grand strategies of concentration, market development, and product development.

Chapter 7 Discussion Case

BusinessWeek

VW's New Strategic Plan for the United States—Part 1: *Crispin Porter + Bogusky's Plan to Rekindle Our Love Affair with VW*

1 Remember the Volkswagen Rabbit? The boxy, fuel-efficient hatchback was launched in 1974 to replace the legendary Beetle as the company's big seller and was the first VW made in the United States. It also became known for catching fire and breaking down, and thus became the symbol of VW's collapse in America through the 1980s. At the insistence of VW's German parent, the Rabbit name was killed in 1985, and the Westmoreland (Pennsylvania) assembly plant was shuttered soon after.

2 So it was audacious indeed when Alex Bogusky, chief creative officer of Crispin Porter + Bogusky, which took over the VW advertising account last December, suggested resurrecting the Rabbit name. In a March 20, 2006, meeting at the Auburn Hills (Michigan) headquarters of VW of America, with company brass and two members of its dealer council, Bogusky reasoned that the redesigned Golf launching in the United States this year had already been selling in Europe for two years, so auto writers probably wouldn't pay much attention to the stateside debut. "So let's change the story," offered the 42-year-old ad director before the assembled group. Nervous laughter followed. VW supervisory board chairman Ferdinand K. Piech, known for his bad temper and for insisting that VW have global model names, was certain to disapprove. But VW's U.S. chief, Adrian M. Hallmark, bought in and took the idea to the carmaker's German headquarters in Wolfsburg on March 25, 2006. Worldwide brand chief Wolfgang Bernhard said yes and ordered new signs, photography, and press releases to be rushed for the New York International Auto Show on April 12, despite whispers that Piech, already gunning for Bernhard's boss, management board chairman Bernd Pischetsrieder, was unhappy.

HATE MAIL

3 Many love the Rabbit idea, but plenty hate it. That's just the kind of strong, polarized reaction Bogusky and his partners like to provoke. VW's U.S. dealer council supports the move. But consider some of the hostile reaction: Peter M. DeLorenzo, founder and publisher of influential Webzine Autoextremist.com Inc., called the decision to return to the Rabbit name "pure, unadulterated lunacy," and wrote that if U.S. VW marketing chief Kerri Martin and her agency weren't stopped, they would "destroy the brand in the U.S. once and for all." Steven Wilhite, former VW marketing chief and current global chief marketing officer at Nissan Motor Co., pronounced the idea "brain-dead." Rance E. Crain, editor-in-chief of *Advertising Age*, editorialized that Crispin's first

work for VW has been "so horrendously awful that [it] smoothes the way for [VW's] quick and complete withdrawal [from the American market]." Says a habitually cool Bogusky, wearing a Kiss T-shirt and stabbing his fork in the air as he scarfed banana pancakes at Greenstreet's, a cafe near his Miami office: "I like that they are talking about the work. If they aren't talking, then your brand is dead."

4 Indeed, Volkswagen is trying to avoid the kind of near-death experience it had in the early 1990s, when sales sank so low that German managers seriously pondered pulling up U.S. stakes altogether. At 224,000 cars sold last year, VW is a long way from the nadir of 49,000 in 1992. But to insiders who have watched the numbers drop by 131,000 sales per year since a peak of 355,648 in 2001, this period has felt eerily like the dark days a decade ago, before the New Beetle lifted the entire brand out of quicksand. Internal research shows a lasting loss of confidence in the brand after costly, repetitive quality problems: VW's U.S. division has lost more than $1 billion in each of the past two years, and this year could be nearly as bad. On May 2, 2006, Pischetsrieder had his contract renewed for six years, but only after intense pressure by the supervisory board to deliver better results with fewer job cuts than the 20,000 he wants. "No question about it, it's a five-alarm fire," says Crispin president Jeff Hicks.

5 Enter Crispin Porter + Bogusky, the eccentric ad shop in Miami that's known for using viral marketing and creating nutty characters like the Subservient Chicken for Burger King Holdings Inc.'s ailing franchises. VW had been through three years of coolly received ad efforts as it juggled a failed luxury sedan (the tony Phaeton, priced at more than $75,000) and the $50,000 Touareg SUV, alongside $20,000 Golfs and Jettas. Former agency Arnold Worldwide, saddled with temporary VW ad directors before marketing chief Kerri Martin arrived, struggled to make sense of it all. A year ago, Martin got the heady title of director of brand innovation, having been the celebrated marketing whiz at MINI USA and Harley-Davidson Inc. Crispin worked with her at MINI to create the kind of B-school case-study advertising excitement for which VW used to be known.

6 As Crispin tries to douse the flames engulfing the VW brand, it has to prove that it won the VW assignment on merit, not just as Martin's pet agency. Situated 1,300 miles south of Madison Avenue's groupthink, Crispin stands apart. Whether it was running MINI Cooper hatchbacks around cities atop Ford Excursion SUVs or getting teens to dump some 1,200 faux body bags at the door of a tobacco company for an antismoking campaign, Crispin has been changing the industry's playbook. It famously helped solve Burger King's

irrelevancy problem, especially with consumers aged 14 to 25, with the Subservient Chicken Web site, where a visitor could make a chicken do almost anything on command—dust furniture or play air guitar.

7   That simple, inexpensive, wacky idea has generated a staggering 460 million-plus hits in two years and helped Burger King post its first string of positive growth quarters in a decade. The agency's relaunch of the MINI brand helped the unit of BMW surpass sales targets by 80 percent. Crispin's success has fueled growth in its own staff from 105 in 2000 to 438. As it transforms marketing messages into entertainment time and again, "the agency has been redefining what consumers even recognize as advertising," says rival and admirer Jeff Goodby, co-chairman of Goodby, Silverstein & Partners in San Francisco.

8   It's early days, but it looks as if Crispin's style of marketing is working once more. Since its ads started running, VW sales are up, dealers are enthusiastic, Internet chatter about VW is as high as it has been since the public relations bonanza around the New Beetle in 1998. Just about every aspect of Crispin's work in its first five months on the job has been covered in major media outlets. As the agency and Martin have challenged many of VW's old ways and ignored some of the company's internal political trip-wires, the brand is being talked about again around the water cooler, a must for any consumer company today that hopes to not just survive but thrive.

WEB ALLURE

9   Volkswagen, of course, has its own special place in advertising history. Two separate agencies defined themselves, and advertising as a whole, in two different decades working for VW. In the 1960s it was Doyle Dane Bernbach, which created the headlines "Think Small" and "Lemon," pioneering the use of self-deprecating humor and wit to sell cars. "It was the first time ever that people talked about ads at cocktail parties and at work," says Andrew Langer, vice chairman of Lowe & Partners Worldwide, who worked at DDB then. In the 1990s, VW and Boston's Arnold Fortuna Lawner & Cabot, before it was Arnold Worldwide, ignited a new genre of storytelling mixed with independent rock music: the "Da Da Da" ad, playing the German song of the same title while two slackers drove around town in their Golf. "It fits your life," went the ad's voiceover, "or your complete lack thereof." Now it's Crispin's turn to make history—or humiliate itself trying—by taking on America's favorite advertising account for yet another comeback.

10   It certainly didn't take long for Crispin to get people talking again. In place of a subservient chicken, Crispin invented a German-accented, dominatrix-type blonde bombshell named Helga. She appears in ads with an effete German engineer named Wolfgang, whose message to introduce the GTI hatchback is "Unpimp Your Auto," a swipe at the over-accessorized, high-performance small Japanese cars often dubbed "rice rockets." Billboards for the GTI read "Auf Wiedersehen, sucka" and "Fast as Schnell."

Schnell, and then some. Day One on the account, December 6, 2005 the agency began to perform triage on the ailing carmaker. Bogusky, a Miami native who dropped out of art school though both parents are graphic artists, met with creative director Andrew Keller, 35, and more than 40 writers, art directors, and researchers in the agency's big conference room. The brief for the GTI read: "How does GTI regain its position as the original hot hatch?" By the way, Keller told the crowd, "we have to figure this out and execute a plan in time to launch during the Winter Olympics [on] February 6." That gave the team fewer than 60 days, with a Christmas holiday in the middle.   **11**

Crispin's cognitive anthropologists went to work. Two-hour in-home interviews with two dozen GTI buyers, all men 18 to 30, were done in five cities. The researchers sent the subjects an assignment in advance of visits: Make a collage with magazine pictures to illustrate how they felt about Japanese "tuner" cars, like Honda Civics, on which owners tack thousands of dollars in speed-enhancing and cosmetic accessories. Then cut out pictures representing the European tuner cars like GTI and BMW M cars that are accessorized at the German factories. One GTI fan contrasted cutouts of Tweety Bird and a tuner "dude" wearing a chrome dollar-sign necklace to represent the Asian tuner "posers" with images of a black wolf and Ninja warrior depicting the "more authentic and serious" Euro tuner crowd.   **12**

Crispin's researchers then asked them to write epitaphs on paper tombstones after the phrase "Here Lies the Japanese Hot Hatch," and recipes that begin with, "My perfect recipe for driving is . . ." One recipe reads: "One S-curve, a pinch of fishtail, two parts turbo toast, an ounce of hard rock music. Combine and bring to a boil." The strategy drawn from all this was to flog the GTI as tuned in Germany by speed-happy engineers rather than at some U.S. neighborhood retail joint.   **13**

In launching the GTI and reviving the Volkswagen brand in general, Crispin faced two challenges. First, since the debut of the New Beetle, the VW brand has become feminized, says Keller. Loyal young males who were hanging on to VW by a thread needed to be reassured. Too many men had come to view VW as a "chick's brand." Worse, women were turning away from VW because of quality issues. Second, VW loyalists had become baffled about the pricey Phaeton and Touareg and loaded Jettas with price tags topping $30,000. A decade into the popularity of small SUVs priced under $25,000, VW has none. "Affordable German engineering is a huge part of VW's DNA, and these decisions really confused customers," says Tom Birk, Crispin vice president for research and planning.   **14**

Crispin's employee handbook says advertising is "anything that makes our clients famous." So for the GTI, Bogusky and Keller are pulling no punches. This is a car built for driving fast and having fun. And for men, that inevitably leads to a certain amount of sex, they reckoned. That led to Helga, an over-the-top parody of a German nightclubbing valkyrie. She is in ads—and stars in VW's GTI Web site. Anyone configuring a GTI, choosing interior, wheels, engine, and the like, can take a   **15** virtual test drive with the boot-wearing siren, who comments about each driver's selections. "I see from your paddle shifters, you're ready to go." And, "I luf leather." There are some 500 variations of GTI, and Helga can talk you through them all.

16   Helga and Wolfgang, says Hicks, are an example of taking an audience to a place they didn't know they wanted to go. "A lot of advertisers try and mirror what the research tells them. What we do is try and make the brand part of the pop culture." Ads featuring Helga and Wolfgang ran on TV in March and April 2006, but now enthusiasts all over the Net are downloading them. In one, engineer Wolfgang is consulting a young owner with an oversized intake port on his hood that sucks air into the engine compartment. Says Helga: "It's definitely sucking." Thanks to the Internet, VW has been fielding requests for copies of these ads from media outlets and VW clubs as far away as India.

17   A spike in Net chatter will go only so far. Although VW ranked third from the bottom in J. D. Power & Associates' 2005 Initial Quality Survey, it improved from the year before—by 10 percent fewer glitches per 100 cars. VW's quality woes have spread around the Net as fast as Helga's double entendres. This month, says VW, it will post another big improvement, while dealers are reporting half as many warranty repairs on new models as they did in 2004.

SEXY SYMBOL

18   Despite its hasty execution, the campaign has already achieved what Martin hoped it would. "We needed to ignite a new conversation with owners," she says. The viral dimension has worked well. For about two weeks, VW ads were the top download from video-sharing site YouTube.com. Wolfgang and Helga have become part of the new VW story. They have sites on MySpace.com, where more than 7,500 fans have signed up as Helga's "friends" and are downloading a printable life-size Helga. "Bachelor parties, maybe," quips Keller.

19   Can Crispin's edgy playfulness go over the line? With the suggestive content, charges of sexism have followed. TV ads for the Winter Olympics depicted young men so into their GTIs that one refused to roll up the window to shield his girlfriend's wind-blown hair and told her to stop "yackin" so he could enjoy the engine's growl. Another refused to take his girlfriend on an errand in his GTI because her weight would slow him down. Ouch. Nissan's Wilhite says he's all for shaking up VW's message, "but I can't go along with ads that marginalize women like beer commercials often do." Suzanne Farley, a Boston education consultant and owner of a 1999 VW Passat, agrees, saying the ads "made me feel weird, like they were talking right past me." But the agency just introduced its first work for Miller Lite and junked the predictable frat-boy approach. Instead, icons like Burt Reynolds and Pittsburgh Steelers running back Jerome Bettis thoughtfully discuss "man laws," like how long to wait before dating a buddy's ex-girlfriend.

20   There's no doubt that Crispin and Volkswagen's Martin are out to take some risks, and that for now at least they have a long leash from management, which is doing its part to supply the right products. VW is moving fast under Pischetsrieder and Bernhard to bring out several new models in the next 20 months, including a minivan, two light SUVS, and two sports cars—the Eos convertible and a new interpretation of the 1970s and 1980s VW Scirocco—all priced under $30,000. A pricier sedan larger than the Passat is due, too, to try to hold on to aging boomer fans. It's the fastest product proliferation in VW history, and Crispin had better get a coherent strategy to reposition the entire brand before the new models arrive. "We are on a whole new timetable for getting this brand right and will move faster than people around here thought we could," says Bernhard.

21   In an industry that celebrates the slogan, that magical line of ad copy that crystallizes a brand's essence, Crispin hasn't yet hit on one for VW. It did, however, kill off VW's 10-year-old "Drivers wanted" line. "A slogan or tag line is not important if the messaging is right," says Bogusky. Still, Crispin likes the VW logo so much that it came up with a gimmick in the GTI ads in which Wolfgang forms the V and W with his interlocked fingers. That's already sticking online. People selling VWs on eBay, for example, have turned up in pictures in their cars making the hand sign.

22   Crispin may offer a new slogan sometime in 2007. For now, it's giving each model its own campaign. It just relaunched the Jetta with ads that are far from funky or sexy. In an about-face from its usual humorous tack, Crispin spotlights the car's top side-impact safety ratings. And like almost everything else the agency does, even these sober-as-a-judge ads have stirred conversation. In one, two couples are chatting as they drive away from a movie house. The driver is distracted and gets creamed by an SUV in real time. The effect on the TV viewer is jolting. The ad moves from the crash to the people standing by, shaky but unharmed, looking at the crushed car. A survivor says, "Holy . . ." and the ad cuts to a video frame that says "Safe Happens." Requests for Jetta brochures went up 30 percent after the ads' debut. And dozens of newspapers and NBC's *The Today Show* have reported on their jarring quality. "When [*Today Show* host] Matt Lauer talks for seven minutes about our ads, I know it's right," says Santa Monica (California) VW dealer Mike Sullivan. GTI sales are at 20-year highs, and VW sales overall are up 20 percent this year since Crispin's ads began.

Source: Reprinted with special permission from David Kiley, "The Craziest Ad Guys in America," *BusinessWeek,* May 22, 2006. Copyright © 2007 The McGraw-Hill Companies.

DISCUSSION QUESTIONS

1. How would you describe VW's new intended business strategy?

2. How would you describe VW's new advertising strategy?

3. Explain how effective you believe that the advertising strategy will be in helping to achieve the business strategy of VW in the long term.

4. Do you agree with Martin (paragraph 18) when he concludes that the advertising campaign achieved its goal of "igniting a new conversation with owners"?

5. If ad copy "crystallizes a brand's essence," what is the essence of VW? If it can be easily changed with a new ad campaign, what do we know about VW's business strategy?

VW's New Strategic Plan for the United States—Part 2

1 Volkswagen's experience in the United States has always been one of highs and lows. But rarely have its fortunes sunk so low as now. Less than a decade ago, the quirky reinvented Beetle helped VW come roaring back from a previous crisis. But for the past three years, its U.S. operations have lost close to $1 billion annually.

2 Now it's trying again to save the brand in the United States. To head U.S. operations, it's bringing in Stefan Jacoby, a German with close ties to VW chairman Martin Winterkorn and supervisory board chairman Ferdinand K. Piech, who took control of the company this year after a shakeup that left Porsche as VW's controlling shareholder. Jacoby, 49, an accountant by training, made his mark as head of VWs global sales and marketing. Since Jacoby took charge, the company boosted its European market share to 20.3 percent from 18.1 percent, helping keep it solidly in place as the Continent's leading brand. With its U.S. fortunes in long-term decline, Jacoby is facing his biggest challenge yet. His mission: to meet Winterkorn's target of breaking even in the United States by 2009.

3 Only a year ago, VW was gearing up a huge marketing campaign to relaunch a revamped Rabbit and Jetta in a bid to recapture its niche as the affordable, stylish European car of choice for younger buyers. VW hired former MINI USA marketing chief Kerri Martin, who recruited super-hot U.S. ad agency Crispin Porter + Bogusky. The plan, as chronicled in Part 1 of this case study, was to create a VW renaissance.

4 It didn't work out that way. A string of attention-grabbing adds—one campaign showed people surviving crashes unscathed and another starred a German dominatrix named Helga—did little to juice sales of VW's two most important models, the Jetta and the Passat. "I've never seen a brand struggle so hard to understand the U.S. market and fail so miserably," says Rebecca Lindland, a director at consulting firm Global Insight Inc. VW's sales slid to 235,000 last year, from 338,000 in 2002. Martin left in December 2006, part of a shakeup when Porsche took over.

5 Making matters worse is the perception in the United States that VW's quality lags versus its Japanese rivals. VW's interiors, for example, don't stand up to the kind of abuse they get from U.S. drivers, who do a lot more eating, drinking coffee, and applying makeup in their cars than Europeans do. That's one factor in J. D. Power & Associates Inc. ranking VW in the bottom 20 percent for reliability, quality, and service. "That really hurts VW when its young customer base does so much online comparative shopping," says Power Information Network analyst Tom Libby.

6 To turn operations around, Jacoby has to battle the punishingly high euro and VW's limited manufacturing presence in North America. Even more important, the company needs to introduce new models that build on its long tradition of quirkiness and connect with U.S. consumers. Instead, the carmaker's more recent offerings feel bland. Dealers think VW blew a golden opportunity when it chose not to introduce an updated version of the wildly popular Microbus from the 1960s and 1970s. Instead, the company is launching a repackaged, Volkswagen-branded, Chrysler minivan. Casey Gunther, VW's top-selling U.S. dealer, in Coconut Creek, Florida, is worried. "We're missing the funkiness" that U.S. buyers expect from VW, he says. "The Germans don't understand." And unlike in Europe, affluent buyers don't see VW as an aspirational brand.

7 Winterkorn vows the turnaround of the U.S. business is his "no. 1 priority." But there's only so long any management can put up with nearly $1 billion annual losses. Says one executive close to VW: "For the first time in some time, the phrase 'If we are to stay in the U.S.' precedes a lot of conversations at VW."

Source: Reprinted with special permission from David Kiley and Gail Edmondson, "Can VW Finally Find Its Way In America? A Last-Ditch Drive Must Correct Disastrous Turns to Make the U.S. Profitable Again," *BusinessWeek,* July 23, 2007. Copyright © 2007 The McGraw-Hill Companies.

DISCUSSION QUESTIONS

1. Does the trouble at VW suggest that VW executives confused business strategy with advertising (a non-strategic marketing activity)?

2. What are three essential elements that you would prefer to see in an ad campaign which would parallel the message in VW's business strategy?

3. To help answer the question of whether VW should plan to stay in the U.S., what information would executives need to consider?

4. How do you explain the relative success of VW in Europe (paragraph 2) given its failure in the U.S.?

5. Does this case teach us something about the classic debate over "style versus substance"? If it does, how does what you learned apply generally to formulating a business strategy?

Chapter **Eight**

Business Strategy

After reading and studying this chapter, you should be able to

1. Determine why a business would choose a low-cost, differentiation, or speed-based strategy.

2. Explain the nature and value of a market focus strategy.

3. Illustrate how a firm can pursue both low-cost and differentiation strategies.

4. Identify requirements for business success at different stages of industry evolution.

5. Determine good business strategies in fragmented and global industries.

6. Decide when a business should diversify.

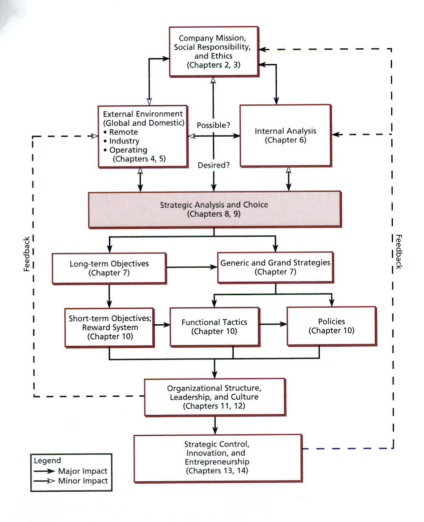

Strategic analysis and choice is the phase of the strategic management process in which business managers examine and choose a business strategy that allows their business to maintain or create a sustainable competitive advantage. Their starting point is to evaluate and determine which competitive advantages provide the basis for distinguishing the firm in the customer's mind from other reasonable alternatives. Businesses with a dominant product or service line must also choose among alternate grand strategies to guide the firm's activities, particularly when they are trying to decide about broadening the scope of the firm's activities beyond its core business. This chapter examines strategic analysis and choice in single- or dominant-product/service businesses by addressing two basic issues:

1. **What strategies are most effective at building sustainable competitive advantages for single business units?** What competitive strategy positions a business most effectively in its industry? For example, Scania, the most productive truck manufacturer in the world, joins its major rival Volvo as two anchors of Sweden's economy. Scania's return on sales of 9.9 percent far exceeds Mercedes (2.6 percent) and Volvo (2.5 percent), a level it has achieved most of the last 60 years. Scania has built a sustainable competitive advantage with a strategy of focusing solely on heavy transport vehicles in three geographic markets—Europe, Latin America, and Asia—by providing vehicles customized to specific tasks yet built using modularized components (20,000 components per vehicle versus 25,000 for Volvo and 40,000 for Mercedes). Scania is a low-cost producer of a differentiated heavy transport vehicle that can be custom-manufactured quickly and sold to a regionally focused market.

2. **Should dominant-product/service businesses diversify to build value and competitive advantage?** For example, Dell and Coca-Cola managers have examined the question of diversification and apparently concluded that continued concentration on their core products and services and development of new markets for those same core products and services are best. IBM and Pepsi examined the same question and concluded that concentric diversification and vertical integration were best. Why?

EVALUATING AND CHOOSING BUSINESS STRATEGIES: SEEKING SUSTAINED COMPETITIVE ADVANTAGE

Business managers evaluate and choose strategies that they think will make their business successful. Businesses become successful because they possess some advantage relative to their competitors. The two most prominent sources of competitive advantage can be found in the business's cost structure and its ability to differentiate the business from competitors. DisneyWorld in Orlando offers theme park patrons several unique, distinct features that differentiate it from other entertainment options. Costco offers retail customers the lowest prices on popular consumer items because they have created a low-cost structure that results in a competitive advantage over most competitors.

Businesses that create competitive advantages from one or both of these sources usually experience above-average profitability within their industry. Businesses that lack a cost or differentiation advantage usually experience average or below-average profitability. Two well-recognized studies found that businesses that do not have either form of competitive advantage perform the poorest among their peers, while businesses that possess both forms of competitive advantage enjoy the highest levels of profitability within their industry.[1]

[1] G. G. Dess and G. T. Lumpkin, "Emerging Issues in Strategy Process Research," in *Handbook of Strategic Management,* M. A. Hitt, R. E. Freeman, and J. S. Harrison (eds) (Oxford: Blackwell, 2001), pp. 3–34; and R. B. Robinson and J. A. Pearce, "Planned Patterns of Strategic Behavior and Their Relationship to Business Unit Performance," *Strategic Management Journal* 9, no. 1 (1988), pp. 43–60.

The average return on investment for more than 2,500 businesses across seven industries looked like this:

Differentiation Advantage	Cost Advantage	Overall Average ROI across Seven Industries
High	High	35.0%
Low	High	26.0
High	Low	22.0
Low	Low	9.5

Initially, managers were advised to evaluate and choose strategies that emphasized one type of competitive advantage. Often referred to as generic strategies, firms were encouraged to become either a differentiation-oriented or low-cost-oriented company. In so doing, it was logical that organizational members would develop a clear understanding of company priorities and, as these studies suggest, likely experience profitability superior to competitors without either a differentiation or low-cost orientation.

The studies mentioned here, and the experience of many other businesses, indicate that the highest profitability levels are found in businesses that possess both types of competitive advantage at the same time. In other words, businesses that have one or more resources/capabilities that truly differentiate them from key competitors and also have resources/capabilities that let them operate at a lower cost will consistently outperform their rivals that don't. So the challenge for today's business managers is to evaluate and choose business strategies based on core competencies and value chain activities that sustain both types of competitive advantage simultaneously. Exhibit 8.1, Strategy in Action, shows Honda Motor Company attempting to do just this in Europe.

Evaluating Cost Leadership Opportunities

Business success built on cost leadership requires the business to be able to provide its product or service at a cost below what its competitors can achieve. And it must be a sustainable cost advantage. Through the skills and resources identified in Exhibit 8.2, a business must be able to accomplish one or more activities in its value chain activities—procuring materials, processing them into products, marketing the products, and distributing the products or support activities—in a more cost-effective manner than that of its competitors or it must be able to reconfigure its value chain so as to achieve a cost advantage. Exhibit 8.2 provides examples of such **low-cost strategies.**

low-cost strategies
Business strategies that seek to establish long-term competitive advantages by emphasizing and perfecting value chain activities that can be achieved at costs substantially below what competitors are able to match on a sustained basis. This allows the firm, in turn, to compete primarily by charging a price lower than competitors can match and still stay in business.

Strategists examining their business's value chain for low-cost leadership advantages evaluate the sustainability of those advantages by benchmarking (refer to Chapter 6 for a discussion of this comparison technique) their business against key competitors and by considering the effect of any cost advantage on the five forces in their business's competitive environment. Low-cost activities that are sustainable and that provide one or more of these advantages relative to key industry forces should become a key basis for the business's competitive strategy:

Low-cost advantages that reduce the likelihood of pricing pressure from buyers When key competitors cannot match prices from the low-cost leader, customers pressuring the leader risk establishing a price level that drives alternate sources out of business.

Truly sustained low-cost advantages may push rivals into other areas, lessening price competition Intense, continued price competition may be ruinous for all rivals, as seen occasionally in the airline industry.

Strategy in Action

Honda Pursues Young Buyers via Low-Cost Leadership and Differentiation Strategies

BusinessWeek

Honda is hot. In the United States, the Tokyo company can barely keep up with demand for models like the Acura MDX sport utility vehicle and the Odyssey minivan. North American sales have grown 60 percent in the last decade and its cost leadership is legendary: Honda earned $1,581 on every car sold in North America last year, versus $701 for General Motors.

But the road is not entirely smooth for the Japanese car maker. Honda Motor Co. has suffered a serious breakdown in Europe.

So Honda managers have gone into overdrive to repair the European business. Their game plan includes cost leadership initiatives: boosting capacity at two plants in Britain, heeding European calls for cars with diesel engines, and implementing a hard-nosed cost-cutting program that targets parts suppliers . . . and differentiation opportunities: launching an all-new car for the subcompact market.

The European problem, even against the background of record results in the United States, underscores Honda's fragility. Although less than 10 percent of Honda's global volume—and far less revenue—comes from Europe, the region has outsized importance to Honda executives. Why? Because Honda has no safe harbor if its sales in the United States begin to flag. The company earns some 90 percent of its profits in America, a far higher percentage than other Japanese car makers. "Honda is the least globally diverse Japanese automobile manufacturer," says Chris Redl, director of equity research at UBS Warburg's office in Tokyo. "It's a minor problem for now, but with the U.S. market heading down, it could become a major problem." So a closer look at the cost leadership and differentiation approach at Honda Europe, their confident answer, is as follows:

COST LEADERSHIP

Honda's struggles in Europe are partly the result of a key strategic error it made when it started making cars in Britain 10 years ago. Company officials didn't foresee the huge runup in the value of the British pound against Europe's single currency, the euro, which made its cars more expensive than competing models manufactured on the Continent. Subpar sales cut output in Britain last year to levels near 50 percent of capacity: it's impossible to make money at that production level. "Europe is definitely an Achilles' heel for Honda," says Toru Shimano, an analyst at Okasan Securities Co. in Tokyo.

So Honda is increasing purchases of cheaper parts from suppliers outside Britain and moving swiftly to freshen its lineup. Earlier in 2005, a remodeled and roomier five-door Civic hatchback with improved fuel efficiency rolled off production lines in Britain. To goose output at its British operations, Honda started exporting perky three-door Civic sedans built at its newest plant to the United States and Japan in 2005 and in 2007 began to export its British-made CR-V compact SUV to America to augment the Japan-made CR-Vs now being sold there.

DIFFERENTIATION

All of that will help, but Honda's big issue is the hole in its lineup: subcompacts. While one-liter-engine cars sell poorly in the United States, Europeans and Japanese can't get enough of them. "Honda does not have a product for Europe yet," says UBS Warburg's Redl. It missed out with its one-liter Logo. "It didn't stand out from the crowd," Honda executives admit.

So the Logo is history, and Honda's initial solution in Europe was a five-door hatchback called the Fit. At 1.3 liters, its engine outpowers Toyota's competing Vitz-class line of cars. Honda says the sporty Fit also boasts a number of nifty features, including that owners are able to flatten all four seats, including the driver's, at the flick of a switch—a selling point for youths keen to load bikes or sleep in it on long road trips. It recently added a compact hybrid Sports Concept car to target young European buyers interested in safe, sporty driving.

Sources: Reprinted with special permission from "Honda's Sporty Hybrid," *BusinessWeek,* March 14, 2007; and David Welch, "Honda's Drive for Young Buyers," *BusinessWeek,* February 21, 2005. Copyright © 2007 The McGraw-Hill Companies

---

New entrants competing on price must face an entrenched cost leader without the experience to replicate every cost advantage EasyJet, a British start-up with a Southwest Airlines copycat strategy, entered the European airline market with much fanfare and low-priced, city-to-city, no-frills flights.

Analysts have cautioned for some time that British Airways, KLM's no-frills off-shoot (Buzz), and Virgin Express will simply match fares on easyJet's key routes and let high

Exhibit 8.2

Evaluating a Business's Cost Leadership Opportunities

Source: Based on Michael Porter, *On Competition*, 1998, Harvard Business School Press.

A. Skills and Resources That Foster Cost Leadership

Sustained capital investment and access to capital
Process engineering skills
Intense supervision of labor or core technical operations
Products or services designed for ease of manufacture or delivery
Low-cost distribution system

B. Organizational Requirements to Support and Sustain Cost Leadership Activities

Tight cost control
Frequent, detailed control reports
Continuous improvement and benchmarking orientation
Structured organization and responsibilities
Incentives based on meeting strict, usually quantitative targets

C. Examples of Ways Businesses Achieve Competitive Advantage via Cost Leadership

Technology Development	Process innovations lower production costs		Product redesign reduces the number of components		
Human Resource Management	Safety training for all employees reduces absenteeism, downtime, and accidents				
General Administration	Reduced levels of management cut corporate overhead		Computerized, integrated information system reduces errors and administrative costs		
Procurement	Favorable long-term contracts; captive suppliers or key customer for supplier.				
	Global, online suppliers provide automatic restocking of orders based on our sales.	Economy of scale in plant reduces equipment costs and depreciation.	Computerized routing lowers transportation expense.	Cooperative advertising with distributors creates local cost advantage in buying media space and time.	Subcontracted service technicians repair product correctly the first time or they bear all costs.
	Inbound logistics	Operations	Outbound logistics	Marketing and Sales	Service

Profit Margin

landing fees and flight delays take their toll on the British upstart. Yet first-mover easyJet has survived and solidified its leadership position in the European airline industry's low-cost segment.[2]

Low-cost advantages should lessen the attractiveness of substitute products   A serious concern of any business is the threat of a substitute product in which buyers can meet their original need. Low-cost advantages allow the holder to resist this happening because it allows them to remain competitive even against desirable substitutes, and it allows them to lessen concerns about price facing an inferior, lower-priced substitute.

Higher margins allow low-cost producers to withstand supplier cost increases and often gain supplier loyalty over time   Sudden, particularly uncontrollable increases in the costs suppliers face can be more easily absorbed by low-cost, higher-margin producers. Severe

[2] "EasyJet Expands as Profits Soar," *BBC News,* November 14, 2006; and "Demand Boost Cuts easyJet Losses," *BBC News,* May 9, 2007.

droughts in California quadrupled the price of lettuce—a key restaurant demand. Some chains absorbed the cost; others had to confuse customers with a "lettuce tax." Furthermore, chains that worked well with produce suppliers gained a loyal, cooperative "partner" for possible assistance in a future, competitive situation.

Once managers identify opportunities to create cost advantage–based strategies, they must consider whether key risks inherent in cost leadership are present in a way that may mediate sustained success. The key risks with which they must be concerned are discussed next.

Many cost-saving activities are easily duplicated Computerizing certain order entry functions among hazardous waste companies gave early adopters lower sales costs and better customer service for a brief time. Rivals quickly adapted, adding similar capabilities with similar effects on their costs.

Exclusive cost leadership can become a trap Firms that emphasize lowest price and can offer it via cost advantages where product differentiation is increasingly not considered must truly be convinced of the sustainability of those advantages. Particularly with commodity-type products, the low-cost leader seeking to sustain a margin superior to lesser rivals may encounter increasing customer pressure for lower prices with great damage to both leader and lesser players.

Obsessive cost cutting can shrink other competitive advantages involving key product attributes Intense cost scrutiny can build margin, but it can reduce opportunities for or investment in innovation, processes, and products. Similarly, such scrutiny can lead to the use of inferior raw materials, processes, or activities that were previously viewed by customers as a key attribute of the original products. Some mail-order computer companies that sought to maintain or enhance cost advantages found reductions in telephone service personnel and automation of that function backfiring with a drop in demand for their products even though their low prices were maintained.

Cost differences often decline over time As products age, competitors learn how to match cost advantages. Absolute volumes sold often decline. Market channels and suppliers mature. Buyers become more knowledgeable. All of these factors present opportunities to lessen the value or presence of earlier cost advantages. Said another way, cost advantages that are not sustainable over a period of time are risky.

Once business managers have evaluated the cost structure of their value chain, determined activities that provide competitive cost advantages, and considered their inherent risks, they start choosing the business's strategy. Those managers concerned with differentiation-based strategies, or those seeking optimum performance incorporating both sources of competitive advantage, move to evaluating their business's sources of differentiation.

Evaluating Differentiation Opportunities

differentiation
A business strategy that seeks to build competitive advantage with its product or service by having it be "different" from other available competitive products based on features, performance, or other factors not directly related to cost and price. The difference would be one that would be hard to create and/or difficult to copy or imitate.

Differentiation requires that the business have sustainable advantages that allow it to provide buyers with something uniquely valuable to them. A successful differentiation strategy allows the business to provide a product or service of perceived higher value to buyers at a "differentiation cost" below the "value premium" to the buyers. In other words, the buyer feels the additional cost to buy the product or service is well below what the product or service is worth compared with other available alternatives.

Differentiation usually arises from one or more activities in the value chain that create a unique value important to buyers. Perrier's control of a carbonated water spring in France, Stouffer's frozen food packaging and sauce technology, Apple's control of iTunes download software that worked solely with iPods at first, American Greeting Card's automated

Exhibit 8.3

Evaluating a Business's Differentiation Opportunities

Source: Based on Michael Porter, *On Competition,* 1998, Harvard Business School Press.

A. Skills and Resources That Foster Differentiation

Strong marketing abilities
Product engineering
Creative talent and flair
Strong capabilities in basic research
Corporate reputation for quality or technical leadership
Long tradition in an industry or unique combination of skills drawn from other businesses
Strong cooperation from channels
Strong cooperation from suppliers of major components of the product or service

B. Organizational Requirements to Support and Sustain Differentiation Activities
Strong coordination among functions in R&D, product development, and marketing
Subjective measurement and incentives instead of quantitative measures
Amenities to attract highly skilled labor, scientists, and creative people
Tradition of closeness to key customers
Some personnel skilled in sales and operations—technical and marketing

C. Examples of Ways Businesses Achieve Competitive Advantage via Differentiation

Technology Development	Use cutting-edge production technology and product features to maintain a "distinct" image and actual product.				
Human Resource Management	Develop programs to ensure technical competence of sales staff and a marketing orientation of service personnel.				
General Administration	Develop comprehensive, personalized database to build knowledge of groups of customers and individual buyers to be used in "customizing" how products are sold, serviced, and replaced.				
Procurement	Maintain quality control presence at key supplier facilities; work with suppliers' new-product development activities.				
	Purchase superior quality, well-known components, raising the quality and image of final products.	Carefully inspect products at each step in production to improve product performance and lower defect rate.	Coordinate JIT with buyers; use own or captive transportation service to ensure timeliness.	Build brand image with expensive, informative advertising and promotion.	Allow service personnel considerable discretion to credit customers for repairs.
	Inbound logistics	Operations	Outbound logistics	Marketing and Sales	Service

Profit Margin

inventory system for retailers, and Federal Express's customer service capabilities are all examples of sustainable advantages around which successful differentiation strategies have been built. A business can achieve differentiation by performing its existing value activities or reconfiguring in some unique way. And the sustainability of that differentiation will depend on two things: a continuation of its high perceived value to buyers and a lack of imitation by competitors.

Exhibit 8.3 provides examples of the types of key skills and resources on which managers seeking to build differentiation-based strategies would base their underlying, sustainable competitive advantages. Examples of value chain activities that provide a differentiation advantage are also provided.

Strategists examining their business's resources and capabilities for differentiation advantages evaluate the sustainability of those advantages by benchmarking (refer to Chapter 6 for a discussion of this comparison technique) their business against key competitors and by considering the effect of any differentiation advantage on the five forces in their business's competitive environment. Sustainable activities that provide one or more of the following opportunities relative to key industry forces should become the basis for differentiation aspects of the business's competitive strategy:

Rivalry is reduced when a business successfully differentiates itself   BMW's Z4, made in Greer, South Carolina, does not compete with Saturns made in central Tennessee. A Harvard education does not compete with an education from a local technical school. Both situations involve the same basic needs—transportation or education. However, one rival has clearly differentiated itself from others in the minds of certain buyers. In so doing, they do not have to respond competitively to that competitor.

Buyers are less sensitive to prices for effectively differentiated products   The Highlands Inn in Carmel, California, and the Ventana Inn along the Big Sur charge a minimum of $600 and $900, respectively, per night for a room with a kitchen, fireplace, hot tub, and view. Other places are available along this beautiful stretch of California's spectacular coastline, but occupancy rates at these two locations remain over 90 percent. Why? You can't get a better view and a more relaxed, spectacular setting to spend a few days on the Pacific Coast. Similarly, buyers of differentiated products tolerate price increases low-cost-oriented buyers would not accept. The former become very loyal to certain brands. Harley Davidson motorcycles continue to rise in price, and its buyer base continues to expand worldwide, even though many motorcycle alternatives more reasonably priced are easily available.

Brand loyalty is hard for new entrants to overcome   Many new beers are brought to market in the United States, but Budweiser continues to gain market share. Why? Brand loyalty is hard to overcome! And Anheuser-Busch has been clever to extend its brand loyalty from its core brand into newer niches, such as nonalcohol brews, that other potential entrants have pioneered.

Managers examining differentiation-based advantages must take potential risks into account as they commit their business to these advantages. Some of the more common ways risks arise are discussed next.

Imitation narrows perceived differentiation, rendering differentiation meaningless   AMC pioneered the Jeep passenger version of a truck 40 years ago. Ford created the Explorer, or luxury utility vehicle, in 1990. It took luxury car features and put them inside a jeep. Ford's payoff was substantial. The Explorer became Ford's most popular domestic vehicle. However, virtually every vehicle manufacturer offered a luxury utility in 2006, with customers beginning to be hard pressed to identify clear distinctions between lead models. Ford's Explorer managers have sought to shape a new business strategy for the next decade that relies both on new sources of differentiation and placing greater emphasis on low-cost components in their value chain.

Technological changes that nullify past investments or learning   The Swiss controlled more than 95 percent of the world's watch market into the 1970s. The bulk of the craftspeople, technology, and infrastructure resided in Switzerland. U.S.-based Texas Instruments decided to experiment with the use of its digital technology in watches. Swiss producers were not interested, but Japan's SEIKO and others were. In 2009, the Swiss will make less than 3 percent of the world's watches.

The cost difference between low-cost competitors and the differentiated business becomes too great for differentiation to hold brand loyalty   Buyers may begin to choose to sacrifice some of the features, services, or image possessed by the differentiated business for large cost savings. The rising cost of a college education, particularly at several "premier" institutions, has caused many students to opt for lower-cost destinations that offer very similar courses without image, frills, and professors who seldom teach undergraduate students anyway.

Evaluating Speed as a Competitive Advantage

The cool design of the iPod is often cited as prima facie evidence of the product's greatness. But what you hear less about are the scores of little strategic decisions that were equally important in its speed-related tactics that ultimately made it a phenomenon. For instance, Apple licensed key technologies for the gadget's guts to accelerate its readiness for prototype availability; it acquired, rather than wrote, the software that became iTunes for the same reason; and chief executive Steve Jobs set a demanding nine-month time line to get the first version done, which focused internal attention throughout the organization on the device and ensured speed to market. Altogether, those steps systematically "de-risked" the iPod launch by placing a key emphasis on *speed* and enabled the phenomenal success of Apple's $100 million bet.[3]

speed-based strategies
Business strategies built around functional capabilities and activities that allow the company to meet customer needs directly or indirectly more rapidly than its main competitors.

Speed-based strategies, or rapid responses to customer requests or market and technological changes, have become a major source of competitive advantage for numerous firms in today's intensely competitive global economy. Speed is certainly a form of differentiation, but it is more than that. Speed involves the *availability of a rapid response* to a customer by providing current products quicker, accelerating new-product development or improvement, quickly adjusting production processes, and making decisions quickly. While low cost and differentiation may provide important competitive advantages, managers in tomorrow's successful companies will base their strategies on creating speed-based competitive advantages. Exhibit 8.4 describes and illustrates key skills and organizational requirements that are associated with speed-based competitive advantage. Jack Welch, the now-retired CEO who transformed General Electric from a fading company into one of Wall Street's best performers over the past 25 years, had this to say about speed:

> Speed is really the driving force that everyone is after. Faster products, faster product cycles to market. Better response time to customers. . . . Satisfying customers, getting faster communications, moving with more agility, all these things are easier when one is small. And these are all characteristics one needs in a fast-moving global environment.[4]

Speed-based competitive advantages can be created around several activities:

Customer Responsiveness All consumers have encountered hassles, delays, and frustration dealing with various businesses from time to time. The same holds true when dealing business to business. Quick response with answers, information, and solutions to mistakes can become the basis for competitive advantage—one that builds customer loyalty quickly.

Product Development Cycles Japanese automakers have focused intensely on the time it takes to create a new model because several experienced disappointing sales growth in the last decade in Europe and North America competing against new vehicles like Ford's Explorer and Renault's Megane. VW had recently conceived, prototyped, produced, and marketed a totally new 4-wheel-drive car in Europe within 12 months. Honda, Toyota, and Nissan lowered their product development cycle from 24 months to 9 months from conception to production. This capability is old hat to 3M Corporation, which is so successful at speedy product development that one-fourth of its sales and profits each year are from products that didn't exist five years earlier.

Product or Service Improvements Like development time, companies that can rapidly adapt their products or services and do so in a way that benefits their customers or creates new customers have a major competitive advantage over rivals that cannot do this.

Speed in Delivery or Distribution Firms that can get you what you need when you need it, even when that is tomorrow, realize that buyers have come to expect that level of

[3] "Don't Worry, Be Ready," *BusinessWeek,* May 28, 2007.
[4] "Jack Welch: A CEO Who Can't Be Cloned," *BusinessWeek,* September 17, 2001.

Exhibit 8.4 **Evaluating a Business's Rapid Response (Speed) Opportunities**

A. Skills and Resources That Foster Speed

Process engineering skills
Excellent inbound and outbound logistics
Technical people in sales and customer service
High levels of automation
Corporate reputation for quality or technical leadership
Flexible manufacturing capabilities
Strong downstream partners
Strong cooperation from suppliers of major components of the product or service

B. Organizational Requirements to Support and Sustain Rapid Response Activities

Strong coordination among functions in R&D, product development, and marketing.
Major emphasis on customer satisfaction in incentive programs
Strong delegation to operating personnel
Tradition of closeness to key customers
Some personnel skilled in sales and operations—technical and marketing
Empowered customer service personnel

C. Examples of Ways Businesses Achieve Competitive Advantage via Speed

Technology Development	Use companywide technology sharing activities and autonomous product development teams to speed new-product development.				
Human Resource Management	Develop self-managed work teams and decision making at the lowest levels to increase responsiveness.				
General Administration	Develop highly automated and integrated information processing system. Include major buyers in the "system" on a real-time basis.				
Procurement	Integrate preapproved online suppliers into production.				
	Work very closely with suppliers to include their choice of warehouse location to minimize delivery time.	Standardize dies, components, and production equipment to allow quick changeover to new or special orders.	Ensure very rapid delivery with JIT delivery plus partnering with express mail services.	Use of laptops linked directly to operations to speed the order process and shorten the sales cycle.	Locate service technicians at customer facilities that are geographically close.
	Inbound logistics	Operations	Outbound logistics	Marketing and Sales	Service

Profit Margin

responsiveness. Federal Express's success reflects the importance customers place on speed in inbound and outbound logistics.

Information Sharing and Technology Speed in sharing information that becomes the basis for decisions, actions, or other important activities taken by a customer, supplier, or partner has become a major source of competitive advantage for many businesses. Telecommunications, the Internet, and networks are but a part of a vast infrastructure that is being used by knowledgeable managers to rebuild or create value in their businesses via information sharing.

These rapid response capabilities create competitive advantages in several ways. They create a way to lessen rivalry because they have *availability* of something that a rival may not have. It can allow the business to charge buyers more, engender loyalty, or otherwise enhance the business's position relative to its buyers. Particularly where impressive customer response is involved, businesses can generate supplier cooperation and concessions because their business ultimately benefits from increased revenue. Finally, substitute products and new entrants find themselves trying to keep up with the rapid changes rather than introducing them. Exhibit 8.5, Strategy in Action, provides examples of how "speed" can become a source of competitive advantage for your business or your customer.

While the notion of speed-based competitive advantage is exciting, it has risks managers must consider. First, speeding up activities that haven't been conducted in a fashion that prioritizes rapid response should only be done after considerable attention to training, reorganization, and/or reengineering. Second, some industries—stable, mature ones that have very minimal levels of change—may not offer much advantage to the firm that introduces some forms of rapid response. Customers in such settings may prefer the slower pace or the lower costs currently available, or they may have long time frames in purchasing such that speed is not that important to them.

Evaluating Market Focus as a Way to Competitive Advantage

market focus
This is a generic strategy that applies a differentiation strategy approach, or a low-cost strategy approach, or a combination—and does so solely in a narrow (or "focused") market niche rather than trying to do so across the broader market. The narrow focus may be geographically defined or defined by product type features, or target customer type, or some combination of these.

Small companies, at least the better ones, usually thrive because they serve narrow market niches. This is usually called **market focus,** the extent to which a business concentrates on a narrowly defined market. Take the example of Soho Beverages, a business former Pepsi manager Tom Cox bought from Seagram after Seagram had acquired it and was unable to make it thrive. The tiny brand, once a healthy niche product in New York and a few other East Coast locations, languished within Seagrams because its sales force was unused to selling in delis. Cox was able to double sales in one year. He did this on a lean marketing budget that didn't include advertising or database marketing. He hired Korean- and Arabic-speaking college students and had his people walk into practically every deli in Manhattan in order to reacquaint owners with the brand, spot consumption trends, and take orders. He provided rapid stocking services to all Manhattan-area delis, regardless of size. The business has continued sales growth at more than 50 percent per year. Why? Cox says, "It is attributable to focusing on a niche market, delis; differentiating the product and its sales force; achieving low costs in promotion and delivery; and making rapid, immediate response to any deli owner request its normal practice."[5]

Two things are important in this example. First, this business focused on a narrow niche market in which to build a strong competitive advantage. But focus alone was not enough to build competitive advantage. Rather, Cox created several capabilities, resources, and value chain activities that achieved differentiation, low-cost, and rapid response competitive advantages within this niche market that would be hard for other firms, particularly mass market–oriented firms, to replicate.

Market focus allows some businesses to compete on the basis of low cost, differentiation, and rapid response against much larger businesses with greater resources. Focus lets a business "learn" its target customers—their needs, special considerations they want accommodated—and establish personal relationships in ways that "differentiate" the smaller firm or make it more valuable to the target customer. Low costs can also be achieved, filling niche needs in a buyer's operations that larger rivals either do not want to bother with or cannot do as cost effectively. Cost advantage often centers around the high level of customized service the focused, smaller business can provide. And perhaps the greatest competitive weapon that can arise is rapid response. With enhanced knowledge of its customers and intricacies of their operations, the small, focused company builds up organizational knowledge about timing-sensitive ways to work with a customer. Often the needs of that narrow

[5] Michael Porter, *On Competition* (Boston: Harvard Business School Press, 1998), p. 57.

The Pitch for Speed

BusinessWeek

Time is money, sure. But customers are increasingly more interested in saving time than they are in saving money. Incorporating one or more of the six benefits below in what you sell, or what your customer seeks to sell, is a potential source of competitive advantage for one or both of you.

1. **Faster to Market.** If you can show how your offering will help your customer get a new product or service ready to sell faster than competitive offerings, you will be giving them a competitive advantage. Don't forget that you may be competing against their in-house resources, too. Portal Player helped accelerate the launch of the iPod and iTunes by selling Apple its software to manage music via the net. Portal Player helped Apple gain competitive advantage. Apple's programmers may have had better ideas, but time to market was the key consideration.

2. **Faster Results.** Customers want instant results. Perhaps you can show them how they can measure the results of a marketing campaign or manufacturing process faster than before by using your offering. You can explain that by speeding up the process, they can make corrections sooner, which decreases error rates and waste. Many online advertisers sell this benefit, but you can apply it to almost any process. Many a kiosk was bought by an airline, a bank, or other users because it offered them the benefit of offering their customer faster results.

3. **Faster to Operate.** If you sell equipment that can produce more widgets per hour, offer it as a valuable benefit to your customer. Find out if your customers need more production power at certain peak times, such as over holidays or during the summer months. You could offer to save them costly overtime or outsourcing expenses.

4. **Faster to Train.** If your customer's business has high employee turnover, sell the offering based on its learning curve and ease of use. After all, if your customers have to wait to train their employees, they're losing precious efficiency and productivity. For an offering that takes more time to learn to use, offer a training DVD or a Webinar employees can watch any time. It may be enough to win the order for you.

5. **Faster to Modify, Upgrade, or Customize.** Customers know their needs will change over time, but they want to get the longest useful life out of their purchases. If you sell accounting software, for example, show your customers how easy it is to upgrade when tax rates or withholding tables change. Apply the same idea to all types of equipment.

6. **Faster to Deliver or Install.** Sometimes, the first seller to be able to deliver wins the order. I've bought expensive items simply because they were in stock, and you probably have, too. If your customer can begin saving money or earning more revenue very soon after they buy from you, use this benefit to close them.

Source: Reprinted with special permission from "The Pitch for Speed," *BusinessWeek,* May 7, 2007. Copyright © 2007 The McGraw-Hill Companies.

set of customers represent a large part of the small, focused business's revenues. Exhibit 8.6, Top Strategist, illustrates how Ireland's Ryanair has become the European leader in discount air travel via the focused application of low cost, differentiation, and speed.

The risk of focus is that you attract major competitors who have waited for your business to "prove" the market. Domino's proved that a huge market for pizza delivery existed and now faces serious challenges. Likewise, publicly traded companies built around focus strategies become takeover targets for large firms seeking to fill out a product portfolio. And perhaps the greatest risk of all is slipping into the illusion that it is focus itself, and not some special form of low cost, differentiation, or rapid response, that is creating the business's success.

Managers evaluating opportunities to build competitive advantage should link strategies to resources, capabilities, and value chain activities that exploit low cost, differentiation, and rapid response competitive advantages. When advantageous, they should consider ways to use focus to leverage these advantages. One way business managers can enhance their likelihood of identifying these opportunities is to consider several different "generic" industry environments from the perspective of the typical value chain activities most often linked to sustained competitive advantages in those unique industry situations. The next section discusses key generic industry environments and the value chain activities most associated with success.

Stages of Industry Evolution and Business Strategy Choices

The requirements for success in industry segments change over time. Strategists can use these changing requirements, which are associated with different stages of industry evolution, as a way to isolate key competitive advantages and shape strategic choices around them. Exhibit 8.7 depicts four stages of industry evolution and the typical functional capabilities that are often associated with business success at each of these stages.

Competitive Advantage and Strategic Choices in Emerging Industries

Emerging industries are newly formed or re-formed industries that typically are created by technological innovation, newly emerging customer needs, or other economic or sociological changes. **Emerging industries** of the last decade have been the Internet social networking, satellite radio, surgical robotics, and online services industries.

emerging industry
An industry that has growing sales across all the companies in the industry based on growing demand for the relatively new products, technologies, and/or services made available by the firms participating in this industry.

From the standpoint of strategy formulation, the essential characteristic of an emerging industry is that there are no "rules of the game." The absence of rules presents both a risk and an opportunity—a wise strategy positions the firm to favorably shape the emerging industry's rules.

Business strategies must be shaped to accommodate the following characteristics of markets in emerging industries:

- Technologies that are mostly proprietary to the pioneering firms and technological uncertainty about how product standardization will unfold.
- Competitor uncertainty because of inadequate information about competitors, buyers, and the timing of demand.
- High initial costs but steep cost declines as the experience curve takes effect.
- Few entry barriers, which often spurs the formation of many new firms.
- First-time buyers requiring initial inducement to purchase and customers confused by the availability of a number of nonstandard products.
- Inability to obtain raw materials and components until suppliers gear up to meet the industry's needs.
- Need for high-risk capital because of the industry's uncertainty prospects.

For success in this industry setting, business strategies require one or more of these features:

1. The ability to *shape the industry's structure* based on the timing of entry, reputation, success in related industries or technologies, and role in industry associations.
2. The ability to *rapidly improve product quality* and performance features.
3. *Advantageous relationships* with key suppliers and promising distribution channels.
4. The ability to *establish the firm's technology as the dominant one* before technological uncertainty decreases.
5. The early acquisition of *a core group of loyal customers* and then the expansion of that customer base through model changes, alternative pricing, and advertising.
6. The ability to *forecast future competitors* and the strategies they are likely to employ.

A firm that has had repeated successes with business in emerging industries is 3M Corporation. In each of the past 20 years, more than 25 percent of 3M's annual sales have come

Top Strategist
Michael O'Leary, CEO of Ryanair

**Exhibit
8.6**

Michael O'Leary, CEO of Ryanair

It was vintage Michael O'Leary. Outfitting his staff in full combat gear, O'Leary drove an old World War II tank to England's Luton airport and demanded access to the base of archrival easyJet Airline Co. With military theme music blaring, O'Leary declared he was "liberating the public from easyJet's high fares." When security—surprise!—refused to let the Ryanair armor roll in, O'Leary led the troops in his own rendition of a platoon march song: "I've been told and it's no lie. easyJet's fares are way too high!"

Buffoonery? Of course. But "O'Leary and his management team are absolutely the best at adopting a focus strategy and sticking to it relentlessly," said Ryanair's chairman David Bonderman.

Ryanair's focus strategy has key differentiation, low cost, and speed elements allowing it to far out-pace European airline competitors. They are as follows:

DIFFERENTIATION

Ryanair flies to small, secondary airports outside major European cities. Often former military bases are attractive access points to European tourists, which the airports and small towns encourage. Virtually all of its rivals, including discount rival easyJet, focus on business travelers and major international airports in Europe's largest cities. Its fares average 30 percent less than rival easyJet and are far lower than major European airlines. And Ryanair, one of Europe's leading e-tailers, Ryanair.com, sells more than 95 percent of its tickets online and has hooked

(continued)

from products that did not exist five years earlier. Start-up companies enhance their success by having experienced entrepreneurs at the helm, a knowledgeable management team and board of directors, and patient sources of venture capital. Steven Jobs's dramatic unveiling of Apple's iPod came to be seen by many as the catalyst for the emergence of a new personalized digital music industry. Jobs and Apple certainly took advantage by building a strategy that shaped the industry's structure, established the firm's technology as a dominant one, endeared themselves to a core group of loyal customers, and rapidly improved the product quality and Internet-based music service.

Competitive Advantages and Strategic Choices in Growing Industries

growth industry strategies
Business strategies that may be more advantageous for firms participating in rapidly growing industries and markets.

Rapid growth brings new competitors into the industry. Oftentimes, those new entrants are large competitors with substantial resources who have waited for the market to "prove" itself before they committed significant resources. At this stage, **growth industry strategies** that emphasize brand recognition, product differentiation, and the financial resources to support both heavy marketing expenses and the effect of price competition on cash flow can be key strengths. Accelerating demand means scaling up production or service capacity to meet the growing demand. Doing so may place a premium on being able to adapt product design and production facilities to meet rapidly increasing demand effectively. Increased investment in plant and equipment, in research and development (R&D), and especially marketing efforts to target specific customer groups along with developing strong distribution capabilities place a demand on the firm's capital resources.

Exhibit 8.6 cont.

up with hotel chains, car rentals, life insurers, and mobile phone companies to offer one-stop shopping to the European leisure traveler.

LOW COST

Ryanair bought 100 new Boeing 737-800s less than a year after placing an order for 150 next-generation 737s. Boeing offered Ryanair 40 percent off list price, significantly lowering Ryanair's cost of capital, maintenance costs, and operating expenses. Ryanair's differentiation choice of flying mainly to small, secondary airports outside major European cities has led to sweetheart deals on everything from landing and handling fees to marketing support. Less congestion lets Ryanair significantly lower personnel costs and the time a plane stays on the ground compared with rivals. Ryanair sells snacks and rents the back of seats and overhead storage to advertisers.

SPEED

Ryanair's Ryanair.com sells more than 95 percent of its tickets quickly and conveniently for customers

seeking simplicity, speed, and convenience. Its large purchases from Boeing allow it to grow to additional airports at a rate of about 30 percent annually. Its use of less congested airports allows Ryanair to get its planes back in the air in 25 minutes—half the time it takes competitors at major airports. This lets Ryanair provide significantly more frequent flights, which simplifies and adds time-saving convenience for the leisure traveler and business traveler.

FOCUS

O'Leary continues to focus like a light beam on small outlying airports and leisure travelers with speedy, low-cost services. "I've always been a transport innovator," he jokes. Millions of Europeans flying Ryanair planes would agree.

Sources: Reprinted with special permission from "Wal-Mart With Wings," *BusinessWeek,* November 27, 2006; "Ryanair Down Amid Dispute with Pilots," *BusinessWeek,* March 30, 2005; Stanley Holmes, "An Updraft for Boeing and Airbus," *BusinessWeek,* October 20, 2004 and Kerry Capell, "Ryanair Rising," *BusinessWeek,* June 2, 2003. Copyright © 2006 The McGraw-Hill Companies.

For success in this industry setting, business strategies require one or more of these features:

1. The ability to *establish strong brand recognition* through promotional resources and skills that increase selective demand.
2. The ability and resources to *scale up to meet increasing demand,* which may involve production facilities, service capabilities, and the training and logistics associated with that capacity.
3. *Strong product design skills* to be able to adapt products and services to scaled operations and emerging market niches.
4. The ability to *differentiate the firm's product[s]* from competitors entering the market.
5. *R&D resources and skills* to create product variations and advantages.
6. The ability to *build repeat buying from established customers* and attract new customers.
7. Strong capabilities in *sales and marketing.*

IBM entered the personal computer market—which Apple pioneered in the growth stage—and was able to rapidly become the market leader with a strategy based on its key strengths in brand awareness and possession of the financial resources needed to support consumer advertising. Many large technology companies today prefer exactly this approach: to await proof of an industry or product market and then to acquire small pioneer firms with first-mover advantage as a means to obtain an increasingly known

EXHIBIT 8.7 **Sources of Distinctive Competence at Different Stages of Industry Evolution**

Functional Area	Introduction	Growth	Maturity	Decline
Marketing	Resources/skills to create widespread awareness and find acceptance from customers; advantageous access to distribution	Ability to establish brand recognition, find niche, reduce price, solidify strong distribution relations, and develop new channels	Skills in aggressively promoting products to new markets and holding existing markets; pricing flexibility; skills in differentiating products and holding customer loyalty	Cost-effective means of efficient access to selected channels and markets; strong customer loyalty or dependence; strong company image
Production operations	Ability to expand capacity effectively, limit number of designs, develop standards	Ability to add product variants, centralize production, or otherwise lower costs; ability to improve product quality; seasonal subcontracting capacity	Ability to improve product and reduce costs; ability to share or reduce capacity; advantageous supplier relationships; subcontracting	Ability to prune product line; cost advantage in production, location or distribution; simplified inventory control; subcontracting or long production runs

Unit sales

Growth rate ≤ 0

Profit (dollars)

brand, or to acquire technical know-how and experience behind which the firms can put its resources and distribution strength to build brand identify and loyalty. In 2005 as the PC market matured, IBM sold its PC division to a Chinese company and now outsources its PCs.

Competitive Advantages and Strategic Choices in Mature Industry Environments

As an industry evolves, its rate of growth eventually declines. This "transition to maturity" is accompanied by several changes in its competitive environment: Competition for market share becomes more intense as firms in the industry are forced to achieve sales growth at one another's expense. Firms working with the **mature industry strategies** sell increasingly to experienced, repeat buyers who are now making choices among known alternatives. Competition becomes more oriented to cost and service as knowledgeable buyers expect similar price and product features. Industry capacity "tops out" as sales growth ceases to cover up poorly planned expansions. New products and new applications are harder to come by. International competition increases as cost pressures lead to overseas production advantages. Profitability falls, often permanently, as a result of pressure to lower prices and the increased costs of holding or building market share. Exhibit 8.8, Strategy in Action, looks at how American Patricia Russo is trying to craft a turnaround

mature industry strategies
Strategies used by firms competing in markets where the growth rate of that market from year to year has reached or is close to zero.

EXHIBIT 8.7 *(continued)*

Functional Area	Introduction	Growth	Maturity	Decline
Finance	Resources to support high net cash overflow and initial losses; ability to use leverage effectively	Ability to finance rapid expansion, to have net cash outflows but increasing profits; resources to support product improvements	Ability to generate and redistribute increasing net cash inflows; effective cost control systems	Ability to reuse or liquidate unneeded equipment; advantage in cost of facilities; control system accuracy; stream-lined management control
Personnel	Flexibility in staffing and training new management; existence of employees with key skills in new products or markets	Existence of an ability to add skilled personnel; motivated and loyal workforce	Ability to cost effec-tively, reduce workforce, increase efficiency	Capacity to reduce and reallocate personnel; cost advantage
Engineering and research and development	Ability to make engi-neering changes, have technical bugs in product and process resolved	Skill in quality and new feature develop-ment; ability to start developing successor product	Ability to reduce costs, develop variants, differentiate products	Ability to support other grown areas or to apply product to unique customer needs
Key functional area and strategy focus	Engineering: market penetration	Sales: consumer loyalty; market share	Production efficiency; successor products	Finance; maximum investment recovery

strategy for French-based Alcatel-Lucent in the maturing global telecommunications equipment industry.

These changes necessitate a fundamental strategic reassessment. Strategy elements of successful firms in maturing industries often include the following:

1. *Product line* pruning, or dropping unprofitable product models, sizes, and options from the firm's product mix.
2. *Emphasis on process innovation* that permits low-cost product design, manufacturing methods, and distribution synergy.
3. *Emphasis on cost reduction* through exerting pressure on suppliers for lower prices, switching to cheaper components, introducing operational efficiencies, and lowering administrative and sales overhead.
4. *Careful buyer selection* to focus on buyers who are less aggressive, more closely tied to the firm, and able to buy more from the firm.
5. *Horizontal integration* to acquire rival firms whose weaknesses can be used to gain a bargain price and that are correctable by the acquiring firms.
6. *International expansion* to markets where attractive growth and limited competition still exist and the opportunity for lower-cost manufacturing can influence both domestic and international costs.

Hard Times at Alcatel-Lucent

BusinessWeek

Alcatel-Lucent Chief Executive Patricia Russo is running out of time. Less than a year after the American woman took the top job at the Paris telecom equipment maker, she leads and Alcatel that is in free fall. Five years after the global telecom meltdown and in a maturing telecom equipment industry, news from Alcatel just keeps getting worse, and Alcatel's board called an emergency meeting to ask Russo to present a turnaround plan within 30 days.

Can Russo, the U.S.-born former boss of Lucent, pull the merged company out of this tailspin? Can she even hold onto her job? What are key elements of their strategy in a maturing industry that might work, or that may not?

HORIZONTAL INTEGRATION AND INTERNATIONAL EXPANSION

French Alcatel and U.S.-based Lucent agreed to merge a few years ago as a mutual horizontal integration strategy seeking to become more competitive in a maturing industry. Second, each represented a chance to reach international markets already served by the other partner. Five years later, the combined company has yet to see the benefits hoped for in this original combination. A decision made on Russo's watch—the recent acquisition of Nortel's next-generation wireless business—has compounded the problems in Europe, because integrating the new business has hampered Alcatel-Lucent's ability to fight off aggressive competitors.

COST REDUCTION

Russo has embarked on a cost-cutting plan to save $2.5 billion over the next three years. Only a day before the recent profit warning, the company concluded negotiations with French unions to cut more than 1,400 jobs. But cost-cutting won't remedy the worsening problem of its wireless business, whose troubles first emerged after the acquisition of the additional wireless business.

PRODUCT LINE PRUNING

Already, some industry watchers are talking about jettisoning big parts of the company—and Russo herself. "There are serious questions about Pat's viability as CEO," says Richard Windsor, a London-based analyst. There's growing consensus that the company will have to sell off its wireless business, including European operations formerly held by Alcatel, and U.S. holdings that once belonged to Lucent. Some analysts are calling for even more drastic steps. Per Lindberg, a London analyst, says the company should sell Bell Labs—which it inherited from Lucent—while eliminating 30,000 jobs, more than twice the 12,000 layoffs that the company has already forecast.

Business strategists in maturing industries must avoid several pitfalls. First, they must make a clear choice among the three generic strategies and avoid a middle-ground approach, which would confuse both knowledgeable buyers and the firm's personnel. Second, they must avoid sacrificing market share too quickly for short-term profit. Finally, they must avoid waiting too long to respond to price reductions, retaining unneeded excess capacity, engaging in sporadic or irrational efforts to boost sales, and placing their hopes on "new" products, rather than aggressively selling existing products.

Competitive Advantages and Strategic Choices in Declining Industries

declining industry
An industry in which the trend of total sales as an indicator of total demand for an industry's products or services among all the participants in the industry have started to drop from the last several years with the likelihood being that such a trend will continue indefinitely.

Declining industries are those that make products or services for which demand is growing slower than demand in the economy as a whole or is actually declining. This slow growth or decline in demand is caused by technological substitution (such as the substitution of electronic calculators for slide rules), demographic shifts (such as the increase in the number of older people and the decrease in the number of children), and shifts in needs (such as the decreased need for red meat).

Firms in a declining industry should choose strategies that emphasize one or more of the following themes:

1. *Focus* on segments within the industry that offer a chance for higher growth or a higher return.

2. *Emphasize product innovation and quality improvement,* where this can be done cost effectively, to differentiate the firm from rivals and to spur growth.

3. *Emphasize production and distribution efficiency* by streamlining production, closing marginal production facilities and costly distribution outlets, and adding effective new facilities and outlets.

4. *Gradually harvest the business*—generate cash by cutting down on maintenance, reducing models, and shrinking channels and make no new investment.

Strategists who incorporate one or more of these themes into the strategy of their business can anticipate relative success, particularly where the industry's decline is slow and smooth and some profitable niches remain. Penn Tennis, the nation's no. 1 maker of tennis balls, watched industrywide sales steadily decline over the last decade. In response it started marketing tennis balls as "dog toys" in the rapidly growing pet products industry. It secondly made Penn balls the official ball at major tournaments. Third, it created three different quality levels; then, as sales revived, Penn Sports sold its tennis ball business to Head Sports.

Competitive Advantage in Fragmented Industries

Fragmented industries are another setting in which identifiable types of competitive advantages and the strategic choices suggested by those advantages can be identified. A **fragmented industry** is one in which no firm has a significant market share and can strongly influence industry outcomes. Fragmented industries are found in many areas of the economy and are common in such areas as professional services, retailing, distribution, wood and metal fabrication, and agricultural products. The funeral industry is an example of a highly fragmented industry. Business strategists in fragmented industries pursue low-cost or differentiation strategies or focus competitive advantages in one of five ways:

fragmented industry
An industry in which there are numerous competitors (providers of the same or similar products or services the industry involves) such that no single firm or small group of firms controls any significant share of the overall industry sales.

Tightly Managed Decentralization   Fragmented industries are characterized by a need for intense local coordination, a local management orientation, high personal service, and local autonomy. Recently, however, successful firms in such industries have introduced a high degree of professionalism into the operations of local managers.

"Formula" Facilities   This alternative, related to the previous one, introduces standardized, efficient, low-cost facilities at multiple locations. Thus, the firm gradually builds a low-cost advantage over localized competitors. Fast-food and motel chains have applied this approach with considerable success.

Increased Value Added   The products or services of some fragmented industries are difficult to differentiate. In this case, an effective strategy may be to add value by providing more service with the sale or by engaging in some product assembly that is of additional value to the customer.

Specialization   Focus strategies that creatively segment the market can enable firms to cope with fragmentation. Specialization can be pursued by

1. *Product type.* The firm builds expertise focusing on a narrow range of products or services.

2. *Customer type.* The firm becomes intimately familiar with and serves the needs of a narrow customer segment.

3. *Type of order.* The firm handles only certain kinds of orders, such as small orders, custom orders, or quick turnaround orders.
4. *Geographic area.* The firm blankets or concentrates on a single area.

Although specialization in one or more of these ways can be the basis for a sound focus strategy in a fragmented industry, each of these types of specialization risks limiting the firm's potential sales volume.

Bare Bones/No Frills Given the intense competition and low margins in fragmented industries, a "bare bones" posture—low overhead, minimum wage employees, tight cost control—may build a sustainable cost advantage in such industries.

Competitive Advantage in Global Industries

global industry
Industry in which competition crosses national borders.

Global industries present a final setting in which success is often associated with identifiable sources of competitive advantage. A **global industry** is one that comprises firms whose competitive positions in major geographic or national markets are fundamentally affected by their overall global competitive positions. To avoid strategic disadvantages, firms in global industries are virtually required to compete on a worldwide basis. Oil, steel, automobiles, apparel, motorcycles, televisions, and computers are examples of global industries.

Global industries have four unique strategy-shaping features:

- Differences in prices and costs from country to country due to currency exchange fluctuations, differences in wage and inflation rates, and other economic factors.
- Differences in buyer needs across different countries.
- Differences in competitors and ways of competing from country to country.
- Differences in trade rules and governmental regulations across different countries.

These unique features and the global competition of global industries require that two fundamental components be addressed in the business strategy: (1) the approach used to gain global market coverage and (2) the generic competitive strategy. Three basic options can be used to pursue global market coverage:

1. *License* foreign firms to produce and distribute the firm's products.
2. *Maintain a domestic production base* and export products to foreign countries.
3. *Establish foreign-based plants and distribution* to compete directly in the markets of one or more foreign countries.

Along with the market coverage decision, strategists must scrutinize the condition of the global industry features identified earlier to choose among four generic global competitive strategies:

1. *Broad-line global competition*—directed at competing worldwide in the full product line of the industry, often with plants in many countries, to achieve differentiation or an overall low-cost position.
2. *Global focus* strategy—targeting a particular segment of the industry for competition on a worldwide basis.
3. *National focus* strategy—taking advantage of differences in national markets that give the firm an edge over global competitors on a nation-by-nation basis.
4. *Protected niche* strategy—seeking out countries in which governmental restraints exclude or inhibit global competitors or allow concessions, or both, that are advantageous to localized firms.

Old World French Steelmaker Vallourec Crafts a New Global Focus Strategy

BusinessWeek

With sky-high labor costs, a 35-hour workweek, and a surging currency, France hardly seems the kind of place where an export-focused manufacturer might prosper. Yet specialty steelmaker Vallourec, based just outside Paris, is not only beating the odds, it's performing so well that it landed the top spot on the European BW50 list.

Vallourec, which traces its roots to nineteenth-century mill towns in Burgundy and northern France, illustrates how some of Europe's quintessentially old economy companies are learning to compete in the new, globalized world. Until the 1990s, Vallourec was a hodgepodge of businesses ranging from construction and engineering to metallurgy and steelmaking, and its growth was anemic. Since then, it has shed peripheral operations to focus on its most profitable products: steel pipes used in oil drilling and electric power plants. "We have oriented ourselves to the high end of the market," says Pierre Verluca, chairman of Vallourec's management board.

Vallourec has also gone global. Seven years ago, all its factories were in Europe. But it now makes some 35 percent of its pipes in Texas and in Brazil and is expanding operations in China and India. That offers it a crucial hedge against the strong euro because about 60 percent of its sales are outside of Europe.

The result: earnings last year rose 58 percent, to $1.36 billion, on sales that were up 29 percent, to $7.5 billion. That has helped boost shares more than sixfold over the past two years, to 280 from 38. Recent rumors that Vallourec could be a takeover target for newly merged Arcelor Mittal have added bounce to its share price, although neither company has confirmed talks.

Of course, Vallourec has profited from high oil prices that fueled a boom in oil exploration. But it is also offering new services such as pipe installation and maintenance. Innovation is another key to Vallourec's success. The company has invested millions to develop high-pressure piping for the next generation of power plants. Expanding this business, which now accounts for 16 percent of sales, hedges against the possibility of an oil and gas slump.

Still, Vallourec can't afford to rest. It is keeping a close eye on China, where a quickly modernizing steel industry could provide a low-cost challenge. For now, though, oil companies are willing to pay extra for Vallourec's quality and reliability. "The cost of the pipe, even though it's expensive, is a fraction of the cost of a failure" in the oil field. So, an Old World company that makes steel pipes. It may not sound that exciting—unless, that is, you're a Vallourec investor who has ridden its success to riches.

Source: Reprinted with special permission from Carol Matlack, "Steel Beats the Odds," *BusinessWeek, Europe*, May 3, 2007. Copyright © 2007 The McGraw-Hill Companies.

Competing in a global context has become a reality for most businesses in virtually every economy around the world. So most firms must consider among the global competitive strategies identified above. Exhibit 8.9, Strategy in Action, describes how an "Old World" French steelmaker did just this to craft a global focus strategy selling steel pipe worldwide and in the process increase its market value sevenfold in five short years.

DOMINANT PRODUCT/SERVICE BUSINESSES: EVALUATING AND CHOOSING TO DIVERSIFY TO BUILD VALUE

McDonald's has frequently looked at numerous opportunities to diversify into related businesses or to acquire key suppliers. Its decision has consistently been to focus on its core business using the grand strategies of concentration, market development, and product development. Rival Yum Brands, on the other hand, has chosen to diversify into related businesses and vertical integration as the best grand strategies for it to build long-term value. Both firms experienced unprecedented success during the last 20 years.

Many dominant product businesses face this question as their core business proves successful: What grand strategies are best suited to continue to build value? Under what circumstances should they choose an expanded focus (diversification, vertical integration); steady

Exhibit 8.10 **Grand Strategy Selection Matrix**

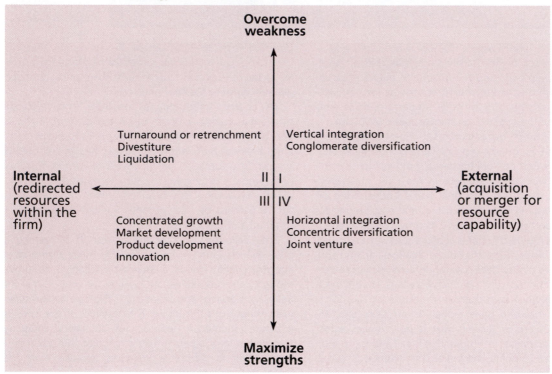

grand strategy selection matrix
A four-cell guide to strategies based upon whether the business is (1) operating from a position of strength or weakness and (2) rely on its own resources versus having to acquire resources via merger or acquisition.

continued focus (concentration, market or product development); or a narrowed focus (turnaround or divestiture)? This section examines two ways you can analyze a dominant product company's situation and choose among 12 grand strategies identified in Chapter 7.

Grand Strategy Selection Matrix

One valuable guide to the selection of a promising grand strategy is the **grand strategy selection matrix** shown in Exhibit 8.10. The basic idea underlying the matrix is that two variables are of central concern in the selection process: (1) the principal purpose of the grand strategy and (2) the choice of an internal or external emphasis for growth or profitability.

In the past, planners were advised to follow certain rules or prescriptions in their choice of strategies. Now, most experts agree that strategy selection is better guided by the conditions of the planning period and by the company strengths and weaknesses. It should be noted, however, that even the early approaches to strategy selection sought to match a concern over internal versus external growth with a desire to overcome weaknesses or maximize strengths.

The same considerations led to the development of the grand strategy selection matrix. A firm in quadrant I, with "all its eggs in one basket," often views itself as over-committed to a particular business with limited growth opportunities or high risks. One reasonable solution is **vertical integration,** which enables the firm to reduce risk by reducing uncertainty about inputs or access to customers. Another is **conglomerate diversification,** which provides a profitable investment alternative with diverting management attention from the original business. However, the external approaches to overcoming weaknesses usually result in the most costly grand strategies. Acquiring a second business demands large

vertical integration
Acquisition of firms that supply inputs such as raw materials, or customers for its outputs, such as warehouses for finished products.

conglomerate diversification
Acquiring or entering businesses unrelated to a firm's current technologies, markets, or products.

investments of time and sizable financial resources. Thus, strategic managers considering these approaches must guard against exchanging one set of weaknesses for another.

More conservative approaches to overcoming weaknesses are found in quadrant II. Firms often choose to redirect resources from one internal business activity to another. This approach maintains the firm's commitment to its basic mission, rewards success, and enables further development of proven competitive advantages. The least disruptive of the quadrant II strategies is **retrenchment,** pruning the current activities of a business. If the weaknesses of the business arose from inefficiencies, retrenchment can actually serve as a *turnaround* strategy—that is, the business gains new strength from the streamlining of its operations and the elimination of waste. However, if those weaknesses are a major obstruction to success in the industry and the costs of overcoming them are unaffordable or are not justified by a cost-benefit analysis, then eliminating the business must be considered. **Divestiture** offers the best possibility for recouping the firm's investment, but even **liquidation** can be an attractive option if the alternatives are bankruptcy or an unwarranted drain on the firm's resources.

A common business adage states that a firm should build from strength. The premise of this adage is that growth and survival depend on an ability to capture a market share that is large enough for essential economies of scale. If a firm believes that this approach will be profitable and prefers an internal emphasis for maximizing strengths, four grand strategies hold considerable promise. As shown in quadrant III, the most common approach is **concentrated growth,** that is, market penetration. The firm that selects this strategy is strongly committed to its current products and markets. It strives to solidify its position by reinvesting resources to fortify its strengths.

Two alternative approaches are **market development** and **product development.** With these strategies, the firm attempts to broaden its operations. Market development is chosen if the firm's strategic managers feel that its existing products would be well received by new customer groups. Product development is chosen if they feel that the firm's existing customers would be interested in products related to its current lines. Product development also may be based on technological or other competitive advantages. The final alternative for quadrant III firms is **innovation.** When the firm's strengths are in creative product design or unique production technologies, sales can be stimulated by accelerating perceived obsolescence. This is the principle underlying the innovative grand strategy.

Maximizing a firm's strengths by aggressively expanding its base of operations usually requires an external emphasis. The preferred options in such cases are shown in quadrant IV. **Horizontal integration** is attractive because it makes possible a quick increase in output capability. Moreover, in horizontal integration, the skills of the managers of the original business often are critical in converting newly acquired facilities into profitable contributors to the parent firm; this expands a fundamental competitive advantage of the firm—its management.

Concentric diversification is a good second choice for similar reasons. Because the original and newly acquired businesses are related, the distinctive competencies of the diversifying firm are likely to facilitate a smooth, synergistic, and profitable expansion.

The final alternative for increasing resource capability through external emphasis is a **joint venture** or **strategic alliance.** This alternative allows a firm to extend its strengths into competitive arenas that it would be hesitant to enter alone. A partner's production, technological, financial, or marketing capabilities can reduce the firm's financial investment significantly and increase its probability of success.

Model of Grand Strategy Clusters

A second guide to selecting a promising strategy is the **grand strategy cluster** shown in Exhibit 8.11. The figure is based on the idea that the situation of a business is defined

retrenchment
Cutting back on products, markets, operations because the firm's overall competitive and financial situation cannot support commitments needed to sustain or build its operations.

divestiture
The sale of a firm or a major component.

liquidation
Closing down the operations of a business and selling its assets and operations to pay its debts and distribute any gains to stockholders.

concentrated growth
Aggressive market penetration where a firm's strong position and favorable market growth allow it to "control" resources and effort for focused growth.

market development
Selling present products, often with only cosmetic modification, to customers in related marketing areas by adding channels of distribution or by changing the content of advertising or promotion.

Exhibit 8.11 **Model of Grand Strategy Clusters**

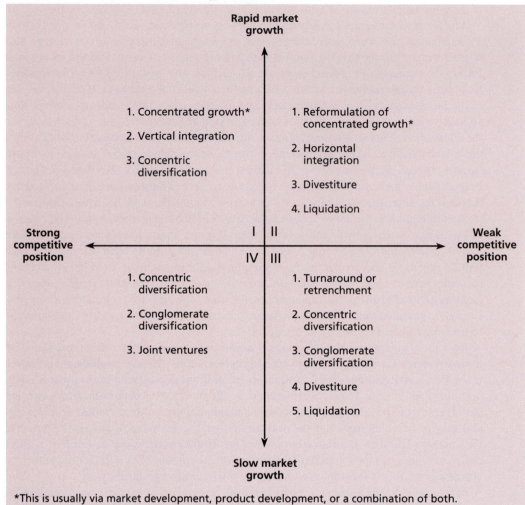

*This is usually via market development, product development, or a combination of both.

**product
development**
The substantial modi-
fication of existing
products or the creation
of new but related
products that can be
marketed to current
customers through
established channels.

in terms of the growth rate of the general market and the firm's competitive position in
that market. When these factors are considered simultaneously, a business can be broadly
categorized in one of four quadrants: (I) strong competitive position in a rapidly growing
market, (II) weak position in a rapidly growing market, (III) weak position in a slow-growth
market, or (IV) strong position in a slow-growth market. Each of these quadrants suggests
a set of promising possibilities for the selection of a grand strategy.

Firms in quadrant I are in an excellent strategic position. One obvious grand strategy for
such firms is continued concentration on their current business as it is currently defined.
Because consumers seem satisfied with the firm's current strategy, shifting notably from it
would endanger the firm's established competitive advantages. McDonald's Corporation has
followed this approach for 25 years. However, if the firm has resources that exceed the demands
of a concentrated growth strategy, it should consider vertical integration. Either forward or
backward integration helps a firm protect its profit margins and market share by ensuring better
access to consumers or material inputs. Finally, to diminish the risks associated with a narrow
product or service line, a quadrant I firm might be wise to consider concentric diversification;
with this strategy, the firm continues to invest heavily in its basic area of proven ability.

innovation
A strategy that seeks to reap the initially high profits associated with customer acceptance of a new or greatly improved product.

horizontal integration
Growth through the acquisition of one or more similar firms operating at the same stage of the production-marketing chain.

concentric diversification
Acquisition of businesses that are related to the acquiring firm in terms of technology, markets, or products.

joint ventures
Commercial companies created and operated for the benefit of the co-owners; usually two or more separate companies that form the venture.

strategic alliances
Partnerships that are distinguished from joint ventures because the companies involved do not take an equity position in one another.

grand strategy clusters
Strategies that may be more advantageous for firms to choose under one of four sets of conditions defined by market growth rate and the strength of the firm's competitive position.

Firms in quadrant II must seriously evaluate their present approach to the marketplace. If a firm has competed long enough to accurately assess the merits of its current grand strategy, it must determine (1) why that strategy is ineffectual and (2) whether it is capable of competing effectively. Depending on the answers to these questions, the firm should choose one of four grand strategy options: formulation or reformulation of a concentrated growth strategy, horizontal integration, divestiture, or liquidation.

In a rapidly growing market, even a small or relatively weak business often is able to find a profitable niche. Thus, formulation or reformulation of a concentrated growth strategy is usually the first option that should be considered. However, if the firm lacks either a critical competitive element or sufficient economies of scale to achieve competitive cost efficiencies, then a grand strategy that directs its efforts toward horizontal integration is often a desirable alternative. A final pair of options involves deciding to stop competing in the market or product area of the business. A multiproduct firm may conclude that it is most likely to achieve the goals of its mission if the business is dropped through divestiture. This grand strategy not only eliminates a drain on resources but also may provide funds to promote other business activities. As an option of last resort, a firm may decide to liquidate the business. This means that the business cannot be sold as a going concern and is at best worth only the value of its tangible assets. The decision to liquidate is an undeniable admission of failure by a firm's strategic management and, thus, often is delayed—to the further detriment of the firm.

Strategic managers tend to resist divestiture because it is likely to jeopardize their control of the firm and perhaps even their jobs. Thus, by the time the desirability of divestiture is acknowledged, businesses often deteriorate to the point of failing to attract potential buyers. The consequences of such delays are financially disastrous for firm owners because the value of a going concern is many times greater than the value of its assets.

Strategic managers who have a business in quadrant III and expect a continuation of slow market growth and a relatively weak competitive position will usually attempt to decrease their resource commitment to that business. Minimal withdrawal is accomplished through retrenchment; this strategy has the side benefits of making resources available for other investments and of motivating employees to increase their operating efficiency. An alternative approach is to divert resources for expansion through investment in other businesses. This approach typically involves either concentric or conglomerate diversification because the firm usually wants to enter more promising arenas of competition than integration or concentrated growth strategies would allow. The final options for quadrant III businesses are divestiture, if an optimistic buyer can be found, and liquidation.

Quadrant IV businesses (strong competitive position in a slow-growth market) have a basis of strength from which to diversify into more promising growth areas. These businesses have characteristically high cash flow levels and limited internal growth needs. Thus, they are in an excellent position for concentric diversification into ventures that utilize their proven acumen. A previous example in this chapter described how the no. 1 tennis ball maker, Penn Racquet Sports, chose concentric diversification from humans to dogs as their best option. A second option is conglomerate diversification, which spreads investment risk and does not divert managerial attention from the present business. The final option is joint ventures, which are especially attractive to multinational firms. Through joint ventures, a domestic business can gain competitive advantages in promising new fields while exposing itself to limited risks.

Opportunities for Building Value as a Basis for Choosing Diversification or Integration

The grand strategy selection matrix and model of grand strategy clusters are useful tools to help dominant product company managers evaluate and narrow their choices among alternative grand strategies. When considering grand strategies that would broaden the scope of their company's business activities through integration, diversification, or joint venture strategies, managers must examine whether opportunities to build value are present. Opportunities to build value via diversification, integration, or joint venture strategies are usually found in market-related, operating-related, and management activities. Such opportunities center around reducing costs, improving margins, or providing access to new revenue sources more cost effectively than traditional internal growth options via concentration, market development, or product development. Major opportunities for sharing and value building as well as ways to capitalize on core competencies are outlined in the next chapter, which covers strategic analysis and choice in diversified companies.

Dominant product company managers who choose diversification or integration eventually create another management challenge. That challenge is charting the future of a company that becomes a collection of several distinct businesses. These distinct businesses often encounter different competitive environments, challenges, and opportunities. The next chapter examines ways managers of such diversified companies attempt to evaluate and choose corporate strategy. Central to their challenge is the continued desire to build value, particularly shareholder value.

Summary

This chapter examined how managers in businesses that have a single or dominant product or service evaluate and choose their company's strategy. Two critical areas deserve their attention: (1) their business's value chain, and (2) the appropriateness of 12 different grand strategies based on matching environmental factors with internal capabilities.

Managers in single-product-line business units examine their business's value chain to identify existing or potential activities around which they can create sustainable competitive advantages. As managers scrutinize their value chain activities, they are looking for three sources of competitive advantage: low cost, differentiation, and rapid response capabilities. They also examine whether focusing on a narrow market niche provides a more effective, sustainable way to build or leverage these three sources of competitive advantage.

Managers in single- or dominant-product/service businesses face two interrelated issues: (1) They must choose which grand strategies make best use of their competitive advantages. (2) They must ultimately decide whether to diversify their business activity. Twelve grand strategies were identified in this chapter along with three frameworks that aid managers in choosing which grand strategies should work best and when diversification or integration should be the best strategy for the business. The next chapter expands the coverage of diversification to look at how multibusiness companies evaluate continued diversification and how they construct corporate strategy.

Key Terms

concentrated growth, *p. 267*
concentric diversification, *p. 269*
conglomerate diversification, *p. 266*
declining industry, *p. 262*
differentiation, *p. 250*
divestiture, *p. 267*
emerging industry, *p. 257*
fragmented industry, *p. 263*

global industry, *p. 264*
grand strategy cluster, *p. 269*
grand strategy selection matrix, *p. 266*
growth industry strategies, *p. 258*
horizontal integration, *p. 269*
innovation, *p. 269*
joint ventures, *p. 269*
liquidation, *p. 267*

low-cost strategies, *p. 247*
market development, *p. 267*
market focus, *p. 255*
mature industry strategies, *p. 260*
product development, *p. 268*
retrenchment, *p. 267*
speed-based strategies, *p. 253*
strategic alliances, *p. 269*
vertical integration, *p. 266*

Questions for Discussion

1. What are three activities or capabilities a firm should possess to support a low-cost leadership strategy? Use Exhibit 8.2 to help you answer this question. Can you give an example of a company that has done this?
2. What are three activities or capabilities a firm should possess to support a differentiation-based strategy? Use Exhibit 8.3 to help you answer this question. Can you give an example of a company that has done this?
3. What are three ways a firm can incorporate the advantage of speed in its business? Use Exhibit 8.4 to help you answer this question. Can you give an example of a company that has done this?
4. Do you think it is better to concentrate on one source of competitive advantage (cost versus differentiation versus speed) or to nurture all three in a firm's operation?
5. How does market focus help a business create competitive advantage? What risks accompany such a posture?
6. Using Exhibits 8.10 and 8.11, describe situations or conditions under which horizontal integration and concentric diversification would be preferred strategic choices.

Chapter 8 Discussion Case

DHL's American Strategy

BusinessWeek

1   No question, those cheeky DHL ads seemed to be everywhere, from the New York City subways to the World Series. In one TV pitch, a FedEx worker goes on holiday, enjoying parasailing and golf—only to see DHL trucks speeding parcels to their destinations. Then there was the bus stop poster that took a swipe at UPS: "Yellow. It's the new Brown." And a print ad proclaimed what DHL hopes is inevitable: "The Roman empire, the British empire, the FedEx empire. Nothing lasts forever."

2   In short, it was war, as DHL, the $35 billion delivery and logistics company started in San Francisco and acquired in 2002 by Deutsche Post World Net—the privatized German postal service—fought to become a credible alternative in the United States to FedEx Corp. and United Parcel Service Inc. DHL is the largest express carrier in Europe with a 40 percent share, and the largest international express carrier in Asia, also with 40 percent. Now DHL, whose U.S. base is in Plantation, Florida, is seeking to build its presence by expanding its trucking routes, creating air hubs, and advertising heavily to raise awareness of its brand in a country where it has only 7 percent of the air and ground parcel market.

3   With North American express traffic accounting for nearly half the worldwide total, no carrier with global ambitions can afford to ignore it. And DHL has set its sights on the small- and medium-size U.S. businesses that are increasingly involved in foreign trade. "It's a global economy now," says Hans Hickler, CEO of DHL-USA Inc. "You have to be everywhere."

4   But taking on FedEx and UPS, which together command 78 percent of the U.S. parcel market, is a daunting task. For example, it took more than two years before the company won a bruising legal battle, when regulators turned aside

challenges by FedEx and UPS that the planes DHL contracted to use here constituted illegal foreign control of an airline. Completing the integration of Airborne Inc., the Seattle carrier that merged with DHL, was a massive job. And DHL's limited ground network has hurt its ability to attract domestic customers who want to cut costs by sending parcels overland rather than by air. In fact, until 2005, DHL had almost no ground network in much of the Midwest and Rocky Mountain states.

5   The result: DHL, with $8 billion in American revenues, projects it will break even with its U.S. operations in 2009. Even after reaching profitability, Hickler says that DHL's return on investment is unlikely to top 4 percent for the next few years.

Can DHL Deliver?
It aims to be a strong No. 3 among U.S. couriers.
How it plans to get there:

Get Better Known
DHL has spent $150 million annually on an ad campaign that tweaks UPS and FedEx

Improve the Infrastructure
Build stronger trucking network in Rocky Mountain and Midwest regions; open West Coast air hub

Target the Little Guy
Focus on midmarket and smaller businesses by offering more personal service

Boost Market Share
In five years, DHL wants 12 percent to 14 percent of the market, up from 7 percent in 2005.

CROWN JEWELS

6 It's clearly going to take a lot more than a snappy ad campaign to turn DHL into a winner. Analysts have raised substantial doubts about whether DHL can be a viable no. 3 in the United States. Since the mid-1990s, Deutsche Post has acquired over 100 logistics, transport, and freight-forwarding services, and expertly integrated them to build its worldwide business. DHL and Airborne were to be the crown jewels, the acquisitions that extended its grasp into the world's richest economy. But Deutsche Post "underestimated the challenges," said Raimund Saxinger, a fund manager at Frankfurt Trust in Frankfurt.

7 Chief among those challenges has been the lack of ground transport capability. DHL had virtually none when it was acquired by Deutsche Post, while Airborne was just getting started. Now, with high fuel prices boosting the cost of air shipment, the parcel market in the United States is shifting toward ground transport, which is DHL's weakest link. So DHL is investing $1.2 billion over the next three years in sorting centers, drop-off points, and other network improvements. Nationally, for instance, DHL has only 16,000 drop-off points—about one-third FedEx's number. "It takes a lot of money and a lot of talent to build a high-quality network. That's a big hurdle," says Kurt Kuehn, senior vice president of worldwide sales and marketing for UPS.

8 But DHL is determined to build out its network. "If we did not have an efficient pickup and delivery system in the U.S., it would be very tough for us to hold on to our no. 1 position in Europe and Asia," says Klaus Zumwinkel, chief executive of parent Deutsche Post and the mastermind behind its global strategy.

9 DHL is better situated in terms of air transport. In the past five years, it and Airborne have collectively invested $1.9 billion in the United States and Canada, much of it on projects such as the consolidation of air operations at its Wilmington (Ohio) hub and its four strategically located gateways in New York, Miami, Los Angeles, and San Francisco. But those outlays only begin to get DHL into the game. "It does not close the gap," said Satish Jindel, president of transportation consultant SJ Consulting Group Inc. Over the same period, FedEx and UPS each spent more than $6 billion in North America.

10 While investing $1.9 billion to increase infrastructure along with a $150 million media campaign is part of DHL's strategy to compete with UPS and FedEx, rolling out a strategy to differentiate itself from these key competitors is the other. DHL is counting on improved customer service to build its U.S.-based business. While the company knows that it won't be easy to separate customers from their UPS drivers, it's trying to mold a more customer-friendly workforce. Analysts say that task was neglected by Airborne. And in one survey, DHL rated even lower than Airborne did on customer satisfaction.

11 For DHL, that has meant changing the way customers perceive DHL. Hans Hickler created the "Customer Service Initiative," a strategy to solidify among both customers and employees just who DHL is and what values the company represents. He identified 82 customer "touch points" within DHL to systematically evaluate, change, and monitor changes to solidify the customer-centric DHL difference. "Customers don't just do business with you for one year in this business," Hickler said. "They're buying in to your strategy, especially in the shipping business, which is a very global and international business. People don't switch easily, and so they need to understand that what you stand for is there."

12 Personalized service can be a winning pitch for some customers. Shoemaker Skechers USA Inc. already has shifted about a third of the business from its Manhattan Beach (California) headquarters from FedEx to DHL, which it also uses for international shipments. "I've been responsible for shipping and receiving for 13 years, and it wasn't until this past year that I met my FedEx rep. DHL is constantly out here," says Michael Cardenas, Skechers' office services manager. He also praises DHL's hustle. "UPS and FedEx are more reluctant to go to remote locations. DHL will just do it. If their driver has to sit in the parking lot and fill out the air bills, he'll do it."

13 For now, DHL has modest goals in the United States. The company aims just to raise market share to between 12 percent and 14 percent—a statement that draws derision from competitors. "I don't think that customers will turn over their mission-critical operations to a fledgling operation whose stated goal is to become the No. 3 player," said the vice president for investor relations at FedEx. Even if DHL doesn't break even in the United States by 2009, don't expect it to stop trying. With a deep-pocketed corporate parent, it can keep plugging away for years. "They can afford a U.S. problem," says analyst Markus Hesse at HVB Group in Munich. Good thing, because it looks like a problem that's not going to go away soon.

Sources: Reprinted with special permission from Mark Scott, "Brand Builder," *Smart Business*, Cleveland, OH, February 2007; "DHL: Delivering the Goods," *BusinessWeek,* August 11, 2006; Jack Ewing and Dean Foust, "DHL's American Adventure," *BusinessWeek,* November 29, 2004; and Jack Ewing "A Mercedes in the Parcel Industry," *BusinessWeek,* November 29, 2004. Copyright © 2007 The McGraw-Hill Companies.

AN INTERVIEW WITH DR. KLAUS ZUMWINKEL, CHAIRMAN, DEUTSCHE POST

DHL, a unit of Germany's Deutsche Post, is the dominant express and parcel company in Europe and also the leader in crossborder air express in Asia. In the United States, though, DHL is still tiny compared with market leaders UPS and FedEx. Deutsche Post chairman Klaus Zumwinkel is trying to change that, in part by acquiring Airborne and merging it with

DHL. Mr. Zumwinkel aims to be the transportation services "Mercedes" in the U.S. market.

But gaining ground in the United States is proving tougher than expected. DHL announced that it won't break even in the United States until 2009, instead of 2006 as planned. This is partly because DHL was held up by a regulatory battle after rivals complained that the air fleet used under contract by the German outfit constituted illegal foreign control of an airline. DHL prevailed in the dispute earlier this year. Still, many analysts doubt whether even the revised profit goal is realistic.

Zumwinkel, who has overseen transformation of the German postal service into a global express-courier and logistics company, remains determined. He spoke recently with *BusinessWeek* about how DHL will prove the doubters wrong.

Question: Why is the U.S. worth investing [$1.9] billion in?

Zumwinkel: In an industry like ours, the network has to be complete. Customers inside the U.S. and outside are welcoming an increase in our U.S. presence. If we didn't have an efficient pickup and delivery system in the U.S., it would be very tough for us to hold onto our no. 1 position in Europe and Asia.

Question: Has the U.S. been more difficult than you expected? Have there been any surprises?

Zumwinkel: In the beginning we had a long battle with our competitors because of [regulatory issues regarding] the air fleet used by DHL. . . . We lost some time in streamlining and integrating and restructuring the whole thing. But with all of our acquisitions, we're now experts in integration. We have integrated more than 100 companies.

Question: How big a priority is DHL in the U.S. for you?

Zumwinkel: In such a big group we have several priorities. We had the IPO of Postbank [Deutsche Post's retail banking unit in Germany], and Asia is a very attractive and strong growth area. In Europe, we're integrating heavily in several key countries like Italy, the U.K., [and] France. The U.S. is one of these priorities, it's in this class.

Question: So it's not keeping you up at night?

Zumwinkel: No [laughs].

Question: The U.S. market is moving toward a ground network. Does that increase the amount of investment you have to put into the U.S.?

Zumwinkel: Yes. . . . Airborne had already established a ground-based network. Like everybody else in this industry, Airborne found that if you have a good ground network, why should the customer pay so much for air products?

This is a secular trend. We want to provide the same kind of quality our customers are used to in other parts of the world. We want to be the Mercedes in our industry.

Question: What are your profit goals for DHL in the U.S.? Will you be satisfied to break even?

Zumwinkel: Naturally, management is concentrating on [breaking even] [by 2009] [and on the goals] to restructure [the U.S. business], to integrate two companies, to integrate into the worldwide network, [and] to build a ground network. That will keep everybody busy for the next [few] years. [If we broke even,] we would have 500 million [euros or $750 million] more profit, we would have 500 million [euros] losses less. That is only 10 percent of our whole group profit. That's the main objective. After that, we will see.

Question: Can you foresee that the U.S. will become a major profit center?

Zumwinkel: Sure. We have invested a lot of money in the U.S. Our competitors are earning nice profit rates, double-digit margins—something we're not used to in Europe. We won't get these margins for a while because our competitors have larger economies of scale, but with our economies of scale worldwide, I think we can [realize these margins in the long term].

Question: Is this like the Japanese carmakers coming into the U.S. decades ago where you're willing to invest for a long time in order to get a permanent foothold in the market?

Zumwinkel: I don't compare myself with Japanese carmakers. Here the game is very simple. The express game is an international game. To be international, one has to cover the largest economy in the world—the U.S. Otherwise, one is not thoroughly competitive in Asia or Europe.

We're in the U.S. for the long term. I think the globalization trend will strengthen in the next 10 years. World trade has to be transported, and we're here to provide the transport.

DISCUSSION QUESTIONS

1. What aspects of DHL's strategy for entering the United States reflect a low-cost strategy? A differentiation strategy?

2. Are there any aspects that appear to reflect a focus strategy?

3. How has DHL incorporated "speed" into its overall strategy?

4. What appear to be DHL's most important competitive advantages? Are they best suited to a mature industry or a growth industry? Which way would you characterize the U.S. parcel market and the global parcel market?

5. What appears to be the likelihood that DHL will succeed? What key factors will determine that?

6. DHL comes to you for advice on whether they should continue a global focus on parcels and express mail or diversify their business activities into other types of businesses. What would you advise and why?

Chapter **Nine**

Multibusiness Strategy

After reading and studying this chapter, you should be able to

1. Understand the portfolio approach to strategic analysis and choice in multibusiness companies.

2. Understand and use three different portfolio approaches to conduct strategic analysis and choice in multibusiness companies.

3. Identify the limitations and weaknesses of the various portfolio approaches.

4. Understand the synergy approach to strategic analysis and choice in multibusiness companies.

5. Evaluate the parent company role in strategic analysis and choice to determine whether and how it adds tangible value in a multibusiness company.

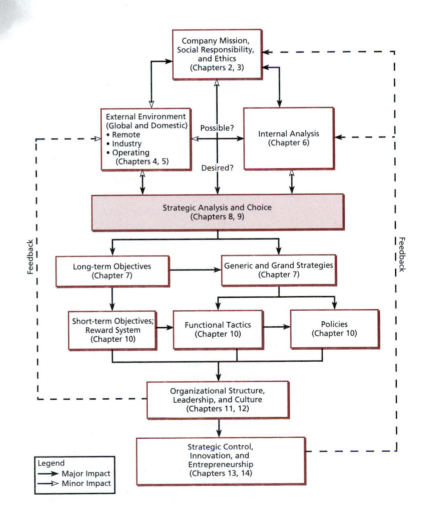

Company Mission, Social Responsibility, and Ethics (Chapters 2, 3)

External Environment (Global and Domestic)
• Remote
• Industry
• Operating
(Chapters 4, 5)

Possible?

Internal Analysis (Chapter 6)

Desired?

Strategic Analysis and Choice (Chapters 8, 9)

Long-term Objectives (Chapter 7)

Generic and Grand Strategies (Chapter 7)

Short-term Objectives; Reward System (Chapter 10)

Functional Tactics (Chapter 10)

Policies (Chapter 10)

Organizational Structure, Leadership, and Culture (Chapters 11, 12)

Strategic Control, Innovation, and Entrepreneurship (Chapters 13, 14)

Feedback

Feedback

Legend
→ Major Impact
⇢ Minor Impact

Jeff Immelt, successor to the globally admired Jack Welch as chairman and CEO of General Electric, said in response to a question about GE's future that his greatest fear for GE was that it would become boring and his top managers would become cowards. His real concern was how to determine what businesses GE should build its future around, and which businesses it should not. Should GE stay in appliances, in lighting, in television with its NBC network, or should it sell some of these businesses? Should he take a risk and move GE into renewable energy equipment, or water, or security, or biomedicine, or making movies? How much of the company should any of these dramatic new businesses represent? So, if you were about to finish this semester and Immelt came to talk at your school, and if he posed this fundamental concern today, singled you out to give him advice, what would you say? What should he do?

General Motors, for so long the world's oldest and largest car company, faces a real dilemma. Does it intentionally and aggressively shrink its number of car brands, its overall car businesses, and reduce its involvement in other businesses such as consumer finance services so that a profitable but much smaller version of its old self becomes the new GM? Or does it seek to build many if not all of it venerable brand names? What would you advise GM's CEO Rick Wagoner? Likewise, rumors abounded just last year that Microsoft and Yahoo! should merge to create a meaningful competitor to all-powerful Google. Suppose any of these executives came to your strategy class to speak and asked each class team to tell him which was the best way to go and why. What would you say?

Strategic analysis and choice is complicated for corporate-level managers because they must create a strategy to guide a company that contains numerous businesses. They must examine and choose which businesses to own and which ones to forgo or divest. They must consider business managers' plans to capture and exploit competitive advantage in each business, and then decide how to allocate resources among those businesses. This chapter covers ways managers in multibusiness companies analyze and choose what businesses to be in and how to allocate resources across those businesses.

The portfolio approach was one of the early approaches for charting strategy and allocating resources in multibusiness companies. It was particularly popular in the 1960s and 1970s, after which corporate managers, concerned with some shortcomings in this type of approach, welcomed new options. Yet while many companies have moved on to use other approaches, the portfolio approach remains a useful technique for some. Indeed, after GE pioneered one form of the approach and subsequently abandoned it under Jack Welch, GE's new leader Jeff Immelt has brought it back and made it the central theme in his corporate strategic decision making and development. Immelt's recent comment to GE shareholders after his first five years leading GE were as follows:

> I would ask investors to think about the progress we have made with our portfolio [of businesses] over the last five years. In 2001, one-third of our earnings were generated by businesses that could not consistently hit our 10 percent earnings growth and 20 percent return goals. Since then, we have executed a disciplined portfolio strategy to create a sustainable competitive advantage based on technology, brand and a valuable installed base. GE now has a portfolio of six strong businesses aligned to grow with the market trends of today and tomorrow. This is not by chance. It is the result of considered, strategic investment in each business over time—and ahead of external realities.[1]

Perhaps, as they say, history repeats itself—or what goes around comes around. Exhibit 9.1, Strategy in Action, provides a more in-depth description of the manifestations of a return to a portfolio approach at General Electric under Immelt's watch.

---

[1] "Letter to Shareholders," *2006 G.E. Annual Report.*

Strategy in Action

Exhibit 9.1

Hum? Is it Back to the Future—GE Returns to the Portfolio Approach

Shuffling the Portfolio
Immelt has spent more than $75 billion to bolster GE's mix of businesses. Some new capabilities:

Media Content	Biosciences	Security	Water	Renewable Energy
Buying Universal gave GE a rich library, film studio, cable networks, and theme parks. Bravo and Telemundo help, too.	With Amersham, GE can bring diagnostics down to the cellular level and be a leader in personalized medicine.	GE bought its way into fire safety and industrial security with Edwards Systems. Ion Track and InVision gave it entrée into homeland security, from bomb detection to screening for narcotics.	Buying Ionics and Osmonics gets GE into desalination, fluid filtration, and other water processing services. The goal: to increase the availability of clean water around the world.	GE moved into solar and wind power and biogas with acquisitions such as Enron Wind.

To lay the groundwork for an organization that grows through innovation, Immelt took steps early on to rejigger the GE portfolio. He sold several profitable businesses such as insurance and GE Plastics while shelling out more than $75 billion in acquisitions to dive into hot areas such as bioscience, cable and film entertainment, security, water processing, and wind power that have better growth prospects. In doing so, he pared the low-margin, slower-growth businesses like appliances or lighting, which he diplomatically calls "cash generators" instead of "losers," down to 10 percent of the portfolio, from 33 percent in 2000. Nicole M. Parent of Credit Suisse First Boston is impressed with "the way they have been able to evolve the portfolio in such a short time" and with so little disruption. "This is a company where managers will do anything to achieve their goals."

That in itself may be a stretch of the imagination for now, but Immelt is trying to recast the company for decades to come. He's spending big bucks to create the kind of infrastructure that can equip and foster an army of dreamers. That means beefing up GE's research facilities, creating something akin to a global brain trust that GE can tap to spur innovation. He has sunk $100 million into overhauling the company's research center in Niskayuna, New York, and forked out for cutting-edge centers in Bangalore, Shanghai, and Munich.

Now that Immelt has repositioned the portfolio and added resources, his main objective is to get more immediate growth out of the businesses he already has. That's where the Imagination Breakthroughs come in. over the past five years, Immelt has invested more than $15 billion in 80 projects that range from creating microjet engines to overhauling the brand image of 3,000 consumer-finance locations. The hope is that the first lot will generate $40 billion in revenue by 2009—cheap, if it works, when you consider what it would cost to acquire something from the outside with that level of sales. In the next year or two, Immelt expects to have 400 such projects under way.

Sources: Reprinted with special permission from "GE and the Global Economy," *BusinessWeek,* April 13, 2007; "The Secret to GE's Success," *BusinessWeek,* January 29, 2007; and "Shuffling the Portfolio," *BusinessWeek,* March 28, 2005. Copyright © 2007 The McGraw-Hill Companies.

Improvement on the portfolio approach focused on ways to broaden the rationale behind pursuit of diversification strategies. This approach centered on the idea that at the heart of effective diversification is the identification of core competencies in a business or set of businesses to then leverage as the basis for competitive advantage in the growth of those businesses and the entry in or divestiture of other businesses. This notion of leveraging core competencies as a basis for strategic choice in multibusiness companies has been a popular one for the past 20 years.

Recent evolution of strategic analysis and choice in this setting has expanded on the core competency notion to focus on a series of fundamental questions that multibusiness companies should address in order to make diversification work. With both the accelerated rates of change in most global markets and trying economic conditions, multibusiness companies have adapted the fundamental questions into an approach called "patching" to map and remap their business units swiftly against changing market opportunities. Finally, as companies have embraced lean organizational structures, strategic analysis in multibusiness companies has included careful assessment of the corporate parent, its role, and value or lack thereof in contributing to the stand-alone performance of their business units. This chapter will examine each of these approaches to shaping multibusiness corporate strategy.

THE PORTFOLIO APPROACH: A HISTORICAL STARTING POINT

portfolio techniques
An approach pioneered by the Boston Consulting Group that attempted to help managers "balance" the flow of cash resources among their various businesses while also identifying their basic strategic purpose within the overall portfolio.

The past 30 years we have seen a virtual explosion in the extent to which single-business companies seek to acquire other businesses to grow and to diversify. There are many reasons for this emergence of multibusiness companies: Companies can enter businesses with greater growth potential; enter businesses with different cyclical considerations; diversify inherent risks; increase vertical integration, and thereby reduce costs; capture value added; and instantly have a market presence rather than slower internal growth. As businesses jumped on the diversification bandwagon, their managers soon found a challenge in managing the resource needs of diverse businesses and their respective strategic missions, particularly in times of limited resources. Responding to this challenge, the Boston Consulting Group (BCG) pioneered an approach called **portfolio techniques** that attempted to help managers "balance" the flow of cash resources among their various businesses while also identifying their basic strategic purpose within the overall portfolio. Three of these techniques are reviewed here. Once reviewed, we will identify some of the problems with the portfolio approach that you should keep in mind when considering its use.

The BCG Growth-Share Matrix

market growth rate
The projected rate of sales growth for the market being served by a particular business.

Managers using the BCG matrix plotted each of the company's businesses according to market growth rate and relative competitive position. **Market growth rate** is the projected rate of sales growth for the market being served by a particular business. Usually measured as the percentage increase in a market's sales or unit volume over the two most recent years, this rate serves as an indicator of the relative attractiveness of the markets served by each business in the firm's portfolio of businesses. **Relative competitive position** usually is expressed as the market share of a business divided by the market share of its largest competitor. Thus, relative competitive position provides a basis for comparing the relative strengths of the businesses in the firm's portfolio in terms of their positions in their respective markets. Exhibit 9.2 illustrates the growth-share matrix.

relative competitive position
The market share of a business divided by the market share of its largest competitor.

The **stars** are businesses in rapidly growing markets with large market shares. These businesses represent the best long-run opportunities (growth and profitability) in the firm's portfolio. They require substantial investment to maintain (and expand) their dominant position in a growing market. This investment requirement is often in excess of the funds that they can generate internally. Therefore, these businesses are often short-term, priority consumers of corporate resources.

stars
Businesses in rapidly growing markets with large market shares.

cash cows
Businesses with a high market share in low-growth markets or industries.

Cash cows are businesses with a high market share in low-growth markets or industries. Because of their strong competitive positions and their minimal reinvestment requirements, these businesses often generate cash in excess of their needs. Therefore, they are selectively "milked" as a source of corporate resources for deployment elsewhere (to stars and question marks). Cash cows are yesterday's stars and the current foundation of corporate portfolios. They provide the

EXHIBIT 9.2
The BCG Growth-Share Matrix

Source: The growth-share matrix was originally developed by the Boston Consulting Group.

Description of Dimensions

Market share: Sales relative to those of other competitors in the market (dividing point is usually selected to have only the two to three largest competitors in any market fall into the high market share region)

Growth rate: Industry growth rate in constant dollars (dividing point is typically the GNP's growth rate)

Cash Generation (market share)

	High	Low
High (Cash Use / growth rate)	★ Star	? Problem Child
Low	$ Cash Cow	X Dog

cash needed to pay corporate overhead and dividends and provide debt capacity. They are managed to maintain their strong market share while generating excess resources for corporatewide use. Look back at Exhibit 9.1, which summarizes GE chairman/CEO Jeff Immelt's assessment of GE "cash cows" and "cash generators" to target businesses from which he will generate resources to invest in GE's portfolio of new "start" businesses.

dogs
Low market share and low market growth businesses.

Low market share and low market growth businesses are the **dogs** in the firm's portfolio. Facing mature markets with intense competition and low profit margins, they are managed for short-term cash flow (e.g., through ruthless cost cutting) to supplement corporate-level resource needs. According to the original BCG prescription, they are divested or liquidated once this short-term harvesting has been maximized.

question marks
Businesses whose high growth rate gives them considerable appeal but whose low market share makes their profit potential uncertain.

Question marks are businesses whose high growth rate gives them considerable appeal but whose low market share makes their profit potential uncertain. Question marks are cash guzzlers because their rapid growth results in high cash needs, while their small market share results in low cash generation. At the corporate level, the concern is to identify the question marks that would increase their market share and move into the star group if extra corporate resources were devoted to them. Where this long-run shift from question mark to star is unlikely, the BCG matrix suggests divesting the question mark and repositioning its resources more effectively in the remainder of the corporate portfolio.

The Industry Attractiveness–Business Strength Matrix

Corporate strategists found the growth-share matrix's singular axes limiting in their ability to reflect the complexity of a business's situation. Therefore, some companies adopted a matrix with a much broader focus. This matrix, developed by McKinsey & Company at General Electric, is called the industry attractiveness–business strength matrix. This matrix uses multiple factors to assess industry attractiveness and business strength rather than the single measures (market share and market growth, respectively) employed in the BCG matrix. It also has nine cells as opposed to four—replacing the high/low axes with high/medium/low axes to make finer distinctions among business portfolio positions.

The company's businesses are rated on multiple strategic factors within each axis, such as the factors described in Exhibit 9.3. The position of a business is then calculated by "subjectively" quantifying its rating along the two dimensions of the matrix. Depending on the location of a business within the matrix as shown in Exhibit 9.4, one of the following strategic approaches is suggested: (1) invest to grow, (2) invest selectively and manage for earnings, or (3) harvest or divest for resources. The resource allocation decisions remain quite similar to those of the BCG approach.

EXHIBIT 9.3
Factors Considered in Constructing an Industry Attractiveness–Business Strength Matrix

Industry Attractiveness	Business Strength

Industry Attractiveness

Nature of Competitive Rivalry

Number of competitors
Size of competitors
Strength of competitors' corporate parents
Price wars
Competition on multiple dimensions

Bargaining Power of Suppliers/Customers

Relative size of typical players
Numbers of each
Importance of purchases from or sales to
Ability to vertically integrate

Threat of Substitute Products/New Entrants

Technological maturity/stability
Diversity of the market
Barriers to entry
Flexibility of distribution system

Economic Factors

Sales volatility
Cyclicality of demand
Market growth
Capital intensity

Financial Norms

Average profitability
Typical leverage
Credit practices

Sociopolitical Considerations

Government regulation
Community support
Ethical standards

Business Strength

Cost Position

Economies of scale
Manufacturing costs
Overhead scrap/waste/rework
Experience effects
Labor rates
Proprietary processes

Level of Differentiation

Promotion effectiveness
Product quality
Company image
Patented products
Brand awareness

Response Time

Manufacturing flexibility
Time needed to introduce new products
Delivery times
Organizational flexibility

Financial Strength

Solvency
Liquidity
Break-even point
Cash flows
Profitability
Growth in revenues

Human Assets

Turnover
Skill level
Relative wage/salary
Morale
Managerial commitment
Unionization

Public Approval

Goodwill
Reputation
Image

Although the strategic recommendations generated by the industry attractiveness–business strength matrix are similar to those generated by the BCG matrix, the industry attractiveness–business strength matrix improves on the BCG matrix in three fundamental ways:

1. The terminology associated with the industry attractiveness–business strength matrix is preferable because it is less offensive and more understandable.

2. The multiple measures associated with each dimension of the business strength matrix tap many factors relevant to business strength and market attractiveness besides market share and market growth.

EXHIBIT 9.4   The Industry Attractiveness–Business Strength Matrix

		Business Strength		
		Strong	**Average**	**Weak**
Industry Attractiveness	**High**	***Premium—invest for growth:*** • Provide maximum investment • Diversify worldwide • Consolidate position • Accept moderate near-term profits • Seek to dominate	***Selective—invest for growth*** • Invest heavily in selected segments • Share ceiling • Seek attractive new segments to apply strengths	***Protect/refocus— selectively invest for earnings:*** • Defend strengths • Refocus to attractive segments • Evaluate industry revitalization • Monitor for harvest or divestment timing • Consider acquisitions
	Medium	***Challenge—invest for growth:*** • Build selectively on strengths • Define implications of leadership challenge • Avoid vulnerability—fill weaknesses	***Prime—selectively invest for earnings:*** • Segment market • Make contingency plans for vulnerability	***Restructure—harvest or divest:*** • Provide no unessential commitment • Position for divestment or • Shift to more attractive segment
	Low	***Opportunistic—selectively invest for earnings:*** • Ride market and maintain overall position • Seek niches, specialization • Seek opportunity to increase strength (for example through acquisition) • Invest at maintenance levels	***Opportunistic—preserve for harvest:*** • Act to preserve or boost cash flow • Seek opportunistic sale or • Seek opportunistic rationalization to increase strengths • Prune product lines • Minimize investment	***Harvest or divest:*** • Exit from market or prune product line • Determine timing so as to maximize present value • Concentrate on competitor's cash generators

Source: From N. Paley, *The Manager's Guide to Competitive Marketing Strategies*, 2/e, CRC Press, 1999, p. 155. Copyright © Taylor & Francis Group, Ltd. Via Copyright Clearance Center.

3. In turn, this makes for broader assessment during the planning process, bringing to light considerations of importance in both strategy formulation and strategy implementation.

   Exhibit 9.1 (see page 277) shows GE chairman and CEO Jeff Immelt's surprising return to the use of a portfolio approach in 2006 as he charts GE's future.

BCG's Strategic Environments Matrix

BCG's latest matrix offering (see Exhibit 9.5) took a different approach, using the idea that it was the nature of competitive advantage in an industry that determined the strategies available to a company's businesses, which in turn determined the structure of the industry. Their idea was that such a framework could help ensure that individual businesses' strategies were consistent with strategies appropriate to their strategic environment. Furthermore,

EXHIBIT 9.5
**BCG's Strategic
Environments Matrix**

Source: R. M. Grant, *Contemporary Strategy Analysis*, 2001, p. 327. Reprinted with permission of Blackwell Publishing.

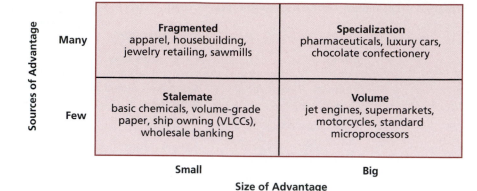

volume businesses
Businesses that have few sources of advantage, but the size is large—typically the result of scale economies.

stalemate businesses
Businesses with few sources of advantage, most of them small. Skills in operational efficiency, low overhead, and cost management are critical to profitability.

fragmented businesses
Businesses with many sources of advantage, but they are all small. They typically involve differentiated products with low brand loyalty, easily replicated technology, and minimal scale economies.

specialization businesses
Businesses with many sources of advantage. Skills in achieving differentiation (product design, branding expertise, innovation, and perhaps scale) characterize winning specialization businesses.

for corporate managers in multiple-business companies, this matrix offered one way to rationalize which businesses they are in—businesses that share core competencies and associated competitive advantages because of similar strategic environments.

The matrix has two dimensions. The number of sources of competitive advantage could be many with complex products and services (e.g., automobiles, financial services) and few with commodities (chemicals, microprocessors). Complex products offer multiple opportunities for differentiation as well as cost, while commodities must seek opportunities for cost advantages to survive.

The second dimension is size of competitive advantage. How big is the advantage available to the industry leader? The two dimensions then define four industry environments as follows:

- **Volume businesses** are those that have few sources of advantage, but the size is large—typically the result of scale economies. Advantages established in one such business may be transferable to another as Honda has done with its scale and expertise with small gasoline engines.

- **Stalemate businesses** have few sources of advantage, with most of those small. This results in very competitive situations. Skills in operational efficiency, low overhead, and cost management are critical to profitability.

- **Fragmented businesses** have many sources of advantage, but they are all small. This typically involves differentiated products with low brand loyalty, easily replicated technology, and minimal scale economies. Skills in focused market segments, typically geographic, the ability to respond quickly to changes, and low costs are critical in this environment.

- **Specialization businesses** have many sources of advantage and find those advantages potentially sizable. Skills in achieving differentiation—product design, branding expertise, innovation, first-mover, and perhaps scale—characterize winners here.

BCG viewed this matrix as providing guidance to multibusiness managers to determine whether they possessed the sources and size of advantage associated with the type of industry facing each business and allowed them a framework to realistically explore the nature of the strategic environments in which they competed or were interested in entering.

Limitations of Portfolio Approaches

Portfolio approaches made several contributions to strategic analysis by corporate managers convinced of their ability to transfer the competitive advantage of professional management across a broad array of businesses. They helped convey large amounts of information about diverse business units and corporate plans in a greatly simplified format. They illuminated similarities and differences between business units and helped convey the logic behind corporate strategies for each business with a common vocabulary. They simplified priorities for sharing corporate resources across diverse business units that generated and used those resources. They provided a simple prescription that gave corporate managers a sense of what they should accomplish—a balanced portfolio of businesses—and a way to control and allocate resources among them. While these approaches offered meaningful contributions, they had several critical limitations and shortcomings:

- A key problem with the portfolio matrix was that it did not address how value was being created across business units—the only relationship between them was cash. Addressing each business unit as a stand-alone entity ignores common core competencies and internal synergies among operating units.
- Truly accurate measurement for matrix classification was not as easy as the matrices portrayed. Identifying individual businesses, or distinct markets, was not often as precise as underlying assumptions required. Comparing business units on only two fundamental dimensions can lead to the conclusion that these are the only factors that really matter and that every unit can be compared fairly on those bases.
- The underlying assumption about the relationship between market share and profitability—the experience curve effect—varied across different industries and market segments. Some have no such link. Some find that firms with low market share can generate superior profitability with differentiation advantages.
- The limited strategic options, intended to describe the flow of resources in a company, came to be seen more as basic strategic missions, which creates a false sense of what each business's strategy actually entails. What do we actually "do" if we're a star? A cash cow? This becomes even more problematic when attempting to use the matrices to conceive strategies for average businesses in average-growth markets.
- The portfolio approach portrayed the notion that firms needed to be self-sufficient in capital. This ignored capital raised in capital markets.
- The portfolio approach typically failed to compare the competitive advantage a business received from being owned by a particular company with the costs of owning it. The 1980s saw many companies build enormous corporate infrastructures that created only small gains at the business level. The reengineering and deconstruction of numerous global conglomerates in the past 10 years reflects this important omission. We will examine this consideration in greater detail later in this chapter.
- Recent research by well-known consulting firm Booz-Allen-Hamilton suggests that "conventional wisdom is wrong. Corporate managers often rely on accounting metrics [based on past performance] to make business decisions." They go on to argue that "past performance is a poor predictor of the future. When performance is assessed over time, greater shareholder value can be created by improving the operations of the company's worst-performing businesses." "The way to thrive," they say, "is to love your dogs." Their point, backed up by impressive research, is that a corporate manager can learn to identify "value assets," hold and nurture them, and produce superior performance ultimately leading to increased shareholder value more so than can be achieved by acquiring and trying to add value to an overvalued "star."[2]

[2] A comprehensive discussion of these ideas to include their research examining the performance of "falling stars" and "rising dogs" can be found at Harry Quaris, Thomas Pernsteiner, and Kasturi Rangan, "Love your 'Dogs,'" *Strategy+Business Magazine,* Booz Allen Hamilton, www.strategy-business.com/resiliencereport/resilience/rr00030, 2007.

EXHIBIT 9.6 **Value Building in Multibusiness Companies**

Opportunities to Build Value or Sharing	Potential Competitive Advantage	Impediments to Achieving Enhanced Value
Market-Related Opportunities		
Shared salesforce activities, shared sales office, or both	Lower selling costs Better market coverage Stronger technical advice to buyers Enhanced convenience for buyers (can buy from single source) Improved access to buyers (have more products to sell)	• Buyers have different purchasing habits toward the products. • Different salespersons are more effective in representing the product. • Some products get more attention than others. • Buyers prefer to multiple-source rather than single-source their purchases.
Shared after-sale service and repair work	Lower servicing costs Better utilization of service personnel (less idle time) Faster servicing of customer calls	• Different equipment or different labor skills, or both, are needed to handle repairs. • Buyers may do some in-house repairs.
Shared brand name	Stronger brand image and company reputation Increased buyer confidence in the brand	• Company reputation is hurt if quality of one product is lower.
Shared advertising and promotional activities	Lower costs Greater clout in purchasing ads	• Appropriate forms of messages are different. • Appropriate timing of promotions is different.
Common distribution channels	Lower distribution costs Enhanced bargaining power with distributors and retailers to gain shelf space, shelf positioning, stronger push and more dealer attention, and better profit margins	• Dealers resist being dominated by a single supplier and turn to multiple sources and lines. • Heavy use of the shared channel erodes willingness of other channels to carry or push the firm's products.
Shared order processing	Lower order processing costs One-stop shopping for buyer to enhance service and, thus, differentiation	• Differences in ordering cycles disrupt order-processing economies.
Operating Opportunities		
Joint procurement of purchased inputs.	Lower input costs Improved input quality Improved service from suppliers	• Input needs are different in terms of quality or other specifications. • Inputs are needed at different plant locations, and centralized purchasing is not responsive to separate needs of each plant.
Shared manufacturing and assembly facilities	Lower manufacturing/assembly costs Better capacity utilization, because peak demand for one product correlates with valley demand for the other Bigger scale of operation to improve access to better technology, resulting in better quality	• Higher changeover costs in shifting from one product to another. • High-cost special tooling or equipment is required to accommodate quality differences or design differences.

EXHIBIT 9.6 *(continued)*

Opportunities to Build Value or Sharing	Potential Competitive Advantage	Impediments to Achieving Enhanced Value
Operating Opportunities (cont.)		
Shared inbound or outbound shipping and materials handling	Lower freight and handling costs Better delivery reliability More frequent deliveries, such that inventory costs are reduced	• Input sources or plant locations, or both, are in different geographic areas. • Needs for frequency and reliability of inbound/outbound delivery differ among the business units.
Shared product and process technologies, technology development, or both.	Lower product or process design costs, or both, because of shorter design times and transfers of knowledge from area to area More innovative ability, owing to scale of effort and attraction of better R&D personnel	• Technologies are the same, but the applications in different business units are different enough to prevent much sharing of real value.
Shared administrative support activities	Lower administrative and operating overhead costs	• Support activities are not a large proportion of cost, and sharing has little cost impact (and virtually no differentiation impact).
Management Opportunities		
Shared management know-how, operating skills, and proprietary information	Efficient transfer of a distinctive competence—can create cost savings or enhance differentiation More effective management as concerns strategy formulation, strategy implementation, and understanding of key success factors	• Actual transfer of know-how is costly or stretches the key skill personnel too thinly, or both. • Increased risks that proprietary information will leak out.

Source: Based on Michael Porter, *On Competition*, Harvard Business School Press.

Constructing business portfolio matrices must be undertaken with these limitations in mind. Perhaps it is best to say that they provide one form of input to corporate managers seeking to balance financial resources. While limitations have meant portfolio approaches are seen as mere historical concepts, seldom recommended, it is interesting that the new chairman of the company that pioneered and subsequently abandoned the portfolio has come full circle in 2006, embracing the concept as a key basis for helping the post-Welch GE rationalize a dramatically new approach to the twenty-first century at GE (see Exhibit 9.1). Perhaps this foretells a continued use of the portfolio approach, recognizing its limitations, to provide a picture of the "balance" of resource generators and users, to test underlying assumptions about these issues in more involved corporate planning efforts, and to leverage core competencies to build sustained competitive advantages. Indeed, the next major approach in the evolution of multibusiness strategic analysis is to leverage shared capabilities and core competencies.

THE SYNERGY APPROACH: LEVERAGING CORE COMPETENCIES

Opportunities to build value via diversification, integration, or joint venture strategies are usually found in market-related, operations-related, and management activities. Each business's basic value chain activities or infrastructure become a source of potential synergy and competitive advantage for another business in the corporate portfolio. Morrison's Cafeterias, once a mainstay of the food-service industry in malls across much of the United States, accelerated its diversification into other restaurant concepts such as Ruby Tuesday's, followed by L&N Seafood Grill, Silver Spoon Café, Mozzarella's, and Tia's Tex-Mex. It also acquired three other food-contract firms. Numerous opportunities for shared operating capabilities and management capabilities drove this decision and, upon repeated strategic analysis, accelerated corporate managers' decision to move Morrison's totally out of the cafeteria segment a few years later. Some of the more common opportunities to share value chain activities and build value are identified in Exhibit 9.6.

Strategic analysis is concerned with whether or not the potential competitive advantages expected to arise from each value opportunity have materialized. Where advantage has not materialized, corporate strategists must take care to scrutinize possible impediments to achieving the synergy or competitive advantage. We have identified in Exhibit 9.6 several impediments associated with each opportunity, which strategists are well advised to examine. Good strategists assure themselves that their organization has ways to avoid or minimize the effects of any impediments, or they recommend against further integration or diversification and consider divestiture options.

Two elements are critical in meaningful shared opportunities:

1. The shared opportunities must be a significant portion of the value chain of the businesses involved. Returning to Morrison's Cafeteria, its purchasing and inbound logistics infrastructure give Ruby Tuesday's operators an immediate cost-effective purchasing and inventory management capability that lowered its cost in a significant cost activity.

2. The businesses involved must truly have shared needs—need for the same activity—or there is no basis for synergy in the first place. Novell, the U.S.-based networking software giant, paid $900 million for WordPerfect, envisioning numerous synergies serving offices globally, not to mention 15 million WordPerfect users. Little more than a year later, Novell would sell WordPerfect for less than $300 million, because, as CEO Bob Frankenberg said, "It is not because WordPerfect is not a business without a future, but for Novell it represented a distraction from our strategy."

Corporate strategies have repeatedly rushed into diversification only to find perceived opportunities for sharing were nonexistent because the businesses did not really have shared needs.

The most compelling reason companies should diversify can be found in situations where core competencies—key value-building skills—can be leveraged with other products or into markets that are not a part of where they were created. Where this works well, extraordinary value can be built. Managers undertaking diversification strategies should dedicate a significant portion of their strategic analysis to this question.

General Cinema was a company that grew from drive-in theaters to eventually dominate the multicinema, movie exhibition industry. Next, they entered soft-drink bottling and became the largest bottler of soft drinks (Pepsi) in North America. Their stock value rose 2,000 percent in 10 years. They found that core competencies in movie exhibition—managing many small, localized businesses; dealing with a few large suppliers; applying central marketing skills locally; and acquiring or crafting a "franchise"—were virtually the same in soft-drink bottling. IBM CEO Sam Palmisano and his management team have done an extraordinary job of creating a virtually new IBM by adapting a multibusiness strategy

IBM Gets a Second Life . . . and Its CEO an Avatar

BusinessWeek

Big Blue's consumer-related business is growing fast thanks to the migration of its technologies from enterprise computing to consumer applications.

IBM may be one of the last tech outfits to come to mind when you think about consumer products. After all, the company severed its direct sales link with consumers when it sold its PC division to Lenovo Group two years ago. Among the glitzy, tricked-out Consumer Electronics Show booths for Sony (SNE), Samsung, and XM Satellite Radio (XMSR), IBM has set up a sprawling showcase for its technologies and services.

No, Big Blue isn't getting into the gadget business. Instead, it makes a host of technologies that go inside other companies' products—whether it's video game consoles, TVs, or even virtual worlds such as Second Life. "There are a lot of ways we can play (in consumer markets) but not necessarily be the game console maker or the YouTube," said IBM chief executive Samuel Palmisano.

Most of IBM's revenue comes from selling powerful computers, software, and services to large corporations, but one of the fastest-growing pieces of its business is the consumer sphere.

ENTERPRISE INVESTMENT, CONSUMER BENEFITS

Some of IBM's competitors belittle its consumer aspirations. Microsoft CEO Steven Ballmer said he doesn't even consider IBM to be a broad-based technology company anymore, because it focuses so much on the enterprise.

Still, analysts credit IBM with crafting a smart and successful corporate strategy designed to leverage and share core competencies across a diverse set of businesses. "A few years ago, nobody would have dreamed that IBM would score the top three game consoles," says analyst Rick Doherty of market researcher Envisioneering Group. "Now there's an opportunity for IBM to do similar things in the digital living room and portable devices. And this isn't just about hardware. They can manage content and security for the entertainment industry."

IBM has found a way to make many of its research investments in enterprise computing also pay off in the consumer realm, and vice versa. The Cell microprocessor, which it co-developed with partners Sony and Toshiba, is being employed by Mercury Computer in so-called blade servers that are used for medical imaging, defense electronics, and, you guessed it, video gaming.

SECOND LIFE—Sam Palmisano, IBM Chairman and CEO
On November 14, Sam Palmisano's avatar made an appearance on the IBM island in Second Life to announce that the computer giant is investing $100 million in a new business unit to explore the potential of new technologies like virtual worlds in commerce, e-learning, and customer services.

SEVERAL DIVISIONS INVOLVED

On the software side, programs designed to manage and safeguard corporate data can be used for movies and music. "You have a convergence between the computer world and the consumer world," says Adalio Sanchez, general manager of IBM's Technology Collaboration Solutions business unit, one of its emerging businesses, which targets the consumer sphere. "In the past, discoveries in the computer world fed the consumer space. That's flipping today."

Other parts of IBM are also instrumental in its consumer play. IBM Research labs provided the real-time speech translation technology being used by the U.S. Army in Iraq and now being targeted by IBM at consumer uses. Its engineering services division helps consumer companies design whole new products and services, including the Joysound Karaoke service being sold by Xing to bars in Japan.

Sources: Reprinted with special permission from Steve Hamm, "IBM at CES: Right at Home," *BusinessWeek,* May 11, 2007; and Steve Hamm, "Palmisano Gets a Second Life," *BusinessWeek,* November 20, 2006. Copyright © 2007 The McGraw-Hill Companies.

centered around finding, sharing, and leveraging core competencies across a seemingly diverse set of businesses and markets. Not only have they done so with existing competencies, but their organization has proven remarkably adept at leveraging newly found technologies and capabilities within each business across other businesses—enterprise focused business competencies deployed in consumer product offerings and vice versa as described in Exhibit 9.7, Strategy in Action.

Each Core Competency Should Provide a Relevant Competitive Advantage to the Intended Businesses

The core competency must assist the intended business in creating strength relative to key competition. This could occur at any step in the business's value chain. But it must represent a major source of value to be a basis for competitive advantage—and the core competence must be transferable. Honda of Japan viewed itself as having a core competence in manufacturing small, internal combustion engines. It diversified into small garden tools, perceiving that traditional electric tools would be much more attractive if powered by a lightweight, mobile, gas combustion motor. Their core competency created a major competitive advantage in a market void of gas-driven hand tools. When Coca-Cola added bottled water to its portfolio of products, it expected its extraordinary core competencies in marketing and distribution to rapidly build value in this business. Ten years later, Coke sold its water assets, concluding that the product did not have enough margin to interest its franchised bottlers and that marketing was not a significant value-building activity among many small suppliers competing primarily on the cost of "producing" and shipping water. In the last few years, however, Coke has reversed its decision and added the Dasani water brand because a rapidly increasing consumer demand has made the value of its extensive distribution network a relevant competitive advantage to the Dasani water product line.

Businesses in the Portfolio Should Be Related in Ways That Make the Company's Core Competencies Beneficial

Related versus unrelated diversification is an important distinction to understand as you evaluate the diversification question. "Related" businesses are those that rely on the same or similar capabilities to be successful and attain competitive advantage in their respective product markets. Earlier, we described General Cinema's spectacular success in both movie exhibition and soft-drink bottling. Seemingly unrelated, they were actually very related businesses in terms of key core competencies that shaped success—managing a network of diverse business locations, localized competition, reliance on a few large suppliers, and centralized marketing advantages. Thus, the products of various businesses do not necessarily have to be similar to leverage core competencies. While their products may not be related, it is essential that some activities in their value chains require similar skills to create competitive advantage if the company is going to leverage its core competence(s) in a value-creating way. Exhibit 9.7 offered an example of IBM's remarkable effectiveness in doing just this the last five years. In fact, their CEO now even has an Avatar on Second Life to build an understanding of ways IBM's core competencies could be related to and leveraged in the emerging virtual world on the Web.

Situations that involve "unrelated" diversification occur when no real overlapping capabilities or products exist other than financial resources. We refer to this as *conglomerate diversification* in Chapter 7. Recent research indicates that the most profitable firms are those that have diversified around a set of resources and capabilities that are specialized enough to confer a meaningful competitive advantage in an attractive industry, yet adaptable enough to be advantageously applied across several others. The least profitable are broadly diversified firms whose strategies are built around very general resources

Six Critical Questions for Diversification

WHAT CAN OUR COMPANY DO BETTER THAN ANY OF ITS COMPETITORS IN ITS CURRENT MARKET(S)?

Managers often diversify on the basis of vague definitions of their business rather than on a systematic analysis of what sets their company apart from its competitors. By determining what they can do better than their existing competitors, companies will have a better chance of succeeding in new markets.

WHAT CORE COMPETENCIES DO WE NEED IN ORDER TO SUCCEED IN THE NEW MARKET?

Excelling in one market does not guarantee success in a new and related one. Managers considering diversification must ask whether their company has every core competency necessary to establish a competitive advantage in the territory it hopes to conquer.

CAN WE CATCH UP TO OR LEAPFROG COMPETITORS AT THEIR OWN GAME?

All is not necessarily lost if managers find that they lack a critical core competency. There is always the potential to buy what is missing, develop it in-house, or render it unnecessary by changing the competitive rules of the game.

WILL DIVERSIFICATION BREAK UP CORE COMPETENCIES THAT NEED TO BE KEPT TOGETHER?

Many companies introduce their time-tested core competencies and capabilities in a new market and still fail. That is because they have separated core competencies and capabilities that rely on one another for their effectiveness and hence are not able to function alone.

WILL WE SIMPLY BE A PLAYER IN THE NEW MARKET OR WILL WE EMERGE AS A WINNER?

Diversifying companies are often quickly outmaneuvered by their new competitors. Why? In many cases, they have failed to consider whether their strategic assets can be easily imitated, purchased on the open market, or replaced.

WHAT CAN OUR COMPANY LEARN BY DIVERSIFYING, AND ARE WE SUFFICIENTLY ORGANIZED TO LEARN IT?

Savvy companies know how to make diversification a learning experience. They see how new businesses can help improve existing ones, act as stepping-stones to industries previously out of reach, or improve organizational efficiency.

Source: Reprinted by permission of *Harvard Business Review*. Exhibit from "To Diversify or Not to Diversify," by C. C. Markides, November–December 1997. Copyright © 1997 by the Harvard Business School Publishing Corporation; all rights reserved.

(e.g., money) that are applied in a wide variety of industries, but that are seldom instrumental to competitive advantage in those settings.[3]

Any Combination of Competencies Must Be Unique or Difficult to Recreate

Skills that corporate strategists expect to transfer from one business to another, or from corporate to various businesses, may be transferable. They may also be easily replicated by competitors. When this is the case, no sustainable competitive advantage is created. Sometimes strategists look for a combination of competencies, a package of various interrelated skills, as another way to create a situation where seemingly easily replicated competencies become unique, sustainable competitive advantages. 3M Corporation has the enviable record of having 25 percent of its earnings always coming from products introduced within the last five years. 3M has been able to "bundle" the skills necessary to

[3] David J. Collis and Cynthia A. Montgomery, *Corporate Strategy* (Chicago: McGraw-Hill/Irwin, 2005), p. 88; "Why Mergers Fail," *McKinsey Quarterly Report,* 2001, vol. 4; and "Deals That Create Value," *McKinsey Quarterly Report,* 2001, vol. 1.

accelerate the introduction of new products so that it consistently extracts early life-cycle value from adhesive-related products that hundreds of competitors with similar technical or marketing competencies cannot touch.

All too often companies envision a combination of competencies that make sense conceptually. This vision of synergy develops an energy of its own, leading CEOs to relentlessly push the merger of the firms involved. But what makes sense conceptually and is seen as difficult for competitors to recreate often proves difficult if not impossible to create in the first place. Exhibit 9.8, Strategy in Action, summarizes six key questions managers should answer to identify the strategic risks and opportunities that diversification presents.

THE CORPORATE PARENT ROLE: CAN IT ADD TANGIBLE VALUE?

Realizing synergies from shared capabilities and core competencies is a key way value is added in multibusiness companies. Research suggests that figuring out if the synergies are real and, if so, how to capture those synergies is most effectively accomplished by business unit managers, not the corporate parent.[4] How then can the corporate parent add value to its businesses in a multibusiness company? We want to acquaint you with two perspectives to use in attempting to answer this question: the parenting framework and the patching approach.

The Parenting Framework

parenting framework
The perspective that the role of corporate headquarters (the "parent") in multibusiness (the "children") companies is that of a parent sharing wisdom, insight, and guidance to help develop its various businesses to excel.

The **parenting framework** perspective sees multibusiness companies as creating value by influencing—or parenting—the businesses they own. The best parent companies create more value than any of their rivals do or would if they owned the same businesses. To add value, a parent must improve its businesses. Obviously there must be room for improvement. Advocates of this perspective call the potential for improvement within a business "a parenting opportunity." They identify 10 places to look for parenting opportunities, which then become the focus of strategic analysis and choice across multiple businesses and their interface with the parent organization.[5] Let's look at each briefly.

Size and Age

Old, large, successful businesses frequently engender entrenched bureaucracies and overhead structures that are hard to dismantle from inside the business. Doing so may add value, and getting it done may be best done by an external catalyst, the parent. Small, young businesses may lack some key functional skills, or outgrow their top managers' capabilities, or lack capital to deal with a temporary downturn or accelerated growth opportunity. Where these are relevant issues within one or more businesses, a parenting opportunity to add value may exist.

Management

Does the business employ managers superior in comparison with its competitors? Is the business's success dependent on attracting and keeping people with specialized skills?

---

[4] Michael Goold, Andrew Campbell, and Marcus Alexander, "The Quest for Parenting Advantage," *Harvard Business Review,* March–April 1995; Michael Goold, Andrew Campbell, and Marcus Alexander, "How Corporate Parents Add Value to the Stand-Alone Performance of Their Businesses," *Business Strategy Review,* Winter 1994.

[5] Ibid, p. 126. These 10 areas of opportunity are taken from an insert entitled "Ten Places to Look for Parenting Opportunities" on this page of the *Harvard Business Review* article.

Are key managers focused on the right objectives? Ensuring that these issues are addressed and objectively assessed and assisting in any resolution may be a parenting opportunity that could add value.

Business Definition

Business unit managers may have a myopic or erroneous vision of what their business should be, which, in turn, has them targeting a market that is too narrow or broad. They may employ too much vertical integration or not enough. Accelerated trends toward outsourcing and strategic alliances are changing the definitions of many businesses. All of this creates a parenting opportunity to help redefine a business unit in a way that creates greater value.

Predictable Errors

The nature of a business and its unique situation can lead managers to make predictable mistakes. Managers responsible for previous strategic decisions are vested in the success of those decisions, which may prevent openness to new alternatives. Older, mature businesses often accumulate a variety of products and markets, which becomes excessive diversification within a particular business. Cyclical markets can lead to underinvestment during downturns and overinvestment during the upswing. Lengthy product life cycles can lead to overreliance on old products. All of these are predictable errors a parent can monitor and attempt to avoid, creating, in turn, added value.

Linkages

Business units may be able to improve market position or efficiency by linking with other businesses that are not readily apparent to the management of the business unit in question. Whether apparent or not, linkages among business units within or outside the parent company may be complex or difficult to establish without parent company help. In either case, an opportunity to add value may exist.

Common Capabilities

Fundamental to successful diversification, as we have discussed earlier, is the notion of sharing capabilities and competencies needed by multiple business units. Parenting opportunities to add value may arise from time to time through regular scrutiny of opportunities to share capabilities or add shared capabilities that would otherwise go unnoticed by business unit managers closer to daily business operations.

Specialized Expertise

There may be situations in which the parent company possesses specialized or rare expertise that may benefit a business unit and add value in the process. Unique legal, technical, or administrative expertise critical in a particular situation or decision point, which is quickly and easily available, can prove very valuable.

External Relations

Does the business have external stakeholders—governments, regulators, unions, suppliers, shareholders—the parent company could manage more effectively than individual business units? If so, a natural parenting opportunity exists that should add value.

Major Decisions

A business unit may face difficult decisions in areas for which it lacks expertise—for example, making an acquisition, entering China, a major capacity expansion, divesting and outsourcing a major part of the business's operations. Obtaining capital externally to fund a major investment may be much more difficult than doing so through the parent

Top Strategist
Indra Nooyi, CEO of PepsiCo

Exhibit
9.9

Keep an eye on Indra Nooyi. Analysts expect this daughter of Chennai, India, to accelerate the beverage and snack giant's efforts to broaden its portfolio and globalize its brands as PepsiCo chairperson and CEO.

At PepsiCo Inc., Indra Nooyi has long been known for two things: a prescient business sense and an irreverent personal style. The combination became obvious soon after she joined the company as its chief strategist 13 years ago. She pushed chief executive Roger Enrico to spin off Taco Bell, Pizza Hut, and KFC in 1997 because she didn't feel PepsiCo could add enough value to the fast-food business. She later was instrumental in the purchase of Tropicana, the spinoff of Pepsi's bottling business, and the $13 billion merger with Quaker Oats Co. Each of these moves has paid off.

All the while, Nooyi has proved comfortable enough with her leadership presence to patrol the office barefoot at times and even sing in the halls, perhaps a holdover from her teen days in an all-girl rock band in her hometown of Chennai, India. She gave Enrico a karaoke machine before he left in 2001 and hired a live "Jam-eoke" band to help senior executives belt out tunes at a management conference earlier this year.

"Indra can drive as deep and hard as anyone I've ever met," Enrico says, "but she can do it with a sense of heart and fun." Enrico praises Nooyi for her practicality, vision, and courage—"This was a woman who was well-known for walking around barefoot and singing songs," he laughs. "She is a mature and seasoned executive, but she hasn't lost her spontaneity and sense of humor."

Nooyi learned early on to embrace rather than hide her differences in the corporate world. Nooyi wore a sari to an interview at Boston Consulting Group and was offered the job. She later held corporate strategy posts at Motorola Inc. and what is now ABB Group. What drew her to PepsiCo was the chance to make a difference in a company that was struggling.

Over the past decade, she says, "PepsiCo has transformed itself to become among the best food companies and one of the better corporations in the world." Since 2000, when she became chief financial officer, the company's annual revenues have risen 72 percent, while net profit more than doubled, to $5.6 billion last year. As chairman and CEO, Nooyi promotes the concept of "performance with purpose," trying to make PepsiCo a ground-breaker in areas like selling healthy food and diversifying its workforce.

With her passion for globalization and sharp eye for acquisitions, Nooyi has been a major force in shaping the direction of PepsiCo for some time now. She brings a rich understanding of emerging markets at a time when they have become critical growth areas for PepsiCo. It was her idea to move south of the border and buy Mexican subsidiary Sabritas, bringing their products into the United States and selling them through smaller mom-&-pop retail outlets in Mexican-dominated areas. It was an immediate hit with the 50 million Hispanic population in the United States.

By defining its mission as serving the customer, a global customer, rather than protecting its venerable brands, PepsiCo under Nooyi's leadership appears to be leveraging its central, corporate parent capabilities in support of opportunities for product and market growth and improvement driven from the consumer end, not the corporate end. And she is doing so on a global scale.

Source: Reprinted with special permission from Diane Brady, "Indra Nooyi: Keeping Cool in Hot Water," *Business-Week*, June 11, 2007. Copyright © 2007 The McGraw-Hill Companies.

company—GE proved this could be a major parenting advantage in the way it developed GE Capital into a major source of capital for its other business units as well as to finance major capital purchases by customers of its own business units.

Major Changes

Sometimes a business needs to make major changes in ways critical to the business's future success yet which involve areas or considerations in which the business unit's management has little or no experience. A complete revamping of a business unit's information management process, outsourcing all that capability to India, or shifting all of a business unit's production operations to another business unit in another part of the world—these are just a few examples of major changes in which the parent may have extensive experience with what feels like unknown territory to the business's management team.

Overlap in some of these 10 sources of parenting opportunities may exist. For example, specialized expertise in China and a major decision to locate or outsource operations there may be the same source of added value. And that decision would involve a major change. The fact that overlap, or redundancy may exist in classifying sources of parenting opportunity is a minor consideration, however, relative to the value of the parenting framework for strategic analysis in multibusiness companies. The portfolio approaches focus on how businesses' cash, profit, and growth potential create a balance within the portfolio. The core competence approach concentrates on how business units are related and can share technical and operating know-how and capacity. The parenting framework adds to these approaches and the strategic analysis in a multibusiness company because it focuses on competencies of the parent organization and on the value created from the relationship between the parent and its businesses. Exhibit 9.9, Top Strategist, shows how PepsiCo's chairwoman and CEO Indra Nooyi has created a significant corporate parenting role as she fosters innovations, acquires new brands, divests certain businesses, all the time building organizational linkages and sharing core competencies across several PepsiCo business units and brands, both domestically and globally.

The Patching Approach

patching
The process by which corporate executives routinely "remap" their businesses to match rapidly changing market opportunities—adding, splitting, transferring, exiting, or combining chunks of businesses.

strategic processes
Decision making, operational activities, and sales activities that are critical business processes.

strategic positioning
The way a business is designed and positioned to serve target markets.

Another approach that focuses on the role and ability of corporate managers to create value in the management of multibusiness companies is called "patching."[6] **Patching** is the process by which corporate executives routinely remap businesses to match rapidly changing market opportunities. It can take the form of adding, splitting, transferring, exiting, or combining chunks of businesses. Patching is not seen as critical in stable, unchanging markets. When markets are turbulent and rapidly changing, patching is seen as critical to the creation of economic value in a multibusiness company.

Proponents of this perspective on the strategic decision-making function of corporate executives say it is the critical, and arguably only, way corporate executives can add value beyond the sum of the businesses within the company. They view traditional corporate strategy as creating defensible strategic positions for business units by acquiring or building valuable assets, wisely allocating resources to them, and weaving synergies among them. In volatile markets, they argue, this traditional approach results in business units with strategies that are quickly outdated and competitive advantages rarely sustained beyond a few years.[7] As a result, they say, strategic analysis should center on **strategic processes** more than **strategic positioning.** In these volatile markets, patchers' strategic analysis focuses on making quick, small, frequent changes in parts of businesses and organizational processes that enable dynamic strategic repositioning rather than building long-term defensible positions. Exhibit 9.10 compares differences between traditional approaches to shaping corporate strategy with the patching approach.

[6] Kathleen M. Eisenhardt and Shona L. Brown, "Patching: Restitching Business Portfolios in Dynamic Markets," *Harvard Business Review,* May–June 1999, pp. 72–82.

[7] Ibid, p. 76; and K. M. Eisenhardt and D. N. Sull, "Strategy as Simple Rules," *Harvard Business Review,* January 2001.

EXHIBIT 9.10   **Three Approaches to Strategy**

Managers competing in business can choose among three distinct ways to fight. They can build a fortress and defend it; they can nurture and leverage unique resources; or they can flexibly pursue fleeting opportunities within simple rules. Each approach requires different skill sets and works best under different circumstances.

	Position	**Resources**	**Patching [Simple Rules]**
Strategic logic	Establish position	Leverage resources	Pursue opportunities
Strategic steps	Identify an attractive market	Establish a vision Build resources	Jump into the confusion Keep moving
	Locate a defensible position	Leverage across markets	Seize opportunities Finish strong
	Fortify and defend		
Strategic question	Where should we be?	What should we be?	How should we proceed?
Source of advantage	Unique, valuable position with tightly integrated activity system	Unique, valuable, inimitable resources	Key processes and unique simple rules
Works best in	Slowly changing, well-structured markets	Moderately changing, well-structured markets	Rapidly changing, ambiguous markets
Duration of advantage	Sustained	Sustained	Unpredictable
Risk	Too difficult to alter position as conditions change	Too slow to build new resources as conditions change	Too tentative in executing promising opportunities
Performance goal	Profitability	Long-term dominance	Growth

Source: Reprinted by permission of *Harvard Business Review.* Exhibit from "Strategy as Simple Rules," by K. M. Eisenhardt and D. N. Sull, January 2001. Copyright © 2001 by the Harvard Business School Publishing Corporation; all rights reserved.

To be successful with a patching approach to corporate strategic analysis and choice in turbulent markets, Eisenhardt and Sull suggest that managers should flexibly seize opportunities—as long as that flexibility is disciplined. Effective corporate strategists, they argue, focus on key processes and *simple rules*. The following example at Miramax helps illustrate the notion of strategy as simple rules:

> Miramax—well known for artistically innovative movies such as *The Crying Game, Life is Beautiful*, and *Pulp Fiction*—has boundary rules that guide the all-important movie-picking process: First, every movie must revolve around a central human condition, such as love *(The Crying Game)* or envy *(The Talented Mr. Ripley)*. Second, a movie's main character must be appealing but deeply flawed—the hero of *Shakespeare in Love* is gifted and charming but steals ideas from friends and betrays his wife. Third, movies must have a very clear story line with a beginning, middle, and end (although in *Pulp Fiction* the end comes first). Finally, there is a firm cap on production costs. Within the rules, there is flexibility to move quickly when a writer or director shows up with a great script. The result is an enormously creative and even surprising flow of movies and enough discipline to produce superior, consistent financial results. *The English Patient*, for example, cost $27 million to make, grossed more than $200 million, and grabbed nine Oscars.[8]

[8] Ibid, Eisenhardt and Sull, p. 111.

EXHIBIT 9.11   Simple Rules, Summarized

In turbulent markets, managers should flexibly seize opportunities—but flexibility must be disciplined. Smart companies focus on key processes and simple rules. Different types of rules help executives manage different aspects of seizing opportunities.

Type	Purpose	Example
How-to rules	Spell out key features of how a process is executed—"What makes our process unique?"	Akami's rules for the customer service process: Staff must consist of technical gurus, every question must be answered on the first call or e-mail, and R&D staff must rotate through customer service.
Boundary rules	Focus on which opportunities can be pursued and which are outside the pale.	Cisco's early acquisitions rule: Companies to be acquired must have no more than 75 employees, 75 percent of whom are engineers.
Priority rules	Help managers rank the accepted opportunities.	Intel's rule for allocating manufacturing capacity: Allocation is based on a product's gross margin.
Timing rules	Synchronize managers with the pace of emerging opportunities and other parts of the company.	Nortel's rules for product development: Project teams must know when a product has to be delivered to the customer to win, and product development time must be less than 18 months.
Exit rules	Help managers decide when to pull out of yesterday's opportunities.	Oticon's rule for pulling the plug on projects in development: If a key team member—manager or not—chooses to leave the project for another within the company, the project is killed.

Source: Reprinted by permission of *Harvard Business Review.* Exhibit from "Strategy as Simple Rules," by K. M. Eisenhardt and D. N. Sull, January 2001. Copyright © 2001 by the Harvard Business School Publishing Corporation; all rights reserved.

Different types of rules help managers and strategists manage different aspects of seizing opportunities. Exhibit 9.11 explains and illustrates five such types of rules. These rules are called "simple" rules because they need to be brief, be axiomatic, and convey fundamental guidelines to decisions or actions. They need to provide just enough structure to allow managers to move quickly to capture opportunities with confidence that the judgments and commitments they make are consistent with corporate intent. At the same time, while they set parameters on actions and decisions, they are not thick manuals or rules and policies that managers in turbulent environments may find paralyze any efforts to quickly capitalize on opportunities. Exhibit 9.12, Strategy in Action, helps explain the simple rules idea behind the patching approach to corporate strategic decision making by explaining what simple rules are not.

The patching approach then relies on simple rules unique to a particular parent company that exist to guide managers in the corporate organization and its business units in making rapid decisions about quickly reshaping parts of the company and allocating time as well as money to capitalize on rapidly shifting market opportunities. The fundamental argument of this approach is that no one can predict how long a competitive advantage will last, particularly in turbulent, rapidly changing markets. While managers in stable markets may be able to rely on complex strategies built on detailed predictions of future trends, managers in complex, fast-moving markets—where significant growth and wealth creation may occur—face constant unpredictability; hence, strategy must be simple, responsive, and dynamic to encourage success.

Strategy in Action

Exhibit 9.12

What Simple Rules Are Not

It is impossible to dictate exactly what a company's simple rules should be. It is possible, however, to say what they should *not* be.

BROAD

Managers often confuse a company's guiding principles with simple rules. The celebrated "HP way," for example, consists of principles like "we focus on a high level of achievement and contribution" and "we encourage flexibility and innovation." The principles are designed to apply to every activity within the company, from purchasing to product innovation. They may create a productive culture, but they provide little concrete guidance for employees trying to evaluate a partner or decide whether to enter a new market. The most effective simple rules, in contrast, are tailored to a single process.

VAGUE

Some rules cover a single process but are too vague to provide real guidance. One Western bank operating in Russia, for example, provided the following guideline for screening investment proposals: all investments must be currently undervalued and have potential for long-term capital appreciation. Imagine the plight of a newly hired associate who turns to that rule for guidance!

A simple screen can help managers test whether their rules are too vague. Ask: could any reasonable person argue the exact opposite of the rule? In the case of the bank in Russia, it is hard to imagine anyone suggesting that the company target overvalued companies with no potential for long-term capital appreciation. If your rules flunk this test, they are not effective.

MINDLESS

Companies whose simple rules have remained implicit may find upon examining them that these rules destroy rather than create value. In one company, managers listed their recent partnership relationships and then tried to figure out what rules could have produced the list. To their chagrin, they found that one rule seemed to be: always form partnerships with small, weak companies that we can control. Another was: always form partnerships with companies that are not as successful as they once were. Again, use a simple test; reverse-engineer your processes to determine your implicit simple rules. Throw out the ones that are embarrassing.

STALE

In high-velocity markets, rules can linger beyond their sell-by dates. Consider Banc One. The Columbus, Ohio–based bank grew to be the seventh-largest bank in the United States by acquiring more than 100 regional banks. Banc One's acquisitions followed a set of simple rules that were based on experience: Banc One must never pay so much that earnings are diluted, it must only buy successful banks with established management teams, it must never acquire a bank with assets greater than one-third of Banc One's, and it must allow acquired banks to run as autonomous affiliates. The rules worked well until others in the banking industry consolidated operations to lower their costs substantially. Then Banc One's loose confederation of banks was burdened with redundant operations, and it got clobbered by efficient competitors.

How do you figure out if your rules are stale? Slowing growth is a good indicator. Stock price is even better. Investors obsess about the future, while your own financials report the past. So if your share price is dropping relative to your competitors' share prices, or if your percentage of the industry's market value is declining, or if growth is slipping, your rules may need to be refreshed.

Source: Reprinted by permission of *Harvard Business Review.* Exhibit from "Strategy as Simple Rules," by K. M. Eisenhardt and D. N. Sull, January 2001. Copyright © 2001 by the Harvard Business School Publishing Corporation; all rights reserved.

Summary

This chapter examined how managers make strategic decisions in multibusiness companies. One of the earliest approaches was to look at the company as a portfolio of businesses. This portfolio was then examined and evaluated based on each business's growth potential, market position, and need for and ability to generate cash. Corporate strategists then allocated resources, divested, and acquired businesses based on the balance across this portfolio of businesses or possible businesses.

The notion of synergy across business units—sharing capabilities and leveraging core competencies—has been another very widely adopted approach to making strategic decisions in multibusiness companies. Sharing capabilities allows for greater efficiencies, enhanced expertise, and competitive advantage. Core competencies that generate competitive advantage can often be leveraged across multiple businesses, thereby expanding the impact and value added from that competitive advantage.

Globalization, rapid change, outsourcing, and other major forces shaping today's economic landscape have ushered in multibusiness strategic decision making that also focuses on the role and value-added contributions, if any, of the parent company itself. Does the parent company add or could it add value beyond the sum of the businesses it owns? Two perspectives that have gained popularity in multibusiness companies' strategic decision making are the parenting framework and the patching approach. The parenting framework focuses on 10 areas of opportunity managers should carefully explore to find ways the parent organization might add value to one or more businesses and the overall company. The patching approach concentrates on multibusiness companies in turbulent markets of the twenty-first century, where managers need to make quick, small shifts and adjustments in processes, markets, and products, and offers five types of "simple rules" that managers use as guidelines to structure quick decisions throughout a multibusiness company on a continuous basis.

Key Terms

cash cows, *p. 278*
dogs, *p. 279*
fragmented businesses, *p. 282*
market growth rate, *p. 278*
parenting framework, *p. 290*
patching, *p. 293*

portfolio techniques, *p. 278*
relative competitive
position, *p. 278*
question marks, *p. 279*
specialization
businesses, *p. 282*

stalemate businesses, *p. 282*
stars, *p. 278*
strategic positioning, *p. 293*
strategic processes, *p. 293*
volume businesses, *p. 282*

Questions for Discussion

1. How does strategic analysis at the corporate level differ from strategic analysis at the business unit level? How are they related?
2. When would multibusiness companies find the portfolio approach to strategic analysis and choice useful?
3. What are three types of opportunities for sharing that form a sound basis for diversification or vertical integration? Give an example of each from companies you have read about.
4. Describe three types of opportunities through which a corporate parent could add value beyond the sum of its separate businesses.
5. What does "patching" refer to? Describe and illustrate two rules that might guide managers to build value in their businesses.

Chapter 9 Discussion Case

eBay's Changing Identity: *Best known for online auctions, the PayPal parent is building a diversified portfolio of Internet businesses. So why aren't investors happier?*

Meg Whitman, CEO, eBay

1 In its television ads, eBay describes itself as the place to get "it," whatever it may be. The company deliberately leaves "it" undefined to emphasize the immense variety of goods available for auction on its site. "It" is anything a consumer can imagine. But as eBay expands into myriad new businesses—from telecommunications to social networking—some investors are puzzling over what it (eBay) is becoming.

2 Since shelling out $1.5 billion in 2002 to acquire online payment processor PayPal, eBay has aggressively expanded into areas well beyond its core business of charging people fees to auction off goods via the Internet. Over the last five years, a spate of acquisitions—some of which are just now generating significant profits—has made the company into something of an enigma. EBay is a Web auctioneer. It's an online payment processor and bank of sorts (PayPal). It's a ticket seller (StubHub). It's a global Internet telephone service (Skype). It's a classified ad service (Kijiji).

3 Now eBay is said to be moving into the social search business. Tech industry blogs such as GigaOm and TechCrunch are buzzing that eBay is in talks to acquire StumbleUpon, a popular site that lets users find other Web sites based on their interests and the recommendations of others. Both eBay and StumbleUpon declined comment.

CORE CONCERNS

4 The difficulty of defining eBay and how its businesses fit together partially explains the subdued reaction to the company's 2007 earnings, a 52 percent increase over the prior year. Much of the growth stemmed from eBay's new businesses: "Our diverse portfolio of businesses that we began to build a few years ago is showing sustainable traction. We're extremely

pleased with their results this quarter," eBay chief executive Meg Whitman told analysts during a conference call.

5 Such growth would typically impress investors. Particularly when Wall Street was predicting lower growth than the revenues eBay reported. But investors didn't show much enthusiasm. The stock declined slightly after the announcement.

6 What's troubling investors is a slowdown in the company's "core" auction business, even as other businesses post gains. EBay's auction business accounts for 69 percent of its revenue. That business grew 23 percent, but investors have been used to growth rates of 40 percent. Active auction users grew 10 percent—a significant drop considering the category grew 25 percent during 2006 compared to the prior year. "Our concern is the core eBay business has been in a pretty steady downward spiral for several years now and it doesn't seem to be reversing itself," says Derek Brown, an analyst at Cantor Fitzgerald. Brown is recommending investors shed the stock.

7 The trouble with that view, say some analysts, is that it fails to see what eBay is evolving into. Tim Boyd, an analyst at American Technology Research who correctly anticipated eBay's revenues would beat the Street's expectations, sees eBay as an e-commerce and online advertising company that uses each business to fuel the other. "It doesn't make sense to look at this thing as solely an auction company anymore," says Boyd.

POSITIVE PRUNING?

8 Whitman attributed the year, in part, to more product listings turning into actual sales on eBay's site. The company's core auction business had suffered last year from sellers dumping slow-selling and patently unwanted merchandise in their eBay stores, as well as pricing some items too high for eBay's bargain-hunting audience. The result was a poorer experience for buyers and inventory that sat on the site far longer than desired, Whitman explained.

9 Last spring and summer, eBay raised fees by roughly 6 percent in order to encourage merchants to sell items people want and to price them to move. So far, the plan seems to be working. The site saw declines in the inventory that languished in eBay stores before selling or that didn't sell at all. "We are moving toward a better eBay marketplace," Whitman said during the call, cautioning that there was still work to do this year. Company CFO Bob Swan said that conversion rates have yet to reach their 2005 levels, but that they markedly improved since 2006.

10 In a note to investors, Goldman Sachs analyst Anthony Noto indicated he was pleased with eBay's efforts to "prune" low-quality listings. "EBay's focus on successful listings, as opposed to listings at any cost, is the key focus and driver of growth for eBay at this juncture," he wrote, adding "improved revenue-per-listing trends reinforce our view that eBay is at the early stages of a multi-quarter period of stabilizing-to-accelerating growth."

A PAL THAT PAYS

11 Indeed, eBay sees itself as a portfolio of companies that encompasses all the activities people perform on the Internet: trade, communicate, shop, search, and entertain. The eBay bulls see it as a diversified company with a hand in each one of the Internet's cash pots.

12 The newer members of eBay's portfolio are gaining momentum. PayPal revenue grew 31 percent in 2007. Its user base expanded 36 percent, to 143 million accounts. For eBay, an initial attraction of PayPal was its potential to enable sellers and buyers to share one trusted payment service instead of registering and working with multiple merchant bank cards. Facilitating transactions is important for eBay, which makes most of its money from taking a cut of sales.

13 PayPal's largest growth, however, has come from outside eBay. In the first quarter of 2007, it processed roughly $11.4 billion in transactions—about $4.4 billion was on non-eBay sites. That amount was a 51 percent increase from the prior year. For PayPal users, the service functions as something of an online bank, delivering interest, processing transactions, and even wiring money to friends through eBay's Internet phone service Skype. "The company [PayPal] has a lot of potential," says Matthew Kelmon, a portfolio manager at Kelmoore Investment, which owns eBay shares.

14 The big surprise of the season, however, was the strength of PayPal's services, which were supposed to be suffering at the hands of Google. PayPal posted revenues of $417 million, a 37 percent growth rate compared with 2005's fourth quarter. The payment-service company handled a record $11 billion in transactions, up 57 percent.

15 In fact, Whitman said that all the hype over Google Checkout actually boosted sales for market-leading PayPal, which reaped publicity amid the coverage of Google's foray. "I think we have disproportionately benefited from news in this category," Whitman said. She added that PayPal has an advantage over Google Checkout in that it's not just "a wrapper for Visa and Mastercard" but functions as an independent payment service.

16 Scott Devitt, an analyst at Stifel, Nicolaus & Company, says that acquiring PayPal was one of eBay's best moves. EBay purchased the payment company for $1.5 billion in 2002. "PayPal has just been phenomenal," says Devitt. "It is one of the best acquisitions in the history of the Internet in terms of the returns."

BRANCHING OUT

17 EBay jumped into the communications business by acquiring Skype in September 2005, for $2.6 billion plus stock. The service posted its first profitable quarter in 2007, growing 123 percent, to sales of $79 million, and adding 101 million new users. (Skype now has nearly 250 million customers.) EBay uses Skype to lubricate transactions by making it easier for consumers to talk to sellers, ask questions, and build trust. Skype also is a leader in the market for Web phones.

18 Despite the positive glow overall, the jury is still out on the eBay acquisition of Skype. While many analysts agree that the service has potential, they worry about eBay's ability to make money off of Skype's growing number of users. One positive sign: Google is working with Skype in developing click-to-call ads, says Devitt. The move may show that Google isn't so confident about being able to effectively challenge Skype for pay-per-call ads with its own competing service.

19 In the future, eBay could merge Skype with its classified advertising businesses to serve click-to-call ads, tapping into the market for local advertising. EBay is currently exploring such a service with Google and Yahoo! separately. Market researcher Borrell Associates estimates that about $8.6 billion will be spent on local Web ads in 2010.

20 EBay's advertising business and other small services also posted significant growth, swelling 65 percent to $60 million. This business is perhaps the most complicated of all because it is not confined to simply one kind of advertising. EBay has been serving classified ads through a network of foreign ad sites, such as Kijiji and Marktplaats, as well as via its 25 percent stake in Craigslist. It shares advertising revenue with Google, which serves search-related text ads on its non-U.S. auction pages. The company also has a wide-ranging advertising deal with Yahoo! By 2010, Internet advertising is expected to become a $27.8 billion market in the United States and a $29.5 billion market outside the United States, according to a January Oppenheimer & Co. report.

STUBHUB

21 In terms of acquisitions, Devitt also believes eBay picked a winner, for $310 million, in ticket reseller StubHub. EBay expects that the site will bring in between $105 and $120 million in 2007. That would help boost the company's overall revenues this year. During the call, eBay raised its revenue estimates for 2007 to between $7.05 and $7.3 billion for the full year. It predicts earnings-per-share growth of between 20 and 23 percent in the range of $1.25 to $1.29.

22 "StubHub has been extremely successful in the online tickets segment, and it's a perfect complement to eBay's tickets business," said Bill Cobb, president, eBay North America Marketplaces. "Together we can strengthen both businesses and provide fans with more choice and better service."

23 Standard & Poor's equity analyst Scott Kessler says Whitman is buying smart, for a price valuing StubHub at around three times what he estimates were its 2006 revenues. "We think this is a sound strategic move for eBay, which already has what we view as a strong tickets category," Kessler said in a research note. "We foresee notable business opportunities where StubHub would work with eBay, as well as PayPal, Shopping.com, and even Skype."

24   "StubHub's business model is an excellent fit with eBay, a company we've admired for a long time," StubHub CEO Jeff Fluhr said in the press release. "StubHub exists to serve passionate fans—and we feel great knowing our customers will benefit from the power of eBay and its community of users."

25   The 30-something Fluhr co-founded StubHub in March 2000, after getting the idea at Stanford Business School to resell hard-to-find tickets online for everything from concerts to sporting events. When asked in 2005 how he felt about going up against an 800-pound gorilla like eBay, he said he wouldn't underestimate them. But he also pointed out that his company has things like guaranteed fulfillment and integration with FedEx.

STUMBLING UPON NEW OPPORTUNITIES

26   With such large markets available for eBay's new businesses, it is not difficult to imagine a future in which eBay's auction business no longer dominates the company. EBay sees that long-term potential, though company executives underscore that a chief objective is to "reinvigorate" the core business. An acquisition such as StumbleUpon could help eBay's auction business by leveraging its recommendation technology to suggest other specific items related to goods sellers are bidding on or have bought. Currently, eBay recommends related categories of products.

27   Of course, eBay also could integrate Skype with StumbleUpon, using the call features to strengthen the networking aspects of both. It could potentially integrate the service with its classified ad business, using it to recommend ads related to products people are looking for.

28   Share gains aside, eBay thinks the stock merits a higher value and announced a plan to repurchase $2 billion in stock over the next two years. The plan shows the company's confidence in its ability to grow, says Devitt. He adds that he thinks the company will show mid- to upper-teens growth on a three-year basis.

29   With the variety of businesses that are now part of the company, what is eBay? More than just auctions—that's for sure.

Sources: Reprinted with special permission from Catherine Holahan, "eBay's Changing Identity," *BusinessWeek,* April 23, 2007; Catherine Holahan, "eBay Holds Its Turf Against Google," *BusinessWeek,* January 25, 2007; and "Is StubHub the Ticket for eBay?" *BusinessWeek,* January 11, 2007. Copyright © 2007 The McGraw-Hill Companies.

DISCUSSION QUESTIONS

1. What does eBay's corporate or multibusiness strategy for the twenty-first century appear to be?
2. List the businesses eBay is emphasizing and deemphasizing.
3. Which framework in this chapter—portfolio approach, leveraging core competencies, or parenting/patching—best helps explain what eBay is doing today in its corporate strategy? Why?
4. What appears to be the major advantage of this new eBay strategy and the major disadvantage or risk?
5. What would you advise Meg Whitman to do differently, and why?
6. Do you agree with her/eBay's approach and the logic of eBay moving from being an online auction–based company to being a broader, Internet services–based company? Why?

Part Three

Strategy Implementation, Control, and Innovation

The last section of this book examines what is often called the action phase of the strategic management process: implementation of the chosen strategy. Up to this point, three phases of that process have been covered—strategy formulation, analysis of alternative strategies, and strategic choice. Although important, these phases alone cannot ensure success.

To ensure success, the strategy must be translated into carefully implemented action. This means that

1. The strategy must be translated into guidelines for the daily activities of the firm's members.
2. The strategy and the firm must become one—that is, the strategy must be reflected in
   a. The way the firm organizes its activities.
   b. The key organization leaders.
   c. The culture of the organization.
3. The company's managers must put into place "steering" controls that provide strategic control and the ability to adjust strategies, commitments, and objectives in response to ever-changing future conditions.
4. Increasingly, organizations must make a serious commitment to be innovative and must consider bringing the entrepreneurship process into their company to survive, grow, and prosper in a vastly more competitive and rapidly changing global business arena.

Chapter 10 explains how organizational action is successfully initiated in four interrelated steps:

1. Creation of clear *short-term objectives* and *action plans*.
2. Development of specific *functional tactics*, to include *outsourcing*, that create competitive advantage.
3. Empowerment of operating personnel through *policies* to guide decisions.
4. Implementation of effective *reward systems*.

Short-term objectives and action plans guide implementation by converting long-term objectives into short-term actions and targets. Functional tactics, whether done internally or outsourced to other partners, translate the business strategy into activities that build advantage. Policies empower operating personnel by defining guidelines for making decisions. Reward systems encourage effective results.

Today's competitive environment requires careful analysis in designing the organizational structure most suitable to build and sustain competitive advantage. Chapter 11 examines traditional organizational structures—their pros and cons. It looks at the pervasive trend toward outsourcing, along with outsourcing's pros and cons. It concludes with examination of the latest developments in creating ambidextrous, virtual, boundaryless organizations designed to adapt in a highly interconnected, lightning-speed, global business environment.

There can be no doubt that effective organizational leadership and the consistency of a strong organizational culture reinforcing norms and behaviors best suited to the organization's mission are two central ingredients in enabling successful execution of a firm's strategies and objectives. Chapter 12 examines leadership, the critical things good leaders do, and how to nurture effective operating managers as they become outstanding future organizational leaders. Chapter 12 then examines the organizational culture, how it is shaped, and creative ways of managing the strategy-culture relationship.

Because the firm's strategy is implemented in a changing environment, successful implementation requires strategic control—an ability to "steer" the firm through an extended future time period when premises, sudden events, internal implementation efforts, and general economic and societal developments will be sources of change not anticipated or predicted when the strategy was conceived and initiated. Chapter 13 examines how to set up strategic controls to deal with the important steering function during the implementation process. The chapter also examines operational control functions and the balanced scorecard approach to integrating strategic and operational control.

The overriding concerns in executing strategies and leading a company are survival, growth, and prosperity. In a global economy that allows everyone everywhere instant information and instant connectivity, change often occurs at lightning speed. Thus, leaders are increasingly encouraging their firms to embrace innovation and entrepreneurship as key ways to respond to such overwhelming uncertainty. Chapter 14 examines innovation in general, different types of innovation, and the best ways to bring more innovative activity into a firm. It examines the entrepreneurship process as another way to build innovative responsiveness and opportunity recognition into a firm, both in new-venture settings and in large business organizations.

Implementation is "where the action is." It is the arena that most students enter at the start of their business careers. It is the strategic phase in which staying close to the customer, achieving competitive advantage, and pursuing excellence become realities. These five chapters in Part Three will help you understand how this is done and how to prepare to take your place as a future leader of successful, innovative business organizations.

Chapter **Ten**

Implementation

After reading and studying this chapter, you should be able to

1. Understand how short-term objectives are used in strategy implementation.

2. Identify and apply the qualities of good short-term objectives to your own experiences.

3. Illustrate what is meant by functional tactics and understand how they are used in strategy implementation.

4. Gain a general sense of what outsourcing is and how it becomes a choice in functional tactics decisions for strategy implementation.

5. Understand what policies are and how to use policies to empower operating personnel in implementing business strategies and functional tactics.

6. Understand the use of financial reward in executive compensation.

7. Identify different types of executive compensation and when to use each in strategy implementation.

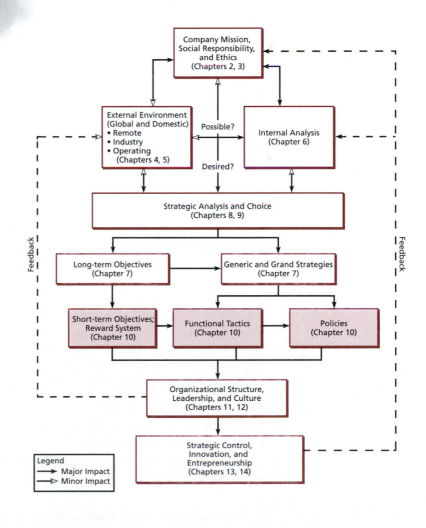

Xerox and Hewlett-Packard faced difficult times as this decade began. For Xerox, bankruptcy was a real possibility given its $14 billion debt and its serious problems with the U.S. Securities and Exchange Commission. Hewlett-Packard was falling behind in the computer business while living solely on profits from its printer division. Anne Mulcahy became Xerox CEO during this time. Carly Fiorina became HP's CEO. Five years later, Anne Mulcahy was celebrated for the success of her strategy at Xerox while Carly Fiorina was dismissed for the failure of the path she chose. Two legendary technology companies and two celebrated CEOs who shattered the "glass ceiling" in being selected to lead two legendary companies back to glory: why did one succeed and the other fail?

Analysts suggest that the "devil is in the detail." Fiorina's strategy was to acquire Compaq, build the size of HP's PC business, and use profits from HP's venerable printer business to sustain a reorganization of the combined companies. Mark Anderson, an investment analyst who has followed HP for more than 20 years, said this about Carly Fiorina's strategy:

> I would say it stinks, but it isn't even a strategy. A few bullet points don't make a strategy.
> Such an approach lacks the technical and market understanding necessary to drive HP.[1]

In other words, Carly Fiorina's strategy was a glitzy combination of two large computer companies, but it was less clear exactly what key actions and tactics would bring about a reinvented, "new," profitable HP.

Anne Mulcahy took a different approach, in part reflecting her 28 years inside Xerox. She set about to "reinvent" Xerox as well, but made four functional tactics and their respective short-term objectives very clear building blocks for reinventing Xerox: (1) She prioritized aggressive cost cutting—30 percent—throughout the company to restore profitability. (2) She emphasized a productivity increase in each Xerox division. (3) She quickly settled Xerox's SEC litigation about its accounting practices, and she refinanced Xerox's massive debt. (4) She made a major point of continued heavy R&D funding even as every other part of Xerox suffered through severe cost cutting. This, she felt, sent a message of belief in Xerox's future. It clearly established her priorities.

Mulcahy's articulation of specific tactical efforts, and the short-term objectives they were intended to achieve, turned Xerox around in three short years. As she proudly pointed out:

> Probably one of the hardest things was to continue investing in the future, in growth. One of the most controversial decisions we made was to continue our R&D investment. When you're drastically restructuring in other areas, that's a tough decision. It makes it harder for the other businesses to some extent. But it was important for the Xerox people to believe we were investing in the future. Now two-thirds of our revenue is coming from products and services introduced in the last two years.[2]

The reason Anne Mulcahy succeeded while Carly Fiorina did not, the focus of this chapter, involves translating strategic thought into organizational action. In the words of two well-worn phrases, they move from "planning their work" to "working their plan." Anne Mulcahy successfully made this shift at Xerox when she did these five things well:

1. Identify short-term objectives.
2. Initiate specific functional tactics.
3. Outsource nonessential functions.
4. Communicate policies that empower people in the organization.
5. Design effective rewards.

[1] "The Only HP Way Worth Trying," Viewpoint, *BusinessWeek,* March 9, 2005.
[2] "She Put the Bounce Back in Xerox," *BusinessWeek,* January 10, 2005.

Short-term objectives translate long-range aspirations into this year's targets for action. If well developed, these objectives provide clarity, a powerful motivator and facilitator of effective strategy implementation.

Functional tactics translate business strategy into daily activities people need to execute. Functional managers participate in the development of these tactics, and their participation, in turn, helps clarify what their units are expected to do in implementing the business's strategy.

Outsourcing nonessential functions normally performed in-house frees up resources and the time of key people to concentrate on leveraging the functions and activities critical to the core competitive advantages around which the firm's long range strategy is built.

Policies are empowerment tools that simplify decision making by empowering operating managers and their subordinates. Policies can empower the "doers" in an organization by reducing the time required to decide and act.

Rewards that align manager and employee priorities with organizational objectives and shareholder value provide very effective direction in strategy implementation.

SHORT-TERM OBJECTIVES

short-term objective
Measurable outcomes achievable or intended to be achieved in one year or less.

Chapter 7 described business strategies, grand strategies, and long-term objectives that are critically important in crafting a successful future. To make them become a reality, however, the people in an organization who actually "do the work" of the business need guidance in exactly what they need to do. Short-term objectives help do this. **Short-term objectives** are measurable outcomes achievable or intended to be achieved in one year or less. They are specific, usually quantitative, results operating managers set out to achieve in the immediate future.

Short-term objectives help implement strategy in at least three ways:

1. Short-term objectives "operationalize" long-term objectives. If we commit to a 20 percent gain in revenue over five years, what is our specific target or objective in revenue during the current year, month, or week to indicate we are making appropriate progress?

2. Discussion about and agreement on short-term objectives help raise issues and potential conflicts within an organization that usually require coordination to avoid otherwise dysfunctional consequences. Exhibit 10.1 illustrates how objectives within marketing, manufacturing, and accounting units within the same firm can be very different even when created to pursue the same firm objective (e.g., increased sales, lower costs).

3. Finally, short-term objectives assist strategy implementation by identifying measurable outcomes of action plans or functional activities, which can be used to make feedback, correction, and evaluation more relevant and acceptable.

Short-term objectives are usually accompanied by action plans, which enhance these objectives in three ways. First, action plans usually identify functional tactics and activities that will be undertaken in the next week, month, or quarter as part of the business's effort to build competitive advantage. The important point here is *specificity*—what exactly is to be done. We will examine functional tactics in a subsequent section of this chapter. The second element of an action plan is a clear *time frame for completion*—when the effort will begin and when its results will be accomplished. A third element action plans contain is identification of *who is responsible* for each action in the plan. This accountability is very important to ensure action plans are acted upon.

Because of the particular importance of short-term objectives in strategy implementation, the next section addresses how to develop meaningful short-term objectives. Exhibit 10.2, Top Strategist, provides a *BusinessWeek* interview with Symantec CEO John Thompson about the nature and importance of short-term objectives to Symantec's success.

EXHIBIT 10.1
Potential Conflicting Objectives and Priorities

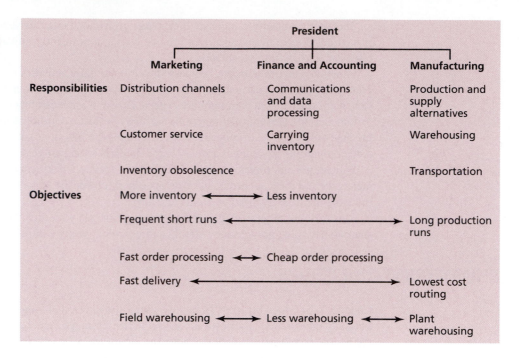

Qualities of Effective Short-Term Objectives

Measurable

Short-term objectives are more consistent when they clearly state *what* is to be accomplished, *when* it will be accomplished, and *how* its accomplishment will be *measured*. Such objectives can be used to monitor both the effectiveness of each activity and the collective progress across several interrelated activities. Exhibit 10.3 illustrates several effective and ineffective short-term objectives. Measurable objectives make misunderstanding less likely among interdependent managers who must implement action plans. It is far easier to quantify the objectives of *line* units (e.g., production) than of certain *staff* areas (e.g., personnel). Difficulties in quantifying objectives often can be overcome by initially focusing on *measurable activity* and then identifying *measurable outcomes*.

Priorities

Although all annual objectives are important, some deserve priority because of a timing consideration or their particular impact on a strategy's success. If such priorities are not established, conflicting assumptions about the relative importance of annual objectives may inhibit progress toward strategic effectiveness. Anne Mulcahy's turnaround of Xerox described at the beginning of this chapter emphasized several important short-term objectives. But it was clear throughout Xerox that her highest priority in the first two years was to dramatically lower overhead and production costs so as to satisfy the difficult challenge of continuing to invest heavily in R&D while also restoring profitability.

Priorities are established in various ways. A simple ranking may be based on discussion and negotiation during the planning process. However, this does not necessarily communicate the real difference in the importance of objectives, so such terms as primary, top, and secondary may be used to indicate priority. Some firms assign weights (e.g., 0 to 100 percent) to establish and communicate the relative priority of objectives. Whatever the method, recognizing priorities is an important dimension in the implementation value of short-term objectives.

Top Strategist
John Thompson, Chairman and CEO of Symantec

**Exhibit
10.2**

**John Thompson, Chairman
and CEO of Symantec**

"If you could only monitor five objectives to run/steer your business, what would they be and why?" is a question *BusinessWeek* posed to John Thompson, chairman and CEO of Symantec, a Cupertino (California)-based Internet security outfit that makes antivirus and firewall technology as it implemented a merger with Veritas in 2005. Since Thompson joined Symantec as top exec, revenues have grown eightfold, from $632 million to more than $5.3 billion in 2007.

Q: So what would be your critical objectives, and why?

A: Let's define what objectives are: They are vectors for how you are performing now, but also indicators for how you will do in the future. Here are five critical objectives I use to manage Symantec. Our most critical objectives are customer satisfaction and market share.

CUSTOMER SATISFACTION
We use an outside firm to poll customers on a continuous basis to determine their satisfaction with our products and services. This needs to be an anonymous relationship—a conversation between our pollster and our customers. Polling is done by product area: firewall, antivirus, services, and other product lines.

MARKET SHARE
There are a couple of ways we look at this. We have our own views based on relevant markets. Then we use industry analysts such as Gartner, IDC, and Giga as benchmarks for annualized results on market share. On a quarterly basis, we look at our revenue performance and growth rates, and that of our competitors. We compare against actual realized growth rates, as compared to growth rates of relevant competitors in similar segments.

The purpose is to get trending data. That gives us a sense of market changes and market growth. We also use a blended (rating) of analyst companies in the same space. Each industry-analyst firm counts things a bit differently, based on its methodology. The numbers don't have to be spot on or Six Sigma precise.

REVENUE GROWTH
You have to consider if revenue is growing at a rate equal to or greater than the market rate. If you look at the antivirus market, for example, industry analysts projected growth in the high teens while our enterprise antivirus sector grew at a rate of 32 percent. This indicates that we are gaining market share faster than the market growth rate for the industry.

We can then assess how we had planned to grow. Did we plan to grow at 32 percent or less—or more? You have to gauge your growth relative to the market for your product or service and your own internal expectations of your performance.

EXPENSES
It is important to always plan for how much money will have to be spent to generate a certain level of revenue. This enables you to monitor funds flow in the company. Did I plan to spend $10 or $12, and what did I get for that expense in return? The purpose is to keep expenses in equilibrium to revenue generation.

EARNINGS
Two keys to watch here—operating margins and earnings per share (EPS). A business running efficiently is improving its operating margins. If you are efficient in your operating margins, this should produce a strong EPS, which is a strong objective that Wall Street looks at all the time.

Q: What problems do tracking objectives solve for a corporation? How does maintaining objectives help you manage and steer the direction of the corporation?

A: I am a little old-fashioned—I don't believe you can manage what you don't measure. The importance of objectives becomes more important as the enterprise grows in size and scale. Objectives also serve as an indication for

(continued)

Exhibit 10.2 cont.

the team about what you are paying attention to. If employees know you are measuring market growth and customer satisfaction, they will pay attention to those considerations and will behave based on indicators that you, as the leader, provide to the organization. Objectives helps the team focus on what's important for an organization.

Q: How should companies consider industry-specific objectives versus broad financial objectives: P/E [price to earnings] ratio, etc?

A: This is an issue for all of us. I am on the board of a utility company. The company has achieved modest single-digit revenue growth. They are quite proud of that, while I would be quite concerned if that were to be the growth rate for a software firm. For example: An important consideration may be what you are spending in R&D in comparison to your peer group. Or, for a software firm, what is the license revenue mix?

I couldn't care less about the performance of Symantec relative to that of a financial-services company. But I would care about the performance of Symantec in comparison with an enterprise software company or with another securities software firm. Whatever measures you choose should give you the ability to measure your performance against like-industry companies.

Q: What do new managers need to keep in mind as they consider/reevaluate the use of objectives for their companies?

A: Live by the adage that you can't manage what you can't measure. The best objectives are simple to understand, simple to communicate, and relatively easy for everyone to get access to the data that represents the results. That makes your objectives an effective management tool. If you make your objectives difficult to gather, manage, or communicate, they won't be effective. Simplicity is key.

My experience has proven to me the importance of picking the few objectives that are the most critical for the running of the business. Stick with them—and communicate them to both internal and external audiences.

Sources: Reprinted with special permission from "Symantec's CEO Takes the Long View," *BusinessWeek,* February 28, 2007; Sarah Lacy, "Symantec's John Thompson: I Can't Wait to Compete," *BusinessWeek,* March 21, 2005; and Sarah Lacy, "A Revolution in John Thompson's Head," *BusinessWeek,* April 28, 2005. Copyright © 2007 The McGraw-Hill Companies.

Cascading: From Long-Term Objectives to Short-Term Objectives

The link between short-term and long-term objectives should resemble cascades through the firm from basic long-term objectives to specific short-term objectives in key operation areas. The cascading effect has the added advantage of providing a clear reference for communication and negotiation, which may be necessary to integrate and coordinate objectives and activities at the operating level.

3M's recent refocus on growth, particularly in international markets, provides a good example of cascading objectives. 3M's CEO, George Buckley, has had to aggressively seek to turn around the company's declining performance by accelerating sales growth while financing the growth internally by improving cash flow and profitability. Currently, 60 percent of 3M's sales come from outside the United States and Buckley expects that to rise to 75 percent in two years. At the same time, only 35 percent of their manufacturing and distribution facilities are located outside the United States. To achieve 3M's sales goals, and growth abroad, operating managers have set an objective of 18 new plants or major expansions online within the next two years, with 11 new plants being outside the United States and four of those in China alone. Managers of 3M's logistic chain have identified lowering the number of "days 3M products spend traveling through its supply lines" as a critical objective to increase cash flow, which in turn helps free up cash to build these new plants. Currently, a typical product might be extruded in Canada, machined in France, packaged

EXHIBIT 10.3
Creating Measurable
Objectives

Examples of Deficient Objectives	Examples of Objectives with Measurable Criteria for Performance
To improve morale in the division (plant, department, etc.)	To reduce turnover (absenteeism, number of rejects, etc.) among sales managers by 10 percent by January 1, 2008. *Assumption:* Morale is related to measurable outcomes (i.e., high and low morale are associated with different results).
To improve support of the sales effort	To reduce the time lapse between order data and delivery by 8 percent (two days) by June 1, 2008. To reduce the cost of goods produced by 6 percent to support a product price decrease of 2 percent by December 1, 2008. To increase the rate of before- or on-schedule delivery by 5 percent by June 1, 2008.
To improve the firm's image	To conduct a public opinion poll using random samples in the five largest U.S. metropolitan markets to determine average scores on 10 dimensions of corporate responsibility by May 15, 2008. To increase our score on those dimensions by an average of 7.5 percent by May 1, 2008.

in Mexico, and sold in Japan—tying up a sizable inventory around the world just sitting on boats, in trucks, and in warehouses—currently averaging 100 days. Supply chain managers have the objective of freeing up $1 billion in working capital, and $200 million in cost savings annually from a more efficient supply chain. Buckley will be monitoring working capital as a percent of sales which, as it declines, provides the needed internal cash flow to achieve the overall goal of international plant and facilities expansion.[3]

FUNCTIONAL TACTICS THAT IMPLEMENT BUSINESS STRATEGIES

functional tactics
Detailed statements of the "means" or activities that will be used by a company to achieve short-term objectives and establish competitive advantage.

Functional tactics are the key, routine activities that must be undertaken in each functional area—marketing, finance, production/operations, R&D, and human resource management—to provide the business's products and services. In a sense, functional tactics translate thought (grand strategy) into action designed to accomplish specific short-term objectives. Every value chain activity in a company executes functional tactics that support the business's strategy and help accomplish strategic objectives.

Exhibit 10.5 Strategy in Action, illustrates the difference between functional tactics and business strategy. It also shows that functional tactics are essential to implement business strategy. It explains the situation at California Pizza Kitchen, where consultants were brought in to identify specific tactical things employees needed to do or deal with to implement an overall business strategy to differentiate the growing pizza chain from many other restaurant competitors. The business strategy outlined the competitive posture of its operations in the restaurant industry. To increase the likelihood that these strategies would be successful, specific functional tactics were needed for the firm's operating components. These functional tactics clarified the business strategy, giving specific,

[3] Brian Hindo, "3M Chief Plants a Money Tree," *BusinessWeek Online,* June 11, 2007.

EXHIBIT 10.4
The Value-Added Benefit of Short-Term Objectives and Action Plans

Source: Reprinted with special permission from Brian Hindo, "3M Chief Plants a Money Tree," *BusinessWeek Online,* June 11, 2007. Copyright © 2007 The McGraw-Hill Companies.

- They give operating personnel a better understanding of their role in the firm's mission.
- The process of developing them becomes a forum for raising and resolving conflicts between strategic intent and operational reality.
- They provide a basis for developing budgets, schedules, trigger points, and other sources of strategic control.
- They can be powerful motivators, especially when connected to the reward system.

short-term guidance to operating managers and employees in the areas of marketing, operations, and finance.

Differences between Business Strategies and Functional Tactics

Functional tactics are different from business or corporate strategies in three fundamental ways:

1. Time horizon.
2. Specificity.
3. Participants who develop them.

Time Horizon

Functional tactics identify activities to be undertaken "now" or in the immediate future. Business strategies focus on the firm's posture three to five years out. Exhibit 10.6, Strategy in Action, shows functional tactics turnaround CEO Alan Mulally seeks to implement in five strategic areas of concern at Ford Motor Company.

The shorter time horizon of functional tactics is critical to the successful implementation of a business strategy for two reasons. First, it focuses the attention of functional managers on what needs to be done *now* to make the business strategy work. Second, it allows functional managers like those at 3M to adjust to changing current conditions.

Specificity

Functional tactics are more specific than business strategies. Business strategies provide general direction. Functional tactics identify the specific activities that are to be undertaken in each functional area and thus allow operating managers to work out *how* their unit is expected to pursue short-term objectives. Exhibit 10.5, Strategy in Action, illustrated the nature and value of specificity in functional tactics versus business strategy at California Pizza Kitchen.

Specificity in functional tactics contributes to successful implementation by

- Helping ensure that functional managers know what needs to be done and can focus on accomplishing results.
- Clarifying for top management how functional managers intend to accomplish the business strategy, which increases top management's confidence in and sense of control over the business strategy.
- Facilitating coordination among operating units within the firm by clarifying areas of interdependence and potential conflict.

Participants

Different people participate in strategy development at the functional and business levels. Business strategy is the responsibility of the general manager of a business unit. That manager typically delegates the development of functional tactics to subordinates charged with running the operating areas of the business. The manager of a business unit must

The Nature and Value of Specificity in Functional Tactics versus Business Strategy

A restaurant business was encountering problems. Although its management had agreed unanimously that it was committed to a business strategy to differentiate itself from other competitors based on concept and customer service rather than price, California Pizza Kitchen continued to encounter inconsistencies across different store locations in how well it did this. Consultants indicated that the customer experience varied greatly from store to store. The conclusion was that while the management understood the "business strategy," and the employees did too in general terms, the implementation was inadequate because of a lack of specificity in the functional tactics—what everyone should do every day in the restaurant—to make the vision a reality in terms of the customers' dining experience. The following breakdown of part of their business strategy into specific functional tactics just in the area of customer service helps illustrate the value specificity in functional tactics brings to strategy implementation.

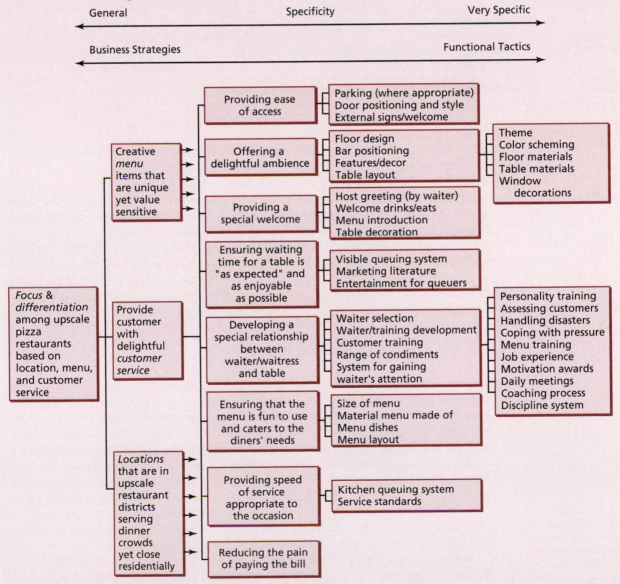

Sources: Adapted from Dennis Milton, "California Pizza Kitchen: Say Cheese!," *BusinessWeek*, July 15, 2003; and A. Campbell and K. Luchs, Eds., *Core Competency – Based Strategy* (London: Thompson, 1997).

The Mulally Difference in Key Tactics to Save Ford Motor Company

How Things Are Changing at Ford Now That the New Boss Has Arrived

	Before	After
Organization	Regional fiefdoms. Every global market has had its own strategy and products.	Mulally wants to break down geographic hierarchies and create a single worldwide organization.
Division chief meetings	Held monthly. Lots of happy talk. Little information sharing.	Held weekly. Discussing problems is encouraged. Goal is to spot red flags early.
Product mix	Emphasis on trucks, SUVs, niche sports cars.	Focus is shifting to passenger cars and or crossovers.
Brand vision	To diversify away from ford brand. The company acquired dysfunctional luxury brands.	Strengthen the traditional blue oval Ford brand. Sell off or close poor-performing brands.
Promotions	Managers changed jobs frequently to develop their skills.	Executives stay in place, winning only promotions that are deserved.

Source: Reprinted with special permission from "The Mulally Difference," *BusinessWeek*, June 7, 2007. Copyright © 2007 The McGraw-Hill Companies.

establish long-term objectives and a strategy that corporate management feels contributes to corporate-level goals. Similarly, key operating managers must establish short-term objectives and operating strategies that contribute to business-level goals. Just as business strategies and objectives are approved through negotiation between corporate managers and business managers, so, too, are short-term objectives and functional tactics approved through negotiation between business managers and operating managers.

Involving operating managers in the development of functional tactics improves their understanding of what must be done to achieve long-term objectives and, thus, contributes to successful implementation. It also helps ensure that functional tactics reflect the reality of the day-to-day operating situation. And perhaps most important, it can increase the commitment of operating managers to the strategies developed.

OUTSOURCING FUNCTIONAL ACTIVITIES

A generation ago, it was conventional wisdom that a business has a better chance of success if it controls the doing of everything necessary to produce its products or services. Referring back to Chapter 6's value chain approach, the "wise" manager would have sought to maintain control of virtually all the "primary" activities and the "support" activities associated with the firm's work. Not any longer. Starting for most firms with the outsourcing of producing payroll each week, companies worldwide are embracing the idea that the best way to implement their strategies is to retain responsibility for executing some functions while seeking outside people and companies to do key support and key primary activities where they can do so more effectively and more inexpensively. **Outsourcing,** then, is acquiring an activity, service, or product necessary to provide a company's products or services from "outside" the people or operations controlled by that acquiring company.

outsourcing
Obtaining work previously done by employees inside the companies from sources outside the company.

DuPont Co. has always run corporate training and development out of its Wilmington (Delaware) head office. But these days, Boston-based Forum Corp. handles it instead. In Somers, New York, PepsiCo Inc. employees, long used to receiving personal financial planning from their employer, now get that service from KPMG Peat Marwick. Denver's TeleTech Holdings Inc. is taking customer-service calls from AT&T customers and books seat reservations for Continental Airlines.

Wyck Hay's first entrepreneurial effort was a smashing success: The co-founder of herbal tea maker Celestial Seasonings helped sell the company to Kraft Foods for $40 million in 1984. But Hay found managing 300 employees a headache. So when he launched Woodside (California)-based Kaboom Beverages a few years ago, he kept a decidedly small payroll: himself. In lieu of a workforce, Hay assembled a team of contractors to perform every task at his $2 million business—from label design to manufacturing of his "power juice" drinks. Hay said outsourcing saves him at least 30 percent, while minimizing his daily distractions. "I don't know that I ever plan to hire any employees," he mused.[4]

Relentless cost cutting is the main force behind the trend. BellSouth Corp., which shed 13,200 employees over two years, outsourced about $60 million in services to replace them. Companies are parceling out everything from mailroom management to customer service, from pieces of human resources departments to manufacturing and distribution. "We're at the beginning of an explosion," predicts Scott Hartz, managing partner of Price-waterhouseCoopers consulting group. "Many of the firms doing more outsourcing aren't troubled corporations trying to save a nickel. They are often the corporate leaders." All major corporations now outsource at least some services.[5] Exhibit 10.7 provides a summary of the increase in outsourcing.

It's hardly just rote work that's being outsourced—even such key functions as marketing are now up for bidding. "Some CEOs say they'd rather focus on operations and finance," says Dave Camp, the director of creative services at Bellevue (Washington)-based Out-source Marketing. The 12-person company originally provided basic marketing support to small clients. Today, it acts as the full marketing department for some clients.[6]

The hype over outsourcing's benefits, however, disguises numerous problems. General Electric Co. stubbed its toe when the introduction of a new washing machine was delayed by production problems at a contractor to whom it had farmed out key work. GE only lost three weeks as a result of the glitches, but it could have been worse. Southern Pacific Rail Corp. suffered through myriad computer breakdowns and delays after outsourcing its internal computer network to IBM.

The important point to recognize at this point is that functional activities long associated with doing the work of any business organization are increasingly subject to be outsourced if they can be done more cost effectively by other providers. So it becomes critical for managers implementing strategic plans to focus company activities on functions deemed central to the company's competitive advantage and to seek others outside the firm's structure to provide the functions that are necessary, but not within the scope of the firm's core competencies. And, increasingly, this decision considers every organizational activity fair game—even marketing, product design, innovation. We will explore this in greater detail in Chapter 11.

EMPOWERING OPERATING PERSONNEL: THE ROLE OF POLICIES

Specific functional tactics provide guidance and initiate action implementing a business's strategy, but more is needed. Supervisors and personnel in the field have been charged in today's competitive environment with being responsible for customer value—for being

---

[4] Dean Foust, et al., "The Outsourcing Food Chain," *BusinessWeek Online,* March 11, 2004.

[5] Steven Goldman, "Dynamism as the Norm," *BusinessWeek Online,* April 18, 2005.

[6] Ibid.

EXHIBIT 10.7
Outsourcing Is Increasing

Source: Estimated based on various articles in *BusinessWeek* on outsourcing.

ORDERING OUT... Companies That Say They Outsource Some Functional Activity		
	Yes	No
2008	98%	2%
2000	75	25
1995	52	48
1990	23	77
. . . FOR EVERYTHING Functional Activities Most Frequently Outsourced		
Payroll	75%	
Manufacturing	72	
Maintenance	68	
Warehousing/transportation/distribution	62	
Information technology	52	
Travel	48	
Temporary service	48	
HR activities (varied)	40	
Product design	35	
R&D	25	
Marketing	22	

the "front line" of the company's effort to truly meet customers' needs. Meeting customer needs is a buzzword regularly cited as a key priority by most business organizations. Efforts to do so often fail because employees that are the real contact point between the business and its customers are not empowered to make decisions or act to fulfill customer needs. One solution has been to empower operating personnel by pushing down decision making to their level. General Electric allows appliance repair personnel to decide about warranty credits on the spot, a decision that used to take several days and multiple organizational levels. American Air Lines allows customer service personnel and their supervisors wide range in resolving customer ticket pricing decisions. Federal Express couriers make decisions and handle package routing information that involves five management levels in the U.S. Postal Service.

empowerment
The act of allowing an individual or team the right and flexibility to make decisions and initiate action.

Empowerment is the act of allowing an individual or team the right and flexibility to make decisions and initiate action. It is being expanded and widely advocated in many organizations today. Training, self-managed work groups, eliminating whole levels of management in organizations, and aggressive use of automation are some of the ways and ramifications of this fundamental change in the way business organizations function. At the heart of the effort is the need to ensure that decision making is consistent with the mission, strategy, and tactics of the business while at the same time allowing considerable latitude to operating personnel. One way operating managers do this is through the use of policies.

policies
Broad, precedent-setting decisions that guide or substitute for repetitive or time-sensitive managerial decision making.

Policies are directives designed to guide the thinking, decisions, and actions of managers and their subordinates in implementing a firm's strategy. Sometimes called *standard operating procedures,* policies increase managerial effectiveness by standardizing many routine decisions and clarifying the discretion managers and subordinates can exercise in implementing functional tactics. Logically, policies should be derived from functional

Selected Policies That Aid Strategy Implementation

3M Corporation has a *personnel policy,* called the *15 percent rule,* that allows virtually any employee to spend up to 15 percent of the workweek on anything that he or she wants to, as long as it's product related. (This policy supports 3M's corporate strategy of being a highly innovative manufacturer, with each division required to have a quarter of its annual sales come from products introduced within the past five years.)

Wendy's has a *purchasing policy* that gives local store managers the authority to buy fresh meat and produce locally, rather than from regionally designated or company-owned sources. (This policy supports Wendy's functional strategy of having fresh, unfrozen hamburgers daily.)

General Cinema has a *financial policy* that requires annual capital investment in movie theaters not to exceed annual depreciation. (By seeing that capital investment is no greater than depreciation, this policy supports General Cinema's financial strategy of maximizing cash flow—in this case, all profit—to its growth areas. The policy also reinforces General Cinema's financial strategy of leasing as much as possible.)

Crown, Cork, and Seal Company has an *R&D policy* of not investing any financial or people resources in basic research. (This policy supports Crown, Cork, and Seal's functional strategy, which emphasizes customer services, not technical leadership.)

Bank of America has an *operating policy* that requires annual renewal of the financial statement of all personal borrowers. (This policy supports Bank of America's financial strategy, which seeks to maintain a loan-to-loss ratio below the industry norm.)

tactics (and, in some instances, from corporate or business strategies) with the key purpose of aiding strategy execution.[7] Exhibit 10.8, Strategy in Action, illustrates selected policies of several well-known firms.

Creating Policies That Empower

Policies communicate guidelines to decisions. They are designed to control decisions while defining allowable discretion within which operational personnel can execute business activities. They do this in several ways:

1. *Policies establish indirect control over independent action* by clearly stating how things are to be done *now.* By defining discretion, policies in effect control decisions yet empower employees to conduct activities without direct intervention by top management.

2. *Policies promote uniform handling of similar activities.* This facilitates the coordination of work tasks and helps reduce friction arising from favoritism, discrimination, and the disparate handling of common functions—something that often hampers operating personnel.

---

[7] The term *policy* has various definitions in management literature. Some authors and practitioners equate policy with strategy. Others do this inadvertently by using "policy" as a synonym for company mission, purpose, or culture. Still other authors and practitioners differentiate policy in terms of "levels" associated, respectively, with purpose, mission, and strategy. "Our policy is to make a positive contribution to the communities and societies we live in" and "Our policy is not to diversify out of the hamburger business" are two examples of the breadth of what some call policies. This book defines *policy* much more narrowly as specific guides to managerial action and decisions in the implementation of strategy. This definition permits a sharper distinction between the formulation and implementation of functional strategies. And, of even greater importance, it focuses the tangible value of the policy concept where it can be most useful—as a key administrative tool to enhance effective implementation and execution of strategy.

3. *Policies ensure quicker decisions* by standardizing answers to previously answered questions that otherwise would recur and be pushed up the management hierarchy again and again—something that requires unnecessary levels of management between senior decision makers and field personnel.

4. *Policies institutionalize basic aspects of organization behavior.* This minimizes conflicting practices and establishes consistent patterns of action in attempts to make the strategy work—again, freeing operating personnel to act.

5. *Policies reduce uncertainty in repetitive and day-to-day decision making,* thereby providing a necessary foundation for coordinated, efficient efforts and freeing operating personnel to act.

6. *Policies counteract resistance to or rejection of chosen strategies by organization members.* When major strategic change is undertaken, unambiguous operating policies clarify what is expected and facilitate acceptance, particularly when operating managers participate in policy development.

7. *Policies offer predetermined answers to routine problems.* This greatly expedites dealing with both ordinary and extraordinary problems—with the former, by referring to these answers; with the latter, by giving operating personnel more time to cope with them.

8. *Policies afford managers a mechanism for avoiding hasty and ill-conceived decisions in changing operations.* Prevailing policy can always be used as a reason for not yielding to emotion-based, expedient, or temporarily valid arguments for altering procedures and practices.

Policies may be written and formal or unwritten and informal. Informal, unwritten policies are usually associated with a strategic need for competitive secrecy. Some policies of this kind, such as promotion from within, are widely known (or expected) by employees and implicitly sanctioned by management. Managers and employees often like the latitude granted by unwritten and informal policies. However, such policies may detract from the long-term success of a strategy. Formal, written policies have at least seven advantages:

1. They require managers to think through the policy's meaning, content, and intended use.
2. They reduce misunderstanding.
3. They make equitable and consistent treatment of problems more likely.
4. They ensure unalterable transmission of policies.
5. They communicate the authorization or sanction of policies more clearly.
6. They supply a convenient and authoritative reference.
7. They systematically enhance indirect control and organizationwide coordination of the key purposes of policies.

The strategic significance of policies can vary. At one extreme are such policies as travel reimbursement procedures, which are really work rules and may not have an obvious link to the implementation of a strategy. Exhibit 10.9, Strategy in Action, provides an interesting example of how the link between a simple policy and strategy implementation regarding customer service can have serious negative consequences when it is neither obvious to operating personnel nor well thought out by bank managers. At the other extreme are organizationwide policies that are virtually functional strategies, such as Wendy's requirement that every location invest 1 percent of its gross revenue in local advertising.

Policies can be externally imposed or internally derived. Policies regarding equal employment practices are often developed in compliance with external (government) requirements, and policies regarding leasing or depreciation may be strongly influenced by current tax regulations.

Regardless of the origin, formality, and nature of policies, the key point to bear in mind is that they can play an important role in strategy implementation. Communicating specific policies will help overcome resistance to strategic change, empower people to act, and foster commitment to successful strategy implementation.

Policies empower people to act. Compensation, at least theoretically, rewards their action. The last decade has seen many firms realize that the link between compensation, particularly executive management compensation, and value-building strategic outcomes within their firms was uncertain. The recognition of this uncertainty has brought about increased recognition of the need to link management compensation with the successful implementation of strategies that build long-term shareholder value. The next section examines this development and major types of executive bonus compensation plans.

BONUS COMPENSATION PLANS[8]

Major Plan Types

Company shareholders typically believe that the goal of a bonus compensation plan is to motivate executives and key employees to achieve maximization of shareholder wealth. Because shareholders are both owners and investors of the firm, they desire a reasonable return on their investment. Because they are absentee landlords, shareholders expect their board of directors to ensure that the decision-making logic of their firm's executives to be concurrent with their own primary motivation.

However, the goal of shareholder wealth maximization is not the only goal that executives may pursue. Alternatively, executives may choose actions that increase their personal compensation, power, and control. Therefore, an executive compensation plan that contains

---

[8] We wish to thank Roy Hossler for his assistance on this section.

EXHIBIT 10.10 **Types of Executive Bonus Compensation**

Bonus Type	Description	Rationale	Shortcomings
Stock option grants	Right to purchase stock in the future at a price set now. Compensation is determined by "spread" between option price and exercise price.	Provides incentive for executive to create wealth for shareholders as measured by increase in firm's share price.	Movement in share price does not explain all dimensions of managerial performance.
Restricted stock plan	Shares given to executive who is prohibited from selling them for a specific time period. May also include performance restrictions.	Promotes longer executive tenure than other forms of compensation.	No downside risk to executive, who always profits unlike other shareholders.
Golden handcuffs	Bonus income deferred in a series of annual installments. Deferred amounts not yet paid are forfeited with executive resignation.	Offers an incentive for executive to remain with the firm.	May promote risk-averse decision making due to downside risk borne by executive.
Golden parachute	Executives have right to collect the bonus if they lose position due to takeover, firing, retirement, or resignation.	Offers an incentive for executive to remain with the firm.	Compensation is achieved whether or not wealth is created for shareholders. Rewards either success or failure.
Cash based on internal business performance using financial measures	Bonus compensation based on accounting performance measures such as return on equity.	Offsets the limitations of focusing on market-based measures of performance.	Weak correlation between earnings measures and shareholder wealth creation. Annual earnings do not capture future impact of current decisions.

a bonus component can be used to orient management's decision making toward the owners' goals. The success of bonus compensation as an incentive hinges on a proper match between an executive bonus plan and the firm's strategic objectives. As one author has written, "Companies can succeed by clarifying their business vision or strategy and aligning company pay programs with its strategic direction."[9] Exhibit 10.10 summarizes five types of executive compensation plans we will now explore in more detail.

Stock Options

A common measure of shareholder wealth creation is appreciation of company stock price. Therefore, a popular form of bonus compensation is stock options. Stock options have typically represented more than 50 percent of a chief executive officer's average pay

[9] James E. Nelson, "Linking Compensation to Business Strategy," *The Journal of Business Strategy* 19, no. 2 (1998), pp. 25–27.

stock options
The right, or "option," to purchase company stock at a fixed price at some future date.

package.[10] **Stock options** provide the executive with the right to purchase company stock at a fixed price in the future. The precise amount of compensation is based on the difference, or "spread," between the option's initial price and its selling, or exercised, price. As a result, the executive receives a bonus only if the firm's share price appreciates. If the share price drops below the option price, the options become worthless.

Stock options were the source of extraordinary wealth creation for executives, managers, and rank-and-file employees in the technology boom of the last decade. Behind using options as compensation incentives was the notion that they were essentially free. Although they dilute shareholders' equity when they're exercised, taking the cost of stock options as an expense against earnings was not required. That, in turn, helped keep earnings higher than actual costs to the company and its shareholders. The bear market and corporate scandals of the last few years brought increased scrutiny on the use of and accounting for stock options. Recent changes in SEC guidelines have encouraged expensing stock options to more accurately reflect company performance. The following table shows the effect expensing stocks options would have on the net earnings of Standard & Poor's (S&P) 500 firms in recent years. "Stock options were a free resource, and because of that, they were used freely," said BankOne CEO James Dimon, who voluntarily began to expense stock options in 2003. "But now," he said, "when you have to expense options, you start to think, 'Is it an effective cost? Is there a better way?' " The Financial Accounting Standards Board issued a new ruling in 2004 that required expensing of stock options beginning in 2006.[11]

A Big Hit to Earnings

If options had been expensed the past 10 years, earnings would have been whacked as their popularity grew as shown below:

Options Expense as a Percent of Net Earnings for S&P 500 Companies

1996	1998	2000	2002	2005
2%	5%	8%	23%	22%

Source: *The Analysis Accounting Observer,* R. G. Associates Inc.

Microsoft shocked the business world in 2003 by announcing it would discontinue stock options, eliminating a form of pay that made thousands of Microsoft employees millionaires and helped define the culture of the tech industry. Starting in September 2003, the company began paying its 54,000 employees with restricted stock, a move that will let employees make money even if the company's share price declines. Like options, the restricted stock will vest gradually over a five-year period, and grants of restricted stock are counted as expenses and charged against earnings. Said CEO Steven Ballmer, "We asked: Is there a smarter way to compensate our people, a way that would make them feel even more excited about their financial deal at Microsoft and at the same time be something that was at least as good for the shareholders as today's compensation package?" At the time of Ballmer's announcement, more than 20,000 employees who had joined Microsoft in the past three years held millions of stock options that were "under water," meaning the market value of Microsoft stock was far below the stock price of their stock options.

Restricted stock has the advantage of offering employees more certainty, even if there is less potential for a big win. It also means shareholders don't have to worry about massive

[10] Louis Lavelle, Frederick Jespersen, and Spencer Ante, "Executive Pay," *BusinessWeek,* April 21, 2003.

[11] U.S. GAAP (generally accepted accounting principles) required expensing of stock options using one of two acceptable valuation methods starting in the first fiscal year after June 15, 2005. (www.wikipedia.org/wiki/employee_stock_options)

dilution after employees exercise big stock gains, as happened in the 1990s. Another advantage is that grants of restricted stock are much easier to value than options because restricted stock is equivalent to a stock transfer at the market price. That improves the transparency of corporate accounting.[12]

Research suggests that stock option plans lack the benefits of plans that include true stock ownership. Stock option plans provide unlimited upside potential for executives, but limited downside risk because executives incur only opportunity costs. Because of the tremendous advantages to the executive of stock price appreciation, there is an incentive for the executive to take undue risk. Thus, supporters of stock ownership plans argue that direct ownership instills a much stronger behavioral commitment, even when the stock price falls, because it binds executives to their firms more than do options.[13] Additionally, "Executive stock options may be an efficient means to induce management to undertake more risky projects."[14]

Options may have been overused and indeed abused in the last two bull markets,[15] but evidence suggests that the smart use of options and other incentive compensation does boost performance. Companies that spread ownership throughout a large portion of their workforce deliver higher returns than similar companies with more concentrated ownership. If options seemed for a time to be the route that enriched CEOs, employees, and investors alike, it still appears they will be used, although with less emphasis than a mix of options, restricted stock, and cash bonuses. Whatever the exact mix, they are likely to be more closely tied to achieving specific operating goals. The next section examines restricted stock and cash bonuses in greater detail.

Restricted Stock

restricted stock
Stock given to an employee who is prohibited or "restricted" from selling the stock for a certain time period and not at all if they leave the company before that time period.

A **restricted stock** plan is designed to provide benefits of direct executive stock ownership. In a typical restricted stock plan, an executive is given a specific number of company stock shares. The executive is prohibited from selling the shares for a specified time period. Should the executive leave the firm voluntarily before the restricted period ends, the shares are forfeited. Therefore, restricted stock plans are a form of deferred compensation that promotes longer executive tenure than other types of plans.

In addition to being contingent on a vesting period, restricted stock plans may also require the achievement of predetermined performance goals. Price-vesting restricted stock plans tie vesting to the firm's stock price in comparison to an index or to reaching a predetermined goal or annual growth rate. If the executive falls short on some of the restrictions, a certain amount of shares are forfeited. The design of these plans motivates the executive to increase shareholder wealth while promoting a long-term commitment to stay with the firm.

If the restricted stock plan lacks performance goal provisions, the executive needs only to remain employed with the firm over the vesting period to cash in on the stock. Performance provisions make sure executives are not compensated without achieving some

---

[12] Many argue that stock options are critical to start-up firms as a way to motivate and retain talented employees with the promise of getting rich should the new venture succeed. Among them appear to be FASB chairman Robert Herz, who favors sentiment to make special exceptions in the expensing of options in pre-IPO firms.

[13] Jeffrey Pfeffer, "Seven Practices of Successful Organizations," *California Management Review,* Winter 1998.

[14] Richard A. DeFusco, Robert R. Johnson, and Thomas S. Zorn, "The Effect of Executive Stock Option Plans on Stockholders and Bondholders," *Journal of Finance* 45, no. 2 (1990), pp. 617–35.

[15] Erik Lie and Randall A. Heron, "Does Backdating Explain the Stock Price Pattern Around Stock Option Grants," *Journal of Financial Economics* 83, (2007) pp. 271–95. Lie and Heron found 30 percent of all U.S. publicly traded firms apparently manipulated (backdated) stock option grants to increase the payoff to executives receiving the grants. See the Chapter 10 Discussion Case Part II for more details.

level of shareholder wealth creation. Like stock options, restricted stock plans offer no downside risk to executives because the shares were initially gifted to the executive. Unlike options, the stock retains value tied to its market value once ownership is fully vested. Shareholders, on the other hand, do suffer a loss in personal wealth resulting from a share price drop.

Golden Handcuffs

golden handcuffs
A form of executive compensation where compensation is deferred (either a restricted stock plan or bonus income deferred in a series of annual installments).

The rationale behind plans that defer compensation forms the basis for another type of executive compensation called golden handcuffs. **Golden handcuffs** refer to either a restricted stock plan, where the stock compensation is deferred until vesting time provisions are met, or to bonus income deferred in a series of annual installments. This type of plan may also involve compensating an executive a significant amount upon retirement or at some predetermined age. In most cases, compensation is forfeited if the executive voluntarily resigns or is discharged before certain time restrictions.

Many boards consider their executives' skills and talents to be their firm's most valuable assets. These "assets" create and sustain the professional relationships that generate revenue and control expenses for the firm. Research suggests that the departure of key executives is unsettling for companies and often disrupts long-range plans when new key executives adopt a different management strategy.[16] Thus, the golden handcuffs approach to executive compensation is more congruent with long-term strategies than short-term performance plans, which offer little staying-power incentive.

Firms may turn to golden handcuffs if they believe stability of management is critical to sustained growth. Jupiter Asset Management recently tied 10 fund managers to the firm with golden handcuffs. The compensation scheme calls for a cash payment in addition to base salaries if the managers remain at the firm for five years. In the first year of the plan, the firm's pretax profits more than doubled, and their assets under management increased 85 percent. The firm's chairman has also signed a new incentive deal that will keep him at Jupiter for four years.

Deferred compensation is worrisome to some executives. In cases where the compensation is payable when the executives are retired and no longer in control, as when the firm is acquired by another firm or a new management hierarchy is installed, the golden handcuff plans are considerably less attractive to executives.

Golden handcuffs may promote risk averseness in executive decision making due to the huge downside risk borne by executives. This risk averseness could lead to mediocre performance results from executives' decisions. When executives lose deferred compensation if the firm discharges them voluntarily or involuntarily, the executive is less likely to make bold and aggressive decisions. Rather, the executive will choose safe, conservative decisions.

Golden Parachutes

golden parachute
A form of bonus compensation that guarantees a substantial cash payment if the executive quits, is fired, or simply retires.

Golden parachutes are a form of bonus compensation that guarantees a substantial cash payment to an executive if the executive quits, is fired, or simply retires. In addition, the golden parachute may also contain covenants that allow the executive to cash in on noninvested stock compensation.

The popularity of golden parachutes grew with the increased popularity of takeovers, which often led to the ouster of the acquired firm's top executives. In these cases, the golden parachutes encouraged executives to take an objective look at takeover offers. The executives could decide which move was in the best interests of the shareholders, having been personally protected in the event of a merger. The "parachute" helps soften the fall

---

[16] William E. Hall, Brian J. Lake, Charles T. Morse, and Charles T. Morse, Jr., "More Than Golden Handcuffs," *Journal of Accountancy* 184, no. 5 (1997), pp. 37–42.

of the ousted executive. It is "golden" because the size of the cash payment often varies from several to tens of millions of dollars.

AMP Incorporated, the world's largest producer of electronic connectors, had golden parachutes for several executives. When Allied Signal proclaimed itself an unsolicited suitor for AMP, the action focused attention on the AMP parachutes for its three top executives. Robert Ripp became AMP's chief executive officer during this time. If Allied Signal ousted him, he stood to receive a cash payment of three times the amount of his salary as well as his highest annual bonus from the previous three years. His salary at the time was $600,000 and his previous year's bonus was $200,000. The cash payment to Ripp would therefore exceed $2 million. Parachutes would also open for the former chief executive officer and the former chairman who were slated to officially retire a year later. They stood to receive their parachutes if they were ousted before their respective retirement dates with each parachute valued at more than $1 million.

In addition to cash payments, these three executives' parachutes also protect existing blocks of restricted stock grants and nonvested stock options. The restricted stock grants were scheduled to become available within three years. Should the takeover come to fruition, the executives would receive the total value of the restricted stock even if it was not yet vested. The stock options would also become available immediately. Some of the restricted stock was performance restricted. Under normal conditions this stock would not be available without the firm reaching certain performance levels. However, the golden parachutes allow the executives to receive double the value of the performance-restricted stock.

Golden parachutes are designed in part to anticipate hostile takeovers like this. In AMP's case, Ripp's position is to lead the firm's board of directors in deciding if Allied Signal's offer is in the long-term interests of shareholders. Because Ripp is compensated heavily whether AMP is taken over or not, the golden parachute has helped remove the temptation that Ripp could have of not acting in the best interests of shareholders.

By design, golden parachutes benefit top executives whether or not there is evidence that value is created for shareholders. In fact, research has suggested that since high-performing firms are rarely taken over, golden parachutes often compensate top executives for abysmal performance.[17] Recent stockholder reactions to excessive executive compensation regardless of company performance are seen in Exhibit 10.11, Strategy in Action.

Cash

Executive bonus compensation plans that focus on accounting measures of performance are designed to offset the limitations of market-based measures of performance. This type of plan is most usually associated with the payment of periodic (quarterly or annual) cash bonuses. Market factors beyond the control of management, such as pending legislation, can keep a firm's share price repressed even though a top executive is exceeding the performance expectations of the board. In this situation, a highly performing executive loses bonus compensation due to the undervalued stock. However, accounting measures of performance correct for this problem by tying executive bonuses to improvements in internally measured performance.

Traditional accounting measures, such as net income, earnings per share, return on equity, and return on assets, are used because they are easily understood, are familiar to senior management, and are already tracked by firm data systems.[18] Sears bases annual

---

[17] Graef S. Crystal, *In Search of Excess* (New York: W. W. Norton & Company, 1991).

[18] Francine C. McKenzie and Matthew D. Shilling, "Avoiding Performance Measurement Traps: Ensuring Effective Incentive Design and Implementation," *Compensation and Benefits Review,* July–August 1998, pp. 57–65.

bonus payments on such performance criteria, given an executive's business unit and level with the firm. The measures used by Sears include return on equity, revenue growth, net sales growth, and profit growth.

Critics argue that because of inherent flaws in accounting systems, basing compensation on these figures may not result in an accurate gauge of managerial performance. Return on equity estimates, for example, are skewed by inflation distortions and arbitrary cost allocations. Accounting measures are also subject to manipulation by firm personnel to artificially inflate key performance figures. Firm performance schemes, critics believe, need to be based on a financial measure that has a true link to shareholder value creation.[19] This issue led to the creation of the Balanced Scorecard, which emphasizes not only financial measures, but also such measures as new-product development, market share, and safety as discussed in Chapter 12.

Matching Bonus Plans and Corporate Goals

Exhibit 10.12 provides a summary of the five types of executive bonus compensation plans. The figure includes a brief description, a rationale for implementation, and the identification of possible shortcomings for each of the compensation plans. Not only do compensation plans differ in the method through which compensation is rewarded to the executive, but they also provide the executive with different incentives.

Exhibit 10.12 matches a company's strategic goal with the most likely compensation plan. On the vertical axis are common strategic goals. The horizontal axis lists the main compensation types that serve as incentives for executives to reach the firm's goals. A rationale is provided to explain the logic behind the connection between the firm's goal and the suggested method of executive compensation.

Researchers emphasize that fundamental to these relationships is the importance of incorporating the level of strategic risk of the firm into the design of the executive's

[19] William Franklin, "Making the Fat Cats Earn Their Cream," *Accountancy,* July 1998, pp. 38–39.

EXHIBIT 10.12   **Compensation Plan Selection Matrix**

Strategic Goal	Cash	Golden Handcuffs	Golden Parachutes	Restricted Stock Plans	Stock Options	Rationale
Type of Bonus Compensation					
Achieve corporate turnaround					X	Executive profits only if turnaround is successful in returning wealth to shareholders.
Create and support growth opportunities					X	Risk associated with growth strategies warrants the use of this high-reward incentive.
Defend against unfriendly takeover			X			Parachute helps takeover remove temptation for executive to evaluate takeover based on personal benefits.
Evaluate suitors objectively			X			Parachute compensates executive if job is lost due to a merger favorable to the firm.
Globalize operations					X	Risk of expanding overseas requires a plan that compensates only for achieved success.
Grow share price incrementally	X					Accounting measures can identify periodic performance benchmarks.
Improve operational efficiency	X					Accounting measures represent observable and agreed-upon measures of performance.
Increase assets under management				X		Executive profits proportionally as asset growth leads to long-term growth in share price.
Reduce executive turnover		X				Handcuffs provide executive tenure incentive.
Restructure organization					X	Risk associated with major change in firm's assets warrants the use of this high-reward incentive.
Streamline operations				X		Rewards long-term focus on efficiency and cost control.

compensation plan. Incorporating an appropriate level of executive risk can create a desired behavioral change commensurate with the risk level of strategies shareholders and their firms want.[20] To help motivate an executive to pursue goals of a certain risk-return level, the compensation plan can quantify that risk-return level and reward the executive accordingly.

[20] Lavelle, Jespersen, and Ante, "Executive Pay."

The links we show between bonus compensation plans and strategic goals were derived from the results of prior research. The basic principle underlying Exhibit 10.12 is that different types of bonus compensation plans are intended to accomplish different purposes; one element may serve to attract and retain executives; another may serve as an incentive to encourage behavior that accomplishes firm goals.[21] Although every strategy option has probably been linked to each compensation plan at some time, experience shows that there may be scenarios where a plan type best fits a strategy option. Exhibit 10.12 attempts to display the "best matches."

Once the firm has identified strategic goals that will best serve shareholders' interests, an executive bonus compensation plan can be structured in such a way as to provide the executive with an incentive to work toward achieving these goals.

Summary

The first concern in the implementation of business strategy is to translate that strategy into action throughout the organization. This chapter discussed five considerations for accomplishing this.

Short-term objectives are derived from long-term objectives, which are then translated into current actions and targets. They differ from long-term objectives in time frame, specificity, and measurement. To be effective in strategy implementation, they must be integrated and coordinated. They also must be consistent, measurable, and prioritized.

Functional tactics are derived from the business strategy. They identify the specific, immediate actions that must be taken in key functional areas to implement the business strategy.

Outsourcing of selected functional activities has become a central tactical agenda for virtually every business firm in today's global economy. Can we get that activity done more effectively—and more inexpensively—outside our company? This question has become a regular one managers ask as they seek to make their business strategies work.

Employee empowerment through policies provides another means for guiding behavior, decisions, and actions at the firm's operating levels in a manner consistent with its business and functional strategies. Policies empower operating personnel to make decisions and take action quickly.

Compensation rewards action and results. Once the firm has identified strategic objectives that will best serve stockholder interests, there are five bonus compensation plans that can be structured to provide the executive with an incentive to work toward achieving those goals.

Objectives, functional tactics, policies, and compensation represent only the start of the strategy implementation. The strategy must be institutionalized—it must permeate the firm. The next chapter examines this phase of strategy implementation.

[21] Nelson, "Linking Compensation to Business Strategy."

Key Terms

empowerment, *p.314*	golden parachute, *p.321*	restricted stock, *p. 320*
functional tactics, *p. 309*	outsourcing, *p.312*	short-term objective, *p. 305*
golden handcuffs, *p. 321*	policies, *p. 314*	stock options, *p. 319*

Questions for
Discussion

1. How does the concept "translate thought into action" bear on the relationship between business strategy and operating strategy? Between long-term and short-term objectives?
2. How do functional tactics differ from corporate and business strategies?
3. What key concerns must functional tactics address in marketing? finance? production/operations management? personnel?
4. What is "outsourcing?" Why has it become a key element in shaping functional tactics within most business firms today?
5. How do policies aid strategy implementation? Illustrate your answer.
6. Use Exhibits 10.9 and 10.11 to explain five executive bonus compensation plans.
7. Illustrate a policy, an objective, and a functional tactic in your personal career strategy.
8. Why are short-term objectives needed when long-term objectives are already available?

Chapter 10 Discussion Case 1

BusinessWeek

A Better Look at the Boss's Pay

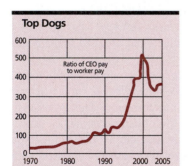

Top Dogs

Ratio of CEO pay to worker pay

Since 1993, CEO pay has increased faster than the cost of gasoline, Ivy League tuition, residential real estate prices, and a whole lot else. Your boss may have an inflated ego, but it's probably not nearly as inflated as his paycheck. In 1993, chief executives' salaries averaged $2.6 million, and by 2005 they had skyrocketed to $10.5 million—a 304 percent increase over 12 years.

1 No topic inflames the passions of business leaders and shareholders like executive pay. Companies and compensation consultants argue that, in a free market, they'd be foolish not to pay the going rate for top talent. Investors demand that compensation be tied to performance and complain loudly when pay rises while share prices don't.

2   The perennial battle is about to reach a new level of contentiousness. The proxy season, just getting started, will be the first under new Securities and Exchange Commission reporting rules that force companies to disclose more about executive pay than ever before—from the hundreds of millions some executives stand to gain in severance, pensions, and deferred pay, to any perk worth more than $10,000. Golden parachutes and sybaritic benefits such as club memberships and personal use of company jets won't score many

points against a backdrop of the options-backdating scandal and increasingly empowered activist investors.

Thanks to recent blowups like that at Home Depot, **3** shareholder-rights groups hold a distinct advantage in the public-relations war. Former Chief Executive Robert L. Nardelli walked away from Home Depot Inc. in early January with a $210 million severance package, shocking shareholders unhappy with the company's flagging stock. And the timing couldn't have been worse for companies nervously preparing to reveal their own pay practices. "Home Depot is a preview of things to come," says Michael S. Melbinger, a compensation lawyer with Winston & Strawn in Chicago. "It's the perfect example of the rich payout that would have been buried before, but which everyone now must disclose."

Governance advocates and politicians gain even more **4** public support when they point out that in 2005 the average CEO in the Standard & Poor's 500-stock index took home 369 times the pay of the average worker, up from 28 times the average in 1970. The counterargument, that the ratio is down from the 514 multiple in 2000, doesn't get much traction.

THE LITTLE THINGS

Some boards have been looking hard at executive contracts **5** and even tried to renegotiate them. Such minor perks as the personal driver and financial planning services are often on the table. But most boards plan to do little more.

In many cases, they can't. Almost all CEOs have contracts **6** guaranteeing their big payouts. And the fear of angering a CEO over a pay issue has made directors reluctant to push harder. "No one wants to be responsible for seeing the CEO walk," says Jannice L. Koors, a managing director of pay consultants Pearl Meyer & Partners. In a survey of 110 companies at year-end, Mercer Human Resource Consulting found that 70 percent planned only minimal changes to their executive compensation programs as a result of the new SEC rules; just 15 percent said the impact would be more substantial. Cutbacks in executives' packages are "just not terribly widespread," says Mark A. Borges, a former SEC official who is a principal at Mercer. Chicago lawyer Melbinger, who has sat in on recent board meetings, echoes Borges' view: "Yes, there's pressure to get rid of these deals, but I have not seen a single situation where an executive was willing to give one up."

7   To avoid provoking shareholders, companies are most commonly shifting pay out of categories that raise questions. Late last year aerospace giant Lockheed Martin Corp. said it would stop paying for a car and driver as well as club dues for CEO Robert J. Stevens. Instead, it hiked his $1.48 million salary $40,000. A spokesman says ending perks was in the company's best interests.

8   Some items, however, are too large to move or obscure. The biggest fights are likely to be over multimillion-dollar deferred pay and retirement accounts, as well as guaranteed payments for executives who are fired or who leave when the company is acquired. Such items have been focal points of recent firestorms, from the Nardelli flap to the $82 million pension Pfizer Inc. paid outgoing CEO Hank McKinnell last year.

9   The surprise this proxy season, predicts Shekhar Purohit, a principal of pay consultants James F. Reda & Associates, will be just how common, and lucrative, these severance packages are. Typically they include a payment of three times salary and bonus, immediate vesting of options and restricted stock awards, and, in many cases, payment of taxes owed. Purohit says dozens of executives could have payouts of $100 million or more.

10   Revelations of extra-sweet deferred-compensation deals are sure to raise eyebrows, too. Such plans usually allow executives to sock away money tax-free, often with a company match—much like 401(k) accounts, only with no limit on the contributions. And some companies guarantee better-than-market interest for executives. American Express Co. gave CEO Kenneth I. Chenault $1.1 million in above-market returns on his deferred compensation account in 2005. The company won't divulge the rate it gave that year, but in 2006 it paid 13 percent on executives' deferred balances. In late January, AmEx said it would continue to pay 13 percent to 16 percent on money they set aside between 1994 and 2004 if the company meets or beats financial targets, and will pay 9 percent to 11 percent on money deferred after 2005. A spokesman says the plan is consistent with industry practice.

RICH RETIREES

11   Pension plans will likely draw attention, too. Whereas regular workers typically retire on one-half to two-thirds of their average salary in their last three to five years, some CEOs get far more. Pfizer's deal with McKinnell was unusually

rich: in calculating his final pay, Pfizer counted not only salary and bonus, but stock awards that vested through 2004. That notched his annual pension up from roughly $3.5 million to $6.6 million. The company says it stopped including new stock awards in pension calculations in 2001, but earlier grants were grandfathered in. Huge bonuses issued just before retirement can also pump up pensions. "It's the gift that keeps on giving," says Kevin J. Murphy, a professor at the University of Southern California's Marshall School of Business.

12   Governance activists are already targeting such practices. The United Brotherhood of Carpenters has identified 14 companies, including AT&T and Johnson & Johnson, where it believes the inclusion of large incentive bonuses in pension calculations has led to excessive benefits. So far, the union can claim one small victory. In January, American Express also announced further limits on retirement benefits. Rather than basing them on total salary and bonus—which for Chenault were $1.1 million and $6 million, respectively, in 2005—earnings used in calculating retirement will be capped at twice the annual salary. The AmEx spokesman says the changes, long in the works, stem from the shift away from traditional defined benefit pensions to 401(k)-type defined contribution plans.

13   As for the smaller perks, companies maintain that some are born of legitimate need. For example, many argue that use of a company jet even for personal flights is a must in the post-9/11 era. Ditto home alarm systems and other security measures. The practice isn't universal. Intel Corp. and Goldman Sachs & Co. both forbid personal use of company jets.

14   Even so, in a study of 2005 proxies filed by the 100 largest U.S. companies, compensation research firm Equilar Inc. found that the median value of personal travel on corporate jets rose 21.7 percent, to $109,000, while execs got roughly $37,000 to safeguard themselves, up 69 percent. The numbers for individuals can fly much higher. United Technologies Corp. chief George David ran up a $581,396 tab for "personal use of the corporate aircraft for security reasons," according to SEC filings. The company declined to comment. FedEx Corp. gave CEO Frederick W. Smith $833,000 in jet use and security services on top of his $1.3 million salary in fiscal 2006. FedEx, which requires the CEO to use the jet for all travel, says an independent security consultant determined the need for the benefits.

15   Still, jet travel irks some. Richard C. Breeden, a former SEC chairman who runs a hedge fund, criticized restaurant chain Applebee's International Inc. over the issue. He found that, over a 10-month period, Applebee's jet made 29 trips to Galveston, Texas, where Lloyd Hill, who stepped down as CEO in September but remains chairman, has a beach house. A spokeswoman for Applebee's, which said on February 13 it will explore a sale, says its plane policy is disclosed.

16   One thing is clear: it is increasingly tough for boards to keep everyone happy. Retired General Hugh Shelton, the former chairman of the U.S. Joint Chiefs of Staff who heads

the compensation committee of software maker Red Hat Inc., says boards are focused more on finding the right balance between shareholder demands to link pay to performance and the company's need to ensure good executives have the right incentives. "You try to be fair, and give appropriate rewards for performance," he says. But ultimately, "you compensate them so that they're not desperate to go to work for someone else."

Discussion Case 2

BusinessWeek

He's Making Hay as CEOs Squirm: *Erik Lie Uncovered*
Widespread Backdating of Stock Options. Now He's Reaping Rewards

17 Erik Lie loves academic life. The University of Iowa associate finance professor is free to research whatever topic intrigues him, and his $160,000-plus income goes a nice long way in Iowa City. Summers off means that Lie (rhymes with "key"), his wife, and two kids can travel back to his parents' vacation home in Norway. During the rest of the year, he's free to take off after class for a run or some cross-country skiing. "Life as a professor is good," says the lanky 38-year-old.

18   It's particularly good now that Lie's research is having a major impact on Corporate America. His mid-2005 research first suggested that hundreds of companies may have routinely manipulated stock-option accounting rules to sweeten top executives' paydays. A later study done with his research partner, Indiana University associate professor Randall Heron, puts the number at 2,000, or 29 percent of all public corporations. Five executives face criminal indictments for such alleged backdating, more than 100 companies face civil charges and shareholder suits, and hundreds more are neck-deep in comprehensive investigations of their books to try to make sure the Feds don't add them to the list.

19   The scandal is creating a financial windfall for Lie. He and Heron have created a limited partnership now that the initial crush of calls from reporters has given way to people willing to actually pay for their insights. Lie says he has earned around $100,000 from hedge funds and other investors, who pay him to handicap whether a company's options irregularities are harmless paperwork errors or the kinds of fraud that lead to CEO ousters and big civil penalties. He'll probably draw $400 an hour or more doing consulting work for law firms, and still more as an expert witness. He's now a senior adviser at the Brattle Group, a consultancy in Washington. All told, Lie figures he could make $250,000 before the options scandal fades from memory.

20   Lie may be underestimating his prospects. An elite business professor can make tens of thousands for a one-day consulting gig. Notre Dame University professor Paul H. Schultz, who in the mid-1990s discovered that NASDAQ market makers were skimming pennies from investors on stock trades, says he earned $250,000 over three years, charging $250 an hour to work with plaintiffs' attorneys. "But Erik can do quite a bit better, if he wants to," Schultz says. "There are more lawsuits, and he should be charging a higher rate."

LUCKY TIMING?

21 Rarely has an academic had such an outsize, real-time impact on the business world. Academics had long known that companies tended to grant options with remarkable acuity—just before big rises that gave those options immediate value, at least on paper. But Lie and Heron were first to suggest that this could only have happened with the help of hindsight. That's because those favorable trading patterns appeared only in cases where companies had delayed their options paperwork for months, giving them the ability to look back and cherry-pick the most lucrative grant dates. That's a violation of federal law—and of many corporate options plans—if not properly disclosed.

22   Lie helped make sure the scandal exploded, notifying the Securities and Exchange Commission of his work and showing *The Wall Street Journal* how to interpret a particular company's options records, although he insists he never identified companies himself. He's clearly proud of his work's resonance but insists the attendant financial opportunities are a low priority. He limits his consulting time, he says, to less than one day a week. "I did not start this line of research for the money, and I am still not in this for the money," Lie says.

23   Now he's turning away many opportunities, he says—particularly from plaintiffs' lawyers who would like to tailor his findings to suit their cases. But he is helping "less pushy" plaintiffs' attorneys prepare potential cases against three dozen companies, diving into details of specific transactions. Indeed, he says he'll probably take the stand as an expert witness in some high-profile cases. He won't name any names, in part because it's too early to know which companies will settle rather than make it into court, but does say that he "may become involved in litigations" against Apple Computer.

24   Lie is also open to working with defendants facing options-related allegations, although none have taken him up on the offer. "People tend to think I'm against all companies," he says, "but I think some of the companies identified in the media are innocent"—perhaps a dozen or so of the 200 companies that have announced options irregularities. He says some guiltless CEOs are likely to lose their jobs simply because they were at the helm when mistakes were made by others. Still, "it's one of those necessary evils; a small price to pay to get more transparency into the system. How much is good governance worth to the economy? I don't know, but it's billions and billions."

25 Lie grew up the son of left-leaning parents in southern Norway. His father, Rolf, a retired construction engineer, thinks Lie is imbued with the economic egalitarianism they taught him. "Erik doesn't like that people have gotten money they didn't deserve," says the elder Lie. The son briefly considered a career in law but later caught the academic bug while doing a finance research project at the University of Oregon.

SERENDIPITY

26 When he began researching stock options as a young professor in 2002, it wasn't to find a scandal. "Shareholders were giving executives options so they'd work harder to change corporate behavior," he says. "I just wanted to see how it manifested itself"—say, by companies repurchasing more shares. Even after Lie began to suspect backdating, it took a while for anyone to listen. An initial paper in 2004 was slammed by a reviewer who said that Lie was "overreaching" and that his conclusions "made little economic sense." After Sarbanes-Oxley regulations were imposed, however, all option grants had to be reported to the SEC within two days. By comparing the new grants with pre-Sarbanes-Oxley grants, Lie and Heron were able to document a disappearance of the windfall obtained by execs at companies that had taken months to file in the past.

27 Defense lawyers dismiss Lie's analysis because it doesn't consider legitimate explanations for how options may have been granted at low stock prices. For example, CEOs during the boom routinely granted options on days when their stocks were down because of unfounded rumors. That way, they could provide some extra incentive to employees before cranking up their investor relations efforts to refute the rumor. "His analysis is simplistic," says Richard Marmaro of Skadden, Arps, Slate, Meagher & Flom, who is representing indicted former Brocade Communications Systems CEO Greg Reyes. "There are people whose job it is to grant options, who are expert in understanding what they perceived to be low prices."

28 Lie says he's going into this next phase of the scandal with his eyes wide open, expecting to have his motives criticized, and ready for persuasive arguments about why a specific company, board, or executive did nothing wrong. He figures that the bulk of backdaters have yet to be identified, and that just 10 percent will ever be punished in any way. "I don't anticipate I'll be able to create something of this magnitude again," he says. "But it's not necessary for me that there is a consequence for every single firm. My research has already helped curb this behavior. That's the most important thing."

Source: Reprinted with special permission from "He's Making Hay as CEOs Squirm," *BusinessWeek,* January 15, 2007. Copyright © 2007 The McGraw-Hill Companies.

Discussion Case 3

BusinessWeek

Google Gives Employees Another Option: *The Search Giant's Innovative Program Offers Workers Another Way to Realize the Value of Their Stock Options*

29 In a bid to breathe new life into scandal-tainted stock options, Google plans to give employees a novel method of cashing in their options starting next April. The search giant will let employees sell their vested stock options, which give the holder the right to reap the difference between the initial price and the current price, to selected financial institutions in an auction marketplace it's setting up with Morgan Stanley.

30 The program is a unique stab at unlocking for employees the underlying value of these securities that have been a favored method of luring and keeping employees, particularly among technology companies. In the past year or so, as rules requiring the expensing of stock options kicked in, employers have been cutting back on the number of options they grant, or doling out new incentives such as restricted stock, in a bid to avoid a hit to reported profits.

31 That has some observers worrying about the possible demise of a classic performance incentive tool. While options continue to be granted by many companies, some 30 percent

have cut back their options grants, and 25 percent of employees who once received options and other equity awards now do not, according to the National Center for Employee Ownership, a nonprofit research group in Oakland, California. And for those getting grants, the value of their options is about a third lower than it used to be.

HOW IT WORKS

32 Under Google's Transferable Stock Option program, employees could sell their stock options on the semi-private marketplace much the way public options are sold today. That would let employees potentially reap more than if they merely exercised and then sold the securities. Say an employee holds an option with a strike price of $400, meaning it can be purchased for $400 and then resold at a higher price. If Google's stock is trading at $500, an investor might pay $150 for that option, betting that the stock will rise well past $500 during

the life of the option. The employee selling the option could net an immediate $150. An employee exercising and then selling the same option would net only $100, the difference between the strike price and the current price.

33   The impetus for the new approach is Google's volatile stock, which can change substantially in the space of a month or even days. Google's stock has been on a long if volatile rise since the company's initial public offering in 2004 at $85 a share. Just since September 1, 2006, the shares have risen 27 percent, to $481.78 on December 12, after rising above $500 in November.

34   As a result, many recent and incoming employees may feel the options don't have much value, given how high Google's stock already is. Moreover, an employee who joins one week ultimately may end up having very different compensation than another hired a few weeks later. That difference can raise pay equity issues and potentially reduce the incentive for employees to stick around. "This goes a long way toward solving recruiting and retention issues," says Dave Rolefson, Google's equity and executive compensation manager.

"VERY INNOVATIVE"

35   If Google's plan works—an open question at this point—other companies once again might find options an attractive offering for hiring and keeping talent. "I think it's a very good idea," says James Glassman, resident fellow at the American Enterprise Institute, who was briefed on the plan. "It achieves Google's goal of making the value of options more apparent to people who get them."

36   There could also be some unpredictable consequences to the plan. Investors buying these options no doubt will want to hedge their bets, possibly through a short sale—a bet that Google's stock will fall. That's not usually something companies like to see. But Google believes the overall impact of the program on the company will be positive. Former Securities and Exchange Commission chairman Arthur Levitt, now a senior advisor to the Carlyle Group, says he's not sure what all the implications will be. "But on balance, it's a very innovative program," he says.

37   The plan is only for employees, not executives, who Google says are already adequately compensated. So on its face the plan doesn't address some of the recent problems surrounding stock options, including manipulation of the date on which the securities are granted, so-called backdating, that have landed companies other than Google in legal hot water. But it does offer a different—and possibly more accurate—way to value stock options, an area of great debate even now, nearly a year after options were required to be logged as expenses on a company's books.

NO BENEFIT TO THE BOTTOM LINE

38   Google's program isn't aimed at minimizing the impact to its bottom line, however. Indeed, the company expects to incur a larger expense on its books as the plan rolls out. That's because the fair market value of the options will be greater under the new plan than the current one. The reason: the options, which are estimated to have a four-year average life before employees exercise them, will convert to two-year options when they're sold to investors. So their expected life will be essentially extended by two years—making them more valuable because investors will have two more years for Google's stock potentially to rise, and thus more of an impact on Google's bottom line.

39   If Google's stock doesn't rise, or even falls, the options may well still have value, because investors may assume that over a two-year period the stock has a good chance to rise again. So employees may be able to sell even underwater options—those whose strike price is higher than the current stock price—and reap gains. "Underwater options lose their value as retention tools," notes Levitt. Even under Google's new plan, however, if its stock price drops well below options' strike prices, investors may not want to pay for them, and the options will still be worthless.

40   Google said it's not implementing the new plan because it's having problems attracting and retaining employees—at least not yet. "We're not having any problem recruiting people to work at Google," says Rolefson. "Attrition rates are very low." The idea, in an increasingly competitive business, is to keep it that way.

Source: Reprinted with special permission from "Google Gives Employees Another Option," *BusinessWeek*, December 13, 2006. Copyright © 2006 The McGraw-Hill Companies.

DISCUSSION QUESTIONS

1. What has been the compensation of CEOs relative to their "line" workers the past few years?

2. Do you think it is deserved? Why?

3. Do executives and related compensation/incentives appear key to effective implementation, or unrelated?

4. Regarding Case 2, does it seem reasonable for executives and employees to "backdate" stock option grants so that their grants are priced at the lowest daily stock price within a two- to four-month time period? Why?

5. Regarding Case 3, does it appear Google has found a way to add liquidity and simplicity to employee stock options designed to reward effective implementation and performance? Why?

Chapter 10 Appendix

Functional Tactics

FUNCTIONAL TACTICS THAT IMPLEMENT BUSINESS STRATEGIES

Functional tactics are the key, routine activities that must be undertaken in each functional area—marketing, finance, production/operations, R&D, and human resource management—to provide the business's products and services. In a sense, functional tactics translate thought (grand strategy) into action designed to accomplish specific short-term objectives. Every value chain activity in a company executes functional tactics that support the business's strategy and help accomplish strategic objectives.

The next several sections will highlight key tactics around which managers can build competitive advantage and add value in each of the various functional areas.

FUNCTIONAL TACTICS IN PRODUCTION/OPERATIONS

Basic Issues

Production/operations management (POM) is the core function of any organization. That function converts inputs (raw materials, supplies, machines, and people) into value-enhanced output. The POM function is most easily associated

with manufacturing firms, but it also applies to all other types of businesses (e.g., service and retail firms). POM tactics must guide decisions regarding (1) the basic nature of the firm's POM system, seeking an optimum balance between investment input and production/operations output, and (2) location, facilities design, and process planning on a short-term basis. Exhibit 10.A1 highlights key decision areas in which the POM tactics should provide guidance to functional personnel.

POM facility and equipment tactics involve decisions regarding plant location, size, equipment replacement, and facilities utilization that should be consistent with grand strategy and other operating strategies. In the mobile home industry, for example, the facilities and equipment tactic of Winnebago was to locate one large centralized, highly integrated production center (in Iowa) near its raw materials. On the other extreme, Fleetwood Inc., a California-based competitor, located dispersed, decentralized production facilities near markets and emphasized maximum equipment life and less-integrated, labor-intensive production processes. Both firms are leaders in the mobile home industry, but have taken very different tactical approaches.

The interplay between computers and rapid technological advancement has made flexible manufacturing systems (FMS) a major consideration for today's POM tacticians. FMS allows managers to automatically and rapidly shift production systems to retool for different products or other steps

EXHIBIT 10.A1   Key Functional Tactics in POM

Functional Tactic	Typical Questions That the Functional Tactic Should Answer
Facilities and equipment	How centralized should the facilities be? (One big facility or several small facilities?)
	How integrated should the separate processes be?
	To what extent should further mechanization or automation be pursued?
	Should size and capacity be oriented toward peak or normal operating levels?
Sourcing	How many sources are needed?
	How should suppliers be selected, and how should relationships with suppliers be managed over time?
	What level of forward buying (hedging) is appropriate?
Operations planning and control	Should work be scheduled to order or to stock?
	What level of inventory is appropriate?
	How should inventory be used, controlled, and replenished?
	What are the key foci for control efforts (quality, labor cost, downtime, product use, other)?
	Should maintenance efforts be oriented to prevention or to breakdown?
	What emphasis should be placed on job specialization? Plant safety? The use of standards?

in a manufacturing process. Changes that previously took hours or days can be done in minutes. The result is decreased labor cost, greater efficiency, and increased quality associated with computer-based precision.

Sourcing has become an increasingly important component in the POM area. Many companies now accord sourcing a separate status like any other functional area. Sourcing tactics provide guidelines about questions such as, Are the cost advantages of using only a few suppliers outweighed by the risk of overdependence? What criteria (e.g., payment requirements) should be used in selecting vendors? Which vendors can provide "just-in-time" inventory, and how can the business provide it to our customers? How can operations be supported by the volume and delivery requirements of purchases?

POM planning and control tactics involve approaches to the management of ongoing production operations and are intended to match production/operations resources with longer-range, overall demand. These tactical decisions usually determine whether production/operations will be demand oriented, inventory oriented, or outsourcing oriented to seek a balance between the two extremes. Tactics in this component also address how issues such as maintenance, safety, and work organization are handled. Quality control procedures are yet another focus of tactical priorities in this area.

Just-in-time (JIT) delivery, outsourcing, and statistical process control (SPC) have become prominent aspects of the way today's POM managers create tactics that build greater value and quality in their POM system. JIT delivery was initially a way to coordinate with suppliers to reduce inventory carrying costs of items needed to make products. It also became a quality control tactic because smaller inventories made quality checking easier on smaller, frequent deliveries. It has become an important aspect of supplier-customer relationships in today's best businesses.

Outsourcing, or the use of a source other than internal capacity to accomplish some task or process, has become a major operational tactic in today's downsizing-oriented firms. Outsourcing is based on the notion that strategies should be built around the core competencies that add the most value in the value chain and that functions or activities that add little value or that cannot be done cost effectively should be done outside the firm—outsourced. When done well, the firm gains a supplier that provides superior quality at lower cost than it could provide itself. JIT and outsourcing have increased the strategic importance of the purchasing function. Outsourcing must include intense quality control by the buyer. ValuJet's tragic 1996 crash in the Everglades was caused by poor quality control over its outsourced maintenance providers.

The Internet and e-commerce have begun to revolutionize functional tactics in operations and marketing. How we sell, where we make things, how we logistically coordinate what we do—all of these basic business functions and questions have new perspectives and ways of being addressed because of the technological effect of the globally emerging ways we link together electronically, quickly, and accurately.

FUNCTIONAL TACTICS IN MARKETING

The role of the marketing function is to achieve the firm's objectives by bringing about the profitable sale of the business's products/services in target markets. Marketing tactics should guide sales and marketing managers in determining who will sell what, where, to whom, in what quantity, and how. Marketing tactics at a minimum should address four fundamental areas: products, price, place, and promotion. Exhibit 10.A2 highlights typical questions marketing tactics should address.

In addition to the basic issues raised in Exhibit 10.A2, marketing tactics today must guide managers addressing the effect of the communication revolution and the increased diversity among market niches worldwide. The Internet and the accelerating blend of computers and telecommunications has facilitated instantaneous access to several places around the world. A producer of plastic kayaks in Easley, South Carolina, receives orders from somewhere in the world about every 30 minutes over the Internet without any traditional distribution structure or global advertising. It fills the order within five days without any transportation capability. Speed linked to the ability to communicate instantaneously is causing marketing tacticians to radically rethink what they need to do to remain competitive and maximize value.

Diversity has accelerated because of communication technology, logistical capability worldwide, and advancements in flexible manufacturing systems. The diversity that has resulted is a virtual explosion of market niches—adaptations of products to serve hundreds of distinct and diverse customer segments that would previously have been served with more mass-market, generic products or services. Where firms used to rely on volume associated with mass markets to lower costs, they now encounter smaller niche players carving out subsegments they can serve more timely *and* more cost effectively. These new, smaller players lack the bureaucracy and committee approach that burdens the larger firms. They make decisions, outsource, incorporate product modifications, and make other agile adjustments to niche market needs before their larger competitors get through the first phase of committee-based decision making.

FUNCTIONAL TACTICS IN ACCOUNTING AND FINANCE

While most functional tactics guide implementation in the immediate future, the time frame for functional tactics in the area of finance varies because these tactics direct the use of financial resources in support of the business strategy, long-term goals, and annual objectives. Financial tactics with longer time perspectives guide financial managers in long-term capital investment, debt financing, dividend allocation, and leveraging. Financial tactics designed to manage working

EXHIBIT 10.A2 Key Functional Tactics in Marketing

Functional Tactic	Typical Questions That the Functional Tactic Should Answer
Product (or service)	Which products do we emphasize? Which products/services contribute most to profitability? What product/service image do we seek to project? What consumer needs does the product/service seek to meet? What changes should be influencing our customer orientation?
Price	Are we competing primarily on price? Can we offer discounts on other pricing modifications? Are our pricing policies standard nationally, or is there regional control? What price segments are we targeting (high, medium, low, and so on)? What is the gross profit margin? Do we emphasize cost/demand or competition-oriented pricing?
Place	What level of market coverage is necessary? Are there priority geographic areas? What are the key channels of distribution? What are the channel objectives, structure, and management? Should the marketing managers change their degree of reliance on distributors, sales reps, and direct selling? What sales organization do we want? Is the salesforce organized around territory, market, or product?
Promotion	What are the key promotion priorities and approaches? Which advertising/communication priorities and approaches are linked to different products, markets, and territories? Which media would be most consistent with the total marketing strategy?

EXHIBIT 10.A3 Key Functional Tactics in Finance and Accounting

Functional Tactic	Typical Questions That the Functional Tactics Should Answer
Capital acquisition	What is an acceptable cost of capital? What is the desired proportion of short- and long-term debt? Preferred and common equity? What balance is desired between internal and external funding? What risk and ownership restrictions are appropriate? What level and forms of leasing should be used?
Capital allocation	What are the priorities for capital allocation projects? On what basis should the final selection of projects be made? What level of capital allocation can be made by operating managers without higher approval?
Dividend and working capital management	What portion of earnings should be paid out as dividends? How important is dividend stability? Are things other than cash appropriate as dividends? What are the cash flow requirements? The minimum and maximum cash balances? How liberal/conservative should the credit policies be? What limits, payment terms, and collection procedures are necessary? What payment timing and procedure should be followed?

capital and short-term assets have a more immediate focus. Exhibit 10.A3 highlights some key questions that financial tactics must answer.

Accounting managers have seen their need to contribute value increasingly scrutinized. Traditional expectations centered around financial accounting; reporting requirements from bank and SEC entities and tax law compliance remain areas in which actions are dictated by outside governance. Managerial accounting, where managers are responsible for keeping records of costs and the use of funds within their company, has taken on increased strategic significance in the last decade. This change has involved two tactical areas: (1) how to account for costs of creating and providing their business's products and services and (2) valuing the business, particularly among publicly traded companies.

Managerial cost accounting has traditionally provided information for managers using cost categories like those shown on the left side of the following table. However, value chain advocates have been increasingly successful getting managers to seek activity-based cost accounting information like that shown on the right side. In so doing, accounting is becoming a more critical, relevant source of information that truly benefits strategic management.

Traditional Cost Accounting in a Purchasing Department		Activity-Based Cost Accounting in the Same Purchasing Department	
Wages and salaries	$350,000	Evaluate supplier capabilities	$135,750
Employee benefits	115,000	Process purchase orders	82,100
Supplies	6,500	Expedite supplier deliveries	23,500
Travel	2,400	Expedite internal processing	15,840
Depreciation	17,000	Check quality of items purchased	94,300
Other fixed charges	124,000	Check incoming deliveries against purchase orders	48,450
Miscellaneous operating expenses	25,250		
	$640,150	Resolve problems	110,000
		Internal administration	130,210
			$640,150

Source: From Terence P. Pare, "A New Tool for Managing Costs," *Fortune*, June 14, 1993, pp. 124–29. Copyright, © 1993, Time, Inc. All rights reserved.

FUNCTIONAL TACTICS IN RESEARCH AND DEVELOPMENT

With the increasing rate of technological change in most competitive industries, research and development has assumed a key strategic role in many firms. In the technology-intensive computer and pharmaceutical industries, for example, firms typically spend between 4 and 6 percent, respectively, of their sales dollars on R&D. In other industries, such as the hotel/motel and construction industries, R&D spending is less than 1 percent of sales. Thus, functional R&D tactics may be more critical instruments of the business strategy in some industries than in others.

Exhibit 10.A4 illustrates the types of questions addressed by R&D tactics. First, R&D tactics should clarify whether basic research or product development research will be emphasized. Several major oil companies now have solar energy subsidiaries in which basic research is emphasized, while the smaller oil companies emphasize product development research.

The choice of emphasis between basic research and product development also involves the time horizon for R&D efforts. Should these efforts be focused on the near term or the long term? The solar energy subsidiaries of the major oil companies have long-term perspectives, while the smaller oil companies focus on creating products now in order to establish a competitive niche in the growing solar industry.

R&D tactics also involve organization of the R&D function. For example, should R&D work be conducted solely within the firm, or should portions of that work be contracted out? A closely related issue is whether R&D should be centralized or decentralized. What emphasis should be placed on process R&D versus product R&D?

Decisions on all of these questions are influenced by the firm's R&D posture, which can be offensive or defensive, or both. If that posture is offensive, as is true for small high-technology firms, the firm will emphasize technological innovation and new-product development as the basis for its future success. This orientation entails high risks (and high payoffs) and demands considerable technological skill, forecasting expertise, and the ability to quickly transform innovations into commercial products.

A defensive R&D posture emphasizes product modification and the ability to copy or acquire new technology. Converse Shoes is a good example of a firm with such an R&D posture. Faced with the massive R&D budgets of Nike and Reebok, Converse placed R&D emphasis on

EXHIBIT 10.A4 **Key Functional Tactics in R&D**

R&D Decision Area	Typical Questions That the Functional Tactics Should Answer
Basic research versus product and process development	To what extent should innovation and breakthrough research be emphasized? In relation to the emphasis on product development, refinement, and modification? What critical operating processes need R&D attention? What new projects are necessary to support growth?
Time horizon	Is the emphasis short term or long term? Which orientation best supports the business strategy? The marketing and production strategy?
Organizational fit	Should R&D be done in-house or contracted out? Should R&D be centralized or decentralized? What should be the relationship between the R&D units and product managers? Marketing managers? Production managers?
Basic R&D posture	Should the firm maintain an offensive posture, seeking to lead innovation in its industry? Should the firm adopt a defensive posture, responding to the innovations of its competitors?

EXHIBIT 10.A5 **Key Functional Tactics in HRM**

Functional Tactic	Typical Questions That HRM Tactics Should Answer
Recruitment, selection, and orientation	What key human resources are needed to support the chosen strategy? How do we recruit these human resources? How sophisticated should our selection process be? How should we introduce new employees to the organization?
Career development and training	What are our future human resource needs? How can we prepare our people to meet these needs? How can we help our people develop?
Compensation	What levels of pay are appropriate for the tasks we require? How can we motivate and retain good people? How should we interpret our payment, incentive, benefit, and seniority policies?
Evaluation, discipline, and control	How often should we evaluate our people? Formally or informally? What disciplinary steps should we take to deal with poor performance or inappropriate behavior? In what ways should we "control" individual and group performance?
Labor relations and equal opportunity requirements	How can we maximize labor-management cooperation? How do our personnel practices affect women/minorities? Should we have hiring policies?

bolstering the product life cycle of its prime products (particularly canvas shoes).

Large companies with some degree of technological leadership often use a combination of offensive and defensive R&D strategy. GE in the electrical industry, IBM in the computer industry, and Du Pont in the chemical industry all have a defensive R&D posture for currently available products *and* an offensive R&D posture in basic, long-term research.

FUNCTIONAL TACTICS IN HUMAN RESOURCE MANAGEMENT

The strategic importance of human resource management (HRM) tactics received widespread endorsement in the 1990s. HRM tactics aid long-term success in the development of managerial talent and competent employees, the creation of systems to manage compensation or regulatory concerns, and guiding the effective utilization of human resources to achieve both the firm's short-term objectives and employees' satisfaction and development. HRM tactics are helpful in the areas shown in Exhibit 10.A5. The recruitment, selection, and orientation should establish the basic parameters for bringing new people into a firm and adapting them to "the way things are done" in the firm. The career development and training component should guide the action that personnel take to meet the future human resources needs of the overall business strategy. Merrill Lynch, a major brokerage firm whose long-term corporate strategy is to become a diversified financial service institution, has moved into such areas as investment banking, consumer credit, and venture capital. In support of its long-term objectives, it has incorporated extensive early-career training and ongoing career development programs to meet its expanding need for personnel with multiple competencies. Larger organizations need HRM tactics that guide decisions regarding labor relations; Equal Employment Opportunity Commission requirements; and employee compensation, discipline, and control.

Current trends in HRM parallel the reorientation of managerial accounting by looking at their cost structure anew. HRM's "paradigm shift" involves looking at people expense as an investment in human capital. This involves looking at the business's value chain and the "value" of human resource components along the various links in that chain. One of the results of this shift in perspective has been the downsizing and outsourcing phenomena of the last quarter century. While this has been traumatic for millions of employees in companies worldwide, its underlying basis involves an effort to examine the use of "human capital" to create value in ways that maximize the human contribution. This scrutiny continues to challenge the HRM area to include recent major trends to outsource some or all HRM activities not regarded as part of a firm's core competence. The emerging implications for human resource management tactics may be a value-oriented perspective on the role of human resources in a business's value chain as suggested here:

Traditional HRM Ideas	Emerging HRM Ideas
Emphasis solely on physical skills	Emphasis on total contribution to the firm
Expectation of predictable, repetitive behavior	Expectation of innovative and creative behavior
Comfort with stability and conformity	Tolerance of ambiguity and change
Avoidance of responsibility and decision making	Accepting responsibility for making decisions
Training covering only specific tasks	Open-ended commitment; broad continuous development
Emphasis placed on outcomes and results	Emphasis placed on processes and means
High concern for quantity and throughput	High concern for total customer value
Concern for individual efficiency	Concern for overall effectiveness
Functional and subfunctional specialization	Cross-functional integration
Labor force seen as unnecessary expense	Labor force seen as critical investment
Workforce is management's adversary	Management and workforce are partners

Source: From A. Miller and G. Dess, *Strategic Management,* 2002, p. 400. Copyright © 2002 The McGraw-Hill Companies, Inc. Reprinted with permission.

To summarize, functional tactics reflect how each major activity of a firm contributes to the implementation of the business strategy. The specificity of functional tactics and the involvement of operating managers in their development help ensure understanding of and commitment to the chosen strategy. A related step in implementation is the development of policies that empower operating managers and their subordinates to make decisions and to act autonomously.

Chapter Eleven

Organizational Structure

After reading and studying this chapter, you should be able to

1. Identify five traditional organizational structures and the pros and cons of each.

2. Describe the product-team structure and explain why it is a prototype for a more open, agile organizational structure.

3. Explain five ways improvements have been sought in traditional organizational structures.

4. Describe what is meant by agile, virtual organizations.

5. Explain how outsourcing can create agile, virtual organizations, along with its pros and cons.

6. Describe boundaryless organizations and why they are important.

7. Explain why organizations of the future need to be ambidextrous learning organizations.

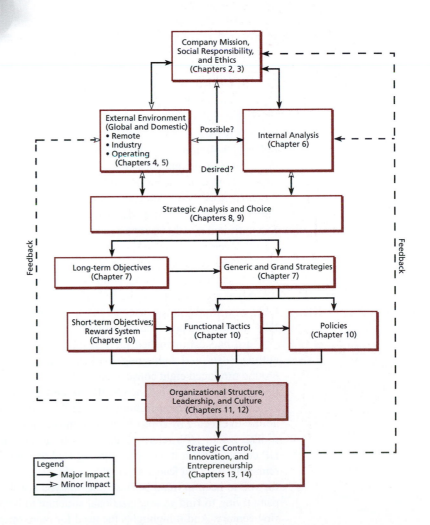

337

Until this point in the strategic management process, managers have maintained a decidedly market-oriented focus as they formulate strategies and begin implementation through action plans detailing the tactics and actions that will be taken in each functional activity. Now the process takes an organizational focus—getting the work of the business done efficiently and effectively so as to make the strategy work. What is the best way to organize people and tasks to execute the strategy effectively? What should be done "in-house" and what activities should be "outsourced" for others to do?

What has happened at Hewlett-Packard over the course of this decade? It began with new CEO Carly Fiorina taking over HP in the midst of a global recession. The unfortunate reality for her: HP's lumbering organization was losing touch with its global customers. Her response: as illustrated in Exhibit 11.1, Strategy in Action, Fiorina immediately dismantled the decentralized structure honed throughout HP's 64-year history. Pre-Fiorina, HP was a collection of 83 independently run units, each focused on a product such as scanners or security software. Fiorina collapsed those into four sprawling organizations. One so-called back-end unit developed and built computers; another focused on printers and imaging equipment. The back-end divisions were to hand products off to the two "front-end" sales and marketing groups to peddle the wares—one to consumers, the other to corporations. The theory: the new structure would boost collaboration, giving sales and marketing execs a direct pipeline to engineers so products were developed from the ground up to solve customer problems. This was the first time a company with thousands of product lines and scores of businesses attempted a front-back approach, a structure that requires laser focus and superb coordination.

Fiorina believed she had little choice lest the company experience a near-death experience like Xerox or, 10 years earlier, IBM. The conundrum: how could HP put the full force of the company behind winning in its immediate fiercely competitive technology business when they must also cook up brand-new megamarkets? It's a riddle Fiorina said she could solve only by sweeping structural change that would ready HP for the next stage of the technology revolution, when companies latch on to the Internet to transform their operations. At its core lay a conviction that HP must become "ambidextrous and boundaryless," excelling at short-term execution while pursuing long-term visions that create new markets.

Did it work? No. After five years, Fiorina was dismissed. The chairman of the HP board of directors, Patricia Dunn, said at that time that the board did not intend to change HP's strategy. She indicated that the board was confident in HP's overall strategy even though, she acknowledged, several analysts and stockholders disagreed with the board on this. Confident that the strategy was correct, she indicated that the HP board concluded it had been execution of that strategy, particularly with regard to the "new" HP organizational structure, that the board felt was a major contributor to the lack of success at HP. So, Dunn said, the board wanted a new CEO who would simply execute better. Two months later, Mark Hurd, a 25-year veteran of NCR's sprawling portfolio of businesses, became HP's new chief executive.

Hurd had distinguished himself turning around NCR over the previous two years by cutting costs and tightening marketing and increasing accountability. His NCR turnaround produced eight consecutive profitable quarters at NCR. His organizational structure preference—smaller independently run units, each with a narrow product focus—allowed a clear sense of responsibilities, measurable accountability, tight spending controls, and the ability to execute by controlling their units production-to-sales activities.

The result: HP's return to smaller, semi-autonomous units led to exceptional success at HP culminating in it recently eclipsing Dell as the world's largest computer company, while remaining a global leader and highly profitable printer company. The HP saga is a useful one for you to keep in mind because it shows you a well-known, major, global technology company trying to find an organizational structure to help if be more competitive in the twenty-first century. And it highlights the need for more openness in an organizational structure—a "boundaryless" organization, as management icon Jack Welch called his approach—but also

Fiorina Gives Way to Hurd at Hewlett-Packard

When Carly Fiorina arrived at HP, the company was a confederation of 83 autonomous product units reporting through four groups. She radically revamped the structure into two "back-end" divisions—one developing printers, scanners, and the like, and the other computers. These report to "front-end" groups that market and sell HP's wares. Here's how the overhaul went:

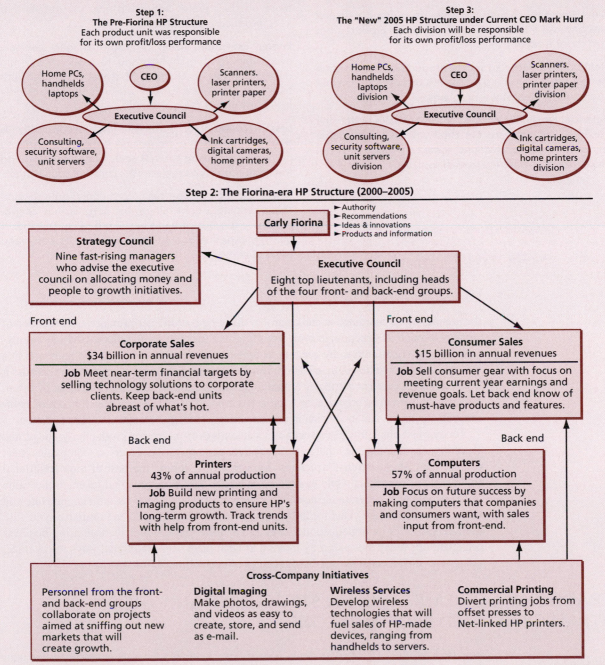

Step 1:
The Pre-Fiorina HP Structure
Each product unit was responsible for its own profit/loss performance

Step 3:
The "New" 2005 HP Structure under Current CEO Mark Hurd
Each division will be responsible for its own profit/loss performance

Step 2: The Fiorina-era HP Structure (2000–2005)

Carly Fiorina

- ► Authority
- ► Recommendations
- ► Ideas & innovations
- ► Products and information

Strategy Council
Nine fast-rising managers who advise the executive council on allocating money and people to growth initiatives.

Executive Council
Eight top lieutenants, including heads of the four front- and back-end groups.

Front end

Corporate Sales
$34 billion in annual revenues
Job Meet near-term financial targets by selling technology solutions to corporate clients. Keep back-end units abreast of what's hot.

Front end

Consumer Sales
$15 billion in annual revenues
Job Sell consumer gear with focus on meeting current year earnings and revenue goals. Let back end know of must-have products and features.

Back end

Printers
43% of annual production
Job Build new printing and imaging products to ensure HP's long-term growth. Track trends with help from front-end units.

Back end

Computers
57% of annual production
Job Focus on future success by making computers that companies and consumers want, with sales input from front-end.

Cross-Company Initiatives

Personnel from the front- and back-end groups collaborate on projects aimed at sniffing out new markets that will create growth.

Digital Imaging Make photos, drawings, and videos as easy to create, store, and send as e-mail.

Wireless Services Develop wireless technologies that will fuel sales of HP-made devices, ranging from handhelds to servers.

Commercial Printing Divert printing jobs from offset presses to Net-linked HP printers.

(continued)

Exhibit 11.1 cont.

Fiorina's Expectations
The Assessment

Happier Customers Clients should find HP easier to deal with, since they'll work with just one account team.

Sales Boost HP should maximize its selling opportunities because account reps will sell all HP products, not just those from one division.

Real Solutions HP can sell its products in combination as "solutions"—instead of just PCs or printers—to companies facing e-business problems.

Financial Flexibility With all corporate sales under one roof, HP can measure the total value of a customer, allowing reps to discount some products and still maximize profits on the overall contract.

What Actually Happened over Fiorina's 5 Years
The Assessment

Overwhelmed with Duties With so many products being made and sold by just four units, HP execs have more on their plates and could miss the details that keep products competitive.

Poorer Execution When product managers oversaw everything from manufacturing to sales, they could respond quickly to changes. That will be harder with front- and back-end groups synching their plans only every few weeks.

Less Accountability Profit-and-loss responsibility is shared between the front- and back-end groups so no one person is on the hot seat. Finger-pointing and foot-dragging could replace HP's collegial cooperation.

Fewer Spending Controls With powerful division chiefs keeping a tight rein on the purse strings, spending rarely got out of hand in the old HP. In the fourth quarter, expenses soared as those lines of command broke down.

the importance of coordination and control of the organization's performance and execution of strategy through its structure. In some ways Fiorina's structure more reflected the way twenty-first-century organizations are seeking to organize themselves, while Hurd's approach is a return to a more traditional organization. Hurd's approach has found success in part because it is an attempt to combine attributes of traditional organizational structures and those of newer, boundaryless or virtual organization approaches in an effort to balance a need for control, coordination, openness, and innovation in implementing a strategy best suited to HP's situation.

Today's fast-changing, global economy demands ever-increasing productivity, speed, and flexibility from companies that seek to survive, perhaps thrive. To do so, companies must change their organizational structures dramatically, retaining the best of their traditional (hierarchical) structures while embracing radically new structures that leverage the value of the people who generate ideas, collaborate with colleagues and customers, innovate and therein generate future value for the company. So this chapter seeks to familiarize you with both perspectives on organizational structure and the major trends in structuring business organizations today. Let's start by looking at what have been traditional ways to organize, along with the advantages and disadvantages of each organizational structure.

TRADITIONAL ORGANIZATIONAL STRUCTURES AND THEIR STRATEGY-RELATED PROS AND CONS

You may be one of several students who choose to start your own business rather than take a job with an established company when you finish your current degree program.

Or perhaps you are currently in a full-time job position but soon plan to leave that job and start your own company. Like millions of others who have done or will soon do the same thing, usually with a few other "partners," your group will be faced with the question of how to organize your work and the activities and tasks necessary to do the work of your new company. What you are looking for is an organizational structure. We do not mean, here, the "legal" structure of your company such as a proprietorship, corporation, limited liability corporation, or limited partnership to mention a few. **Organizational structure** refers to the formalized arrangement of interaction between and responsibility for the tasks, people, and resources in an organization. It is most often seen as a chart, often a pyramidal chart, with positions or titles and roles in cascading fashion. The organizational structure you and your partners would have in this start-up of which you are a part would most likely be a "simple" organization.

organizational structure
Refers to the formalized arrangements of interaction between and responsibility for the tasks, people, and resources in an organization.

Simple Organizational Structure

In the smallest business enterprise, a simple structure usually prevails. A **simple organizational structure** is one where there is an owner and, usually, a few employees and where the arrangement of tasks, responsibilities, and communication is highly informal and accomplished through direct supervision. All strategic and operating decisions are made by the owner, or a small owner-partner team. Because the scope of the firm's activities are modest, there is little need to formalize roles, communication, and procedures. With the strategic concern primarily being survival, and the likelihood that one bad decision could seriously threaten continued existence, this structure maximizes the owner's control. It can also allow rapid response to product/market shifts and the ability to accommodate unique customer demands without major coordination difficulties. This is in part because the owner is directly involved with customers on a regular basis. Simple structures encourage employees to multitask, and they are efficacious in businesses that serve a simple, local product/market or narrow niche.

simple organizational structure
Structure in which there is an owner and a few employees and where the arrangement of tasks, responsibilities, and communication is highly informal and accomplished through direct supervision.

The simple structure can be very demanding on the owner-manager. If it is successful, and starts to grow, this can cause the owner-manager to give increased attention to day-to-day concerns, which may come at the expense of time invested in stepping back and examining strategic questions about the company's future. At the same time, the company's reliance on the owner as the central point for all decisions can limit the development of future managers capable of assuming duties that allow the owner time to be a strategist. And, this structure usually requires a multitalented, resourceful owner, good at producing and selling a product or service—and at controlling scarce funds.

Most businesses in this country and around the world are of this type. Many survive for a period of time, then go out of business because of financial, owner, or market conditions. Some grow, having been built on an idea or capability that taps a great need for what the company does. As they grow, the need to "get organized" is increasingly heard among owners and a growing number of employees in the growing company. That fortunate circumstance historically led to the need for a functional organizational structure.

Functional Organizational Structure

Continuing our example, you and your partners, no doubt being among the successful ones, find increased demand for your product or service. Your sales have grown substantially—and so have the number of people you employ to do the work of your business. Once you reach 15 to 25 people in the organization, you will experience a need to have some people handle sales, some operations, a financial accounting person or two—that is, you will need to have different people focus on different functions within the business to become better organized and efficient, and to achieve control and coordination.

functional organizational structure
Structure in which the tasks, people, and technologies necessary to do the work of the business are divided into separate "functional" groups (e.g., marketing, operations, finance) with increasingly formal procedures for coordinating and integrating their activities to provide the business's products and services.

A **functional organizational structure** is one in which the tasks, people, and technologies necessary to do the work of the business are divided into separate "functional" groups (such as marketing, operations, finance) with increasingly formal procedures for coordinating and integrating their activities to provide the business's products and services.

Functional structures predominate in firms with a single or narrow product focus and that have experienced success in their marketplace, leading to increased sales and an increased number of people needed to do the work behind those sales. Such firms require well-defined skills and areas of specialization to build competitive advantages in providing their products or services. Dividing tasks into functional specialties enables the personnel of these firms to concentrate on only one aspect of the necessary work. This allows use of the latest technical skills and develops a high level of efficiency.

Product, customer, or technology considerations determine the identity of the parts in a functional structure. A hotel business might be organized around housekeeping (maids), the front desk, maintenance, restaurant operations, reservations and sales, accounting, and personnel. An equipment manufacturer might be organized around production, engineering/ quality control, purchasing, marketing, personnel, and finance/accounting. Two examples of functional organizations are illustrated in Exhibit 11.2.

The strategic challenge presented by the functional structure is effective coordination of the functional units. The narrow technical expertise achieved through specialization can lead to limited perspectives and to differences in the priorities of the functional units. Specialists may see the firm's strategic issues primarily as "marketing" problems or "production" problems. The potential conflict among functional units makes the coordinating role of the chief executive critical. Integrating devices (such as project teams or planning committees) are frequently used in functionally organized firms to enhance coordination and to facilitate understanding across functional areas.

Divisional Structure

When a firm diversifies its product/service lines, covers broad geographic areas, utilizes unrelated market channels, or begins to serve heterogeneous customer groups, a functional structure rapidly becomes inadequate. If a functional structure is retained under these circumstances, production managers may have to oversee the production of numerous and varied products or services, marketing managers may have to create sales programs for vastly different products or sell through vastly different distribution channels, and top management may be confronted with excessive coordination demands. A new organizational structure is often necessary to meet the increased coordination and decision-making requirements that result from increased diversity and size, and the divisional structure is the form often chosen.

divisional organizational structure
Structure in which a set of relatively autonomous units, or divisions, are governed by a central corporate office but where each operating division has its own functional specialists who provide products or services different from those of other divisions.

A **divisional organizational structure** is one in which a set of relatively autonomous units, or divisions, are governed by a central corporate office but where each operating division has its own functional specialists who provide products or services different from those of other divisions. For many years, global automobile companies have used divisional structures organized by product groups. Manufacturers often organize sales into divisions based on differences in distribution channels.

A divisional structure allows corporate management to delegate authority for the strategic management of distinct business entities—the division. This expedites decision making in response to varied competitive environments and enables corporate management to concentrate on corporate-level strategic decisions. The division usually is given profit responsibility, which facilitates accurate assessment of profit and loss. Exhibit 11.3 illustrates a divisional organizational structure and specifies the strategic advantages and disadvantages of such structures.

EXHIBIT 11.2
Functional Organization Structures

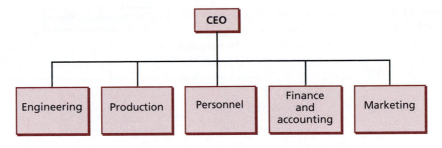

A process-oriented functional structure (an electronics distributor):

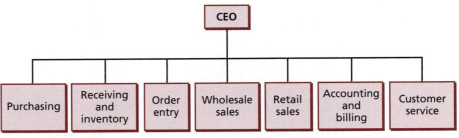

Strategic Advantages	Strategic Disadvantages
1. Achieves efficiency through specialization	1. Promotes narrow specialization and functional rivalry or conflict
2. Develops functional expertise	2. Creates difficulties in functional coordination and interfunctional decision making
3. Differentiates and delegates day-to-day operating decisions	3. Limits development of general managers
4. Retains centralized control of strategic decisions	4. Has a strong potential for interfunctional conflict—priority placed on functional areas, not the entire business
5. Tightly links structure to strategy by designating key activities as separate units	5. May cost more to do a function than it does "outside" the company, unless outsourced

Strategic Business Unit

Some firms encounter difficulty in controlling their divisional operations as the diversity, size, and number of these units continues to increase. Corporate management may encounter difficulty in evaluating and controlling its numerous, often multi-industry divisions. Under these conditions, it may become necessary to add another layer of management in order to improve implementation, promote synergy and gain greater control over the diverse business interests. The **strategic business unit** (SBU) is an adaptation of the divisional structure whereby various divisions or parts of divisions are grouped together based on some common strategic elements, usually linked to distinct product/market differences. General Foods, after originally organizing itself along product lines (which served overlapping markets), created an SBU organization along menu lines with SBUs for breakfast foods, beverages, main meals, desserts, and pet foods. This change allowed General Foods to adapt a vast divisional organization into five strategic business areas with a distinct market focus for each unit and the divisions each contained.

strategic business unit
An adaptation of the divisional structure in which various divisions or parts of divisions are grouped together based on some common strategic elements, usually linked to distinct product/market differences.

EXHIBIT 11.3
Divisional
Organizational
Structure

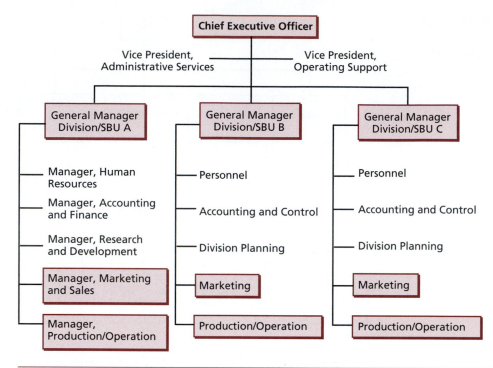

Strategic Advantages	Strategic Disadvantages
1. Forces coordination and necessary authority down to the appropriate level for rapid response	1. Fosters potentially dysfunctional competition for corporate-level resources
2. Places strategy development and implementation in closer proximity to the unique environments of the division	2. Presents the problem of determining how much authority should be given to division managers
3. Frees chief executive officer for broader strategic decision making	3. Creates a potential for policy inconsistencies among divisions
4. Sharply focuses accountability for performance	4. Presents the problem of distributing corporate overhead costs in a way that's acceptable to division managers with profit responsibility
5. Retains functional specialization within each division	5. Increases costs incurred through duplication functions
6. Provides good training ground for strategic managers	6. Creates difficulty maintaining overall corporate image
7. Increases focus on products, markets, and quick response to change	

   The advantages and disadvantages of the SBU form are very similar to those identified for divisional structures in Exhibit 11.3. Added to its potential disadvantages would be the increased costs of coordination with another "pricy" level of management.

Holding Company

A final form of the divisional organization is the **holding company structure,** where the corporate entity is a broad collection of often unrelated businesses and divisions such

holding company structure
Structure in which the corporate entity is a broad collection of often unrelated businesses and divisions such that it (the corporate entity) acts as financial overseer "holding" the ownership interest in the various parts of the company, but has little direct managerial involvement.

that it (the corporate entity) acts as financial overseer "holding" the ownership interest in the various parts of the company but has little direct managerial involvement. Berkshire Hathaway owns a wide variety of businesses in full or in part. Essentially, at the corporate level, it provides financial support and manages each of these businesses, or divisions, through financial goals and annual review of performance, investment needs, etc. Otherwise, strategic and operating decisions are made in each separate company or division, which operates autonomously. The corporate office acts simply as a holding company.

This approach can provide a cost savings over the more active SBU approach since the additional level of "pricy" management is not that much. The negative, of course, becomes the degree to which the corporate office is dependent on each business unit's management team and the lack of control over the decisions those managers make in terms of being able to make timely adjustments or corrections.

Matrix Organizational Structure

In large companies, increased diversity leads to numerous product and project efforts of major strategic significance. The result is a need for an organizational form that provides skills and resources where and when they are most vital. For example, a product development project needs a market research specialist for two months and a financial analyst one day per week. A customer site application needs a software engineer for one month and a customer service trainer one day per month for six weeks. Each of these situations is an example of a matrix organization that has been used to temporarily put people and resources where they are most needed. Citicorp, Matsushita, Microsoft, Dow Chemical, and Accenture are firms that now use some form of matrix organization.

matrix organizational structure
The matrix organization is a structure in which functional and staff personnel are assigned to both a basic functional area and to a project or product manager. It provides dual channels of authority, performance responsibility, evaluation, and control.

The **matrix organizational structure** is one in which functional and staff personnel are assigned to both a basic functional area and to a project or product manager. It provides dual channels of authority, performance responsibility, evaluation, and control, as shown in Exhibit 11.4. The matrix form is intended to make the best use of talented people within a firm by combining the advantages of functional specialization and product-project specialization.

The matrix structure also increases the number of middle managers who exercise general management responsibilities (through the project manager role) and, thus, broaden their exposure to organizationwide strategic concerns. In this way, the matrix structure overcomes a key deficiency of functional organizations while retaining the advantages of functional specialization.

Although the matrix structure is easy to design, it is difficult to implement. Dual chains of command challenge fundamental organizational orientations. Negotiating shared responsibilities, the use of resources, and priorities can create misunderstanding or confusion among subordinates. These problems are heightened in an international context with the complications introduced by distance, language, time, and culture.

Product-Team Structure

product-team structure
Assigns functional managers and specialists to a new product, project, or process team that is empowered to make major decisions about their product. Team members are assigned permanently in most cases.

To avoid the deficiencies that might arise from a permanent matrix structure, some firms are accomplishing particular strategic tasks, by means of a "temporary" or "flexible" *overlay structure*. This approach, used recently by such firms as Motorola, Matsushita, Philips, and Unilever, is meant to take *temporary* advantage of a matrix-type team while preserving an underlying divisional structure. This adaptation of the matrix approach has become known as the "product-team structure." The **product-team structure** seeks to simplify and amplify the focus of resources on a narrow but strategically important product, project, market, customer, or innovation. Exhibit 11.5 illustrates how the product-team structure looks.

EXHIBIT 11.4

Matrix Organizational Structure

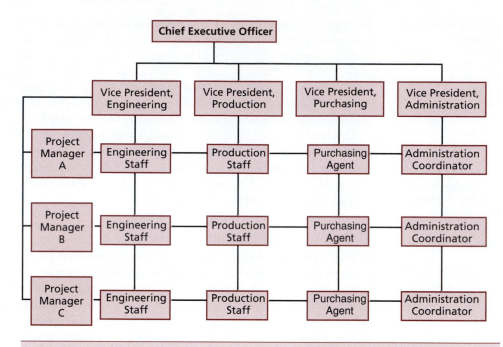

Strategic Advantages	Strategic Disadvantages
1. Accommodates a wide variety of project-oriented business activities	1. May result in confusion and contradictory policies
2. Provides good training ground for strategic managers	2. Necessitates tremendous horizontal and vertical coordination
3. Maximizes efficient use of functional managers	3. Can proliferate information logjams and excess reporting
4. Fosters creativity and multiple sources of diversity	4. Can trigger turf battles and loss of accountability
5. Gives middle management broader exposure to strategic issues	

The product-team structure assigns functional managers and specialists (e.g., engineering, marketing, financial, R&D, operations) to a new product, project, or process team that is empowered to make major decisions about their product. The team is usually created at the inception of the new-product idea, and they stay with it indefinitely if it becomes a viable business. Instead of being assigned on a temporary basis, as in the matrix structure, team members are assigned permanently to that team in most cases. This results in much lower coordination costs and, because every function is represented, usually reduces the number of management levels above the team level needed to approve team decisions.

It appears that product teams formed at the beginning of product-development processes generate cross-functional understanding that irons out early product or process design problems. They also reduce costs associated with design, manufacturing, and marketing, while typically speeding up innovation and customer responsiveness because authority rests with the team allowing decisions to be made more quickly. That ability to make speedier, cost-saving decisions has the added advantage of eliminating the need for one or more management layers above the team level, which would traditionally have been in place to review and control these types of decisions. While seemingly obvious, it has only recently become apparent that those additional management layers were also making these decisions with

EXHIBIT 11.5
The Product-Team Structure

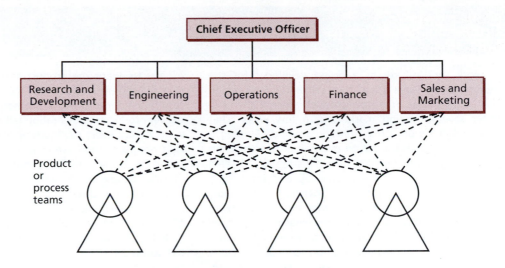

less firsthand understanding of the issues involved than the cross-functional team members brought to the product or process in the first place. Exhibit 11.6, Strategy in Action, gives examples of a product-team approach at several well-known companies and some of the advantages that appear to have accrued.

WHAT A DIFFERENCE A CENTURY MAKES

Exhibit 11.7 offers a useful perspective for designing effective organizational structures in tomorrow's global economy. In contrasting twentieth- and twenty-first-century corporations on different characteristics, it offers a historical or evolutionary perspective on organizational attributes associated with successful strategy execution today and just a few years ago. Successful organizations once required an internal focus, structured interaction, self-sufficiency, a top-down approach. Today and tomorrow, organizational structure reflects an external focus, flexible interaction, interdependency, and a bottom-up approach, just to mention a few characteristics associated with strategy execution and success. Three fundamental trends are driving decisions about effective organizational structures in the twenty-first century: globalization, the Internet, and speed of decision making.

Globalization

Pulitzer Prize–winning author Thomas Friedman[1] described the first 10 years of the twenty-first century as "Globalization 3.0." This, he says, is a whole new era in which the world is shrinking from a size "small" to a size "tiny" and flattening the global playing field for everyone at the same time. He describes it as follows:

> Globalization 1.0 was countries globalizing;
> Globalization 2.0 was companies globalizing;
> Globalization 3.0 is the newfound power for *individuals*
> To collaborate and compete globally, instantly;
> Individuals from every corner of the flat world are
> Being empowered to enter a wide open, global marketplace.[2]

---

[1] Thomas L. Friedman, *The World Is Flat* (New York: Farrar, Straus and Giroux, 2005).
[2] Ibid, p. 10.

Cross-Functional Teams

BusinessWeek

"I work for Unilever as a brand developer for the beauty brand Dove Soap. I am currently working on the initial stages of a new-product concept that will enter several foreign markets in a few years. That means that I work on everything from developing a product and packaging it to creating a retail marketing strategy with the help of a cross-functional team made up of international, regional, and local R&D, market research, promotions, finance, legal, supply chain and sales people. These members of my team have other responsibilities in their specialty, but they are responsible to me in helping develop this concept into a profitable new addition to Unilever's Dove brand of products." . . . Jason Levin, MBA graduate, Georgetown University.

"At Electronic Arts, innovations happen from small, cross-functional teams of programmers, designers, artists, development and marketing people. And we have found that the best way to avoid the usual conflict between development/programming [our "operations"] and marketing is to have a cross-functional team leader with experience in both camps. The next best is a leader with great empathy for the other function. In the video game business, that means that marketing leaders should be awesome game-players, and game-makers should be awesome tv-commercial makers." . . . Bing Gordon, CEO, Electronic Arts.

"I'm a Workplace Solutions Domain Engineer at IBM in Cambridge, Mass. As part of a cross-functional, software product development team, I manage product requirements by working with clients, analysts, and experts to adapt the product and strengthen its position and differentiation. As the external communicator for my team, I talk with customers, press, analysts and deliver product demonstration talks to audiences worldwide. Almost every day I turn on Sametime, our internal chat program, and have regular meetings and conversations with my cross-functional team members which includes people in Massachusetts, North Carolina and many in China. Questions, requests, and can-you-join-a-conference-call-right-now are normal pings." . . . Sally McSwiney, MBA graduate, Bentley College.

In his 20-year career at BMW, CEO Norbert Reithofer has worked his way up from maintenance planner to head of production and, by 2007, CEO. Along the way, he has built an informal network of associates across the company. Five years ago, he and Development Chief Burkhard Goeschel wanted to halve the time it took to reach full production on a next generation 3 series. They reached deep into the organization to assemble a cross-functional team of R&D and production aces who then worked for three years to reach their goal. The car was introduced in March, with full production of 800 cars daily in June. The cross-functional team had defied the skeptics. . . . Norbert Reithofer, Head of Production and now CEO, BMW, Germany.

Sources: Reprinted with special permission from "Always on the Go at Big Blue," *BusinessWeek,* May 17, 2007; "A Role Model for the Team Player," *BusinessWeek,* October 16, 2006; "Managing a Brand: Concept to Product," *BusinessWeek,* October 16, 2006; and "Bing Gordon's Game Revealed," *BusinessWeek,* June 26, 2007. Copyright © 2007 The McGraw-Hill Companies.

This means that companies in virtually every industry either operate globally (e.g., computers, aerospace) or will soon do so. In the past 10 years, the percentage of sales from outside the home market for these five companies grew dramatically:

	1995	2000	2005	2010 est.
General Electric	16%	35%	41%	55%
Wal-Mart	0	18	32	43
McDonald's	46	65	71	79
Nokia	85	98	99	99+
Toyota	44	53	61	78

The need for global coordination and innovation is forcing constant experimentation and adjustment to get the right mix of local initiative, information flow, leadership, and corporate culture. At Swedish-based Ericsson, top managers scrutinize compensation schemes to make managers pay attention to global performance and avoid turf battles, while also

EXHIBIT 11.7
What a Difference a Century Can Make

Source: Reprinted with special permission from "21st Century Corporation," *BusinessWeek*, August 28, 2000. Copyright © 2000 The McGraw-Hill Companies.

Contrasting Views of the Corporation:		
Characteristic	**20th Century**	**21st Century**
Organization	The pyramid	The Web or network
Focus	Internal	External
Style	Structured	Flexible
Source of strength	Stability	Change
Structure	Self-sufficiency	Interdependencies
Resources	Atoms—physical assets	Bits—information
Operations	Vertical integration	Virtual integration
Products	Mass production	Mass customization
Reach	Domestic	Global
Financials	Quarterly	Real time
Inventories	Months	Hours
Strategy	Top-down	Bottom-up
Leadership	Dogmatic	Inspirational
Workers	Employees	Employees and free agents
Job expectations	Security	Personal growth
Motivation	To compete	To build
Improvements	Incremental	Revolutionary
Quality	Affordable best	No compromise

attending to their local operations. Companies such as Dutch electronics giant Philips regularly move headquarters for different businesses to the hottest regions for new trends—the "high voltage" markets. Its digital set-top box is now in California; its audio business moved from Europe to Hong Kong.[3]

Global once meant selling goods in overseas markets. Next was locating operations in numerous countries. Today companies will call on talents and resources wherever they can be found around the globe, just as they now sell worldwide. Such companies may be based in the United States, do their software programming in New Delhi, their engineering in Germany, and their manufacturing in Indonesia. The ramifications for organizational structures are revolutionary.

The Internet

The Net gives everyone in the organization, or working with it—from the lowest clerk to the CEO to any supplier or customer—the ability to access a vast array of information—instantaneously, from anywhere. Ideas, requests, and instructions zap around the globe in the blink of an eye. The Net allows the global enterprise with different functions, offices, and activities dispersed around the world to be seamlessly connected so that far-flung customers, employees, and suppliers can work together in real time. The result—coordination, communication, and decision-making functions are accomplished quickly and easily, making traditional organizational structures look slow, inefficient, and noncompetitive.

Speed

Technology, or digitization, means removing human minds and hands from an organization's most routine tasks and replacing them with computers and networks. Digitizing everything from employee benefits to accounts receivable to product design cuts cost, time, and payroll, resulting in cost savings and vast improvements in speed. "Combined with the Internet,

[3] Wendy Zellner, "See the World, Erase Its Borders," *BusinessWeek,* August 28, 2000.

the speed of actions, deliberations, and information will increase dramatically," says Intel's Andy Grove. "You are going to see unbelievable speed and efficiencies," says Cisco's John Chambers, "with many companies about to increase productivity 20 percent to 40 percent per year." Leading-edge technologies will enable employees throughout the organization to seize opportunity as it arises. These technologies will allow employees, suppliers, and freelancers anywhere in the world to converse in numerous languages online without need for a translator to develop markets, new products, new processes. Again, the ramifications for organizational structures are revolutionary.

Whether technology assisted or not, globalization of business activity creates a potential velocity of decision making that challenges traditional hierarchical organizational structures. A company like Cisco, for example, may be negotiating 50 to 60 alliances at one time due to the nature of its diverse operations. The speed at which these negotiations must be conducted and decisions made requires a simple and accommodating organizational structure lest the opportunities may be lost. Consider these recent observations by *BusinessWeek* editors at the end of a year-long research effort asking just the same question:

> The management of multinationals used to be a neat discipline with comforting rules and knowable best practices. But globalization and the arrival of the information economy have rapidly demolished all the old precepts. The management of global companies, which must innovate simultaneously and speed information through horizontal, global-spanning networks, has become a daunting challenge. Old, rigid hierarchies are out—and flat, speedy, virtual organizations are in. Teamwork is a must and compensation schemes have to be redesigned to reward team players. But aside from that bit of wisdom, you can throw out the textbooks.
>
> CEOs will have to custom-design their organizations based on their industry, their own corporate legacy, and their key global customers—and they may have to revamp more than once to get it right. Highly admired companies such as General Electric, Hewlett-Packard, ABB Ltd., and Ericsson have already been through several organizational reincarnations in the past decade to boost global competitiveness.[4]

Faced with these and other major trends, what are managers doing to structure effective organizations? Let's examine this question two ways. First, we will summarize some key ways managers are changing traditional organizational structures to make them more responsive to this new reality. Second, we will examine current ideas for creating agile, virtual organizations.

INITIAL EFFORTS TO IMPROVE THE EFFECTIVENESS OF TRADITIONAL ORGANIZATIONAL STRUCTURES

Major efforts to improve traditional organizational structures seek to reduce unnecessary control and focus on enhancing core competencies, reducing costs, and opening organizations more fully to outside involvement and influence. One key emphasis in large organizations has been corporate headquarters.

Redefine the Role of Corporate Headquarters from Control to Support and Coordination

The role of corporate management in multibusiness and multinational companies increasingly face a common dilemma: How can the resource advantages of a large company be exploited, while ensuring the responsiveness and creativity found in the small companies

---

[4] John Byrne, "The 21st Century Corporation," *BusinessWeek,* August 28, 2000.

against which each of their businesses compete? This dilemma constantly presents managers with conflicting priorities or adjustments as corporate managers:[5]

- Rigorous financial controls and reporting enable cost efficiency, resource deployment, and autonomy across different units; flexible controls are conducive to responsiveness, innovation and "boundary spanning."
- Multibusiness companies historically gain advantage by exploiting resources and capabilities across different businesses and markets, yet competitive advantage in the future increasingly depends on the creation of new resources and capabilities.
- Aggressive portfolio management seeking maximum shareholder value is often best achieved through independent businesses; the creation of competitive advantage increasingly requires the management—recognition and coordination—of business interdependencies.

Increasingly, globally engaged, multibusiness companies are changing the role of corporate headquarters from one of control, resource allocation, and performance monitoring to one of coordinator of linkages across multiple businesses, supporter, and enabler of innovation and synergy. One way this has been done is to create an executive council comprised of top managers from each business, usually including four to five of their key managers, with the council then serving as the critical forum for corporate decision, discussions, and analysis. IBM's Sam Palmisano uses this approach today at IBM to cross-fertilize ideas and opportunities across its software, enterprise services, chip design, and now virtual world business activities. These councils replace the traditional corporate staff function of overseeing and evaluating various business units, replacing it instead with a forum to share business unit plans, to discuss problems and issues, to seek assistance and expertise, and to foster cooperation and innovation.

Jack Welch's experience at GE provides a useful example. Upon becoming chairman, he viewed GE headquarters as interfering too much in GE's various businesses, generating too much paperwork, and offering minimal value added. He sought to "turn their role 180 degrees from checker, inquisitor, and authority figure to facilitator, helper, and supporter of GE's 13 businesses." He said, "What we do here at headquarters . . . is to multiply the resources we have, the human resources, the financial resources, and the best practices . . . Our job is to help, it's to assist, it's to make these businesses stronger, to help them grow and be more powerful." GE's Corporate Executive Council was reconstituted from predominantly a corporate level group of sector managers (which was eliminated) into a group comprised of the leaders of GE's 13 businesses and a few corporate executives. They met formally two days each quarter to discuss problems and issues and to enable cooperation and resource sharing. This has expanded to other councils throughout GE intent on greater coordination, synergy, and idea sharing.

Balance the Demands for Control/Differentiation with the Need for Coordination/Integration

Specialization of work and effort allows a unit to develop greater expertise, focus, and efficiency. So it is that some organizations adopt functional, or similar, structures. Their strategy depends on dividing different activities within the firm into logical, common groupings—sales, operations, administration, or geography—so that each set of activities can be done most efficiently. Control of sets of activities is at a premium. Dividing activities in this manner, sometimes called "differentiation," is an important structural decision. At the same time, these separate activities, however they are differentiated, need to be coordinated and integrated back together as a whole so the business functions effectively.

[5] Robert M. Grant, *Contemporary Strategy Analysis* (Oxford: Blackwell, 2001), p. 503.

Demands for control and the coordination needs differ across different types of businesses and strategic situations.

The rise of a consumer culture around the world has led brand marketers to realize they need to take a multidomestic approach to be more responsive to local preferences. Coca-Cola, for example, used to control its products rigidly from its Atlanta headquarters. But managers have found in some markets consumers thirst for more than Coke, Diet Coke, and Sprite. So Coke has altered its structure to reduce the need for control in favor of greater coordination/integration in local markets where local managers independently launch new flavored drinks. At the same time, GE, the paragon of new-age organization, had altered its GE Medical Systems organization structure to allow local product managers to handle everything from product design to marketing. This emphasis on local coordination and reduced central control of product design led managers obsessed with local rivalries to design and manufacture similar products for different markets—a costly and wasteful duplication of effort. So GE reintroduced centralized control of product design, with input from a worldwide base of global managers and their customers, resulting in the design of several single global products produced quite cost competitively to sell worldwide. GE's need for control of product design out-weighed the coordination needs of locally focused product managers.[6] At the same time, GE obtained input from virtually every customer or potential customer worldwide before finalizing the product design of several initial products, suggesting that it rebalanced in favor of more control, but organizationally coordinated input from global managers and customers so as to ensure a better potential series of medical scanner for hospitals worldwide. Virtually all companies serving global markets face a similar organizational puzzle—how does the company integrate itself with diverse markets yet ensure adequate control and differentiation of internal units so that it executes profitably and effectively? We will examine some ways to do so later in this chapter.

Restructure to Emphasize and Support Strategically Critical Activities

restructuring
Redesigning an organizational structure with the intent of emphasizing and enabling activities most critical to a firm's strategy to function at maximum effectiveness.

Restructuring is redesigning an organizational structure with the intent of emphasizing and enabling activities most critical to the firm's strategy to function at maximum effectiveness. At the heart of the restructuring trend is the notion that some activities within a business's value chain are more critical to the success of the business's strategy than others. Wal-Mart's organizational structure is designed to ensure that its impressive logistics and purchasing competitive advantages operate flawlessly. Coordinating daily logistical and purchasing efficiencies among separate stores lets Wal-Mart lead the industry in profitability yet sell retail for less than many competitors buy the same merchandise at wholesale. Motorola's organizational structure is designed to protect and nurture its legendary R&D and new-product development capabilities—spending over twice the industry average in R&D alone each year. Motorola's R&D emphasis continually spawns proprietary technologies that support its technology-based competitive advantage. Coca-Cola emphasizes the importance of distribution activities, advertising, and retail support to its bottlers in its organizational structure. All three of these companies emphasize very different parts of the value chain process, but they are extraordinarily successful in part because they have designed their organizational structures to emphasize and support strategically critical activities. Two developments that have become key ways many of these firms have sought to improve their emphasis and support of strategic activities are business process reengineering and downsizing/self-management.

---

[6] Zellner, "See the World, Erase Its Borders."

business process reengineering
A customer-centric restructuring approach. It involves fundamental rethinking and radical redesigning of a business process so that a company can best create value for the customer by eliminating barriers that create distance between employees and customers.

Business process reengineering (BPR) was originally advocated by consultants Michael Hammer and James Champy[7] as a "customer-centric" restructuring approach. BPR is intended to place the decision-making authority that is most relevant to the customer closer to the customer, in order to make the firm more responsive to the needs of the customer. This is accomplished through a form of empowerment, facilitated by revamping organizational structure.

Business reengineering reduces fragmentation by crossing traditional departmental lines and reducing overhead to compress formerly separate steps and tasks that are strategically intertwined in the process of meeting customer needs. This "process orientation," rather than a traditional functional orientation, becomes the perspective around which various activities and tasks are then grouped to create the building blocks of the organization's structure. This is usually accomplished by assembling a multifunctional, multilevel team (the product-team approach discussed earlier) that begins by identifying customer needs and how the customer wants to deal with the firm. Customer focus must permeate all phases. Companies that have successfully reengineered their operations around strategically critical business processes have pursued the following steps[8]

• Develop a flowchart of the total business process, including its interfaces with other value chain activities.

• Try to simplify the process first, eliminating tasks and steps where possible and analyzing how to streamline the performance of what remains.

• Determine which parts of the process can be automated (usually those that are repetitive, time-consuming, and require little thought or decision); consider introducing advanced technologies that can be upgraded to achieve next-generation capability and provide a basis for further productivity gains down the road.

• Evaluate each activity in the process to determine whether it is strategy-critical or not. Strategy-critical activities are candidates for benchmarking to achieve best-in-industry or best-in-world performance status—and ones to emphasize in reengineered organizational structures.

• Weigh the pros and cons of outsourcing activities that are noncritical or that contribute little to organizational capabilities and core competencies.

• Design a structure for performing the activities that remain; reorganize the personnel and groups who perform these activities into the new structure.

When asked about his BPR-derived networking-oriented structure that helped revitalize IBM, former IBM CEO Gerstner responded: "It's called *reengineering*. It's called *getting competitive*. It's called *reducing cycle time and cost, flattening organizations, increasing customer responsiveness*. All of these require a collaboration with the customer and with suppliers and with vendors."[9] Ten years later IBM is still at it as we see in Exhibit 11.8, Strategy in Action, about which current CEO Sam Palmisano said:

> IBM has developed a system that lets it shift work to the areas with available skills at the lowest-available costs. The goal is to deliver higher-quality services at competitive prices. Clearly one opportunity associated with globalization is costs. You have access to expertise wherever it is in the world—if you have the infrastructure and the relationships to take advantage of it.[10]

[7] Michael Hammer, *The Agenda* (New York: Random House, 2001); and Michael Hammer and James Champy, *Reengineering the Corporation* (New York: HarperBusiness, 1993).
[8] Judy Wade, "How to Make Reengineering Really Work," *Harvard Business Review* 71, no. 6 (November–December 1993), pp. 119–31.
[9] Ira Sager, "How IBM Became a Growth Company Again," *BusinessWeek Online,* Dec. 9, 1996.
[10] Steve Hamm, "Big Blue Wields the Knife Again," *BusinessWeek,* May 30, 2007.

IBM Continuously Reengineers Its BPO Business

BusinessWeek

Job reductions are nothing new for IBM's huge global-IT services business, still the No. 1 tech services company in the world. The cuts started when IBM, shocked by very poor results two years ago, began a major restructuring in Europe and the United States that eliminated 15,000 jobs in a matter of months. Ever since then, every few months, a new batch of jobs is trimmed from high-cost countries, including 700 in the first quarter of this year.

The trend is likely to continue. In the first quarter, the largest chunk of the services business, called Global Technology Services, grew a relatively healthy 7 percent, but its operating margin narrowed, shrinking by 2.5 points to just 7.8 percent. In comparison, the top Indian services outfits have operating profits of between 25 percent and 30 percent.

To improve its efficiency, IBM has adopted the business process reengineering approach called the "Lean Operations discipline" developed by Toyota Motor for manufacturing cars. It's adapting Lean so it applies to a global service organization, something the top Indian companies began two years ago. The basic principle of Lean Operations is that a company should be making continuous, incremental improvements in its business processes. That's one of the ways IBM figures out where it can eliminate work. The company also keeps a master database, nicknamed "Blue Monster," of all of its services employees. Supervisors use the information to track who is working on what project and when they'll be available for another assignment. In this way, the company hopes to minimize the amount of time people are between assignments.

All of this cost-cutting is the task of Robert Moffat, senior vice president for integrated operations. His goal is to make the Global Technology Services workforce 10 to 15 percent more efficient each year. The key for him is to take costs out of the equation through a combination of workforce globalization, process improvements, and replacing manual labor with software. In a little more than six months, Moffat said at the May 17, 2007, analysts' meeting, he has rolled out the new formula for 22 of IBM's largest clients in seven countries. In some cases, he said, the clients have seen up to a 50 percent improvement in productivity. Now, Moffat is extending the new system to 600 more accounts.

All of this huffing and puffing over efficiency won't calm the frazzled nerves of IBM's 155,000-strong services workforce. True, there are still abundant employment opportunities in the company. About 30 percent of the people whose jobs are eliminated find other jobs within the behemoth, and, in the first four months of this year alone, IBM hired more than 19,000 people. But a lot of those hires were made in India. For the U.S. workforce, there is always fear that jobs will be lost to foreigners.

downsizing
Eliminating the number of employees, particularly middle management, in a company.

self-management
Allowing work groups or work teams to supervise and administer their work as a group or team without a direct supervisor exercising the supervisory role. These teams set parameters of their work, make decisions about work-related matters, and perform most of the managerial functions previously done by their direct supervisor.

Downsizing and self-management at operating levels are additional ways companies restructure critical activities. **Downsizing** is eliminating the number of employees, particularly middle management, in a company. The arrival of a global marketplace, information technology, and intense competition caused many companies to reevaluate middle management activities to determine just what value was really being added to the company's products and services. The result of this scrutiny, along with continuous improvements in information processing technology, has been widespread downsizing of the number of management personnel in thousands of companies worldwide. *BusinessWeek*'s survey of companies worldwide that have been actively downsizing are shown in Exhibit 11.9, Strategy in Action.

One of the outcomes of downsizing was increased **self-management** at operating levels of the company. Cutbacks in the number of management people left those who remained with more work to do. The result was that remaining managers had to give up a good measure of control to operating personnel. Spans of control, traditionally thought to maximize under 10 people, have become much larger due to information technology, running "lean and mean," and delegation to lower levels. Ameritech, one of the Baby Bells, has seen its spans of control rise to as much as 30 to 1 in some divisions because most of the people who did staff work—financial analysts, assistant managers, and so on—have disappeared.

How Lean Is Your Company?

Company Characteristic	Analysis
1. Layers of management between CEO and the shop floor	Some companies, such as Ameritech, now have as few as 4 or 5 where as many as 12 had been common. More than 6 is most likely too many.
2. Number of employees managed by the typical executive	At lean companies, spans of control range up to 1 manager to 30 staffers. A ratio lower than 1:10 is a warning of arterial sclerosis.
3. Amount of work cut out by your downsizing	Eliminating jobs without cutting out work can bring disaster. A downsizing should be accompanied by at least a 25 percent reduction in the number of tasks performed. Some lean companies have hit 50 percent.
4. Skill levels of the surviving management group	Managers must learn to accept more responsibility and to eliminate unneeded work. Have you taught them how?
5. Size of your largest profit center by number of employees	Break down large operating units into smaller profit centers—less than 500 employees is a popular cutoff—to gain the economies of entrepreneurship and offset the burdens of scale.
6. Post-downsizing size of staff at corporate headquarters	The largest layoffs, on a percentage basis, should be at corporate headquarters. It is often the most over-staffed—and the most removed from customers.

Source: Reprinted with special permission from John Byrne, "The 21st Century Corporation," *BusinessWeek,* August 28, 2000. Copyright © 2000 The McGraw-Hill Companies.

This delegation, also known as *empowerment,* is accomplished through concepts such as self-managed work groups, reengineering, and automation. It is also seen through efforts to create distinct businesses within a business—conceiving a business as a confederation of many "small" businesses, rather than one large, interconnected business. Whatever the terminology, the idea is to push decision making down in the organization by allowing major management decisions to be made at operating levels. The result is often the elimination of up to half the levels of management previously existing in an organizational structure.

CREATING AGILE, VIRTUAL ORGANIZATIONS

virtual organization
A temporary network of independent companies—suppliers, customers, subcontractors, and even competitors—linked primarily by information technology to share skills, access to markets, and costs.

Corporations today are increasingly seeing their "structure" become an elaborate network of external and internal relationships. This organizational phenomenon has been termed the **virtual organization,** which is defined as a temporary network of independent companies—suppliers, customers, subcontractors, even competitors—linked primarily by information technology to share skills, access to markets, and costs.[11] An **agile organization** is one that identifies a set of business capabilities central to high-profitability operations and then builds a virtual organization around those capabilities, allowing the agile firm to build its business around the core, high-profitability information, services, and products. Creating an agile, virtual organization structure involves outsourcing, strategic alliances, a boundaryless structure,

[11] W. H. Davidow and M. S. Malone, *The Virtual Corporation* (New York: Harper, 1992); and Steven Goldman, *Agile Competitors and Virtual Organizations* (New York: Van Nostrand Reinhold, 1995).

agile organization
A firm that identifies a set of business capabilities central to high-profitability operations and then builds a virtual organization around those capabilities.

outsourcing
Obtaining work previously done by employees inside the companies from sources outside the company.

modular organization
An organization structured via outsourcing where the organization's final product or service is based on the combination of several companies' self-contained skills and business capabilities.

an ambidextrous learning approach, and Web-based organization. Let's examine each of the approaches to creating a virtual organization in more detail.

Outsourcing—Creating a Modular Organization

Outsourcing was an early driving force for the virtual organization trend. Dell does not make PCs. Cisco doesn't make its world renowned routers. Motorola doesn't make cell phones. Sony makes Apple's low-end PowerBook computers. **Outsourcing** is simply obtaining work previously done by employees inside the companies from sources outside the company. Managers have found that as they attempt to restructure their organizations, particularly if they do so from a business process orientation, numerous activities can often be found in their company that are not "strategically critical activities." This has particularly been the case of numerous staff activities and administrative control processes previously the domain of various middle management levels in an organization. But it can also refer to primary activities that are steps in their business's value chain—purchasing, shipping, manufacturing, and so on. Further scrutiny has led managers to conclude that these activities either add little or no value to the product or services, or that they can be done much more cost effectively (and competently) by other businesses specializing in these activities. If this is so, then the business can enhance its competitive advantage by outsourcing the activities.

Choosing to outsource activities has been likened to creating a "modular" organization. A **modular organization** provides products or services using different, self-contained specialists or companies brought together—outsourced—to contribute their primary or support activity to result in a successful outcome. Dell is a "modular" organization because it uses outsourced manufacturers and assemblers to provide parts and assemble its computers. It also uses outsourced customer service providers in different parts of the world to provide most of its customer service and support activities. These outsourced providers are independent companies, many of which offer similar services to other companies including, in some cases, Dell's competitors. Dell remains the umbrella organization and controlling organization in fact and certainly in the customers' mind, yet it is able to do so based on putting together a variety of "modules" or parts because of its ability to provide computers and related services through extensive dependence on outsourcing.

Many organizations long ago started outsourcing functions like payroll and benefits administration—routine administrative functions more easily and cost effectively done by a firm specializing in that activity. But outsourcing today has moved into virtually every aspect of what a business does to provide the products and services it exists to provide. Exhibit 11.10, Top Strategist, shows the biggest sectors for outsourcing so far. And not only large companies are involved. Veteran entrepreneur and co-founder of Celestial Seasonings, Wyck Hay, has returned from retirement to build a new company, Kaboom Beverages, in California. What is interesting is that Hay, like many entrepreneurs today, is building a totally modular organization. Every function in Kaboom Beverages is outsourced to a variety of specialists and specialized companies. Indeed, one of the drivers for outsourcing to create a modular organization is to be able to combine world-class talent, wherever it resides, into a company's ability to deliver the best product and service it can.

Boeing opened its own engineering center in Moscow, where it employs 1,100 skilled but relatively inexpensive aerospace engineers to design parts of the 787 Dreamliner. It also has Japanese, Korean, and European companies making various parts of that critical new plane. Chicago-based law firm Baker and Mckenzie has its own English-speaking team in Manila that drafts documents and does market research. Bank of America (BOA) has its own India subsidiary, but also teamed up with InfoSys and Tata Consultancies—BOA estimates that

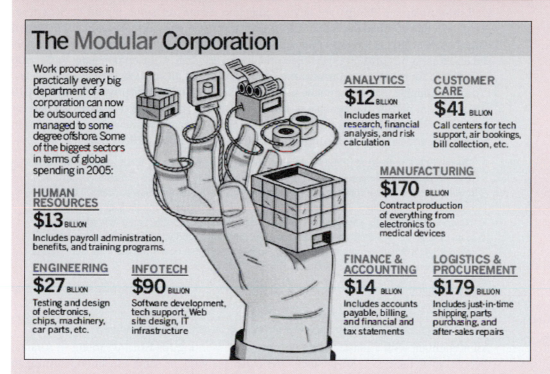

The Modular Corporation

Work processes in practically every big department of a corporation can now be outsourced and managed to some degree offshore. Some of the biggest sectors in terms of global spending in 2005:

ANALYTICS
$12 BILLION
Includes market research, financial analysis, and risk calculation

CUSTOMER CARE
$41 BILLION
Call centers for tech support, air bookings, bill collection, etc.

MANUFACTURING
$170 BILLION
Contract production of everything from electronics to medical devices

HUMAN RESOURCES
$13 BILLION
Includes payroll administration, benefits, and training programs.

ENGINEERING
$27 BILLION
Testing and design of electronics, chips, machinery, car parts, etc.

INFOTECH
$90 BILLION
Software development, tech support, Web site design, IT infrastructure

FINANCE & ACCOUNTING
$14 BILLION
Includes accounts payable, billing, and financial and tax statements

LOGISTICS & PROCUREMENT
$179 BILLION
Includes just-in-time shipping, parts purchasing, and after-sales repairs

Source: Reprinted with special permission from "The Modular Corporation," *BusinessWeek*, January 30, 2006. Copyright © 2006 The McGraw-Hill Companies.

it has saved almost $200 million in IT work the last two years, while improving product quality at the same time.

Outsourcing IT services, call center services, and routine computer programming services—and managing a company's IT systems—have become major industries unto themselves. IT outsourcing to companies in India alone reached $20 billion in 2005 and is projected to top $50 billion by 2008. India's Infosys and Wipro (India's GE) are multi-billion-dollar revenue providers of IT outsourced services.

Business process outsourcing (BPO) is the most rapidly growing segment of the outsourcing services industry worldwide, and it is expected to reach more than $200 billion in revenues in 2008. BPO includes a broad array of administrative functions—HR, supply procurement, finance and accounting, customer care, supply-chain logistics, engineering, research and development, sales and marketing, facilities management and even management training and development.[12] IBM strategist Bruce Harreld estimates that the world's companies spend about $19 trillion each year on sales, general, and administrative expenses. Only $14 trillion-worth of this, he estimates, has been outsourced to other firms. He further expects that many of the advantages in scale, wage rates, and productivity found when manufacturing was outsourced will quickly emerge driving a rapid increase in BPO over the next 10 years.[13] Many big companies estimate they could outsource half or more

business process outsourcing
Having an outside company manage numerous routine business management activities previously done by employees inside the company such as HR, supply procurement, finance and accounting, customer care, supply-chain logistics, engineering, R&D, sales and marketing, facilities management, and management/development.

[12] Pete Engardio and Bruce Einhorn, "Outsourcing Innovation," *BusinessWeek,* March 21, 2005.
[13] "A World of Work," *The Economist,* November 11, 2004.

of this work currently done in-house. Similarly, banking services currently deliver less than 1 percent of their services remotely—a major global outsourcing opportunity.[14]

Perhaps the more controversial outsourcing trends involve product design and even innovation activities. Particularly in consumer electronics markets, companies such as Dell, Motorola, and Philips are buying complete designs of some digital devices from Asian developers, tweaking them to their own specifications, and just adding their brand name before selling or having a more effective sales channel sell the product for them. This trend seems to be spreading. Boeing works with an Indian software company to develop its software for landing gear, navigation systems, and cockpit controls in its newest planes. Procter & Gamble, the consummate innovator, wants half of its new-product ideas by 2010 to come from outside the company—outsourced R&D or innovation—versus 20 percent right now. Eli Lilly has outsourced selected biotech research for new drugs to an Asian biotech research firm. Consider this comment in a recent *BusinessWeek* article:

> The result is a rethinking of the structure of the modern corporation. What, specifically, has to be done in-house anymore? At a minimum, most leading Western companies are turning toward a new model of innovation, one that employs global networks of partners. These can include U.S. chipmakers, Taiwanese engineers, Indian software developers, and Chinese factories. IBM is even offering the smarts of its famed research labs and a new global team of 1,200 engineers to help customers develop future products using next-generation technologies. When the whole chain works in sync, there can be a dramatic leap in the speed and efficiency of product development.[15]

Outsourcing as a means to create an agile, virtual organization has many potential advantages:

1. *It can lower costs incurred when the activity outsourced is done in-house.*

An accountant with a masters degree from UGA working for Ernst & Young in Atlanta, George, costs E&Y $75,000 annually. Her colleague with the same education returning to her native Philippines to live, works on a similar E&Y audit team in Southeast Asia and via the Internet in the United States—$7,000 annual salary.

2. *It can reduce the amount of capital a firm must invest in production or service capacity.*

Lenovo will cover the capital expenditure for its new Chinese PC manufacturing facilities; IBM will not. IBM will sell Lenovo its existing PC manufacturing facilities around the world, freeing up that capital for investment in IBM's development of its own core competencies, and just buy PCs very cheaply from Lenovo as it needs them. It will include a markup in doing so to pass along to its IT management services clients.

3. *The firm's managers and personnel can concentrate on mission-critical activities.*

As noted in the preceding example, not only does IBM free up capital, but it frees up its people and remaining capital to focus more intensely on its new emphasis on IT systems, BPO, and consulting.

4. *This concentration and focus allow the firm to control and enhance the source of its core competitive advantage.*

Dell outsources the manufacture of its computers. It carefully controls and continuously improves its Web-based direct sales capability so that it increasingly distances itself from the closest competitors. It is able to build such a strong direct sales capability because that is virtually all it concentrates on, even though it is a computer company.

---

[14] "Time to Bring It Back," *The Economist,* March 3, 2005.
[15] Engardio and Einhorn, "Outsourcing Innovation."

5. *Careful selection of outsourced partners allows the firm to potentially learn and develop its abilities through ideas and capabilities that emerge from the growing expertise and scope of work done by the outsource partner for several firms.*

Outsourced cell phone manufacturers in Korea and Taiwan have become large providers to several large, global cell phone companies. Their product design prototypes and improvements for one client quickly find their way to the attention of other clients. Their improvement in logistics with some firms becomes knowledge incorporated in their dealings with another client.

Outsourcing is not without its "cons," however. There are several:

1. *Outsourcing involves loss of some control and reliance on "outsiders."*

By definition, outsourcing places control of that function or activity "outside" the requesting firm. This loss of control can result in many future problems such as delays, quality issues, customer complaints, and loss of competitor-sensitive information. Recent thefts of personal ID information from U.S.-based bank clients using major information management outsourcing services from Indian companies have caused major problems for the banks obtaining these services.

2. *Outsourcing can create future competitors.*

Companies that supply the firm with basic IT services or software programming assistance or product design services may one day move "up the chain" to undertake the higher level work the firm was attempting to reserve for itself. IBM has outsourced considerable work to Indian companies related to its "value-added" IT system management services—its strategic future. It now is experiencing competition from some of these former suppliers of programming support that have become multi-billion-dollar software and IT service providers in their own right.

3. *Skills important to a product or service are "lost."*

While things a company does may not be considered essential to its core competency, they still may be quite important. And as it continues over time to outsource that activity, it loses any capacity in the firm of being able to do it effectively. That, potentially, leaves the company vulnerable.

4. *Outsourcing may cause negative reaction from the public and investors.*

Outsourcing manufacturing, tech support, and back-office work may make sense to investors, but product design and innovation? Asking what value the company is providing and protecting will be an obvious potential reaction. Publicly, the loss of jobs from home country to low-cost alternative locations represents difficult job losses and transitions for people who bring political heat.

5. *Crafting good legal agreements, especially for services, is difficult.*

When outsourced manufacturers send product, you take delivery, inspect, and pay. When service providers supply a service, it is a continuous process. Bottom line: It takes considerable trust and cross-cultural understanding to work.

6. *The company may get locked into long-term contracts at costs that are no longer competitive.*

Multiyear IT management contracts can be both complex and based on costs that are soon noncompetitive because of other sources providing much more cost-effective solutions.

7. *Cost aren't everything: What if my supplier underbids?*

EDS (Dallas, Texas) has a multiyear contract as an outsource provider to the U.S. Navy to provide IT services and consolidate 70,000 different IT systems. Two years into the contract, in 2005, it was $1.5 billion in the red. It hopes to make that heavy loss up over the life of the contract. But what if it was a smaller company and couldn't afford to carry a loss for a contract it poorly bid?

8. *Outsourcing can lead to increasingly fragmented work cultures where low-paid workers get the work done with little initiative or enthusiasm.*

"A mercenary may shoot a gun the same as a soldier, but he will not create a revolution, build a new society, or die for the homeland," says a Silicon Valley manager who objects to his company's turning to contract workers for services.[16]

Its potential disadvantages not withstanding, outsourcing has become a key, standard means by which agile, virtual organization structures are built. It has become an essential building block; most firms in any market anywhere in the world structure some of their business activities to allow them to remain cost competitive, dynamic, and able to develop their future core competencies. As outsourcing moves from sourcing manufacturing and IT management to all business management processes, careful attention and efforts to build trust and cross-cultural understanding will be important as will effective contractual arrangements to govern multiyear, ongoing relationships.

Strategic Alliances

strategic alliances
Alliances with suppliers, partners, contractors, and other providers that allow partners in the alliance to focus on what they do best, farm out everything else, and quickly provide value to the customer.

Strategic alliances are arrangements between two or more companies in which they both contribute capabilities, resources, or expertise to a joint undertaking, usually with an identity of its own, with each firm giving up overall control in return for the potential to participate in and benefit from the joint venture relationship. They are different from outsourcing relationships because the requesting company usually retains control when outsourcing, whereas strategic alliances involve firms giving up overall control to the joint entity, or alliance, in which they become a partner. Texas-based EDS was awaiting word at the time of this writing on whether the "Atlas Consortium" would be awarded a 10-year, $7.6 billion contract to manage 150,000 computers and networking software for British military personnel. The Atlas Consortium is a strategic alliance, formed by EDS as the "lead" firm with the Dutch firm LogicaCMG and a British subsidiary of the defense company, EADS, as full partners. While EDS is the "lead" member of the alliance, final control of the alliance rests not in EDS but in the governance that all three partners have the right to influence and shape.

This is a good example of a strategic alliance—three different firms all with other major business commitments and activities. They have joined together, investing time, analysis resources, and negotiations so as to be in a position to bid as a team (or alliance) on a major 10-year contract. In a few weeks they will know. If they get the contract, then their alliance will have a lengthy commitment to the British military and their firms to the Atlas Consortium. If they don't, then they may or may not work together to pursue other deals. But this relationship allowed each firm to seek work it could not have otherwise pursued independently because of restrictions imposed by the British government, the limitations of each firm individually, or both. It expanded the exposure of each firm to the other, to selected markets, to the building of relationships that may be usefully leveraged in each company's interests in the future.

Strategic alliances can be for long-term or for very short periods. Engaging in alliances, whether long-term or one time, lets each participant take advantage of fleeting opportunities quickly, usually without tying up vast amounts of capital. Strategic alliances allow companies with world-class capabilities to partner together in a way that combines different core competencies so that within the alliance each can focus on what they do best, but the alliance can pull together what is necessary to quickly provide superior value to the customer. FedEx and the U.S. Postal Service have formed an alliance—FedEx planes carry USPS

[16] "Time to Bring It Back," *The Economist*, March 3, 2005.

EXHIBIT 11.11
**General Motors:
Alliances with
Competitors**

Source: General Motors
Corporation annual reports;
"Carmakers Take Two Routes
to Global Growth," *Financial
Times* (July 11, 2000), p. 19.

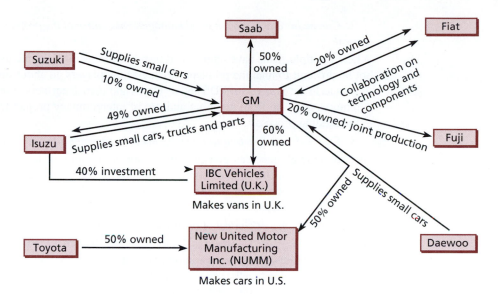

next-day letters and USPS delivers FedEx ground packages—to allow both to challenge their common rival, UPS.

Strategic alliances sometimes put competitors together as partners in some settings while they remain competitors in others. EDS competes with LogicaCMG in some situations, but they are close partners in the Atlas Consortium. Exhibit 11.11 shows how General Motors, in its effort to become more competitive globally, entered into numerous alliances with competitors.

Strategic alliances have the following pros and cons for firms seeking agile, responsive organizational structures:

Advantages

1. *Leverages several firms' core competencies.*
This allows alliance members to be more competitive in seeking certain project work or input.

2. *Limits capital investment.*
One partner firm does not have to have all the resources necessary to do the work of the alliance.

3. *Is flexible.*
Alliances allow a firm to be involved yet continue to pursue its other, "regular" business opportunities.

4. *Leads to networking and relationship building.*
Alliances get companies together, sometimes even competitors. They allow key players to build relationships that are valuable, even if the present alliance doesn't "pan out." Alliance partners learn more about each others' capabilities and gain advantage or benefit from referrals and other similar behaviors, creating win–win situations.

Disadvantages

1. *Can result in loss of control.*
A firm in an alliance by definition cedes ultimate control to the broader alliance for the undertaking for which the alliance is formed. This can prove problematic if the alliance doesn't work out as planned—or is not well planned.

2. *Can be hard to establish good management control of the project—loss of operational control.*

Where multiple firms have interrelated responsibilities for a sizable joint project, it should not be difficult to imagine problems arising as the players go about implementing a major project as in the example of EDS and its Dutch and British partners in the Atlas Consortium. It requires good up-front planning and use of intercompany project team groups early on in the bidding process.

3. *Can distract a participating company's management and key players.*

One strategic alliance can consume the majority attention of key players essential to the overall success of the "home" company. Whether because of their technical skills, managerial skills, key roles, or all three, the potential for lost focus or time to devote to key responsibilities exists.

4. *Raises issues of control of proprietary information and intellectual property.*

Where technology development is the focus of the alliance, or maybe part of it, firms partnered together may also compete in other circumstances. Or they may have the potential to do so. So partnering together gives each the opportunity to learn much more about the other, their contacts, capabilities, and unique skills or trade secrets.

Strategic alliances have proven a very popular mechanism for many companies seeking to become more agile competitors in today's dynamic global economy. They have proven a major way for small companies to become involved with large players to the benefit of both—allowing the smaller player to grow in a way that builds its future survival possibilities and the larger player to tap expertise and knowledge it can no longer afford to retain or develop in-house.

Toward Boundaryless Structures

boundaryless organization
Organizational structure that allows people to interface with others throughout the organization without need to wait for a hierarchy to regulate that interface across functional, business, and geographic boundaries.

Management icon Jack Welch coined the term **boundaryless organization** to characterize his vision of what he wanted GE to become: to be able to generate knowledge, share knowledge, and get knowledge to the places it could be best used to provide superior value. A key component of this concept was erasing internal divisions so the people in GE could work across functional, business, and geographic boundaries to achieve an integrated diversity—the ability to transfer the best ideas, the most developed knowledge, and the most valuable people quickly, easily, and freely throughout GE. Here is his description:

> Boundaryless behavior is the soul of today's GE … Simply put, people seem compelled to build layers and walls between themselves and others, and that human tendency tends to be magnified in large, old institutions like ours. These walls cramp people, inhibit creativity, waste time, restrict vision, smother dreams and above all, slow things down … Boundaryless behavior shows up in actions of a woman from our Appliances Business in Hong Kong helping NBC with contacts needed to develop satellite television service in Asia … And finally, boundaryless behavior means exploiting one of the unmatchable advantages a multibusiness GE has over almost any other company in the world. Boundaryless behavior combines 12 huge global businesses—each number one or number two in its markets—into a vast laboratory whose principal product is new ideas, coupled with a common commitment to spread them throughout the Company.

> —*Letter to Shareholders, Jack Welch, chairman, General Electric Company, 1981–2001*

horizontal boundaries
Rules of communication, access, and protocol for dealing with different departments or functions or processes within an organization.

Boundaries, or borders, arise in four "directions" based on the ways we traditionally structure and run organizations:

1. **Horizontal boundaries**—between different departments or functions in a firm. Salespeople are different from administrative people or operating people or engineering people. One division is separate from another.

vertical boundaries
Limitations on interaction, contact, and access between operations and management personnel; between different levels of management; and between different organizational parts like corporate versus divisional units.

geographic boundaries
Limitations on interaction and contact between people in a company based on being at different physical locations domestically and globally.

external interface boundaries
Formal and informal rules, locations, and protocol that separate and/or dictate the interaction between members of an organization and those outside the organization—customers, suppliers, partners, regulators, associations, and even competitors.

2. **Vertical boundaries**—between operations and management, and levels of management; between "corporate" and "division," in virtually every organization.

3. **Geographic boundaries**—between different physical locations; between different countries or regions of the world (or even within a country) and between cultures.

4. **External interface boundaries**—between a company and its customers, suppliers, partners, regulators, and, indeed, its competitors.

Outsourcing, strategic alliances, product-team structures, reengineering, restructuring—all are ways to move toward boundaryless organization. Culture and shared values across an organization that value boundaryless behavior and cooperation help enable these efforts to work.

As we noted at the beginning of this section, globalization has accelerated many changes in the way organizations are structured, and that is certainly driving the recognition by many organizations of their need to become more boundaryless, to become an agile, virtual organization. Technology, particularly driven by the Internet, has and will be a major driver of the boundaryless organization. Commenting on technology's effect on Cisco, John Chambers observed that with all its outsourcing and strategic alliances, roughly 90 percent of all orders come into Cisco without ever being touched by human hands. "To my customers, it looks like one big virtual plant where my suppliers and inventory systems are directly tied into our virtual organization," he said. "That will be the norm in the future. Everything will be completely connected, both within a company and between companies. We will become boundaryless. The people who get that will have a huge competitive advantage."[17]

The Web's contribution electronically has simultaneously become the best analogy in explaining the future boundaryless organization. And it is not just the Web as in the Internet, but a weblike shape of successful organizational structures in the future. If there are a pair of images that symbolize the vast changes at work, they are the pyramid and the web. The organizational chart of large-scale enterprise had long been defined as a pyramid of ever-shrinking layers leading to an omnipotent CEO at its apex. The twenty-first-century corporation, in contrast, is far more likely to look like a web: a flat, intricately woven form that links partners, employees, external contractors, suppliers, and customers in various collaborations. The players will grow more and more interdependent. Fewer companies will try to master all the disciplines necessary to produce and market their goods but will instead outsource skills—from research and development to manufacturing—to outsiders who can perform those functions with greater efficiency.[18]

Exhibit 11.12 illustrates this evolution in organization structure to what it calls the B-Web, a truly Internet-driven form of organization designed to deliver speedy, customized, service-enhanced products to savvy customers from an integrated boundaryless B-Web organization, pulling together abundant, world-class resources digitally. Take Colgate-Palmolive. The company needed a more efficient method for getting its toothpaste into the tube—a seemingly straightforward problem. When its internal R&D team came up empty-handed, the company posted the specs on InnoCentive, one of many new marketplaces that link problems with problem-solvers. A Canadian engineer named Ed Melcarek proposed putting a positive charge on fluoride powder, then grounding the tube. It was an effective application of elementary physics, but not one that Colgate-Palmolive's team of chemists had ever contemplated. Melcarek was duly rewarded with $25,000 for a few hours' work. Today, some 120,000 scientists like Melcarek have registered with InnoCentive and hundreds of companies pay annual fees of roughly $80,000 to tap the talents of a global

[17] Peter Burrows, "Can Cisco Shift into Higher Gear?" *BusinessWeek Online*, October 4, 2004.
[18] Byrne, "The 21st Century Organization."

EXHIBIT 11.12
From Traditional Structure to B-Web Structure

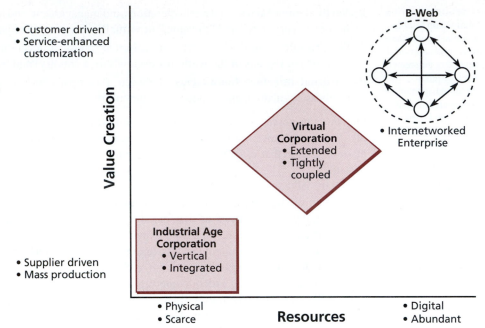

scientific community. Launched as an e-business venture by U.S. pharmaceutical giant Eli Lilly in 2001, the company now provides on-demand solutions to innovation-hungry titans such as Boeing, Dow, DuPont, P&G, and Novartis.[19]

Managing this intricate network of partners, spin-off enterprises, contractors, and free-lancers will be as important as managing internal operations. Indeed, it will be hard to tell the difference. All of these constituents will be directly linked in ways that will make it nearly impossible for outsiders to know where an individual firm begins and where it ends. "Companies will be much more molecular and fluid," predicts Don Tapscott, co-author of *Digital Capital.* "They will be autonomous business units connected not necessarily by a big building but across geographies all based on networks. The boundaries of the firm will be not only fluid or blurred but in some cases hard to define.[20]

learning organization
Organization structured around the idea that it should be set up to enable learning, to share knowledge, to seek knowledge, and to create opportunities to create new knowledge. It would move into new markets to learn about those markets rather than simply to bring a brand to it, or find resources to exploit in it.

Ambidextrous Learning Organizations

The evolution of the virtual organizational structure as an integral mechanism managers use to implement strategy has brought with it recognition of the central role knowledge plays in this process. *Knowledge* may be in terms of operating know-how, relationships with and knowledge of customer networks, technical knowledge upon which products or processes are based or will be, relationships with key people or a certain person that can get things done quickly, and so forth. Exhibit 11.13, Strategy in Action, shares how McKinsey organizational expert Lowell Bryan sees this shaping future organizational structure with managers becoming knowledge "nodes" through which intricate networks of personal relationships—inside and outside the formal organization—are constantly coordinated to bring together relevant know-how and successful action.

A shift from what Subramanian Rangan calls *exploitation to exploration* indicates the growing importance of organizational structures that enable a **learning organization** to

[19] Don Tapscott and Anthony Williams, "Ideagora, a Marketplace for Minds," *BusinessWeek,* February 15, 2007.

[20] Ibid.

Q&A with McKinsey's Lowell Bryan about Organizational Structures

BusinessWeek

Lowell Bryan, a senior partner and director at consultancy McKinsey & Co., leads McKinsey's global industries practice and is the author of *Race for the World: Strategies to Build a Great Global Firm* and *Market Unbound: Unleashing Global Capitalism.*

Q: How will global companies be managed in the twenty-first century?

A: Describing it is hard because the language of management is based on command-and-control structures and "who reports to whom." Now, the manager is more of a network operator. He is part of a country team and part of a business unit. Some companies don't even have country managers anymore.

Q: What is the toughest challenge in managing global companies today?

A: Management structures are now three-dimensional. You have to manage by geography, products, and global customers. The real issue is building networked structures between those three dimensions. That is the state of the art. It's getting away from classic power issues. Managers are becoming nodes, which are part of geographical structures and part of a business unit.

Q: What are the telltale questions that reflect whether a company is truly global?

A: CEOs should ask themselves four questions: First, how do people interact with each other—do employees around the world know each other and communicate regularly? Second, do management processes reflect a network or an old-style hierarchy? Third, is information provided to everyone simultaneously? And fourth, is the company led from the bottom up, not the top down?

Q: Why do multinationals that have operated for decades in foreign markets need to overhaul their management structures?

A: The sheer velocity of decisions that must be made is impossible in a company depending on an old-style vertical hierarchy. Think of a company [like] Cisco that is negotiating 50 to 60 alliances at one time. The old corporate structures [can't] integrate these

decisions fast enough. The CEO used to be involved in every acquisition, every alliance. Now, the role of the corporate center is different. Real business decisions move down to the level of business units.

Q: If there is not clear hierarchy, and managers have conflicting opinions, how does top management know when to make a decision? Doesn't that raise the risk of delay and inaction?

A: In the old centralized model, there was no communication. If you have multiple minds at work on a problem, the feedback is much quicker. If five managers or "nodes" in the network say something is not working right, management better sit up and take notice.

Q: Are there any secrets to designing a new management architecture?

A: Many structures will work. [H]aving the talent and capabilities you need to make a more fluid structure work [is key]. [But] it's much harder to do. The key is to create horizontal flow across silos to meet customers' needs. The question is how you network across these silos. [G]etting people to work together [is paramount]. That's the revolution that is going on now.

Q: What is the role of the CEO?

A: The CEO is the architect. He puts in place the conditions to let the organization innovate. No one is smart enough to do it alone anymore. Corporate restructuring should liberate the company from the past. As you break down old formal structures, knowledge workers are the nodes or the glue that hold different parts of the company together. They are the network. Nodes are what it is all about.

Q: How do you evaluate performance in such a squishy system?

A: The role of the corporate center is to worry about talent and how people do relative to each other. Workers build a set of intangibles around who they are. If they are not compensated for their value-added, they will go somewhere else.

ambidextrous organization

Organization structure most notable for its lack of structure wherein knowledge and getting it to the right place quickly are the key reasons for organization. Managers become knowledge "nodes" through which intricate networks of personal relationships—inside and outside the formal organization—are constantly, and often informally, coordinated to bring together relevant know-how and successful action.

allow global companies the chance to build competitive advantage.[21] Rather than going to markets to exploit brands or for inexpensive resources, in Rangan's view, the smart ones are going global to learn. This shift in the intent of the structure, then, is to seek information, to create new competences. Demand in another part of the world could be a new-product trendsetter at home. So a firm's structure needs to be organized to enable learning, to share knowledge, to create opportunities to create it. Others look to companies like 3M or Procter & Gamble that allow slack time, new-product champions, manager mentors—all put in place in the structure to provide resources, support, and advocacy for cross-functional collaboration leading to innovation in new-product development, and the generation and use of new ideas. This perspective is similar to the boundaryless notion—accommodate the speed of change and therefore opportunity by freeing up historical constraints found in traditional organizational approaches. So having structures that emphasize coordination over control, that allow flexibility (are **ambidextrous**), that emphasize the value and importance of informal relationships and interaction over formal systems, techniques, and controls are all characteristics associated with what are seen as effective structures for the twenty-first century.

Summary

This chapter has examined ways organizations are structured and ways to make those structures most effective. It described five traditional organizational structures–simple organization, functional structure, divisional structure, matrix structure, and product-team structure. Simple structures are often found in small companies, where tight control is essential to survival. Functional structures take advantage of the specialization of work by structuring the organization into interconnected units like sales, operations, and accounting/finance. This approach generates more efficiency, enhances functional skills over time, and is perhaps the most pervasive organizational structure. Coordination and conflict across functional units are the perpetual challenge in functional structures.

As companies grow they add products, services, and geographic locations, which leads to the need for divisional structures which divide the organization into units along one or more of these three lines. This division of the business into units with common settings increases focus and allows each division to operate more like an independent business itself. That in turn can generate competition for corporate level resources and potentially loose consistency and image corporatewide. Companies that work intensely with certain clients or projects created the matrix organization structure to temporarily assign functional specialists to those activities while having them remain accountable to their "home" functional unit. The product-team structure has evolved from the matrix approach, where functional specialists' assignments can be for an extended time and usually center around creating a functionally balanced team to take charge of a new-product idea from generation to production, sales, and market expansion. This approach has been found to create special synergy, teamwork, and cooperation since these specialists are together building a new revenue stream from its inception through its success and expansion.

The twenty-first century has seen an accelerating move away from traditional organizational structures toward hybrid adaptations that emphasize an external focus, flexible interaction, interdependency, and a bottom-up approach. Organizations have sought to adapt their traditional structures in this direction by redefining the role of corporate headquarters, rebalancing the need for control versus coordination, adjusting and reengineering the structure to emphasize strategic activities, downsizing and moving toward self-managing operational activities.

---

[21] Subramanian Rangan, *A Prism on Globalization* (Fountainebleau, France: INSEAD, 1999).

More successful organizations are becoming agile, virtual organizations—temporary networks of independent companies linked by information technology to share skills, markets, and costs. Outsourcing has been a major way organizations have done this. They retain certain functions, while having other companies take full responsibility for accomplishing other functions necessary to provide the product or services of this host organization. Strategic alliances are arrangements between two or more companies who typically contribute resources or skills to a joint undertaking where the joint entity is a separate, distinct organization itself and usually created to seek a particular contract or activities that represent too great an undertaking for any one player in the alliance.

Twenty-first century leaders have increasingly spoken about making their organizations boundaryless, by which they mean the absence of internal and external "boundaries" between units, levels, and locations that lessen their company's ability to generate knowledge, share knowledge, and get knowledge to the places it can be best used to create value. Forward thinkers describe ambidextrous learning organizations as ones that innately share knowledge, enable learning within and across organizations, and nurture informal relationships within and outside organizations to foster opportunities to be at the forefront of creating new knowledge.

Key Terms

agile organization, *p. 356*

ambidextrous organization, *p. 366*

boundaryless organization, *p. 362*

business process outsourcing, *p. 357*

business process reengineering, *p. 353*

divisional organizational structure, *p. 342*

downsizing, *p. 354*

external interface boundaries, *p. 363*

functional organizational structure, *p. 342*

geographic boundaries, *p. 363*

holding company structure, *p. 345*

horizontal boundaries, *p. 362*

learning organization, *p. 364*

matrix organizational structure, *p. 345*

modular organization, *p. 356*

organizational structure, *p.341*

outsourcing, *p. 356*

product-team structure, *p. 345*

restructuring, *p. 352*

self-management, *p. 354*

simple organizational structure, *p. 341*

strategic alliances, *p. 360*

strategic business unit, *p. 343*

vertical boundaries, *p. 363*

virtual organization, *p. 355*

Questions for Discussion

1. Explain each traditional organizational structure.
2. Select a company you have worked for or research one in the business press that uses one of these traditional structures. How well suited is the structure to the needs and strategy of the organization? What seems to work well, and what doesn't?
3. What organizations do you think are most likely to use product-team structures? Why?
4. Identify an organization that operated like a twentieth-century organization but has now adopted a structure that manifests twenty-first-century characteristics. Explain how you see or detect the differences.
5. How would you use one or more of the ways to improve traditional structures to improve the company you last worked in? Explain what might result.
6. What organization are you familiar with that you would consider the most agile, virtual organization? Why?
7. What situation have you personally seen outsourcing benefit?
8. What "boundary" would you first eliminate or change in an organization you are familiar with? Explain what you would do to eliminate it or change it and how that should make it more effective.

Chapter 11 Discussion Case

BusinessWeek

The Secret of BMW's Success: *BMW's Success Can Be Traced to Its Speed, Organizational Agility, and Lateral Management Techniques*

1 At 4:00 p.m. on a Friday afternoon, when most German workers have long departed for the weekend, the mini-cafés sprinkled throughout BMW's sprawling R&D center in Munich are jammed with engineers, designers, and marketing managers deliberating so intently it's hard to hear above the din. Even the cappuccino machine is running on empty. It's an atmosphere far more Silicon Valley than Detroit.

2 "At lunch and breaks everyone is discussing ideas and projects all the time. It's somewhat manic. But it makes things move faster," says BMW chief designer Adrian van Hooydonk.

3 The intense employee buzz at BMW is hot management theory in action. Top consultants and academics say the kind of informal networks that flourish at BMW and the noise and borderline chaos they engender in big organizations are vital for innovation—especially in companies where knowledge sits in the brains of tens of thousands of workers and not in a computer server. Melding that brain power, they say, is essential to unleashing the best ideas.

HANDS ACROSS DIVISIONS

4 "Cross-functional teams look messy and inefficient, but they are more effective at problem solving," says James M. Manyika, a partner at McKinsey & Co. in San Francisco who has studied the effectiveness of such networks. Companies such as BMW that leverage workers' tacit knowledge through such networks "are widely ahead of their competitors," Manyika adds.

5 BMW is one of a handful of global companies including Nokia and Raytheon that have turned to networks to manage day-to-day operations, superseding classic hierarchies. Those pioneering companies still turn to management hierarchies to set strategic goals, but workers have the freedom to forge teams across divisions and achieve targets in the best way possible—even if that way is unconventional.

6 And they are encouraged to build ties across divisions to speed change. "Good companies have this lateral ability to communicate across divisions and silos, not just up and down the hierarchy. That's what makes BMW tick," says chief financial officer Stefan Krause.

LIGHTNING-FAST CHANGES

7 Speed and organizational agility is increasingly vital to the auto industry, since electronics now make up some 20 percent of a car's value—and that level is rising. BMW figures some 90 percent of the innovations in its new models are electronics-driven. That requires once-slow-moving automakers to adapt to the lightning pace of innovation and change driving the semiconductor and software industries. Gone is the era of the 10-year model cycle.

8 Now automakers must ram innovation into high gear to avoid being overtaken by the competition. That's especially true in the luxury-auto leagues, where market leaders must pulse new innovations constantly onto the market, from podcasting for cars to infrared night vision systems.

9 By shifting effective management of day-to-day operations to such human networks, which speed knowledge laterally through companies faster and better than old hierarchies can, BMW has become as entrepreneurial as a tech start-up, consultants say. "Not many large companies take on lateral communications the way BMW does. It's a knocking down of barriers, like Jack Welch did at General Electric to make a boundaryless corporation," says Jay Galbraith, a Breckenridge (Colorado)-based management consultant.

Deep-six the egos Rigorously screen new hires for their ability to thrive as part of a team. Promote young talent but hold back perks until they've shown their stuff.

Build a share mythology New hires learn about 1959, when BMW nearly went bankrupt. Its recovery remains the centerpiece of company lore, inspiring a deep commitment to innovation.

Worship the network Teams from across the company work elbow to elbow in open, airy spaces, helping them to create informal networks where they hatch ideas quickly and resolve disagreements.

Work outside the system The sleek Z4 coupe exists because a young designer's doodle inspired a team to push his concept even though management had already killed the program.

Keep the door open From the factory floor to the executive suite, everyone is encouraged to speak out. Ideas bubble up freely, and even the craziest proposals will get a hearing.

MOBILE-PHONE MESSAGES

10 BMW's ability to drive innovation even pervades its marketing division. "People talk about innovation in products, but what's underestimated is innovation in processes and organization,"

says Ernst Baumann, head of personnel at BMW, which has its share of radical new ideas.

11   To reach a younger crowd of potential buyers for its new 1 Series launch in 2004, BMW used mobile-phone messages as the main source of buzz, directing interested people to signups on BMW's Web site for pre-launch test drives in August that year—something unheard of in the industry at the time. The experimental tactic worked: BMW sparked responses from 150,000 potential customers—and sales of the 1 Series took off when it was launched in September, 2004.

12   In 2001, BMW stunned the advertising world by investing ad spending normally set aside for Super Bowl spots in short films that had nothing to do with telling consumers about its cars. The slick, professionally made films were pure entertainment, like its series of short films, *The Hire,* starring Clive Owens, and they cost a bundle: $25 million.

BALANCING ACT

13   The risky bet triggered serious consternation at BMW's Munich headquarters. "You have to worry when your marketing team goes into the business of making films," says Krause, who noted that Internet-driven businesses were imploding left and right in 2001. Given those conditions, "Who cares how many clicks you get."

14   Few large companies are willing to embrace the lack of organizational clarity and nebulous structures that drive innovative ideas. At most companies, headquarters would have put the kibosh on the short-film idea, which has since been widely imitated. Researchers say most experiment with networks on a small scale and very few use the practice to full effect since doing so means an uncomfortable balancing act between hierarchy and discipline on one hand, and free-wheeling networks that can veer toward near-chaos.

15   But for innovation-driven companies, networks that enable entrepreneurial risk-taking are a silver bullet. "The ideas are richer, they implement more effectively, and there is less resistance to change," says Rob Cross, assistant professor of management at the University of Virginia.

IDEAS FIRST

16   How does BMW manage discipline with creativity and keep the anarchy of networks from careening out of control? Workers at the Bavarian automaker are encouraged from their first day on the job to build a network or web of personal ties to speed problem-solving and innovation, be it in R&D, design, production, or marketing. Those ties run across divisions and up and down the chain of command.

17   When it comes to driving innovation, forget formal meetings, hierarchy, and stamps of approval. Each worker learns quickly that pushing fresh ideas is paramount. "It's easier to ask forgiveness for breaking the rules than to seek permission," says Richard Gaul, a 33-year veteran at BMW and former head of communications at the $60 billion automaker.

18   BMW's complex customized production system, the polar opposite of Toyota's standardized lines, is easier to manage if workers feel empowered to drive change. Like Dell Computer, BMW configures its cars to customers' orders, so each auto moving down the production line is different.

FORGET OLD-SCHOOL RIGIDITY

19   Making sure the system works without a hitch requires savvy workers who continually suggest how to optimize processes. "Networks can do things that hierarchies cannot, because hierarchies lack the freedom. With a network you get the powerful ability to leverage knowledge quickly to bear on solving problems," says Karen Stephenson, management consultant and Harvard professor. "A network is the only way to effectively manage BMW's kind of complexity."

20   By contrast, companies that don't have lateral nimbleness are crippled in fast-moving technology-driven industries. Rigid hierarchies that stifle fresh ideas and slow reaction times are one problem facing General Motors and Ford Motor.

21   Once giants like GM were king, dominating the market with their huge volume and purchasing muscle. Big is no longer the ticket to success, and the slow-moving bureaucracies that big companies are saddled with are now a major handicap. "Lean is passé. What is in is lean and agile: the ability to shift and adjust as circumstances in the market change," says David Cole, partner at the Center for Automotive Research in Ann Arbor, Michigan.

KNOW THY CONSUMER

22   BMW managers, by contrast, even talk about the "physics of chaos" and how to constantly nurture innovation and creativity by operating on the very edge of chaos without getting out of control. "Discipline and creativity are not a paradox, there is a borderline case of self-controlling systems," says Gaul. "Where you break rules you have to be very disciplined." That's the industry's next *kaizen*—the art automakers will be forced to master in the twenty-first century.

23   The novel advertising scheme developed back in 2001 is a good example. Jim McDowell, then U.S. vice president of marketing, was confident the project, dubbed "Big Idea," and kept under tight security in "War Room" No. 6 at BMW USA's Woodlake (New Jersey) headquarters, would create just the kind of consumer buzz that BMW wanted—and would ultimately be more cost-effective for BMW than Super Bowl advertising. The idea was to give film directors a BMW car around which a compelling short film was to be made. Many of the tales centered on life-and-death chase scenes, but several were humorous or even melancholy.

24   McDowell figured if *The Hire* took off and the films were downloaded from BMW's Web site by more than 2 million viewers, BMW would chalk up the same number of eyeballs as a snappy advertising campaign aired during the Super Bowl, but would reach a higher percentage of BMW-type customers, progressives with a nose for cinema, technology,

and high bandwidth. "If you really understand your consumer, you can be very clever about how to communicate. You can change the whole paradigm," says McDowell, who is now executive vice president at Mini.

SNOWBALL EFFECT

25 McDowell didn't take any half-measures. He went after talented directors such as John Frankenheimer (*The French Connection*) and Ang Lee (*Crouching Tiger, Hidden Dragon*), and signed up stars such as Madonna, Clive Owens, and Gary Oldman—giving them complete artistic freedom, aside from the BMW model that starred in each film. No advance advertising heralded the Internet launch of the films.

26   The buzz started slowly with the first film but grew to avalanche proportions by the time Madonna's short comedy film about a cranky diva was released, overwhelming BMW's expectations and forcing the automaker to add servers as fast as it could.

27   But it didn't stop there. As the short-film gambit rocketed around the blogosphere, national TV broadcasters flooded McDowell's office with requests for interviews on CBS, *Entertainment Tonight*, and Fox News. The novelty of an automaker producing films fanned public interest and stoked downloads.

"EXPERIMENTAL ENVIRONMENT"

28 After one year, the number of viewers who had visited BMW's Web site to download *The Hire* shot to more than 21 million, and with three more films added in 2002, it rocketed to 100 million, sparking a Harvard Business School case study. One million enthusiasts ordered a DVD with all eight films.

29 McKinsey's Manyika, who has studied networks extensively, says knowledge forced through a company top-down drives "conformity, consistency, and efficiency." That's better suited to companies that make a standardized widget than a complex, electronics-driven product that requires constant innovation.

30 Companies such as BMW have to tap into tacit knowledge to spark fresh ideas. "It's more of a learning and experimental environment. It's building on what people know. It's learning instead of instruction," says Manyika.

HOW IDEAS TRAVEL

31 For academics and consultants studying the phenomenon of corporate networks, the most fascinating element is the "node" or the broker individual who can join two separate clusters with different pools of knowledge. Such a broker may have once worked in purchasing but now sits in R&D. As such, he or she can bridge the two worlds by "reaching across the white space of disconnected people," says Ronald S. Burt, a sociologist at the University of Chicago, who is studying the impact corporate networks have on performance.

32 That linkage speeds learning throughout companies—a vital tool to industries that should continually innovate. "People exposed to a diversity of information are at higher risk of seeing a new angle, a better way to frame ideas," says Burt. And companies that recognize and tap such social capital "have better growth rates and better patent rates. Formal structures decide whom to blame. Informal structures decide how to get things done," he says.

Extra: An Interview with Helmut Panke, newly retired CEO, who talks about why BMW is the world's greatest automobile company

33 Helmut Panke became chief executive at BMW in 2001 as the company was recovering from the failed 1994 acquisition of Rover. He has since powered the German automaker through the fastest model expansion in its history. Panke recently turned 60, the mandatory retirement age at BMW, handing over the job as CEO to production chief Norbert Reithofer. His legacy is a company that churns out top profits but nonetheless continues to question its own success—and innovate at a breakneck pace.

34   Panke, a PhD-holding physicist who did brief stints as a physics professor and a consultant at McKinsey before joining BMW, epitomized the automaker's bottom-up culture throughout his 24-year career. His easy-going, walk-around management style encouraged staffers to express opinions, challenge the views of associates or superiors, and even engage in debate with Panke himself.

35   Unlike the Sun King CEOs who dominate many large corporations with their oversize egos, Panke loves to engage in arguments that test his preconceptions and make him see things differently. "I hate to admit it, but you're right," says Panke, when he's won over—according to managers who work closely with him.

PERFORMANCE CLASS

36 The trim, energetic, detail-obsessed manager constantly set an example for breaking down silos to speed the transfer of knowledge throughout the company—one of the secrets of BMW's success.

37 Like many archetype BMW chiefs, Panke, who sits on Microsoft's board of directors, gathered his own intelligence about the $60 billion automaker by showing up in factories, sales offices, company cafeterias, research labs, and test tracks to ask a lot of questions. His personal knowledge about everything from new engine technology to electronics software and market trends runs deep. His favorite tactic in the boardroom was throwing out intelligence he gathered from "the machinery room," a German idiom meaning the

deepest levels of the company's operations—his own secret sources—and sparking debate.

38   Even as a member of Germany's industrial elite, Panke remained a low-key manager who avoided hobnobbing with politicians, preferring to spar with his own employees, test-drive the company's cars, or escape the official routine to do his own market sleuthing in Asia. A top priority for Panke is spending one day a month behind the wheel of new BMW prototypes or rivals' cars, together with the entire management board, scrutinizing everything from handling to interiors to design.

Question: *How does the BMW organization balance creative freedom with the discipline needed for building high-performance cars?*

Helmut Panke: Our philosophy is to get recommendations and then take decisions on the level where the competence lies, which by definition is not always at the top of the company. If expertise sits at the level of a department manager, he or she should decide—whether you are an engineer for R&D, or marketing expert, or technical planner—the archetype BMW associate has more freedom and authority to decide what he or she does than in most companies.

Despite our focus on innovation, on technology, and on marketing, we have a culture of strong cost controls, and we are driven by cost targets, even in the early stages of developing a car. Still, the individual has more room to decide how he or she will reach the targets that have been agreed on.

Question: *Can you give an example?*

Helmut Panke: The freedom BMW associates have can be exemplified by major capital investment decisions that don't reach the board of management but are decided one or two levels lower in the organization. Projects with a value of up to several hundred million dollars don't need 10 stamps of approval. In other organizations they would go to the board.

Question: *So where are the controls?*

Helmut Panke: No individual is in a position to decide alone. We have the four-eye principle. Contracts with binding agreements must be approved and signed by at least two people.

Question: *BMW has been a pioneer in implementing new management concepts and organizational models. You were very quick, for example, to jump on the idea of creating a "skunkworks" to spur innovation outside the corporate organization. How*

did a German-based company decide in the early 1980s to be among the first to test a newfangled approach to innovation?

Helmut Panke: BMW was among the first companies to create its own skunkworks. We heard that Lockheed took engineers out of the regular organization to work on special projects. We thought the approach interesting and created BMW Technik GmbH—which was designed to bring together engineers with different technological backgrounds.

Their work was not specifically project-based or budget-based. They could play. Out of playing around, they created the Z1 concept car, with downward moving doors. They explored the possibilities of working with different materials and engines. [Today's Aston Martin CEO] Ulrich Bez ran it in the beginning. We set up the company in a different building [in Munich] and created an entirely different HR and compensation system. BMW's contracts and work-time limits didn't apply. To give an example, employees were allowed to work at night if they wanted to.

Question: *How would you describe BMW's management structure?*

Helmut Panke: It is a much more informal, open, nonhierarchical way to work. I get e-mails from associates deep down in the organization with creative proposals or simple comments. My door is open. It's not uncommon to have managers below my immediate reports to call me [directly]. There is no structured hierarchical process communication. We have become more open. In 1982, it was a no-no to call another division. You wrote memos that went up and down the chain of command.

Question: *BMW encourages employees to speak out and defend their ideas—even to the point of prompting open conflicts. How do you manage that process effectively?*

Helmut Panke: It's a positive handling of different opinions and judgments. One good example is the process of tangible discussions, step-by-step, in designing a new model. Design starts at the beginning of the concept phase. You start by defining proportions, such as the front overhang, the rear overhang, the height, the width, the length. We look at proportions independent from what an engineer might say about whether it can or can't be done.

The participants in the discussions can't just say they don't like it. They have to argue and explain. We debate and express differences. Maybe the amount of metal compared to glass is too much. Maybe the design is too round, too smooth, or has too many lines. You express, argue, and explain as you go from six to seven versions to two to three models. The differences in opinion are expressed and backed up by clear argumentation. We don't move forward until it's clear there is mutual agreement. Yet, we have a culture of conflict. But if something is easy, it becomes routine. It's part of BMW's culture to push the limits. The challenge is to make a best seller even better.

Question: *BMW is big on encouraging informal networks of employees to work across divisions, spurring innovative ideas and solving problems. And you spend a fair amount of time soliciting ideas and input from all ranks at the company. Do you have your own personal network that you use in managing BMW?*

Helmut Panke: Yes, I like to go into the belly of the organization. One interest of mine is to stay informed through my network of former colleagues. Two weeks ago I met someone I knew in my first job at BMW as product planner and chatted with him. I still have a network, and I get information from it. I don't just talk to board members. It's fun to talk with department managers. The information is much less filtered, cleansed, or politicized.

Sources: Reprinted with special permission from Gail Edmondson, "The Secret of BMW's Success," *BusinessWeek,* October 16, 2006; and "Danke Panke," *BusinessWeek,* October 16, 2006. Copyright © 2006 The McGraw-Hill Companies.

DISCUSSION QUESTIONS

1. How does BMW use cross-functional teams?
2. What role does "speed" play in BMW's structure?
3. How has the role of electronics in cars influenced the way BMW's organization works?
4. What appear to be the strengths, and weaknesses, of BMW's approach?
5. Does outsourcing play a role at BMW?
6. How is BMW an ambidextrous organization?

Chapter **Twelve**

Leadership and Culture

After reading and studying this chapter, you should be able to

1. Describe what good organizational leadership involves.

2. Explain how vision and performance help leaders clarify strategic intent.

3. Explain the value of passion and selection/development of new leaders in shaping an organization's culture.

4. Briefly explain seven sources of power and influence available to every manager.

5. Define and explain what is meant by organizational culture, and how it is created, influenced, and changed.

6. Describe four ways leaders influence culture.

7. Explain four strategy-culture situations.

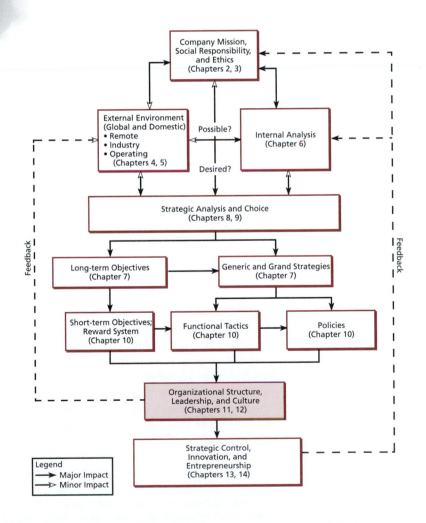

Company Mission, Social Responsibility, and Ethics (Chapters 2, 3)

External Environment (Global and Domestic)
• Remote
• Industry
• Operating
(Chapters 4, 5)

Possible?

Internal Analysis (Chapter 6)

Desired?

Strategic Analysis and Choice (Chapters 8, 9)

Long-term Objectives (Chapter 7)

Generic and Grand Strategies (Chapter 7)

Short-term Objectives; Reward System (Chapter 10)

Functional Tactics (Chapter 10)

Policies (Chapter 10)

Organizational Structure, Leadership, and Culture (Chapters 11, 12)

Strategic Control, Innovation, and Entrepreneurship (Chapters 13, 14)

Feedback

Feedback

Legend
→ Major Impact
⇒ Minor Impact

The job of leading a company has never been more demanding, and it will only get more challenging amidst the global dynamism businesses face today. The CEO will retain ultimate authority, but the corporation will depend increasingly on the skills of the CEO and a host of subordinate leaders to lead, coordinate, make decisions, and act quickly. The accelerated pace and complexity of business will continue to force corporations to push authority down through increasingly horizontal, flattened management structures. As we saw in the last chapter, these organizations will also need to be more and more open, agile, and boundaryless. This will require all the more emphasis on able leadership and a strong culture to shape decisions that must be made quickly, even when the stakes are big. In the future, every line manager will have to exercise leadership's prerogatives—and bear its burdens—to an extent unthinkable 20 years ago.[1]

John Kotter, a widely recognized leadership expert, predicted this evolving role of leadership in an organization when he distinguished between management and leadership:

> Management is about coping with complexity. Its practices and procedures are largely a response to one of the most significant developments of the twentieth century: the emergence of large organizations. Without good management, complex enterprises tend to become chaotic in ways that threaten their very existence. Good management brings a degree of order and consistency to key dimensions like the quality and profitability of products.
>
> Leadership, by contrast, is about coping with change. Part of the reason it has become so important in recent years is that the business world has become more competitive and more volatile. . . . The net result is that doing what was done yesterday, or doing it 5 percent better, is no longer a formula for success. Major changes are more and more necessary to survive and compete effectively in this new environment. More change always demands more leadership.[2]

organizational leadership
The process and practice by key executives of guiding and shepherding people in an organization toward a vision over time and developing that organization's future leadership and organization culture.

Organizational leadership, then, involves action on two fronts. The first is in guiding the organization to deal with constant change. This requires CEOs who embrace change, and who do so by clarifying strategic intent, who build their organization and shape their culture to fit with opportunities and challenges change affords. The second front is in providing the management skill to cope with the ramifications of constant change. This means identifying and supplying the organization with operating managers prepared to provide operational leadership and vision as never before. Thus, organizational leadership is guiding and shepherding toward a vision over time and developing that organization's future leadership and organizational culture.

Consider the challenge currently facing Ford Motor Company CEO Alan Mulally as he seeks to transform Ford's culture and return the company to profitability after years of accelerating decline. He was brought in by CEO Bill Ford, great-grandson of the founder, who finally threw up his arms in frustration and concluded that an insider could no longer fix Ford. Mulally was not Bill Ford's first choice, but Ford concluded Mulally was someone who knows how to shake the company to its foundations.

Mulally inherited virtually all the managers he must work through. Ford was losing from $3,000 to $5,000 on most every car it sold. There is a legacy within the company of placing a premium on personal ties to the Ford family, sometimes trumping actual performance in promotion decisions. Mulally had no experience in the automobile industry and was viewed with suspicion as an outsider in a town that places a premium on lifelong association with the industry. On Mulally's first meeting with his inherited management team, one manager asked early on: "How are you going to tackle something as complex and unfamiliar as the auto business when we are in such tough financial shape?"

[1] Larry Bossidy, "What Your Leader Expects of You," *Harvard Business Review,* June 2007; and Anthony Bianco, "The New Leadership," *BusinessWeek,* August 28, 2000.

[2] John P. Kotter, "What Leaders Really Do," *Harvard Business Review* (May–June 1990), p. 104.

Wall Street was skeptical early on. Of 15 analysts surveyed by Bloomberg.com, only two rated it a buy. The other 13's opinion: fixing Ford will require much more than simply whacking expenses and replacing a few key people. The company will have to figure out how to produce more vehicles consumers actually want. And doing that requires addressing the most fundamental problem of all: Ford's dysfunctional, often defeatist, culture. Once a model of efficiency, it has degenerated into a symbol of inefficiency, and its managers seem comfortable with the idea of losing money.

If you were Alan Mulally, how would you lead the dramatic change that appears to be needed at Ford Motor Company? How would you seek to move Ford's 300,000-plus employees and managers in a direction that abandons ingrained, and to some "sacred," cultural and leadership norms, quickly.

Consider another example. Jeff Immelt took the reins of leadership of GE from Jack Welch, recognized worldwide as one of the truly great business leaders of the twentieth century and faced a leadership and organizational culture challenge quite different in some ways from what Alan Mulally is addressing. GE under Welch built more value for its stockholders than any other company in the history of global commerce. That legacy alone would be pressure enough on a new leader, wouldn't you think?

Fortunately, some would quickly answer, Immelt had trained for many years under and in Welch's shadow. He was Welch's choice as successor. He was deeply schooled in the GE way and the Jack Welch leadership approach, as were all the other 300,000 GE employees over the prior 20 years. That Welch/GE way valued, above all, executives who could cut costs, cut deals, and generate continuous improvement in their business units. They were evaluated personally by Welch on an annual basis, in front of each other at the GE School.

But a storm was brewing. Shortly after Immelt became CEO, the 9/11 tragedy unfolded. A major recession and stock market drop soon followed. The option to continue mega deal making was slowing down with fewer candidates. The ability to generate GE-caliber earnings growth via sales growth combined with relentless efficiency was slowing down. So Immelt concluded that he could not continue with the old strategy. Rather, he would have to embark on virtually a new direction at GE that would dramatically change what he needed GE executives as leaders to prioritize and become. Instead of being experts in deal making and continuous improvement, they needed, in Immelt's vision, to become creative, innovators of internal growth generated by identifying new markets and technologies and needs as yet unknown.

With a slower-growing domestic economy, less tolerance among investors for buying your way to growth, and more global competitors, Immelt, like many of his peers, is being forced to shift the emphasis from deals and cost-cutting to new products, services, and markets. "It's a different world," says Immelt, than the one Welch knew. And so, he inherited one of the world's greatest companies yet faced a situation he concluded required dramatic changes in the way GE would be led, in the nature of the culture it needed, and in the fundamental priorities its managers would build GE's future.

If you were Jeff Immelt, how would you lead such a change? How would you seek to move GE's 300,000 people in a direction that abandons "sacred" cultural and leadership norms that were well used and entrenched under Welch's watch to make GE great? How would you quickly and convincingly lead those people to accept massive change throughout this special company and very quickly have that uncertain change produce the growth and profitability investors understandably expect?

The challenges Immelt and Mulally faced were different, but both were nothing short of a revolution. Indeed, the case at the end of this chapter will examine how Mulally is attempting to revolutionize Ford Motor Company. The bottom line is that Immelt and Mulally as well as all good executives, focus intensely and aggressively on the organizational leadership and organizational culture elements we will now examine.

STRATEGIC LEADERSHIP: EMBRACING CHANGE

The blending of telecommunications, computers, the Internet, and one global marketplace has increased the pace of change exponentially during the past 10 years. All business organizations are affected. Change has become an integral part of what leaders and managers deal with daily. The opening example about Jeff Immelt shows a manager normally able to celebrate 20 years of historically unmatched accomplishment, only to face the need for dramatic change at a GE employees and investors had come to believe was infallible.

The leadership challenge is to galvanize commitment among people within an organization as well as stakeholders outside the organization to embrace change and implement strategies intended to position the organization to succeed in a vastly different future. Leaders galvanize commitment to embrace change through three interrelated activities: clarifying strategic intent, building an organization, and shaping organizational culture.

Clarifying Strategic Intent

strategic intent
Leaders' clear sense of where they want to lead their company and what results they expect to achieve.

Leaders help their company embrace change by setting forth their **strategic intent**—a clear sense of where they want to lead the company and what results they expect to achieve. They do this by concentrating simultaneously and very clearly on two very different issues: vision and performance.

Vision

leader's vision
An articulation of a simple criterion or characterization of what a leader sees the company must become in order to establish and sustain global leadership.

A leader needs to communicate clearly and directly a fundamental vision of what the business needs to become. Traditionally, the concept of vision has been a description or picture of what the company could be that accommodates the needs of all its stakeholders. The intensely competitive, rapidly changing global marketplace has refined this to be targeting a very narrowly defined **leader's vision**—an articulation of a simple criterion or characterization of what the leader sees the company must become to establish and sustain global leadership. Former IBM CEO Lou Gerstner is a good example of a leader in the middle of trying to shape strategic intent when he began to try to change IBM from a computer company to a business solutions management company. He said at the time: "One of the great things about this industry is that every decade or so, you get a chance to redefine the playing field." He further commented, "We're in that phase of redefinition right now, and winners or losers are going to emerge from it. We've got to become the leader in 'network-centric computing.' It's a shift brought about by telecommunications-based change that is changing IBM more than semiconductors did in the last decade." Said Gerstner, "I sensed there were too many people inside IBM who wanted to fight the war we lost," referring to PCs and PC software, so he aggressively instilled network-centric computing as the strategic intent for IBM in the next decade. It is a comment on his sense of vision that his successor, Sam Palmisano, sold IBM's PC business to China's Lenovo, creating the world's third-largest PC company, and is aggressively pushing his IBMers to concentrate on newer IBM businesses in IT services, software, and servers—and seriously examining IBM's future in the online digital world, the 3D Internet.

Keep the Vision Simple The late Sam Walton's vision for Wal-Mart, *value to the consumer,* lives on in that amazing global company, guiding its development in a vastly changed world. Meg Whitman's leadership of eBay has produced explosive growth, keeping everyone committed to a vision that eBay simply exists to help you buy or sell anything, anywhere, anytime. Coca-Cola's legendary former CEO and chairman Roberto Goizueta said, "Our company is a global business system for which we raise capital to make concentrate and sell it at an operating profit. Then we pay the cost of that capital. Shareholders pocket the difference." Coke averaged 27 percent annual return on stockholder equity for 18 years under his leadership. Exhibit 12.1, Top Strategist, shows how Mayor Michael Bloomberg articulated a radical yet simple vision of New York City that has resonated with New York's famously cynical citizenry, who give him a 75 percent approval rating. All four of these organizations are very different, but their leaders were each effective in shaping and communicating a vision that clarified strategic intent in a way that helped everyone understand, or at least have a sense of, where the organization needed to go and, as a result, created a better sense of the rationale behind any new, and often radically changing, strategy. When you read the discussion case at the end of the chapter about Mulally at Ford, examine this issue and whether Mulally communicates a clear vision for a new Ford Motor Company.

Performance

Clarifying strategic intent must also ensure the survival of the enterprise as it pursues a well-articulated vision, and after it reaches the vision. So a key element of good organizational leadership is to make clear the performance expectations a leader has for the organization, and managers in it, as they seek to move toward that vision.

Oftentimes this can create a bit of a paradox, because the vision is a future picture and performance is now and tomorrow and next quarter and this year. Steven Reinemund, former CEO of PepsiCo and responsible for its impressive performance the last several years, offered an insightful way to think about this role of a good leader in clarifying strategic intent. "As I am looking to select other leaders, it's important to remember that results count. If you can't get the results over the goal line, are you really a leader?" The job of a good leader, in clarifying strategic intent, is to do so by painting a picture of that intent in future terms, and in setting sound performance expectations while moving toward that vision and as the vision becomes a reality.[3]

Jim McNerney, Boeing CEO and GE alumnus, described how he handles this paradox at Boeing and 3M as a contrast between an encouraging style (visioning) and setting expectations (performance).

> I think the harder you push people, the more you have to encourage them. Some people feel you either have a demanding, command-and-control management style or you have a nurturing, encouraging management style. I believe you have to have both. If you're only demanding, without encouraging, eventually that runs out of gas. And if you're only encouraging, without setting high expectations, you're not getting as much out of people. It's not either/or. You can't have one without the other.[4]

A real challenge for Alan Mulally at Ford is changing managers' mindsets about being profitable. When he was reviewing Ford's 2008 product line as the new CEO, he was told that Ford loses close to $3,000 every time a customer buys a Focus compact. "Why haven't you figured out a way to make a profit?" he asked. Executives explained that Ford needed the high sales volume to maintain the company's CAFÉ, or corporate average fuel economy, rating and that the plant that makes the car is a high-cost UAW factory in Michigan. "That's not what I asked," he shot back. "I want to know why no one figured out a way to build this car at a profit, whether it has to be built in Michigan or China or India, if that's what it takes." Nobody had a good answer.[5]

Building an Organization

The previous chapter examined alternative structures to use in designing the organization necessary to implement strategy. Leaders spend considerable time shaping and refining

---

[3] Diane Brady, "The Six "Ps" of PepsiCo's Chief," *BusinessWeek Online,* January 10, 2005.

[4] Michael Arndt, "The Hard Work in Leadership," *BusinessWeek Online,* April 12, 2004.

[5] David Kiley, "New Heat on Ford," *BusinessWeek,* June 4, 2007.

Top Strategist
Mike Bloomberg, The CEO Mayor

**Exhibit
12.1**

Applying lessons from an early career on Wall Street and from two decades building his eponymous financial information and media empire, New York City Mayor Michael R. Bloomberg is using technology, marketing, data analysis, and results-driven incentives to manage what is often seen as an unmanageable city of 8 million.

Bloomberg sees New York City as a corporation; its citizens as customers; its sanitation workers, police officers, clerks, and deputy commissioners as talent. He is the chief executive. Call him a technocrat all you want; he's O.K. with that. "I hear a disparaging tone, like there's something wrong with accountability and results," he says. "What was I hired for?"

Yet his checklist-obsessed operating style has resonated with New York's famously cynical citizenry—75 percent approval ratings attest to that—and well beyond Gotham. "People see that this can be done in a place like New York, effectively managing something so large and complex," says Time Warner CEO Richard D. Parsons, a Bloomberg friend and someone mentioned as a possible mayoral candidate himself. "And they think, 'Hey, this can be done elsewhere.'"

THE CITY IS A BRAND

Put yourself in Bloomberg's size $9\frac{1}{2}$ loafers on January 1, 2002, the day he was sworn in as New York's 108th mayor. The city was grappling with the psychological and financial impact of the terrorist attacks. It faced a budget gap of nearly $6 billion. On Wall Street, there was talk of abandoning Manhattan for the safer precincts of New Jersey or Connecticut.

Bloomberg had three options: cut services, raise taxes, or both. He did what no mayor had dared to do in more than a decade: he jacked up property taxes. And he didn't agonize over the decision a bit. "It [was] easy to make that choice," he recalls.

Some of his aides tried to talk him out of it, fearing the move amounted to political suicide. And by the following summer, Bloomberg's approval ratings had plunged, to 31 percent. But the novice mayor was undeterred. Where most politicians would have seen only a fiscal solution to the budget gap, he spotted a marketing opportunity. He was protecting the New York City "brand." Bloomberg saw a low crime rate, good public transportation, and clean streets as indispensable to selling New York. Cutting back on services, he felt, would send the wrong message to the business community and the outside world.

At the same time, Bloomberg boosted New York's promotional efforts. First, he consolidated three existing operations under a not-for-profit entity called NYC & Co. He tripled the city's contribution to the annual marketing budget, to $22 million. Then he went out and hired as CEO a veteran ad man, George Fertitta, whose branding and marketing firm had handled the likes of Coca-Cola, Perry Ellis, and Disney. All cities have marketing arms. But Fertitta's operation is essentially an advertising agency with an in-house creative services unit that uses various media, from bus shelters to the city's cable channel, to help sell the Big Apple.

Ever the metric junkie, Bloomberg set a goal for NYC & Co.: lure 50 million visitors a year by 2015. And knowing that foreign tourists spend three times as much as U.S. visitors, he ordered Fertitta to open more branch offices around the world. Today, NYC & Co. has a presence in 14 cities, with new offices set to open in Seoul, Tokyo, and Shanghai in coming months.

Since 2003, New York says it has added 151,100 new private sector jobs, boosting the economy and fueling a construction boom. And last year [2006], partly owing to a weak U.S. dollar, the city reports attracting 44 million visitors, up from 35 million in 2002. As for that 18.5 percent property tax hike, it got a whole lot easier to swallow when the average value of a single family home surged by 55 percent. Now, with the city in surplus, Bloomberg plans to hand out $1.3 billion in tax cuts not only to homeowners but also to businesses and shoppers.

THE VOTERS ARE CUSTOMERS

Bloomberg the executive was obsessive about catering to his customers, establishing 24-hour call lines,

(continued)

Exhibit 12.1 cont.

collecting data to help develop new products, and sending his executives out into the field to solicit feedback directly from clients. "Good companies listen to their customers, No. 1," he says. "Then they try to satisfy their needs, No. 2. But don't let [them] drive the internal decisions of the company."

As daunting as it may sound in a city never shy about complaining, Bloomberg decided New York needed its own 24-hour customer-service line. Yes, other cities had deployed 311 numbers, but never on such a grand scale. The benefit, beyond giving the public a new outlet to vent, would be making city government more efficient.

One month after being sworn in, Bloomberg proposed a 311 line that would allow New Yorkers to report everything from noise pollution to downed power lines. More important, 311 would give the mayor unprecedented access to what was on his constituents' minds. Bloomberg sees the weekly reports and gets a sense of the citizenry's angst—and whether problems are getting solved and how quickly.

Since it launched in March 2003, at a start-up cost of $25 million, 311 has received 49 million calls. The service employs 370 round-the-clock call takers. And New York has done an impressive job of data-mining the calls and quickly responding, says Stephen Goldsmith, the former mayor of Indianapolis and now a professor at Harvard's Kennedy School of Government. "Something special is going on in New York," he says. As far as the mayor is concerned, the numbers tell the story. Emergency 911 traffic is down by 1 million calls since 311's inception, meaning first responders are being called to fewer nonemergencies. The Buildings Department uses 311 to streamline the permit process and the review of plans by inspectors. The average wait time for an appointment with a building inspector has dropped from 40 days to less than a week. Two years after 311 launched, inspections for excessive noise were up 94 percent; rodent exterminations, 36 percent.

Heather Schwartz, a 30-year-old graduate student, is a regular user of the 311 line and says she became a big fan last year when she called about graffiti in a northern Manhattan subway station. Within days, the walls were painted over. Each time the graffiti artists returned, the city would paint over their handiwork. Finally the vandals gave up. Now Schwartz calls 311 for everything from elevator inspections to trash in the streets. "I am thrilled with it," she says. "It professionalizes the city."

THE MORE LIGHT, THE BETTER
Earlier this year, during a morning meeting with top staffers, Bloomberg noticed the large doors to the ornate conference room in City Hall. They were wooden. How could that be? Bloomberg thought he'd made City Hall "see-through." All meeting rooms had glass windows, so you could look inside. His desk and those of his staff were clustered in a room without walls to facilitate better and faster communication. By week's end the room had glass doors.

Bloomberg has tried to make the government and its agencies more open, too. In a task that previously fell to city budget directors, Bloomberg himself each year makes three budget presentations in the same day: one to city council, another for other elected officials, and one to the press. He uses easy-to-follow charts and tables, much like a CEO's PowerPoint presentation to analysts. His hope is that, by explaining the forces shaping the city's economy, a better understanding of his tax and spending priorities will emerge. The approach has not only helped him in budget negotiations with city council but also fostered a smoother relationship with civic and advocacy groups, says Mitchell Moss, an urban policy and planning professor at New York University.

What's more, citizens can get a closer look at their city government than ever before. The semiannual mayor's management report once exceeded 1,000 pages in three printed volumes. Today, the report—which reviews the delivery of city services—is 186 pages, is available online, and includes many more features than before, including neighborhood data and five-year trends that allow New Yorkers to compare past and present. In addition, the city plans and budget, once convoluted fiscal documents with only summaries available online, are now fully accessible on the city's Web site. Before, a New Yorker could never see a specific agency's overhead costs—its pensions and legal claims, say. The costs were pooled as a single number. Now each agency breaks them out.

HIRE SMART AND DELEGATE
The first thing most politicians do upon winning office is fill top jobs with people to whom they owe their support or who have long-standing ties

(continued)

Exhibit 12.1 cont.

to the political establishment. Bloomberg arrived at City Hall with no such debts. That's partly because he financed his own campaign. But even if he hadn't, Bloomberg says, he still would have recruited his lieutenants based on their ability to set targets and hit them. One of them was Katherine Oliver. Bloomberg had a turnaround mission in mind for her at the city's Office of Film, Theatre & Broadcasting. Oliver was working in London, overseeing Bloomberg global radio and television operations, when she got the call. Her marching orders from the mayor were simple: build a customer-service organization. She wasn't prepared for how much the film office needed modernizing and refocusing. Toronto and Louisiana, among other places, were stealing business from New York. Production companies were required to visit the office and fill out permit applications on paper. And to Oliver's astonishment, the agency had only one computer. Most staff were tapping away on electric typewriters.

Within a month of her arrival, her 22 employees had new Dell flat-screens, and production companies were able to file for permits online. Approvals have since surged to 200 a day, up from 200 a week in 2002. Oliver also put a photo library on the Web site, letting producers scout locations from their desks. She began offering a combined 15 percent tax credit to film and TV productions that complete at least 75 percent of their stage work in the city. Oliver says the program has generated $2.4 billion in new business and 10,000 new jobs since 2005. She offered filmmakers free advertising space on public property. And she set up a dedicated team of 33 police officers to ease shoots in the city.

"We tried to look at this as B to B," says Oliver. "This is a microcosm of what Michael wanted to do for the entire city."

BE BOLD, BE FEARLESS
"A major part of the CEO's responsibilities is to be the ultimate risk-taker and decision-maker. Truman ('The buck stops here') had it right." So wrote Bloomberg in his 1997 autobiography *Bloomberg By Bloomberg*. The mayor has embraced risk with an almost reckless disregard for political repercussions. Sometimes it has worked out: His controversial smoking ban in bars and restaurants is being replicated in other cities. Sometimes it hasn't: in a crushing defeat, he lost the 2012 Olympics bid to London.

Bloomberg recently reflected on the rare setback. "In business, you reward people for taking risks. When it doesn't work out, you promote them because they were willing to try new things. If people come back and tell me they skied all day and never fell down, I tell them to try a different mountain." He adds: "I have always joked that [the difference between] having the courage of your convictions and being pigheaded is in the results."

What has Bloomberg learned as mayor? "The real world, whether in business or government, requires that you don't jump to the endgame [or] to success right away," he says. "You do it piece by piece. Some people get immobilized when they come to a roadblock. My answer is, 'you know, it's a shame it's there, but now where else can we go? Let's just do it.'"

Source: Reprinted with special permission from Tom Lowry, "The CEO Mayor," *BusinessWeek*, June 25, 2007. Copyright © 2007 The McGraw-Hill Companies.

their organizational structure and making it function effectively to accomplish strategic intent. Because leaders are attempting to embrace change, they are often rebuilding or remaking their organization to align it with the ever-changing environment and needs of a new strategy. And because embracing change often involves overcoming resistance to change, leaders find themselves addressing problems such as the following as they attempt to build or rebuild their organization:

- Ensuring a common understanding about organizational priorities.
- Clarifying responsibilities among managers and organizational units.
- Empowering newer managers and pushing authority lower in the organization.

- Uncovering and remedying problems in coordination and communication across the organization and across boundaries inside and outside the organization.
- Gaining the personal commitment to a shared vision from managers throughout the organization.
- Keeping closely connected with what's going on inside and outside the organization and with its customers.

There are three ways good leaders go about building the organization they want and dealing with problems and issues like those listed: education, principles, and perseverance.

leadership development

The effort to familiarize future leaders with the skills important to the company and to develop exceptional leaders among the managers employed.

Education and **leadership development** is the effort to familiarize future leaders with the skills important to the company and to develop exceptional leaders among the managers you employ. Jack Welch was legendary for the GE education center in Croton-on-Hudson, New York, and its role in allowing the GE leader to educate current and future GE managers on the ways of GE and the vision of its future. It allowed a leader to shape future leaders, thereby building an organization. His successor, Jeff Immelt, uses the same facility to interact with and discuss GE's future with a new crop of future leaders.

Leaders do this in many ways. Larry Bossidy, former chairman of Honeywell and co-author of the best seller, *Execution,* spent 50 percent of his time each year flying to Allied Signal's various operations around the world, meeting with managers and discussing decisions, results, and progress. Bill Gates at Microsoft reportedly spent two hours each day reading and sending e-mail to any of Microsoft's 36,000 employees who want to contact him. All managers adapt structures, create teams, implement systems, and otherwise generate ways to coordinate, integrate, and share information about what their organization is doing and might do. Once again, here is what Jim McNerney had to say:

> It comes down to personal engagement. I spend a lot of time out with our people. I probably do 30 major events a year with 100 people or more, where I spend time debating things and pushing my ideas, telling them what I am thinking and soliciting feedback. Most CEOs are smart enough to figure out where to go with a company. The hard work is engaging everyone in doing it. That's the hard work in leadership.[6]

Others create customer advisory groups, supplier partnerships, R&D joint ventures, and other adjustments to build an adaptable, learning organization that buys into the leader's vision and strategic intent and the change driving the future opportunities facing the business. These, in addition to the fundamental structural guidelines described in the previous chapter for restructuring to support strategically critical activities, are key ways leaders constantly attempt to educate and build a supportive organization.

principles (of a leader)

A leader's fundamental personal standards that guide her sense of honesty, integrity and ethical behavior.

Principles are your fundamental personal standards that guide your sense of honesty, integrity, and ethical behavior. If you have a clear moral compass guiding your priorities and those you set for the company, you will be a more effective leader. This observation is repeatedly one of the first thing effective leaders interviewed by researchers, business writers, and students mention when they answer a question about what they think is most important in explaining their success as leaders and the success of leaders they admire. Steven Reinemund, PepsiCo's very successful (former) CEO, said it this way:

> It starts with basic beliefs and values. It's important to make clear to the people in the organization what those are, so you're transparent. They have to be consistent with the values of the organization, or there will be a problem. If you look at all the issues that have happened in the corporate world of the last few years, . . . it all boils down to a basic lack of a moral compass and checks and balances among leaders. We as leaders have to check each other. We're going to make mistakes. If we don't check each other on them, you

[6] Ibid.

get in trouble. Most of the companies that got into trouble had a set of stated principles, but the leaders didn't check each other on those principles.[7]

Principle boils down to a personal philosophy we all deal with at an individual level—choices involving honesty, integrity, ethical behavior. Indeed Exhibit 12.2, Strategy in Action, gives you the chance to "test" *your* personal principles in comparison with the actions of some of your business school peers at Duke university's MBA program, and *BusinessWeek*'s thoughts too. The key thing to remember as a future leader is that your personal philosophies, or choices, manifest themselves exponentially for you or any key leaders of any organization. The people who do the work of any organization watch their leaders and what their leaders do, sanction, or stand for. So do people outside that organization who deal with it. These people then reflect those principles in what they do or come to believe is the way to do things in or with that organization. An effective organization is better built—is stronger—when its leaders show by example what they want their people to do and the principles they want their people to operate by on a day-to-day basis and in making decisions shaped by values and principles—a clear sense of right or wrong. "Values," "Lead by example," "Do as I say AND as I do"—these are very basic notions that good leaders find great strength in using. *BusinessWeek*'s "The Ethics Guy" says simply that principles should boil down to "five easy principles," which are:[8]

1. Do no harm
2. Make things better
3. Respect others
4. Be fair
5. Be compassionate

The value of that kind of clarity, and transparency, as PepsiCo's Reinemund described it, can become a major force by which a leader will shape and move his or her organization.

perseverance (of a leader)

The capacity to see a commitment through to completion long after most people would have stopped trying.

Perseverance is the capacity to see a commitment through to completion long after most people would have stopped trying. The opening example about Jeff Immelt conjures up images of some people in GE being hesitant to follow him because of their longtime loyalty to Jack Welch and his ways. Immelt will need to have patience and perseverance to deal with these people, to help them gradually shift their loyalty and accept the new. The example also conjures up another image, one of people excited to embrace Immelt's effort to take GE in a new direction—just because of the excitement of the moment along with some sense that a change is needed. But imagine that the first signs are not good, that it is unclear whether the radical new approach will work or not. It is relatively easy to then imagine a significant negative shift in the enthusiasm and faith of this group—again, Immelt must call on considerable perseverance to simply continue to bring them along and build their commitment over the long term.

PepsiCo's Reinemund talked about perseverance and says it is "sticking with it through the good and the bad times, mostly the bad." He goes on to credit his predecessor with having the perseverance at PepsiCo to stick with a vision that didn't "take" right away but that has proven to be exactly the vision PepsiCo needed to pursue to create a favorable future.

Shaping Organizational Culture

Leaders know well that the values and beliefs shared throughout their organization will shape how the work of the organization is done. And when attempting to embrace

---

[7] Brady, "The Six Ps."

[8] Bruce Weinstein, "Five Easy Principles," *BusinessWeek,* January 10, 2007.

On April 27, 2007, the dean of Duke's business school had the unfortunate task of announcing that nearly 10 percent of the Class of 2008 had been caught cheating on a take-home final exam. The scandal, which has cast yet another pall over the leafy, Gothic campus, is already going down as the biggest episode of alleged student deception in the business school's history.

Almost immediately, the questions started swirling. The accused MBAs were, on average, 29 years old. They were the cut-and-paste generation, the champions of Linux. Before going to business school, they worked in corporations for an average of six years. They did so at a time when their bosses were trumpeting the brave new world of open source, where one's ability to aggregate (or rip off) other people's intellectual property was touted as a crucial competitive advantage.

It's easy to imagine the explanations these MBAs, who are mulling an appeal, might come up with. Teaming up on a take-home exam: that's not academic fraud, it's postmodern learning, wiki style. Text-messaging exam answers or downloading essays onto iPods: that's simply a wise use of technology.

One can understand the confusion. This is a generation that came of age nabbing music off Napster and watching bootlegged Hollywood blockbusters in their dorm rooms. "What do you mean?" you can almost hear them saying. "We're not supposed to share?"

GO ALONG OR GO SOLO

That's not to say that university administrators should ignore unethical behavior, if it in fact occurred. But in this wired world, maybe the very notion of what constitutes cheating has to be reevaluated. The scandal at Duke points to how much the world has changed, and how academia and corporations are confused about it all, sending split messages.

We're told it's all about teamwork and shared information. But then we're graded and ranked as individuals. We assess everybody as single entities. But then we plop them into an interdependent world and tell them their success hinges on creative collaboration.

The new culture of shared information is vastly different from the old, where hoarding information was power. But professors—and bosses, for that matter—need to be able to test individual ability. For all the talk about workforce teamwork, there are plenty of times when a person is on his or her own, arguing a case, preparing a profit and loss statement, or writing a research report.

Still, many believe that a rethinking of the assessment process is in store. The Stanford University Design School, for example, is so collaborative that "it would be impossible to cheat," says design school professor Robert I. Sutton. "If you found somebody to help you write a group project, in our view that's a sign of an inventive team member who gets stuff done. If you found someone to do work for free who was committed to open source, we'd say, 'Wow, that was smart.' One group of students got the police to help them with a school project to build a roundabout where there were a lot of bike accidents. Is that cheating?"

That's food for thought at a time when learning is becoming more and more of a social process embedded in a larger network. This is in no way a pass on those who consciously break the rules. With countries aping American business practices, a backlash against an ethically rudderless culture can't happen soon enough. But the saga at Duke raises an interesting question: In the age of Twitter, a social network that keeps users in constant streaming contact with one another, what is cheating?

So, what do you think? Is what the Duke MBAs did "cheating," or is it simply collaborative learning as *BusinessWeek* posits?

accelerated change, reshaping their organization's culture is an activity that occupies considerable time for most leaders. Elements of good leadership—vision, performance, principles, perseverance, which have just been described—are important ways leaders shape organizational culture as well. Leaders shape organizational culture through their passion for the enterprise and the selection/development of talented managers to be future leaders. We will examine these two ideas and then cover the notion of organizational culture in greater detail.

**passion
(of a leader)**
A highly motivated
sense of commitment
to what you do and
want to do.

Passion, in a leadership sense, is a highly motivated sense of commitment to what you do and want to do. PepsiCo's Reinemund described it this way:

> I remember when I was a kid, Kennedy made the announcement that he wanted to put a man on the moon and bring him back safely to earth. That was so motivating and passionate. Nobody believed it could happen, but he inspired them to do it with his passion.[9]

Like many other traits of good leaders, passion is best seen through the leaders' intermittent behaviors while in the throws of the challenging times of the organizations they lead. They must use special moments to convey a sincere passion for and delight in the work of the company they lead. These observations by and about Ryanair CEO Michael O'Leary about competing in the increasingly competitive European airline industry and archrival easyJet provide a useful example:

> It was vintage Michael O'Leary. On May 13, the 42-year-old CEO of Dublin-based discount airline Ryanair outfitted his staff in full combat gear, drove an old World War II tank to England's Luton airport, an hour north of London, then demanded access to the base of archrival easyJet Airline Co. With the theme to the old television series *The A-Team* blaring, O'Leary declared he was "liberating the public from easyJet's high fares." When security—surprise!—refused to let the Ryanair armor roll in, O'Leary led the troops in his own rendition of a platoon march song: "I've been told and it's no lie. EasyJet's fares are way too high!" So it is that there are new rivals for O'Leary to conquer. "When we were a much smaller company, we compared ourselves to British Airways. But they are such a mess, most people just feel sorry for them," O'Leary says. "Now we're turning the guns on easyJet."[10]

It was readily apparent to anyone on this scene that O'Leary was passionate about Ryanair, and that example sent a clear message that he wanted an organizational culture that was aggressive, competitive, and somewhat free-wheeling in order to take advantage of change in the European airline industry. He did this by passionate example, by expectations felt by his managers, and in the way decision making is approached within Ryanair.

Sam Walton used to lead cheers at every Wal-Mart store he visited each year before and long after Wal-Mart was an overwhelming success. Kathy Mulhany at Xerox, a 28-year company veteran when she assumed the presidency with Xerox close to bankruptcy, started and continues to travel to every Xerox location worldwide twice annually just to convey her passion for Xerox as a way of rallying veteran Xerox employees to continue to buy into her vision and continue its extraordinary turnaround. GE's Jeff Immelt is described by a board member as a natural salesman who still happily recounts the days when he drove around his territory in a Ford Taurus while at GE Plastics. "He knows the world looks to GE as a harbinger of future trends," says Ogilvy & Mather Worldwide CEO Rochelle Lazarus, who sits on the board. "He really feels GE has a responsibility to the world to get out in front and play a leadership role." Immelt, it would seem, is passionate about GE and its future opportunities. Indeed, at the most recent gathering of GE's top 650 executives, amidst a situation where GE stock price is down 20 percent from last year, Immelt insisted that "there's never been a better day, a better time, or a better place to be," meaning than GE. That's passion.

Leaders also use reward systems, symbols, and structure among other means to shape the organization's culture. Travelers' Insurance Co.'s notable turnaround was accomplished in part by changing its "hidebound" culture through a change in its agent reward system. Employees previously on salary with occasional bonuses were given rewards that involved substantial cash bonuses and stock options. A major Travelers' customer and risk management director at drug-maker Becton Dickinson said: "They're hungrier now. They want to make deals. They're different than the old, hidebound Travelers' culture." Jeff Immelt is doing something similar to reshape the ingrained GE culture—tying executive compensation

---

[9] Ibid.

[10] "Ryanair Rising," *BusinessWeek,* June 2, 2003.

to their ability to come up with new ideas that show improved customer service, generate cash growth, and boost sales instead of simply meeting bottom-line targets.[11]

As leaders clarify strategic intent, build an organization, and shape their organization's culture, they look to one key element to help—their management team throughout their organization. As Honeywell's chairman Larry Bossidy candidly observed when asked about how after 42 years at General Electric, Allied Signal, and now Honeywell, with seemingly drab businesses, he could expect exciting growth: "There's no such thing as a mature market. What we need is mature executives who can find ways to grow."[12] Leaders look to managers they need to execute strategy as another source of leadership to accept risk and cope with the complexity that change brings about. So selection and development of key managers become major leadership roles.

Recruiting and Developing Talented Operational Leadership

As we noted at the beginning of this section on organizational leadership, the accelerated pace and complexity of business will increase pressure on corporations to push authority down in their organizations, ultimately meaning that every line manager will have to exercise leadership's prerogatives to an extent unthinkable a generation earlier. We also defined one of the key roles of good organizational leadership as building the organization by educating and developing new leaders. They will each be global managers, change agents, strategists, motivators, strategic decision makers, innovators, and collaborators if the business is to survive and prosper. So we want to examine this more completely by looking at key competencies these future managers need to possess or develop. Exhibit 12.3, Strategy in Action, provides an interesting perspective on this reality showing IBM's use of Internet-based, three-dimensional (3D) games to train and develop future global leaders in today's fast-paced, global marketplace.

Today's need for fluid learning organizations capable of rapid response, sharing, and cross-cultural synergy place incredible demands on young managers to bring important competencies to the organization. Exhibit 12.4 describes the needs organizations look to managers to meet and then identifies the corresponding competencies managers would need to do so. Ruth Williams and Joseph Cothrel drew this conclusion in their research about competencies needed from managers in today's fast-changing business environment.

> Today's competitive environment requires a different set of management competencies than we traditionally associate with the role. The balance has clearly shifted from attributes traditionally thought of as masculine (strong decision making, leading the troops, driving strategy, waging competitive battle) to more feminine qualities (listening, relationship-building, and nurturing). The model today is not so much "take it on your shoulders" as it is to "create the environment that will enable others to carry part of the burden." The focus is on unlocking the organization's human asset potential.[13]

Researcher David Goleman addressed the question of what types of personality attributes generate the type of competencies described in Exhibit 12.4. His research suggested that a set of four characteristics commonly referred to as emotional intelligence play a key role in bringing the competencies needed from today's desirable manager:[14]

- *Self-awareness* in terms of the ability to read and understand one's emotions and assess one's strengths and weaknesses, underlain by the confidence that stems from positive self-worth.

- *Self-management* in terms of control, integrity, conscientiousness, initiative, and achievement orientation.

[11] Howard Gleckman, "A Golden Opportunity," *BusinessWeek Online*, March 29, 2003.

[12] Diane Brady, "The Immelt Revolution," *BusinessWeek Online*, October 18, 2005.

[13] Ruth Williams and Joseph Cothrel, *Current Trends in Strategic Management* (New York: Blackwell Publishing, 2007).

[14] D. Goleman "What Makes a Leader?" *Harvard Business Review* (November–December 1998), pp. 93–102.

IBM's Management Games

BusinessWeek

Thunder crashes, lightning flashes, and a camera zooms in on a shadowy, futuristic-looking, gray-and-black office. The camera follows a female avatar in slacks and a button-down shirt as she jogs from one cubicle to the next, up a spiral staircase, and across a high gangplank as dramatic classical music plays in the background. This YouTube trailer could easily be a plug for a new shoot-'em-up video game, or a slasher flick. Instead, it's promoting a video game called Innov8, which IBM will start selling in September 2007.

Yes, IBM. The computer giant says it received dozens of calls from potential customers after showing the video clip at a recent conference for clients. Designed to help tech managers better understand the roles of businesspeople, and vice versa, players go into a virtual business unit to test their hand at ventures such as redesigning a call center, opening a brokerage account, or processing an insurance claim.

WAR OF THE WORLDS

The game will be available free of charge to universities around the world. No price has been set yet for corporate customers because it will depend on how much IBM has to change the game to accommodate a particular business process a client might want to improve. The game will be available online and will also be able to run on standalone PCs.

Innov8 is only one of several initiatives afoot at Big Blue to incorporate features of online games into business. IBM recently launched an internal competition,

dubbed "War of the Worlds," to encourage employees to, for instance, start virtual businesses or meet with real clients through a slew of online games. Each member of the winning team will receive a Nintendo Wii. The company hopes to use the exercise to determine which virtual ventures are best for specific business tasks or processes.

Why is one of the world's most buttoned-down organizations encouraging its people—and customers—to play games? IBM says that the skills honed playing massive multiplayer dragon-slaying games like "World of Warcraft" can be useful when managing modern multinationals. The company says its research supports that claim and it will release its findings the same day as its War of the Worlds contest.

DEVELOPING LEADERSHIP

While IBM's research may be aimed at helping to build its own consulting business, it comes at a time when there's a flurry of corporate experimentation in games. McKinsey & Co. is using video games to test recruits for leadership potential and assess their team-building style. Royal Philips Electronics and Johnson & Johnson, meanwhile, are using multiplayer games to improve collaboration between far-flung divisions, as well as between managers and their overseas underlings.

What distinguishes the latest corporate forays into the gaming world is the degree to which companies are tapping virtual environments to hone the leadership skills of their workers. By 2011, 80 percent

- *Social awareness* in relation to sensing others' emotions (empathy), reading the organization (organizational awareness), and recognizing customers' needs (service orientation).

- *Social skills* in relation to influencing and inspiring others; communicating, collaborating, and building relationships with others; and managing change and conflict.

A key way these characteristics manifest themselves in a manager's routine activities is found in the way they seek to get the work of their unit or group done over time. How do they use power and influence to get others to get things done? Effective leaders seek to develop managers who understand they have many sources of power and influence, and that relying on the power associated with their position in an organization is often the least effective means to influence people to do what is needed. Managers have available seven sources of power and influence (see Exhibit 12.5).

Organizational sources of power are derived from a manager's role in the organization. **Position power** is formally established based on the manager's position in the organization. By virtue of holding that position, certain decision-making authorities and responsibilities

position power
The ability and right to influence and direct others based on the power associated with your formal position in the organization.

reward power
The ability to influence and direct others that comes from being able to confer rewards in return for desired actions or outcomes.

of Internet users will have avatars, or digital versions of themselves, for work and play, according to market researcher Gartner. By the end of 2012, half of all U.S. companies will also have digital offices or "networked virtual environments," adds Gartner. The online game world will become an important place to hold meetings, orient new hires, and communicate across the globe.

For IBM's new research, the computer giant tracked the leadership qualities of gamers with the help of Seriosity (a company that develops enterprise software inspired by multiplayer games), Stanford, and the Massachusetts Institute of Technology (MIT). IBM also surveyed more than 200 game-playing managers at the company over a seven-month period. Besides IBM, there are several others, such as Joi Ito, a tech entrepreneur, looking at how managing fast-expanding "guilds," or teams, in multiplayer games provides a forum for trying out different corporate management styles.

MANAGEMENT FLIGHT SIMULATORS

The IBM researchers found that those who are deeply immersed in online worlds that link millions of players, such as "World of Warcraft," were ideally suited to manage in the new millennium. They were particularly savvy at gathering information from far-flung sources, determining strategic risks, failing fast, and moving on to the next challenge quickly. "If you want to see what business leadership will look like in three to five years, look at what's happening in online games," says Byron Reeves, a Stanford University communications professor and co-founder of Seriosity.

One of the key findings from the research, says Thomas Malone, an MIT professor of management and Seriosity board member, is that companies need to create more opportunities for flexible, project-oriented leadership. In fast-paced games, people can jump in to manage a team for as little as 10 minutes, if they have the needed skills for the task at hand. "Games make leaders from lemmings," says Tony O'Driscoll, an IBM learning strategist and one of the authors of the study. "Since leadership happens quickly and easily in online games, otherwise reserved players are more likely to try on leadership roles."

The study points out that games can become "management flight simulators" of sorts, letting employees manage a global workforce in cyberspace before they do so in the real world. More than half of the managers surveyed say playing massive multiplayer games had helped them lead at work. Three-quarters of those surveyed believed that specific game tools, such as expressive avatars that can communicate via body language, as well as by voice and typing, would help manage remote employees in the real world.

Source: Reprinted with special permission from Ali McCannon, "IBM's Management Games," *BusinessWeek*, June 14, 2007. Copyright © 2007 The McGraw-Hill Companies.

information power
The ability to influence others based on your access to information and your control of dissemination of information that is important to subordinates and others yet not otherwise easily obtained.

punitive power
Ability to direct and influence others based on your ability to coerce and deliver punishment for mistakes or undesired actions by others, particularly subordinates.

are conferred that the manager is entitled to use to get things done. It is the source of power many new managers expect to be able to rely on, but often the least useful. **Reward power** is available when the manager confers rewards in return for desired actions and outcomes. This is often a power source. **Information power** can be particularly effective and is derived from a manager's access to and control over the dissemination of information that is important to subordinates yet not easily available in the organization. **Punitive power** is the power exercised via coercion or fear of punishment for mistakes or undesired actions by a manager's subordinates.

Leaders today increasingly rely on their personal ability to influence others perhaps as much, if not more so, than organizational sources of power. Personal influence, a form of "power," comes mainly from three sources. **Expert influence** is derived from a leader's knowledge and expertise in a particular area or situation. This can be a very important source of power in influencing others. **Referent influence** comes from having others want to identify with the leader. We have all seen or worked for leaders who have major influence over others based simply on their charisma, personality, empathy, and other personal

EXHIBIT 12.4
What Competencies Should Managers Possess?

Source: Ruth L. Williams and Joseph P. Cothrel, "Building Tomorrow's Leaders Today," *Strategy and Leadership* 26, October 1997. Reprinted with permission of Emerald Group Publishing Limited.

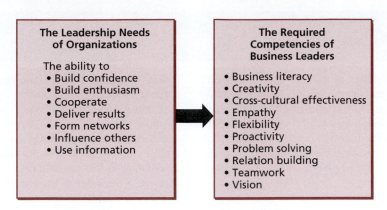

The Leadership Needs of Organizations

The ability to
- Build confidence
- Build enthusiasm
- Cooperate
- Deliver results
- Form networks
- Influence others
- Use information

The Required Competencies of Business Leaders

- Business literacy
- Creativity
- Cross-cultural effectiveness
- Empathy
- Flexibility
- Proactivity
- Problem solving
- Relation building
- Teamwork
- Vision

expert influence
The ability to direct and influence others because they defer to you based on your expertise or specialized knowledge that is related to the task, undertaking, or assignment in which they are involved.

referent influence
The ability to influence others derived from their strong desire to be associated with you, usually because they admire you, gain prestige or a sense of purpose by that association, or believe in your motivations.

peer influence
The ability to influence individual behavior among members of a group based on group norms, a group sense of what is the right thing or right way to do things, and the need to be valued and accepted by the group.

attributes. And finally, **peer influence** can be a very effective way for leaders to influence the behavior of others. Most people in organizations and across an organization find themselves put in groups to solve problems, serve customers, develop innovations, and perform a host of other tasks. Leaders can use the assignment of team members and the charge to the team as a way to enable peer-based influence to work on key managers and the outcomes they produce.

Effective leaders make use of all seven sources of power and influence, very often in combination, to deal with the myriad situations they face and need others to handle. The exact best source(s) of power and influence are often shaped by the nature of the task, project, urgency of an assignment, or the unique characteristics of specific personnel, among myriad factors. Organizational leaders such as Jeff Immelt at GE draw on all these sources and, equally important, seek to develop their organizations around subordinate leaders and managers who insightfully and effectively make use of all their sources of power and influence.

One final perspective on the role of organizational leadership and management selection is found in the work of Bartlett and Ghoshal. Their study of several of the most successful global companies in the last decade suggests that combining flexible responsiveness with integration and innovation requires rethinking the management role and the distribution of management roles within a twenty-first-century company. They see three critical management roles: the *entrepreneurial process* (decisions about opportunities to pursue and resource deployment), the *integration process* (building and deploying organizational capabilities), and the *renewal process* (shaping organizational purpose and enabling change). Traditionally viewed as the domain of top management, their research suggests that these functions need to be shared and distributed across three management levels as suggested in Exhibit 12.6.[15]

ORGANIZATIONAL CULTURE

organizational culture
The set of important assumptions and beliefs (often unstated) that members of an organization share in common.

Organizational culture is the set of important assumptions (often unstated) that members of an organization share in common. Every organization has its own culture. An organization's culture is similar to an individual's personality—an intangible yet ever-present theme that provides meaning, direction, and the basis for action. In much the same way as personality influences the behavior of an individual, the shared assumptions

[15] C. A. Barlett and S. Ghoshal, "The Myth of the General Manager: New Personal Competencies for New Management Roles," *California Management Review* 40 (Fall 1997), pp. 92–116; "Beyond Structure to Process," *Harvard Business Review* (January–February 1995).

EXHIBIT 12.5
Sources of Power and Influence

Organizational Power	Personal Influence
Position power	Expert influence
Reward power	Referent influence
Information power	Peer influence
Punitive power	

(beliefs and values) among a firm's members influence opinions and actions within that firm. Exhibit 12.7, Strategy in Action, shows the results of a *BusinessWeek* survey conducted by Staffing.org to identify how employees view their company's culture in the context of various TV shows or cartoon characters.

A member of an organization can simply be aware of the organization's beliefs and values without sharing them in a personally significant way. Those beliefs and values have more personal meaning if the member views them as a guide to appropriate behavior in the organization and, therefore, complies with them. The member becomes fundamentally committed to the beliefs and values when he or she internalizes them; that is, comes to hold them as personal beliefs and values. In this case, the corresponding behavior is *intrinsically rewarding* for the member—the member derives personal satisfaction from his or her actions in the organization because those actions are congruent with corresponding personal beliefs and values. *Assumptions become shared assumptions through internalization among an organization's individual members.* And those shared, internalized beliefs and values shape the content and account for the strength of an organization's culture.

The Role of the Organizational Leader in Organizational Culture

The previous section of this chapter covered organizational leadership in detail. Part of that coverage discussed the role of the organizational leader in shaping organizational culture. Several points in that discussion apply here. We will not repeat them, but it is important to emphasize that the leader and the culture of the organization s/he leads are inextricably intertwined. The leader is the standard bearer, the personification, the ongoing embodiment of the culture (Steve Jobs, Jeff Immelt) or the new example (Alan Mulally, Mike Bloomberg) of what it should become. As such, several of the aspects of what a leader does or should do represent influences on the organization's culture, either to reinforce it or to exemplify the standards and nature of what it needs to become. How the leader behaves and emphasizes those aspects of being a leader become what all the organization sees are "the important things to do and value."

Build Time in the Organization

Some leaders have been with the organization for a long time. If they have been in the leader role for an extended time, then their association with the organization is usually strongly entrenched. They continue to reinforce the current culture, are empowered by it, and understandably go to considerable lengths to reinforce it as a key element in sustaining continued success. The problematic long-time leaders are those who have built a successful enterprise that also sustains a culture that appears unethical or worse. Exhibit 12.8, Strategy in Action, describes just such a situation at AIG. Either type of long-time leader is often a widely known figure in today's media-intense business world. And in their setting, while the culture may be exceptionally strong, their role in creating it usually means they seemingly hold sway over the culture rather than the other way around.

Many leaders in recent years, and inevitably in any organization, are new to the top post of the organization. Their relationship with the organization's culture is perhaps more complex. Those who built a management career within that culture—Jeff Immelt at GE, Anne Mulcahy at Xerox, Alan Lafley at P&G—have the benefit of knowledge of the culture and credibility

EXHIBIT 12.6

Management Processes and Levels of Management

Sources: C. A. Bartlett and S. Ghoshal, "The Myth of the General Manager: New Personal Competencies for New Management Roles," *California Management Review* 40 (Fall, 1997); R. M. Grant, *Contemporary Strategy Analysis* (Oxford: Blackwell, 2001), p. 529.

	RENEWAL PROCESS	
Attracting resources and capabilities and developing the business	Developing operating managers and supporting their activities; maintaining organizational trust	Providing institutional leadership through shaping and embedding corporate purpose and challenging embedded assumptions
	INTEGRATION PROCESS	
Managing operational interdependencies and personal networks	Linking skills, knowledge, and resources across units; reconciling short-term performance and long-term ambition	Creating corporate direction; developing and nurturing organizational values
	ENTREPRENEURIAL PROCESS	
Creating and pursuing opportunities; managing continuous performance improvement	Reviewing, developing, and supporting initiatives	Establishing performance standards

Front-Line Management   Middle Management   Top Management

as an "initiated" member of that culture. This may be quite useful in helping engender confidence as they take on the task of leader of that culture or, perhaps more difficult (as with these three), as change agent for parts of that culture as the company moves forward.

In the other situation, a new leader who is not an "initiated" member of the culture or tribe faces a much more challenging task. Quite logically, they must earn credibility with the "tribe," which is usually somewhat resistant to change. And, very often, they are being brought in with a board of directors desiring change in the strategy, company, and usually culture. That becomes a substantial challenge for these new leaders to face. Some make it happen, others find the strength of the organization's culture far more powerful than their ability to change it.

Exhibit 12.9, Strategy in Action, provides an interesting example of these two perspectives as viewed through the experience of the same founder/CEO of successful companies with two very different cultures. It explains how Netflix founder and CEO Reed Hastings sought to dramatically change the culture and way of doing things at Netflix, his second company, after his experience with the nature of the culture that his first start-up, Pure Software, grew into as it became a part of IBM through a series of acquisitions and mergers. Hastings said of Pure, "We got more bureaucratic as we grew," and that it went from being a place that was fast-paced and the "where-everybody-wanted-to-be" place to a "dronish, when-does-the-day-end" software factory. After leaving Pure, Hastings spent about two years thinking about how to build a culture in his next start-up that would not have "big company creep."

At Netflix, Hastings has instilled a very unique "freedom and responsibility" culture that seeks to revolutionize both the way people rent movies and, perhaps more important to Hastings, how his managers work. In the face of Blockbuster, Wal-Mart, Amazon, the cable companies, and Apple, Hastings is attempting to create a culture so unique at Netflix that it is an "A" talent magnet, ensuring the best players in the business line up to help Netflix outsmart these very sizable competitors. And in doing so, Hastings is a "new" leader of a new company with a different business model that is trying to outlast and outcompete other, well established, major players in selling movie rentals. So in a sense, Hastings is a new leader, but with solid experience as a successful entrepreneur and innovator in similarly competitive, large, firmly entrenched, industry niches.

It may suggest that one way new leaders coming to established cultures can improve their chances of succeeding (where changing that culture is desired) is if they bring a similar background such that they establish credibility quicker, lower resistance easier, or simply

THE BIG PICTURE

THINK YOUR WORKPLACE is like a sitcom? In an online survey, Staffing.org, a performance research firm, asked 300 people to describe their company's culture using one of four fictional touchstones. The results:

"A lot like *The Office*" 57%	"More like *Dilbert* than I'd like to admit" 24%	"*M*A*S*H*, on a good day" 14%	"Like *Leave It to Beaver*" 5%

Source: Reprinted with special permission from "The Big Picture," *BusinessWeek*, May 25, 2007. Copyright © 2007 The McGraw-Hill Companies.

have a better basis for understanding the situation. At the same time, examples such as former R. J. Reynolds executive Lou Gerstner, who took over and pulled a declining IBM from the ashes, suggest that it can also be done if you come from an entirely different industry. So it may be that the skills of the leader and other relevant experience in the strategic dynamics at previous assignments are both critical to new leaders facing established cultures they must change.

ethical standards
A person's basis for differentiating right from wrong.

Ethical standards are a person's basis for differentiating right from wrong. An earlier section of this chapter emphasized the importance of "principles" in defining what a leader needs to incorporate in his or her recipe to become an effective leader. We need not repeat those points in the context of being a leader, but it is critical to recognize that the culture of an organization, and particularly the link between the leader and the culture's very nature, is inextricably tied to the ethical standards of behavior, actions, decisions, and norms that leader personifies. Enron, WorldCom, Qwest, Computer Associates, Ken Lay, Jeff Skillings, Sanjay Kumar, Joseph Nacchio, Bernie Ebbers, and Martha Stewart are companies, people, and situations we discussed in Chapter 3—they are all imprinted in each of our minds (see Exhibit 12.10, Strategy in Action). They speak volumes about this very point: Leaders, and their key associates, play a key role in shaping and defining the ethical standards that become absorbed into and shape the culture of the organizations they lead. Those ethical standards then become powerful, informal guidelines for the behaviors, decisions, and dealings of members of that culture or tribe. Exhibit 12.8 provided an example of where ethical standards shape culture and the challenges they present to insurance giant AIG's new CEO, Martin Sullivan, when the culture was led by a leader whose standards were rather unethical. An interesting question to ask yourself when you read the Exhibit 12.8 example is whether or not Martin Sullivan, in your opinion, is the right person to lead AIG toward a new culture and, if so, what the best relationship between AIG and Mr. Greenberg should be.

Searching for a New Culture, Even Though Business Is Great!

BusinessWeek

Wall Street cheered Martin Sullivan in late 2007: "AIG has emerged from a tumultuous period as a stronger, more disciplined, and more transparent company," Bank of America analyst Tamara Kravec said in a research note. "With the issue of regulatory settlement behind the company, we believe investors can now focus on improving fundamentals across AIG's businesses, particularly in its foreign life operations." Kravec made AIG Bank of America's top pick in financial services for 2007. Just a few years ago, Sullivan's cheers were few. The company he assumed leadership of had to change. And the problem wasn't its profitable, core business.

Instead, the problem was the archaic style and opaque business practices of Sullivan's former boss, the legendary Maurice R. "Hank" Greenberg, who resigned under pressure. For almost 40 years, no one challenged Greenberg's iron rule. While the 79-year-old chairman, president, and CEO delivered great results, he was frequently bellicose, known to yell at staffers with such intensity that at least one insider jokingly compared his tenure to a reign of terror. More significant, he was slow to embrace efforts to improve corporate governance, even characterizing the expenses of the Sarbanes-Oxley law as "an enormous burden."

Sullivan, 50, a witty charmer who eschews his predecessor's confrontational style, promised to cooperate fully with regulators. While the findings of the latest investigation were yet to be determined, they raised concerns about whether AIG may have used techniques to elevate results in the past, especially given its record of consistently outperforming industry peers.

A far harder job for Sullivan: yanking this mystery-shrouded organization's culture into the twenty-first century by pushing for greater transparency and a stronger board. About half of the AIG board was independent, and the company strengthened that contingent with the addition of former Merrill Lynch executive Stephen L. Hammerman. But investors like the AFL-CIO preferred to see a two-thirds majority of truly independent directors.

One item that Sullivan was expected to place high on his agenda: breaking down two little-known Byzantine private entities, Starr International and C.V. Starr & Co. These companies, which held shares in AIG, seemed to do little more than grossly enrich senior executives. Starr International, in which Greenberg still held a directorship, was much like a private partnership used to compensate senior managers. Getting a stake equates with winning entrance to an elite club. C.V. Starr & Co. was essentially a broker that did business with AIG. Several of its board members were also senior AIG executives, including Greenberg and Sullivan. Both entities stayed largely immune from public scrutiny but had drawn the ire of shareholders and regulators alike.

Last but not least: Sullivan was encouraged to speed up the exit of Greenberg, who sought to stay on as nonexecutive chairman and, within the private entities, exert enormous control. Having him hang around would make it tougher to speed through reform and restore the confidence of investors.

Sullivan inherited a strong global franchise, but he also headed a company that bears the stamp of Greenberg, a brilliant but tone-deaf autocrat who continued to complain about increased regulation even as AIG was immersed in scandal. Says Patrick McGurn, of Institutional Shareholder Services: "Was there a reform he ever put in place that he liked?" Investors' hope that Sullivan would embrace the reforms needed to bring AIG and its culture into the twenty-first century was eventually rewarded, and AIG is now in Wall Street's good graces.

Sources: Reprinted with special permission from "Investors Cheer AIG Results," *BusinessWeek*, March 2, 2007; and Diane Brady, "AIG Needs New Policies," *BusinessWeek*, March 17, 2005. Copyright © 2005 The McGraw-Hill Companies.

Leaders use every means available to them as an organizational leader to influence an organization's culture and their relationship with it. It bears repeating in this regard that reward systems, assignment of new managers from within versus outside the organization, composition of the firm's board of directors, reporting relationships, and organizational structure—each of these fundamental elements of executing a company's vision and strategy are also a leader's key "levers" for attempting to shape organizational culture in a direction she or he sees it needing to go. Because we have already discussed these levers, we move on to other ways leaders have sought to shape and reinforce their organization's culture.

Netflix Builds a Revolutionary, Unique Culture

BusinessWeek

I had the great fortune of doing a mediocre job at my first company," says Netflix Inc. founder Reed Hastings. He's talking about his 1990s start-up Pure Software, a wildly successful maker of debugging programs that, through a series of mergers, became part of IBM. Hastings says Pure, like many other outfits, went from being a heat-filled, everybody-wants-to-be-here place to a dronish, when-does-the-day-end sausage factory. "We got more bureaucratic as we grew," says Hastings.

After Pure, the Stanford-trained engineer spent two years thinking about how to ensure his next endeavor wouldn't suffer the same big-company creep.

The resulting sequel is Netflix, where Hastings is trying to revolutionize not only the way people rent movies but also how his managers work. Hastings pays his people lavishly, gives them unlimited vacations, and lets them structure their own compensation packages. In return, he expects ultra-high performance. His 400 salaried employees are expected to do the jobs of three or four people. Netflix is no frat party with beer bashes and foosball tables. Nor does the company want to play cruise director to its employees. Rather, Netflix is a tough, fulfilling, "fully formed adult" culture, says marketing manager Heather McIlhany. "There's no place to hide at Netflix."

Hastings calls his approach "freedom and responsibility." And as one might expect, employees get all cinematic when describing the vibe. Netflix is the workplace equivalent of *Ocean's 11,* says Todd S. Yellin, hired to perfect the site's movie-rating system. Hastings is Danny Ocean, the bright, charismatic leader who recruits the best in class, gives them a generous cut, and provides the flexibility to do what they *do best*, all while uniting them on a focused goal. The near-impossible mission, in this case, is trying to outmaneuver Blockbuster, Amazon, the cable companies, and Apple in the race to become the leading purveyor of online movies.

The tension has never been higher. Last quarter, for the first time in Netflix's history, the company lost customers in its bloody, fight-to-the-death battle with Blockbuster Inc. Netflix shares cratered and have yet to recover. Some analysts are talking doom.

Netflix executives like to point out, though, that the company has been pronounced dead more than once before. When Wal-Mart started offering online movie rentals in 2002, for example, analysts started referring to Netflix as *The Last Picture Show*. But by 2005, Wal-Mart had closed shop. It referred all its customers to Netflix.

Today, Netflix is embroiled in an even tougher, two-front war: competing with Blockbuster for online supremacy in DVD rentals while also inaugurating a digital streaming service to compete with the likes of Apple. That's one mighty gang of entrenched competitors. "There's usually room in a marketplace for more than one," says Wedbush Morgan Securities analyst Michael Pachter. "But in this case there really isn't."

Hastings is betting on Netflix's *culture* to get the company out of this corner. The plan includes continuing to increase what Hastings calls "talent density." Most companies go to great scientific lengths to ensure they are paying just enough to attract talent but not a dollar more than they need to. Netflix, which hands out salaries that are typically much higher than what is customary in Silicon Valley, is unabashed in its we-pay-above-market swagger. "We're unafraid to pay high," says Hastings.

To ensure that the company is constantly nabbing A players, company talent hunters are told that money is no object. Each business group has what amounts to an internal boutique headhunting firm. Employees often recommend people they bonded with at work before (that *Ocean's 11* effect again).

Gibson Biddle, who runs the Web site, knew that Yellin, who had both deep tech and film expertise, was the perfect guy to help Netflix improve how it recommends movies to customers on its site. Yellin had worked for Biddle at a family entertainment site during the boom. The snag was that Yellin, also a filmmaker, was finishing up his first feature film, *Brother's Shadow,* in Los Angeles. He also was allergic to anything corporate or publicly traded.

Impossible sell, right? But Netflix threw so much cash and flexibility at Yellin that he couldn't turn it down. During his first three months he flew back and forth between L.A. and San Francisco doing his Netflix job and finishing his movie. "This company is *über*-flexible," says Yellin. "I'm given the freedom to do what I do well without being micromanaged."

NO GOLDEN HANDCUFFS

Pay is not tied to performance reviews, nor to some predetermined raise pool, but to the job market. Netflix bosses are constantly gleaning market compensation data from new hires and then amping up salaries when needed. And what happens when someone doesn't live up to expectations? "At most companies, average

(continued)

Exhibit 12.9 cont.

BusinessWeek

performers get an average raise," says Hastings. "At Netflix, they get a generous severance package." Why? Because Hastings believes that otherwise managers feel too guilty to let someone go.

When it comes to paychecks, Netflix is arguably going where no public company has gone before. Employees are free to choose annually how much of their compensation they want in cash versus stock. Unlike the case at most companies, options vest immediately. Netflix doesn't want golden-handcuffs types. One engineer got so excited that he told human resources head Patty McCord to give him half his pay in stock. When McCord saw him drive away in an old minivan, she wasn't surprised when he popped into her office the next day and told her he wanted to make it more cash: 80–20.

Good thing for him. With great choice comes great risk. Netflix employees who loaded up on stock this year have gotten hammered, leaving some to pine for the paternalism that has long shielded employees from the vagaries of stock market volatility. But great risk also means great freedom, as in: "Take as much vacation as you want." Last year, engineering manager Aroon Ramadoss took off five weeks to go to Europe with his girlfriend. He plans on taking another extended vacation next year in Brazil. "I like to travel in bigger chunks rather than take five days off and rush right back," says Ramadoss.

Source: Reprinted with special permission from "Netflix Flees to the Max," *BusinessWeek*, September 24, 2007. Copyright © 2007 The McGraw-Hill Companies.

Emphasize Key Themes or Dominant Values

Businesses build strategies around distinct competitive advantages they possess or seek. Quality, differentiation, cost advantages, and speed are four key sources of competitive advantage. Insightful leaders nurture key themes or dominant values within their organization that reinforce competitive advantages they seek to maintain or build. Key themes or dominant values may center around wording in an advertisement. They are often found in internal company communications. They are most often found as a new vocabulary used by company personnel to explain "who we are." At Xerox, the key themes include respect for the individual and services to the customer. At Procter & Gamble (P&G), the overarching value is product quality; McDonald's uncompromising emphasis on QSCV—quality, service, cleanliness, and value—through meticulous attention to detail is legendary; Southwest Airlines is driven by the "family feeling" theme, which builds a team spirit and nurtures each employee's cooperative attitude toward others, cheerful outlook toward life, and pride in a job well done. Du Pont's safety orientation—a report of every accident must be on the chairman's desk within 24 hours—has resulted in a safety record that was 27 times better than the chemical industry average and 68 times better than the all-manufacturing average.

Encourage Dissemination of Stories and Legends about Core Values

Companies with strong cultures are enthusiastic collectors and tellers of stories, anecdotes, and legends in support of basic beliefs. Frito-Lay's zealous emphasis on customer service is reflected in frequent stories about potato chip route salespeople who have slogged through sleet, mud, hail, snow, and rain to uphold the 99.5 percent service level to customers in which the entire company takes great pride. Milliken (a textile leader) holds "sharing" rallies once every quarter at which teams from all over the company swap success stories and ideas. Typically, more than 100 teams make five-minute presentations over a two-day period. Every rally is designed around a major theme, such as quality, cost reduction, or customer service. No criticisms are allowed, and awards are given to reinforce this

Strategy in Action

Exhibit 12.10

CEOs as Founders, Felons, Convicted of Fraud, Conspiracy, and Securities Violations

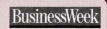

The "I-knew-nothing-about-the-books" defense failed to persuade juries. "This is absolutely going to raise the level of expectation that CEOs should know everything that's going on inside their companies, because they will be held responsible for it," says Dan Reingold, a CSFB analyst. The collapse of WorldCom, Enron, and significant damage to Qwest, Computer Associates, and Martha Stewart OmniMedia have profoundly affected the business climate in the United States. They were major reasons lawmakers passed the Sarbanes-Oxley Act. Five important lessons can be gleaned from the testimony in their trials for investors, business school students, and aspiring execs alike:

1. **Beware of companies with cult-like corporate cultures.**

   From the start, most of these companies functioned more like a tribe than a business. Their operations centered around a charismatic leader, who also had a close relationship with the company's chief financial officer. Together, they exercised unquestioned authority and demanded unquestioned loyalty from employees.

   Company stock was imbued with enormous symbolism. Each employee received a grant of stock, a form of initiation into the tribe. But the culture created by these key leaders often prevented them from selling the stock, lest the employees be ostracized from the group.

2. **Beware of too much corporate reliance on Washington.**

   WorldCom, Qwest, Enron, and other companies, spent an enormous amount of time and energy lobbying regulators and elected officials. The telecom boom led by WorldCom was driven mostly by the government-ordered breakup of AT&T in 1984 and the Telecom Act of 1996. WorldCom, Qwest, and Enron benefited from rules that helped it compete. But when the rules unexpectedly changed, it found itself in trouble, ultimately pulling out of the consumer market.

3. **Beware of companies that rely too heavily on mergers and acquisitions.**

   There's no question that M&A is a legitimate means of growth for many companies. But when a corporation bases its business plan on aggressively acquiring companies (e.g., WorldCom did nearly 70 deals in less than five years), that's a flashing yellow light. It's a strong signal that the other engines of growth, such as product development, sales, and marketing, aren't very strong. The constant write-offs of good will, which reflects the premium that an acquiring company pays on a purchase, distorts quarterly earnings and can lead to confusion. If it is too good, it just may be.

4. **Beware of close personal ties between management and the board.**

   Most of the directors in these companies had been with the company for years. Many of them invested in the company at the founding, or led companies that were subsequently acquired. All of them received significant amounts of stock and in some cases enjoyed perks like the use of corporate jets. Yes, their share values dropped, too, like everyone else's, when the companies hit the skids, and there's no suggestion that any were aware of fraud. Still, close ties didn't help those boards when it came to asking tough questions about their company's accounting, or probing the wisdom of a CEO's strategy, or offering hundreds of millions of dollars in loans to CEOs who are also their personal benefactors.

5. **The biggest lesson.**

   The most haunting of them all, is the image of each executive sitting in an old courtroom, stoically contemplating his or her fate before the jury returned its verdict. It's no place you want to be!

Sources: Reprinted with special permission from "Cornered in the Corner Office," *BusinessWeek*, June 25, 2007; "Corporate Justice," December 18, 2006; and Steven Rosenbush, "Five Lessons of the WorldCom Debacle," *BusinessWeek Online*, March 16, 2005. Copyright © 2007 The McGraw-Hill Companies.

institutionalized approach to storytelling. L. L. Bean tells customer service stories; 3M tells innovation stories; P&G, Johnson & Johnson, IBM, and Maytag tell quality and innovation stories. These stories are very important in developing an organizational culture, because organization members identify strongly with them and come to share the beliefs and values they support.

Institutionalize Practices That Systematically Reinforce Desired Beliefs and Values

Companies with strong cultures are clear on what their beliefs and values need to be and take the process of shaping those beliefs and values very seriously. Most important, the values espoused by these companies underlay the strategies they employ. For example, McDonald's has a yearly contest to determine the best hamburger cooker in its chain. First, there is a competition to determine the best hamburger cooker in each store; next, the store winners compete in regional championships; finally, the regional winners compete in the "All-American" contest. The winners, who are widely publicized throughout the company, get trophies and All-American patches to wear on their McDonald's uniforms.

Adapt Some Very Common Themes in Their Own Unique Ways

The most typical beliefs that shape organizational culture include (1) a belief in being the best (or, as at GE, "better than the best"); (2) a belief in superior quality and service; (3) a belief in the importance of people as individuals and a faith in their ability to make a strong contribution; (4) a belief in the importance of the details of execution, the nuts and bolts of doing the job well; (5) a belief that customers should reign supreme; (6) a belief in inspiring people to do their best, whatever their ability; (7) a belief in the importance of informal communication; and (8) a belief that growth and profits are essential to a company's well-being. Every company implements these beliefs differently (to fit its particular situation), and every company's values are the handiwork of one or two legendary figures in leadership positions. Accordingly, every company has a distinct culture that it believes no other company can copy successfully. And in companies with strong cultures, managers and workers either accept the norms of the culture or opt out from the culture and leave the company.

The stronger a company's culture and the more that culture is directed toward customers and markets, the less the company uses policy manuals, organization charts, and detailed rules and procedures to enforce discipline and norms. The reason is that the guiding values inherent in the culture convey in crystal-clear fashion what everybody is supposed to do in most situations. Poorly performing companies often have strong cultures. However, their cultures are dysfunctional, being focused on internal politics or operating by the numbers as opposed to emphasizing customers and the people who make and sell the product.

Manage Organizational Culture in a Global Organization[16]

The reality of today's global organizations is that organizational culture must recognize cultural diversity. *Social norms* create differences across national boundaries that influence how people interact, read personal cues, and otherwise interrelate socially. *Values* and *attitudes* about similar circumstances also vary from country to country. Where individualism is central to a North American's value structure, the needs of the group dominate the value structure of their Japanese counterparts. *Religion* is yet another source of cultural differences. Holidays, practices, and belief structures differ in very fundamental ways that must be taken into account as one attempts to shape organizational culture in a global setting. Finally, *education,* or ways people are accustomed to learning, differs across national borders. Formal classroom learning in the United States may teach things that are only learned via apprenticeship in other cultures. Because the process of shaping an organizational

[16] Differing backgrounds, often referred to as *cultural diversity,* is something that most managers will certainly see more of, both because of the growing cultural diversity domestically and the obvious diversification of cultural backgrounds that result from global acquisitions and mergers. For example, Harold Epps, manager of a computer keyboard plant in Boston, manages 350 employees representing 44 countries of origin and 19 languages.

culture often involves considerable "education," leaders should be sensitive to global differences in approaches to education to make sure their cultural education efforts are effective. Henning Kagermann, CEO of German-based global software company SAP, spoke to this issue recently when he said: "If you are a big company, you need to tap into the global talent pool. It's foolish to believe the smartest people are in one nation. In Germany, we now have this big public debate about there being a shortage of engineers in the country. Well, I don't care, or at least not as CEO of SAP. We are a collection of talented engineers in Germany, India, China, the U.S., Israel, Brazil, and the diversity therein represented enriches the culture, creativity, and market responsiveness of SAP."[17] Kagermann seeks significant representation of cultures and communities worldwide so that SAP truly reflects the vast global settings in which it does business.

Manage the Strategy-Culture Relationship

Managers find it difficult to think through the relationship between a firm's culture and the critical factors on which strategy depends. They quickly recognize, however, that key components of the firm—structure, staff, systems, people, style—influence the ways in which key managerial tasks are executed and how critical management relationships are formed. And implementation of a new strategy is largely concerned with adjustments in these components to accommodate the perceived needs of the strategy. Consequently, managing the strategy-culture relationship requires sensitivity to the interaction between the changes necessary to implement the new strategy and the compatibility or "fit" between those changes and the firm's culture. Exhibit 12.11 provides a simple framework for managing the strategy-culture relationship by identifying four basic situations a firm might face.

Link to Mission

A firm in cell 1 is faced with a situation in which implementing a new strategy requires several changes in structure, systems, managerial assignments, operating procedures, or other fundamental aspects of the firm. However, most of the changes are potentially compatible with the existing organizational culture. Firms in this situation usually have a tradition of effective performance and are either seeking to take advantage of a major opportunity or are attempting to redirect major product-market operations consistent with proven core capabilities. Such firms are in a very promising position: They can pursue a strategy requiring major changes but still benefit from the power of cultural reinforcement.

Four basic considerations should be emphasized by firms seeking to manage a strategy-culture relationship in this context:

1. *Key changes should be visibly linked to the basic company mission.* Because the company mission provides a broad official foundation for the organizational culture, top executives should use all available internal and external forums to reinforce the message that the changes are inextricably linked to it.

2. *Emphasis should be placed on the use of existing personnel* where possible to fill positions created to implement the new strategy. Existing personnel embody the shared values and norms that help ensure cultural compatibility as major changes are implemented.

3. *Care should be taken if adjustments in the reward system are needed.* These adjustments should be consistent with the current reward system. If, for example, a new product-market thrust requires significant changes in the way sales are made, and, therefore, in incentive compensation, common themes (e.g., incentive oriented) should be emphasized. In this way, current and future reward approaches are related, and the changes in the reward system are justified (encourage development of less familiar markets).

[17] "Tapping Global Talent in Software," *BusinessWeek,* June 9, 2007.

EXHIBIT 12.11
Managing the Strategy-Culture Relationship

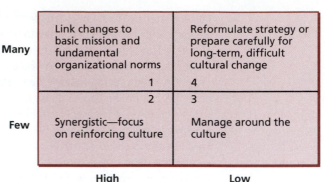

Changes in key organizational factors that are necessary to implement the new strategy

	High	**Low**
Many	Link changes to basic mission and fundamental organizational norms — 1	Reformulate strategy or prepare carefully for long-term, difficult cultural change — 4
Few	2 — Synergistic—focus on reinforcing culture	3 — Manage around the culture

Potential compatibility of changes with existing culture

4. *Key attention should be paid to the changes that are least compatible with the current culture,* so current norms are not disrupted. For example, a firm may choose to subcontract an important step in a production process because that step would be incompatible with the current culture.

P&G's new innovation approach under Alan Lafley, described in Exhibit 12.12, Strategy in Action, offers an excellent example of a company in this situation. P&G's long-standing mission as a consumer products company had been one of innovative product design and development. Alan Lafley was very careful to push for a more open culture in terms of who would help P&G innovate more effectively, but he was also emphatic about linking these new efforts at changing how the "great innovator" innovated with the core notion that P&G people, and P&G's 100-year-old tradition or mission was still *THE* global consumer products innovator. He linked changes to the basic P&G mission. Lafley next emphasized speaking positively about P&G people and getting them to buy in to the changes he sought. He placed emphasis on existing personnel. Third, he included new rewards to encourage acceptance of the different way of doing things. And fourth, he made sure on changes that were "stretching people too much" to use what he called an accelerator and a throttle approach. He identified himself as the accelerator, pushing aggressively for change. And he assigned his managers as his throttle, to regularly meet and discuss and perhaps alter the pace of change, depending on their assessment of whether the changes were taking or whether people were being pushed to change too quickly. So in this way Lafley made sure to monitor changes least compatible with P&G's current culture.

Maximize Synergy

A firm in cell 2 needs only a few organizational changes to implement its new strategy, and those changes are potentially quite compatible with its current culture. A firm in this situation should emphasize two broad themes:

1. *Take advantage of the situation to reinforce and solidify the current culture.*
2. *Use this time of relative stability to remove organizational roadblocks to the desired culture.*

3M's current effort to reacquire its culture of innovation illustrates this situation. Earlier this decade, James McNerney became the first outsider to lead 3M in its 100-year history. He had barely stepped off the plane before he announced he would change the DNA of the place. His playbook was classic pursuit of efficiency: he axed 8,000 workers (about 11 percent of the workforce), intensified the performance-review process, tightened the purse strings, and implemented a Six Sigma program to decrease production defects and increase efficiency. Five years later, McNerney abruptly left for a bigger opportunity—Boeing. His successor, George Buckley, faced a challenging question: whether the relentless emphasis on efficiency had made 3M a less creative company. That's a vitally important issue for a company whose very identity is built on innovation—the company that has always prided itself on drawing at least one-third of sales from products released in the past five years; today that fraction has slipped to only one-quarter.

Those results are not coincidental. Efficiency programs such as Six Sigma are designed to identify problems in work processes—and then use rigorous measurement to reduce variation and eliminate defects. When these types of initiatives become ingrained in a company's culture, as they did at 3M, creativity can easily get squelched. After all, a break-through innovation is something that challenges existing procedures and norms. "Invention is by its very nature a disorderly process," says CEO Buckley, who has dialed some key McNerney's initiatives as he attempts to return 3M to its roots and its culture of innovation. "You can't put a Six Sigma process into that area and say, well, I'm getting behind on invention, so I'm going to schedule myself for three good ideas on Wednesday and two on Friday. That's not how creativity works." While process excellence demands precision, consistency, and repetition, innovation calls for variation, failure, and serendipity.[18] Buckley is taking advantage of this difficult situation to reinforce and solidify 3M's "re"-embrace of its former, innovation culture by bringing back flexible funding for innovative ideas among other traditions. At the same time, he is using the general embrace of a return to its old culture to make some key changes in manufacturing practices and plant locations outside the United States to make 3M more cost effective and competitive in a global economy.

Manage around the Culture

A firm in cell 3 must make a few major organizational changes to implement its new strategy, but these changes are potentially inconsistent with the firm's current organizational culture. The critical question for a firm in this situation is whether it can make the changes with a reasonable chance of success.

A firm can manage around the culture in various ways: create a separate firm or division; use task forces, teams, or program coordinators; subcontract; bring in an outsider; or sell out. These are a few of the available options, but the key idea is to create a method of achieving the change desired that avoids confronting the incompatible cultural norms. As cultural resistance diminishes, the change may be absorbed into the firm.

IBM's recent sale of its PC business to China's Lenovo, creating the third-largest global PC firm behind Dell and HP, was a strategic decision it took three years to conclude. IBM management became increasingly concerned with the problem that the PC business, and the culture surrounding it, were incompatible with the culture and direction IBM's core business had been taking for some time. The conflict, and the inability to reconcile different cultural needs, led IBM executives to explore the sale of the PC division almost three years ago to Lenovo. At the time IBM's PC division was in disarray and losing $400 million annually. Lenovo's reaction was to send IBM packing out of China with a sense they had tried to take Lenovo's executives for fools who would buy a "pig in a poke." But IBM executives, still desperately concerned about the fundamental and cultural difference between the PC business and the rest of IBM set about an intense 18-month effort to wring costs out of the PC's supply chain, bring it back to profitability, and then go to call on Lenovo again. They achieved both in 18 months and, in their next business, found a more receptive Lenovo management team—ultimately concluding the deal a few months later. In so doing, IBM worked feverishly even to include creating a profitable global PC business only to then sell it quickly and cheaply so that it could "manage around a culture" in the sense of allowing IBM to unify around a different business model and remove the business it was most known

---

[18] "At 3M, a Struggle Between Efficiency and Creativity," *BusinessWeek,* June 11, 2007.

Recreating P&G and Its 170-Year-Old Culture

BusinessWeek

Lafley is changing Procter & Gamble. He's undertaking the company's most sweeping remake since it was founded in 1837. Nothing is sacred any longer at the Cincinnati-based maker of Tide, Pampers, and Crest. And in the process, he has made P&G one of the world's top five innovation companies in 2007.

Lafley has inverted the invent-it-here mentality by turning outward for innovation. He's broadening P&G's definition of brands and how it prices goods. He's moving P&G deep into the beauty-care business with several large acquisitions over five years. And he's redefining P&G's core business by outsourcing operations—like information technology and bar-soap manufacturing.

What's surprising is that at the start, Lafley was perceived as a tame pair of hands—far from a person who would conduct a radical makeover. He followed a forceful change agent, Durk Jager, who had tried to jump-start internal innovation, launching a host of new brands. Jager also criticized P&G's insular culture, which he sought to shake up. In the end, though, he overreached, as P&G missed earnings forecasts and employees bucked under his leadership.

Lafley answered some questions recently about his views on leading change at P&G:

Q: When you started, you weren't perceived as a forceful change agent like your predecessor. Yet you're making more dramatic changes. Can you discuss that?

A: Durk and I had believed very strongly that the company had to change and make fundamental changes in a lot of the same directions. There are two simple differences: One is I'm very externally focused. I expressed the change in the context of how we're going to serve consumers better,

how we're going to win with the retailer, and how we're going to defeat the competitor in the marketplace.

The most important thing—I didn't attack. I avoided saying P&G people are bad. I thought that was a big mistake [on Jager's part]. The difference is, I preserved the core of the culture and pulled people where I wanted to go. I enrolled them in change. I didn't tell them.

Q: Why did you both see a need for change?

A: We were looking at slow growth. An inability to move quickly, to commercialize on innovation and get full advantage out of it. We were looking at new technologies that were changing competition in our industry, retailers, and the supply base. We were looking at a world that all of a sudden was going to go 24/7, and we weren't ready for that kind of world.

Q: Was the view on the need for change widely held within P&G?

A: It depends on who you ask. Without a doubt, Durk and I and a few others were in the camp of "We need a much bigger change."

Q: Jager says he tried to change P&G too fast. What do you think about that?

A: I think he's right.

Q: Are you concerned about the same thing?

A: I'm worried that I will ask the organization to change ahead of its understanding, capability, and commitment, because that's a problem. I have been a catalyst of change and encourager of change and a coach of change management.

for, the IBM-PC business, from its organization along with the cultural incompatibility it represented.

Reformulate the Strategy or Culture

A firm in cell 4 faces the most difficult challenge in managing the strategy-culture relationship. To implement its new strategy, such a firm must make organizational changes that are incompatible with its current, usually entrenched, values and norms. A firm in this situation faces the complex, expensive, and often long-term challenge of changing its culture; it is a challenge that borders on impossible.

When a strategy requires massive organizational change and engenders cultural resistance, a firm should determine whether reformulation of the strategy is appropriate.

And I've tried not to drive change for the sake of change.

Q: How do you pace change?

A: I have tremendous trust in my management team. I let them be the brake. I am the accelerator. I help with direction and let them make the business strategic choices.

Q: Did the fact that P&G was in crisis when you came in help you implement change?

A: It was easier. I was lucky. When you have a mess, you have a chance to make more changes.

Q: Jager tried to drive innovation from within. You would like P&G to ultimately get 50 percent of its ideas from outside. Why?

A: Durk and I both wanted more innovation. We both felt we absolutely, positively had to get more innovation. We had to get more innovation commercialized and more innovation globalized. So we were totally together.

He tried to drive it all internally. He tried to rev the R&D organization, supercharge them, and hoped that enough would come out of there that we would achieve the goals of commercializing more of it and globalizing more of it. We got in trouble 'cause we pulled stuff out that was half-baked or that was never going to be successful. We hadn't developed it far enough.

The difference is that my hypothesis is that innovation and discovery are likely to come from anywhere. What P&G is really good at is developing innovations and commercializing them. So what I said is, "We need an open marketplace."

We're probably as good as the next guy at inventing. But we are not absolutely and positively better than everybody else at inventing. There are a lot of good inventors out there.

Q: How hard will it be to shift P&G's R&D focus outwards, given that it has historically focused inwards?

A: It will be a challenge, but I think we'll get there. It's like a flywheel. That first turn is really difficult. Then the second turn is a little bit easier. This has been like turning a flywheel. We will have failures. We will have to celebrate that failure.

Q: When you couple your outward focus on innovation with your moves toward outsourcing, it seems you're making P&G a less vertically integrated company.

A: I don't believe in vertical integration. I think it's a trap. I believe in horizontal networked organizations.

Our core capability is to develop and commercialize. Branding is a core capability. Customer business development is a core capability. We concluded in a lot of areas that manufacturing isn't. Therefore, I let the businesses go do more outsourcing. We concluded that running a back room wasn't a core capability. You do what you do best and can do world-class.

Sources: Reprinted with special permission from Jean McGregor, "P&G Asks: What's the Big Idea," *BusinessWeek*, May 4, 2007; and Jay Greene and Mike France, "P&G: New & Improved," *BusinessWeek*, July 7, 2003. Copyright © 2007 The McGraw-Hill Companies.

Are all of the organizational changes really necessary? Is there any real expectation that the changes will be acceptable and successful? If these answers are yes, then massive changes are often necessary. When you study the chapter case about Alan Mulally's actions at Ford over the last few years you will see him making major changes in an attempt to change Ford's culture to suit its new strategy: bringing outsiders in as top execs, changing long-standing executive compensation programs, emphasizing sales and marketing over the traditional, patronage-based culture as, sadly, Ford's most "prized" cultural element. These are elements through which Ford, under Mulally, is undergoing massive change as he tries to build a different culture compatible with a new vision and strategy.

Merrill Lynch faced the challenge of strategy-culture incompatibility in the last decade. Seeking to remain no. 1 in the newly deregulated financial services industry, it chose to pursue a product development strategy in its brokerage business. Under this strategy, Merrill Lynch would sell a broader range of investment products to a more diverse customer base and would integrate other financial services, such as real estate sales, into the Merrill Lynch organization. The new strategy could succeed only if Merrill Lynch's traditionally service-oriented brokerage network became sales and marketing oriented. Initial efforts to implement the strategy generated substantial resistance from Merrill Lynch's highly successful brokerage network. The strategy was fundamentally inconsistent with long-standing cultural norms at Merrill Lynch that emphasized personalized service and very close broker-client relationships. Merrill Lynch ultimately divested its real estate operation, reintroduced specialists who supported broker/retailers, and refocused its brokers more narrowly on basic client investment needs.

Summary

This chapter has examined organizational leadership and organization culture—two factors essential to the successful implementation and execution of a company's strategic plan. Organizational leadership is guiding and shepherding an organization over time and developing that organization's future leadership and its organization culture.

We saw that good organizational leadership involves three considerations: clarifying strategic intent, building an organization, and shaping the organization's culture. Strategic intent is clarified through the leader's vision, a broad picture of where he or she is leading the firm, and candid attention to and clear expectations about performance.

Leaders use education, principles, and perseverance to build their organization. Education involves familiarizing managers and future leaders with an effective understanding of the business and the skills they need to develop. Principles are the leader's personal standards that guide her or his sense of honesty, integrity and ethical behavior. They are more essential than ever in today's world as key building blocks for the type of organization for which a leader's principles reflect and are watched with great interest by every manager, employee, customer, and supplier of the organization. Perseverance, the ability to stick to the challenge when most others falter, is an unquestionable tool for leaders to instill faith in the vision they seek when times are hard.

Leaders start to shape organizational culture by the passion they bring to their role, and their choice and development of young manager and future leaders. Passion, a highly motivated sense of commitment to what you do and want to do, is a force that permeates attitudes throughout an organization and helps them buy into your cultural aspirations. Combining those with the skills, aspirations, and inclinations you seek to make the vision a reality—and then helping them develop—is a key way to build a culture over the long term. One of the key skills of these rising leaders is to learn how to motivate, lead, and get others to do what they need.

Understanding seven sources of power and influence, rather than just the power of position and punishment, is a critical skill for effective future leaders to grasp.

Organizational culture is the set of important assumptions, values, beliefs, and norms that members of an organization share in common. The organizational leader plays a critical role in developing, sustaining, and changing organizational culture. Ethical standards, the leader's basis for differentiating right from wrong, quickly spread as a centerpiece between the leader and the organization's culture. Leaders use many means to reinforce and develop their organization's culture—from rewards and appointments to story telling and rituals. Managing the strategy-culture relationship requires different approaches, depending on the match between the demands of the new strategy and the compatibility of the culture with that strategy. This chapter examined four different scenarios.

Key Terms

ethical standards, *p. 391*
expert influence, *p. 388*
information power, *p. 387*
leadership development, *p. 381*
leader's vision, *p. 376*
organizational culture, *p. 388*

organizational leadership, *p. 374*
passion (of a leader), *p. 384*
peer influence, *p. 388*
perseverance (of a leader), *p. 382*
position power, *p. 386*
principles (of a leader), *p. 381*

punitive power, *p. 387*
referent influence, *p. 388*
reward power, *p. 386*
strategic intent, *p. 376*

Questions for Discussion

1. Think about any two leaders you have known, preferably one good and one weak. They can be businesspersons, coaches, someone you work(ed) with, and so forth. Make a list of five traits, practices, or characteristics that cause you to consider one good and the other weak. Compare the things you chose with the seven factors used to differentiate effective organizational leadership in the first half of this chapter.

2. This chapter describes seven attributes that enable good leadership—vision, performance, principles, education of subordinates, perseverance, passion, and leader selection/development. Which one have you found to be the most meaningful to you in the leaders you respond to the best?

3. Consider the following situation and determine whether the VC group is engaging in something that would violate your principles, or be totally acceptable to you. Explain why.

   Who likes those ubiquitous online pop-up ads planted by intrusive spyware? Technology Crossover Ventures is betting few do. The Silicon Valley venture-capital firm helped to finance the anti-spyware company Webroot Software. But it appears to hedge that bet with a sizable investment in Claria, a company vilified for spreading spyware.

   More than 40 million Web surfers viewed Claria ads. TCV pumped at least $13 million into Claria, but it has removed the company from a list of investments on its Web site.

   Critics wonder why TCV would make dual investments. "Users are rubbed the wrong way by even the suggestion that the same companies that made this mess are now profiting from helping to clean it up," says Harvard University researcher and spyware expert Ben Edelman. TCV declined to comment. There is a similar element in both ventures: the potential to make money.

4. Read Exhibit 12.2. What would you do if you were asked to serve as an Ethics Review Arbitrator and render a decision on what should happen to the Duke MBA students? Summarize the key reasons supporting your ruling.

5. Do you think Martin Sullivan is a good CEO candidate for AIG right now? See Exhibit 12.8.

6. Do you think Alan Lafley is a good organizational leader? What is his most important contribution to his organizational culture in your opinion?

7. What three sources of power and influence are best suited to you as a manager?

8. Describe two organizations you have been a part of based on differences in their organizational cultures.

9. What key things is Alan Mulally doing at Ford (see the following case) as an organizational leader to shape Ford's organizational culture? Do you think he will succeed? Why?

Chapter 12 Discussion Case

The New Heat on Ford

The Mulally Difference: How things are changing at Ford now that the new boss has arrived

	Before	After
Organization	Regional fiefdoms. Every global market has had its own strategy and products.	Mulally wants to break down geographic hierarchies and create a single worldwide organization.
Division chief meetings	Held monthly. Lots of happy talk. Little information sharing.	Held weekly. Discussing problems is encouraged. Goal is to spot red flags early.

(continued)

The Mulally Difference: How things are changing at Ford now that the new boss has arrived   *cont.*

	Before	After
Production mix	Emphasis on trucks, SUVs, niche sports cars.	Focus is shifting to passenger cars and crossovers.
Brand vision	To diversify away from Ford brand, the company acquired dysfunctional luxury brands.	Strengthen the traditional blue oval Ford brand. Sell off or close poor-performing brands.
Promotions	Managers changed jobs frequently to develop their skills.	Executives stay in place, winning only promotions that are deserved.

1 On a chilly morning in February, the new chief executive of Ford Motor Co., Alan R. Mulally, boarded one of the company's Falcon twin-turbo jets and flew to *Consumer Reports* magazine's automobile testing facility in East Haddam, Connecticut. He was joined by two senior engineers. Their mission: to spend half a day with the publication's staff getting detailed evaluations of every model made by Ford, Lincoln, and Mercury.

2 It wasn't a fun trip, according to a source close to the company. At one point, the *Consumer Reports* team criticized the new Ford Edge crossover SUV for lacking an electric opener triggered by the key fob—or at least a handle on the rear hatch. Both are standard equipment on many of its rivals. A woman on the magazine's staff demonstrated how she, at five feet tall, struggled to open the rear of the SUV as she carried two bags of groceries. Had it been a rainy day, she would have had to set her purchases down on the wet pavement and then muscle up the hatch. Once she'd done that, she'd face another hurdle: she was too short to shut it.

3 After a couple of hours on the firing line, Ford's engineers got defensive. Interrupting the testers, they started airing their side of the story in front of the new boss. Sensing that the meeting was deteriorating, Mulally says he handed each one a pad and pen. "You know what? Let's just listen and take notes," he said. The episode was a perfect illustration of what Mulally considers one of Ford's major problems: the tendency of employees to rationalize mistakes instead of fixing them. "We seek to be understood more than we seek to understand," he observes.

4 It's no secret Ford is fighting for its life. After losing $12.7 billion last year, it had to endure the indignity of pledging its factories, headquarters, and the rights to the iconic blue oval logo to the banks and bondholders just to get enough money to finance its turnaround plan. Those were all tough steps. But these are tough times for the U.S. auto industry. With Cerberus Capital Management taking over at Chrysler, the status quo is no longer an option in Detroit, a town infamous for incremental change.

5 For Mulally to have any chance of making Ford profitable by 2009, he'll have to strike a tough deal with the United Auto Workers (UAW) this summer [2007]. He will also likely ditch a struggling brand such as Jaguar or Mercury. But fixing Ford will require more than simply whacking expenses. One way or another, the company will also have to figure out how to produce more vehicles that consumers actually want. And doing that will require addressing the most fundamental problem of all: Ford's dysfunctional, often defeatist culture.

6 Although Ford once exemplified corporate efficiency—it is the birthplace of the assembly line and home of the celebrated Whiz Kids, who pioneered many modern management techniques in the 1960s—it has degenerated into a symbol of inefficiency. Weary corporate lifers have become all too comfortable with the idea of losing money. Mediocrity is acceptable. The company's complacency shows up in the very language it uses internally to rate its own models. It uses the designations "L" for Leader, "AL" for Among Leaders, and "C" for Competitive. Too many executives simply strive for Cs, says William C. "Bill" Ford Jr., executive chairman of the board. When asked about the grading system, the great-grandson of Henry Ford mimes putting a gun to his head and pulling the trigger. "We still do that?" he asks in disbelief. "I don't know where that came from."

FEET TO THE FIRE

7 Last September, the 50-year-old family scion, who had served as chief executive for nearly five years, threw up his arms in frustration and concluded that an insider could no longer fix Ford. The job required the emotional detachment of an outsider. While Mulally was not his first choice, the former chief of Boeing Co.'s commercial airlines division had impressive turnaround credentials. He helped the aerospace giant bounce back from the September 11, 2001, terrorist attacks by axing 27,000 workers, cutting jet production in half, repairing the company's antiquated production lines, and making a courageous bet on the 787 Dreamliner. That remarkable performance earned the 61-year-old ex-engineer recognition as one of *BusinessWeek*'s top managers of the year in 2005. The hard-nosed Mulally is somebody, Ford promises, "who knows how to shake the company to its foundations."

8 Just eight months into the job, Mulally is working hard to change institutional work habits that took years to develop. He wants managers to think more about customers than their own careers. He has made it a top priority to encourage his team to admit mistakes, to share more information, and to cooperate across divisions. He's holding everybody's feet to the fire

Ford: A Brief History of Management Evolution

Henry Ford era: 1902–1940	The company founder invented modern manufacturing. He was innovative and dictatorial.
Whiz Kids era: 1940s–1950s	Home to some of the most creative business thinkers in the postwar era. Ford evolved into a management lab.
"Hank the Deuce" era: 1960–1980	The imperious Henry Ford II pitted managers against one another. He often clashed with the Whiz Kids.
OPEC era: 1970s	Ford became more political under the autocratic Lee Iacocca, president from 1970 to 1978.
Global competition era: 1980s–1990s	While Ford had some huge hits, its passenger car business foundered and it lost ground to foreign rivals.
"Way forward" era: 2001-Present	Henry's great-grandson, Bill Ford, failed to transform the culture. He recruited Alan Mulally to instill discipline.

with tough operational oversight and harsh warnings about Ford's predicament. "We have been going out of business for 40 years," Mulally told a group of 100 information technology staffers at a "town meeting" in February. He has repeated the message to every employee group that he has addressed.

9   It is far from guaranteed, of course, that any of his cultural reforms will be enough to rescue Ford. Far-reaching as they are, they may not go far enough to do the job. And now that Cerberus is in the process of buying Chrysler, Mulally can no longer claim the title of most feared outsider in town. He may very well have to develop an even more radical rebuilding plan to stay ahead of his crosstown rival.

10   Mulally has yet to convince Wall Street that he can reach his goal of profitability by 2009. Of 15 analysts surveyed by Bloomberg.com News recently, only two rate the stock a buy. "They're in a precarious situation," says John Novak, an analyst with Morningstar Investment Service Inc. in Chicago. "Mulally's honeymoon period isn't going to last."

11   History provides ample basis for such skepticism. Ford is a place that's notorious for destroying auto industry outsiders—and Mulally is admittedly no car guy. Despite Bill Ford's strong backing, Mulally has run into plenty of internal resistance. Nearly all of his managers have been inherited, and some of them snickered when he received a $28 million paycheck for his first four months' work. On Mulally's first meeting with his inherited team, one manager asked: "How are you going to tackle something as complex and unfamiliar as the auto business when we are in such tough financial shape?"

12   The questioner discovered that the wiry former Boy Scout from Lawrence, Kansas, a veteran of many bruising political battles at Boeing, is hard to intimidate. Unfazed by the challenge, he looked the questioner directly in the eye and said: "An automobile has about 10,000 moving parts, right? An airplane has 2 million, and it has to stay up in the air."

GLADIATOR ARENA

13   Although Mulally lacks in-depth auto industry knowledge, he is also free of many of the intellectual biases and habits that have gotten Detroit into so much trouble. "He doesn't know what he doesn't know," says Ford Americas President Mark Fields. When Mulally was reviewing the company's 2008 product line last September, for example, he was told that Ford loses close to $3,000 every time a customer buys a Focus compact, according to one executive. "Why haven't you figured out a way to make a profit?" he asked. Executives explained that Ford needed the high sales volume to maintain the company's CAFE, or corporate average fuel economy, rating and that the plant that makes the car is a high-cost UAW factory in Michigan. "That's not what I asked," he shot back. "I want to know why no one figured out a way to build this car at a profit, whether it has to be built in Michigan or China or India, if that's what it takes." Nobody had a good answer.

14   How did Ford evolve from one of the most admired companies in the world into one where losing money has seemingly lost nearly all of its stigma? Until the mid-1960s, it was considered a management shrine. Under U.S. Defense Secretary Robert S. McNamara, one of a celebrated group of military veterans at the company dubbed the Whiz Kids, Ford developed scientific consumer research techniques that are now commonplace throughout the business world. It was one of the first auto companies to create products that were based on hard data rather than the personal tastes of executives.

15   But after McNamara exited in 1961, Henry Ford II (Bill's uncle) gradually assumed a bigger role in management. He built a high-testosterone culture where rising stars like successive Ford Presidents Lee Iacocca and Semon "Bunkie" Knudson were often pitted against one another like gladiators to prove themselves. As the auto industry's postwar growth slowed, limiting opportunities for a swelling cadre of managers, executives turned on one another. They also became more cautious. "The bureaucracy at Ford grew, and managers took refuge in the structure when things got tough rather than innovate or try new ideas that seemed risky," says Allan Gilmour, a retired chief financial officer at Ford who has met twice with Mulally, at Bill Ford's behest, to offer historical perspective on the company's woes.

16   Personal ties with the Ford family, always important at the company, sometimes trumped genuine performance in promotion decisions. So ambitious managers focused increasingly on kissing the right rings instead of racking up results. It became "something of a palace atmosphere," says Gerald C. Meyers, a professor at the University of Michigan School of Business. Some critics also blame the family, which has many members who depend on dividends as their main source of income, for encouraging a focus on current profits rather than long-term planning over the decades.

17   In the royal hierarchy at Ford, an elaborate system of employment grades clearly established an employee's rank in the pecking order. The grades also had the unintentional effect of quashing ideas and keeping information tightly controlled. When Fields, now president of Ford Americas, first arrived at the company from IBM in 1989, he couldn't make a lunch date with an executive who held a higher grade. People asked him what his grade was "as a condition of including me or socializing with me," Fields recalls. And he was discouraged from airing problems at meetings unless his boss approved first.

TOO MANY FIEFDOMS

18   The company's unusual approach to grooming leaders also discouraged collaboration. Ford has a long tradition of rapidly cycling executives through new posts every two years or so. In fact, managers refer to their posts as "assignments" rather than jobs. But one consequence of employees' need to make their mark in such a short time was to discourage cooperation with other divisions and regions, whose products were often on a different timetable. And no engineer ever got noticed by carrying over his predecessor's design or idea—even if it saved big money. Mulally, who is moving to lengthen job tenures, finds this system appalling. "I had the same job at Boeing for seven years," he says. "You can't hold somebody accountable for a job they've held for nine months."

19   Thus did Ford become what it is today: a balkanized mess. It has four parallel operating units worldwide, each with its own costly bureaucracy, factories, and product development staff. According to a Mulally audit designed to uncover cost-cutting opportunities, no two vehicles in Ford's lineup share the same mirrors, headlamps, or even such mundane pieces as the springs and hinges for the hood. And that's just taking into account the Ford brand. Add Volvo, Jaguar, and Land Rover to the mix, and the company has more than 30 engineering platforms worldwide. That leaves Ford at a big cost disadvantage in engineering and parts compared with General Motors, Chrysler, Toyota, and Honda. Mulally wants to get that number down to five or six platforms, similar to Honda. "There's no global company I know of that can succeed with the level of complexity we have at Ford," he says.

20   Examples of Ford losing opportunities because of its byzantine corporate structure abound. A recent example involves Sync, a system that allows voice-command control of a cell phone and MP3 player. It was a big success at last January's North American International Auto Show. Ford developed it with Microsoft Corp. last year and will start rolling it out this fall. Although Volvo and Land Rover are also dying to offer Sync, neither will get the system because the electrical architectures of the Swedish and British cars are incompatible with Ford's. Mulally finds that incomprehensible, considering that Ford has owned the European brands for nearly a decade.

21   To try to eliminate all of Ford's unnecessary duplication, Mulally is asserting more control over the product line. Now he personally approves every new vehicle worldwide. Production is now coordinated by Derrick M. Kuzak, Ford's first-ever chief of global product development.

22   Kuzak's team is already hard at work designing cars that can be easily adapted to appeal to worldwide markets. They've developed a global small car that Ford will build in two or three plants starting in 2010, and which will sell in the United States for $10,000 to $12,000. It will differ only slightly from the version that will sell in South America, Europe, and Asia. Another key goal in the near future is to create a midsize sedan that could serve both North America and Europe. Today, for example, the European Mondeo sedan and the North American Fusion are built independently of one another. Kuzak is overseeing an attempt to coordinate the future designs of those vehicles.

23   But Mulally knows that changing the organizational chart won't cure Ford. The company's deeply ingrained hierarchical culture needs to be blown up. So for the first time ever he's forcing every operating group to share all its financial data with every other group. That information used to be closely guarded. Shortly after he ordered the change, three separate executives called him to make sure they had heard right. Says Mulally: "You can't manage a secret."

24   To spread his new religion, Mulally has turned the traditional monthly meeting of divisional chiefs into a weekly affair. Every executive has to attend in person or by videoconference. No subordinates can be sent. To ensure focus, the BlackBerrys that used to be common at these meetings are now banned. So are side conversations when someone is talking, even if by video link. But the most radical change is that operating chiefs are now encouraged to bring a different subordinate to every meeting—a big step at a company where underlings formerly were not privy to sensitive data. Mulally wants staffers to start buzzing about his ideas through unofficial e-mail, blog, and watercooler channels.

HEALTH CARE MINEFIELD

25   He is also taking symbolic steps to treat white-collar and blue-collar employees more equitably. This year many workers on the shop floor will receive bonuses of $300 to $800, based on a new formula that is also being applied to executives. Of course, his popularity with union workers will depend a lot on this summer's contract negotiations with the UAW. The new deal will give Mulally an opportunity to cut his workforce's costly health benefits. That's expected to lead to divisiveness.

The arrival at Chrysler of Cerberus, though it increases the competitive pressure on Mulally, may turn out to be a blessing in this arena. Cerberus has sent a message to labor leaders that the old ways of doing business are no longer acceptable. Partially for that reason, the Cerberus deal "is good for us," Mulally says.

26   Ford's new CEO is fond of talking about how he is breaking long-standing company taboos, such as the one about never admitting when you don't know something. At a meeting last fall, one of Mulally's operating chiefs chattered on for several minutes trying to answer a question to which he clearly did not have the answer. After the meeting, Mulally asked Fields why the executive droned on for so long. "Because 'I don't know' isn't in Ford's vocabulary," Fields explained.

27   Now it is. To reinforce the point, Mulally has actually banned the thick background binders executives used to bring to the weekly meetings. That means they sometimes can't immediately summon the necessary details to answer Mulally's questions. That's fine with him: "I know that if they don't have the answer one week, they'll have it next week," he says.

28   As a longtime observer of the auto industry, David E. Cole, chairman of the Center for Automotive Research in Ann Arbor, Michigan, is not sure that Mulally will succeed in his mission. But he has concluded that Ford's culture is beyond fixing by anyone who has spent a long time inside the company, or any of the "usual candidates" at other automakers. "Ford employees feel very paternalistic toward Ford," says Cole, "and the only way Bill was going to convince them that the company was truly at risk was by bringing in someone they'd never heard of to break the cycle."

Sources: Reprinted with special permission from "The New Heat on Ford," *BusinessWeek,* June 7, 2007; and "The Mulally Difference," *BusinessWeek,* June 24, 2007. Copyright © 2007 The McGraw-Hill Companies.

DISCUSSION QUESTIONS

1. What attributes of good organizational leadership do you see Alan Mulally display?
2. What changes is he making in rewards, skills, and selection of key leaders that are most different from Ford's past?
3. Do you think they will be embraced? And work?
4. How is he changing the Ford culture?
5. What will be his hardest task?
6. Do you sense he operates at the margin, ethically speaking, or that his principles are transparent? Why?

Chapter **Thirteen**

Strategic Control

After reading and studying this chapter, you should be able to

1. Describe and illustrate four types of strategic control.

2. Summarize the balanced scorecard approach and how it integrates strategic and operational control.

3. Illustrate the use of controls to guide and monitor strategy implementation.

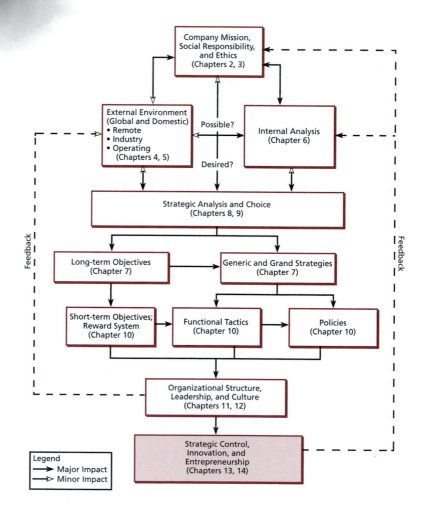

Company Mission, Social Responsibility, and Ethics (Chapters 2, 3)

External Environment (Global and Domestic)
• Remote
• Industry
• Operating (Chapters 4, 5)

Possible?

Internal Analysis (Chapter 6)

Desired?

Strategic Analysis and Choice (Chapters 8, 9)

Long-term Objectives (Chapter 7)

Generic and Grand Strategies (Chapter 7)

Short-term Objectives; Reward System (Chapter 10)

Functional Tactics (Chapter 10)

Policies (Chapter 10)

Organizational Structure, Leadership, and Culture (Chapters 11, 12)

Strategic Control, Innovation, and Entrepreneurship (Chapters 13, 14)

Feedback

Feedback

Legend
→ Major Impact
⇢ Minor Impact

STRATEGIC CONTROL

Strategies are forward looking, designed to be accomplished several years into the future. They are based on management assumptions about numerous events that have not yet occurred. How should executives "control" a strategy, and its execution?

Consider the recent experiences of Motorola and Dell Computer. Motorola's CEO Ed Zander looked like a genius in early 2007, executing his strategy of cranking out "wow" products like the Razr phone and delivering them via an even-more-efficient supply chain. Then, quickly, Motorola ran into a cell-phone price war, and its profit margins sank dramatically, revealing an outsourced manufacturing process that was much less efficient and more costly than rival Nokia's in-house operations were steadily delivering. Motorola's stock quickly dropped almost 50 percent in value, and CEO Zander faced some serious challenges to his leadership and the efficacy of the Motorola strategy.

Dell Computer saw its rival Hewlett-Packard struggle with a poorly integrated acquisition of Compaq and a confusing reorganization of HP a few years ago. IBM sold its PC business to China's Lenovo, admitting it couldn't compete with the Dell approach. Dell was a world leader in PCs and was broadening its offerings into printers and other electronic devices. But within two years, HP's new CEO Mark Hurd had HP much more focused, and it soon eclipsed Dell as the world's largest seller of PCs. Lenovo was gaining strength in the Asia-Pacific area. And Dell found itself losing market share and experiencing declining profitability, excess inventory, and problems with its outsourced customer service. Founder Michael Dell has recently returned to the CEO role after firing his handpicked former successor, Ken Rollins, and is attempting to rebuild Dell and its strategy.

So we see two great companies with seemingly solid strategies that deteriorated very quickly. What could they have done or done better? How could Motorola and Dell have adjusted their strategies and actions when key premises, technology, competitors, or sudden events changed everything for them? How could they have established better "strategic control" and reduced the impact of negative events or taken advantage of new opportunities?

strategic control
Management efforts to track a strategy as it is being implemented, detect problems or changes in its underlying premises, and make necessary adjustments.

Strategic control is concerned with tracking a strategy as it is being implemented, detecting problems or changes in its underlying premises, and making necessary adjustments. In contrast to postaction control, strategic control is concerned with guiding action on behalf of the strategy as that action is taking place and when the end result is still several years off. Managers responsible for the success of a strategy typically are concerned with two sets of questions:

1. Are we moving in the proper direction? Are key things falling into place? Are our assumptions about major trends and changes correct? Are we doing the critical things that need to be done? Should we adjust or abort the strategy?

2. How are we performing? Are objectives and schedules being met? Are costs, revenues, and cash flows matching projections? Do we need to make operational changes?

The rapidly accelerating level of change in the global marketplace has made the need for strategic control key in managing a company. This chapter examines strategic control.

ESTABLISHING STRATEGIC CONTROLS

The control of strategy can be characterized as a form of "steering control." As time elapses between the initial implementation of a strategy and achievement of its intended results, investments are made and numerous projects and actions are undertaken to implement the strategy. Also, during that time, changes are taking place in both the environmental situation and the firm's internal situation. Strategic controls are necessary to steer the firm through these events. They must provide the basis for adapting the firm's strategic actions and directions in response to these developments and changes. The four basic types of strategic control summarized in Exhibit 13.1 are

1. Premise control.
2. Strategic surveillance.
3. Special alert control.
4. Implementation control.

Premise Control

premise control
Management process of systematically and continuously checking to determine whether premises upon which the strategy is based are still valid.

Every strategy is based on certain planning premises—assumptions or predictions. **Premise control** is designed to check systematically and continuously whether the premises on which the strategy is based are still valid. If a vital premise is no longer valid, the strategy may have to be changed. The sooner an invalid premise can be recognized and rejected, the better are the chances that an acceptable shift in the strategy can be devised. Planning premises are primarily concerned with environmental and industry factors.

Environmental Factors

Although a firm has little or no control over environmental factors, these factors exercise considerable influence over the success of its strategy, and strategies usually are based on key premises about them. Inflation, technology, interest rates, regulation, and demographic/social changes are examples of such factors.

The second generation Internet, known as Web 2.0, and its intersection with rapid globalization, is spawning a global youth culture that presents both a challenge to the old ways of doing business and an opportunity to gain tremendous leverage via the right goods and services. "Flying blind" is how some executives describe their effort to adapt to it: the tens of millions of digital elite who are the vanguard of a fast-emerging global culture based on smartphones, blogs, instant messaging, Flickr, MySpace, Skype, YouTube, dig, and de.lic.ious, to mention a few. These highly influential young people are sharing ideas and information across borders that will drive products, employment, services, food, fashion, and ideas—rapidly. Savvy companies are recognizing this phenomenon as perhaps the most critical environmental factor/phenomenon they need to monitor and understand.[1]

Industry Factors

The performance of the firms in a given industry is affected by industry factors. Competitors, suppliers, product substitutes, and barriers to entry are a few of the industry factors about which strategic assumptions are made.

Rubbermaid has long been held up as a model of predictable growth, creative management, and rapid innovation in the plastic housewares and toy industry. Its premise in its most recent strategic plan was that large retail chains would continue to prefer its products over competitors' because of this core competence. This premise included continued receptivity to regular price increases when necessitated by raw materials costs. Retailers, most notably Wal-Mart, recently balked at Rubbermaid's attempt to raise prices to offset the doubling of petroleum-based resin costs. Furthermore, traditionally overlooked competitors have begun to make inroads with computerized stocking services. Rubbermaid is moving aggressively to adjust its strategy because of the response of Wal-Mart and other key retailers.

Strategies are often based on numerous premises, some major and some minor, about environmental and industry variables. Tracking all of these premises is unnecessarily

---

[1] Steve Hamm, "Children of the Web," *BusinessWeek,* July 2, 2007.

EXHIBIT 13.1 Four Types of Strategic Control

Source: From Academy of Management Review by G. Schreyogg and H. Steinmann. Copyright © 1987 by Academy of Management. Reproduced with permission of Academy of Management via Copyright Clearance Center.

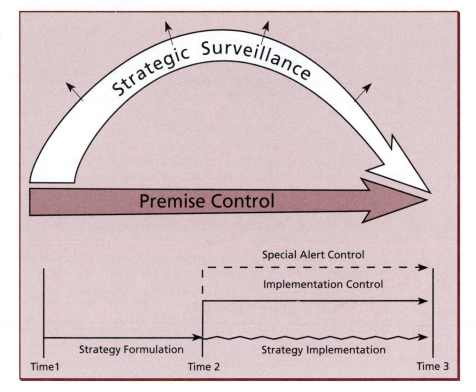

Characteristics of the Four Types of Strategic Control

Basic Characteristics	Types of Strategic Control			
	Premise Control	**Implementation Control**	**Strategic Surveillance**	**Special Alert Control**
Objects of control	Planning premises and projections	Key strategic thrusts and milestones	Potential threats and opportunities related to the strategy	Occurrence of recognizable but unlikely events
Degree of focusing	High	High	Low	High
Data acquisition:				
Formalization	Medium	High	Low	High
Centralization	Low	Medium	Low	High
Use with:				
Environmental factors	Yes	Seldom	Yes	Yes
Industry factors	Yes	Seldom	Yes	Yes
Strategy-specific factors	No	Yes	Seldom	Yes
Company-specific factors	No	Yes	Seldom	Seldom

Source: From *Academy of Management Review* by G. Schreyogg and H. Steinmann. Copyright © 1987 by Academy of Management. Reproduced with permission of Academy of Management via Copyright Clearance Center.

expensive and time consuming. Managers must select premises whose change (1) is likely and (2) would have a major impact on the firm and its strategy.

Strategic Surveillance

strategic surveillance
Management efforts to monitor a broad range of events inside and more often outside the firm that are likely to affect the course of its strategy over time.

By their nature, premise controls are focused controls; strategic surveillance, however, is unfocused. **Strategic surveillance** is designed to monitor a broad range of events inside and outside the firm that are likely to affect the course of its strategy.[2] The basic idea behind strategic surveillance is that important yet unanticipated information may be uncovered by a general monitoring of multiple information sources.

Strategic surveillance must be kept as unfocused as possible. It should be a loose "environmental scanning" activity. Trade magazines, *The Wall Street Journal,* trade conferences, conversations, and intended and unintended observations are all subjects of strategic surveillance. Despite its looseness, strategic surveillance provides an ongoing, broad-based vigilance in all daily operations that may uncover information relevant to the firm's strategy. P&G has used strategic surveillance of Europe's private label trend to shape an aggressive response minimizing any effect on its European sales compared with the dramatically negative effect the trend has had by blindsiding many European consumer products giants like Nestlé, Unilever, and L'Oreal, as discussed in Exhibit 13.2, Strategy in Action.

Special Alert Control

special alert control
Management actions undertaken to thoroughly, and often very rapidly, reconsider a firm's strategy because of a sudden, unexpected event.

Another type of strategic control, really a subset of the other three, is special alert control. A **special alert control** is the thorough, and often rapid, reconsideration of the firm's strategy because of a sudden, unexpected event. The tragic events of September 11, 2001; an outside firm's sudden acquisition of a leading competitor; an unexpected product difficulty, like the fingertip in a bowl of Wendy's chili—events of these kinds can drastically alter the firm's strategy.

Such an event should trigger an immediate and intense reassessment of the firm's strategy and its current strategic situation. In many firms, crisis teams handle the firm's initial response to unforeseen events that may have an immediate effect on its strategy. IBM's shock at the precipitous decline in the sales growth and profitability of its core IT services business in 2005 resulted in a special alert and ongoing focus on this business's strategy as summarized in Exhibit 13.2. Increasingly, firms have developed contingency plans along with crisis teams to respond to circumstances such as United Airlines did on September 11, 2001, and JetBlue did after its snow-storm fiasco at New York's JFK International Airport in the winter of 2007.

Implementation Control

implementation control
Management efforts designed to assess whether the overall strategy should be changed in light of results associated with the incremental actions that implement the overall strategy. These are usually associated with specific strategic thrusts or projects and with predetermined milestone reviews.

Strategy implementation takes place as a series of steps, programs, investments, and moves that occur over an extended time. Special programs are undertaken. Functional areas initiate strategy-related activities. Key people are added or reassigned. Resources are mobilized. In other words, managers implement strategy by converting broad plans into the concrete, incremental actions and results of specific units and individuals.

Implementation control is the type of strategic control that must be exercised as those events unfold. **Implementation control** is designed to assess whether the overall strategy should be changed in light of the results associated with the incremental actions that implement the overall strategy. The two basic types of implementation control are (1) monitoring strategic thrusts and (2) milestone reviews.

---

[2] G. Schreyogg and H. Steinmann, "Strategic Control: A New Perspective," *Academy of Management Review* 12, no. 1 (1987), p. 101.

Examples of Strategic Control

BusinessWeek

PREMISE CONTROL AT BANK OF AMERICA

Bank of America, and other financial service companies, recently lobbied aggressively in Washington, D.C., opposing Wal-Mart's application for a bank charter. Most were surprised and somewhat blindsided by Wal-Mart's sudden attempt to add financial services—and particularly, banking—for its retail customers at its thousands of locations throughout the U.S.

Wal-Mart has come back with an announcement that it will not be a bank but that it will offer a host of financial services at more than 1,000 stores by 2008, which will include check cashing, bill payments, international money transfers, and a pre-paid Wal-Mart Money Card. Bank of America is examining Wal-Mart's move into limited financial services and reworking key premises that underlie its current strategic plan. One key premise is whether or not there is a whole generation of consumers—Gen Y in particular—who are going to form their opinions of what bank to use based on where they shop now. Some experts argue that banks have focused on longstanding customers, "seniors and boomers," and not so much on younger patrons or potential patrons. So Bank of America is much more closely monitoring its premises based on Wal-Mart's moves.

IMPLEMENTATION CONTROL AT BOEING

All eyes are on Boeing as it begins the final assembly of the first 787 Dreamliner. Rollout for the first jet is slated for July 8, 2007, and the first flight is scheduled for mid-August, provided the plane is ready to fly. Boeing's first customer, All Nippon Airways, should receive its first Dreamliner in May 2008. Meeting those deadlines is key, as delivery is when Boeing collects most of its money, and faces penalties if delayed. "Today, we begin assembling the first airplane of a new generation, and a new way of building airplanes," boasted Scott Strode, 787 VP of airline production. The actual snapping together of enormous composite parts built by different companies in Asia, Europe, and North America is the first milestone of this new airplane, and Boeing's strategy that is built on the concept of outsourcing components and even sections of the fuselage worldwide—a revolutionary new approach to building airplanes.

STRATEGIC SURVEILLANCE AT P&G

It was not long ago that big global brands among consumer products companies did not lose sleep over private labels. Indeed retail's worst-kept secret is that house brands in many grocery stores are often produced by Nestlé, Cadbury Schweppes, and H. J. Heinz. But over the last few years, Europe's private-label business has taken off due to the rapid growth of discounters such as Germany's Aldi and France's Leader Price. Their no-frills stores, which stock almost entirely private labels that usually cost consumers up to 40 percent less than comparable global brands, have lured customers away from established retailers. Some of Europe's big names—Nestlé, L'Oreal, and Unilever—have been getting clobbered. Not Procter & Gamble. It picked up on this trend in the course of its ongoing strategic surveillance in the European publications looking at consumer lifestyles. As a result, P&G says sales are growing as planned. P&G flexed its pricing muscle causing a British private-label competitor to write off a $1.5 billion invested in Ontex, a disposable diaper, after P&G clobbered Ontex by slashing prices on Pampers in selected markets. P&G's European CEO said, "We have surveyed this general trend in Europe for some time and concluded that discounters don't need to be a threat, rather, they can be an opportunity!"

SPECIAL ALERT CONTROL AT IBM

The $48-billion-a-year information technology services business that saved IBM from ruin in the 1990s is becoming a slow-growing, low-margin drag on the rest of the company. The special alert control attention to the IT services business and its strategy started in 2005, when IBM was shocked by the poor profit results in the first quarter of that year. IBM's growth and profit margin both declined substantially during that time, due in large part to the accelerated growth and success of India's Tata Consultancy Services and Infosys, which have seen steady 30 percent growth with profit margins three to four times what IBM achieves. IBM's reaction was to cut 15,000 jobs in Europe and the United States in a matter of months of that first shocking result. Even though IBM remains the No. 1 tech services company in the world, with 7.2 percent market share in 2007, it has a regular special alert review of its sales growth and profit levels in the IT services business each quarter, which has resulted in the elimination of approximately 700 to 1,500 jobs in North America and Europe each quarter since that initial shock as it attempts to reorganize this business and the nature of the way it does work around the globe.

Sources: Reprinted with special permission from Steve Hamm, "Big Blue Wields the Knife Again," *BusinessWeek,* May 30, 2007; Stanley Holmes, "Crunch Time for Boeing," *BusinessWeek,* May 22, 2007; "How P&G Skips the Middle Man," *BusinessWeek,* January 8, 2007; and Pallavi Gogoi, "Why Wal-Mart Will Help Finance Customers," *BusinessWeek,* June 20, 2007. Copyright © 2007 The McGraw-Hill Companies.

Monitoring Strategic Thrusts or Projects

strategic thrusts or projects
Special efforts that are early steps in executing a broader strategy, usually involving significant resource commitments yet where predetermined feedback will help management determine whether continuing to pursue the strategy is appropriate or whether it needs adjustment or major change.

As a means of implementing broad strategies, narrow strategic projects often are undertaken—projects that represent part of what needs to be done if the overall strategy is to be accomplished. These **strategic thrusts** provide managers with information that helps them determine whether the overall strategy is progressing as planned or needs to be adjusted.

Although the utility of strategic thrusts seems readily apparent, it is not always easy to use them for control purposes. It may be difficult to interpret early experience or to evaluate the overall strategy in light of such experience. One approach is to agree early in the planning process on which thrusts or which phases of thrusts are critical factors in the success of the strategy. Managers responsible for these implementation controls will single them out from other activities and observe them frequently. Another approach is to use stop/go assessments that are linked to a series of meaningful thresholds (time, costs, research and development, success, and so forth) associated with particular thrusts. Exhibit 13.2 describes Boeing's current effort to do this as it coordinates globally diverse outsourcing partners' production of various parts of the revolutionary new 787 Dreamliner fuselage and its components.

Milestone Reviews

milestone reviews
Points in time, or at the completion of major parts of a bigger strategy, where managers have predetermined they will undertake a go–no go type of review regarding the underlying strategy associated with the bigger strategy.

Managers often attempt to identify significant milestones that will be reached during strategy implementation. These milestones may be critical events, major resource allocations, or simply the passage of a certain amount of time. The **milestone reviews** that then take place usually involve a full-scale reassessment of the strategy and of the advisability of continuing or refocusing the firm's direction.

A useful example of implementation control based on milestone review is offered by an earlier Boeing's product-development strategy of entering the supersonic transport (SST) airplane market. Boeing had invested millions of dollars and years of scarce engineering talent during the first phase of its SST venture, and competition from the British/French Concorde effort was intense. Because the next phase represented a billion-dollar decision, Boeing's management established the initiation of the phase as a milestone. The milestone reviews greatly increased the estimates of production costs; predicted relatively few passengers and rising fuel costs, thus raising the estimated operating costs; and noted that the Concorde, unlike Boeing, had the benefit of massive government subsidies. These factors led Boeing's management to scrap its SST strategy in spite of high sunk costs, pride, and patriotism. Only an objective, full-scale strategy reassessment could have led to such a decision. A similar decision by Boeing regarding its current strategic "bet" on the new 787 Dreamliner is very unlikely as it nears final assembly and initial test flights of this revolutionary, next-generation, composite airplane (see Exhibit 13.2).

In the SST example, a milestone review occurred at a major resource allocation decision point. Milestone reviews may also occur concurrently when a major step in a strategy's implementation is being taken or when a key uncertainty is resolved. Managers even may set an arbitrary period, say, two years, as a milestone review point. Whatever the basis for selecting that point, the critical purpose of a milestone review is to thoroughly scrutinize the firm's strategy so as to control the strategy's future.

Implementation control is also enabled through operational control systems like budgets, schedules, and key success factors. While strategic controls attempt to steer the company over an extended period (usually five years or more), operational controls provide postaction evaluation and control over short periods—usually from one month to one year. To be effective, operational control systems must take four steps common to all postaction controls:

1. Set standards of performance.
2. Measure actual performance.

EXHIBIT 13.3 **Monitoring and Evaluating Performance Deviations**

Key Success Factors	Objective, Assumption, or Budget	Forecast Performance at This Time	Current Performance	Current Deviation	Analysis
Cost control: Ratio of indirect overhead cost to direct field and labor costs	10%	15%	12%	+3 (ahead)	Are we moving too fast, or is there more unnecessary overhead than was originally thought?
Gross profit	39%	40%	40%	0%	
Customer service: Installation cycle in days	2.5 days	3.2 days	2.7 days	+0.5 (ahead)	Can this progress be maintained?
Ratio of service to sales personnel	3.2	2.7	2.1	−0.6 (behind)	Why are we behind here? How can we maintain the installation-cycle progress?
Product quality: Percentage of products returned	1.0%	2.0%	2.1%	−0.1% (behind)	Why are we behind here? What are the ramifications for other operations?
Product performance versus specification	100%	92%	80%	−12% (behind)	
Marketing: Monthly sales per employee	$12,500	$11,500	$12,100	+$600 (ahead)	Good progress. Is it creating any problems to support?
Expansion of product line	6	3	5	+2 products (ahead)	Are the products ready? Are the perfect standards met?
Employee morale in service area: Absenteeism rate	2.5%	3.0%	3.0%	(on target)	Looks like a problem!
Turnover rate	5%	10 %	15%	−8% (behind)	Why are we so far behind?
Competition: New-product introductions (average number)	6	3	6	−3 (behind)	Did we underestimate timing? What are the implications for our basic assumptions?

3. Identify deviations from standards set.
4. Initiate corrective action.

Exhibit 13.3 illustrates a typical operational control system. These indicators represent progress after two years of a five-year strategy intended to differentiate the firm as a customer-service–oriented provider of high-quality products. Management's concern is to compare *progress to date* with *expected progress*. The *current deviation* is of particular interest because it provides a basis for examining *suggested actions* (usually suggested by subordinate managers) and for finalizing decisions on changes or adjustments in the firm's operations.

From Exhibit 13.3, it appears that the firm is maintaining control of its cost structure. Indeed, it is ahead of schedule on reducing overhead. The firm is well ahead of its delivery cycle target, while slightly below its target service-to-sales personnel ratio.

Its product returns look OK, although product performance versus specification is below standard. Sales per employee and expansion of the product line are ahead of schedule. The absenteeism rate in the service area is on target, but the turnover rate is higher than that targeted. Competitors appear to be introducing products more rapidly than expected.

After deviations and their causes have been identified, the implications of the deviations for the ultimate success of the strategy must be considered. For example, the rapid product-line expansion indicated in Exhibit 13.3 may have been a response to the increased rate of competitors' product expansion. At the same time, product performance is still low, and, while the installation cycle is slightly above standard (improving customer service), the ratio of service to sales personnel is below the targeted ratio. Contributing to this substandard ratio (and perhaps reflecting a lack of organizational commitment to customer service) is the exceptionally high turnover in customer service personnel. The rapid reduction in indirect overhead costs might mean that administrative integration of customer service and product development requirements have been cut back too quickly.

This information presents operations managers with several options. They may attribute the deviations primarily to internal discrepancies. In that case, they can scale priorities up or down. For example, they might place more emphasis on retaining customer service personnel and less emphasis on overhead reduction and new-product development. On the other hand, they might decide to continue as planned in the face of increasing competition and to accept or gradually improve the customer service situation. Another possibility is reformulating the strategy or a component of the strategy in the face of rapidly increasing competition. For example, the firm might decide to emphasize more standardized or lower-priced products to overcome customer service problems and take advantage of an apparently ambitious salesforce.

This is but one of many possible interpretations of Exhibit 13.3. The important point here is the critical need to monitor progress against standards and to give serious in-depth attention to both the causes of observed deviations and the most appropriate responses to them. After the deviations have been evaluated, slight adjustments may be made to keep progress, expenditure, or other factors in line with the strategy's programmed needs. In the unusual event of extreme deviations—generally because of unforeseen changes—management is alerted to the possible need for revising the budget, reconsidering certain functional plans related to budgeted expenditures, or examining the units concerned and the effectiveness of their managers.

The Balanced Scorecard Methodology

An alternative approach linking operational and strategic control, developed by Harvard Business School professors Robert Kaplan and David Norton, is a system they named the **balanced scorecard.** Recognizing some of the weaknesses and vagueness of previous implementation and control approaches, the balanced scorecard approach was intended to provide a clear prescription as to what companies should measure in order to "balance" the financial perspective in implementation and control of strategic plans.[3]

The balanced scorecard is a management system (not only a measurement system) that enables companies to clarify their strategies, translate them into action, and provide

balanced scorecard
A management control system that enables companies to clarify their strategies, translate them into action, and provide quantitative feedback as to whether the strategy is creating value, leveraging core competencies, satisfying the company's customers, and generating a financial reward to its shareholders.

[3] This methodology is covered in great detail in a number of books and articles by R. S. Kaplan and D. P. Norton. It is also the subject of frequent special publications by the *Harvard Business Review* that provided updated treatment of uses and improvements in the balanced scorecard methodology. Some useful books include *Balanced Scorecard: Translating Strategies into Action* (Boston: Harvard Business School Press, 1996); *The Strategy-Focused Organization* (Boston: Harvard Business School Press, 2001). HBR offers "Using the Balanced Scorecard as a Strategic Management System," *Harvard Business Review*, January–February 1996. Numerous useful Web sites also exist such as www.bscol.com.

meaningful feedback. It provides feedback around both the internal business processes and external outcomes in order to continuously improve strategic performance and results. When fully deployed, the balanced scorecard is intended to transform strategic planning from a separate top management exercise into the nerve center of an enterprise. Kaplan and Norton describe the innovation of the balanced scorecard as follows:

> The balanced scorecard retains traditional financial measures. But financial measures tell the story of past events, an adequate story for industrial age companies for which investments in long-term capabilities and customer relationships were not critical for success. These financial measures are inadequate, however, for guiding and evaluating the journey that information age companies must make to create future value through investment in customers, suppliers, employees, processes, technology, and innovation.[4]

The balanced scorecard methodology adapts the total quality management (TQM) ideas of customer-defined quality, continuous improvement, employee empowerment, and measurement-based management/feedback into an expanded methodology that includes traditional financial data and results. The balanced scorecard incorporates feedback around internal business process *outputs,* as in TQM, but also adds a feedback loop around the *outcomes* of business strategies. This creates a "double-loop feedback" process in the balanced scorecard. In doing so, it links together two areas of concern in strategy execution—quality operations and financial outcomes—that are typically addressed separately yet are obviously critically intertwined as any company executes its strategy. A system that links shareholder interests in return on capital with a system of performance management that is linked to ongoing, operational activities and processes within the company is what the balanced scorecard attempts to achieve.

Exhibit 13.4 illustrates the balanced scorecard approach drawing on the traditional Du Pont formula discussed in Chapter 5 and historically used to examine drivers of stockholder-related financial performance across different company activities. The balanced scorecard seeks to "balance" shareholder goals with customer goals and operational performance goals, and Exhibit 13.4 shows that they are interconnected: shareholder value creation is linked to divisional concerns for return on capital employed, which, in turn, is driven by functional outcomes in sales, inventory, capacity utilization, that, in turn, come about through the results of departments' and teams' daily activities throughout the company. The balanced scorecard suggests that we view the organization from four perspectives and to develop metrics, collect data, and analyze it relative to each of these perspectives:

1. *The learning and growth perspective: How well are we continuously improving and creating value?* The scorecard insists on measures related to innovation and organizational learning to gauge performance on this dimension—technological leadership, product development cycle times, operational process improvement, and so on.

2. *The business process perspective: What are our core competencies and areas of operational excellence?* Internal business processes and their effective execution as measured by productivity, cycle time, quality measures, downtime, and various cost measures, among others, provide scorecard input here.

3. *The customer perspective: How satisfied are our customers?* A customer satisfaction perspective typically adds measures related to defect levels, on-time delivery, warranty

EXHIBIT 13.4
**Integrating
Shareholder Value
and Organizational
Activities across
Organizational
Levels**

Source: From R. M. Grant,
*Contemporary Strategy
Analysis*, 2001, p. 56.
Reprinted with permission of
Wiley-Blackwell.

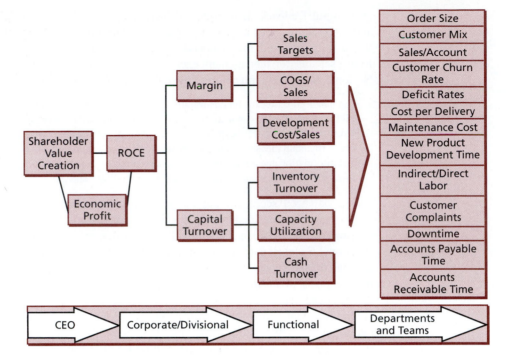

support and product development, among others, that come from direct customer input and are linked to specific company activities.

4. *The financial perspective: How are we doing for our shareholders?* A financial perspective typically uses measures like cash flow, return on equity, sales, and income growth.

Through the integration of goals from each of these four perspectives, the balanced scorecard approach enables the strategy of the business to be linked with shareholder value creation while providing several measurable short-term outcomes that guide and monitor strategy implementation. The integrating power of the balanced scorecard can be seen at Mobil Corporation's North American Marketing and Refining business (NAM&R). NAM&R's scorecard is shown in Exhibit 13.5. Assisted by Kaplan and Norton, an unprofitable NAM&R adopted the scorecard methodology to better link its strategy with financial objectives and to translate these into operating performance targets tailored to outcomes in each business unit, functional departments and operating process within them. They included measures developed with key customers from their perspective. The result was an integrated system in which scorecards provided measurable outcomes through which the performance of each department and operating unit, team, or activity within NAM&R was monitored, adjusted, and used to determine performance-related pay bonuses.[5]

dashboard
A user interface that
organizes and presents
information from
multiple digital sources
simultaneously in a
user-designed format
on the computer screen.

Executives and CEOs are increasingly monitoring specific measurable outcomes related to the execution of their strategies. Now, thanks to the Internet and new Web-based software tools known as **dashboards,** accessing this type of specific information is as easy as clicking a mouse. Exhibit 13.6, Top Strategists, shows how a few well-known CEOs embrace the dashboard as a key management tool for timely strategic and operational control. So, for example, an executive at Mobil Corporation might now use a dashboard to monitor updated information on where the company stands on some of the key measures

[5] "How Mobil Became a Strategy-Focused Organization," Chapter 2 in R. Kaplan and D. Norton, *The Strategy-Focused Organization* (Boston: Harvard Business School Press, 2001). For an online version of the Mobil NAM&R case study, see www.bscol.com.

EXHIBIT 13.5
Balanced Scorecard for Mobil Corporation's NAM&R

Source: Reprinted by permission of *Harvard Business Review*. Exhibit from "Putting the Balanced Scorecard to Work," by R. Kaplan and D. Norton, September–October 1993. Copyright © 1993 by the Harvard Business School Publishing Corporation; all rights reserved.

		Strategic Objectives	Strategic Measures
Financially Strong	Financial	F1 Return on Capital Employed F2 Cash Flow F3 Profitability F4 Lowest Cost F5 Profitable Growth F6 Manage Risk	• ROCE • Cash Flow • Net Margin • Full cost per gallon delivered to customer • Volume growth rate vs. industry • Risk index
Delight the Consumer **Win–Win Relationship**	Customer	C1 Continually delight the targeted consumer C2 Improve dealer/distributor profitability	• Share of segment in key markets • Mystery shopper rating • Dealer/distributor margin on gasoline • Dealer/distributor survey

Safe and Reliable
 	
Competitive Supplier
 	
Good Neighbor
 	
On Spec On Time
	Internal	I1 Marketing
		  1. Innovative products and services
		  2. Dealer/distributor quality
		
		I2 Manufacturing
		  1. Lower manufacturing costs
		  2. Improve hardware and performance
		I3 Supply, Trading, Logistics
		  1. Reducing delivered cost
		  2. Trading organization
		  3. Inventory management
		
		I4 Improve health, safety, and environmental performance
		I5 Quality
			• Non-gasoline revenue and margin per square foot
			• Dealer/distributor acceptance rate of new programs
			• Dealer/distributor quality ratings
			• ROCE on refinery
			• Total expenses (per gallon) vs. competition
			• Profitability index
			• Yield index
			Delivered cost per gallon vs. competitors
			• Trading margin
			• Inventory level compared to plan and to output rate
			• Number of incidents
			• Days away from work
			• Quality index

Motivated and Prepared	Learning and growth	L1 Organization involvement L2 Core competencies and skills L3 Access to strategic information	• Employee survey • Strategic competitive availability • Strategic information availability

generated through their balanced scorecard process as shown in Exhibit 13.5. The opportunity to react, take action, ask questions, and so forth approaches real time with the advent of the dashboard software options. That is, of course, when there is a high level of confidence in the reliability of the data that appear—both for the CEO and the managers who might expect a question or expression of concern. The variety of ways the four executives in Exhibit 13.6 report they use their dashboards gives an interesting look at the different

Top Strategists
Using a Dashboard for Strategic Control

Exhibit 13.6

STEVE BALLMER, MICROSOFT

Ballmer requires his top officers to bring their dashboards with them into one-on-one meetings. Ballmer zeroes in on such metrics as sales, customer satisfaction, and status of key products under development.

JEFF IMMELT, GENERAL ELECTRIC

Many GE executives use dashboards to run their day-to-day operations, monitoring profits per product line and fill rates for orders. Immelt occasionally looks at a dashboard. But he relies on his managers to run the businesses so he can focus on the big picture.

IVAN SEIDENBERG, VERIZON

Seidenberg and others can choose from more than 300 metrics to put on their dashboards, from broadband sales to wireless defections. Managers pick the metrics they want to track, and the dashboard flips the pages 24 hours a day.

LARRY ELLISON, ORACLE

A fan of dashboards, Ellison uses them to track sales activity at the end of a quarter, the ratio of sales divided by customer service requests, and the number of hours that technicians spend on the phone solving customer problems.

Source: Reprinted with special permission from "What's on Your Dashboard?" *BusinessWeek*, February 13, 2006. Copyright © 2007 The McGraw-Hill Companies.

ways they might use them, and the different types of information they would choose as key indicators about the unfolding success of their strategies.

Strategic controls and comprehensive control programs like the balanced scorecard bring the entire management task into focus. Organizational leaders can adjust or radically change their firm's strategy based on feedback from a balanced scorecard approach as well as other strategic controls. Other, similar approaches like Six Sigma, which is described in Chapter 14, can also be sources of information and specific measurable outcomes useful in strategic and operational control efforts. The overriding goal is to enable the survival and long-term success of the business. In addition to using controls, leaders are increasingly embracing innovation and entrepreneurship as a way to accomplish this overriding goal in rapidly changing environments. They look to young business graduates, like you, to bring a fresh sense of innovativeness and entrepreneurship with you as you join their companies. We will examine innovation and entrepreneurship in the next chapter.

Summary

Strategies are forward looking, usually designed to be accomplished over several years into the future. They are often based in part on management assumptions about numerous events and factors that have not yet occurred. Strategic controls are intended to steer a company toward its long-term strategic goals under uncertain, often changing, circumstances.

Premise controls, strategic surveillance, special alert controls, and implementation controls are four types of strategic controls. All four types are designed to meet top management's needs to track a strategy as it is being implemented; to detect underlying problems, circumstances, or assumptions surrounding that strategy; and to make necessary adjustments. These strategic controls are linked to environmental assumptions and the key operating requirements necessary for successful strategy implementation. Ever-present forces of change fuel the need for and focus of strategic control.

Operational control systems require systematic evaluation of performance against pre-determined standards and targets. A critical concern here is identification and evaluation of performance deviations, with careful attention paid to determining the underlying reasons for and strategic implications of observed deviations before management reacts. Approaches like the balanced scorecard and Six Sigma (discussed in the next chapter) have emerged as comprehensive control systems that integrate strategic goals, operating outcomes, customer satisfaction, and continuous improvement into an ongoing strategic management system.

The emergence of the Internet has led to innovative software that further assists executives in more closely and carefully monitoring outcomes in real time as a strategy is being implemented. This allows executives and managers to have *dashboards* on their computers, laptops, or mobile devices that further enhance their ability to control and adjust strategies as they are being executed.

A central goal with any strategy is the survival, growth, and improved competitive position of the company in the face of ever-accelerating rates of change. Executives, as they seek to control the execution of their strategy, are also increasingly aware of the need for innovation and entrepreneurial thinking as a companion to their emphasis on control as a means to accomplish these key goals in the face of rapid global change. The next chapter will examine innovation and entrepreneurship.

Key Terms

balanced scorecard, *p. 416*	milestone reviews, *p. 414*	strategic control, *p. 409*
dashboard, *p. 418*	premise control, *p. 410*	strategic surveillance, *p. 412*
implementation control, *p. 412*	special alert control, *p. 412*	strategic thrusts or projects, *p. 414*

Questions for Discussion

1. Distinguish between strategic control and operating control. Give an example of each.
2. Select a business whose strategy is familiar to you. Identify what you think are the key premises of the strategy. Then select the key indicators that you would use to monitor each of these premises.
3. Explain the differences between implementation controls, strategic surveillance, and special alert controls. Give an example of each.
4. Why are budgets, schedules, and key success factors essential to operations control and evaluation?
5. What are the key considerations in monitoring deviations from performance standards?
6. How is the balanced scorecard related to strategic and operational control?
7. Read the first chapter discussion case. How would strategic controls be used to help those three situations?
8. What is a dashboard?

Chapter 13 Discussion Cases

BusinessWeek

Case 13-1: Big Blue Wields the Knife Again: *To Wrest Profits from Its Ailing IT Services Business, IBM Is Slashing Its North American Workforce and Finding Efficiencies Overseas*

1 On the surface, IBM seems to be cruising. Its stock is trading near a six-year high, at almost $106, and its overall financial performance has been improving steadily for more than a year. The company raised this year's per-share earnings forecast after stepping up a stock repurchase plan.

2 Yet the company is battling a bugbear that keeps it from breaking out and prevents the stock from really soaring. Ironically, its problem is with the $48 billion-a-year business that saved it from ruin in the 1990s: IT services. What was once IBM's growth engine seems to be turning into a chronically slow-growing, low-margin drag on the rest of the company.

3 Fresh evidence of IBM's trouble with services came May 30, when the company revealed that it had just eliminated 1,573 services jobs, mostly in North America, bringing to 3,023 the total jobs cut in the high-cost region this quarter alone. That's a small percentage of the company's total workforce of more than 355,000. Yet when weighed against rapid growth in low-cost India, where the staff topped 53,000 at the beginning of the year, the cuts underscore the biggest challenge facing Big Blue: the Indian tech industry.

INDIAN RIVALS FORCE CHANGE

4 IBM remains the No. 1 tech services company in the world, with 7.2 percent of the market last year, but its share slipped from 7.5 percent in 2005. India's tech services exports grew 32 percent, to $31 billion last fiscal year, ended in March, and are expected by analysts to top $60 billion by 2010. With a combination of low labor costs, high quality, and efficiency in how it handles jobs, the Indian companies have forced IBM and other Western services giants to fundamentally restructure the way they do business and massively shift work offshore. "The Indians are doing to the world's IT processes what the Japanese did to manufacturing," says analyst John McCarthy of Forrester Research.

5 IBM's answer isn't as simple as moving more jobs offshore. The company has developed a system that lets it shift work to the areas with available skills at the lowest available costs. The goal is to deliver higher-quality services at competitive prices. "Clearly one opportunity associated with globalization is costs," IBM chief executive Samuel Palmisano told a gathering of stock analysts on May 17, 2007. "You have access to expertise wherever it is in the world—if you have the infrastructure and the relationships to take advantage of it."

CONTINUING TREND

6 Job reductions are nothing new for IBM's huge global-services workforce, which has been under the knife continuously in the past two years. The cuts started when IBM, shocked by very poor results for the first quarter of 2005, began a major restructuring in Europe and the United States that eliminated 15,000 jobs in a matter of months. Ever since then, every few months, a new batch of jobs is trimmed from high-cost countries, including 700 in the first quarter of this year.

7 The trend is likely to continue. In the first quarter, the largest chunk of the services business, called Global Technology Services, grew a relatively healthy 7 percent, but its operating margin narrowed, shrinking by 2.5 points to just 7.8 percent. In comparison, the top Indian services outfits have operating profits of between 25 and 30 percent.

8 And their quarterly revenues are growing 30 to 40 percent year over year. IBM "is in a transition," says S. Padmanabhan, an executive vice president at Tata Consultancy Services, India's largest IT services firm. "We have been doing this for over 35 years, and it has taken a lot of intellectual capital to fine-tune the process. It's taking these companies time to reach our level of maturity."

LEANER AND LEANER

9 Meanwhile, the Indians are taking on larger and larger contracts and doing evermore sophisticated work. Even IBM's seemingly most solid relationships can become unstuck. For instance, when China's Lenovo Group bought IBM's personal computer business two years ago, IBM became a major supplier of services for Lenovo's operations. Yet Lenovo is now undertaking a massive cost-cutting campaign, and, according to a source familiar with the situation, the company has opened up bidding on its effort to integrate all of its operations using run-the-business software from SAP.

10 Why are the Indian companies able to underprice IBM and still make a much better profit? Partly—geography. The Indians typically employ about 80 percent of their staffs in low-cost countries and place the remaining 20 percent near their clients in the United States and Europe.

11 To improve its efficiency, IBM has adopted the so-called Lean Operations discipline developed by Toyota Motor for manufacturing cars. It's adapting Lean so it applies to a global service organization, something the top Indian companies began two years ago. The basic principle of Lean Operations is that a company should be making continuous, incremental improvements in its business processes. That's one of the ways IBM figures out where it can eliminate work. The company also keeps a master database, nicknamed "Blue Monster," of all of its services employees. Supervisors use the information to track who is working on what project and when they'll be available for another assignment. In this way, the company hopes to minimize the amount of time people are between assignments.

MOFFAT'S MISSION

12 All of this cost-cutting is the task of Robert Moffat, senior vice president for integrated operations. His goal is to make the Global Technology Services workforce 10 to 15 percent more efficient each year. The key for him is to take costs out of the equation through a combination of workforce globalization, process improvements, and replacing manual labor with software. In a little more than six months, Moffat said at the May 17, 2007, analysts' meeting, he has rolled out the new formula for 22 of IBM's largest clients in seven countries. In some cases, he said, the clients have seen up to a 50 percent

improvement in productivity. Now, Moffat is extending the new system to 600 more accounts.

13 All of this huffing and puffing over efficiency won't calm the frazzled nerves of IBM's 155,000-strong services workforce. True, there are still abundant employment opportunities in the company. About 30 percent of the people whose jobs are eliminated find other jobs within the behemoth, and, in the first four months of this year alone, IBM hired more than 19,000 people. But a lot of those hires were made in India. For the U.S. workforce, there is always fear that jobs will be lost to foreigners.

14 For investors, the fear is just the opposite—that IBM won't make the shift quickly enough. Only then will its massive services business be healthy again.

Source: Reprinted with special permission from Steve Hamm, "Big Blue Wields the Knife Again," *BusinessWeek*, May 30, 2007. Copyright © 2007 The McGraw-Hill Companies.

CASE 13-2: Crunch Time for Boeing: *As an August Deadline Looms for the 787 Dreamliner, Company Executives Insist It's on Target, Despite Supplier Delays*

1 All eyes are on Boeing as it begins the final assembly of the first 787 Dreamliner.

2 Even Washington Governor Christine Gregoire joined the official ceremony that kicked off the process on May 21, 2007, at the company's sprawling new state-of-the-art aircraft plant in Everett, Washington. A lot is at stake, of course, for all interested parties, including the state. The Dreamliner has notched 568 firm orders from 44 airlines, making it the fastest selling new airplane in aviation history, and it is partly responsible for reviving the once fading fortunes of Boeing's commercial airplane division.

3 But now Boeing actually has to begin building the complicated composite jets and still faces the crucial test: seeing if it can make the plane fly. "If there are going to be problems—and every new airplane program has some—it's going to start appearing now and over the next 9 to 12 months," says Richard Aboulafia, aerospace analyst for the Teal Group. "So far, so good. But you can bet that few senior Boeing executives are going to be sleeping well over the next few months."

EXECUTIVE ENTHUSIASM

4 Rollout for the first jet is slated for July 8, 2007, and the first flight is scheduled for mid-August, provided the airplane is ready to fly. Boeing's first customer, All Nippon Airways, should receive its first Dreamliner in May 2008. Meeting those deadlines is key, as delivery is when Boeing collects most of its money.

5 Boeing executives, as expected, put on a brave face May 21, 2007, and gushed enthusiastically about progress so

far. The large composite fuselage sections, the first set of carbon-fiber wings, and the horizontal stabilizer have all been delivered safely to the staging area at Boeing's stripped-down assembly space. Boeing is transporting the big airplane component parts to Everett on modified 747s, called Dreamlifters, from factories in Japan, Italy, South Carolina, and Kansas.

6 "Today, we begin assembling the first airplane of a new generation," boasted Scott Strode, 787 vice president of airplane production. "The 787 not only will revolutionize air travel, it represents a new way of building airplanes."

CONTINGENCY PLAN

7 As final assembly has drawn closer, people inside Boeing say some challenges are emerging. The actual snapping together of enormous composite parts built by different companies in Asia, Europe, and North America is the first test of this new system. Boeing's supplier partners did not install many of the electronic and hydraulic systems into their respective fuselage sections as planned. Boeing is shifting workers—known as "travelers" in airplane production argot—from other airplane programs, such as the 777 Jetliner, to make up for the unfinished work. That is sure to boost overtime pay, push workers harder, and create havoc as employees frantically try to catch up on the unfinished work.

8 But on May 21, Strode downplayed some of the production challenges, saying they were typical of a new airplane program. He said suppliers did not integrate the systems in the first fuselage sections as they focused on producing their first composite structures. He said the company has it under control. In the future, however, fuselage sections will come stuffed with the electronics and hydraulic systems, so that Boeing workers will just have to connect the wiring and piping to the other sections and then snap the plane together.

9   Strode said one challenge is that fuselage sections are currently being held together by temporary fasteners. The cause, he said, is a global shortage of fasteners—the bolts that hold the airplane together—as a result of the boost in jet production at Boeing and Airbus. Mike Bair, Boeing vice president of the 787, had said earlier during a conference call with reporters that "the fastener industry is stretched tighter than a rubber band."

SUPPLIER DELAYS

10   The other continuing challenge has been production delays from Italy. Alenia Aeronautica, which builds the 62-foot composite horizontal stabilizer and the center fuselage, had fallen behind on creating its first barrel section. This caused concern for people in the 787 program. Although Alenia Aeronautica delivered its horizontal stabilizer early, the quality of the part had many defects that Strode said were caused by the early manufacturing challenges Alenia faced. He says the Italians now have a handle on the production issue and expects to see much improved stabilizers in the near future. But such design and manufacturing fixes cost more money.

11   In an earlier quarterly financial call with analysts, Boeing executives said the company is spending an additional $1 billion to cover contingencies that could occur as production of the 787 gears up. Some of that money is earmarked for the development of the 747-8 Intercontinental.

12   Still, the making of the 787 represents a new way to produce commercial jetliners, and the changes could be positive for Boeing, if not the entire industry.

PRODUCTION LINE

The biggest change is the outsourcing of much of the   **13** manufacturing work to global suppliers. The Japanese are making the composite wings and wing box. Dallas-based Vought Aircraft Industries and Spirit AeroSystems of Wichita, Kansas, are making fuselage and nose sections. Italy's Alenia is making the center fuselage and the horizontal stabilizer.

The 787 production system has been designed using lean   **14** manufacturing techniques honed on other Boeing airplane programs, resulting in a simplified final assembly process. A huge advantage of using composites on the airframe is that Boeing and its suppliers build the wing or the nose section in just one unified piece. This means the final assembly workers will only have to fasten together six major items—the forward, center, and aft fuselage sections, the wings, the horizontal stabilizer, and the vertical fin, Boeing officials say. That drastically cuts production time compared to other current programs, where workers have to attach many more component parts to the different aircraft sections.

Portable tools, designed with ergonomics in mind, move   **15** the assemblies into place. No overhead cranes are used to move the different airplane structures. Although the first airplane will take about seven weeks to assemble, executives say production flow time will increase to where mechanics in final assembly are producing a Dreamliner in six days. Ultimately, the goal is to roll out a 787 every three days.

Source: Reprinted with special permission from Stanley Holmes, "Crunch Time for Boeing," *BusinessWeek,* May 22, 2007. Copyright © 2007 The McGraw-Hill Companies.

Case 13-3: Unproductive Uncle Sam: *To Boost Performance, Government Needs to Measure and Set Targets for Its Programs*

1   The past decade has been one of America's finest in terms of productivity growth. Yet a crucial 20 percent of our economy appears to have been left behind: government. Despite numerous attempts at management reform and a panoply of opportunities to transfer best practices between the private and public sectors, government seems to have missed out on the productivity boom seen in the private sector. That's a shame, because while there are important differences between the public and private sectors, government does an abundance of grant making, procurement, property management, customer service, and other jobs ripe for productivity improvement.

2   So just how far behind is government? We can't say with any certainty because the Bureau of Labor Statistics, which used to measure its productivity, stopped in 1996. Our analysis shows that government kept up with the private sector until

1987, when a gap emerged. It went on widening until 1994, when the data ran out. We believe it has widened further still.

This public productivity deficit couldn't come at a worse   **3** moment. Americans today say they want to limit the cost of government, but they also want more homeland security, better-managed borders, more disaster readiness, extra help in the face of global trade, cheaper health care, and better public schools. These demands sit uncomfortably with our budget deficit and our natural desire not to pay more taxes. In short, we are stuck in a productivity bind: we want more output but no more input.

In a white paper our firm, McKinsey & Co., published this   **4** week, "How Can American Government Meet Its Productivity Challenge?", we map out an agenda inspired by lessons from the private sector. Having studied productivity growth around the world for more than 15 years, the McKinsey Global

Institute has shown that competitive intensity at the industry sector level is the prime catalyst for productivity growth. It forces managers to improve performance and allows innovation to diffuse quickly across the sector.

5 Make no mistake, government is a sector—structured and regulated in ways that can foster or stunt productivity growth at its "firms" (agencies). And while it may not be possible to use competition in government to exert pressure to perform, Congress and the White House or state legislators and governors have plenty of tools to improve public agencies.

6 The most natural tool is the budget process, but the reality in Washington and many state capitals is that performance remains a secondary factor in budget decision making. Congressmen fight for their district or their passions, and accordingly, agencies privately admit that you budget for what you can get, not what you need or deserve. Yet when government performance, or the lack thereof, is highly visible (witness the response after Katrina), everyone takes action.

7 That's why we think a radical new approach to transparency of how government programs are performing is required. Only this will push Congress to exert performance pressure on government agencies. First, government should measure public productivity again and set national targets for productivity growth against which everyone can be held accountable. Next, political leaders should create a body we call "GovStar," modeled after fund-rating agency Morningstar Inc., to provide completely independent measurement of government program performance; to develop comparable program data over time—between programs, between governments, and with the private sector; and to make the data and their implications clear to appropriators and citizens.

8 But in government, pressure without support can yield demoralization and underperformance. So we also need to adopt key transformation initiatives: incentives that allow agencies to reinvest savings to the top line of programs; the introduction of chief operating officers at public agencies, to be appointed based on management experience in government or leading corporations; and a SWAT team of management experts at the Office of Management and Budget to help lagging agencies.

9 It's a long list. But if we want our government to do more and do better, we must take public management and productivity more seriously. Otherwise, citizen demands for effective government in the future will go unheeded.

Source: Reprinted with special permission from Nancy Killefer and Lenny Mendonca, "Unproductive Uncle Sam," *BusinessWeek*, August 14, 2007. Copyright © 2007 The McGraw-Hill Companies. Nancy Killefer, a senior partner at McKinsey & Co., is former Assistant Treasury Secretary for Management. Lenny Mendonca is a senior partner and chairman of the McKinsey Global Institute.

Questions for Discussion
Case 13-1: IBM

1. What is the strategy IBM is monitoring and controlling within its IT business?
2. What implementation controls (measures) and industry comparison measures does IBM appear to be using to evaluate and control its ongoing implementation and execution?

Case 13-2: Boeing

1. How is Boeing using milestones and other implementation measures to gauge its 787 Dreamliner strategy's successful implementation?
2. How could a dashboard approach help the vice president for Dreamliner production control strategy execution?
3. What complications do so many outsourced partners create for Boeing?

Case 13-3: Uncle Sam

1. How might strategic and operational controls help increase implementation effectiveness among government programs?
2. Is it realistic to expect that doing so is feasible?
3. How would you apply strategic control or operational control to a specific government program?

Chapter **Fourteen**

Innovation and Entrepreneurship

After reading and studying this chapter, you should be able to

1. Summarize the difference between incremental and breakthrough innovation.
2. Explain what is meant by continuous improvement and how it contributes to incremental innovation.
3. Summarize the risks associated with an incremental versus a breakthrough approach to innovation.
4. Describe the three key elements of the entrepreneurship process.
5. Explain intrapreneurship and how to enable it to thrive.

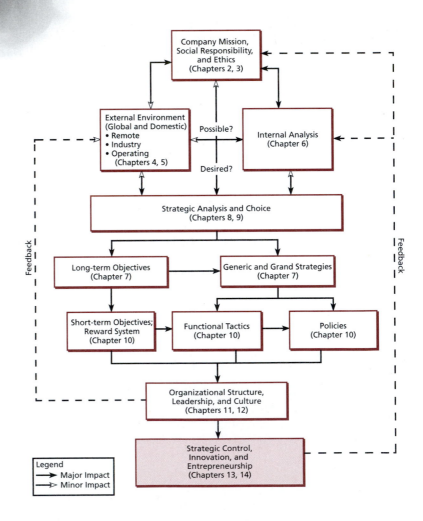

Company Mission, Social Responsibility, and Ethics (Chapters 2, 3)

External Environment (Global and Domestic)
• Remote
• Industry
• Operating
(Chapters 4, 5)

Possible?

Internal Analysis (Chapter 6)

Desired?

Strategic Analysis and Choice (Chapters 8, 9)

Feedback

Long-term Objectives (Chapter 7)

Generic and Grand Strategies (Chapter 7)

Short-term Objectives; Reward System (Chapter 10)

Functional Tactics (Chapter 10)

Policies (Chapter 10)

Organizational Structure, Leadership, and Culture (Chapters 11, 12)

Strategic Control, Innovation, and Entrepreneurship (Chapters 13, 14)

Feedback

Legend
→ Major Impact
⇒ Minor Impact

Survival and long-term success in a business enterprise eventually come down to two outcomes: sales growth or lower costs, and hopefully both. Rapid change, globalization, and connectivity in the global economy have led to impressive growth across many sectors of the global economy. Most companies have spent the last decade or two putting continuous pressure on their organizations to drive out excessive costs and inefficiencies so as to compete in this increasingly price sensitive global arena. Increasingly, executives in these same companies see growth, particularly growth via innovation, as the key priority to their firm's long-term survival and prosperity.

Recent studies by four prominent consulting organizations have documented the critical importance of innovation for CEOs of companies large and small around the globe as these CEOs seek to chart the destinies of their companies into the next decade. IBM's study of almost 800 CEOs found innovation in three ways to be the central focus among today's CEOs:—product/service/market innovation, business model innovation, and operational innovation.[1] Accenture and the Center for Strategy Research surveyed executives in the *Fortune* 1000 companies and found innovation to be very important to 95 percent of the firms represented, with innovation being most important when it results in improvements to existing products or services, decreases in costs, or improvements in meeting customer needs.[2] The Boston Consulting Group surveyed senior executives from 500 companies in 47 countries and found that almost 75 percent of those companies would increase their spending on innovation the next few years an average of 15 percent each year; more than 90 percent of these companies said that generating growth through innovation had become essential for success in their industry.[3]

The other interesting finding in the study was that fewer than half of these executives were satisfied with the returns on their investments to date in innovation. "Unless companies improve their approach to innovation," BCG Senior Vice President Jim Andrew said, "increased investment may in fact lead to increased disappointment." These executives indicated their three biggest problems with innovation were

1. Moving quickly from the idea generation to initial sales.
2. Leveraging suppliers for new ideas.
3. Appropriately balancing risks, timeframes, and returns.

Yet these executives were anxious to become more innovative. After identifying Apple, 3M, GE, Microsoft, and Sony as the innovators they most admire—the "most innovative" companies worldwide, 80 percent of these executives indicated that they anticipated even higher innovation spending by 2007.[4]

WHAT IS INNOVATION?

invention
The creation of new products or processes through the development of new knowledge or from new combinations of knowledge.

Common to the vocabulary of most business executives is a distinction between *invention* and *innovation*. We define the two using this common perspective:

Invention is the creation of new products or processes through the development of new knowledge or from new combinations of existing knowledge. The jet engine was patented in 1930, yet the first commercial jet airplane did not fly until 1957. Computers were based on three different sets of knowledge created decades before the first computer.

[1] *IBM Global CEO Study,* IBM Global Business Services, www-935.ibm.com/services, 2007.
[2] Toni Langlinais and Bruce Bendix, "Moving from Strategy to Execution to High Performance," *Accenture Outlook,* No. 2, (October 2006).
[3] "Global Firms Will Increase Their Spending on Innovation," *PRNewswire,* December 8, 2004.
[4] Ibid.

innovation
The initial commercialization of invention by producing and selling a new product, service, or process.

Innovation is the initial commercialization of invention by producing and selling a new product, service, or process. As executives across each of the surveys summarized earlier typically put it, "Innovation is turning ideas into profits."[5]

Apple's iPod was a *product innovation* that applied Apple's chip storage technology with sleek device styling to create an innovation within six months in 2001 at Apple. Steven Jobs then worked intensely for almost two years negotiating digital music rights with a recalcitrant music industry, culminating in the launching of iTunes in 2003—a music download *service innovation* with 200,000 digital songs to choose from for your iPod. That quickly became more than 1 million songs, and Apple had a $1 billion revenue stream added to its business. Starbucks added the simple service of wireless access free to its customers at most of its 8,000 stores in what turned out to be a highly successful *service innovation* that resulted in customers using the service staying nine times longer than regular customers, and doing so during off-peak hours.

While these two leading innovators are creating profitable product and service innovations, Toyota is perhaps the most envied business *process innovator* worldwide due to its meticulous attention to business and operating processes. Several years ago, Toyota made one change to its production lines, using a single brace to hold auto frames together instead of the 50 it previously took. While a minute part of Toyota's overall production process, this "global body line" system slashed 75 percent off the cost of refitting a production line. It is the reason behind Toyota's ability to make different models on a single production line, estimated to save Toyota more than $2.6 billion in 2005 alone.

To some business managers, "innovation seems as predictable as a rainbow and as manageable as a butterfly. Penicillin, Teflon, Post-it-notes—they sprang from such accidents as moldy Petri dishes, a failed coolant, and a mediocre glue." Not surprisingly, many managers forgo trying to harness innovation systematically. "Our approach has always been very simple, which is to try not to manage innovation," says Michael Moritz, a partner with world-renowned venture capital firm Sequoia Capital. "We prefer to just let the market manage it."[6] Exhibit 14.1 outlines a typical innovation process. For those managers who try to manage innovation, it is important to distinguish two types of innovations: incremental innovation and breakthrough innovation.

incremental innovation
Simple changes or adjustments in existing products, services, or processes.

Incremental Innovation

Incremental innovation refers to simple changes or adjustments in existing products, services, or processes. There is growing evidence that companies seeking to increase the payoff from innovation investments best do so by focusing on incremental innovations. We will examine the payoff research more completely in a subsequent section on risks associated with innovation. First, however, we need to examine how companies are seeking incremental innovation. A major driver of incremental innovation in many companies the last several years has come from programs aimed at continuous improvement, cost reduction and quality management.

continuous improvement
The process of relentlessly trying to find ways to improve and enhance a company's products and processes from design through assembly, sales, and service. It is called *kaizen* in Japanese. It is usually associated with incremental innovation.

Continuous improvement, what in Japanese is called *kaizen,* is the process of relentlessly trying to find ways to improve and enhance a company's products and processes from design through assembly, sales, and service. This approach, or really an operating philosophy, seeks to always find slight improvements or refinements in every aspect of what

---

[5] Ibid.

[6] Robert Hof, Steve Hamm, Diane Brady, and Ian Rowley, "Building an Idea Factory," *BusinessWeek,* October 11, 2004.

EXHIBIT 14.1 Genesis of an Innovation

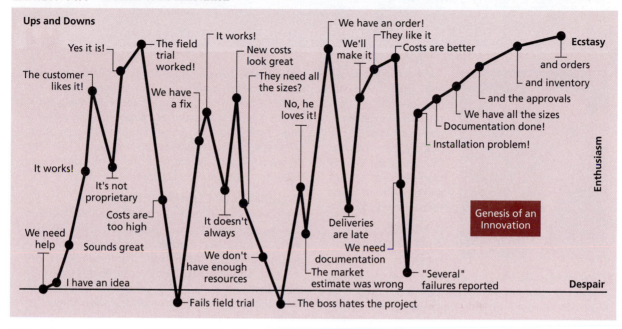

CCC21
A world-famous, cost-oriented continuous improvement program at Toyota (Construction of Cost Competitiveness for the 21st Century).

Six Sigma
A continuous improvement program adopted by many companies in the last two decades that takes a very rigorous and analytical approach to quality and continuous improvement with an objective to improve profits through defect reduction, yield improvement, improved customer satisfaction, and best-in-class performance.

a company does so that it will result in lower costs, higher quality and speed, or more rapid response to customer needs.[7]

Toyota's extraordinary success the last five years is one good example of a cost-oriented continuous improvement effort (see Exhibit 14.2, Top Strategist). Named **CCC21** (Construction of Cost Competitiveness for the 21st Century), Toyota embarked on this intense scrutiny of every product it purchases or builds to include in the assembly of its automobiles in response to growing concern about the relative cost advantage to be derived from a surge in global automobile company mergers starting with Daimler-Chrysler. The result: a stunning $10 billion in cost savings over the past five years in the parts it buys, while also improving quality significantly. Taking the Japanese perspective, 1001 small innovations or improvements together have become something transformative. A good example would be Toyota engineers disassembling the horns made by a Japanese supplier and finding ways to eliminate 6 of 28 horn components, saving 40 percent in costs and improving quality. Or, interior assist grips above each door—once there were 35 different grips but now, across 90 different Toyota models, there are only 3. Toyota engineers call this process *kawaita zokin wo shiboru*, or "wringing drops from a dry towel," which means an excruciating, unending process essential to Toyota's continuous improvement success.

Six Sigma is another continuous improvement approach widely used by many companies worldwide to spur incremental innovation in their businesses. Six Sigma is a rigorous and analytical approach to quality and continuous improvement with an objective to improve profits through defect reduction, yield improvement, improved consumer satisfaction, and best-in-class performance. Six Sigma complements TQM philosophies such as

[7] TQM, total quality management, is the initial continuous improvement philosophy used worldwide to focus managers and employees on customer defined quality since starting in Japan in the 1970s.

<table>
<tr><td>

Top Strategist
Katsuaki Watanabe, President, Toyota Motor Corp.

</td><td>

**Exhibit
14.2**

</td></tr>
</table>

There are milestones—and then there are ground-shifting, era-smashing milestones, like word that Toyota dislodged General Motors as the world's biggest seller of cars and trucks for the first time ever in 2007.

A FANATICAL ATTENTION TO DETAIL

Even more daunting, though, is Toyota's deeply ingrained commitment to manufacturing excellence that runs throughout this sprawling global operation. That work ethic seems to reside in the collective gene pool of company executives decade after decade, and dates back to founder Kiichiro Toyoda, who launched the company some 70 years ago.

Toyota's Katsuaki Watanabe may be self-effacing to the extreme—ever-smiling and somewhat colorless—but his sole focus in good years and so-so ones is that Toyota never lose its fanatical attention to detail, corrective adjustment, frugality, process redesign, and market adaptation.

Watanabe, and every 20-something-year-old factory hand and designer, are mindful of the heritage bestowed upon them by Taiichi Ohno, a leader still revered inside the company as the father of the fabled Toyota production system. Decades ago, Ohno established a set of in-house precepts on efficient and lean manufacturing that evolved to include just-in-time delivery; continuous improvement (*kaizen*); mistake proofing (*pokayoke*); and *obeya,* or face-to-face brainstorming sessions among engineers, designers, marketing pros, and suppliers. Toyota didn't just revolutionize car making—but pretty much global manufacturing as well.

Visit any Toyota plant in Japan, and you will see a high-tech ballet of a half dozen separate car models—from the Corolla compact to the youth-oriented models like the Scion xB—gliding along a single production line in any of a half-dozen colors. Overhead, car doors flow by on a conveyor belt that descends to floor level and drops off the right door in the correct color for each vehicle.

AVOIDING BIG-COMPANY DISEASE

The same exacting efficiency and quality standards are expected at Toyota plants anywhere in the world. Toyota's best workers are trained by in-house quality gurus at their local plant—or flown off to Japan to learn the Toyota way of double- and triple-checking parts and processes for trouble and immediately signaling to superiors when things go wrong.

Above all, Toyota workers value frugality—whether it's turning down the heat at company-owned dormitories during working hours back in Japan or spending weeks jawboning with suppliers to figure out ways to redesign a key component and shave another 10 percent from production costs.

Toyota is scarcely a flawless organization, but it has managed, so far, to avoid what Watanabe and others have called the "big-company disease"—and by that what they really mean (though will never say it) is the GM disease. "The scariest symptom," Watanabe said in an interview with *BusinessWeek,* "is that complacency will breed in the company. To be satisfied with becoming the top runner, and to become arrogant, is the path we must be most fearful of." If Toyota can manage to keep that sentiment in mind, it's going to be leading the global industry for a very long time to come.

management leadership, continuous education and customer focus while deploying a disciplined and structured approach of hard-nosed statistics.[8]

Companies such as Honeywell, Motorola, BMW, GE, Polaroid, SAP, IBM, and Texas Instruments have adopted the Six Sigma discipline as a major business initiative. Many of these companies invested heavily in and pursued this model initially to create products and services that were of equal and higher quality than those of its competitors and to improve relationships with customers. A Six Sigma program at many organizations simply means a measure of quality that strives for near perfection in every facet of the business including every product, process, and transaction:

How the Six Sigma Statistical Concept Works

Six Sigma means a failure rate of 3.4 parts per million or 99.9997 percent. At the sixth standard deviation from the mean under a normal distribution, 99.9996 percent of the population is under the curve with not more than 3.4 parts per million defective. The higher the sigma value, the less likely a process will produce defects as excellence is approached.

If you played 100 rounds of golf per year and played at:
2 Sigma: You'd miss 6 putts per round.
3 Sigma: You'd miss 1 putt per round.
4 Sigma: You'd miss 1 putt every 9 rounds.
5 Sigma: You'd miss 1 putt every 2.33 years.
6 Sigma: You'd miss 1 putt every 163 years!

Source: From John Petty, "When Near Enough Is Not Good Enough," *Australian CPA* (May 2000), pp. 34–35.

Many frameworks, management philosophies, and specific statistical tools exist for implementing the Six Sigma methodology and its objective to create a near-perfect process or service. One such method for improving a system for existing processes falling below specification while looking for incremental improvement is the DMAIC process (define, measure, analyze, improve, control) shown in Exhibit 14.3.

Incremental innovation via continuous improvement programs is viewed by most proponents as virtually a new organizational culture and way of thinking. It is built around an intense focus on customer satisfaction; on accurate measurement of every critical variable in a business's operation; on continuous improvement of products, services, and processes; and on work relationships based on trust and teamwork. One useful explanation of the continuous improvement philosophy suggests 10 essential elements that lead to meaningful incremental innovation:

1. *Define quality and customer value.* Rather than be left to individual interpretation, company personnel should have a clear definition of what *quality* means in the job, department, and throughout the company. It should be developed from your customer's perspective and communicated as a written policy. Thinking in terms of customer value broadens the definition of *quality* to include efficiency and responsiveness. Said another way, quality to your customer often means that the product performs well; that it is priced competitively (efficiency); and that you provide it quickly and adapt it when needed (responsiveness). Customer value is found in the combination of all three—quality, price, and speed.

2. *Develop a customer orientation.* Customer value is what the customer says it is. Don't rely on secondary information—talk to your customers directly. Also recognize your "internal" customers. Usually less than 20 percent of company employees come into

[8] ISO certification, from the International Standards Organization, is another widely used means of encouraging rigorous and analytically based assessment and confirmation of meeting quality and building continuous improvement into the way the organization functions.

EXHIBIT 14.3   **The DMAIC Six Sigma Approach**

Define

- Project definition
- Project charter
- Gathering voice of the customer
- Translating customer needs into specific requirements

Measure

- Process mapping (as-is process)
- Data attributes (continuous vs. discrete)
- Measurement system analysis
- Gauge repeatability and reproducibility
- Measuring process capability
- Calculating process sigma level
- Visually displaying baseline performance

Analyze

- Visually displaying data (histogram, run chart, pareto chart, scatter diagram)
- Value-added analysis

- Cause-and-effect analysis (a.k.a. Fishbone, Ishikawa)
- Verification of root causes
- Determining opportunity (defects and financial) for improvement
- Project charter review and revision

Improve

- Brainstorming
- Quality function deployment (house of quality)
- Failure modes and effects analysis (FMEA)
- Piloting your solution
- Implementation planning
- Culture modification planning for your organization

Control

- Statistical process control (SPC) overview
- Developing a process control plan
- Documenting the process

contact with external customers, while the other 80 percent serve internal customers—other units with real performance expectations—in a process that looks like this:

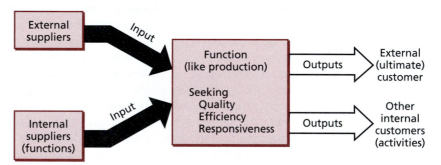

3. *Focus on the company's business processes.* Break down every minute step in the process of providing the company's product or service, and look at ways to improve it, rather than focusing simply on the finished product or service. Each process contributes value in some way, which can be improved or adapted to help other processes (internal customers) improve. Here are several examples of ways customer value is enhanced across business processes in several functions:

	Quality	**Efficiency**	**Responsiveness**
Marketing	Provides accurate assessment of customer's product preferences to R&D	Targets advertising campaign at customers, using cost-effective medium	Quickly uncovers and reacts to changing market trends
Operations	Consistently produces goods matching engineering design	Minimizes scrap and rework through high-production yield	Quickly adapts to latest demands with production flexibility

(continued)

	Quality	Efficiency	Responsiveness
Research and development	Designs products that combine customer demand and production capabilities	Uses computers to test feasibility of idea before going to more expensive full-scale prototype	Carries out parallel product/process designs to speed up overall innovation
Accounting	Provides the information that managers in other functions need to make decisions	Simplifies and computerizes to decrease the cost of gathering information	Provides information in "real time" (as the events described are still happening)
Purchasing	Selects vendors for their ability to join in an effective "partnership"	Given the required vendor quality, negotiates prices to provide good value	Schedules inbound deliveries efficiently, avoiding both extensive inventories and stock-outs
Personnel	Trains workforce to perform required tasks	Minimizes employee turnover, reducing hiring and training expenses	In response to strong growth in sales, finds large numbers of employees and quickly teaches needed skills

4. *Develop customer and supplier partnerships.* Organizations have a destructive tendency to view suppliers and even customers adversarially. It is better to understand the horizontal flow of a business—outside suppliers to internal suppliers/customers (a company's various departments) to external customers. This view suggests suppliers are partners in meeting customer needs, and customers are partners by providing input so the company and suppliers can meet and exceed those expectations.

Ford Motor Company's Dearborn, Michigan, plant is linked electronically with supplier Allied Signal's Kansas City, Missouri, plant. A Ford computer recently sent the design for a car's connecting rod to an Allied Signal factory computer, which transformed the design into instructions that it fed to a machine tool on the shop floor. The result: quality, efficiency, and responsiveness.

5. *Take a preventive approach.* Many organizations reward "fire fighters" not "fire preventers" and identify errors after the work is done. Management, instead, should be rewarded for being prevention oriented and seeking to eliminate non-value-added work as CCC21 does quite well at Toyota.

6. *Adopt an error-free attitude.* Instill an attitude that "good enough" is not good enough anymore. "Error free" should become each individual's performance standard, with managers taking every opportunity to demonstrate and communicate the importance of this Six Sigma–type imperative.

7. *Get the facts first.* Continuous improvement–oriented companies make decisions based on facts, not on opinions. Accurate measurement, often using readily available statistical techniques, of every critical variable in a business's operation—and using those measurements to trace problems to their roots and eliminate their causes—is a better way.

8. *Encourage every manager and employee to participate.* Employee participation, empowerment, participative decision making, and extensive training in quality techniques, statistical techniques, and measurement tools are the ingredients continuous improvement companies employ to support and instill a commitment to customer value.

9. *Create an atmosphere of total involvement.* Quality management cannot be the job of a few managers or of one department. Maximum customer value cannot be achieved unless all areas of the organization apply quality concepts simultaneously.

10. *Strive for continuous improvement.* Stephen Yearout, director of Ernst & Young's Quality Management Center, recently observed that "Historically, meeting your customers' expectations would distinguish you from your competitors. The twenty-first century will require that you anticipate customer expectations and deliver quality service faster than the competition."

Quality, efficiency, and responsiveness are not one-time programs of competitive response because they create a new standard to measure up to. Organizations quickly find that continually improving quality, efficiency, and responsiveness in their processes, products, and services is not just good business; it's an excellent means to identify incremental innovations that become foundations for long-term survival.

Disciplines like Six Sigma are systematic ways to improve customer service and quality; the added benefit that emerged has been its effectiveness in cutting costs and improving profitability. That has made it a powerful tool, but the notion that Six Sigma is a survival cure-all is subsiding. Once a company has created incremental innovations that maximize profitability, some argue that "kick-starting the top line" becomes paramount, which in turn means acquisition or dramatic, revenue-generating product or service innovations. And that, they argue, calls less for Six Sigma's "define, measure, analyze, improve, control" regiment and more for a "fuzzier" front-end, creative-idea-generation type of orientation.[9] That calls for a more disruptive form of innovation, which we call *breakthrough innovation.*

Breakthrough Innovation

breakthrough innovation
An innovation in a product, process, technology, or the cost associated with it that represents a quantum leap forward in one or more of these ways.

Clayton Christensen of Harvard Business School makes the distinction between "sustaining" technologies, which are incremental innovations that improve product or process performance, and "disruptive" technologies, which revolutionize industries and create new ones.[10] Rather than an innovation that reduces the cost of a mirror on a car by 40 percent, Christensen is focusing when speaking of disruptive technologies on the product idea that works 10 times better than existing ones or costs less than half what the existing ones do to make—a breakthrough innovation. A **breakthrough innovation**, then, is an innovation in a product, process, technology, or the cost associated with it that represents a quantum leap forward in one or more of those ways.

Apple's innovation with iPod and iTunes is a breakthrough innovation. It was not an incremental improvement in Apple's computer offerings. It was an application of the microprocessor technology associated with Apple's computers, applied in a totally different industry. Apple, which only has a 2 percent market share in the personal computer industry, now has positioned itself as a dominant force in the emerging digital music and entertainment industries based on this breakthrough innovation.

Breakthrough innovations, which Christensen calls "disruptive," often shake up the industries with which they are associated, even though many times they may come from totally different origins or industry settings than the industry to start with. Apple seems to make a habit of creating new industries; Apple's original innovation 20 years earlier in Jobs's and Wozniak's garage that created the first Apple computer was viewed as a toy by most players in the computer industry at the time, but it quickly tore the mainstream computer industry apart and almost brought down the mighty IBM. Texas Instrument's digital watch resulted in the virtual destruction of the dominant Swiss watch industry. Breakthrough innovations can also be appreciated by some fringe (often new) customer group for features such as being cheap, simple, easy to use, or smaller, which is seen as underperforming the

[9] Brian Hindo and Brian Grow, "Six Sigma: So Yesterday?" *BusinessWeek,* June 11, 2007.
[10] Clayton M. Christensen, *The Innovator's Dilemma* (Boston: HBS Press, 1997).

EXHIBIT 14.4
From Idea to Profitable Reality

Source: Industrial Research Institute, Washington, D.C.

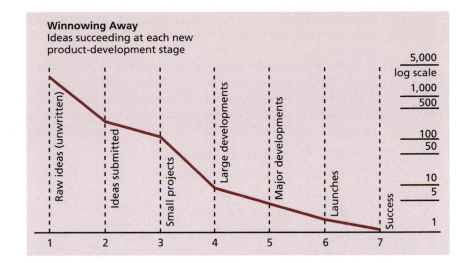

mainstream products. Sony's Walkman, Wal-Mart's discount retailing, and health insurance industry HMOs are all examples of breakthrough innovations that ultimately caused the demise of or significant reduction in key industry participants. Former Digital Equipment Company CEO Ken Olsen, a leading industry figure and a leading computer manufacturer at the time, said of Apple and the idea of a personal computer in your home when the early Apple computers were being sold: "I can think of no reason why an individual should wish to have a computer in his own home."[11]

Breakthrough approaches to innovation are inherently more risky than incremental innovation approaches. The reason can be seen in Exhibit 14.4, which is provided by the Industrial Research Institute in Washington, D.C. Their conclusion is that firms committed to breakthrough innovation must first have the ability to explain clearly to all employees, at every level, just how critical the breakthrough project is to the company's future. The second is to set next-to-impossible goals for those involved. The third is to target only "rich domains"—areas of investigation where plenty of answers are still waiting to be found. The fourth, and maybe the most important, is to move people regularly between laboratories and business units, to ensure that researchers fully understand the needs of the marketplace. These thoughts, of course, apply more to larger firms and particularly ones where breakthrough efforts are concentrated in laboratories and other separate R&D units.

Smaller firms are often sources for breakthrough innovation because they have less invested in serving a large, established customer base and gradually improving on the products, services, or processes used to serve them. We will explore these differences more completely in the section on entrepreneurship. Regardless of the size of a firm, it is important to consider risks associated with incremental versus breakthrough innovation.

Risks Associated with Innovation[12]

Innovation involves creating something that doesn't now exist. It may be a minor creation or something monumental. In either case, there is risk associated with it. Exhibit 14.4 shows the conclusions of the Industrial Research Institute's examination of breakthrough

[11] Robert M. Grant, *Contemporary Strategic Analysis* (Oxford: Blackwell, 2002), p. 330.

[12] See Morten Hansen and Julian Birkinshaw, "The Innovation Value Chain," *Harvard Business Review,* June 2007, for an interesting use of a value chain "breakdown" of innovation to use in assessing risks and sources of problems in innovation efforts.

innovation outcomes, which suggests that you need to start with 3,000 "bright" ideas, which are winnowed down to four product launches, then one major success emerges. Long odds for sure.

A recent study of 197 product innovations, 111 of which were successes and 86 failures, sought to compare the two groups in order to see what might explain differences between innovation success and innovation failure. They first sought to examine what was common to successful innovations and what was common to failing innovations First, they found that successful innovations had some, or all, of the following five characteristics:[13]

- Moderately new to the marketplace.
- Based on tried and tested technology.
- Saved money for users of the innovation.
- Reportedly met customer needs.
- Supported existing practices.

In contrast, product innovations that failed were based on cutting-edge or untested technology, followed a "me-too" approach, or were created with no clearly defined problem or solution in mind.

The second set of findings from this study emerged from the researchers' examination of what they called "idea factors." Idea factors were concerned with how the idea for the innovation originated. They identified six idea factors:

- *Need spotting*—actively looking for an answer to a known problem.
- *Solution spotting*—finding a new way of using an existing technology.
- *Mental inventions*—things dreamed up in the head with little reference to the outside world.
- *Random events*—serendipitous moments when innovators stumbled on something they were not looking for but immediately recognized its significance.
- *Market research*—traditional market research techniques to find ideas.
- *Trend following*—following demographic and other broad trends and trying to develop ideas that may be relevant and useful.

The researchers then compared the "success-to-failure" ratio of these six idea factors to see which idea factors were more often associated with success or failure of the related innovation. The two most failure-prone idea factors were trend following and mental inventions, both producing three times as many failures as successes. Need spotting produced twice as many successes as failures. Market research produced four times as many, and solution spotting seven times more successes than failures. Taking advantage of random events was the clear winner, generating 13 times more successes than failures. Their conclusion: focus on eliminating bad ideas early in the process, emphasize market research and technology application/ solution spotting efforts, while being open to serendipitous outcomes in the process.

Inherent in their analysis is the presence of two key risks associated with innovation— market risks and technology risks. Market risks come from uncertainty with regard to the presence of a market, its size, and its growth rate for the product or service in question: do customers exist and will they buy it? Technology risks derive from uncertainty about how the technology will evolve and the complexity through which technical standards and dominant designs or approaches emerge: will it work?

Research by Michael Treacy of GEN3 Partners reported in the *Harvard Business Review* suggests that incremental innovation is far more effective than breakthrough innovation in managing the market and technology risk associated with innovation. Exhibit 14.5 provides

---

[13] "Expect the Unexpected," *The Economist,* September 4, 2004.

EXHIBIT 14.5   **Risks Associated with Innovation**

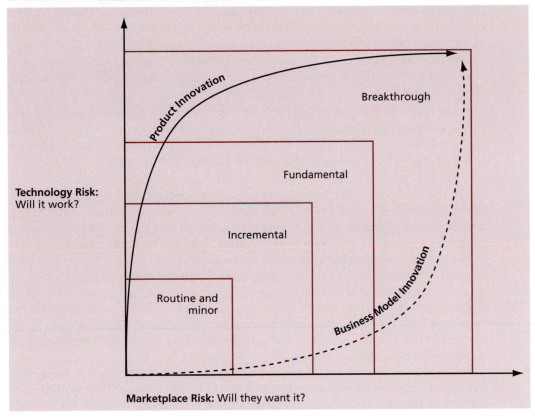

a visual portrayal of his research.[14] In it he suggests that technology risk is primary and marketplace risk secondary in product innovations; the reverse is true for business model or process innovations.

The point that emerges from this graph is that breakthrough innovation, while glamourous and exciting, is very risky compared with incremental innovation. Breakthrough innovations, according to Treacy's examination of much of the research to date on innovation, usually get beaten down or outperformed by the slow and steady approach of incremental innovation. He makes several useful points about managing the resulting risks:

• Remember, *the point of innovation is growth.* So ask the question, Can I increase revenue without innovation? Retain existing customers and improve targeted coverage of existing and similar new customers, where innovation isn't necessary to keep existing customers.

• *Get the most out of minimum innovation.* Tweaking a business process doesn't incur much technology risk. Incremental product or service innovation does not incur nearly the market risk that a radical one would. So emphasize an incremental approach to most innovation efforts.

• Incremental product innovations can be particularly good at *locking in existing customers.* Every saved customer is an additional source of revenue.

[14] Michael Treacy, "Innovation as a Last Resort," *Harvard Business Review,* July 1, 2004.

• Incremental business process innovations can *generate more revenue gain or cost savings with less risk* than radical ones. The earlier example about Toyota's single brace to hold auto frames is a dramatic example of the payoff—$2.6 billion annually—from one simple, incremental business process innovation.

• Radical innovations are often *too radical for existing markets,* and customers will balk at paying for that new approach, product, process, or technology. So it will fail with existing customers.

• The time to launch breakthrough innovations is not when they are necessary, important, or of interest to your business, but *when they are essential to the marketplace.* And that usually takes time, like the 10 years it has taken for car buyers to become interested in the electric/hybrid vehicles that have been available for more than 10 years.

The case for incremental innovation as a less risky approach than breakthrough innovation is widely advocated. Clayton Christensen offers a word of caution in this regard, arguing that as important as incremental improvements are, steady improvements to a company's product do not conquer new markets. Nor do they guarantee survival. He argues that while **disruptive** (breakthrough) **innovations** may underperform established products in mainstream markets, they often offer features or capabilities appreciated by some fringe (usually new) customer group—like being easier to use, cheaper, smaller, or more versatile. Often, his research suggests, those fringe customers swell in numbers to become the mainstream market, absorbing the newly informed old mainstream in the process. And in so doing, they "disrupt" or bring about the downfall of leading existing industry players.

Not surprisingly, many companies are experimenting with new ways to lower risks and improve chances for failure regardless of the innovation approach they use. For years the idea of product teams and cross-functional groups within the company has played a major role in trying to improve the odds that innovations will succeed, or that bad ideas are eliminated much earlier in the innovation management process. This approach broadens to include several more:

• *Joint ventures* with other firms that have an interest in the possible innovation share the costs and risks associated with the effort. Toyota is now negotiating with General Motors to share its hybrid vehicle technology and jointly build a manufacturing facility in the United States to lower both companies' risk associated with this innovation.

• *Cooperation with lead users* is increasingly used in both types of innovation. Nike tests new shoes with inner-city street gangs; software companies beta-test their new software with loyal users; GE works with railroad companies to create a new, ecofriendly locomotive.

• *"Do it yourself"* innovation allows a company to work directly with key existing or expected customers, further allowing these customers to play a lead role in developing a product, service, or process—not just get a sense of their reaction to developments. This approach allows a company to go beyond the traditional market research model or simply cooperating with lead users. Instead, it has customers actually conceptualize or make design proposals which become the starting point for developing a new innovation. BMW sent 1,000 customers a "toolkit" that let them develop ideas, showing how the firm could take advantage of telematics and in-car online services. BMW chose 15 submissions, brought them to Germany from all over the world, and worked further with them to flesh out those ideas. Four ideas are now in prototype stage, and BMW anticipates several will emerge in new models along with an increased use of this new customer-innovation effort.

---

disruptive innovation
A term to characterize breakthrough innovation popularized by Harvard Professor Clayton Christensen; usually shakes up or revolutionizes industries with which they are associated even though they often come from totally different origins or industry settings than the industry they "disrupt."

Microsoft's Last Best Hope in Search

BusinessWeek

Microsoft executives like to say they're still in the early stages of the lucrative business of Internet search, contending that as wide as Google's lead may seem now, it's not insurmountable. But for all of Microsoft's protestations, only 8.4 percent of all searches among U.S. Web surfers went through Microsoft compared with Google's 56.3 percent share in 2007.

Microsoft isn't going to give up the fight any time soon. Rather, Microsoft has been spending money to boost its efforts in what's known as vertical search, those niche markets where Netizens go when they're looking for specialized information.

Microsoft's vertical search acquisitions aren't that well known, but they may form the foundation of a different way to keep Google in check. Microsoft bought MotionBridge, a Paris-based provider of search technology for mobile phones. A few weeks later, Microsoft picked up Medstory, a small Foster City (California) start-up focused on dishing up health care information. And then Microsoft announced it bought voice-recognition leader Tellme Networks, whose technology could help Microsoft bake voice recognition into its mobile search efforts. Finally, a $6 billion acquisition of Web advertising giant aQuantive confirms Microsoft's taste for buying search innovations rather than doing it in-house to survive or thrive in search, which ultimately means finding a chink in Google's seemingly impenetrable armor.

That's why analysts think that if Google is vulnerable it may be in those specialized areas where there isn't an established leader. And despite Microsoft's best efforts to compete in generic search, vertical search may prove more strategic. "You've got to find a way to change the rules of the game," says Eric Enge, founder of Stone Temple Consulting, a search engine optimization business in Southborough, Massachusetts.

• *Acquiring innovation* has become a major way larger companies bring innovation into their firm while mitigating the risk/reward trade-off in the process. Exhibit 14.6, Strategy in Action, describes Microsoft's recent use of this approach as its "last, best hope" to compete with Google in the Internet search business. CISCO has built itself into a dominant player in the computer and networking equipment industries in large part by buying smaller companies that had developed and tentatively proven new market niches but who needed capital and distribution to rapidly exploit the new technological advantage. CISCO acquired these companies for a premium using stock, but it invested little or nothing in the early development of the technology. Thus, the smaller firm bore all the early risk of failure, and those that succeeded were rewarded in the price of the sale of their company, but CISCO got to avoid the losses associated with the majority of the innovations attempted but not successful.

• *Outsourcing innovation,* particularly product design, has become a major part of the "modular" organizational structure of today's global technology companies. Nokia, Samsung, and Motorola—cell phone giants—get proposed new-product design prototypes from HTC, Flextronics and Cellon—unknown global, billion-dollar-plus companies that create new designs and sell them to cell phone and other electronics brand-name companies annually at the biggest trade shows around the world. To Nokia and it competitors, this shifts the risk of product design innovation to these emerging technology outsourcing powerhouses.

Procter & Gamble, under Alan Lafley, has radically changed that company's culture so that it accepts as a matter of corporate strategy that 50 percent of its consumer product innovations will come from outside P&G. The resulting growth and profitability due to new-product innovations at P&G over the last five years have made it the new model of open source product/service/market innovation worldwide.[15]

ideagoras
Web-enabled, virtual marketplaces which connect people with unique ideas, talents, resources, or capabilities with companies seeking to address problems or potential innovations in a quick, competent manner.

Ideagoras, defined as places where millions of ideas and solutions change hands in something akin to an eBay for innovation, reflects one of the newest approaches to open innovation, which leverages the value of the Internet to access talent worldwide, instantly. Companies seeking solutions to seemingly insoluble problems can tap the insights of hundreds of thousands of enterprising scientists without having to employ any of them full time. Take, for example, Colgate-Palmolive, which needed a more efficient method for getting its toothpaste into the tube—a seemingly straightforward problem. When its internal R&D team came up empty-handed, the company posted the specs on InnoCentive, one of many ideagoras or marketplaces that link problems with problem solvers. A Canadian engineer named Ed Melcarek proposed putting a positive charge on fluoride powder, then grounding the tube. It was an effective solution, an application of elementary physics, but not one that Colgate-Palmolive's team of chemists had ever contemplated.[16] Melcarek earned $25,000 for a few hours work, and a timely innovation from outside the company accrued to another client company.

Today more than 150,000 scientists like Melcarek have registered with InnoCentive, and hundreds of companies pay annual fees of roughly $80,000 to tap the talents of this global scientific community. Launched as a e-business by Eli Lilly in 2001, the company now provides solutions to some of the world's most well-known and innovation-hungry companies. The reason? Mature companies cannot keep up with the speed of innovation nor the demands for growth by relying on internal capabilities alone. This approach creates a much more flexible, free-market mechanism; secondly, it taps a vastly changing global landscape where the talent to generate disruptive or path-breaking innovation will increasingly reside in China, India, Brazil, Eastern Europe, or Russia. P&G figures that for every one of its 9,000 top-notch scientists, there are another 200 outside who are just as good. That's a total of 1.8 million talented people it could potentially tap, using ideagoras to seek out ideas, innovations, and uniquely qualified minds on a global scale quickly, efficiently, and productively.[17]

Such openness in seeking new, key innovations that determine a company's future survival and growth—as opposed to doing innovation on a closely guarded, internal basis—is viewed with skepticism and as a risk that cuts at the very core of what a company essentially exists to do. Product design, major innovations, even incremental innovations, have long been viewed as key, secret core competencies and competitive advantages that generate the long-term success of the company that possesses them. Outsourcing these activities, or doing so via ideagoras, puts the whole firm at risk in the minds of observers opposed to this open type of innovation. That said, the example of Canada's Goldcorp and Switzerland's Novartis in Exhibit 14.7, Strategy in Action, seems to be reflective of a broadening embrace of Web-enabled, wide-open collaboration in breakthrough innovation.

Another way of looking at the notion of innovation, and an organization's ability to manage it effectively, is found in the argument that innovation is associated with entrepreneurial behavior. And so, to be more innovative, a firm has to become more entrepreneurial.

[15] "P&G: What's the Big Idea," *BusinessWeek,* May 4, 2007.

[16] Don Tapscott and Anthony D. Williams, "Ideagora, a Marketplace for Minds," *BusinessWeek,* February 15, 2007.

[17] Ibid. See also "Innovation in the Age of Mass Collaboration," *BusinessWeek,* February 1, 2007; "The New Science of Sharing," *BusinessWeek,* March 2, 2007; *Wikinomics,* by Don Tapscott and Anthony Williams; and Satish Nambisan and M. Sawhney, "A Buyer's Guide to the Innovation Bazaar," *Harvard Business Review,* June 2007, p. 109.

Strategy in Action

Exhibit 14.7

The Mass Collaboration Approach to Breakthrough Innovation

BusinessWeek

A few years back, Toronto-based gold mining company Goldcorp was in trouble. Besieged by strikes, lingering debts, and an exceedingly high cost of production, the company had terminated mining operations. Without evidence of substantial new gold deposits, Goldcorp was likely to fold. Chief executive officer Rob McEwen needed a miracle. Frustrated that his in-house geologists couldn't reliably estimate the value and location of the gold on his property, McEwen did something unheard of in his industry: he published his geological data on the Web for all to see and challenged the world to do the prospecting. The "Goldcorp Challenge" made a total of $575,000 in prize money available to participants who submitted the best methods and estimates. Every scrap of information (some 400 megabytes worth) about the 55,000-acre property was revealed on Goldcorp's Web site. News of the contest spread quickly around the Internet, and more than 1,000 virtual prospectors from 50 countries got busy crunching the data.

Mining is one of the world's oldest industries, and it's governed by some pretty conventional thinking. Take Industry Rule No. 1: don't share your proprietary data. The fact that McEwen went open-source was a stunning gamble.

Within weeks, submissions from around the world were flooding into Goldcorp headquarters. There were entries from graduate students, management consultants, mathematicians, military officers, and a virtual army of geologists. "We had applied math, advanced physics, intelligent systems, computer graphics, and organic solutions to inorganic problems. There were capabilities I had never seen before in the industry," says McEwen. "When I saw the computer graphics, I almost fell out of my chair."

The contestants identified 110 targets on the Red Lake property, more than 80 percent of which yielded substantial quantities of gold. In fact, since the challenge was initiated, an astounding 8 million ounces of gold have been found—worth well over $3 billion. Not a bad return on a half-million-dollar investment.

Today, Goldcorp is reaping the fruits of its radical approach to exploration. McEwen's willingness to open-source the prospecting process not only yielded copious quantities of gold, it introduced Goldcorp to state-of-the-art technologies and exploration methodologies, including new drilling techniques, data collection procedures, and more advanced approaches to geological modeling. This catapulted his underperforming $100 million company into a $9 billion juggernaut while transforming a backward mining site in Northern Ontario into one of the most innovative and profitable properties in the industry. McEwen and his shareholders are happy miners—$100 invested in the company in 1993 is worth more than $3,000 today.

Swiss drugmaker Novartis recently did something similar—again, almost unheard of in the high-stakes, highly competitive world of Big Pharma. After investing millions trying to unlock the genetic basis of type 2 diabetes, the company released all of its raw data on the Internet. This means anyone (or any company) with the inclination is free to use the data—no strings attached.

Type 2 diabetes and related cardiovascular risk factors—including obesity, high blood pressure, and high cholesterol—are among the most common and most costly public health challenges in the industrialized world. Pinpointing their precise genetic origins could unlock a treasure trove of new medicines and result in a major windfall for Novartis shareholders.

So why the giveaway? "These discoveries are but a first step," says Mark Fishman, president of the Novartis Institute for BioMedical Research. "To translate this study's provocative identification of diabetes-related genes into the invention of new medicines will require a global effort."

In other words, the research conducted by Novartis and its university partners at the Massachusetts Institute of Technology and Lund University in Sweden merely sets the stage for the more complex and costly drug identification and development process. According to researchers, there are far more leads than any one lab could possibly follow up alone. So by placing its data in the public domain, Novartis hopes to leverage the talents and insights of a global research community to dramatically scale and speed up its early-stage R&D activities.

Sources: Reprinted with special permission from "Innovation in the Age of Mass Collaboration," *BusinessWeek*, February 1, 2007; and "The New Science of Sharing," *BusinessWeek*, March 2, 2007. Copyright © 2007 The McGraw-Hill Companies.

EXHIBIT 14.8
Who Is the Entrepreneur?

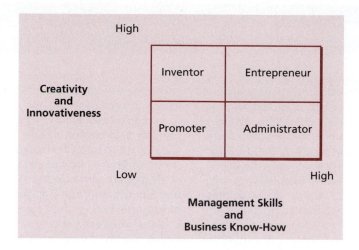

The example of CISCO and the acquiring innovation approach is one way smart companies have targeted the reality that breakthrough innovation occurs very often in the smallest of firms, where focus, intensity, and total survival depend on that innovation succeeding. Advocates of this perspective make the point that many industry-creating and paradigm-changing breakthrough innovations (e.g., personal computers; digital file sharing), as well as seemingly obvious incremental innovations ignored by large industry players (e.g., Paychex serving small businesses), came from start-up or small companies—entrepreneurs—that have since become major industry leaders.

Taking this perspective has led some other forward-thinking large companies to seek ways to make themselves more entrepreneurial and to enable their "entrepreneurs within" to emerge and succeed in building new businesses around innovative ideas. Such people, termed "intrapreneurs" in the business and academic press, have proven to be effective champions of innovation-based growth in many companies that have sincerely encouraged their emergence. But whether it is through the entrepreneurs within, or becoming or teaming with independent entrepreneurs, ensuring the presence of entrepreneurship in an organization is central to innovation, long-term survival, and renewal.

WHAT IS ENTREPRENEURSHIP?

entrepreneurship
The process of bringing together the creative and innovative ideas and actions with the management and organizational skills necessary to mobilize the appropriate people, money, and operating resources to meet an identifiable need and create wealth in the process.

The Global Entrepreneurship Monitor estimates that 11 percent of all working adults are self-employed, a number they project is steadily growing.[18] New entrepreneurial ventures are recognized globally as key drivers of economic development, job creation, and innovation. So what is entrepreneurship? What does it involve?

Entrepreneurship is the process of bringing together creative and innovative ideas and actions with the management and organizational skills necessary to mobilize the appropriate people, money, and operating resources to meet an identifiable need and create wealth in the process. Whether the process is undertaken by a single individual or a team of individuals, there is mounting evidence that growth-minded entrepreneurs possess not only a creative and innovative flair but also solid management skills and business know-how—or they ensure the presence of both in the fledgling organizations they start. Exhibit 14.8

[18] The Global Entrepreneurship Monitor is a not-for-profit research consortium that is the largest single study of entrepreneurial activity in the world. Initiated in 1999 by Babson College and London Business School, it now involves research teams at universities and other organizations worldwide. It provides annual and quarterly GEM updates at www.gemconsortium.org.

Frederick W. Smith: No Overnight Success

BusinessWeek

Frederick W. Smith, founder of FedEx Corp., has transportation in his blood. His grandfather was a steamboat captain, and his father built from scratch a regional bus line that became the Southern backbone of the Greyhound Bus system. Smith learned to fly as a teenager, a skill he turned to cash by working weekends as a charter pilot while a student at Yale University in the 1960s. While flying students and other passengers around, Smith had the insight that led him to revolutionize the delivery business. He noticed that he was also frequently ferrying spare parts for computer companies such as IBM that didn't want to wait for the passenger airlines to get critical components to customers.

Smith, an economics major, first broached his idea for an express delivery service in what became one of the most infamous term papers in Corporate America. Lore has it that he received a modest C, though Smith doesn't think that was the case. Whatever the grade, he wasn't deterred. "I knew the idea was profound," he said.

After a hitch with the Marines in Vietnam, Smith set up Federal Express Corp. in 1971 and guaranteed overnight delivery of critical goods between any two points in an 11-city network. Hardly an overnight success, Smith secured just seven packages for the first night's run.

Sparse initial volume wasn't the only headache. Until the late 1970s, the postal monopoly stopped FedEx from delivering documents. By 1973, Smith was so desperate for cash that he flew to Las Vegas to play the blackjack tables. He wired the $27,000 he won back to FedEx. Smith's persistence paid off. By the late 1970s, America came to rely on FedEx's ability to deliver goods overnight. Merrill Lynch & Co. execs even discovered employees were using FedEx to deliver documents between floors of its Manhattan headquarters building because it was faster and more reliable than the interoffice mail. These days, FedEx is a linchpin of the just-in-time deliveries revolution—its planes and trucks serving as mobile warehouses—that has helped companies around the globe cut costs and boost their productivity.

Its fleet of 675 aircraft and 72,000 trucks carry an average of 6.5 million shipments in 220 countries each day. And all because a college kid could see a market that others couldn't.

Sources: Reprinted with special permission from "FedEx Delivers," *BusinessWeek,* June 20, 2007; and Dean Foust, "Frederick Smith: No Overnight Success," *BusinessWeek,* September 20, 2004. Copyright © 2007 The McGraw-Hill Companies.

illustrates the fundamental skills associated with being entrepreneurial versus those suitable for promoters, managers, and inventors.

Inventors are exceptional for their technical talents, insights, and creativity. But their creations and inventions often are unsuccessful in becoming commercial or organizational realities because their interests and skills are lacking in terms of reading a market and bringing products or services to creation and then marketing and selling them effectively. *Promoters* are in some way just the opposite—clever at devising schemes or programs to push a product or service, but aimed more at a quick payoff than a profitable, business-building endeavor for the longer term.

Administrators, the good ones, develop strong management skills, specific business know-how, and the ability to organize people. They usually take pride in overseeing the smooth, efficient functioning of operations largely as they are. Their administrative talents are focused on creating and maintaining efficient routines and organization—creative and innovative behavior may actually be counterproductive within the organizations they operate.

The ideal *entrepreneur* has that unusual combination of talent: strength in both creativity and management. In a new venture, these strengths enable the entrepreneur to conceive and launch a new business as well as make it grow and succeed. In a large organization, these talents enable strong players to emerge and build new ideas into impressive new revenue streams and profitability for a larger company. Because these strengths so rarely coexist in one individual, entrepreneurship is increasingly found to involve teams of people that combine their strengths to build the business they envision. Exhibit 14.9, Strategy in Action, tells the story of just such a rare entrepreneur, Fred Smith, founder and chairman of Federal Express.

New ventures and small, growth-oriented business entrepreneurs are able to achieve success from effectively managing three elements central to the entrepreneurial process in creating and sustaining new ventures. Those three elements are opportunity, the entrepreneurial team, and resources:

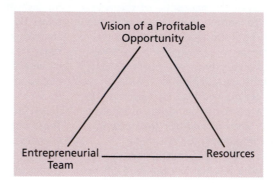

Opportunity

The most frequent cause of failure of new ventures, as reported by Dun & Bradstreet (D&B) in its yearly failure record, is lack of sales; the second is competitive weakness. Both causes stem from the lack of appreciation of the necessity for a market orientation as the basis of any new venture. In other words, failure among new ventures, is heavily linked to ventures started because someone had the idea for such a business but did not identify a concrete market opportunity.

Entrepreneurs doomed to learn from their all too frequent failure conceive an idea for a product or service and immediately become enamored of it. They invest time, money, and energy in developing the idea into a commercial reality. And, tragically, they make only a minimum investment in identifying the customers, the customers' needs, and their willingness to buy the product or service as an answer to those needs. Such entrepreneurs are focused inward, perhaps satisfying their own personal ego needs. The result is often a product or service that few customers will buy. The customers are seeking to buy benefits, and the ineffective entrepreneur is consumed with selling his/her product.

The effective entrepreneur is more likely to assume a marketing orientation and look outward at a target market to identify or confirm the presence of a specific need or desired solution. Here the entrepreneur is focused on potential customers and on seeking to understand their need. The effective entrepreneur seeks to confirm an opportunity defined by what the customer wants and is willing to pay. It is interesting that the most effective approach in the way firms seek to innovate is to bring customers into the innovation process to help shape the solution they seek. In essence, customers define what they want. The design of an effective entrepreneur's product or service comes in response to an opportunity, not the other way around.

Another way to determine if an entrepreneur is focused on simply an idea or a good opportunity is to apply the same criteria venture capitalists use to evaluate new venture investment opportunities. It is important to recognize that these criteria are applied by investors interested primarily in high-growth ventures. The criteria for smaller ventures would be less demanding in scope (e.g., a minimum $200 million market) but similar in the types of concerns that should be addressed in an effort to determine whether the opportunity is a good one. Let's look at each criterion individually:

1. *The venture team can clearly identify its customers and the market segment(s) it plans to capture.* Exactly who are the target customers? Who makes the buying decision?

Does the entrepreneur have evidence that these customers are enthusiastic about the product or service and will act favorably (e.g., pay in advance) on that enthusiasm? Firm purchase orders or other tangible purchase commitments help confirm the timing is right.

2. *A minimum market as large as $200 million.* A market this size suggests that the firms can achieve significant sales without having to attain a dominant share of its market. That, in turn, means the new venture can grow without attracting much competitive reaction. It is important to recognize that this threshold pertains to high-growth opportunities, not smaller, lifestyle ventures.

3. *A market growing at a rate of 30 to 50 percent.* This is another indicator that the timing is right to act on an opportunity; it means new entrants can enter the fray without evoking defensive reactions from established competitors. On the other hand, if the market is static or growing only marginally, then either the opportunity must offer a realistic chance of revolutionizing the industry—a rare occurrence—or the timing is bad.

4. *High gross margins (selling price less direct, variable costs) that are durable.* When entrepreneurs can sell their product or service at gross margins in the 50+ percent range, there is an attractive cushion built in that covers the mistakes they are likely to make while developing a new enterprise. When margins are small, the margin for error is too.

5. *There is no dominant competitor in the market segments representing the venture opportunity.* A market share of 40 to 60 percent usually translates into significant power over suppliers, customers, pricing, and costs. The absence of such a competitor means more room for the newcomer to maneuver, without fear of serious retaliation.

6. *A significant response time, or lead time, in terms of technical superiority, propri-etary protection, distribution, or capacity.* When a new venture possesses this type of legitimate "unfair advantage," the new firm should be able to create barriers to entry or expansion by others who are aware of the profitable opportunity. When an entrepreneur can take advantage of this sort of proprietary edge, and the edge will last, the timing is right.

7. *An experienced entrepreneur or team capable of enthusiastically and professionally building a company to exploit the profitable opportunity.* Venture capitalists universally identify this as an essential ingredient for the timing to be right to invest in a proposed venture. Aspiring entrepreneurs should likewise use it as a criterion for whether it is wise to pursue the new venture opportunity they are considering. Let's examine this last point more fully.

Entrepreneurial Teams

Successful entrepreneurs and entrepreneurial teams bring several competencies and char-acteristics to their new ventures. Let's examine both.

• *Technical competence.* The entrepreneur or team must possess the knowledge and skill necessary to create the products or services the new venture will provide. It may be that some of those competencies exist outside the entrepreneur or team, in which case meaning-ful arrangements to outsource them become part of the technical competence equation. But know-how and capability are essential to success.

• *Business management skills.* The survival and growth of a technically viable new ven-ture depend on the ability of the entrepreneur to understand and manage the economics of the business. Financial and accounting know-how in areas of cash flow, liquidity, costs and contributions, record keeping, pricing, structuring debt, and asset acquisition are essential. People management skills, marketing, organizational skills, sales, computer literacy, and planning skills are just some of those essential to success.

Technical and business skills being critical, they alone are not enough. Observers identify several behavioral and psychological characteristics that are usually associated with successful entrepreneurs:

• *Endless commitment and determination.* Ask any number of entrepreneurs the secret of their success, and they inevitably cite this one. Entrepreneurs' level of commitment can usually be gauged by their willingness to jeopardize personal economic well-being, to tolerate a lower standard of living than they would otherwise enjoy early in the enterprise, and even to sacrifice time with their family.

• *A strong desire to achieve.* Need to achieve is a strong entrepreneurial motivator. Money is a way to keep score, but outdoing their own expectations is an almost universal driver.

• *Orientation toward opportunities and goals.* Good entrepreneurs always like to talk about their customers and their customers' needs. They can readily respond when asked what their goals are for this week, month, and year.

• *An internal locus of control.* Successful entrepreneurs are self-confident. They believe they control their own destiny. To use a sports analogy, they want the ball for the critical last-second shot.

• *Tolerance for ambiguity and stress.* Start-up entrepreneurs face the need to meet payroll when revenue has yet to be received, jobs are constantly changing, customers are ever new, and setbacks and surprises are inevitable.

• *Skills in taking calculated risks.* Entrepreneurs are like pilots: they take calculated risks. They do everything possible to reduce or share risks. They prepare or anticipate problems; confirm the opportunity and what is necessary for success; create ways to share risk with suppliers, investors, customers, and partners; and are typically obsessed with controlling key roles in the execution of the firm's operations.

• *Little need for status and power.* Power accrues to good entrepreneurs, but their focus is on opportunities, customers, markets, and competition. They may use that power in these settings, but they do not often seek status for the sake of having it.

• *Problem solvers.* Good entrepreneurs seek out problems that may affect their success and methodically go about overcoming them. Not intimidated by difficult situations, they are usually decisive and capable of enormous patience.

• *A high need for feedback.* "How are we doing?" The question is ever-present in an entrepreneur's mind. They seek feedback. They nurture mentors to learn from and expand their network of contacts.

• *Ability to deal with failure.* Entrepreneurs love to win, but they accept failure and aggressively learn from it as a way to better manage their next venture.

• *Boundless energy, good health, and emotional stability.* Their challenges are many, so good entrepreneurs seem to embrace their arena and pursue good health to build their stamina and emotional well-being.

• *Creativity and innovativeness.* New ways of looking at things, tinkering, staying late to talk with a customer or employee—all these are typical of entrepreneurs' obsession with doing things better, more efficiently, and so forth. They see an opportunity instead of a problem, a solution instead of a dilemma.

• *High intelligence and conceptual ability.* Good entrepreneurs have "street smarts," a special sense for business, and the ability to see the big picture. They are good strategic thinkers.

• *Vision and the capacity to inspire.* The capacity to shape and communicate a vision in a way that inspires others is a valuable skill entrepreneurs need in themselves or from someone in their core team.

Resources

The third element in new venture entrepreneurship involves *resources*—money and time. Let's summarize money first. A vital ingredient for any business venture is the capital necessary to acquire equipment, facilities, people, and capabilities to pursue the targeted opportunity. New ventures do this in two ways. **Debt financing** is money provided to the venture that must be repaid at some point in time. The obligation to pay is usually secured by property or equipment bought by the business, or by the entrepreneur's personal assets. **Equity financing** is money provided to the venture that entitles the provider to rights or ownership in the venture and which is not expected to be repaid. It entitles the source to some form of ownership in the venture, for which the source usually expects some future return or gain on that investment.

Debt financing is generally obtained from a commercial bank to pay for property, equipment, and maybe provide working capital—all available only after there is proven revenue coming into the business. Family and friends are debt sources, as are leasing companies, suppliers, and companies that lend against accounts receivable. Entrepreneurs benefit when using debt capital because they retain ownership and increase the return on their investment if things go as planned. If not, debt financing can be a real problem for new ventures because rapid growth requires steady cash flow (to pay salaries, bills, interest), which creates a real dilemma if interest rates rise and sales slow down. Most new ventures find early debt capital hard to get anyway, so gradually nurturing a relationship with a commercial lender, letting them get to know the entrepreneur and the business, is a wise approach for the new entrepreneur.

Equity financing is usually obtained from one or more of three sources: friendly sources, informal venture investors, or professional venture capitalists. In each case, it is often referred to as "patient money," meaning it does not have to be paid back immediately or on any particular schedule. *Friendly sources* are prevalent early in many new ventures—friends, family, wealthy individuals who know the entrepreneur. *Informal venture investors,* usually wealthy individuals, or what are now called "angel" investors (for obvious reasons), are increasingly active and accessible as possible equity investors. *Professional venture capitalists* seek investment in the truly high-growth potential ventures. They have stringent criteria as we have seen, and expect a return of five times their money in three to five years! A fourth source of equity capital, *public stock offerings,* is available for a very select few new ventures. They are usually firms that have gone through the other three sources first.

Regardless of the source, equity capital is money that does not have to be repaid on an immediate, regular basis as debt capital requires. So when a firm is rapidly growing and needs to use all its cash flow to grow, not having to repay makes equity more attractive than debt. The unattractive aspect of equity financing for some people is that it constitutes selling part of the ownership of the business and, with it, a say in the decisions directing the venture.

The other resource is time—time of the entrepreneur(s) and key players in the business venture's chance for success. The entrepreneur is the catalyst, the glue that holds the fledgling business together and oftentimes the critical source of energy to make success happen. As we noted earlier, determination is a key characteristic of entrepreneurs. And time is the most critical resource, combined with determination, to virtually "will" the new venture's success at numerous junctures in its early development.

Successful entrepreneurs are impressive growth and value building innovators. Their success often comes at the expense of large firms with which they compete, do business, obtain supplies, and such. Their success in commercializing new ideas has drawn the attention of many larger companies leading to the question, Can a big firm be more entrepreneurial? The conclusion has been a tentative yes, that larger firms can increase their level of innovation and subsequent commercialization success if they encourage

debt financing
Money "loaned" to an entrepreneur or business venture that must be repaid at some point in time.

equity financing
Money provided to a business venture that entitles the provider to rights or ownership in the venture and which is not expected to be repaid.

entrepreneurship and entrepreneurs within their organizations. Understanding and encouraging entrepreneurship in large organizations to improve future survival and growth has become a major agenda in thousands of large companies today. The ideas behind these efforts, which have been called *intrapreneurship,* are examined in the next section.

Intrapreneurship

intrapreneurship
A term associated with entrepreneurship in large, established companies; the process of attempting to identify, encourage, enable, and assist entrepreneurship within a large, established company so as to create new products, processes, services, or improvements that become major new revenue streams and/or sources of cost savings for the company.

intrapreneurship freedom factors
Ten characteristics identified by Dr. Gordon Pinchot and elaborated upon by others that need to be present in large companies seeking to encourage and increase the level of intrapreneurship within their company.

Intrapreneurship, or entrepreneurship in large companies, is the process of attempting to identify, encourage, enable, and assist entrepreneurship within a large, established company so as to create new products, processes, or services that become major new revenue streams and sources of cost savings for the company. Gordon Pinchot, founder of a school for intrapreneurs and creator of the phrase itself, suggests 10 **freedom factors** that need to be present in large companies seeking to encourage intrapreneurship:

1. *Self-selection.* Companies should give innovators the opportunity to bring forth their ideas, rather than making the generation of new ideas the designated responsibility of a few individuals or groups.

2. *No hand-offs.* Once ideas surface, managers should allow the person generating the idea to pursue it rather than instructing him or her to turn it over ("hand it off") to someone else.

3. *The doer decides.* Giving the originator of an idea some freedom to make decisions about its further development and implementation, rather than relying on multiple levels of approval for even the most minor decision, enhances intrapreneurship.

4. *Corporate "slack."* Firms that set aside money and time ("slack") facilitate innovation.

5. *End the "home run" philosophy.* Some company cultures foster an interest in innovative ideas only when they represent major breakthroughs. Intrapreneurship is restricted in that type of culture.

6. *Tolerance of risk, failure, and mistakes.* Where risks and failure are damaging to their careers, managers carefully avoid them. But innovations inherently involve risks, so calculated risks and some failures should be tolerated and chalked up to experience.

7. *Patient money.* The pressure for quarterly profits in many U.S. companies stifles innovative behavior. Investment in intrapreneurial activity may take time to bear fruit.

8. *Freedom from turfness.* In any organization, people stake out turf. Boundaries go up. Intrapreneurship is stifled by this phenomenon because cross-fertilization is often central to innovation and successful entrepreneurial teams.

9. *Cross-functional teams.* Organizations inhibit cross-functional interaction by insisting that communication flow upward. That inhibits sales from learning from operations and company people from interacting with relevant outsiders.

10. *Multiple options.* When an individual with an idea has only one person to consult or one channel to inquire into for developing the idea, innovation can be stifled. Intrapreneurship is encouraged when people have many options for discussing or pursuing innovative ideas.

When you read Pinchot's 10 freedom factors, they sound very much like characteristics associated with entrepreneurs or the nature of the types of resources—money and time—that we identified as being central to the entrepreneurship process. And that, obviously, is exactly what intrapreneurship is trying to do—replicate the presence of entrepreneurs (small undertakings) inside a large enterprise that offers the potential advantage of easier money, expertise, facilities, distribution, and so forth. Exhibit 14.10, Strategy in Action, describes how Yahoo! is trying to launch its own intrapreneurs in just this manner at a facility it calls

BusinessWeek

Yahoo!'s mash-up service, Pipes, was the first product to come out of "Brickhouse," Yahoo!'s answer to the tiny, nimble shops that have nipped at its heels and chewed away at its revenues in recent years. Brickhouse marks a dramatic break from the old ways of doing things at Yahoo!. It's designed to feel completely different from its established—and yes, older—online parent. The 14,000-square-foot offices are located in the hip South of Market neighborhood in San Francisco, 40 miles away from Yahoo! headquarters in strip-mall-laden Sunnyvale. The facility is bereft of Yahoo! logos. Purple, the company's signature color, is noticeably absent.

The staff is made up of Yahoo! employees with the kind of ideas that, in theory at least, would have venture capitalists whipping out their checkbooks. Teams are built around ideas. And the whole effort is led by a genuine star of the Web 2.0 movement, Caterina Fake, who co-founded the innovative photo-sharing site Flickr, which Yahoo! acquired two years ago. The idea is that Brickhouse will give Yahoo! a way to push the envelope and develop brand-new projects, while employees have the chance to experiment with ideas far from their day-to-day jobs.

Brickhouse was born out of the notion that Yahoo!'s employees come up with ideas for new ventures, but they haven't had an effective way to execute them. Bradley Horowitz, vice-president for product strategy, points to a recent experience stemming from Yahoo!'s Hack Day, a two-day event held the last weekend of September 2006, during which all Yahoo! employees were given the ability to hack into the company's programs to develop new features and applications. One employee designed a tool that would leave behind users' fingerprints, in the form of their image or profile, when they visited a page. Yahoo! executives realized the program could be useful to publishers and warrant development. However, the employee had another assignment and there wasn't a good way, at the time, to allow him to easily leave his current project to work on the idea.

Yahoo!'s brand is another challenge. People associate the company and its trademark yodel with one of the Web's prime destinations for mail, news, entertainment, and search. But Yahoo!'s status as an established, family-oriented, commercial brand can turn away some cutting-edge users. That's why, with Brickhouse, Yahoo! is going to launch many more products off-brand than it has done in the past. That he says will let the company float new, edgier ideas without having an adverse impact on the Yahoo! brand, and it may attract users who have negative associations with Yahoo!'s brand.

OUTLET FOR CREATIVE EMPLOYEES

Yahoo! is treating the site as an outlet of sorts for entrepreneurial and creative employees. It wants them to have the ability, as they would if they started their own company, to give things their best shot and then, if they don't really work, walk away.

In this way, Horowitz and others hope Brickhouse serves to help retain employees who otherwise would go off on their own in search of funding. Brickhouse developers whose ideas succeed would receive additional financial compensation for their work. He said the figure would be somewhere between a pat on the back and an acquisition-size bonus. "The idea is they would enjoy some upside," he says.

Whether Brickhouse will succeed remains to be seen. But the scope of Yahoo!'s ambition is clear. Sometimes to think big, you have to act small.

"Brickhouse." Even with all the advantages noted earlier, it is still a challenge for larger organizations to attract, allow, and retain true entrepreneurial behavior within their midst, as Yahoo! readily acknowledges even as it attempts to enhance innovation via intrapreneurship in its Brickhouse.[19] Nine specific ways companies are attempting to enable intrapreneurs and intrapreneurship to flourish in their companies are given here:[20]

[19] Catherine Holahan, "Yahoo! Taps Its Inner Startup," *BusinessWeek,* February 9, 2007.

[20] For elaboration on these and other ideas, see "Lessons from Apple," *The Economist,* June 7, 2007; "Remember to Forget, Borrow, and Learn," *BusinessWeek,* March 28, 2007; "Clayton Christensen's Innovation Brain," *BusinessWeek,* June 15, 2007; and www.Businessweek.com/innovation.

• *Designate intrapreneurship "sponsors."* Formally identify several people with credibility and influence in the company to serve as facilitators of new ideas. These "sponsors" usually have discretionary funds to allocate on the spot to help innovators develop their ideas.

• *Allow innovation time.* 3M was know for its "15 percent rule," which means that members of its engineering group can spend 15 percent of their time tinkering with whatever idea they think has market potential. Google gives employees one day a week to work on their own projects.

• *Accommodate intrapreneurial teams.* 3M calls it "tin cupping." American Cement calls it "innovation volunteers." P&G sets up teams across product divisions to intentionally cross-pollinate new business. The idea is for companies to give managers interdepartmental or unit flexibility to let informal idea-development teams (a marketing person, an engineer, and an operations person) interact about promising ideas and develop them as though they were an independent business.

• *Provide intrapreneurial forums.* Owens Corning calls them "skunkworks, innovation boards, and innovation fairs." 3M has "technical forums," annual "technical review fairs," and "sales clubs." P&G, eBay, and Amazon bring in outsiders, customers especially, to help form the basis for interaction about new ideas where ones that gain traction can quickly move to more serious pursuit using other specific ways described here.

• *Use intrapreneurial controls.* Quarterly profit contribution does not work with intrapreneurial ventures at their early stages. Milestone reviews like we discussed earlier in this chapter—key timetables, resource requirements—provide a type of control more suited to early, innovative activity.

• *Provide intrapreneurial rewards.* Recognition for success, financial bonuses if successful, and most importantly the opportunity to "do it again," with even greater freedom in developing and implementing the next idea are extremely important to this type of venture.

• *Articulate specific innovation objectives.* Clearly setting forth organizational objectives that legitimize and indeed call for intrapreneurship and innovation helps encourage an organizational culture to support this activity. 3M is the "granddaddy" of this approach, having long held to a corporate objective, which they have hit every year since 1970, that "25 percent of annual sales each year will come from products introduced within the last five years." P&G has a corporate goal that 50 percent of its innovations originate outside the company to encourage collaborative, "open," innovative behavior.

• *Create a culture of intrapreneurship.* Jeff Bezos of Amazon.com calls it a "culture of divine discontent," in which everyone itches to improve things. P&G calls it letting outsiders into P&G to innovate, and CEO Lafley is working to ensure that more than half of P&G new products will come from outsiders teamed with inside intrapreneurs. GE's Immelt hires successful intrapreneurs from other companies to become leaders in a usually insider-promoted organization, both to get the intrapreneur involved and even more importantly to send a message of fundamental cultural change toward intrapreneurship. Other firms create internal "banks" to invest in new internal start-ups. Intel has its own venture capital arm investing aggressively in entrepreneurial ventures inside and outside the company, often spinning them off.

• *Encourage innovation from without as well as within.* Apple is widely assumed to be an innovator "within." In fact, its real skill lies in stitching together its own ideas with technologies from outside and then wrapping the results in elegant software and simple, stylish designs.

Innovation and entrepreneurship are intertwined phenomena and processes. Organizations seeking to control their destiny, which most all seek to do, increasingly "get it" that even having a destiny may be the issue. And to have that opportunity or chance, organizations need leaders who embrace the importance of being innovative and entrepreneurial to give their companies the chance to find ways to adapt, be relevant, to position themselves in a future that, to use a trite phrase, has but one real constant—change.

Summary

A central goal with any strategy is the survival, growth, and improved competitive position of the company in the future. Executives seek ways to make their organizations innovative and entrepreneurial because these are increasingly seen as essential capabilities for survival, growth, and relevance. Incremental innovation—where companies increasingly, in concert with their customers, seek to steadily refine and improve their products, services, and processes—has proven to be a very effective approach to innovation. The continuous improvement philosophy, and programs such as CCC21 and Six Sigma, are key ways firms make incremental innovation a central part of their organization's ongoing work activities.

Breakthrough innovation involves far more risk than the incremental approach yet brings high reward when successful. Firms with this approach need a total commitment and are often going against mainstream markets in the process. Large, well-known global companies are increasingly embracing "open" approaches to innovation, including breakthrough innovation, in ways that would have been unthinkable 20 years ago. They have embraced the outsourcing of much product design innovation in recent years and are rapidly adopting Web-enabled forums for tapping expertise located around the globe to gain assistance and collaboration in generating breakthrough innovation. They also increasingly look to innovate by acquiring small, entrepreneurial firms that often generate breakthrough innovations because they have a narrow focus, tolerate risks, have a passion for what they are doing, and benefit greatly if they succeed.

Entrepreneurship is central to making businesses innovative and fresh. New-venture entrepreneurship is the source of much innovation, and it is really a process involving opportunity, resources, and key people. Opportunity is focusing intensely on solving problems and benefits to customers rather than product or service ideas someone just dreams up. Resources involve money and time. Key people, the entrepreneurial team, need to bring technical skill, business skill, and key characteristics to the new venture endeavor for it to succeed.

Intrapreneurship is entrepreneurship in large organizations. Many firms now claim that they seek to encourage intrapreneurship. For intrapreneurship to work, individual intrapreneurs need freedom and support to pursue perceived opportunities, be allowed to fail, and do more of the same more easily if they succeed.

Key Terms

breakthrough innovation, *p. 434*
CCC21, *p. 429*
continuous improvement, *p. 428*
debt financing, *p. 447*
disruptive innovation, *p. 438*

entrepreneurship, *p. 442*
equity financing, *p. 447*
ideagoras, *p. 440*
incremental innovation, *p. 428*
innovation, *p. 428*

intrapreneurship, *p. 448*
intrapreneurship freedom factors, *p. 448*
invention, *p. 427*
Six Sigma, *p. 429*

<table>
</table>

Questions for Discussion

1. What is the difference between incremental and breakthrough innovation? What risks are associated with each approach?
2. Why is continuous improvement, and programs such as CCC21 and Six Sigma, a good way to develop incremental innovation?
3. What is an ideagora?
4. How are big, global companies looking "outward" to accelerate their innovativeness and break-through innovations?
5. Why do most breakthrough innovations occur in smaller firms?
6. What are the three key elements in the entrepreneurship process in new ventures?
7. What is intrapreneurship, and how is it best enabled?

Chapter 14 Discussion Case

At 3M, a Struggle between Efficiency and Creativity

3M and Innovation: George Buckley, 3M's chief executive, wants to jump-start sales growth with breakthrough products and return the company to its risk-taking roots

- 3M has built a reputation for being an outstanding corporate innovator over its 100-plus-year history. In looking back at some of the company's "greatest hits," it's striking how serendipity played a big role in the birth of the breakthrough ideas. For a long while, it was a matter of 3M corporate policy to encourage risk-taking and to tolerate failure.
- By the late 1990s, though, the company had become bloated and sluggish. Profits were erratic, and its stock price languished. In December 2000, CEO Jim McNerney brought much-needed managerial discipline to the company before leaving to take the CEO job at Boeing in 2005. Some critics, however, argue that the Six Sigma mindset he inculcated had an unintended side-effect: crowding out the creative culture needed to innovate. Current CEO George Buckley has shifted the corporate mandate back to sales growth, eased up on Six Sigma, and is looking for more innovative breakthroughs on his watch.

---

1 Not too many years ago, the temple of management was General Electric. Former CEO Jack Welch was the high priest, and his disciples spread the word to executive suites throughout the land. One of his most highly regarded followers, James McNerney, was quickly snatched up by 3M after falling short in the closely watched race to succeed Welch. 3M's board considered McNerney a huge prize, and the company's stock jumped nearly 20 percent in the days after December 5, 2000, when his selection as CEO was announced. The mere mention of his name made everyone richer.

2 McNerney was the first outsider to lead the insular St. Paul (Minnesota) company in its 100-year history. He had barely stepped off the plane before he announced he would change the DNA of the place. His playbook was vintage GE. McNerney axed 8,000 workers (about 11 percent of the workforce), intensified the performance-review process, and tightened the purse strings at a company that had become a profligate spender. He also imported GE's vaunted Six Sigma program—a series of management techniques designed to decrease production defects and increase efficiency. Thousands of staffers became trained as Six Sigma "black belts." The plan appeared

to work: McNerney jolted 3M's moribund stock back to life and won accolades for bringing discipline to an organization that had become unwieldy, erratic, and sluggish.

3 Then, four and a half years after arriving, McNerney abruptly left for a bigger opportunity, the top job at Boeing. Now his successors face a challenging question: whether the relentless emphasis on efficiency had made 3M a less creative company. That's a vitally important issue for a company whose very identity is built on innovation. After all, 3M is the birthplace of masking tape, Thinsulate, and the Post-it note. It is the invention machine whose methods were consecrated in the influential 1994 best-seller *Built to Last* by Jim Collins and Jerry I. Porras. But those old hits have become distant memories. It has been a long time since the debut of 3M's last game-changing technology: the multilayered optical films that coat liquid-crystal display screens. At the company that has always prided itself on drawing at least one-third of sales from products released in the past five years, today that fraction has slipped to only one-quarter.

4 Those results are not coincidental. Efficiency programs such as Six Sigma are designed to identify problems in work processes—and then use rigorous measurement to reduce variation and eliminate defects. When these types of initiatives become ingrained in a company's culture, as they did at 3M, creativity can easily get squelched. After all, a breakthrough innovation is something that challenges existing procedures and norms. "Invention is by its very nature a disorderly process," says current CEO George Buckley, who has dialed back many of McNerney's initiatives. "You can't put a Six Sigma process into that area and say, well, I'm getting behind on invention, so I'm going to schedule myself for three good ideas on Wednesday and two on Friday. That's not how creativity works." McNerney declined to comment for this story.

PROUD CREATIVE CULTURE

5 The tension that Buckley is trying to manage—between innovation and efficiency—is one that's bedeviling CEOs everywhere. There is no doubt that the application of lean and mean work processes at thousands of companies, often through programs with obscure-sounding names such as ISO 9000 and total quality management, has been one of the most important business trends of past decades. But as once-bloated U.S. manufacturers have shaped up and become profitable global competitors, the onus shifts to growth and innovation, especially in today's idea-based, design-obsessed economy. While process excellence demands precision, consistency, and repetition, innovation calls for variation, failure, and serendipity.

6 Indeed, the very factors that make Six Sigma effective in one context can make it ineffective in another. Traditionally, it uses rigorous statistical analysis to produce unambiguous data that help produce better quality, lower costs, and more efficiency. That all sounds great when you know what outcomes you'd like to control. But what about when there are few facts to go on—or you don't even know the nature of the problem you're trying to define? "New things look very bad on this scale," says MIT Sloan School of Management professor Eric von Hippel, who has worked with 3M on innovation projects that he says "took a backseat" once Six Sigma settled in. "The more you hardwire a company on total quality management, [the more] it is going to hurt breakthrough innovation," adds Vijay Govindarajan, a management professor at Dartmouth's Tuck School of Business. "The mindset that is needed, the capabilities that are needed, the metrics that are needed, the whole culture that is needed for discontinuous innovation, are fundamentally different."

7 The exigencies of Wall Street are another matter. Investors liked McNerney's approach to boosting earnings, which may have sacrificed creativity but made up for it in consistency. Profits grew, on average, 22 percent a year. In Buckley's first year, sales approached $23 billion and profits totaled $1.4 billion, but two quarterly earnings misses and a languishing stock made it a rocky ride. In 2007, Buckley seems to have satisfied many skeptics on the Street, convincing them he can ignite top-line growth without killing the McNerney-led productivity improvements. Shares are up 12 percent since January.

8 Buckley's street cred was hard-won. He's nowhere near the management rock star his predecessor was. McNerney could play the President on TV. He's tall and athletic, with charisma to spare. Buckley is of average height, with a slight middle-age paunch, an informal demeanor, and a scientist's natural curiosity. In the office he prefers checked shirts and khakis to suits and ties. He's bookish and puckish, in the way of a tenured professor.

9 Buckley, in short, is just the kind of guy who has traditionally thrived at 3M. It was one of the pillars of the "3M Way" that workers could seek out funding from a number of company sources to get their pet projects off the ground. Official company policy allowed employees to use 15 percent of their time to pursue independent projects. The company explicitly encouraged risk and tolerated failure. 3M's creative culture foreshadowed the one that is currently celebrated unanimously at Google.

10 Perhaps all of that made it particularly painful for 3M's proud workforce to deal with the hard reality the company faced by the late 1990s. Profit and sales growth were wildly erratic. It bungled operations in Asia amid the 1998 financial crisis there. The stock sat out the entire late 1990s boom, budging less than 1 percent from September 1997, to September 2000. The flexibility and lack of structure, which had enabled the company's success, had also by then produced a bloated staff and inefficient workflow. So McNerney had plenty of cause to whip things into shape.

GREEN-BELT TRAINING REGIMEN

11 One of his main tools was Six Sigma, which originated at Motorola in 1986 and became a staple of corporate life in the 1990s after it was embraced by GE. The term is now so widely and divergently applied that it's hard to pin down what it actually means. At some companies, Six Sigma is plainly a euphemism for cost-cutting. Others explain it as a tool for analyzing a problem (e.g., high shipping costs) and then using data to solve each component of it. But on a basic level, Six Sigma seeks to remove variability from a process. In that way you avoid errors, or defects, and increase predictability (technically speaking, Six Sigma quality has come to be accepted as no more than 3.4 defects per million).

12 At 3M, McNerney introduced the two main Six Sigma tools. The first and more traditional version is an acronym known as DMAIC (pronounced "dee-may-ic"), which stands for define, measure, analyze, improve, control. These five steps are the essence of the Six Sigma approach to problem solving. The other flavor is called Design for Six Sigma, or DFSS, which purports to systematize a new-product development process so that something can be made to Six Sigma quality from the start.

13 Thousands of 3Mers were trained as black belts, an honorific awarded to experts who often act as internal consultants for their companies. Nearly every employee participated in a several-day "green-belt" training regimen, which explained DMAIC and DFSS, familiarized workers with statistics, and

showed them how to track data and create charts and tables on a computer program called Minitab. The black belts fanned out and led bigger-scale "black-belt projects," such as increasing production speed 40 percent by reducing variations and removing wasted steps from manufacturing. They also often oversaw smaller "green-belt projects," such as improving the order fulfillment process. This Six Sigma drive undoubtedly contributed to 3M's astronomical profitability improvements under McNerney; operating margins went from 17 percent in 2001 to 23 percent in 2005.

14   While Six Sigma was invented as a way to improve quality, its main value to corporations now clearly is its ability to save time and money. McNerney arrived at a company that had been criticized for throwing cash at problems. In his first full year, he slashed capital expenditures 22 percent, from $980 million to $763 million, and 11 percent more to a trough of $677 million in 2003. As a percentage of sales, capital expenditures dropped from 6.1 percent in 2001 to just 3.7 percent in 2003. McNerney also held R&D funding constant from 2001 to 2005, hovering over $1 billion a year. "If you take over a company that's been living on innovation, clearly you can squeeze costs out," says Charles O'Reilly, a Stanford Graduate School of Business management professor. "The question is, what's the long-term damage to the company?"

15   Under McNerney, the R&D function at 3M was systematized in ways that were unheard of and downright heretical in St. Paul, even though the guidelines would have looked familiar at many other conglomerates. Some employees found the constant analysis stifling. Steven Boyd, a PhD who had worked as a researcher at 3M for 32 years before his job was eliminated in 2004, was one of them. After a couple of months on a research project, he would have to fill in a "red book" with scores of pages worth of charts and tables, analyzing everything from the potential commercial application, to the size of the market, to possible manufacturing concerns.

16   Traditionally, 3M had been a place where researchers had been given wide latitude to pursue research down whatever alleys they wished. After the arrival of the new boss, the DMAIC process was laid over a phase-review process for innovations—a novelty at 3M. The goal was to speed up and systematize the progress of inventions into the new-product pipeline. The DMAIC questions "are all wonderful considerations, but are they appropriate for somebody who's just trying to . . . develop some ideas?" asks Boyd. The impact of the Six Sigma regime, according to Boyd and other former 3Mers, was that more predictable, incremental work took precedence over blue-sky research. "You're supposed to be having something that was going to be producing a profit, if not next quarter, it better be the quarter after that," Boyd says.

17   For a long time, 3M had allowed researchers to spend years testing products. Consider, for example, the Post-it note. Its inventor, Art Fry, a 3M scientist who's now retired, and others fiddled with the idea for several years before the product went into full production in 1980. Early during the Six Sigma effort, after a meeting at which technical employees were briefed on the new process, "we all came to the conclusion that there was no way in the world that anything like a Post-it note would ever emerge from this new system," says Michael Mucci, who worked at 3M for 27 years before his dismissal in 2004. (Mucci has alleged in a class action that 3M engaged in age discrimination; the company says the claims are without merit.)

18   There has been little formal research on whether the tension between Six Sigma and innovation is inevitable. But the most notable attempt yet, by Wharton School professor Mary Benner and Harvard Business School professor Michael L. Tushman, suggests that Six Sigma will lead to more incremental innovation at the expense of more blue-sky work. The two professors analyzed the types of patents granted to paint and photography companies over a 20-year period, before and after a quality improvement drive. Their work shows that, after the quality push, patents issued based primarily on prior work made up a dramatically larger share of the total, while those not based on prior work dwindled.

19   Defenders of Six Sigma at 3M claim that a more systematic new-product introduction process allows innovations to get to market faster. But Fry, the Post-it note inventor, disagrees. In fact, he places the blame for 3M's recent lack of innovative sizzle squarely on Six Sigma's application in 3M's research labs. Innovation, he says, is "a numbers game. You have to go through 5,000 to 6,000 raw ideas to find one successful business." Six Sigma would ask, why not eliminate all that waste and just come up with the right idea the first time? That way of thinking, says Fry, can have serious side effects. "What's remarkable is how fast a culture can be torn apart," says Fry, who lives in Maplewood, Minnesota, just a few minutes south of the corporate campus and pops into the office regularly to help with colleagues' projects. "[McNerney] didn't kill it, because he wasn't here long enough. But if he had been here much longer, I think he could have."

REINVIGORATED WORKFORCE

20   Buckley, a PhD chemical engineer by training, seems to recognize the cultural ramifications of a process-focused program on an organization whose fate and history is so bound up in inventing new stuff. "You cannot create in that atmosphere of confinement or sameness," Buckley says. "Perhaps one of the mistakes that we made as a company—it's one of the dangers of Six Sigma—is that when you value sameness more than you value creativity, I think you potentially undermine the heart and soul of a company like 3M."

21   In recent years, the company's reputation as an innovator has been sliding. In 2004, 3M was ranked No. 1 on Boston Consulting Group's Most Innovative Companies list (now the *BusinessWeek*/BCG list). It dropped to No. 2 in 2005, to No. 3 in 2006, and down to No. 7 this year. "People have kind of forgotten about these guys," says Dev Patnaik, managing associate of innovation consultancy Jump Associates. "When was the last time you saw something innovative or experimental coming out of there?"

Control and Release: The contrasting styles and strategies of Jim McNerney and George Buckley

McNerney		Buckley
Huge. Renowned as a GE über-manager. Was runner-up to Jeff Immelt in the bake-off to succeed Jack Welch.	**Reputation upon Arrival**	Almost nonexistent. Cut his managerial teeth at Emerson Electric and revived boatmaker Brunswick.
Increase profitability at a company that had become a sluggish performer and a disappointment to investors.	**Mandate**	Bring back the legendary creative oomph, while preserving the operating efficiencies McNerney won.
To remake the culture of 3M, instigated one of the most ambitious Six Sigma drives in corporate history.	**Attitude toward Six Sigma**	Dialed back on Six Sigma regime, especially in the research labs, while preserving it in manufacturing.
Clamped down on profligate spending to goose cash flow and improve operating margins.	**Capital Spending**	Worried about underinvestment, plowed $1.5 billion into 18 new plants or major expansions.
Held R&D spending constant and allocated funds to promising new markets such as pharmaceuticals.	**Research Priorities**	Boosted R&D budget. Refocused on "core" research and away from ancillary businesses like pharma.
Instilled a GE-like managerial sensibility.	**Culture**	Reignited the innovation machine by encouraging risk-taking.
From central casting. Former college baseball player is tall, athletic, and charismatic.	**Appearance**	From the research lab. Bespectacled and unassuming, has an informal "call me George" demeanor.

22 Buckley has loosened the reins a bit by removing 3M research scientists' obligation to hew to Six Sigma objectives. There was perhaps a one-size-fits-all approach to the application of Six Sigma as the initial implementation got under way, says Dr. Larry Wendling, a vice president who directs the "R" in 3M's R&D operation. "Since [McNerney] was driving it to the organization, you know, there were metrics established across the organization and quite frankly, some of them did not make as much sense for the lab as they did other parts of the organization," Wendling says. What sort of metrics? Keeping track of how many black-belt and green-belt projects were completed, for one.

23 In fact, it's not uncommon for Six Sigma to become an end unto itself. That may be appropriate in an operations context—at the end of the year, it's easy enough for a line manager to count up all the money he's saved by doing green-belt projects. But what 3Mers came to realize is that these financially definitive outcomes were much more elusive in the context of a research lab. "In some cases in the lab it made sense, but in other cases, people were going around dreaming up green-belt programs to fill their quota of green-belt programs for that time period," says Wendling. "We were letting, I think, the process get in the way of doing the actual invention."

24 To help get the creative juices flowing, Buckley is opening the money spigot—hiking spending on R&D, acquisitions, and capital expenditures. The overall R&D budget will

grow 20 percent this year, to $1.5 billion. Even more significant than the increase in money is Buckley's reallocation of those funds. He's funneling cash into what he calls "core" areas of 3M technology, 45 in all, from abrasives to nanotechnology to flexible electronics. That is another departure from McNerney's priorities; he told *BusinessWeek* in 2004 that the 3M product with the most promise was skin-care cream Aldara, the centerpiece to a burgeoning pharmaceuticals business. In January, Buckley sold the pharma business for $2 billion.

25 Quietly, the McNerney legacy is being revised at 3M. While there is no doubt the former CEO brought some positive change to the company, many workers say they are reinvigorated now that the corporate emphasis has shifted from profitability and process discipline to growth and innovation. Timm Hammond, the director of strategic business development, says "[Buckley] has brought back a spark around creativity." Adds Bob Anderson, a business director in 3M's radio frequency identification division: "We feel like we can dream again."

26 That move already may have had a psychic payoff, as workers at the science-centric company seem newly energized about Buckley's more flexible growth agenda.

27 The big risk comes in the more tangible measurements, such as profit margins. Buckley knows he can't simply undo the profitability and productivity improvements that McNerney won. His challenge is to figure out how to loosen up the organization, but still keep costs under control. How's

he going to do it? "Did Jim take all the money trees?" Buckley asks. His answer, clearly, is no. The big money tree Buckley is eyeing is the company's convoluted supply chain, where he hopes to wring wasted money out of the system.

EXPANSION AND CONTRACTION

28   Buckley plans to spend $1.5 billion on 18 new plants or major expansions around the world, including 11 outside the United States, with four new factories in China alone. The thinking is that the new factories will add much needed capacity—especially abroad, where 3M pulls in more than 60 percent of its revenues, and where it expects to get up to 75 percent over the next several years.

29   Despite a vast, complicated network of 64 international subsidiary companies, just 35 percent of 3M's manufacturing capacity is overseas. In Buckley's view, the plant expansions won't just add capacity—they are an opportunity to make the whole logistics chain more efficient by shortening supply lines and bringing production closer to local markets.

30   How did things get that way at 3M? For a long time, one of the tenets of the 3M catechism was "make a little, sell a little." Once a project was green-lighted, it might receive funding, but the developer or scientist would have to make small quantities of the product in an ad hoc manner by using idle spots of time at factories throughout the 3M system. It was a way to minimize the financial risk of a new product, and it served the company quite well—when its infrastructure and sales were centered mainly in the United States.

KEEPING INVENTORY MOVING

31   Now, "make a little, sell a little" means that a typical product might be extruded in Canada, machined in France, packaged in Mexico, and sold in Japan. That's costly, and it means that half of 3M products spend 100 days traveling through the supply line, according to Buckley, even before it has to jump any local bureaucratic hurdles.

32   The net result is that 3M has a lot of money tied up in inventory around the world that's just sitting on boats, in trucks, and in warehouses. In the fourth quarter of 2006, for instance, sales rose about $500 million. But working capital went up $450 million and receivables increased $250 million, Buckley says. If that trend continues, "You'd be borrowing money to grow," he says.

33   Buckley expects over the next two years to free $1 billion in working capital and to achieve another "hundreds of millions" in cost savings from the more efficient supply chain. "Working capital as a percent of sales is a big metric for CEOs these days," says Jack Kelly, an analyst at Goldman Sachs, "because if you can reduce working capital, you can increase your cash flow." As Buckley explains, "This is the money tree."

Sources: Reprinted with special permission from Brian Hindo, "At 3M, a Struggle Between Efficiency and Creativity," *BusinessWeek,* June 11, 2007; "3M Chief Plants a Money Tree," *BusinessWeek,* June 11, 2007. Copyright © 2007 The McGraw-Hill Companies.

DISCUSSION QUESTIONS

1. Describe the nature of incremental innovations derived at 3M through the adoption of the Six Sigma discipline earlier in the decade under the leadership of James McNerney.

2. How is the approach of George Buckley different? Is it more of a breakthrough type approach to innovation?

3. Does Buckley's approach involve any outside involvement or openness to outside ideas or outside ventures and acquisitions?

4. Are elements of entrepreneurship present under either leader's approach?

5. Which approach to innovation do you think would be best at 3M?

6. Is it seemingly wise to try to have both Six Sigma and incremental innovation alongside a more open, creative breakthrough innovation approach? What challenges may emerge at 3M in attempting to do this?

7. Go to http://images.businessweek.com/ss/07/05/0530_3m_products/index_01.htm for an interesting slide presentation of 3M's innovations and history of innovation.

Glossary

A

adaptive mode   The strategic formality associated with medium-sized firms that emphasize the incremental modification of existing competitive approaches.

adverse selection   An agency problem caused by the limited ability of stockholders to precisely determine the competencies and priorities of executives at the time they are hired.

agency costs   The cost of agency problems and the cost of actions taken to minimize them.

agency theory   A set of ideas on organizational control based on the belief that the separation of the ownership from management creates the potential for the wishes of owners to be ignored.

agile organization   A firm that identifies a set of business capabilities central to high-profitability operations and then builds a virtual organization around those capabilities, allowing the agile firm to build its business around the core, high-profitability information, services, and products. Creating an agile, virtual organization structure involves outsourcing, strategic alliances, a boundaryless learning approach, and web-based organization.

ambidextrous organization   Organization structure most notable for its lack of structure wherein knowledge and getting it to the right place quickly is the key reason for organization. Managers become knowledge "nodes" through which intricate networks of personal relationships—inside and outside the formal organization—are constantly, and often informally, coordinated to bring together relevant know-how and successful action.

B

balanced scorecard   A management control system that enables companies to clarify their strategies, translate them into action, and provide quantitative feedback as to whether the strategy is creating value, leveraging core competencies, satisfying the company's customers, and generating a financial reward to its shareholders. A set of four measures directly linked to a company's strategy: financial performance, customer knowledge, internal business processes, and learning and growth.

bankruptcy   When a company is unable to pay its debts as they become due, or has more debts than assets.

barriers to entry   The conditions that a firm must satisfy to enter an industry.

benchmarking   Evaluating the sustainability of advantages against key competitors. Comparing the way a company performs a specific activity with a competitor or other company doing the same thing.

board of directors   The group of stockholder representatives and strategic managers responsible for overseeing the creation and accomplishment of the company mission.

boundaryless organization   Organizational structure that allows people to interface with others throughout the organization without need to wait for a hierarchy to regulate that interface across functional, business, and geographic boundaries.

breakthrough innovation   An innovation in a product, process, technology, or the cost associated with it that represents a quantum leap forward in one or more of these ways.

business model   A clear understanding of how the firms will generate profits and the strategic actions it must take to succeed over the long term.

business process outsourcing   Having an outside company manage numerous routine business management activities usually done by employees of the company such as HR, supply procurement, finance and accounting, customer care, supply-chain logistics, engineering, R&D, sales and marketing, facilities management, and management/development.

business process reengineering   A popular method by which organizations worldwide undergo restructuring efforts to remain competitive. It involves fundamental rethinking and radical redesigning of a business process so that a company can best create value for the customer by eliminating barriers that create distance between employees and customers.

C

cash cows   Businesses with a high market share in low-growth markets or industries.

CCC21   A world-famous, cost-oriented continuous improvement program at Toyota (Construction of Cost Competitiveness for the 21st Century).

chaebol   A Korean consortia financed through government banking groups to gain a strategic advantage.

company creed   A company's statement of its philosophy.

company mission   The unique purpose that sets a company apart from others of its type and identifies the scope of its operations. The unique purpose that sets a company apart from others of its type and identifies the scope of its operations in product, market, and technology terms.

concentrated growth   A grand strategy in which a firm directs its resources to the profitable growth of a single product, in a single market, with a single dominant technology.

concentration   The extent to which industry sales are dominated by a few firms.

concentric diversification   A grand strategy that involves the operation of a second business that benefits from access to the first firm's core competencies. A strategy that involves the acquisition of businesses that are related to the acquiring firm in terms of technology, markets, or products.

conglomerate diversification   A grand strategy that involves the acquisition of a business because it presents the most promising investment opportunity available. A strategy that involves acquiring or entering businesses unrelated to a firm's current technologies, markets, or products.

consortia Large interlocking relationships between businesses of an industry.

continuous improvement A form of strategic control in which managers are encouraged to be proactive in improving all operations of the firm. The process of relentlessly trying to find ways to improve and enhance a company's products and processes from design through assembly, sales, and service. It is called *kaizen* in Japanese. It is usually associated with incremental innovation.

core competence A capability or skill that a firm emphasizes and excels in doing while in pursuit of its overall mission.

corporate social responsibility The idea that business has a duty to serve society in general as well as the financial interest of stockholders.

D

dashboard a user interface that organizes and presents information from multiple digital sources simultaneously in a user-designed format on the computer screen.

debt financing Money "loaned" to an entrepreneur or business venture that must be repaid at some point in time.

declining industry An industry in which the trend of total sales as an indicator of total demand for an industry's products or services among all the participants in the industry has started to drop from the last several years with the likelihood being that such a trend will continue indefinitely.

differentiation A business strategy that seeks to build competitive advantage with its product or service by having it be "different" from other available competitive products based on features, performance, or other factors not directly related to cost and price. The difference would be one that would be hard to create and/or difficult to copy or imitate.

discretionary responsibilities Responsibilities voluntarily assumed by a business, such as public relations, good citizenship, and full corporate responsibility.

disruptive innovation A term to characterize breakthrough innovation popularized by Harvard Professor Clayton Christensen; usually shakes up or revolutionizes industries with which they are associated even though they often come from totally different origins or industry settings than the industry they "disrupt."

divestiture A strategy that involves the sales of a firm or a major component of a firm.

divestiture strategy A grand strategy that involves the sales of a firm or a major component of a firm.

divisional organization Structure in which a set of relatively autonomous units, or divisions, is governed by a central corporate office but where each operating division has its own functional specialists who provide products or services different from those of other divisions.

dogs Low market share and low market growth businesses.

downsizing Eliminating the number of employees, particularly middle management, in a company.

dynamic The term that characterizes the constantly changing conditions that affect interrelated and interdependent strategic activities.

E

eco-efficiency Company actions that produce more useful goods and services while continuously reducing resource consumption and pollution.

ecology The relationships among human beings and other living things and the air, soil, and water that supports them.

economic responsibilities The duty of managers, as agents of the company owners, to maximize stockholder wealth.

economies of scale The savings that companies achieve because of increased volume.

emerging industry An industry that has growing sales across all the companies in the industry based on growing demand for the relatively new products, technologies, and/or services made available by the firms participating in this industry.

empowerment The act of allowing an individual or team the right and flexibility to make decisions and initiate action.

entrepreneurial mode The informal, intuitive, and limited approach to strategic management associated with owner-managers of smaller firms.

entrepreneurship The process of bringing together the creative and innovative ideas and actions with the management and organizational skills necessary to mobilize the appropriate people, money, and operating resources to meet an identifiable need and create wealth in the process.

equity financing Money provided to a business venture that entitles the provider to rights or ownership in the venture and which is not expected to be repaid.

ethical responsibilities The strategic managers' notion of right and proper business behavior.

ethical standards A person's basis for differentiating right from wrong.

ethics The moral principles that reflect society's beliefs about the actions of an individual or group that are right and wrong.

ethnocentric orientation When the values and priorities of the parent organization guide the strategic decision making of all its international operations.

expert influence The ability to direct and influence others because they defer to you based on your expertise or specialized knowledge that is related to the task, undertaking, or assignment in which they are involved.

external environment The factors beyond the control of the firm that influence its choice of direction and action, organizational structure, and internal processes.

external interface boundaries Formal and informal rules, locations, and protocol that separate and/or dictate the interaction between members of an organization and those outside the organization—customers, suppliers, partners, regulators, associations, and even competitors.

F

feedback The analysis of postimplementation results that can be used to enhance future decision making.

formality The degree to which participation, responsibility, authority, and discretion in decision making are specified in strategic management.

fragmented businesses Businesses with many sources of advantage, but they are all small. They typically involve differentiated products with low brand loyalty, easily replicated technology, and minimal scale economies.

fragmented industry An industry in which there are numerous competitors (providers of the same or similar products or services the industry involves) such that no single firm or small group of firms controls any significant share of the overall industry sales.

functional organization   Structure in which the tasks, people, and technologies necessary to do the work of the business are divided into separate "functional" groups (e.g., marketing, operations, finance) with increasingly formal procedures for coordinating and integrating their activities to provide the business's products and services.

functional tactics   Detailed statements of the "means" or activities that will be used by a company to achieve short-term objectives and establish competitive advantage. Short-term, narrow scoped plans that detail the "means" or activities that a company will use to achieve short-term objectives.

G

generic strategy   A core idea about how a firm can best compete in the marketplace. Fundamental philosophical option for the design of strategies.

geocentric orientation   When an international firm adopts a systems approach to strategic decision making that emphasizes global integration.

geographic boundaries   Limitations on interaction and contact between people in a company based on being at different physical locations domestically and globally.

global industry   An industry in which competition crosses national borders on a worldwide basis. Industry in which competition crosses national borders.

globalization   The strategy of approaching worldwide markets with standardized products.

golden handcuffs   A form of executive compensation where compensation is deferred (either a restricted stock plan or bonus income deferred in a series of annual installments).

golden parachute   A form of bonus compensation designed to retain talented executives that calls for a substantial cash payment if the executive quits, is fired, or simply retires.

grand strategy   A master long-term plan that provides basic direction for major actions directed toward achieving long-term business objectives. The means by which objectives are achieved.

grand strategy cluster   Sets of grand strategies that may be more advantageous for firms to choose under one of four sets of conditions defined by market growth rate and the strength of the firm's competitive position.

grand strategy selection matrix   A four-cell matrix that helps managers choose among different & grand strategies based upon 1) whether the business is operating from a position of strength or weakness and 2) whether it must rely solely on its own internal resources versus having the option to acquire resources externally via merger or acquisition.

growth industry strategies   Business strategies that may be more advantageous for firms participating in rapidly growing industries and markets.

H

holding company   Structure in which the corporate entity is a broad collection of often unrelated businesses and divisions such that it (the corporate entity) acts as financial overseer "holding" the

ownership interest in the various parts of the company, but has little direct managerial involvement.

horizontal boundaries   Rules of communication, access, and protocol for dealing with different departments or functions or processes within an organization.

horizontal integration   A grand strategy based on growth through the acquisition of similar firms operating at the same stage of the production-marketing chain. A strategy based on growth through the acquisition of one or more similar firms operating at the same stage of the production-marketing chain.

I

ideagora   A Web-enabled, virtual marketplace which connects people with unique ideas, talents, resources, or capabilities with companies seeking to address problems or potential innovations in a quick, competent manner.

implementation control   Management efforts designed to assess whether the overall strategy should be changed in light of results associated with the incremental actions that implement the overall strategy. These are usually associated with specific strategic thrusts or projects and with predetermined milestone reviews.

incremental innovation   Simple changes or adjustments in existing products, services, or processes.

industry   A group of companies that provide similar products and services.

industry environment   The general conditions for competition that influence all businesses that provide similar products and services.

information power   The ability to influence others based on your access to information and your control of dissemination of information that is important to subordinates and others yet not otherwise easily obtained.

innovation   A grand strategy that seeks to reap the premium margins associated with creation and customer acceptance of a new product or service. A strategy that seeks to reap the initially high profits associated with customer acceptance of a new or greatly improved product. The initial commercialization of invention by producing and selling a new product, service, or process.

intangible assets   A firm's assets that you cannot touch or see but that are very often critical in creating competitive advantage: brand names, company reputation, organizational morale, technical knowledge, patents an a unique "bundle of resources"—tangible and intangible assets and organizational capabilities to make use of those assets.

intrapreneurship   A term associated with entrepreneurship in large established companies; the process of attempting to identify, encourage, enable, and assist entrepreneurship within a large, established company so as to create new products, processes, services, or improvements that become major new revenue streams and/or sources of cost savings for the company.

intrapreneurship freedom factors   Ten characteristics identified by Dr. Gordon Pinchot and elaborated upon by others that need to be present in large companies seeking to encourage and increase the level of intrapreneurship within their company.

invention   The creation of new products or processes through the development of new knowledge or from new combinations of knowledge.

isolating mechanisms   Characteristics that make resources difficult to imitate. In the RBV context these are physically unique resources, path-dependent resources, causal ambiguity, and economic deterrence.

J

joint venture   A grand strategy in which companies create a co-owned business that operates for their mutual benefit. Commercial companies created and operated for the benefit of the co-owners; usually two or more separate companies that come together to form the venture.

K

keiretsus   A Japanese consortia of businesses that is coordinated by a large trading company to gain a strategic advantage.

L

leadership development   The effort to familiarize future leaders with the skills important to the company and to develop exceptional leaders among the managers employed.

leader's vision   An articulation of a simple criterion or characterization of what a leader sees their company must become in order to establish and sustain global leadership. IBM's former CEO, Lou Gerstner, described IBM as needing to become the leader in "network-centric computing" is an example of such a characterization.

learning organization   Organization structured around the idea that it should be set up to enable learning, to share knowledge, to seek knowledge, and to create opportunities to create new knowledge. It would move into new markets to learn about those markets rather than simply to bring a brand to it, or find resources to exploit in it.

legal responsibilities   The firm's obligations to comply with the laws that regulate business activities.

liquidation   A strategy that involves closing down the operations of a business and selling its assets and operations to pay its debts and distribute any gains to stockholders.

long-term objectives   The results that an organization seeks to achieve over a multiyear period.

low-cost strategies   Business strategies that seek to establish long-term competitive advantages by emphasizing and perfecting value chain activities that can be achieved at costs substantially below what competitors are able to match on a sustained basis. This allows the firm, in turn, to compete primarily by charging a price lower than competitors can match and still stay in business.

M

market development   A grand strategy of marketing present products, often with only cosmetic modification, to customers in related marketing areas. A strategy of marketing present products, often with only cosmetic modification, to customers in related marketing areas by adding channels of distribution or by changing the content of advertising or promotion.

market focus   This is a generic strategy that applies a differentiation strategy approach, or a low-cost strategy approach, or a combination—and does so solely in a narrow (or "focused") market niche rather than trying to do so across the broader market. The narrow focus may be geographically defined, or defined by product type features, or target customer type, or some combination of these.

market growth rate   The projected rate of sales growth for the market being served by a particular business.

matrix organization   The matrix organization is a structure in which functional and staff personnel are assigned to both a basic functional area and to a project or product manager. It provides dual channels of authority, performance responsibility, evaluation, and control.

mature industry strategies   Strategies used by firms competing in markets where the growth rate of that market from year to year has reached or is close to zero.

milestone reviews   Points in time, or at the completion of major parts of a bigger strategy, where managers have predetermined they will undertake a go–no go type of review regarding the underlying strategy associated with the bigger strategy.

modular organization   An organization structured via outsourcing where different parts of the tasks needed to provide the organization's product or service are done by a wide array of other organizations brought together to create a final product or service based on the combination of their separate, independent, self-contained skills and business capabilities.

moral hazard problem   An agency problem that occurs because owners have limited access to company information, making executives free to pursue their own interests.

moral rights approach   Judging the appropriateness of a particular action based on a goal to maintain the fundamental rights and privileges of individuals and groups.

multidomestic industry   An industry in which competition is segmented from country to country.

O

operating environment   Factors in the immediate competitive situation that affect a firm's success in acquiring needed resources.

opportunity   A major favorable situation in a firm's environment.

organizational capabilities   Skills (the ability and ways of combining assets, people, and processes) that a company uses to transform inputs into outputs.

organizational culture   The set of important assumptions and beliefs (often unstated) that members of an organization share in common.

organizational leadership   The process and practice by key executives of guiding and shepherding people in an organization toward a vision over time and developing that organization's future leadership and organization culture.

organizational structure   Refers to the formalized arrangements of interaction between and responsibility for the tasks, people, and resources in an organization.

outsourcing   Obtaining work previously done by employees inside the companies from sources outside the company.

P

parenting framework   The perspective that the role of corporate headquarters (the "parent") in multibusiness (the "children") companies is that of a parent sharing wisdom, insight, and guidance to help develop its various businesses to excel.

passion (of a leader)   A highly motivated sense of commitment to what you do and want to do.

patching   The process by which corporate executives routinely "remap" their businesses to match rapidly changing market opportunities—adding, splitting, transferring, exiting, or combining chunks of businesses.

peer influence   The ability to influence individual behavior among members of a group based on group norms, a group sense of what is the right thing or right way to do things, and the need to be valued and accepted by the group.

perseverance (of a leader)   The capacity to see a commitment through to completion long after most people would have stopped trying.

planning mode   The strategic formality associated with large firms that operate under a comprehensive, formal planning system.

policies   Broad, precedent-setting decisions that guide or substitute for repetitive or time-sensitive managerial decision making. Predetermined decisions that substitute for managerial discretion in repetitive decision making.

pollution   Threats to life-supporting ecology caused principally by human activities in an industrial society.

polycentric orientation   When the culture of the country in which the strategy is to be implemented is allowed to dominate a company's international decision-making process.

portfolio techniques   An approach pioneered by the Boston Consulting Group that attempted to help managers "balance" the flow of cash resources among their various businesses while also identifying their basic strategic purpose within the overall portfolio.

position power   The ability and right to influence and direct others based on the power associated with your formal position in the organization.

premise control   Management process of systematically and continuously checking to determine whether premises upon which the strategy is based are still valid.

primary activities   The activities in a firm of those involved in the physical creation of the product, marketing and transfer to the buyer, and after-sale support.

principles (of a leader)   A leader's fundamental personal standards that guide her sense of honesty, integrity, and ethical behavior.

private equity   Money from private sources that is invested by a venture capital or private equity company in start-ups and other risky—but potentially very profitable—small and medium-size enterprises.

privatization   A restructuring in which the ownership structure of a publicly traded corporation is converted into a privately held company.

process   The flow of information through interrelated stages of analysis toward the achievement of an aim.

product development   A grand strategy that involves the substantial modification of existing products that can be marketed to current customers. A strategy that involves the substantial modification of existing products or the creation of new but related products that can be marketed to current customers through established channels.

product differentiation   The extent to which customers perceive differences among products and services.

product life cycle   A concept that describes a product's sales, profitability, and competencies that are key drivers of the success of that product as it moves through a sequence of stages from development, introduction to growth, maturity, decline, and eventual removal from a market.

product-team structure   Assigns functional managers and specialists (e.g., engineering, marketing, financial, R&D, operations) to a new product, project, or process team that is empowered to make major decisions about their performance responsibility, evaluation, and control.

punitive power   Ability to direct and influence others based on your ability to coerce and deliver punishment for mistakes or undesired actions by others, particularly subordinates.

Q

question marks   Businesses whose high growth rate gives them considerable appeal but whose low market share makes their profit potential uncertain.

R

referent influence   The ability to influence others derived from their strong desire to be associated with you, usually because they admire you, gain prestige or a sense of purpose by that association, or believe in your motivations.

regiocentric orientation   When a parent company blends its own predisposition with those of its international units to develop region-sensitive strategies.

relative competitive position   The market share of a business divided by the market share of its largest competitor.

remote environment   Economic, social, political, technological, and ecological factors that originate beyond, and usually irrespective of, any single firm's operating situation.

resource-based view   A new perspective on understanding a firm's success based on how well the firm uses its internal resources. The underlying premise is that firms differ in fundamental ways because each firm possesses a unique "bundle of resources"—tangible and intangible assets and organizational capabilities to make use of those assets.

restricted stock   Stock given to an employee who is prohibited or "restricted" from selling the stock for a certain time period and not at all if they leave the company before that time period.

restructuring   Redesigning an organizational structure with the intent of emphasizing and enabling activities most critical to a firm's strategy to function at maximum effectiveness.

retrenchment   A business strategy that involves cutting back on products, markets, operations, or other strategic commitments of the firm because its overall competitive position, or its financial situation, or both are not able to support the level of commitments to various markets or the resources needed to sustain or build its operations in some, usually declining or increasingly competitive, markets. Unlike liquidation, retrenchment would have the firm sell some assets, or ongoing operations, to rechannel proceeds to reduce overall debt and to support the firms efforts to rebuild its future competitive posture.

reward power   The ability to influence and direct others that comes from being able to confer rewards in return for desired actions or outcomes.

S

Sarbanes-Oxley Act of 2002   Law that revised and strengthened auditing and accounting standards.

self-management   Allowing work groups or work teams to supervise and administer their work as a group or team without a direct supervisor exercising the supervisory role. These teams set parameters of their work, make decisions about work-related matters, and perform most of the managerial functions previously done by their direct supervisor.

short-term objective   Measurable outcomes achievable or intended to be achieved in one year or less. Desired results that provide specific guidance for action during a period of one year or less.

simple organization   Structure in which there is an owner and a few employees and where the arrangement of tasks, responsibilities, and communication is highly informal and accomplished through direct supervision.

Six Sigma   A continuous improvement program adopted by many companies in the last two decades that takes a very rigorous and analytical approach to quality and continuous improvement with an objective to improve profits through defect reduction, yield improvement, improved customer satisfaction, and best-in-class performance.

social audit   An attempt to measure a company's actual social performance against its social objectives.

social justice approach   Judging the appropriateness of a particular action based on equity, fairness, and impartiality in the distribution of rewards and costs among individuals and groups.

special alert control   Management actions undertaken to thoroughly, and often very rapidly, reconsider a firm's strategy because of a sudden, unexpected event.

specialization businesses   Businesses with many sources of advantage. Skills in achieving differentiation (product design, branding expertise, innovation, and perhaps scale) characterize winning specialization businesses.

speed-based strategies   Business strategies built around functional capabilities and activities that allow the company to meet customer needs directly or indirectly more rapidly than its main competitors.

stakeholder activism   Demands placed on a global firm by the stakeholders in the environments in which it operates.

stakeholders   Influential people who are vitally interested in the actions of the business.

stalemate businesses   Businesses with few sources of advantage, most of them small. Skills in operational efficiency, low overhead, and cost management are critical to profitability.

stars   Businesses in rapidly growing markets with large market shares.

stock options   The right, or "option," to purchase company stock at a fixed price at some future date.

strategic alliances   Alliances with suppliers, partners, contractors, and other providers that allow partners in the alliance to focus on what they do best, farm out everything else, and quickly provide value to the customer. Contractual partnerships because the companies involved do not take an equity position in one another. Partnerships that are distinguished from joint ventures because the companies involved do not take an equity position in one another.

strategic business unit   An adaptation of the divisional structure in which various divisions or parts of divisions are grouped together based on some common strategic elements, usually linked to distinct product/market differences.

strategic control   Management efforts to track a strategy as it is being implemented, detect problems or changes in its underlying premises, and make necessary adjustments. Tracking a strategy as it is being implemented, detecting problems or changes in its underlying premises, and making necessary adjustments.

strategic intent   A leader's clear sense of where they want to lead their company and what results they expect to achieve.

strategic management   The set of decisions and actions that result in the formulation and implementation of plans designed to achieve a company's objectives.

strategic positioning   The way a business is designed and positioned to serve target markets.

strategic processes   Decision making, operational activities, and sales activities that are critical business processes.

strategic surveillance   Management efforts to monitor a broad range of events inside and more often outside the firm that are likely to affect the course of its strategy over time.

strategic thrusts or projects   Special efforts that are early steps in executing a broader strategy, usually involving significant resource commitments yet where predetermined feedback will help management determine whether continuing to pursue the strategy is appropriate or whether it needs adjustment or major change.

strategy   Large-scale, future-oriented plans for interacting with the competitive environment to achieve company objectives.

strength   A resource advantage relative to competitors and the needs of the markets a firm serves or expects to serve.

structural attributes   The enduring characteristics that give an industry its distinctive character.

support activities   The activities in a firm that assist the firm as a whole by providing infrastructure or inputs that allow the primary activities to take place on an ongoing basis.

SWOT analysis   SWOT is an acronym for the internal Strengths and Weaknesses of a firm, and the environmental Opportunities and Threats facing that firm. SWOT analysis is a technique through which managers create a quick overview of a company's strategic situation.

T

tactics   Specific actions that need to be undertaken to achieve short-term objectives, usually by functional areas.

tangible assets   The most easily identified assets, often found on a firm's balance sheet. They include production facilities, raw materials, financial resources, real estate, and computers.

technological forecasting   The quasi-science of anticipating environmental and competitive changes and estimating their importance to an organization's operations.

threat   A major unfavorable situation in a firm's environment.

turnaround   A grand strategy of cost reduction and asset reduction by a company to survive and recover from declining profits.

U

utilitarian approach   Judging the appropriateness of a particular action based on a goal to provide the greatest good for the greatest number of people.

V

value chain   A perspective in which business is seen as a chain of activities that transforms inputs into outputs that customers value. Customer value derives from three basic sources: activities that differentiate the product, activities that lower its cost, and activities that meet the customer's need quickly.

value chain analysis   An analysis that attempts to understand how a business creates customer value by examining the contributions of different activities within the business to that value.

vertical boundaries   Limitations on interaction, contact and access between operations and management personnel; between different levels of management; and between different organizational parts like corporate vs. divisional units.

vertical integration   A grand strategy based on the acquisition of firms that supply the acquiring firm with inputs or new customers for its outputs. A strategy based on the acquisition of firms that supply the acquiring firm with inputs such as raw materials or new customers for its outputs, such as warehouses for finished products.

virtual organization   Corporations whose structure has become an elaborate network of external and internal relationships. In effect, a temporary network of independent companies—suppliers, customers, subcontractors, and businesses around the core, high-profitability information, services, and products. Creating an agile, virtual organization structure involves outsourcing, strategic alliances, a boundaryless learning approach, and web-based organization.

vision statement   A statement that presents a firm's strategic intent designed to focus the energies and resources of the company on achieving a desirable future.

volume businesses   Businesses that have few sources of advantage, but the size is large—typically the result of scale economies.

W

weakness   A limitation or deficiency in one or more resources or competencies relative to competitors that impedes a firm's effective performance.

Photo Credits

Chapter 1

© PRNewsFoto/McDonald's Corporation, p. 9

Chapter 2

Courtesy of Questar Corporation, pg. 30

Chapter 3

© AP Photo/Kirsty Wigglesworth/WPA pool, p. 73

Chapter 4

Courtesy of Robert Half International, p. 95

Chapter 5

Courtesy of Cognizant Technology Solutions, p. 138

Chapter 6

© Julie Cordeiro/Boston Red Sox, p. 158

Chapter 7

© AP Photo/Chuck Burton, p. 205

Chapter 8

© AFP/Getty Images, p. 258

Chapter 9

Courtesy of International Business Machines Corporation. Unauthorized use not permitted, p. 287

© Handout/epa/Corbis, p. 292

© Kim Kulish/Corbis, p. 298

Chapter 10

Courtesy of Symantec Corporation, p. 307

Chapter 12

© AP Photo/Reed Saxon, p. 378

Chapter 13

© AP Photo/Michel Euler, p. 420 (top left)

© AP Photo/Bell Atlantic, p. 420 (bottom left)

© AP Photo/General Electric Company, p. 420 (top right)

© AP Photo/Paul Sakuma, p. 420 (bottom right)

Chapter 14

© ISSEI KATO/Reuters/Corbis, p. 430

Name Index

Dun's Review, 128
Du Pont Co., 59, 192–194, 214, 312, 335, 364, 394, 417
D Wade Sidekick, 206

E

EADS, 360
Earthgrains Co., 227
Eastern Gas and Fuel Associates, 56
Eastman Kodak Co., 105
EasyJet Airline Co., 248–249, 258, 384
eBay, 235, 243, 298–300, 376, 440, 450
Ebbers, Bernie, 57, 391
Economic Indicators, 127
The Economist, 72
Edelman, Ben, 403
Edin, Kathryn, 89
Edmondson, Gail, 140, 207n, 244, 372
EDS, 359–362
Edwards Systems, 277
Einhorn, Bruce, 63, 209, 357n, 358n
Eisenhardt, Kathleen M., 293n, 294, 294n, 295, 296
Electronic Arts, 348
Elgin, Ben, 63
Eli Lilly, 222, 358, 364, 440
Ellison, Larry, 420
EMC Corp., 63, 68, 239
Emerson, Bill, 78, 80
Emerson Electric, 455
EMI, 99, 152
Encyclopedia of Associations, 184
Endust, 226
Engardio, Pete, 54, 111, 357n, 358n
Enge, Eric, 439
Engibous, Tom, 161–162
Enrico, Roger, 292
Enron Corp., 57, 82, 391, 395
Enron Wind, 277
Entertainment Tonight, 370
Entine, Jon, 70n
Entrust, 219
Environmental Defense, 71
Environmental Protection Agency, 56, 80, 99, 101
Envisioneering Group, 287
Epps, Harold, 396n
Epstein, Keith, 92
Equal Employment Opportunity Commission, 336
Equilar Inc., 327
Erbitux, 57
Ericsson, 55, 348, 350
Ernst & Young, 358, 434
Esmark, 227
Estate, 4
Ethics Resource Center (ERC), 83
Étienne Aigner, 31
E*Trade, 133

EUREKA, 235
European Economic Community (EEC), 95, 137
European Free Trade Area, 137
European Strategic Program for Research and Development in Information Technologies, 235
E.W. Scripps, 232
Ewing, Jack, 126, 272
Exelon, 323
Exxon, 59, 69
ExxonMobil, 8, 56, 61, 130, 137

F

Fahrenheit 212, 217
Fake, Caterina, 449
Falcon Waterfree, 61
Fastow, Andrew S., 82
Federal Bureau of Investigation (FBI), 57
Federal Communications Commission (FCC), 97–98
Federal Deposit Insurance Corp. (FDIC), 88, 92, 96
Federal Express. *See* FedEx
Federal Power Commission, 128
Federal Register, 127
Federal Reserve, 88–89
Federal Reserve Bulletin, 127
Federal Trade Commission (FTC), 19, 91, 92
FedEx Corp., 18, 37, 166, 172, 180, 182, 251, 254, 271–272, 314, 327, 360–361, 443–444
Fellowes, Matt, 89
Fenway Park, 158
Ferber, Robert, 128
Ferrari, 207
Fertitta, George, 378
Fiat, 149, 207, 361
Fields, Mark, 405, 407
Financial Accounting Standards Board, 319
Financial Times Stock Exchange (FTSE), 83
Fine, Jon, 232
Fiorina, Carly, 105, 161, 162, 304, 338–340
Firestone, 71
First Coastal Bank, 219
FirstEnergy, 37
Fishman, Mark, 441
Fiyitsue, 133
Fleet-wood Inc., 331
Flextronics, 439
Flickr, 410, 449
Florsheim, 35
Fluhr, Jeff, 300
Fontana, J., 220n
Food and Drug Administration (FDA), 57

Foodmaker, 20
Forbes, 128
Ford, Henry, 71, 404
Ford, William C. "Bill," Jr., 71, 374, 404, 405
Ford Foundation, 127
Ford Motor Company, 14, 35, 37, 39, 71, 90, 139, 149, 150, 214, 241, 252, 253, 310, 312, 369, 374–375, 377, 401, 403–407, 433
Forest, Stephanie Anderson, 82
Forrester Research, 422
Fortune, 70, 72, 131
Fortune 500 Directory, 128
Forum Corp., 312
Foust, Dean, 166, 272, 313n, 443
Fox News, 370
Foxx, Jamie, 207
FPL, 55, 220
France, Mike, 401
Frankenberg, Bob, 286
Frankentheimer, John, 370
Frankfurt Trust, 272
Franklin, William, 323
Frasco, Alyson, 105
Freeman, R. E., 246n
Freescale Semiconductor, 19
Fresenius Medical Care, 55
Friedman, Thomas, 347, 347n
Frigidaire Appliance, 218
Frima, 131
Frito-Lay, 394
Fry, Art, 454
Fry's Electronics, 91
Fuji, 361
Fujitsu, 233
Funk & Scott, 127, 128
Fuqua, 221

G

Galbraith, Jay, 368
Gallardo Spyder, 207
Gannett, 232
Gantt, Roy, 111
Gap Adult, 39
Gap Inc., 39
Garcia, Joey A., 88
Garnier, Jean-Pierre, 72, 73
Gartner, 307, 387
Gates, Bill, 381
Gateway Inc. (GTW), 91
Gaul, Richard, 369
Gaz Metro, 220
GE Appliances (GEA), 29, 362
GE Capital, 292
GE Medical Systems, 352
Genco, 235
General Cinema Corporation, 182, 286, 288, 315

Subject Index